Introduction to Social Psychology

A EUROPEAN PERSPECTIVE

Edited by

Miles Hewstone
Wolfgang Stroebe
Jean-Paul Codol
Geoffrey M. Stephenson

BLACKWELL
Oxford UK & Cambridge USA

Copyright © Basil Blackwell Ltd 1988

First published 1988
Reprinted 1989 (twice), 1990, 1992, 1993, 1994

Blackwell Publishers
108 Cowley Road, Oxford, OX4 1JF, UK

238 Main Street
Cambridge, MA 02142, USA

British Library Cataloguing in Publication Data

A CIP catalogue record for this book is available from the British Library.

Library of Congress Cataloging in Publication Data

Introduction to social psychology.
  Bibliography: p.
  Includes index.
  1. Social psychology.   2. Social psychology—Europe.
I. Hewstone, Miles.
HM251.155   1988   302   87–35508
ISBN 0–631–15163–X
ISBN 0–631–15164–8 (pbk.)

Typeset in 10½ on 12½pt Times
by Colset Private Ltd, Singapore
Printed in Great Britain at the University Press, Cambridge

This book is printed on acid-free paper

Introduction to Social Psychology

Dedicated to those pioneers of European social psychology
who are no longer with us:

Henri Tajfel

and

Jos Jaspars

Contents

Preface   xv

Acknowledgements   xvii

Part I   Introduction   1

1   Introduction to a History of Social Psychology   3
CARL F. GRAUMANN

Introduction: why study history?   3
The long past of social-psychological thought   5
The beginnings of modern social psychology   8
   Völkerpsychologie   8
   Crowd psychology   10
Modern social psychology   12
   Social psychology in America   13
   Social psychology in Europe   16

2   Ethology and Social Psychology   20
ROBERT A. HINDE

Introduction   20
The orienting attitudes of ethology   21
Description: two routes in the analysis of behavioural data   22
The dialectics between successive levels of social complexity   24
The four whys   26
   Function and evolution: pan-cultural characteristics   27
   Function and evolution: variations in human behaviour   31
   The causal why   34
   The developmental why   35
Summary and conclusion   37

3   The Social Nature of Social Development   39
KEVIN DURKIN

Introduction   39

Mutuality and socialization   40

Children as social beings from birth   41
Social interaction and the beginnings of knowledge   42
Social interaction and the beginnings of language   42
Social interaction and the beginnings of interpersonal relations   44

The implications of social development for developmental and
social psychology   46

Social factors and developmental psychology   47
Developmental perspectives on social cognition   52

Summary and conclusion   58

4   Methodology in Social Psychology: Turning Ideas into Actions   60
A.S.R. MANSTEAD and G.R. SEMIN

Introduction   60

Research: descriptive, correlational and experimental   61

Selection of research strategies   62

Experimental methods   66
Experimental designs   70
Threats to validity in experimental research   71

Data collection techniques   74

Observational measures   75
Self-report measures   77
Choosing a measure   79

Problems with experimentation   80

Summary and conclusion   83

Part II   Construction of the Social World   87

5   Social Cognition   89
JACQUES-PHILIPPE LEYENS and JEAN-PAUL CODOL

Introduction   89

Cognition   91

The meaning of cognition   91
Categorization   92
Schemata   93

The field of social cognition   93

Definition   93
The social origin of cognition   94

The content of social cognition   94
Shared social cognitions   97

Five approaches to the person as a social cognizer   99

The consistent or rationalizing person   100
The naive psychologist   100
The data-processing trainee   101
The cognitive miser   104
The cognitive-affective human being   107

Summary and conclusion   108

6   Attribution Theory and Social Explanations   111
MILES HEWSTONE and CHARLES ANTAKI

Introduction   111

Theories of causal attribution   112

The naive analysis of action   112
Correspondent inference theory   113
Covariation and configuration   115

What are common-sense explanations?   119

Internal versus external attributions   119
Is ordinary explanation causal?   120

When do people give explanations?   122

The instigation of causal attributions   123
The pragmatics of explanations   124

How do people make attributions?   125

Errors and biases in the attribution process   125
The process of causal attribution   132

Why do people make attributions – and what are the
consequences?   134

Attributions and motivation   134
Attributions and depression   138

Summary and conclusion   139

7   Attitudes I: Structure, Measurement and Functions   142
DAGMAR STAHLBERG and DIETER FREY

Introduction   142

The attitude construct: definitions and conceptual distinctions   143

Attitude measurements   146

Classic approaches to attitude measurement   146
Other sorts of attitude measurements   150

Functions of attitudes   153

   Motivational functions   153
   Attitudes guiding information processing   154

Attitudes guiding behaviour   158

   Methodological factors   159
   Special characteristics of the attitude   160
   Situational factors   162
   Personality factors   164

Summary and conclusion   164

8   Attitudes II: Strategies of Attitude Change   **167**
WOLFGANG STROEBE and KLAUS JONAS

Introduction   167

The attitudinal effects of direct experience   168

   Direct experience as mere exposure   168
   Direct experience as a source of information   170
   Classical conditioning: the attitudinal impact of the context of
      experience   171
   Summary and conclusions   172

The impact of socially mediated experience   173

   Modelling: forming attitudes from observing the consequences
      of other people's behaviour   173
   Persuasive communications   174
   Summary and conclusions   184

The attitudinal impact of incentive-induced behaviour change   184

   Counter-attitudinal behaviour and attitude change 185
   Pro-attitudinal behaviour and attitude change   191
   Summary and conclusions   192

Strategies of change: an evaluation of their relative effectiveness 193

Part III   Communication and Social Interaction   197

9   Interpersonal Communication   **199**
JOHN M. WIEMANN and HOWARD GILES

Introduction   199

   Communication: its characteristics   199
   Eye contact, distance and affiliation   201

A functional approach to communication   203

   Control   203
   Affiliation   209

The goal: communicative competence 217

Summary and conclusion 219

10 Social Relationships 222
MICHAEL ARGYLE

Introduction 222

Theories of relationships 223

Biological 223
Reinforcement and need satisfaction 224
Exchange theories 224
Equity and fairness 226
Cognitive theories 226
Effects of socialization and culture 227
Social systems 228

The formation, maintenance and dissolution of relationships 228

Acquaintance 228
Build-up and consolidation 229
Decline and breakdown 230

The components of relationships 231

Activities 232
Goals and conflicts 232
Rules 233
Skills 234
Concepts and beliefs 235
Power and roles 235

The distinctive properties of some relationships 237

Marriage 237
Friendship 237
Workmates 237
Kin 239

The effects of relationships 239

Happiness 240
Mental health 240
Physical health 242

Effects of culture and history 243

Summary and conclusion 244

11 Prosocial Behaviour 246
HANS W. BIERHOFF and RENATE KLEIN

Introduction 246

Examples of prosocial behaviour 246

Patterns of prosocial behaviour   250

Pseudo-contingency   250
Asymmetrical contingency   250
Reactive contingency   251
Mutual contingency   252

Normative expectations   252

Norm of social responsibility   253
Personal norms   253
Norm of reciprocity   256
Acquisition of normative beliefs   256

Impulsive helping and emergencies   257

The psychology of receiving help   259

Summary and conclusion   261

12   Aggressive Behaviour   263
AMÉLIE MUMMENDEY
Translated by Miles Hewstone and Claudia Hammer-Hewstone

Introduction   263

Theories of aggression   265

Aggression as instinct   265
Frustration and aggression   268
Aggression as learned behaviour   271

Summary and conclusions   274

Mediating variables in aggression: from internal states to socio-
cultural factors   275

The role of arousal in aggression   275
The social construction of aggression   280
Norms as regulators of aggression   283

Summary and conclusion   286

13   Conflict and Cooperation   288
JANUSZ GRZELAK

Introduction   288

Homo oeconomicus? Maximizing self-interest   289

Theoretical notions and experimental paradigms   289
When do people cooperate? Situational determinants   294
Summary   297

Self-interest revisited: *Homo oeconomicus* socialized?   297

Own benefit versus other's benefit   297
Social orientations   298
Limitations   300

Summary   301

Interpretations of conflict: from situation to representation   301

Perception of interdependence and behaviour   301
Perception of interdependence and social orientations   303
Summary   305

From sophisticated thinking to habitual reactions   305

Deliberate decision-making   305
Learning rules: win/stay, lose/change   306
Summary   307

Me or we? Individual and social identification   308

Mutual trust: community of goals and anticipations   308
Social comparison and social categorization processes   309
Summary   310

Summary and conclusion   310

Part IV   Social Groups   313

14   Group Performance   315
HENK WILKE and AD VAN KNIPPENBERG

Introduction   315

Determinants of productivity   316

Task performance in the presence of others   317

Early social facilitation and inhibition studies   318
Zajonc's explanation of ambiguous SFI results   318
Alternative explanations of SFI   319
*A cognitive-motivational model of group influences on
    individual performance*   321

Performance in interacting groups   324

Steiner's classification of tasks   324
Predicting group productivity   326
Conclusions   332

Group structure   332

Development of structure   333
Status   334
The leadership role   337
Norms   343
Communication networks   346

Summary and conclusion   348

15   Social Influence in Small Groups   350
EDDY VAN AVERMAET

Introduction   350

Conformity or majority influence   351
  Sherif and the autokinetic effect   351
  The surprise of Solomon Asch   352
  Why people conform: normative and informational influence   354
  Normative and informational influence: experimental evidence   355
  The joint effects of normative and informational influence   358
Innovation or minority influence   359
  The power of a consistent minority   359
  *Why and when consistency leads to influence: an attributional
    account*   362
  Majority and minority influence: compliance and conversion   364
Decision-making in groups   368
  Group polarization   368
  *Explaining group polarization: normative and informational
    influence*   370
  Groupthink: an extreme example of group polarization   371
Obeying immoral orders: the social influence of an authority   372
  Milgram's obedience experiment   372
  Situational determinants of obedience   375
  What would you have done?   377
Summary and conclusion   378

16 Intergroup Relations   381
RUPERT BROWN

Introduction   381
Popular notions of intergroup conflict and prejudice   383
  The group as a dehumanizing force   383
  Prejudice as personality type   385
  Interpersonal versus group behaviour   387
Intergroup behaviour as a response to real or imagined group
  interests   389
  Sherif's summer-camp studies   390
Mere group membership as a source of intergroup discrimination   393
  Minimal group experiments   394
  Explanations of intergroup discrimination in minimal groups   396
Group membership and social identity   400
  Who am I? Who are we?   400
  Wage differentials   401
  Ethnolinguistic groups   402
  Occupational groups   403
Subordinate status, intergroup comparisons and social unrest   404

Leaving the group
Social comparisons 405
Cognitive alternatives 405
Relative deprivation 407
Summary and conclusion 408

Epilogue 411

17 Applied Social Psychology 413
GEOFFREY M. STEPHENSON

Introduction 413
Application benefits social psychology 413
Social psychology's social role 414
The pure science model 414
Solving social problems 414
The pure science model in practice 415
Applications may be used to test theory 417
The social science model: addressing social issues 419
Social psychology and health 420
A causal model 420
Behaviourally induced coronary heart disease 422
The effects of stress on health: the example of bereavement 423
Recovering from illness: an attributional analysis 425
Social psychology and health: a model of helping and coping 427
Social-psychological issues of criminal justice 429
The decision-making sequence in criminal justice 429
*The decision-making sequence: brief review of issues and
    research* 430
Juvenile crime as a particular social issue 435
Eye-witness testimony 438
How complex a process is sentencing? 440
Summary and conclusion 442

Glossary 445

References 458

List of Contributors 530

Author index 531

Subject index 549

Preface

The idea for this book grew out of many conversations the editors had with colleagues from all over Europe at various meetings of the European Association of Experimental Social Psychology. Members of the European Association teach social psychology in more than a dozen different countries and often use American textbooks. They typically report that texts which have been highly rated in the United States are not well received by European students. Since these students have to take more psychology courses than are required of American undergraduates they find American texts too basic. They also complain that most American textbooks do not adequately cover work done by European social psychologists and published in European journals. Thus, there seemed to be a need for a social psychology text that would be somewhat more advanced than American undergraduate textbooks and that would present the best of both American and European research in social psychology. Our 'European perspective' refers to the geographical location of our contributors, the literature they cite, and to a lesser extent to their conception of social psychology. There are undoubtedly more similarities than differences between European and North American social psychology, but the present volume is nonetheless distinctive in the attention it gives to such topics as minority influence and intergroup relations, areas in which Europeans have made their most significant contributions.

When we discussed this issue with our American colleagues, we were surprised to learn that many of them shared these views about the limitations of American social psychology texts. They argued that in the United States, there was also a need for a more advanced text that could be assigned in honours courses or in the initial stages of graduate training. Some even believed that such a text could be used in regular undergraduate social psychology classes.

While this idea may seem ambitious, it should be remembered that once upon a time there were textbooks of social psychology that were at the forefront of the field. These books were not only read by students but also by researchers and they were widely quoted in the research literature. Thus, the first generation of textbooks by Asch and Newcomb, and the second generation by Jones and Gerard, Brown, and Secord and Backman offered more than mere reviews. These books helped to shape the field by contributing new theoretical ideas, as well as their unique conceptions of social psychology. They tried to excite the reader with ideas rather than cartoons.

When we decided to produce a textbook in the tradition of those great books, and one that would also offer a representative survey of the field, we soon realized that this had to be an edited volume rather than a book written by the four editors. By making it an edited book, we could for each chapter commission a European social psychologist who was an expert in a given area and could thus be expected to give a 'state of the art' presentation of both European and American work. The danger of uneven writing styles and lack of integration could be avoided by giving explicit and extensive instructions to our authors.

After many discussions about who would be the ideal choice for each of the chapters, we had the gratifying experience of finding that our invitations to collaborate on this text were met with great enthusiasm and that all of our authors tried very hard to incorporate the suggestions made by the editors. We would like to use this opportunity to thank them for the patience with which they worked through several revisions of their initial drafts and for their willingness to accept editorial comments. We hope that they and the readers of this book – whether undergraduates, graduate students or teachers – will enjoy and benefit from the final version. We believe that it conveys a critical knowledge of and enthusiasm for social psychology, whatever its geographical provenance.

We are most grateful to Glynis Hudson, Virginia Heaton, Claudia Hammer-Hewstone, Klaus Jonas, Margaret Stroebe and Eva Walker for their help in proof-reading and in the preparation of the index.

Miles Hewstone
Wolfgang Stroebe
Jean-Paul Codol
Geoffrey M. Stephenson

Acknowledgements

The authors and publishers are grateful to the following for their kind permission to reproduce illustrations: The Associated Press Limited (pp. 175 and 248 bottom); Camera Press (p. 382, top and bottom); Alexandra Milgram (pp. 68 and 374); Pergamon Books Limited (p. 50); Popperfoto/Reuter (p. 264, top); Stuart Nicol Photography (p. 248, top); Syndication International and John Frost (p. 264, bottom).

The authors and publishers wish to thank the following who have kindly given permission to reproduce figures, tables and extracts: Academic Press, Inc. (figure 10.1, from Wilke, H. and Lanzetta, J. T. (1970), The effect of amounts of prior help on subsequent helping behavior, *Journal of Experimental Social Psychology*, 6, figure 1, p. 413; figure 10.2, from Hatfield, E., Utne, M. K. and Traupman, J. (1979), Equity theory and intimate relationships, in R. L. Burgess and T. L. Huston (eds), *Exchange Theory in Developing Relationships*, figure 4.1, p. 118; figure 10.3, from Huston, T. L., Surra, C. A., Fitzgerald, N. M. and Cate, R. M. (1981), From courtship to marriage: mate selection as an interpersonal process, in S. W. Duck and R. Gilmour (eds), *Personal Relationships*, 2, figure 3, P. 77; figure 14.4, from Kerr, S. and Jermier, J. M. (1978), Substitutes for leadership: their meaning and measurement, *Organizational Behavior and Human Performance*, 22, pp. 375–403; figure 16.3, from Brown, R. J. (1978), Divided we fall: an analysis of relations between sections of a factory work-force, in H. Tajfel (ed.), *Differentiation between Social Groups)*; American Journal of Epidemiology (figure 10.8, from Berkman, L. S. and Syme, S. L. (1979), Social networks, host resistance, and mortality: a nine-year follow-up study of Alameda County residents, *American Journal of Epidemiology*, 109, figure 1, p. 190); American Psychological Association (figure 5.2, from Langer, El, Blank, A. and Chanowitz, B. (1978), The mindlessness of ostensibly thoughtful action: the role of placebic information in interpersonal interaction, *Journal of Personality and Social Psychology*, 36, pp. 635–42, copyright © 1978 by the American Psychological Association; figure 5.3 from Ross, L. D., Lepper, M. R. and Hubbard, M. (1975), perserverance in self perception: biased attributional processes in debriefing paradigm, *Journal of Personality and Social Psychology*, 32, pp. 880–92, copyright © 1975 by the American Psychological Association; figure 6.5 from Storms, M. D. (1973), Video tape and the attribution process: reversing actors' and observers' points of view, *Journal of Personality and Social Psychology*, 27, pp. 165–75, copyright © 1973 by the American Psychological Association; figure 13.1, from Deutsch, M. and Krauss, R. M. (1960), The effect of threat on interpersonal bargaining, *Journal of Abnormal and Social Psychology*, 61, pp. 181–9, copyright © 1960 by the American Psychological Association; figure 13.4 adapted from Kuhlman, M. D. and Marshello, A. J. M. (1975), Individual differences in game motivation as moderators of preprogrammed strategy effects in prisoner's dilemma game, *Journal of Personality and Social Psychology*, 32, pp. 912–31, copyright © 1975 by the American Psychological Association; figure 13.6, from Sidowski, J. B., Wyckoff, and Tabory, L. (1956), The influence of reinforcement and punishment in a minimal social situation, *Journal of Abnormal and Social Psychology*, 52, pp. 115–19, copyright © 1956 by the American Psychological Association); The American Sociological Association (figure 9.1, from Argyle, M. and Dean, J. (1956), Eye contact, distance and affiliation, *Sociometry*, 28, p. 300; figure 4.2 from Bales, R. F. (1950), A set of categories for analysis of small group interaction, *Amerian Sociological review*, 15, chart 1, p. 258); Bell Telephone Laboratories, Inc. (figure 10.5, from Wish, M., Deutsch, M. and Kaplan, S. J. (1976), Perceived dimensions of interpersonal relations, *Journal of Personality and Social Psychology*, 33, p. 413); Brooks/Cole Publishing Co. (tables 14.1 and 14.2, from Forsyth, D. R. (1983), *An Introduction to Group Dynamics*, copyright © 1983 by Wadsworth, Inc.); Cambridge University Press (figure 5.4 from Tajfel, H. (1981), *Human Groups and Social Categories: studies in social psychology*); The Eugenics Soceity (figure 10.6, from Walker, C. (1977), Some variations in marital satisfaction, in R. Chester and J. Peel (eds), *Equalities and Inequalities in Family Life*, Academic Press (UK) Ltd, figure 1, p. 131); The Free Press (table 14.3, from Bales, R. F. and Slater, P. E. (1955), Role differentiation in small decision-making groups, in T. Parsons and R. F. Bales (eds) *Family, Socialisation and Interaction Process*, copyright © 1955 by the Free Press, renewed 1983 by Robert F. Bales and Helen W. Parsons); Guilford Press, New York (table 6.3, from Weiner, B. (1986), Attribution, emotion and action, in R. M. Sorrentino and E. T. Higgins, *Handbook of Motivation and Cognition*, p. 294); The Controller of Her Majesty's Stationery Office (figure 17.7, from *Key Data 1986*, CSO); Darwyn E. Linder (figure 8.5, from Linder, D. E., Cooper, J. and Jones, E. E. (1967), Decision freedom as a determinant of the role of incentive magnitude in attitude change, *Journal of Personality and Social Psychology*, 6, pp. 245–54, copyright © 1967 by the American Psychological Association); National Council on Family Relations (figure 10.4, from Argyle, M. and Furnham, A. (1983), Source of satisfaction and conflict in long-term relationships, *Journal of Marriage and the Family*, 45:3, figure 1, p. 486); Richard E. Petty (figure 8.3, from Petty, R. E., Wells, G. L. and Brock, T. C. (1976), Distraction can enhance or reduce yielding to propaganda: thought disruption versus effort justification, *Journal of Personality and Social Psychology*, 34, pp. 874–84; figure 8.4 from Petty, R. E., Cacioppo, J. T. and Goldman, R. (1981), Personal involvement as a determinant of argument-based persuasion, *Journal of Personality and Social Psychology*, 41, pp. 847–55, copyright © 1976 and 1981 by the American Psychological Association); Plenum Publishing Corporation (figures 12.1, 12.2, 12.3, from Baron, R. A. (1977), *Human Aggression*, figure 24, p. 130, figure 29, p. 29 and figure 35, p. 165); Prentice-Hall, Inc. (figure 7.2, from Ajzen, I. and Fishbein, M. (1980), *Understanding Attitudes and Predicting Social Behavior*, p. 8); Random House, Inc. (figure 6.4, from Fiske, S. T. and Taylor, S. E. (1984), *Social Cognition*, p. 78); Philip J. Runkel and Joseph E. McGrath (figure 4.1, from (1972), *Research on Human Behavior: a systematic guide to method*, Holt, Rinehart and Winston); Sage Publications Ltd (table 10.1, from Argyle, M. and Henderson, M. (1984), The rules of friendship, *Journal of Social and Personal Relationships*, 1, table 9, p. 234; figure 10.7, from Kayser, E., Schwinger, T. and Cohen, R. L. (1984), Laypersons' conceptions of social relationships: a test of contract theory, *Journal of Social and Personal Relationships*, 1, figures 3 and 4, pp. 446 and 450); Sage Publications, Inc. (table 7.3, from Frey, D. and Rosch, M. (1984), Information seeking after decisions: the roles of novelty of information and decision reversibility, *Personality and Social Psychology Bulletin*, 10, pp. 91–8; figure 9.3 from Knapp, M. (1983), Dyadic relationship development, in J. M. Wiemann and R. P. Harrison (eds), *Nonverbal Interaction*, p. 193); Times Newspapers Ltd (for extracts from 30 May 1984 and 30 May 1985 issues of *The Times*); John Wiley & Sons, Ltd (figure 14.5, from Fiedler, F. E. and Potter, E. H. (1983), Dynamics of leadership effectiveness, in H. H. Blumburg, A. P. Hare, V. Kent and M. Davies (eds), *Small Groups and Social Interaction*, vol. 1, pp. 407–12; figure 16.1, from Tajfel, H., Flament, C., Billig, M. G. and Bundy, R. P. (1971), Social categorization and intergroup behaviour, *European Journal of Social Psychology*, 1, pp. 149–78); and John Wiley & Sons, Inc. (figure 8.2, from McGuire, W. J. (1978), An information-processing model of advertising effectiveness, in H. J. Davis and A. J. Silk (eds), *Behavioral and Management Science in Marketing*, p. 161); Yale University Press (figure 7.1, from Rosenburg, M. J. and Hovland, C. I. (1960), Cognitive, affective and behavioral components of attitudes, in C. I. Hovland and M. J. Rosenburg (eds), *Attitude Organisation and Change*, p. 3); Mark P. Zanna (figure 8.6, from Zanna, M. P. and Cooper, J. (1974), Dissonance and the pill: an attribution approach to studying the arousal properties of dissonance, *Journal of Personality and Social Psychology*, 29, pp. 703–9, copyright © 1974 by the American Psycholgical Association).

PART I

Introduction

1 Introduction to a History of Social Psychology

CARL F. GRAUMANN

Introduction: Why Study History?

Individuals as well as groups, from families through institutions to nations, have their history. So do science and scientific disciplines. Getting to know any of these is a matter of trying to find out not only who and what they are at present, but what they have been and have done. In general, with social groups and systems we would not fully understand what their members are doing now unless we had some knowledge about what they (or their predecessors) had previously planned for the group to achieve. Social action as goal-directed behaviour can only be accounted for if we know who set the goal, when, and for which purpose. Since social inquiry, including social-psychological research, is a special case of social action, namely a collective enterprise, we should have some knowledge of disciplinary history if we want to understand why social psychologists are doing what they do and how they do it.[1]

What we call 'history' is not something given that can be recorded and studied like other facts, physical or social. History has to be constructed. The data, figures, persons and events may be given. But which of these are to be considered and how they are weighted and related is a matter of construction and of purpose (see Graumann, 1983, 1987a). Although we speak of historiography, i.e. the writing of history, it is important to realize that this writing is construction rather than recording.

One major concern and a plausible reason to construct a discipline's history can be the discipline's *identity*. What, for example, is the identity of social psychology? Is there a definition? There is no agreement, since neither the subject matter nor the methods nor the theories and models that are being traded will yield reliable and valid criteria for definition. We share the topics with neighbouring social, behavioural and biological disciplines. We tend to borrow the models from others, and most of our methods belong to the common arsenal of the social and behavioural sciences. Hence the traditional criteria of theory, method and research do not clearly distinguish social psychology from other fields. Distinction, however, is an important aspect of identity. Furthermore, it is a fact that several different social psychologies exist side by side. At least for the two major variants, namely sociological social psychology (SSP) and psychological social psychology (PSP), it has been shown that they exist without much mutual notice (Wilson and Schafer, 1978). The explanation for this schism is as simple as it is problematic. The members of the two groups, as a rule, take different curricula; study, teach and work at different departments; read and write for different textbooks and journals; have different careers; and may adhere to different views of science. Since this has been going on for several generations of social psychologists we now find that members of SSP and of PSP have different histories, with different 'pioneers' and 'heroes': Lewin, Festinger, Schachter, Asch, Campbell and F.H. Allport for PSP; Mead, Goffman, French, Homans and Bales for SSP (Wilson and Schafer, 1978). It is the different histories that provide and maintain different identities. Hence, while it is the rule that textbooks on social psychology are written from either a psychological or a sociological viewpoint, a comprehensive historiography must account for all major variants of social psychology and their interrelationships.

A third variant of social psychology, relatively independent of PSP and (less so) of SSP, is analytical social psychology as developed within the psycho-analytic framework (see Hall and Lindzey, 1968).

In the establishment and maintenance of social identity, the psychologist recognizes a well-known feature of group formation; and in the display of identity, a technique familiar from the study of intergroup relations (see chapter 16). Hence, it is not surprising that historiography can be conceived as a 'social psychology of the past' (Watson, 1979).

There is one other, closely related function of history construction that has an equally social-psychological character: the *justificatory function*. Agassi (1963), Butterfield (1963) and others have argued that by historiographically relating ourselves and our own present research with 'classical' achievements, with reputed theories of the past or generally with 'great men', we justify our own work and possibly raise our scientific status. Connecting the present with a well-selected past establishes a kind of pedigree whose continuity from the *oeuvre* of a 'classical' ancestor (founding father or the like) to our present research work is interpreted as a mainstream line of progress, of accumulating knowledge (Graumann, 1987a).

Even a brief discussion of the various functions of disciplinary history reveals that we *can* learn from history, if it has not exclusively been written for identificatory and justificatory purposes as is mainly the case in 'presentist' history. In order to be useful a history of a discipline must allow for the dis-continuities, drawbacks, failures and dead ends as well as for continuity, success and progress. It must not pretend unity if there is pluralism as in social psychology. Finally, as with any phenomenon that we may study, we need information about the larger context. For disciplinary history the context is not only the system of sciences, but the social, political and economic system within which an individual discipline develops. That is why the sociology of science has become an essential part of disciplinary historiography (Harvey, 1965; Lepenies, 1977; Woodward, 1980).

The following brief introduction to the history of social psychology cannot meet all these methodological demands. But whoever studies the history of science should have some knowledge of the principles of history construction. This should aid critical reading and the reconsideration of what, after all, is the use of studying the history of social psychology.

The Long Past of Social-Psychological Thought

It has become almost a ritual to refer to the development of what today is called psychology with a quotation from Ebbinghaus (1908, p. 1): 'Psychology has had a long past but only a brief history.' Social psychologists have repeatedly applied this statement to their own discipline. Usually they let 'history' begin in 1908 (or in the 1890s), while the 'past' may extend as far back as Plato (427–347 BC) and Aristotle (384–322 BC) or even the pre-Socratics (seventh to fifth century BC), depending on which philosophy of society and of science a historiographer of social psychology relies most upon and on how broadly an author conceives of social psychology. The decision how far to extend the past or the history of social psychology and whom to include is a function of a writer's present conception of the social and the psychological.

Since there was no social psychology in either form or content before the end of the nineteenth century, our interest in its long past is an interest in the history of social thought or social philosophy. Some of its central issues are:

1 Whether persons are conceived as individuals, each of whom is unique or is essentially like others
2 Whether the individual person is seen as a function of the society or, inversely, society is seen as a product and function of the individuals composing it
3 Whether the relationship between individual and society is at all a meaningful question or is an expression of a hidden ideology
4 Whether the 'nature' of human beings is basically egoistic and needs techniques and processes of education, moralization or socialization to enable people to live together in groups, communes and states, or whether human beings are social by 'nature' and it is good or bad influences that make them social or antisocial
5 Whether men and women are free and responsible agents or are determined by natural and social forces.

These and other anthropological questions have been asked and answered in a variety of ways by philosophers over the centuries. The different solutions offered are still controversial topics in contemporary thought and, inevitably, they become explicit or implicit assumptions of social-psychological theorizing. The primacy of the individual over the social, of mind over matter, of nature over nurture, of rationality over irrational forces, or the inverse positions – there is hardly a large-scale psychological theory that does not answer such questions in its own way. And it is here that the historical foundation of modern social thought is evident and acknowledged.

The acknowledgement may, for example, be seen in the fact that two major strands of social thought have come to be called Platonic and Aristotelian, respectively. Plato had emphasized the primacy of the state over the individual who, in order to become truly social, had to be educated under the responsibility of authorities. For Aristotle, in turn, the human being is social by nature, and nature can be trusted to enable individuals to live together and to enter personal relationships from which families, tribes and ultimately the state will naturally develop. This difference in emphasis between Plato and Aristotle should not be exaggerated; however, they heralded two traditions of social thought which, in modern times, have been distinguished as the **socio-centred approach** and the **individuo-centred approach**. The former emphasizes the determining function of social structures (systems, institutions, groups) for individual experience and behaviour; by contrast, in the latter it is individual processes and functions from which the functions of the social systems are said to be explainable.

In the history of social thought the conception of the primacy of the social has taken many forms. For Hegel (1770–1831), the German idealistic philosopher, the state is not only the ultimate form of society but the incarnation of the (objective) social mind of which individual minds are active participants. Later social-psychological ideas of a (supra-individual) **group mind** have been derived from Hegel's conception. For contemporaries who consider social psychology too exclusively individuo-centred, the philosophy of a social mind is a significant model (see Markova, 1982, 1983). Critical of Hegel but following his emphasis, Marx (1818–83) and Engels (1820–95) developed a theory of history and society according to which the economic level of development in a given society (with the prevalent modes of production and exchange), the resulting division of the society into classes and the struggle between these classes condition social and individual life: 'It is not the consciousness of men that determines their being, but on the contrary, their social being that determines their consciousness' (Marx and Engels, 1962, vol. I, p. 363). A modern social psychology on a Marxist foundation has been developed by Hiebsch and Vorwerg (1980). For a comparison of Soviet and Western perspectives in social psychology see Strickland (1979).

While in the long past of social psychology we may find other important theories of the primacy of the social and of society over the individual, we should now turn to a few examples of the opposite stance: the philosophical antecedents of an individuo-centred social science. Since, broadly speaking, psychology and with it social psychology (PSP) is the study of individual experience and behaviour, we should expect major impacts of the varieties of **individualism** on psychology. Unfortunately, the term 'individualism' has too many different meanings to be useful without conceptual clarification (Lukes,

1973a). One such clarification, crucial for the psychologist, is the notion of the 'abstract individual', according to which the basic human psychological features (be they called instincts, needs, desires or wants) 'are assumed as given, independently of a social context' (1973a, p. 73). Since they are invariant, the group, the whole of society, is a mere union or product of such individual 'faculties'. A large portion of this individualism came historically under the names of hedonism and utilitarianism. The basic tenet of **hedonism** is the *pleasure principle*, according to which we act in order to secure and maintain pleasure and to avoid and reduce pain.

Since Bentham (1748-1832), who theoretically transformed the pleasure principle into a principle of utility, **utilitarianism** – the doctrine that advocates the pursuit of the greatest happiness of the greatest number – has entered social thought to stay there. Over many variations of the doctrine and various combinations of individualism, utilitarianism and liberalism there is one line of tradition leading directly into the foundation of psychology. For most modern theories of conditioning and of motivation, many of which are traded as social-psychological theories, the underlying ideas of individual satisfaction (reinforcement, reward, profit; reduction of tension, of dissonance, of uncertainty; etc.) are variations of the pleasure or utility principle.

There were two other intellectual developments in the nineteenth century that contributed significantly to modern social psychology: sociology and evolutionary theory. As a term and a programme, **sociology** was created by Auguste Comte (1798-1857), who has also been praised and condemned as the father of **positivism**. For Comte (1853) positivism was a system of philosophy that implied a model of evolutionary progress of human knowledge from a theological through a metaphysical to a 'positive' stage of scientific knowledge, in which phenomena are taken to be real and certain, and knowledge is the description of such phenomena and their spatial and temporal order in terms of constancies and variations. Sociology was meant to be the culminating science, which would compare cultures as to their different stages of social evolution. Conventionally, however, Emile Durkheim (1858-1917) is credited with initiating a continuous tradition of sociology. He held that social facts are independent of and exterior to individual consciousness. Hence the 'collective representations' of a given society have an existence of their own. Although they may have emerged from the association of individuals their properties are different from those of individual representations, for which they are a kind of constraint (Durkheim, 1898). While the autonomy of the social from the individual made Durkheim ask for a 'collective psychology' independent of individual psychology, most of the early conceptions of a social psychology around the turn of century were fashioned after the model of a psychology of the individual. Only very much later did the French social psychologist Moscovici (1961) take up and revise Durkheim's theory of collective representations (see Farr and Moscovici, 1984).

Finally, towards the end of the long past there is the impact of the *Theory of evolution*, one of the most powerful, popular, yet controversial intellectual innovations of the nineteenth century. Psychology has been much influenced

by its major protagonist, Charles Darwin (1809–82), as well as by his followers
Darwin's antedated contribution to a social psychology is mainly to be found in
The Descent of Man of 1871 and its sibling volume on *The Expression of the
Emotions in Man and Animals* (1872, 1896). Man is a social animal that has
developed the capacity to adapt physically, socially and mentally to a changing
environment, part of which is social as for example the tribe or group. Hence,
the expression of emotions has its social function in inter- and intraspecies communication. The British philosopher and (early) sociologist Herbert Spencer
(1820–1903) generalized and popularized evolutionary theory, mainly in the
social domain. But since he combined evolutionary theory with the doctrine of
individualism and a *laissez-faire* attitude (let evolution take its course), histo-
rians of social psychology like Karpf (1932) and Hearnshaw (1964) have argued
that Spencer did little to foster a social psychology. Even Darwin's own share in
the establishment of social psychology for a long time went unnoticed (cf. Farr,
1980b) while his direct ancestry has been claimed both by human ethologists
accounting for social behaviour (see Hinde, 1974; and chapter 2) and by socio-
biologists (Wilson, 1975).

The Beginnings of Modern Social Psychology

So far, when we have spoken of social psychology's past it has been to
underline that the positions, briefly discussed, were not social psychologies in
the modern sense of the word. But we saw that some of the doctrines that we
referred to have led to present theorizing. When in this section we do not yet
speak of modern social psychology, but only of its beginning, the reason for
this distinction must be seen in the fact that the research programmes to be
discussed had been given up or given away before the institutionalization of
social psychology was brought about. But they were no longer social
philosophies.

We shall consider only two major approaches toward social psychology:

1   The Völkerpsychologie of Moritz Lazarus (1824–1903), Hermann Steinthal
    (1823–99) and Wilhelm Wundt (1832–1920)
2   The crowd psychology of late-nineteenth-century Italian and French writers
    like Tarde (1843–1904) and LeBon (1841–1931).

Völkerpsychologie

There is no hope of adequately translating this term into English (see Danziger,
1983). Literally, it is a psychology of peoples; in fact, it is a comparative and
historical social and cultural psychology which, in a European textbook, can be
left as the German **Völkerpsychologie**. Instead of a series of definitions, an
outline will be given of its basic rationale.

If, in agreement with Kárpf (1932), we may rightly speak of the 'European background' of social psychology, it is inevitable to consider national traditions of social thought, as for example in Germany, France and England. Völkerpsychologie, then, is the manifestation and prototype of German social-psychological thought, prepared in the eighteenth, elaborated in the nineteenth and brought to an end in the twentieth century. Reference to Germany emphasizes a particular national, i.e. political, social and cultural development as the changing context of social and individual mind. In this tradition the key assumption was that the primary form of human association is the cultural community (*Gemeinschaft*), the *Volk*, in which the formation and education (*Bildung*) of the individual personality takes place. For philosophers and scholars like Herder, Hegel and Wilhelm von Humboldt, language was the medium in which the community shapes its individual members; these, in turn, actively contribute to their language which is to be understood as a social product (Markova, 1983). While today the abstract 'society' is considered to be the social context of experience, action and interaction, in the eighteenth and nineteenth centuries for German scholars it was the national and cultural community of the *Volk*, whose mind or spirit (*Volksgeist*) was taken to be the unifying mental principle or idea.

Both *Volk* and *Volksgeist* became topics of the new discipline when it was institutionalized by and in a professional journal, the *Zeitschrift für Völkerpsychologie und Sprachwissenschaft* in 1860 by M. Lazarus and H. Steinthal. From the beginning there was no doubt that the new discipline was closely connected with and also meant to contribute to the political efforts towards a German nation-state (Eckhardt, 1971a). Many enduring questions in social psychology were raised, but because the framework was national rather than social the questions were different from those of French crowd psychology (see below).

Wilhelm Wundt took up Völkerpsychologie as the equivalent and complement to experimental individual psychology as early as 1863, and with modifications, revocations and confirmations held on to this field until the year of his death in 1920 (Wundt, 1900–20, 1921). Although he was a major critic of Lazarus's and Steinthal's conception, it is possible to outline some common problems that were (or should have been) carried over to modern social psychology. The central question is obviously the nature of the individual–community relationship, which implies a host of theoretical, conceptual and methodological issues. However, there were no doubts about the intrinsically social nature of the individual; a purely individual and therefore experimental psychology is half a psychology.

An equally secular question is whether social psychology, in order to be truly social, must not be a historical discipline, as has recently been postulated again by Gergen (1973, 1985). At least, Völkerpsychologie was a comparative historical study of the objective products of social (or collective) interaction, such as language, myth and custom; it was a cultural-social psychology, in which the study of language had a central place. Except for the most elementary processes, no human experience or activity can (and should) be separated from its socio-cultural context, disregarding the evolutionary history of thought in language. Another feature of Völkerpsychologie that we hardly find in modern social psychology is the interest in the relationship between individuals as they act and interact and the products of their (inter)action – products that, in turn, affect and enrich the individual members' minds. They 'give rise in the individuals to novel accomplishments specific to community life' (Wundt, 1921, vol. I, pp. 20–1).

In a strictly presentist view it is easy to find fault with Völkerpsychologie for its deficiency in empirical methodology and research. But if we try an imaginary inversion of perspective and look at the field of present-day social psychology from Wundt's viewpoint, we may also recognize the degree to which the cultural scope of the field has shrunk while it has methodologically improved (see Jaspars, 1983, 1986). In retrospect one gets the impression that perhaps not the whole idea but many of the major topics of Völkerpsychologie were handed over to neighbouring disciplines, mainly to anthropology and sociology, only to be rediscovered quite recently by European social psychologists. Jaspars (1986, p. 12) even presumed 'a return to the earliest scientific attempt to study social behaviour as advocated by Lazarus and Steinthal'.

Crowd psychology

The intellectual and scientific background of **crowd psychology** is complex. There are, on the one hand, the many techniques and conceptions of **suggestion**, such as the tradition (art, technique, doctrine and cult) of hypnotism, i.e. the induction of a sleep-like condition that subjects its target person, with certain limitations, to the suggestions of the hypnotist. Anton Mesmer (1734–1815), who could put people into a trance, had claimed to control a universal animal force ('magnetism') that would strengthen and enhance life and health. Hypnotic suggestion, as it was called later, was meant to lower a patient's level of consciousness, thus rendering her or his mind more 'primitive'. This technique figured as diagnostic and therapy respectively in the famous controversy between the rivalling French medical schools of Nancy and of the Salpétrière in Paris. But it also became one of the most important models of social influence and was appropriated by early crowd psychologists to account for the alleged irrationality, emotionality and 'primitivism' of the crowds (see Barrows, 1981; Paicheler, 1985).

The other medical model, even more 'pathological' in origin and kind, was taken from epidemiology. In parallel with bacteriological contagion, which had recently become a scientific fact through the research of 'microbe hunters' like Louis Pasteur (1822–95) and Robert Koch (1843–1910), **mental contagion** was considered to be possible and to account for the spread of affect and 'anomie' in mob-like or otherwise agitated crowds.[2] Mental contagion, a key term in LeBon's influential *Crowd Psychology* (LeBon, 1895) though not his own (see Nye, 1975), was later interpreted in terms of 'circular reaction' (Allport, 1924) and 'interstimulation' (Blumer, 1946). It thus theoretically lost its 'infectious disease' character, but the term 'contagion' and its connotative meaning have survived (see Milgram and Toch, 1969). The 'medical' distortions of the image of the crowd in nineteenth-century thought have been excellently documented by Barrows (1981; see also chapter 16).

The second scientific root of crowd psychology was criminology. What was a subconscious and affective state of mind from a medical viewpoint, in the juridical perspective became the *diminished responsibility* of the individual submerged in the crowd or even of the 'delinquent crowd' (Sighele, 1891; Tarde, 1895). The basic assumption of this medico-legal approach is again that in the crowd the individual becomes more primitive, more infantile than when alone, and hence less intelligent, less guided by reason and therefore less responsible. While all these ideas had been pronounced in a series of Italian and French publications before 1895, LeBon popularized them in his best seller without giving credit to the original authors. And it was to LeBon that later students of crowd mind and behaviour referred as the master of crowd psychology (e.g. Freud, 1953; critically Nye, 1975; Moscovici, 1981b).

If we take both sources, the medical and the criminological, together this 'Latin' conception of the crowd is one of non-normalcy, associated with either disease or crime, at best allowing for mitigating circumstances. In order to understand why collective behaviour and its mental correlates were regarded as anomalous or 'anomic', it is necessary to look at the social and political context in which such conceptions developed; this is evident from the texts on the psychology of the crowd. The succession of revolutions (1789, 1830, 1848, 1871 in France); the radical economic and social changes due to rapid industrialization and urbanization; the rise and 'revolt of the masses'; the growing strength of the labour unions and of socialism, with strikes and May demonstrations; the corruption and scandals; the military defeat of France by Prussia in 1871, and the revolutionary Paris Commune and its bloody suppression in the same year; all this taken together became a threat to the established political, social and moral order and mainly to the bourgeoisie. As Barrows (1981) has convincingly argued, there was a general feeling of *décadence* and decline to be accounted for. The masses were 'discovered' (Moscovici, 1981b) and feared as the causes of the general malaise, and science was required to analyse in detail the causal relationship between mass phenomena and the social evils. A criminological as well as a psychiatric or epidemiological 'explanation' suited the prevailing *Zeitgeist*. In spite of the controversial notions of the 'mental unit of the crowd' (LeBon, 1895) and of an entity-like 'crowd mind', which both carried well into the twentieth century (e.g. McDougall, 1920), it is important to see that a major concern of the Latin crowd psychology was the fate of the 'normal' individual who became somehow 'abnormal' under the social condition of the crowd. Whereas LeBon treated of mobs and juries, of mass demonstrations and parliaments, of criminal as well as religious aggregations, all under the category of 'crowds', today we give crowds, social movements, audiences and institutions different treatments (e.g. Milgram and Toch, 1969). One important distinction, however, had already been made by Tarde (1901) and Park (1972), namely that between the crowd and the public. While the former implies physical contact and spatial limitation, the latter, mainly owing to the modern media of communication (the press), transcends spatial contiguity and spreads as 'public opinion'.

Like Völkerpsychologie, crowd psychology did not develop within the context of academic psychology after McDougall (1920) had once more invoked the 'group mind'. But, unlike the former, some of the major topics of crowd psychology were incorporated into the new social psychology after they had been individualized, and thereby become accessible for experimental analysis. Under the topic of social influence we recognize this continuity of what once was understood as effects of suggestion, contagion and imitation (see Moscovici, 1985b; Paicheler, 1985). But only recently the key problems of crowd mind and behaviour were given a fresh look and reinterpretation by Moscovici and others (Moscovici, 1981b; see Graumann and Moscovici, 1986).

Modern Social Psychology

Social psychology as we know it today may be dated from around the turn of the century. American textbook authors prefer to fix the dates for the beginning at 1898 for the first experiment in social psychology and at 1908 for its first two textbooks. As a matter of fact, both 'firsts' are wrong; nor does it make sense to replace them by others 'firsts'. In the late eighteenth century there was not only Völkerpsychologie and crowd psychology. There was also the term 'social psychology', applied to existing and mainly designed studies dealing with the individual in society, or a 'psychology of society' (Lindner, 1871; see Lück, 1987). Yet from the very first programmes of a social psychology we find two different emphases which, in a nutshell, are as follows: (1) as social *psychology* the new discipline should deal with the individual and with intra-individual processes, as does all psychology (e.g. McDougall, 1908; Simmel, 1908); (2) as *social* psychology it should focus on the role of the social (structural) context for individual processes (e.g. Lindner, 1871; Durkheim, see Lukes, 1973b; Ross, 1908). Although the much-cited books of 1908 were not the first textbooks in social psychology, they may well represent the two different emphases. McDougall's *Introduction to Social Psychology* was a (theoretical) book on 'the native propensities and capacities of the individual human mind' (1908, p. 18), i.e. an individualistic approach to social psychology by means of an instinct theory; in modern terms, a theory of motivation (see Farr, 1986). Ross, the sociologist, in *Social Psychology* dealt with the 'planes and currents that come into existence among men in consequence of their association' (1908, p. 1). His topic was the uniformities resulting from social influence due to interaction, partly in the tradition of crowd psychology, mainly a 'heartfelt homage to the genius of Gabriel Tarde' (p. viii). In his reflection on the history of social psychology, Pepitone (1981, p. 974) is right when he states that 'collective social psychology of the sort presented by Ross remained for the most part in sociology', whereas for psychology 'the individual was the only reality' and, hence, for a social psychology developing from it.

Social psychology in America

We have seen that social-psychological individualism had its roots in certain social philosophies. But with the establishment of a (psychological) discipline of social psychology this individualism acquired a methodological note. It may be that the 'emergence of social psychology as a distinctive field of empirical research . . . can be viewed . . . as a generational revolt against the armchair methods of social philosophy' (Cartwright, 1979, p. 83). But it definitely happened that, in the view and work of one of the first modern American social psychologists, F.H. Allport (1924), the individualist conception coincided and coalesced with a methodological orientation, the experimental-behavioural approach. For Allport, the first social psychologist in the behaviourist tradition, social psychology became 'the science which studies the behavior of the individual in so far as his behavior stimulates other individuals, or is itself a reaction to this behavior' (1924, p. 12). Yet while the 'behaviour viewpoint' was only a way of conceiving facts, it is the experimental method that yields them (p. vi). The combination of individualistic approach, 'behaviour viewpoint', and experimental method was meant to make social psychology a scientifically respectable discipline; this effort, according to Cartwright (1979, p. 84), took social psychology the first three or four decades of its existence. While the greater part of this process took place in America and may historically be traced back to the model of F. H. Allport's early experiments on social facilitation (see chapter 14), one should note that Allport (1924) himself leaned heavily on the experimental work of several of Wundt's students (see Graumann, 1986). In this connection, Pepitone (1981, p. 975) speaks of 'the German roots of the experimental tradition in social psychology'. 'European roots' would have been even more precise, since there was not only the overly (and erroneously) cited example of Triplett, who in 1898 reported an experiment on the impact of co-acting others on an individual's working speed and quality (later to become known as 'social facilitation'). As Haines and Vaughan (1979) have shown, there were other experiments before 1898 deserving to be called social psychological, mainly in the context of Binet's and Henri's studies of *suggestibility* (e.g. Binet and Henri, 1894), a topic that had been taken over from the hypnosis tradition discussed earlier.[3] Historically, however, it is less interesting to find the truly first experiment (an arbitrary decision) than to observe that social psychologists are still trying to identify their history with the experimental rather than any other method: a telling example of the identificatory function of historiography (see earlier in this chapter).

In spite of the European roots of experimentalism, it happened mainly in the social and scientific climate of the United States after the First World War that social psychology more than elsewhere became a 'science of the individual' (Allport, 1924, p. 4). The implication of this limitation was that social psychology became largely removed from the study of social issues (Katz, 1978, p. 780). It has, at least in its research practice, isolated its subjects from their social context; until in economic and political crises, such as the Great

Depression and the Second World War, 'the urgency of social problems overwhelmed the purists in their laboratories' (1978, p. 781), as we shall see below.

The major achievement in the 1930s and 1940s was the study and, mainly, the measurement of attitudes (see chapter 7), a preoccupation which was followed in the 1950s, and 1960s by a focus on conceptions of attitude change (see chapter 8). For the historian the many techniques of attitude measurement that have been developed since the mid 1920s are less interesting than the growing certainty, reconfirmed by each new technique, that 'attitudes can be measured' (Thurstone, 1928) and by their measurability, together with a growing sophistication of the experimental method, can enhance the scientific status of social psychology. Today the preference for experimental over field designs and for measurement over observation has been institutionalized in curricula and in criteria for the publication of research papers. In addition, fund-raising and grant-getting depend to no small degree on the level of methodological sophistication. But also what has been called the 'crisis' of social psychology in the 1970s, in which the social meaningfulness and relevance of its major research work was questioned from many angles, was largely attributed to the sovereignty of methods over problems (see Buss, 1979; Israel and Tajfel, 1972).

Historically, there have been deviations from this methodological mainstream whenever pressing social and political problems demanded the cooperation and commitment of social psychologists. This was the case when during the 1930s the Society for the Psychological Study of Social Issues was founded. It happened again when in the 1940s under the impression of Nazi and Fascist domination and terror social psychologists in the free countries not only tried to help win the war, but planned for a better world of democratic societies. One of them was Kurt Lewin (1890–1947), a Jewish refugee from Berlin, a member of the Gestalt group that was to influence social psychology in various direct and indirect ways.

Lewin, fully aware of what happened in Germany and then in Europe, had become a social psychologist when he applied his *field theory* to groups (Lewin, 1948, 1951). Less a theory than a general methodology, this approach focused on the principle of interdependence, emphasizing the primacy of the whole (situation or field) over the parts, and made use of constructive rather than classificatory methods. This broad methodology permitted Lewin and his students to do experiments with groups (as prototypes of 'fields of forces'), but also to work with groups in everyday community life in order to change their conduct, morale, prejudice, style of leadership etc. – an approach that became known as *action research*. The list of his associates and students from his years at the University of Iowa's Child Welfare Research Station (1935–44) to his own foundation, the Research Center for Group Dynamics (then at MIT, now in Ann Arbor), is probably the most impressive and influential ever associated with one individual scholar after Wundt (see Marrrow, 1969; Festinger, 1980). Although Lewin died in 1947 it was largely Lewinians, like Cartwright, Deutsch, Festinger, French, Kelley, Schachter and Thibaut, who shaped social psychology in America after the Second World War and, consequently, in Europe. Marx and Hillix (1979, p. 322) even conclude 'that it is hardly hyperbole to describe American social psychology as a Lewinian development'. If one adds those Americans who came to be influenced by the other emigrants, it is no exaggeration to summarize as did Cartwright (1979, p. 85): 'One can hardly imagine what the field would be like today if such people as Lewin, Heider, Köhler, Wertheimer, Katona, Lazarsfeld, and the Brunswiks had not come to the United States when they did.' It is important to remember this forced transfer of men and ideas from Europe to America if in American texts one repeatedly reads that social psychology has become 'primarily an American product' (p. 85) or 'largely a North American phenomenon' (Jones, 1985, p. 47). The truth in such statements is that after the arrival of the emigrants many ideas had to be and indeed were transformed in a process of adaptation to the new social and scientific context (see Ash, 1985; Graumann, 1976). It is equally true that Hitler had emptied most of Europe of whoever and whatever there was in social psychology. Into this vacuum poured 'American psychology' in the years after 1945; it was not the emigrants returning.

What actually happened in the decades after the Second World War in America and secondarily in Europe was, besides the ongoing methodological refinement, two theoretical changes: *from the behavioural to the cognitive viewpoint* and *from broader to more narrow theory ranges*. Both developments are not restricted to social psychology but apply to psychology in general. While the behavioural approach may be broadly characterized as a mainly American development (which owes key concepts to Pavlovian psychology), it has often been stated that the change or shift to a cognitive approach was brought about, at least facilitated, by the appearance of Gestalt psychology in America. It is a historical fact that the first survey on cognitive theory in a *Handbook of Social Psychology* (Scheerer, 1954) was, in effect, on Gestalt psychology. The situation had changed drastically when, fourteen years later, Zajonc (1968b, p. 391) succeeded Scheerer in the *Handbook*, noting 'with amazement how little in common we have with the previous generation of social psychologists'. Cognitive processes were now understood mainly as the 'underlying dynamics of social behavior' (p. 391). In the meantime, the situation has changed again: cognition has now come to mean the processing of information (for the change of meaning of (social) cognition see Graumann, 1987b; Graumann and Sommer, 1984). Today it is less the (observable) social behaviour that is of interest than its cognitive representation, preceding (e.g. planning), accompanying (e.g. monitoring) and following (e.g. remembering) the behaviour (see chapters 5, 6, 7).

Together with the gradual transformation of the usage of social cognition we witness a proliferation and diminution of social psychological theories. For the historian of psychology a pattern seems to recur. Just as in the heyday of behaviourism the kinds of learning proliferated, it is now the concept of cognition that seems to spawn into many mini-theories which, simultaneously, tend to spread over the whole field of social psychology.

Social psychology in Europe

The situation of social psychology in postwar Europe can hardly be understood without the dialectics of the transatlantic interchange. There is, on the one hand, the American 'naturalization'. For psychology as a whole, Koch (1985, p. 25) made a convincing case that whatever the European contribution may have been historically – British post-Darwinian comparative psychology, Russia's Pavlovian conceptions, the Gestalt emigration, the discovery of Piaget, 'even' phenomenology and, of course, the neo-positivists' philosophy of the Vienna circle – it was all eagerly received, digested and transformed into something American, partly blended with the indigenous behaviourism and thoroughly individualistic. The vigour with which this was done had been made possible by an early and massive institutionalization. Koch, as others before him, is convinced that a cultural atmosphere favouring pragmatism and experimentalism in all walks of life facilitated the rise of psychology as a new science 'that seemed to promise prediction and control of human affairs' (Koch, 1985, p. 22). 'Naturalized' and institutionally strengthened psychology in the United States soon outnumbered and outweighed efforts in other countries. Psychology became an export commodity wherever there was demand, and demand was greatest in postwar Europe although in nationally different degrees and for different reasons. What was later critically called the 'Americanization' of European (e.g. German) psychology (see Cartwright, 1979, p. 85) was originally the much-needed and gratefully received reconstruction and reinternationalization of science with American aid. To the degree, however, that ideas, problems and their solutions were received and communicated in an uncritical attitude, the term 'Americanization' was justified. What was the situation of social psychology in Europe before the war? Without proper institutionalization there were only individual scholars with some interest in social psychology. For example, in England there was Bartlett, whose major work on *Remembering* (1932) has only recently gained interest among cognitive social psychologists. In Switzerland there was Piaget, who in his many volumes on child development also contributed to our present conception of socialization (see chapter 3), mainly by his focus on moral development (Piaget, 1932). In Germany there was Moede, whose early experimental group psychology (Moede, 1920) had already impressed Floyd Allport (1924), and there was Hellpach, the founder of the (short-lived) first Institute for Social Psychology in 1921 and the author of the first systematic German textbook of social psychology (Hellpach, 1933). Yet none of these or other European scholars was founder or mediator of a social-psychological tradition; nor did they form a scientific community of social psychologists. After 1933 Hitler contributed to their separation.

Such was the situation in Europe after 1945. Even after the first centres of social psychology had been established with American help, their members were 'unaware of each other's existence'; 'the lines of communication ran mainly between each centre and the United States', as the first editorial of the

European Journal of Social Psychology states in 1971. It was this isolation that then became one of the motives for a European association of social psychologists, to be founded in the 1960s. For the intellectual history, however, there was a deeper motivation, namely the awareness (of some psychologists) of the growing dependency on the American hegemony in defining the field, the theories, the methods and even the 'crisis' of social psychology.

Among the first to articulate this uneasiness and to search for the identity of social psychology in Europe were Tajfel and Moscovici who, each in his own way, pleaded for a more social social psychology than the one established and developed in America. Critics of the latter have repeatedly maintained that it is wedded to the 'cultural ethos' of 'self-contained individualism' (Sampson, 1977, p. 769). In contrast, Tajfel and his students have emphasized the *social dimension* (Tajfel, 1981, 1984) of individual and group behaviour, i.e. the degree to which our experience and behaviour is embedded in and shaped by the properties of the culture and society we live in. Society, however, 'has its own structure which is not definable in terms of the characteristics of individuals' (Moscovici, 1972, p. 54). Therefore, 'social psychology *can* and *must* include in its theoretical and research preoccupations a direct concern with the relationship between human psychological functioning and the large-scale social processes and events which shape this functioning and are shaped by it' (Tajfel, 1981, p. 7). It may be the diversity of social and cultural backgrounds characteristic of Europe that suggests this greater concern for the social context of both social behaviour and its psychological investigation. The concern for social context is evident, for example, from Tajfel's own studies of stereotypes, prejudice and intergroup behaviour, and from Moscovici's work on social influence, minorities and social representations (see also Israel and Tajfel, 1972; Jaspars, 1986). However, it also belongs to the picture of diversity that many centres of social-psychological research in Europe have not been affected by the European quest for identity, are still 'following at a distance and with due delays the successive ebbs and flows of the mainstream of American social psychology' (Tajfel, 1981, p. 6), and are not noticeably different in their theorizing and research from that of any centre in North America. But whether there is an overall change in orientation in Europe's social psychology or whether it is restricted to some of its prominent protagonists, as Jaspars (1986, p. 12) wonders, the least one can say about the 'Europeanization' of social psychology is that it has succeeded in generating a more frequent and lively interaction among psychologists. The most important forum is the European Association of Experimental Social Psychology, represented in Western and Eastern Europe, and the meetings, the journal and the monographs sponsored by it.[4] Other positive symptoms are the first European textbooks of social psychology, with contributors from several European countries and from North America (Moscovici, 1973, 1984; Tajfel and Fraser, 1978).

It may be an open question whether social psychology's 'coming of age' will be brought about by 'bringing society into the laboratory' (Jaspars, 1980, p. 426) or by venturing into the field of social forces outside the laboratory. Yet since social psychology, as we have tried to show, started off with a much wider scope and agenda but 'narrowed down its task to gain scientific acceptance by employing experimental methods' (Jaspars, 1986, p. 13), it might now gain acceptance as a *social* science by readdressing real social issues.

Notes

1   While this interest in the past for the sake of the present has been called the 'presentist' orientation towards history, there is also a purely historical interest in the past for its own sake, e.g. to find out what the problems of a former period were and which methods of solution were then known and used; this is the 'historicist' attitude (Butterfield, 1963).
2   'Anomie' is Durkheim's term for a state in which dominant social norms are questioned, ignored or repudiated.
3   Haines and Vaughan (1979, p. 332) even wonder 'whether this experient in any way inspired Solomon Asch's famous studies of conformity' (see chapter 15).
4   Another facility is the Laboratoire Européen de Psychologie Sociale at the Maison des Sciences de l'Homme in Paris.

Glossary Terms

Crowd psychology	Positivism
Group mind	Socio-centred approach
Hedonism	Sociology
Individualism	Suggestion
Individuo-centred approach	Utilitarianism
Mental contagion	Völkerpsychologie

Further Reading

There is no history of social psychology in print that is comprehensive, up to date and critically written. The following are second choices.

Allport, G. W. (1968) The historical background of modern social psychology. In G. Lindzey and E. Aronson (eds), *Handbook of Social Psychology* (vol. 1), 2nd edn, Reading, Mass.: Addison-Wesley, 1–80. This chapter appeared in the first edition of the *Handbook* in 1954 and still, though abridged, in the third edition of 1985. In spite of errors and other shortcomings it is the most frequently cited source for the history of social psychology. It sketches the European background of modern American social psychology.

Festinger, L. (ed.) (1980) *Retrospections on Social Psychology*. New York: Oxford University Press. Written by three academic generations of the Research Center for Group Dynamics, founded by Kurt Lewin, this is a very personal and historically limited but highly readable retrospective by some of the leading American figures of modern social psychology.

Jones, E. E. (1985) Major developments in social psychology during the past four decades. In G. Lindzey and E. Aronson (eds), *Handbook of Social Psychology* (vol. 1), 3rd edn, New York: Random House, 47–107. As a necessary addendum to the Allport chapter given above, the article surveys the recent development of social psychology in North America. References to research in Europe are arbitrary and rare.

Karpf, F. B. (1932) *American Social Psychology: its origins, development, and European background*. New York: Macmillan. The most comprehensive and erudite history of the European past of modern social psychology. Recommended to readers with a historical interest. An updating for the period till 1951 was published in 1952 as: American social psychology – 1951. *American Journal of Sociology*, 2, 187–93.

Sahakian, W. S. (1982) *History and Systems of Social Psychology*. 2nd edn Washington: Hemisphere. The only comprehensive history of social psychology in print that reviews not only the mainstream but also the psychoanalytical approach, social ethology and sociobiology. Its historiographical value is greatly diminished by errors and over-simplifications.

2 Ethology and Social Psychology

ROBERT A. HINDE

Introduction

Ethology has been concerned primarily with the behaviour of animals. Such a discipline is, of course, of only limited relevance to the problems posed by human social behaviour. The uniquely human attribute of a spoken language is associated with behaviour of a different order of complexity from that found in animals. In non-human species tradition is of limited importance and institutions non-existent. Nevertheless, in spite of its limitations, the ethological approach to the study of animal behaviour can make some significant contribuions to the understanding of human social behaviour.

Occasionally, such contributions come from direct comparisons between animal and human data. For instance, studies of non-verbal communication in animals have facilitated the understanding of human expressive movements, and physiological studies of the effects of crowding in rats have pointed the way for studies of our own species. But direct comparisons tend to oversimplify the human case. Thus many human non-verbal signals are culture specific or idiosyncratic (Eibl-Eibesfeldt, 1972; Ekman and Friesen, 1969), and the impact of crowding may depend on the subject's ability to make sense of the situation (Chandler, 1985). Furthermore the diversity of animal species and the diversity of human cultures make it only too easy to select cases for comparison that will support any thesis.

Nor is the contribution of ethology to be found in some overarching theory which encompasses the behaviour of all species, including our own. Although the theory of evolution by natural selection is crucial for some questions, ethology has otherwise been restrained in its use of theory. However, ethology is characterized by certain orienting attitudes that could be useful to the social psychologist. Furthermore the *relative* simplicity of the animal case can highlight principles applicable also to our own species, though they are less easily perceived there (or less often stated overtly) because of the complexity. Thus this chapter focuses on the extent to which principles drawn from ethology can be helpful in understanding the human case.

The Orienting Attitudes of Ethology

In part, the strengths of ethology come from its biological heritage. In studying the behaviour of our own species, therefore, ethologists are naturally more interested in its biological bases than are many psychologists. More importantly, however, their orienting attitudes differ markedly from those of many psychologists and especially from those of the experimental psychologists of a few decades ago. Whilst the latter were trying to build a science whose structure would emulate that of classical physics, ethologists pursued a different track. Four issues important in the present context may be mentioned:

1 Behaviour must be described before it can be analysed. Modern biology depends upon the work of generations of taxonomists and systematists who described and classified living organisms, and ethologists likewise emphasize the importance of an initial descriptive phase – not as an end in itself, but as providing a base from which analysis can begin. That task is not always so straightforward as it might seem.
2 Full understanding of social phenomena requires study at more than one level of social complexity. Whilst the scientific method depends upon analysis, this analysis must be accompanied by resynthesis, so that the investigator does not lose touch with the whole. Furthermore there is a continuing **dialectic** between parts and whole: parts contribute to the functioning of the whole, the whole controls the functioning of the parts.
3 Their biological training leads ethologists to treat the four questions of the causation, development, function and evolution of behaviour as equally important, independent, yet interrelated (Tinbergen, 1963). Thus ethologists would stress the importance not only of documenting the existence of racial prejudice or sex stereotypes, and of understanding their development and the conditions that exacerbate or ameliorate them, but also of understanding in evolutionary terms why it is that individuals are prone to hold such views. Indeed ethologists would argue that an understanding of the functions which human propensities had in the social environment in which our species evolved can aid understanding of their dynamics in modern man.
4 Rather than seeking for principles of universal validity, ethologists have sought for concepts and generalizations with a limited range of validity, coupling their generalizations with statements about the limitations of their generality.

These orienting attitudes of ethology will appear throughout the following pages, but we shall start by considering why the description of social behaviour poses special problems and is of particular importance.

Description: Two Routes in the Analysis of Behavioural Data

Social behaviour implies a social context: what the individual does depends in part on that context. Often the data of the social psychologist concern interactions between two (or more) participants: what happens depends on both. Neglect of this fact can cause errors of interpretation. For instance, how quickly a mother goes to a crying baby is not solely a reflection of her maternal responsiveness, but depends on how often the baby has already cried that night. And how often the baby cries depends in part on how quickly the mother goes to it.

Given basic data on interactions, analysis can proceed in two directions. Suppose, for instance, we study mother–child interactions in a number of families. If we wish to make generalizations about a particular type of interaction – for instance about how mothers play with or control their children – we may pool data on that type of interaction from all the families we study. We would then be in a position to assess, for example, how mother–child play changes with age of child, or how techniques of maternal control are related to socio-economic status. A second course involves focusing on individual relationships, for instance by examining the relations between maternal control, maternal warmth and child compliance in each family. This puts us in a position to tackle questions of the type: 'Are children more likely to do what they are told if maternal control is associated with maternal warmth?' This course is more rarely pursued, in part because it requires simultaneous assessment of more than one dimension. Yet if individuals behave differently according to whom they are with, and if (as we shall see to be the case) interactions of different types within the same relationship affect each other, for many purposes this must be the course to pursue. Attempts to understand the dynamics of monkey societies made only limited progress as long as investigators assessed the incidence with which individuals fought, groomed, copulated etc. independently of the partner: a change came when relationships (or types of relationship) were studied separately (chapters in Hinde, 1983). And of course some studies of human behaviour do follow this route: for instance, distinctions between authoritarian, authoritative and permissive parent–child relationships depend on assessments of several types of interaction concerned with parental control and acceptance (Baumrind, 1967; Maccoby and Martin, 1983).

This approach leads us to distinguish a series of levels of social complexity: *interactions*; (dyadic) *relationships*, involving a succession of interactions over time between two individuals known to each other, such that each interaction may influence subsequent ones; and *social groups* (of three or more). At each level, a choice between two routes for analysis is open. By analogy with the interaction level, at the relationship level we can either make generalizations about particular types of relationships (e.g. mother–child relationships) across groups (or in this case families), or see how the relationships within each family affect each other. In the latter case we seek generalizations about how relationships of one type influence others – for instance on how the quality of marriage affects the mother–child relationship (Hinde and Stevenson-Hinde, 1987; 1988).

If we consider only behaviour, then interactions can be described in terms of the content and quality of the behaviour shown, relationships in terms of the content, quality and patterning of the component interactions, and group structure in terms of the nature and patterning of the component relationships. Each level has properties that are not relevant to the level below: for instance, an individual can talk but he or she can converse only in an interaction; properties of relationships that depend on the patterning of interactions over time are not relevant to isolated interactions; and groups but not a particular relationship can be organized linearly or hierarchically, involve a number of individuals independent of each other but all linked to a central focus, and so on.

Whilst these considerations, derived from studies of non-verbal species, apply also to humans, they form only part of the picture. For instance, human relationships continue in the absence of interactions, and include not only what the participants do together, but also the perceptions, fears, expectations and so on that each has about the other and about the future course of the relationship. And human relationships are influenced by the beliefs, values and norms of the society in which they are embedded.

Each of these levels requires study in its own right. This must involve a descriptive base, and a set of principles concerned with the patterning at that level. As an example, we may consider interpersonal relationships. No satisfactory system for describing interpersonal relationships as yet exists, but as a first step the aspects of a relationship likely to be important for its dynamics can be categorized as follows (Hinde, 1979):

1 The content of the interactions – what the participants do together
2 The diversity of the things that they do together
3 The qualities of their interactions
4 Properties arising from the relative frequencies and patterning over time of the interactions within the relationship
5 The patterning of reciprocity and complementarity in the interactions within the relationship, including its power structure
6 The degree of intimacy between the participants
7 Their interpersonal perceptions
8 Their degree of commitment to the relationship.

Such categories are applicable to a wide range of relationships – personal and institutional, cooperative and competitive, close and distant – although much refining of the descriptive tools available is still required (Hinde, 1979). Another approach to the description of relationships, focusing more on the details of interaction patterns, is provided by Kelley et al. (1983).

A descriptive base is important because the explanatory principles concerned with the patterning of interactions are not universally applicable. To take one example, balance theory (see chapter 5) would predict that Jack would be more prone to like Joe if Jack liked jazz and Jack perceived Joe also to like jazz. If Jack perceived Joe not to like jazz he might decide he did not care about it all that much himself, or else that Joe did like jazz, 'really'. However, if Jack likes Jill he is not more likely to like Joe if he perceives that Joe likes Jill. Balance theory, though providing useful generalizations, has exceptions (Newcomb, 1971). A descriptive base is necessary in order to specify these exceptions.

Another approach to the study of relationships, stemming from a different tradition, is provided by Argyle in chapter 10.

The Dialectics between Successive Levels of Social Complexity

Just as the physiological (or quasi-physiological) data yielded by the analysis of individual behaviour must be resynthesized before full understanding of the latter can be achieved, so must the relations between the interactions, between the relationships or between the social groups yielded by the analysis of social phenomena be assessed. Indeed, phenomena at each level of social complexity influence and are influenced by phenomena at other levels (figure 2.1); their understanding thus requires us to come to terms with a series of dialectics or two-way interactions between levels.

For instance, whilst the nature of interactions depends on both individuals involved, the behaviour each shows depends in part on his or her feelings and expectations about the interaction or the relationship of which it forms part. Yet the nature of the relationship, and the participants' feelings and predictions about it, depend on the nature of the interactions. And in the longer run the behaviour individuals *can* show depends in part on the relationships they have experienced in the past. Thus we must come to terms with dialectics between the characteristics of individuals and interactions on the one hand, and between interactions and relationships on the other, with two-way cause–effect influences in each case.

However, that is not all. Each relationship is influenced by the social network of other relationships in which it is embedded, and conversely the

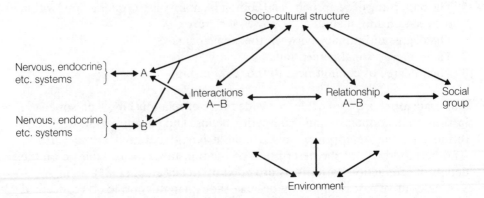

FIGURE 2.1   The dialectics between successive levels of social complexity

characteristics of the social group are determined by the dyadic and higher-order relationships within it. Relationships are affected also by the social norms current in the group: the dynamics of a marriage, for instance, are affected by the expectations and goals of the participants and by the relations between those expectations and perceived reality (Andreyeva and Gozman, 1981). Those norms and values are transmitted and changed through dyadic relationships. The *socio-cultural structure*, used here to refer to the system of institutions, values and beliefs, and the relations between them, shared by the members of the group, in turn both influences and is influenced by individuals, interactions, relationships and the social group. Beyond that, each *group* is juxtaposed with other groups, contact with which affects diverse aspects of the social behaviour of its individuals. Finally each group is set in a physical environment, which affects and is affected by the group members.

Social scientists must therefore come to terms with a series of dialectics between successive levels of social phenomena – interactions, relationships, social structure, socio-cultural structure and intergroup relationships. And at the same time they must remember that each level represents not an entity but a process in continuous creation (Hinde, 1984a).

Whilst some of the social sciences seem to be concerned with one or other of the levels, in practice the dialectics always obtrude. It is rarely possible to study one level in isolation. For example, at the individual level students of personality, finding that supposed traits tended to have low cross-situational consistency, were forced to recognize that behaviour may be affected (to differing extents according to the nature of the individual and the behaviour) by the context. And the most important aspect of the context is the interactional and relationship one, including the meanings that individuals attribute to their relationships according to their sociocultural schemes of reference, and their personal past experience (e.g. Bem and Funder, 1978; Endler and Hunt, 1968; Endler and Magnusson, 1976; Kenrick and Stringfield, 1980; Mischel, 1973).

Developmental psychologists, concerned first with the growing child, have had to come to terms with the interacting influences of parent on child and of child on parent (Bell and Harper, 1977), and to consider the relative importance of parent–child and peer relationships in the development of personality (e.g. Bowlby, 1969; Sullivan, 1938; Youniss, 1980b).

Cognitive psychologists find that how an individual tackles an intellectual problem may change radically with the social context (e.g. Carraher, Carraher and Schliemann, 1985; Doise and Mugny, 1984; Donaldson, 1978; Perret-Clermont and Brossard, 1985).

Amongst social psychologists, some theorists ('symbolic interactionists') describe individuals as having a number of 'role identities' which come into play in different relationships (Goffman, 1959; McCall, 1970, 1974), and other theorists emphasize that interactions within a relationship depend on the participants' perceptions of its past and their expectations about its future (Kelley, 1979).

Anthropologists, concerned with the sociocultural structure, seek to understand the ways in which beliefs, myths and legends affect the lives of individuals, and reciprocally how those beliefs reflect the natures, desires, wishes and frustrations of individuals (Herdt, 1981; Keesing, 1982). And they must also be concerned with the reciprocal influences of societies on each other and with the environment.

Many social scientists focus especially on influences passing from right to left in figure 2.1. Ethologists insist also on influences from left to right. Whilst acknowledging the ubiquitous importance of cultural forces, they emphasize also the role of human characteristics in shaping social phenomena. We shall return to this later.

The Four Whys

Perhaps the issue that has distinguished ethologists most clearly from other students of behaviour is their interest in questions other than causation and development. Thus consider the question: 'Why does your thumb move in a different way from the other fingers?' You could give an answer in terms of the skeleton and muscle insertions (*causation*), or in terms of the ontogeny of the finger rudiments (*development*), or you could say that an opposable thumb makes it easier to pick things up (*function*), or you could give an answer in terms of derivation from monkey-like ancestors (*evolution*). All of these answers would be correct; no one would be complete. In the same way all four types of question can be asked about social behaviour, and all can be revealing.

Because this chapter is concerned with the ethologists' contributions to the human social sciences, we shall concentrate on answers to these four questions which emphasize the interplay between biological and experiential (including cultural) factors. This is perhaps timely, because biological factors have been somewhat neglected by social scientists. Just because experiential factors can be studied and manipulated, social scientists have properly concentrated their attention upon them. But the consequences of changing an individual's experience depend on his or her nature, and thus ultimately in part on genetic factors.

It is important to be clear that this approach does not involve any sort of biological determinism. Every human characteristic of necessity depends on an interaction between characteristics of the individual and aspects of the environment. Furthermore we are mostly concerned not with fixed behavioural responses, but with behavioural propensities that may be expressed differently in different environments and may involve predispositions to learn one thing rather than another, or constraints on what may be learned (Seligman and Hager, 1972; Hinde and Stevenson-Hinde, 1973). An avian example may help here. Chaffinches normally develop a species-characteristic song. Chaffinches reared in isolation produce only a very simple song. However, if chaffinches are allowed to hear another chaffinch singing, even if they hear it before they themselves start to sing, they will produce normal song. But they will not imitate *any* sound that they hear – only songs with a note structure resembling that of chaffinch song. In other species, the constraints are different. For instance, bullfinches are predisposed to imitate the song of the male that reared them, but not that of other males (Thorpe, 1961). Comparable biases in what is learned are widespread in many species, including our own.

Nor does the focus of this chapter on biological factors imply that they are considered more important than cultural ones. Often questions about the relative importance of biological and cultural factors are not sensible questions; sometimes, questions about the nature of differences between societies constituted of genetically similar individuals *require* an answer in terms of cultural factors; but always the range of cultural diversity must be constrained by the genetic endowment of human beings.

It will be convenient to consider first questions of function and evolution.

Function and evolution: pan-cultural characteristics

The issues here are of interest to the social psychologist primarily for their implications about the degree of modifiability in human behaviour, and the manner in which it is adjusted to the social environment.

The biologist is usually concerned with the adaptedness of characters (behavioural or otherwise) in the environment in which the species is now living. Although the human environment has changed so rapidly that evolutionary changes in adaptation to the current environment have probably been at most partial, we can think in terms of adaptations to an 'environment of evolutionary adaptedness' (Bowlby, 1969), i.e. the environment in which the main selective forces determining man's current genetic potential operated. Thus whilst many psychologists regard human behaviour as infinitely malleable, the biologist argues that the behaviour of our ancestors must have been shaped by natural selection, and it is *a priori* likely that our behaviour today may be subject to constraints and predispositions either inherited from our biological past or induced by more recent selective forces. It must be noted, therefore, that the following arguments depend to some degree on speculations about the behaviour of our ancestors and the assumption of evolutionary continuity with them; in this sense questions of function and evolution come together.

How can such influences on behaviour be identified? Genetic influences are normally assessed by comparing the characteristics of individuals who are known to differ genetically. Thus by comparing identical and non-identical twins with siblings, reared in each case either by biological or by adoptive parents, it is possible to attempt to tease apart the relative contributions of genetic and environmental factors to the variance in individuals' behavioural characteristics (Buss and Plomin, 1984; Scarr and Kidd, 1983). That, however, is not our main concern. Rather we shall focus first on pan-cultural behavioural propensities – characteristics whose **heritability** is likely to be zero simply because they are virtually ubiquitous. To what extent can such characteristics be said to have a genetic basis?

There can be no disagreement that our behavioural development must be governed by at least some inherent predispositions. Even a Piagetian must postulate an inherent tendency to make sense of the world, to construct reality, and even culturally determined characteristics depend on propensities to learn from others. The questions concern the bases of such predispositions, and their degree of specificity. We may consider several sources of evidence.

Pan-cultural distribution   Ubiquity of a given characteristic could be due to similarities in the genetic endowment of individuals, or in their environment, or both. In some cases the first seems probable. Expressions of the primary affects, like smiling, laughing and crying, provide a classic example. Any influence of socialization practices on their early form is improbable because they appear in the blind and deaf born, and also in limbless thalidomide babies (e.g. Eibl-Eibesfeldt, 1972). Of course they may be subjected to strong cultural influences from birth onwards; these may affect the factors effective in eliciting them, the extent to which they are accentuated or suppressed, the response to them, and so on. Indeed the form of many other human expressive movements is virtually purely culturally determined (Ekman and Friesen, 1969). But the fact that a given behavioural characteristic is not pan-cultural does not mean that it is not based on biologically influenced propensities which may be revealed to varying extents, or suppressed, according to the prevailing social circumstances.

Functional speculations   A second line of evidence comes from speculations about the probable functions of current human behaviour in our own environment of evolutionary adaptedness. This is especially forceful if we can see behaviour that seems now to be functionless as part of a repertoire that was formerly adaptive. For example what were formerly termed 'the irrational fears of childhood' – fear of the dark, of being left alone, of falling – would make very good sense for infants who were carried by their mothers and for whom maternal proximity was essential for protection and nurturance (Bowlby, 1969). The assumptions are that variations in such behaviour were at least partially genetically determined, that some variants were selected, and have at least not been strongly selected against in more recent times.

This argument can be extended from particular patterns of behaviour to the capacity to vary behaviour adaptively according to circumstances. For example, individuals do not help all others equally, but are especially likely to help relatives (see below) and those who are likely to behave reciprocally. Whilst there is no clear evidence that these tendencies towards differential aiding were produced by natural selection, Essock-Vitale and McGuire (1980) found that predictions about the direction of altruism based on evolutionary theory were confirmed in very nearly all cases (see also Feinman, 1979; Hinde, 1986; Thompson, 1980).

Comparative studies   In some cases, simple similarities between the behaviour of humans and their close relatives support (but do not prove) the case for biological determinants. For example there are similarities in form between the human grin, smile and laugh and those of non-human primates, and reasonable suggestions can be made concerning the course of their evolution (van Hooff, 1972).

The interrelations between diverse aspects of human behaviour This is an extension of the lines of evidence considered previously, but concerns the manner in which many apparently unrelated aspects of human behaviour can be seen as an integrated whole which would have been adaptive in our environment of evolutionary adaptedness.

The argument rests on the biological principle that the characters (anatomical, physiological and behavioural) of every species form a **co-adapted complex** such that evolutionary change in one character may have ramifying effects through the whole. Thus not only do birds have wings, but most of them have behavioural mechanisms for flying and physiological adaptations for flight, and have a lifestyle in which flight is advantageous. In the same way, we can be sure, human anatomy, physiology and behaviour were co-adapted.

For example, many aspects of human mother–child interaction can be seen as parts of an adaptive pattern. The behaviour of the newborn, including the sucking reflex and other responses (such as the **Moro reflex**) formerly related to maintaining contact with the mother, were clearly adapted for infant survival. Comparisons between mammalian species show that the concentration of maternal milk is related to the frequency of suckling, and the dilute nature of human milk is in harmony with the demand feeding practised in most non-Western cultures.

Other aspects of the mother–child relationship can be understood by supposing that, from the point of view of natural selection, it is not only the individual's own reproductive success that matters. Natural selection can also favour behaviour that enhances the reproductive success of the individual's relatives. This arises because the relatives share a high proportion of the individual's genes. Thus a genetic mutation which results in a individual incurring costs (in terms of his or her own reproductive potential) can be selected for if the behaviour in question adequately enhances the reproductive potential of his or her relatives. This is referred to as enhancing 'inclusive fitness'. Selection favours acts that benefit related individuals the more, the closer the degree of relatedness and the smaller the cost to the actor. An individual's offspring are among his or her closest kin, so acts that favour them promote the perpetuation of genes, virtually all of which are identical with the individual's own. Hence selection for parental care. But individuals are equally closely genetically related to their parents and (full) siblings, so altruistic acts directed toward them may also be in an individual's evolutionary interests. This is more the case with siblings than parents since, given two individuals equally closely related, natural selection will favour more strongly altruistic acts directed toward the one with the greater reproductive potential, and this usually means the younger. (This also implies that parents have more interest in the well-being of their young than vice versa.) However, siblings also compete with each other for parental resources, so their relationship is likely to be an ambivalent one (Hinde, 1984b). This selectionist view also suggests that weaning conflict is almost inevitable, since it will be in the mother's interest to conserve resources for future offspring when it is in the current infant's interest to exploit the mother to the full (Trivers, 1974). Thus diverse characteristics of infant, of mother and of other relationships make sense when seen as reflecting possible adaptations to our environment of evolutionary adaptedness.

Perhaps of more interest in the current context is the direction of the differences between the behaviour of males and females in close personal relationships. In a wide range of human cultures, males tend to be more aggressive than females, females to be more concerned with interpersonal relationships. Physical characteristics play a greater role in interpersonal attraction for men than they do for women. When partner choice is mutual, women place more importance than do men on choosing a dependable mate: women prefer mates who are taller, more intelligent and older than themselves, whereas men prefer women who are younger, attractive, and likely to be good home-makers. In a wide range of cultures men tend to be the ones who encourage and females the ones who limit sexual intimacy. The double standard of morality is widespread (Peplau, 1983; Peplau, Rubin and Hill, 1977). Whilst sex differences in behaviour are certainly susceptible to environmental influences, the above tendencies have considerable cross-cultural generality.

Using again the principle of the co-adapted complex, it can be argued that these differences are in the direction that would have been produced by the forces of natural selection in our environment of evolutionary adaptedness if males and females each attempted to maximize their own reproductive success. The issues can be summarized as follows. Comparative study of monkeys and the great apes shows that their sexual anatomy and physiology is related to the social and sexual behaviour they display. It is reasonable to assume that the same was true for the human species in its environment of evolutionary adaptedness. Thus extrapolation of the relations between anatomy, physiology and behaviour from the great apes to the known sexual anatomy and physiology of men and women permits hypotheses about early human socio-sexual behaviour (Short, 1979).

Consider first the difference in body size. In general, in species in which males mate with more than one female the variance in reproductive success is greater amongst males than amongst females. Competition for mates is stronger amongst males, and this leads to selection for attributes leading to success in competition, such as body size and aggression: males tend to be larger and more aggressive than females. Assuming that similar principles applied to our own species in its environment of evolutionary adaptedness, the sex difference in size suggests that our ancestors were mildly **polygynous**.

Considering another aspect of the co-adapted complex, secondary sexual organs amongst the great apes are related to species' differences in copulation patterns and socio-sexual arrangements. For example the chimpanzee female often mates with several males in succession and the males have exceptionally large testes and accessory glands. These probably evolved because sperm competition occurs inside the female, so that it is advantageous to a male to produce many sperm. The gorilla male, who usually has sole access to a number of females, has small testes. The small human testes, the relatively enormous penis and the (in many cultures) sexually attractive female breasts are in harmony with the view that sex was important in maintaining male–female relationships (Short, 1979).

Early man probably lived in small groups, with a marked division of labour, and women bonded to particular males (Mellen, 1981). There would have been selective reasons for women to be more involved in parental care than men because (1) a woman is sure an infant is her own, whereas a man could have been cuckolded, and (2) owing to internal fertilization, a woman is forced to invest more in each infant's early development than is its father, and would thus have to invest more to bring another infant to the same stage than would a male. Thus if successful rearing of the offspring demanded a male presence, an enduring male–female relationship would have been more important to females than to males.

An additional point here is that in women, unlike many other female primates, ovulation is concealed. This could have been adaptive for females in forcing males to form at least a consort relationship with them, for a male could not tell when to mate in order to ensure fertilization, could not desert a female for fear of being cuckolded, and would gain less from philandering himself (Alexander and Norman, 1979). On the other hand promiscuity by a bonded male would matter little to his mate provided it did not detract from his parental care for her offspring, and would be advantageous to the male (from the point of view of natural selection) as it might lead to conception.

Whilst the argument is necessarily much abridged here (see Hinde, 1984a), it will be apparent that the direction of the sex differences in behaviour observed in a wide range of cultures correspond closely with those we should predict natural selection to have produced in our environment of evolutionary adaptedness. The greater importance of the relationship, and of the dependability of the spouse, to the woman, the greater importance of the fidelity of the spouse to the man, and the other issues mentioned earlier are in harmony with the biological predictions. These parallels are of intrinsic interest in providing a way of integrating diverse facts about interpersonal relationships within a relatively simple framework. Of course nothing in this argument should affect our judgement as to the socio-sexual arrangements to be preferred in our society – though if the parallels do reflect differing propensities between the sexes, we should use our knowledge of these differences to help us achieve our aims.

Function and evolution: variations in human behaviour

To the ethologist, the evidence that at least some aspects of human behaviour are to be seen as having been influenced by natural selection is overwhelming. But can *variations* in human behaviour be seen as the result of natural selection? The argument can be divided into two stages.

Are variations in human behavioural propensities adaptive?   It is necessary to phrase the questions asked here precisely, because a selectionist view does not require that every behavioural act should enhance the inclusive fitness of the actor. For example, a propensity which usually leads to adaptive behaviour may sometimes be displayed inappropriately, with neutral or even harmful consequences. Examples of behaviour maladaptive from the point of view of the individual's inclusive fitness can often be explained in terms of propensities adaptive in other contexts. Thus discussion of the adaptive significance of particular manifestations may founder if others are disregarded (Tinbergen, 1956). For instance Kruuk (1972) argues that the killing of prey surplus to their requirements by many carnivores is a trivial disadvantageous consequence of a behavioural propensity otherwise adaptive in obtaining food. Such 'secondary' consequences might be especially likely if a long-term environmental change led to manifestations of the propensity in circumstances other than those in which the propensity was originally adaptive. Possible human examples, such as the eating of the gourmand or the behaviour of an over-protective parent, readily come to mind. However, natural selection acts through the consequences of particular acts, and if any such secondary consequence was markedly disadvantageous it would presumably be selected against.

Some differences between cultures seem to be biologically adaptive. For example, in most human societies males may mate with several females; in a number each male has one mate; but it is rare for one female to have several males. Apart from the industrial societies monogamy occurs principally amongst hunter-gatherers, where a paternal contribution is important for infant survival. Polygyny is more usual in agricultural societies, where wealth can be accumulated and the more successful males can buy brides (van den Berghe, 1979). Thus at least in relatively simple societies there is a broad relation between marriage type and the nature of the economy, and that relation is of the general type that might be expected if individuals were maximizing their reproductive success.

As another case, amongst animals the advantages of territorial defence depend upon the concentration and availability of resources (food, mates), so that it may or may not be worth while to expend energy on territorial defence in order to obtain exclusive access to its resources. A similar model has been applied to three human tribal populations, and accounts for the observed variations in territoriality (Dyson-Hudson and Smith, 1978).

Such examples do not necessarily imply genetic differences between the individuals of the different cultures, because the differences could be based on propensities to select between alternative strategies according to the prevailing conditions. Differences in behaviour amongst *individuals within a culture*, or in individuals over time, may also depend on biologically based propensities which are evoked to different extents according to the situations in which individuals find themselves. An example is provided by Daly and Wilson's (1984) analysis of the killing of infants. These authors view variations in the incidence of infanticide as a manifestation of variations in an abstract parental motivation. It is predicted that the latter varies in an adaptive fashion. An examination of the ethnographic record showed that a high proportion of the circumstances in which infanticide was permitted fell into three categories: (1) the infant was not the putative parents' own; (2) the infant's fitness potential was poor by virtue of deformity, sickness or circumstances; or (3) the parental resources were inadequate (e.g. twins, mother unwed, economic hardship). In each of these cases, it is implied, it is adaptive for parental motivation to be low because further parental investment might not increase the parent's long-term reproductive success in proportion to its costs, and the parent might even do better to abandon this attempt, conserve resources and try again later. Similar conclusions came from an examination of the infanticide statistics in Canada. For instance, the incidence decreases with increase in the child's age, and is greater with mothers who are unmarried, or young, and in the families of step-parents.

From the biological point of view the crucial question is whether variation in the character in question is related to reproductive success. In the cases discussed so far, the correlation is implied but not proven. In a few cases, however, reproductive success has been actually measured. For instance amongst the Turkmen of Persia (Irons, 1979) and the inhabitants of Ifaluk (Turke and Betzig, 1985) in the Western Carolines, wealth is associated with greater reproductive success. This is in harmony with the view that differences in success at acquiring resources are causally related to differences in reproductive success (Turke and Betzig, 1985). Two further deductions seem to be in order. First, the skills and motivations necessary to obtain resources could be the subject of natural selection. Second, the choice of the particular resources towards which those skills are deployed could also be adaptive. Irons (1979, p. 258) suggests that members of a society define their goals to make them correspond with those things which will increase their reproductive success and that of their close relatives.

These examples show that many variations in human behaviour are adaptive in a biological sense. Thus human behavioural propensities, and the capacity to vary their expression in accordance with circumstances, can reasonably be interpreted as having been influenced by natural selection.

This of course does not mean that all aspects of human behaviour can be seen in a similar light. Whilst the behavioural propensities are in general adaptive, the beliefs, values, institutions and other aspects of the socio-cultural structure that result from the dialectics between the successive levels of social complexity are potent determinants of human behaviour, and may lead to actions that are adaptively neutral or even contrary to the reproductive interests of some or most individuals.

What are the bases for adaptive variations in human behavioural propensities? Here we must consider three possibilities.

1 *Genetic differentiation* The first possibility is that the behavioural differences result directly from genetic differences between the populations or individuals. For this, there is as yet no evidence. Whilst genetic predispositions for practices which achieve adaptive ends may be present (e.g. to avoid incest),

it is improbable that the differences between the multitudinous cultural practices by which this is achieved depend upon genetic differences. Furthermore, such a hypothesis cannot account for changes in behaviour through the lifespan, as revealed for instance in the greater probability of infanticide with younger mothers.

2   *Cultural differentiation*   Here the supposition is that the differences are acquired by individuals by imitation of or instruction from their elders, but with no predisposition to acquire one pattern rather than another. Of course we must assume that the capacities that make culture possible, and the particular practices to which at least early cultural evolution gave rise, had selective advantages for individuals. However, a pure *tabula rasa* state would be unstable, since selection would act to produce propensities to learn some practices rather than others (Lumsden and Wilson, 1981; 1982).

3   *Gene–culture differentiation*   In fact there is much empirical evidence against the *tabula rasa* view. For instance, human infants respond selectively to certain stimuli independently of experience of those stimuli, and their learning is channelled by constraints and predispositions. Lumsden and Wilson (1981, 1982) have thus suggested processes of coevolution in genes and culture. The genes prescribe endocrine and neural systems that impose regularities on the development of cognition and behaviour; these regulate into holistic patterns of culture, which could include systems of alternative strategies for coping with diverse circumstances. However, Boyd and Richerson (1986) have shown that social learning from others could be a better strategy than attempts at individual problem-solving in many circumstances, even though it can lead to the spread, through a population, of traits detrimental to individuals: for instance, persons of high status could propagate practices that were taken up by others even though not conducive to their biological fitness. Of course there would be a limit: cultural practices inimical to the reproductive success of a high proportion of individuals could not proceed indefinitely (cf. Hinde, 1987).

The causal why

Given that human behaviour involves biological propensities that influence behaviour, we must take them into account in considering the dialectics between successive levels of social complexity shown in figure 2.1. We may consider two examples, one relatively trivial and the other crucial for the nature of our society.

   The form of human artefacts can be ascribed to the interaction of biological, cultural and environmental factors. For example, a motor car must accommodate human bodies; its shape is influenced by its descent from the horse-drawn carriage, by fashions and by capitalist competition; and it must be moderately streamlined. More interest attaches to cases where the biological factors involve behavioural propensities. One probable example concerns the influence of our tendency to respond parentally to certain facial characteristics – namely to faces with high bulging foreheads, small noses and large cheeks (Fullard and Reiling, 1976; Gardner and Wallach, 1965; Lorenz, 1950; Sternglanz, Gray and Murakami, 1977). This appears to have affected the shape of cartoon characters – Mickey Mouse (Gould, 1983) and teddy bears (Hinde and Barden, 1985). Thus the early teddy bears were modelled on a real bear with a long snout sometimes encased in a leather muzzle. Over the years their snouts have become relatively shorter and their foreheads relatively larger. The change is presumably due to a form of selection, those types most successful in leaving the shop shelves being more numerous there next year.

Less trivially, propensities of individuals, acting through the dialectics in figure 2.1, may place constraints upon, yet not determine, the structure of societies. The cultural practices, rituals and beliefs which symbolize, exacerbate and/or ease the conflicts and problems that individuals face in their lives will not be understood until the natures of those individuals are understood – natures that are themselves the product of dialectics between biological and cultural determinants. On the view that sex differences in behaviour may reflect in part sex differences in biological propensities, we must expect men and women to have differing cognitive models of society, and that myths may reflect the different strands in each sex's perception of the other. Women may be portrayed as evil and dangerous to men (because of their power to cuckold? because they often come from other, hostile, groups?) or as epitomizing all that is good (nurturant for the man's child?). Men may be portrayed as promiscuous self-seekers or as knights errant, the maiden's protector. And within each society socialization practices, values and myths will interact with each other and with environmental factors: thus societies with a female deity tend to have a more favourable female stereotype than those without (Williams and Best, 1982). However, in most societies the norms and gender stereotypes exaggerate and distort the initial differences in behavioural propensities between the sexes. The processes by which this occurs pose a major problem to the social scientist. In part, they are intrinsic to formation of the concept of self; individuals see themselves as belonging to one gender group or the other, tend to see their own group in a more favourable light, and exaggerate the differences between the groups (e.g. Tajfel, 1978a; see chapter 16). There may also be advantages to individuals of both sexes in exaggerating the perceived differences between the sexes (Hinde, 1987).

The developmental why

The development of an individual depends upon a continuing interaction between the individual as he or she is at each point in time and the environment he or she experiences. The latter includes both the physical and social environment, and the social environment can be considered as having both cultural-specific and pan-cultural components. Because individuals selectively perceive and actively seek certain aspects of the environment, and because the way in which they do so is genetically influenced, the pan-cultural components may be more common than superficial inspection would indicate.

Occasionally, children have been brought up in more or less total social isolation. Such children are of course unable to speak, are cognitively very retarded and show bizarre socio-emotional behaviour often involving much fear and hostility. They clearly demonstrate the importance of social interaction in development – as indeed does the fact that social contact can produce marked rehabilitation (e.g. Clarke and Clarke, 1976). The processes whereby social experience affects development are discussed in chapter 3 (see also Doise and Mugny, 1984).

However, one issue which illustrates the integration of biological factors and social experience will be described briefly. This is the development of sex differences in behaviour. In rhesus monkeys, young males show more rough play, threat, aggression and sexual mounting than do females. These differences depend in part on prenatal hormones; genetic females exposed *in utero* to exogenous male hormones show the above patterns almost as frequently as do males. However, these sex differences are affected also by the social conditions of rearing. For example:

1 Male rhesus monkeys reared in restricted environments show deficiencies in mounting behaviour that last into adulthood.
2 Infants reared by the mother show competent sex behaviour and low levels of aggression, but infants reared in peer groups tend to be aggressive.
3 The mounting frequency of males is higher in mother-reared heterosexual groups (i.e. containing both young males and females) than in isosexual ones (i.e. groups of individuals of the same sex), whilst the opposite is true for females.
4 Males reared in heterosexual groups show more aggressive behaviour and less peer behaviour than those reared in isosexual groups: this is probably because the males occupy only the dominant positions in the former case, whilst in isosexual groups they are both dominant and subordinate.
5 Females show less rough play in heterosexual groups than do males, but even less in isosexual groups: this sex difference in heterosexual groups therefore does not depend on suppression by dominant males (Goldfoot and Wallen, 1978).

These results show clearly that, even in monkeys, differences in behaviour between the sexes observed in one situation may not be present in another. Social experience clearly contributes to the acquisition of gender roles. In man the determinants of gender role are even more complex and include hormonal factors (e.g. Money and Ehrhardt, 1972), differences in the ways others treat boys and girls, and differences in their own ideas about behaviour appropriate for the gender they conceive of themselves as having. Furthermore social norms about gender roles may interact with other aspects of personality to produce effects that ramify through the family. For instance, Simpson and Stevenson-Hinde (1985) found that, whilst there were no sex differences in shyness or in most measures of the mother–child relationship in a sample of four-year-olds, shy girls had better mother–child relationships than non-shy girls, whilst the opposite was true for boys. The difference appeared to be related to maternal norms about gender-appropriate behaviour (cf. figure 2.1).

Summary and Conclusion

In this chapter a case has been made for attempts to integrate attitudes and data drawn from ethology into social psychology. The importance of describing social behaviour at various levels of social complexity has been emphasized. As we move from individual behaviour, through interactions and relationships to group structure, description is likely to become more fragmentary because of the more complex nature of the phenomena, but will remain equally important for specifying the limits of generalizations. Whilst the several levels of social complexity must be clearly distinguished, ethologists would argue strongly against isolating their study into distinct subdisciplines of psychology; some of the most important questions concern the dialectics between them.

It has also been suggested that the ethologist's four questions of causation, development, function and evolution are logically distinct and yet interrelated and interfertile and can usefully be applied to the human case. Thus discussion of the possible functions of human behaviour can integrate previously diverse facts and lead to causal hypotheses – hypotheses that must then be tested more directly.

The emphasis on biological determinants in this chapter is in no way incompatible with recognition of the importance of experiential and especially cultural ones. The focus has been on the former only because their influences permeate through the dialectics between the successive levels of social complexity, and the social sciences can therefore not afford to neglect them. Furthermore, as discussed more fully elsewhere (Hinde, 1987), the nature of the socio-cultural structure can ultimately be understood only in terms of behavioural propensities of individuals.

Perhaps it can all be summed up by saying that the ethologist sees us as a species, doing some things less well than our non-human relatives and some things very much better, and with potentials which, though perhaps expanding with every generation, are nevertheless limited by virtue of our nature.

Glossary Terms

Co-adapted complex	Moro reflex
Dialectic	Polygyny
Heritability	

Further Reading

Alexander, R. D. (1977) Natural selection and the analysis of human sociality. In C. E. Gould (ed.), *Changing Scenes in the Natural Sciences, 1776–1976*, Philadelphia: Academy. A discussion of the extent to which biological principles can explain aspects of human sociality.

Bateson, P. and Martin, P. (in press) *Origins of Behaviour*. Cambridge: Cambridge University Press. A recent synthesis of the principles governing the development of behaviour in animals.

Chagnon, N. A. and Irons, W. (eds) (1979) *Evolutionary Biology and Human Social Behavior: an anthropological perspective*. North Scituate, Mass.: Duxbury. Contributions concern the extent to which human behaviour can be understood in terms of biological function.

Hinde, R. A. (1982) *Ethology: its nature and relations with other sciences*. New York: Oxford University Press. A summary of the ethological approach, with chapters on its relations to natural and social sciences.

Hinde, R. A. (1987) *Individuals, Relationships and Culture*. Cambridge: Cambridge University Press. An extended discussion of the issues raised in this chapter.

Kitcher, P. (1985) *Vaulting Ambition: sociobiology and the quest for human nature*. Cambridge, Mass.: MIT Press. A critique of the socio-biological approach.

Wilson, E. O. (1978) *On Human Nature*. Cambridge, Mass.: Harvard University Press. An exposition of the socio-biological approach to human behaviour.

3 The Social Nature of Social Development

KEVIN DURKIN

Introduction

Imagine what kind of knowledge an individual would gather if he or she lived (from birth) in a world without others. Begging the question of survival, presumably most information that our solitary subject could assimilate would be functional, predominantly physical or sensory, and limited to impressions of phenomena directly experienced. Knowledge of other people, means of communication, the possibility of alternative points of view, the necessity for rules of conduct, the benefits of collaboration, the significance of social categories, the transmission of ideas and beliefs; all of these fundamentals of social life, and much more, would be absent from the innocent isolate's life.

Except in cases of wanton neglect or deprivation, the child is dependent upon other people from the outset and is bound to interact with them and to be provided with opportunities and constraints by them through her or his lifespan. These other people and the ways in which they have set up the structures and conventions of life are undoubtedly the most complex phenomena that the normal human being will ever have to deal with. Furthermore, because they are extensively involved in the child's life, by virtue of continuous attempts to transmit information and values, and by the provision of feedback and challenges, they not only are a focus of interest in their own right but are implicated in the ways in which the developing person is able to think, articulate and behave in relation to all aspects of the environment.

This chapter is concerned with the social nature of social development, by which is meant both the development of the child's understanding of social phenomena and the relationship between the child and social phenomena in the development of understanding. It begins with a discussion of the concept of socialization, pointing out that current views of this topic have shifted markedly from earlier assumptions that socialization is something that environmental forces 'do' to the child and now favour approaches which focus on interactive processes. It summarizes evidence which indicates that social interaction is vital to three of the most substantial tasks of early development: the beginnings of knowledge, of language, and of interpersonal relationships. Recognition of the significance of social factors in development raises several issues at the points of intersection between social and developmental psychology. Among these, we will consider new directions in developmental (especially Piagetian-inspired) research; the significance for developmental research of children's understanding of the social context of experiments; and the development of social cognition, with particular reference to knowledge of personal attributes, understanding of social structure, and acquisition of social categories (such as nationality and gender).

The aim of the chapter is to show that it is misleading to imagine we can study the child apart from its social context and that it is an oversimplification to imagine that the child is simply an unwitting product of its environment: instead, we will see that human development is a social achievement in terms of both content and process. To investigate it fruitfully, we need to draw on both developmental and social perspectives, and much of the interest and excitement of developmental social psychology arises from this merger.

Mutuality and Socialization

One of the most important theoretical reformulations influencing much recent work on the nature of social development has been the enrichment of concepts of socialization. In some areas of psychology and neighbouring social science disciplines, socialization has often been taken to refer to processes by which an individual is shaped or restrained so as to fit into the society to which he or she belongs. Current thinking in developmental social psychology has called this notion seriously into question. Discussing some of the conceptual issues, Schaffer (1984) points out that traditionally models of socialization have reflected and nurtured assumptions of external control. Socialization is often thought of as a predominantly *unidirectional* process, with the impetus for change and regulation coming from outside the individual being socialized. In some theories, for example, the child is seen as an ignorant, passive and rather malleable creature whom society fashions into the desired psychological 'shape'. American behaviourism once favoured such accounts of human learning, inspired by Watson's (1928, p. 45) view of the infant as a 'lively squirming bit of flesh' and later endorsed by Skinner's (1953, p. 35) celebrated insistence that 'operant conditioning shapes behaviour as a sculptor shapes a lump of clay.' On the other hand, there are also theories which see the child as arriving in society with a range of instincts and desires which she or he is disposed to vent or gratify with little concern initially for the feelings and desires of others. Schaffer points to Freudian theory as a good example of the latter kind of account: Freud (1933) stressed that young children are impulsive, with easily aroused emotions and little ability to restrain or delay gratification, and he regarded socialization as the process whereby society (primarily represented by the parents) repressed and disciplined the reluctant child into publicly accepted conventions.

Although both of these perspectives have intuitive appeal and have attracted scientific exposition over the years, a wealth of research conducted during the 1970s has consolidated a somewhat different – and more social – view of socialization. Schaffer, whose own research into parent–child interaction (Schaffer, 1977a, 1978) has been particularly influential in the emergence of this new emphasis, identifies as a third view of socialization the *mutuality model* (see Schaffer, 1984). In contrast to the earlier approaches described above, the mutuality model represents the child as an active participant in her or his own social development and it stresses the interdependence of parent and child in much of their social transactions. It does not, of course, maintain that there is no conflict in parent–child relations (a claim which most parents would see as contrary to daily reality) or that there is no influence of adult upon child, but it does stress that the diverse processes that are entailed in social development are from the outset negotiated through mutual exploration and stimulation.

Children as social beings from birth

The strengths of the mutuality model over the unidirectional approaches include its compatibility with the abundant evidence that children are not blank slates at birth, but bring reflexes, capacities and predispositions with them, and that they explore and initiate as well as respond to people and things around them; these social activities often involve synchrony and cooperation with parental behaviour rather than opposition and reluctance. Work on the observation of parent–child interaction during the last decade or so has uncovered intricate and impressively synchronized patterns of mutual behaviour. Micro-analytic study of mothers and babies, made possible by the availability of video recording, has shown that their expressive and communicative behaviours are intermeshed from the simplest burst–pause patterns of feeding through rhythmic qualities of dyadic behaviour to the turn-taking of early dialogue, in which the infant makes vocal, visual and gestural contributions in alternation with the adult in exchanges which have many of the features we would expect of adult–adult conversations (Kaye, 1982; Schaffer, 1977b; Rutter and Durkin, 1987).

Parent–infant exchanges, which to a casual onlooker might appear to be little more than random play and gurgles, are now seen by many developmental social psychologists as richly structured, finely patterned social behaviours in which both parties are making important discoveries about the other and their relationship. The beginnings of social life are to be found in a joint, dynamic enterprise rather than in a unidirectional 'effect' of a mature being upon an empty vessel or a recalcitrant egotist.

As researchers have begun to explore the development of these early social interactions, new light has been cast on the complex activities and achievements involved in entry into the social world. In the following sections, we will consider some aspects of these with reference to three of the central tasks of early childhood: acquiring knowledge about the world, developing one's first language, and learning how to relate to other people, especially peers. In each case, we will see that development depends upon the subtle interplay of the child's initial qualities and competencies and the responsiveness of others in the social environment.

Social interaction and the beginnings of knowledge

A good deal of recent work has attempted to uncover the contributions of social interaction to the cognitive development of the child. Bruner and Sherwood (1981), pointing out that 'an enormous amount of the child's activity during the first year and a half of life is extraordinarily social and communicative' (p. 30), argue that this creates the conditions for the growth of intellectual skill. Particularly useful to the child in the early stages is the opportunity to participate in *games* with the parent. Although ostensibly simple and repetitive, traditional games such as 'peekaboo', 'patacake', 'build and knock down' and 'give and take' allow the child to participate in alternating activities in which the relationships between means and ends, action and reactions can be experienced and practised. During the first year, children become increasingly proficient in these exchanges and their role shifts from recipient to initiator (Camaioni and Laicardi, 1985).

Papousek and Papousek (1977) propose that from very early in life the willingness of the parent to attend carefully to the details of infant activity and to engage in sessions of alternation in which each participant imitates the other's behaviour is invaluable to the child. Such responsiveness provides the child with a 'biological mirror', i.e. the reflections of his or her own actions in the behaviours of another. Henceforth, the child has many opportunities to discover contingency relationships in terms of the effects of his or her actions upon the social environment. Consequently, the kinds of phenomena that present themselves to the young child are socially circumscribed.

We return below to the relationship between social interaction and cognitive development, considering current investigations of social factors and performance in problem-solving tasks among older children. For the moment, we may note that recent work on early cognition points strongly to the conclusion that other people help infants to discover their environment, to determine what is attention-worthy within it, and to explore ways of operating upon it; at the same time, infants' own capacities and interests constrain the kinds of activities and events in which their care-givers attempt to involve them.

Social interaction and the beginnings of language

Very similar conclusions are promoted by recent developments in the field of child language study. It has become increasingly clear from work on early language acquisition that the engagement in conversational activity with more mature language users, whether parents (cf. McShane, 1980; Howe,

1981) or siblings (Dunn and Kendrick, 1982) is central to the developmental achievement. The child and its care-givers are engaged in intentional communication and language is negotiated in the course of meaningful social interaction (Beaudichon, 1982; Camaioni, Volterra and Bates, 1976; Nadel, 1986).

Although contemporary research into language acquisition took its impetus from the focus on intrapsychological (i.e. *within* the individual) processes inspired by work in linguistics and psycho-linguistics, a number of subsequent lines of development within the area converged on the processes of social interaction and their implications for language learning (Durkin, 1987a; Robinson 1984). Once again, research into parent–infant interaction is a key illustration of this: many investigators have attempted to elucidate the ways in which the reciprocal processes mentioned have provided children with a meaningful, shared context for the acquisition of language (cf. Benelli, 1983; Messer, 1983). Bruner has argued that the repetitive routines and games of parent–infant exchanges provide ideal settings or *formats* for the teaching of labelling (Bruner, 1975, 1981, 1983). For example, everyday activities like picturebook reading involve the 'That's an X' format, where useful new information such as the names for things is inserted into a familiar structure:

'That's a lion.'
'That's a gorilla.'
'That's an elephant.'

Once the format is well practised, the routine part of it ('That's a') may signal that an attention-worthy word is forthcoming, giving the child optimal conditions within which to attend to the novel label. There is certainly much evidence that new words can be introduced or stressed in relation to objects and activities which are the current focus of shared attention (cf. Harris, Jones and Grant, 1983; Tomasello and Todd, 1983). Similarly, Bruner and others have argued that the conversation-like qualities of parent–infant interactions (described above) initiate the child into practices which in due course give rise to truly linguistic conversations. In neighbouring work there has been a great deal of interest in the nature of the language made available to children (often referred to as 'motherese' or 'parentese'), with numerous demonstrations that adults modify their normal speech style when talking to young language users by slowing it down, avoiding many of the grammatical complexities of adult speech, raising the pitch and repeating utterances (see contributions to Snow and Ferguson, 1977).

There is extensive evidence, then, that the acquisition of language reflects the social contexts in which it occurs. Nevertheless, it is important to recognize that the processes at stake involve much more than parents skilfully feeding information to the empty learner. First, although parents do speak in distinctive and simpler ways to their children, their motives for so doing are often to communicate with and regulate the behaviour of their child rather than to teach the elements of language (Schaffer and Crook, 1979). Sometimes, these management concerns can conflict with the regularities of conventional syntax and semantics.

For instance, parents often substitute their own name ('mummy', 'daddy') or their child's for pronouns when addressing their youngsters. Thus, we hear parents produce utterances like 'Angie want one?', 'Give mummy a kiss' etc. (see Durkin, Rutter and Tucker, 1982 for further examples). On first sight, this might appear a simplification strategy designed by the parent to help the child get around the problem that the meaning of the personal pronouns ('you', 'me') shifts according to who is speaking. A person can be 'me' as she speaks, 'you' as you reply, and 'her' in a reference by a third party. For a two-year-old, being 'me', 'you' and 'her' in short succession may be a little difficult to follow: far more convenient to be 'Angie' throughout. In fact, however, parents' motives in speaking this way seem to reflect management concerns and the need to control the child; using names is a good way to gain attention quickly, and parents use this pattern from well before the child is able to produce sentences of its own (Durkin, Rutter and Tucker, 1982). But unfortunately, utterances like 'Angie want one?' (where 'Angie' is the addressee) or 'Give mummy a kiss' (where 'mummy' is the speaker) break some of the rules of adult–adult language (you can test this by talking to some adults in this way and observing their reactions).

In short, for social-communicative reasons parents adapt their speech to the child; this has the consequence that the linguistic structures available to the child as a basis for learning about the language contain some irregular properties. Interestingly, children then begin to incorporate these irregular structures in their early utterances – and utterances from children of the form 'Me want one', 'That Angie's' are often taken as 'cute' efforts by parents or as interesting preliminary grammars by students of child language, with little regard to who might have initiated such forms!

Language acquisition reflects the social context of development in *many* ways: sometimes as a joint activity guided by the informed adult; sometimes as a function of communicative failures and cross-purposes between parent and child, which give rise to attempts to reformulate, clarify and recast (cf. Brown, 1980; Durkin, 1987a). Progress depends on both the child and its partners, and it is very unlikely that the hypothetical isolate we considered above would have either the motivation or the opportunity to learn a language. Clearly, other people provide an invaluable context for this task – one of the definitive achievements of human social development. The important point for the moment is that language is not something which is simply donated to the new member of society but something that she or he must discover in the course of varied social exchanges with the available community.

Social interaction and the beginnings of interpersonal relations

It is perhaps not surprising that work by developmental social psychologists interested in the complex unfolding of parent–preschooler interactions exhibits many of the concerns and procedures that an ethologist would see as critical to the investigation of social relationships (see chapter 2). Observational work in naturalistic environments has proven invaluable in this area. Dunn (1984) has stressed the benefits of studying young children in situations of genuine social and emotional significance for them (especially in family settings) and points out that we risk (1) underestimating the child's understanding of others, and (2) neglecting the consequences of individual differences in maternal style for children's emerging social sensitivity. Dunn's work (see also Dunn and Kendrick, 1982) demonstrates this with respect to familial processes and sibling relationships, showing that well before three years of age children are integrated into 'a world of significant others in which they understand and respond with considerable subtlety to the emotions and intentions of those others' (Dunn, 1984; p. 25).

Individual differences in this respect (associated with individual differences in mothers' behaviour towards them) have important implications for the child's early social experiences outside the home. An interesting example is provided by the work of Montagner and his colleagues on the development of early peer interaction (Montagner, 1978, 1979; Montagner et al., 1981). They collect extensive observational data on the behavioural profiles of French pre-school children by filming their spontaneous play in day care centres and kindergartens. They classify items of behaviour as signifying *appeasement* (e.g. smiling, offering, stroking, kissing etc.), *agonistic attitudes* (threatening by clenching the teeth, frowning, assertive noises etc., or aggressive physical acts), *fearfulness/withdrawal* (moving away, crying in response to aggression by others), or *isolation* (sucking fingers or toys, standing alone, crying alone). By calculating the frequency and distribution of these items for a given child, a profile of the individual as he or she relates to the peer group can be determined.

Now, the behavioural items that Montagner studies are all present quite early in life (between six and sixteen months: Montagner et al., 1984, p. 32) and it could be argued that they are innate (see Eibl-Eibesfeldt, 1973). However, the establishment of individual differences in the frequency with which particular modes of behaviour are adopted is closely related to (at least) two important aspects of the social context. The first is the child's relationship with its parents. Montagner et al. (1984) found that changes in maternal behaviour in particular (due for example to physiological factors such as illness, serious modifications of ovarian cycle) or social stresses (at work or in family discord) led to discordant behaviour towards the child which led in turn to changes in the child's behavioural profile. More impatient and aggressive maternal styles were associated with shifts over time in children's classification from 'leaders' to 'dominant aggressives'. Hinde and Tamplin (1983), in a study of British pre-school children, also found that hostile activity towards peers at nursery was positively correlated with relatively poor relations at home with the mother, especially in boys (see also Lutkenhaus, 1984).

The second important aspect of the social context is of course the child's interactions with the peer group. Montagner et al. point out that the tendency to provide a high frequency of a particular type of behaviour, such as aggressive acts, militates against the practice of other ritualized interactions of a more prosocial nature and against invitations to participate in collective activity. In simple terms, it is difficult to greet the girl in the red T-shirt if you have reason to believe that she will respond by hitting you, just as it is difficult to try out your appeasement repertoire when wresting someone else's toys from his grip. On the other hand, the child who favours appeasement acts is likely to approach others and has a higher probability of receiving reciprocal gestures and cooperative acceptance in play. The beginnings of interpersonal relations in these ways illustrate the remark made in chapter 2, that every human characteristic 'depends on an interaction between characteristics of the individual and aspects of the environment'.

The Implications of Social Development for Developmental and Social Psychology

In this preliminary overview of recent research directions in the study of early socialization, we have seen that human beings are from the outset engaged in a social world and learn through interaction with others. When this is pointed out, it may seem almost self-evident. Yet, surprisingly, there are two important areas of psychology which have often tended to neglect or even disregard such considerations. These areas are developmental psychology and social psychology.

Developmental psychologists have overlooked the social contexts of childhood in much of their work through this century because they have been concerned with how the child could come to understand the logical and physical properties of the world. For example, a large amount of developmental research has been focused on seemingly asocial phenomena such as the child's understanding of space, time, causality, mathematical relations and so on: i.e. the child's *material* rather than *personal* environment (Light, 1986, p. 69). This focus is due in part to the influence of the great Swiss psychologist Jean Piaget (1896–1980), whose imaginative and pioneering studies of the development of reasoning in childhood have guided and inspired countless investigations by his followers and critics into the intriguing questions of how children construct their theories of knowledge. It may also reflect the influence of the demands of the educational systems in advanced industrial nations, which promote interest in how children develop literacy, mathematical and technical skills.

Social psychologists, on the other hand, have often overlooked the developmental contexts of human behaviour in much of their work because they have tended to define their concerns as the ways in which social structures and systems affect individual reasoning and action, and vice versa. For example, social psychologists are interested in how group membership influences individual behaviour, how interpersonal processes are mediated, how we perceive others, and so on; the other chapters in this book give a good account of the range of concerns that have motivated the discipline. It is possible and very tempting to tackle these issues by studying adult subjects as though they are ahistorical creatures whose cognitions and behaviours can be examined independently of the processes through which they originated.

Not all developmental psychologists ignore the social aspects of the young person's world, of course, and few social psychologists would pretend that humans arrive in the laboratory or field setting uninfluenced by the complexities of their developmental experiences. What is important to appreciate, though, is that while the convenient academic compartmentalization of social and developmental psychologies helps us to organize study of rich areas of human beings, it can also blinker us to the essential interdependence of the two subdisciplines. As more developmental researchers turn to the social nature of child development, the implications for traditional theories of developmental psychology are becoming particularly evident. At the same time, as social-psychological processes in the young come under scrutiny, the developmental antecedents of phenomena hitherto studied mainly by social psychologists are gaining attention (Chandler, 1982; Shantz, 1983). As a result, the hybrid *developmental social psychology* is becoming an important focus for specialists in both areas. To understand the importance of this overlap, we need in turn to consider the implications of social interaction for developmental theories, and the contribution of developmental research to the investigation of social-psychological processes. In the following, we will consider both perspectives on this overlap.

Social factors and developmental psychology

To understand something of the background to recent interests in developmental social psychology, it is necessary to consider briefly the main emphases of Piagetian developmental psychology which, as we have already noted, has been the guiding framework for much contemporary study of children's thinking. Piaget was interested in how the child could come to know anything and in how knowledge was enriched and revised as a result of new experiences. He drew an analogy between the child and the scientist: both begin with curiosity about some phenomena they encounter, and both conjecture provisional theories to help organize their understanding of the phenomena. As they continue to explore the phenomena, they make new discoveries which lead them to rethink aspects of their theories, and sometimes to change them radically (Kitchener, 1986).

Conceiving of the child as a kind of 'mini-scientist' might seem rather implausible if we hold to notions of the new member of society learning through being moulded by the environment or being disciplined by more mature instructors. But we have already seen that these simplistic models of child development are inadequate – and, from early on, Piaget had in fact rejected such approaches. His theory of how the child constructs and revises its theories of the world is complex and beyond our present scope (see Flavell, 1963 for a comprehensive introduction). For present purposes we will focus on just one important demonstration of progress in children's thought that conveys something of the ingenuity of Piagetian research and that has become the topic of much debate among developmentalists. This is Piaget's famous **conservation** experiment.

The standard conservation experiment   In the technique devised by Piaget (1952) a child is presented with two identical beakers, both containing the same volume of liquid. Once the child has confirmed that they both hold the same amount, the contents of one of the original beakers are transferred to a third beaker of a different shape: say, taller and thinner than the originals. Then, the child is asked whether the new beaker contains the same amount of liquid as the remaining original beaker. Intriguingly, children aged below about six years usually declare that the contents of the new beaker are different – either greater or less than the original. Often they add explanations like 'cos it's taller' or 'cos that one's thinner'. In other words, young children seem to fail to conserve mentally the volume of the transferred liquid, and instead are seduced by the perceptual transformation that makes it look greater or less than the original.

The same effect can be demonstrated with other materials, such as balls of Plasticine rolled up tight or elongated, or rows of counters bunched together or spread out, and so on. Similar responses are obtained: young children will insist that when one of two equal-sized balls of Plasticine is rolled into a sausage shape it is then different *in amount* from the unchanged ball. A child who gives this kind of response is usually termed a 'non-conserver'.

For Piaget the interesting issue here is how the child comes to represent mentally the various dimensions of the task, and he argues that the non-conserving child is failing to perform at least two critical mental operations. First, the child fails to reverse the transformation: that is, he/she fails to consider that if the liquid removed from the first beaker is returned to it, it will fill exactly the same amount of space that is left. Second, the child fails to decentre: that is, he/she focuses on one aspect of the transformed liquid (such as its new height) and ignores the compensating changes on other dimensions (such as its new width). The mental operations involved in representing these aspects of the physical world have not been achieved by the young (say four- to six-year-old) mini-scientist, and Piaget calls the child at this stage **pre-operational**. The slightly older child who can perform such reasoning tasks when dealing with concrete, physical problems (though not yet with more abstract problems) is seen by Piaget as having reached the stage of **concrete operations**.

The shift from preoperational to concrete operational thinking is one of the major cognitive achievements of middle childhood, according to Piaget, and one which underlies changes in children's responses to a wide range of problems. Whether or not Piaget's formulation of these developments is correct, and the extent to which methodological procedures such as the conservation test might distort our impressions of children's underlying abilities, have occasioned much dispute among developmentalists. For the moment, it is useful to note that the focus of this classic experiment, and in fact of much more of Piaget's work, is on how the individual child constructs a logical understanding of the nature of the physical world.

Piaget's studies of matters such as conservation set the scene, then, for what turned out to be decades of research into cognitive development and the spatio-temporal world. In the course of this work, the child's involvement with other people was not always a foremost consideration for many researchers (we consider some exceptions below), and the central question was usually: 'How does the mini-scientist tackle this or that logical or mathematical problem?' Paradoxically, Piaget himself always accorded social interaction an important role in his theory of development, but for various reasons this rarely emerged as a matter for study in Piagetian-inspired research (cf. Chapman, 1986; Light, 1983).

In the 1970s, however, a new group of Genevan psychologists began to renew interest in an early argument of Piaget's (1932) that cognitive disagreement among peers instigated awareness within the child that there could be more than one perspective on a given problem. Taking more perspectives into account could promote decentring, which we saw above might be one of the things pre-operational children fail to do in contexts such as the conservation experiment. Doise, Mugny, Perret-Clermont and their collaborators began an important programme of research concerned with the processes of cognitive conflict in peer interaction, and their work illustrates one of the principal ways in which developmental psychology is beginning to profit from a closer relationship with social psychology. We will consider their research in some detail in the following section, and then go on to consider other recent work on some of the social factors involved in experimental studies of cognitive development.

Peer collaboration and conservation Few investigators would dispute that children aged below seven years frequently do respond erroneously in conservation tasks. In 1975, Doise, Mugny and Perret-Clermont, using a conservation of liquid task, reported the interesting finding that six- to seven-year-olds working together (in twos or threes) to share out liquids performed at a higher level than they had done individually in pre-tests. Furthermore, initially non-conserving children who worked with children who could conserve subsequently performed at a higher level on post-tests than children who did not participate in the collaborative sessions.

It might be argued that, noteworthy as such an outcome is, the children have merely learned to imitate the behaviour of more competent peers, and have not actually advanced their understanding of the cognitive problem posed to them. However, the children were able to provide explanations of their judgements at a higher level than at the outset, making reference now to matters such as reversibility, compensations for changes in height or width and so on – a finding which suggests definite insight had been gained. Furthermore, other work in this tradition has shown that gains acquired through social interaction in Piagetian-type tasks can be generalized, leading to higher performance in other Piagetian tasks (Perret-Clermont, 1980) and to tasks using different material and formats from those used at pre-test (Valiant, Glachan and Emler, 1982).

Doise and his colleagues reason that a critical factor is not imitation but the

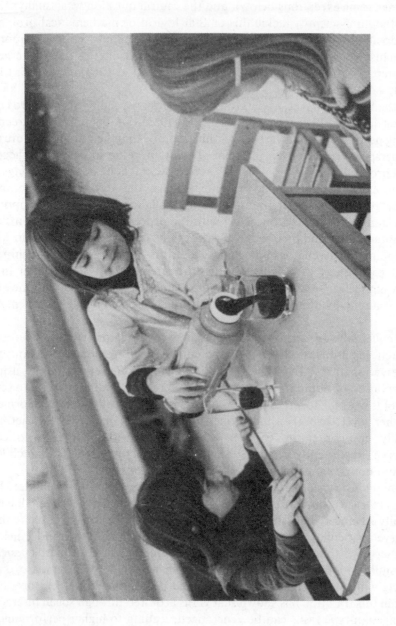

PLATE 3.1   Conservation and social interaction: sharing fruit juice can promote attention and insight (Doise and Mugny, 1984)

resolution of **socio-cognitive conflict** arising from the exposure to contradictory perspectives on the same problem (Mugny and Doise, 1978a, 1979). In a large series of experiments, these investigators have shown that children can profit from social interaction with others of the same, or even lower, level of ability with respect to a particular task if the course of the interaction prompts them to resolve their different perspectives on a problem (see for example Mugny, Levy and Doise, 1978; De Paolis et al., 1981; Rijsman et al., 1980). Improved performance as a result of social interaction on more advanced cognitive tasks has also been demonstrated with older children and adolescents (Gilly and Roux, 1984; Light and Glachan, 1985), and Light and Glachan comment that the peer facilitation effect does not appear to be limited to any particular developmental age or stage. Doise and Mugny maintain that 'social interaction is crucial in the elaboration and indeed the initiation of concept development' because it provides opportunities for awareness of the responses of others so that 'a conflict is created which makes the difference explicit' (1984, p. 160).

For Doise and Mugny, then, the causal links between cognitive development and social development are reciprocal, and they reject views of the latter as dependent upon the former. While debate continues about the role of inter- versus intrapsychological factors (Emler and Valiant, 1982) and of imitation (Fortin, 1985) in children's progress in the kinds of tasks Doise and others study, the fact that social interaction can promote cognitive gains is not in dispute. The increasing sensitivity to these issues brought about by such work has fundamental implications for our conception of child development arising from decades of experiments focused upon the 'individual' child. In fact, contemporaneous developments in developmental research and debate have led to serious questioning of the assumption that traditional experiments really do test the 'individual' child, and we turn to these issues next.

Interpreting the experimenter Another aspect of the relationship between social context and cognitive performance which has become a focus for developmental psychologists in the last decade or so is the way in which the child interprets the point of adult questions. Within child language study, for example, it became increasingly clear that children will generally attempt to provide *some* kind of a response to adult questions, even when these are ambiguous or anomalous (e.g. Wales, 1974). Hughes and Grieve (1980) showed that this predisposition to impose meaning persists even if five- to seven-year-olds are confronted with quite bizarre questions (such as 'Is red wider than yellow?') by an adult. They will almost invariably attempt to answer them (one child, aged six years eight months, explained 'Because yellow's thinner than red': Hughes and Grieve, 1980, p. 150).

A wave of studies has shown that children who fail the classic conservation tests can perform successfully on variants of these tests designed so as to make 'human sense' (Donaldson, 1978). For example, McGarrigle and Donaldson (1975) contrasted four- to six-year-olds' performance in two versions of Piaget's conservation of number task. In the first, the standard procedure was

used: the experimenter presented two equal rows of counters and then spread
one line out. In the alternative version, the two rows were set out as in the
standard procedure, but then a 'naughty teddy' emerged from a box and
wilfully 'messed up' the counters. In the standard version of the test, only 16
per cent of the children conserved (i.e. said that the material remained the same
despite the perceptual transformation), while in the naughty teddy version over
60 per cent conserved (see also Hargreaves, Molloy and Pratt, 1982; Light,
Buckingham and Robbins, 1979).

There is controversy concerning the reasons why children give more conserving responses in certain contexts than others (see Bovet, Parrar-Dayan and
Deshusses-Addor, 1981; Light, 1986; Russell, 1979 for further discussions
from a variety of perspectives). Nonetheless, this line of work has had two
important consequences for views of cognitive development: the first is that the
rather negative assumptions of Piaget about the intellectual capabilities of the
preschool child have been seriously challenged; the second is that investigation
of the social processes in which children's learning is tested or promoted has
moved to 'centre stage' (Light, 1986). In sum, while the dominant traditions of
developmental psychology in this century have attempted to uncover the processes of cognitive development *within* the individual, a radical shift of perspective is under way; the negotiation of cognition *between* individuals is
coming to the fore as a focus of enquiry owing to the increasing interchanges
between developmental and social psychology.

Developmental perspectives on social cognition

The work discussed in the previous section has been focused primarily on the
traditional stuff of developmental psychology (namely tasks involving logical,
physical or mathematical understanding). We have seen that an important
current thrust of developmental social psychology has been to uncover the
social processes implicated in cognitive progress and in the very procedures of
developmental research. But in the meeting of developmental and social psychology there is an equally important contribution in the opposite direction:
namely, the investigation of the developmental antecedents of processes which
are central to the concerns of researchers of social cognition in adults. *Social
cognition* is an umbrella term which includes many aspects of knowledge and
reasoning about the social world (see chapters 5 and 6 for fuller accounts). As
this area of research grows it is becoming increasingly apparent that adequate
theories of how humans engage in these processes cannot rest on the assumption that they arise fully formed in adult life.

In fact, recent work has shown that processes such as causal attribution (cf.
Bar-Tal, 1978; Fincham, 1981; Kassin and Pryor, 1985), social comparison
(Ruble, 1983), attitude formation (Emler and Hogan, 1981) and organization
of social scripts (Nelson, 1985) all have complex developmental histories which
need to be analysed in relation to the interaction of the developing person and
his or her social experiences. To illustrate some of the broader issues attracting
attention from developmental social psychologists, we will consider briefly

three topics each of which bears importantly on how understanding of the social world is acquired: the child's understanding of other people and their attributes; the child's understanding of societal structure; and the child's understanding of social categories. Interestingly, just as we have seen that the dominant (Piagetian) framework of developmental psychology is being reconsidered in the light of greater attention to social factors, fruitful approaches to several topical areas of social psychology have been fashioned in the opposite direction, by adapting Piagetian approaches to social-cognitive issues.

Developing understanding of people's attributes   Knowledge of the personal attributes and mental processes of others is a prerequisite to many tasks in social reasoning. Since cognitive processes are not directly perceptible or manipulable, when and how children acquire theories of mind pose intriguing questions which have been neglected until quite recently (see Durkin, 1987a). The evidence available reveals that insight into psychological properties is acquired gradually over a lengthy developmental period.

For example, Livesley and Bromley (1973) and Peevers and Secord (1973) elicited children's descriptions of others (their friends, or people they knew) and investigated age-related changes in the kinds of characteristics that were focused upon. They found, consistent with Piagetian predictions, that younger children refer most often to peripheral or external phenomena (the person's physical appearance, dress, possessions, kinship status and so on), while from around age seven or eight years there was a notable increase in the amount and sophistication of reference to internal psychological properties (such as traits, needs, motives and attitudes). Subsequent research into children's understanding of interpersonal awareness indicates that children may progress through several levels of increasing sophistication in their thinking about other people, from the simplistic and rather undifferentiated concepts of the five-year-old who takes a 'friend' simply to be whoever she/he is currently playing with, through growing awareness of the qualities and feelings of others through middle childhood, to the greater selectivity of adolescent friendships, and the understanding of reciprocal obligations and expectations between friends (see Selman, 1980; Youniss, 1980a). Clearly, to understand the nature and development of interpersonal relationships among adults, we need to take account of the routes that young people have followed in order to participate in this aspect of social life.

Developing understanding of social structure   Apart from school and church, the young child's relations with societal structure and institutions are rather indirect. Furthermore, the complexity of societal structure and interrelationships is such that it requires correspondingly complex mental operations to grasp them. For these reasons social developmentalists, such as Jahoda (1984), Furth (1980), and Berti and Bombi (1981), have attempted to chart aspects of the development of understanding of societal phenomena (such as the economic system, the government) from a Piagetian stage-sequence theoretical perspective.

Furth's (1980) work provides a good example. Employing Piagetian clinical interview techniques with a sample of English schoolchildren, Furth demonstrated that understanding of both local and remote aspects of societal structure advances in stages and that these stages take several years. For instance, a local societal institution such as the shop is understood in quite simple undifferentiated terms by most five-year-olds, who see shopping as facilitated by adults' apparently unlimited access to money, and by the generosity of the shopkeeper who provides welcome 'change' which can finance future shopping ventures. Over the next few years, theories of how shops operate are enriched as children come to understand the rituals of payment, but even so the notion of profit margins is rarely grasped and the destination of funds in the till is uncertain: seven- to eight-year-olds often suppose it is given to poor or blind people, or collected (in England at least) by the Queen. By age ten to eleven years understanding is fuller, though there is still little or no awareness of considerations such as the expenses of running the shop. Developing understanding of more remote aspects of societal structure, such as the government, is similarly protracted and often limited or inconsistent through childhood and adolescence.

Furth concludes, persuasively, that children's understanding of society must be investigated in relation to cognitive development in general. However, it must be stressed that the converse holds equally: cognitive development needs to be investigated in relation to social experience. Although children may have often fantastic notions about the nature of societal phenomena, it is important to bear in mind that their experience of these processes is very limited (see Jahoda, 1984). A child is likely to construct many different transient understandings of the nature of money through dealings with others (Webley, 1983), and it is through these social interchanges that her or his insights will be acquired and organized. Different cultures afford different experiences in this respect, and Jahoda (1983) found that Zimbabwean nine- to eleven-year-olds, with personal involvement in small-scale trading, showed more sophisticated understanding than European (Scottish, English and Dutch) children in a test of comprehension of the concept of profit. Further, if children are given relevant experience of economic phenomena normally distant from them, their insights can progress. Berti, Bombi and De Beni (1986), for example, devised training games which they found promoted significant improvements in at least some eight-year-olds' understanding of economic profit (one factor which Berti, Bombi and De Beni suggest constrained further improvements was the large figures involved in the Italian currency with which they were working and which made calculations difficult; a Dutch, German or Swiss replication might be illuminating!). For the moment, the evidence of the development of societal understanding echoes the theme above: that cognitive development and social interaction are closely interlinked and have mutual consequences. Once again, there are good grounds for strengthening the link between developmental- and social-psychological perspectives in this area. While studies such as Furth's point to striking limitations in children's accounts of the social order, recent work on *adults'* political knowledge indicates 'dark areas of ignorance' among the general population (see Hewstone, 1986), a finding which suggests that not all citizens manage (or desire) to fulfil their social-cognitive potentialities in the societal domain.

Social cognition and social categories   Knowledge of societal relations is not simply a matter of abstract academic knowledge but has implications for the individual in terms of social identity and intergroup status; as Tajfel has long stressed, cognitive and affective factors become inseparable in this domain (see Tajfel, 1981; see also chapter 16). We will consider here research into two of the major social categories, namely nationality and gender, and then consider some investigations of the implications of social categories for self-determination during the transition to adulthood.

1   *National categorization*   One of the seminal studies in this area was conducted by Piaget himself, who found that among children aged around seven years the concept of nation was very limited and rather confused (Piaget and Weil, 1951), a finding which was supported and extended by Jahoda (1962, 1963). Even earlier, Piaget (1928) had observed that the first thing to interest a child about a country is its name, and it was this point in particular – the possibility that no more than a mere label could elicit children's preferences for some social categories over others – that raised important issues for Tajfel, a social psychologist interested in the influence of groups and group identities upon social judgements. Could the study of children's national preferences contribute to broader understanding of when and how the connotations of social categories are first acquired?

An early study by Tajfel and Jahoda (1966) revealed that by around age six or seven years, although children's empirical knowledge of different countries was minimal (e.g. they knew little of matters such as relative size), their affective orientation was well established; they had quite firm views about which countries they liked or disliked. In a series of studies of six- to twelve-year-olds conducted in England, The Netherlands, Austria, Scotland, Belgium and Italy, Tajfel and Jahoda and their collaborators asked children to identify their likes and dislikes from a set of photographs of young men, and on a separate occasion to distinguish which of the men they believed were members of their own national group (see Jaspars et al., 1973; Simon, Tajfel and Johnson, 1967; Tajfel et al., 1970 for fuller details). They found that the younger children showed a distinct preference for photographs of men they would also categorize as from their own country; the preference was less marked in the older children, though still present in some countries.

The importance of such findings is that they provide 'evidence of the very high sensitivity of young children to the more primitive aspects of the value systems of their societies' (Tajfel, 1981, p. 206). These primitive categorizations of social groups are compatible with low levels of cognitive development in early childhood (see Milner, 1984). Hence, they have the potential for strong influence over the ways in which children think about and behave towards people identified with particular social labels. To understand fully how national categories bear on people's social judgements, then, we may need in many cases to trace their origins to earlier phases of social development.

2   *Gender categorization*   Gender is one of the most fundamental social categories in virtually all societies, and one with profound implications for individuals' opportunities throughout the lifespan. The psychology of gender role has attracted wide interest during the last 20 years, and is an area where the interdependence of developmental- and social-psychological approaches has been most apparent. (For recent discussions of the social psychology of gender see Bem, 1981; Deaux, 1985; Hurtig and Pichevin, 1985.)

Analyses of the social context reveal without difficulty many arrangements whereby differential expectations about the sexes are manifest: in the family (Lewis, 1986), the educational system (Weinreich-Haste, 1979) and the mass media (Durkin, 1986); opportunities in play (Huston, 1985), leisure (Colley, 1986), peer relations (Smith, 1986) and the world of work (Hartnett and Bradley, 1986). This raises many questions about how males and females adapt to environmental indicators of role demands (Durkin, 1987b), and how inequitable social patterns are sustained (e.g. women's limited access to higher-status occupational ranks in most societies).

Echoes of the clay moulding model of socialization are prevalent in everyday discussions of gender roles, and it is often popularly assumed that people are 'conditioned' into particular roles. However, there are good reasons to suppose that gender role development and the perpetuation of gender role differences reflect far more complex processes which can only be investigated from a base which takes account of both developmental- and social-psychological theories.

Developmental approaches to this topic have been particularly influenced by Kohlberg (1966), whose work once more showed the application of Piagetian theory to a social domain. Kohlberg proposed an account of gender role development which located the central processes in 'neither biology nor culture, but with cognition' (p. 82). He and his followers have argued that gender role knowledge, like other areas of cognition, is best understood as developing in stages. The earliest stage is the discovery of gender labels, i.e. learning that one is a 'girl' or a 'boy'. Subsequently children find out the correlates of gender category (i.e. that there are some things that boys and men do or wear, and other things that girls or women do or wear), and that these distinctions are held to be important by other people. Next, they come to recognize that gender membership is a stable feature (i.e. if you are a male now, you will remain one throughout life – an arrangement by no means obvious to a two-year-old). Still later, they gain an understanding that gender is constant despite superficial transformations of dress or hairstyle (again, even five- to seven-year-olds have difficulties with this concept: see Emmerich et al., 1977).

Thinking about gender concepts, and about the origins and rigidity of gender roles, continues to develop from childhood through adolescence (Ullian, 1976) and probably for the rest of life (Worell, 1981). From a developmental perspective, then, the interest of gender role development revolves around questions of how the developing person goes beyond the superficial physical differences between the sexes to an understanding of the abstract associations of gender and the rules governing these aspects of social life. From a social-psychological perspective, however, an equally important question is why do children seize upon this social category as an important one in the first place (Bem, 1983)? What children have to learn in gender role acquisition is not a set of logico-mathematical knowledge from which they are detached (as in the case of a conservation problem), but the traditions of the social structure in which they are participants and which reflect the interests of groups within the society to which they belong (see Huici, 1984).

Do we need to lurch back to clay moulding theories to explain how the social structure has its impact upon the developing person? Probably not. Instead an interactive account, which takes note of the developing abilities and limitations of the child in processing social information, seems a more fruitful basis for investigation. For example, children are well known during certain periods of development to hold starker views about male and female role characteristics than even sex-stereotyped environmental sources would present (see Kohlberg, 1966). Children also show readiness to interpret public messages (such as media content) about gender in accord with their current level of information and their affective orientation towards the message (see Durkin, 1985). These considerations suggest that internal organization is imposed upon the data of experience; it remains the case that the data a given society provide in respect of gender role may be fashioned by the tensions and alignments within the society. To understand how people adjust to definitive role demands such as gender requires that we take account of the developmental and the social constraints, and of their intersection.

Social categories and social differentiation   We have stressed above that many of the discoveries about the social world that the developing person makes demand not only cognitive insight but also affective adjustment. Social categories are particularly important in this respect because they relate very directly to one of the core concerns of development, namely self-definition. As we have seen, working out how the social world operates is a lengthy process, but it is also likely to become a very involving one as the motivations to determine one's own place within the scheme of things intensify.

Adolescence is a major period in this connection, because during this time there are pressing reasons to organize an understanding of prospects and limitations in adult world. Palmonari et al. (1979, 1984) propose that, in the search for a useful set or system of values, adolescents in contemporary Western societies are prompted to create or preserve differentiations among a variety of social groups, and as they do so often adopt powerful socio-cognitive and affective stances towards them. This suggests that the social differentiations of adult society should be seen not simply as imposed by some broader structure (clay moulding or repressing new members of society) but as a creative, functional response to the ways in which young people perceive the opportunities and barriers of the world about them.

The cognitive and the affective are inseparable components of these processes, as Hewstone, Jaspars and Lalljee (1982) have demonstrated in a comparison of the attributions and representations of 16-year-olds attending British public (elite) and comprehensive (state) schools. They found that while the schoolboys from both contexts agreed on the relevance of some descriptive categories, they invested them with differing evaluative connotations. For example, public school boys saw themselves as 'hard working' while the comprehensive boys regarded them as 'swots'; public school boys saw their institutions as providing a 'training for life', while comprehensive school boys regarded the same places as affording contact with 'string pullers'. Similarly, Palmonari (1980) describes the emergence among some sectors of Italian students of groups of people who call themselves 'unguaranteed' (i.e. individuals who lack any effective power or social security). These young people are located in these circumstances by structural forces beyond their control. They can see that they have little prospect of employment because of economic factors; one way of coping with this situation while still preserving a sense of one's own worth is consciously to redefine the situation and abandon the socially ascribed careers that had hitherto been expected of them (Palmonari, 1980, p. 61). Thus, the individual rejects the values and constraints of the status quo and supplants them with strong ingroup attachment and a vigorous, even fanatical, denigration of the outgoing (mainstream) society.

Perhaps the most dramatic outcome of the interaction between social reasoning and social context in development is provided by the potency of the *self* and *other* categorizations as young people participate in constructing social differentiations that mark out their place and their prospects in the social structure.

Summary and Conclusion

From infancy through to adulthood, the young person is immersed in a social world in which the content and the processes of development depend critically upon its interactions with other people. These interactions are multiple and multilevel, involving modes of communication, the emergence of behavioural styles, the formulation of ideas, the transmission of knowledge, cooperation and conflict in problem-solving, and the acquisition of social concepts and categories. As we learn more about these aspects of human development, they expose the inadequacies of traditional approaches which tend to regard the child as a cognitive isolate operating independently upon an objective world. One consequence of this is that recognition of the importance of social factors is leading to a new appraisal of theoretical assumptions in developmental psychology, while another is that the topic of social knowledge is becoming a central concern of students of human development.

As a result, the common ground between social and developmental psychologists is proving to be a fertile and exciting territory to cross. While many specialists have wandered into it from different directions, the growth of social cognition as a research field is drawing several lines of investigation together. This intersection of concerns continues to nurture the young but robust hybrid of developmental social psychology, with implications for both of the parent areas. These advances lead us increasingly to treat the developing person not as an apprentice scientist but as a participant in a social world; correspondingly, to understand how and why people function as they do in the social world requires us to examine the developmental processes through which understanding is acquired and endowed with affective meaning. For these reasons the study of the social nature of social development has to be seen not as a discrete subsection of child study but as the central topic for developmental social investigation. After all, we noted at the beginning of the chapter that it is asocial development which is exceptional, and it may not prove advisable to build our theories of development around metaphors of individual construction or growth which neglect the essence of human existence.

Glossary Terms

Concrete operational stage	Preoperational stage
Conservation	Socio-cognitive conflict

Further Reading

Brehm, S. S., Kassin, S. M. and Gibbons, F. X. (eds) (1981) *Developmental Social Psychology: theory and research*. Oxford: Oxford University Press. A useful collection of review chapters.

Damon, W. (1983) *Social and Personality Development: infancy through adolescence*. New York: Norton. A wide-ranging and insightful account of the integration of social and personality development.

Hargreaves, D. J. and Colley, A. M. (eds) (1986) *The Psychology of Sex Roles* London: Harper and Row. A comprehensive introduction to the study of the development of sex roles through the lifespan.

Higgins, E. T., Ruble, D. N. and Hartup, W. W. (eds) (1983) *Social Cognition and Social Behaviour: developmental perspectives*. Cambridge: Cambridge University Press. A valuable collection of different perspectives on the development of children's social thought.

Turiel, E. (1983) *The Development of Social Knowledge: morality and convention*. Cambridge: Cambridge University Press. An important account of the ways in which children evolve their understanding of the social world, including social rules and conventions.

4 Methodology in Social Psychology: Turning Ideas into Actions

A. S. R. MANSTEAD and G. R. SEMIN

Introduction

Procedures for gathering information in any discipline are known as *methods*. Methods provide a means of translating a researcher's ideas into actions. The researcher's ideas will generally revolve around one or more questions about a phenomenon. An example of such a question in social psychology would be: 'How can a group of intelligent people make a decision that is stupid and could have been shown to be so at the time the decision was taken?' (cf. Janis, 1972). A researcher interested in this question might have a hunch or a theory to explain this phenomenon. For example, it might be thought that the poor decision arises from the fact that the group has a powerful leader who expresses a preference early in the decision-making process and thereby stifles systematic evaluation of superior options. Assessing the correctness of this hunch would necessitate the collection of information about styles of leadership in groups making poor decisions. Methods are the procedures the researcher would follow in gathering that information, and *methodology* is a term used to refer to all aspects of the implementation of methods.

The specific method adopted by a researcher in conducting a particular investigation depends a good deal on the type of question he or she is trying to answer. An analogy may be helpful here. Imagine an individual who wants to cross a river. Various options are available: swimming, rowing or sailing a boat, floating a raft , building a bridge, hang-gliding, flying and so on. The task of crossing the river is analogous to the research question being addressed, and the various means of crossing the river are analogous to the research methods available. The means of crossing chosen by the individual will depend on factors such as the number of people who wish to cross the river, the frequency with which they want to make crossings, the prevailing weather and current conditions, and so on. Similarly, the type of research method chosen by the investigator will depend on the ultimate goal of the research. If the research goal is to *describe* some phenomenon (e.g. whether it exists, how and where it is found, and so on), this implies a different type of method to the one suggested by the research goal of *testing* one or more explanations for or **hypotheses** about a phenomenon.

Research: descriptive, correlational and experimental

It will be useful at this point to distinguish between three different types of research: descriptive, correlational and experimental.

Descriptive research   This is intended to provide the researcher with an accurate description of the phenomenon in question ('Does A occur?'). For example, the researcher may want to know (as did Milgram, 1963) whether the average adult would obey orders from an authority figure to administer painful and potentially lethal electric shocks to a fellow human. The researcher would begin by observing and recording the proportion of adults that obeys an authority's orders. This simply describes the phenomenon. Social-psychological research rarely stops at this point. The researcher typically wants to know *why* people behave as they do. If one finds, as did Milgram, that 65 per cent of a sample of adults are fully obedient to orders to administer shocks, an obvious question is 'Why?'

Correlational research   The correlational approach takes us part of the way to answering this question. The goal here is to describe the extent to which variations in some behaviour, such as obedience, are related systematically to variations in some other factor ('Is A related to B?'). For example, do those who obey the orders tend to be particular *types* of person (men rather than women, introverts rather than extroverts, and so on)? In posing such questions, the researcher is looking for relationships, or *correlations*, in the information that he or she collects. Discovering such a relationship can be helpful in working out why a phenomenon occurs, but correlational information is rarely decisive in this respect. To understand why this is so, let us take the case of a correlational finding from Milgram's (1965) study of obedience. It was found that persons who were more obedient tended also to report experiencing more tension during their participation in the study. How should we interpret this correlation? Is the tension a sign of fear of the consequences of disobedience, which would suggest that obedience is 'caused' by individuals' fears about what might happen to them if they were disobedient? Alternatively, might the tension simply reflect concern about the possible harm befalling the 'victim'? In the first case the relationship between obedience (A) and tension (B) is explained as 'B leads to A'; in the second case, the same relationship is interpreted as 'A leads to B'. In the absence of further information, either interpretation is plausible. This is why it is almost always impossible to infer causality from correlational research.

Experimental research   This is explicitly designed to yield causal information. The goal of an **experiment** is to see what happens to a phenomenon, such as obedience, when the researcher deliberately modifies some feature of the environment in which the phenomenon occurs ('If I change B, will there be resulting changes in A?'). By controlling the variation in B, the researcher can arrive at stronger conclusions about causality if it is found that A and B are related. Instead of simply knowing that more A is associated with more B, the experimental researcher discovers whether A increases when B is increased, decreases when B is reduced, remains stable when B is left unchanged, and so on. Such a pattern of results would suggest that the manipulated variations in B *cause* the observed variations in A. We shall have quite a lot more to say about experimental research below.

The descriptive, correlational and experimental research types are very general kinds of research method, and are by no means specific to psychology or social psychology. Our main purpose in this chapter is to introduce the reader more specifically to the research methods most often employed in social-psychological research. The principal aim is to enable the reader to evaluate social-psychological research; a secondary aim is to provide some preliminary guidance for the conduct of research. To facilitate the process of describing and discussing research methods, we shall consider separately two facets of research methodology. First, we shall describe various *research strategies*; by research strategy we mean the broad orientation one adopts in addressing a question. To pursue our river-crossing analogy, the decision to adopt a research strategy is akin to the decision to swim, float, sail, straddle or fly across the river. Next, we shall describe some of the most popular *data collection techniques*; these are the specific procedures the researcher follows in gathering information. Deciding which technique to adopt is akin to deciding how exactly to construct the raft, boat, bridge or whatever, once a general strategy has been chosen. The selection of a particular technique will be determined partly by the researcher's objectives and partly by the available resources, just as the decision to construct a solid bridge rather than rope bridge depends partly on how many people are expected to use the bridge (and how often), and partly on the availability of skill and raw materials.

Selection of Research Strategies

The strategies available for social-psychological research differ in terms of the degree of control and the amount of precision they offer, the realism of the situations in which data are collected, and so on. In this section, we shall provide an overview of the major research strategies and briefly describe their distinctive attributes, following a scheme devised by Runkel and McGrath (1972, pp. 81ff).

Systematic observations of phenomena in real-life settings are **field studies** (Bickman and Henchey, 1972). If some property of the real-life setting is deliberately modified, as when an interracial housing policy is implemented on a housing estate and levels of prejudice are compared with those on an equivalent housing estate where no such policy is introduced, the strategy is called a **field experiment**. If, however, the ecology of the life setting is contrived, as in a university laboratory, and specific properties of this ecology are deliberately modified, this strategy is known as a **laboratory experiment** (Aronson, Brewer and Carlsmith, 1985). There is also a 'middle road' between field and laboratory experiments in which the investigator devises a situation that simulates key features of a naturally occurring setting (such as an emergency situation) in a laboratory, and this type of strategy is known as an **experimental simulation** (Abelson, 1968). The major difference between a laboratory experiment and an experimental simulation is that in the former the investigator attempts to create a setting which, although contrived, incorporates features believed to be common to a large class of settings. In the experimental simulation, by contrast, the investigator attempts to mimic the essential properties of *one* type of naturally occurring situation.

A different strategy for gathering information is to survey public opinion, either by interview or by questionnaire. Here the investigator is not concerned about the setting in which the data are collected, because this is assumed to be irrelevant. On the other hand, the investigator *is* typically concerned with the extent to which the respondents are representative of a population (such as all adults living in a particular community, region or country). This type of research strategy is known as a **sample survey,** and is well known to us in the form of opinion polls (Schuman and Kalton, 1985).

Another strategy where the setting in which the data are collected is of no great concern to the investigator is referred to by Runkel and McGrath as a **judgement task** (Rosenthal, 1982). Here, as in the sample survey, the investigator is concerned with the subject's report or judgement about some issue or problem. Judgement tasks differ from sample surveys in that the investigator exercises more control over the issues or problems being judged. In a sample survey of attitudes towards different political candidates, for example, the respondent might simply be asked to indicate which candidate he or she likes most, would be likely to vote for, and so on. In a judgement task, by contrast, the respondent might be asked to identify in what way two of three candidates are alike, and in what way they differ from the third candidate. In the first case the investigator's concern is to describe which candidate is most preferred by some population (such as all adults eligible to vote in a particular constituency); in the second case, the investigator's concern is to uncover the dimensions along which respondents distinguish the candidates.

Runkel and McGrath identify two further research strategies, which they term 'formal theory' and 'computer simulation'. These strategies differ from the others we have considered in that they do not involve observation or measurement of actual behaviour; that is they are *non-empirical* strategies. In using **formal theory** the investigator proceeds by building a symbolic system of interconnected statements, assumptions and postulates, and uses deductive logic to derive some consequences which should map on to empirical observations. There are plenty of examples of the use of formal theory in social psychology; one of the better known is Zajonc's (1965) drive theory of social facilitation effects. *Social facilitation* is the impact of the presence of other persons on task performance. Before 1965 researchers were puzzled by the fact that in some experiments this impact was found to be beneficial, but in others it was found to be detrimental. Indeed, research on social facilitation had virtually ground to a halt by the mid 1960s, bogged down in this morass of apparently inconsistent research findings. The utility of theory is demonstrated by the fact that Zajonc's theoretical account for these findings stimulated an upsurge of research interest in this topic (see chapter 14). However, formal theory is rarely, if ever employed by social psychologists as an independent research strategy, because theory is only useful to the extent that it connects with empirical observations.

The other non-empirical research strategy – **computer simulation** – has become increasingly popular, particularly in cognitive science and cognitive psychology. The use of computer simulation is much less common in social psychology, although some cognitively oriented social psychologists (e.g. Abelson, 1968; Schank and Abelson, 1977) have used this strategy. Runkel and McGrath point out that the relationship between formal theory and computer simulation is similar to that between laboratory experiments and experimental simulations, in that computer simulations are in effect formal theories about concrete systems, stated in propositional form. Instead of assessing the applicability of the theory by examining its fit with empirical evidence, the computer simulation attempts to model the properties and dynamics of cognitive or behavioural systems.

A diagrammatic summary of these eight research strategies is shown in figure 4.1. Rather than describing each strategy superficially, we shall confine ourselves to a detailed consideration of experimental methods, on the grounds that experimentation has been the dominant methodology in social psychology for the past three decades.

Before examining experimental methods, however, it is worth noting some points of similarity and dissimilarity between the eight strategies. First, note that the circle shown in figure 4.1 is divided in half, both vertically and horizontally. Beginning with the vertical division, it can be seen that Runkel and McGrath consider the four strategies in the left-hand half of the figure to be ones that deal with *universal* behaviour systems, and the four strategies in the right-hand half of the figure to deal with *particular* behaviour systems. What is meant by this is that strategies of the first type attempt to study behaviour without reference to the particular context in which it is observed or measured; strategies of the latter type, by contrast, are ones in which the investigator studies behaviour in a specific and concrete context, with a view to understanding something about that particular behaviour setting.

Turning now to the horizontal division, it can be seen that the four strategies in the upper half of the figure are classed as **obtrusive research** operations and those in the lower half as **unobtrusive research** operations. What is meant by this is that strategies of the first type intrude into the normal course of events,

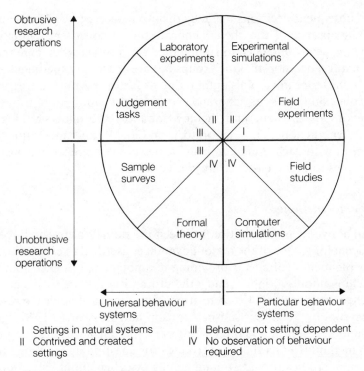

FIGURE 4.1   Research strategies (Runkel and McGrath, 1972)

by manipulating and controlling aspects of the environment in which the subject behaves. Strategies of the latter type, by contrast, are either minimally obtrusive or completely unobtrusive, in that the research process does not disturb the natural course of events.

This brief overview of the alternative strategies available to the social psychologist should provide a general idea of the way in which the different strategies relate to one another, and of their relative advantages and disadvantages. In closing this section, we should point out that the strategies should be regarded as *complementary*. A good example of that complementarity comes from the field of group decision-making, where laboratory experiments (e.g. Fraser, Gouge and Billig, 1971) have revealed a systematic tendency for groups of persons to arrive at a more extreme or polarized decision on some issue than the average of the individual decisions made by those same group members (see chapter 15 for further information). In spite of the obvious real-world applicability of this finding, there has been surprisingly little field research on this issue. In one of the few published field studies, Semin and Glendon (1973) capitalized on the decision-making procedures used by a real managerial team, which happened to correspond very closely to the procedures followed in laboratory experiments on group polarization. Thus they were able to conduct a field experiment without interfering unduly with the normal decision-making procedure of this managerial group. They found *no* differences between the average of the individual decisions made by members of the managerial team and the subsequent decisions made by the group as a whole. In attempting to explain the absence of the phenomenon found so consistently in laboratory experiments, Semin and Glendon pinpointed various factors that are characteristics of natural decision-making groups but are absent in experimental groups studied in the laboratory. This pinpointing of factors permits the researcher to modify the conditions of laboratory experiments until they too yield no evidence of polarization, and thereby enhances the understanding of the general phenomenon. Thus laboratory and field experimentation used in conjunction with each other can provide a more comprehensive answer to a research question than either strategy used alone.

Experimental methods

As noted above, experimentation has been the dominant research method in social psychology. One of the major advantages ascribed to experimentation is that it is the ideal method for providing unambiguous evidence about causal relationships among variables, and is therefore without parallel as a method for testing theories that predict such relationships. Standard guides to research in social psychology (e.g. Carlsmith, Aronson and Ellsworth, 1976; Aronson, Brewer and Carlsmith, 1985) tend to treat experimentation as the preferred research method. In fact there are grounds for questioning the extent to which experimental studies provide unambiguous evidence about causation, as we shall see. However, first we shall describe the principal features of the experimental approach to social-psychological research.

To assist the process of description, we shall use one experiment as an illustrative example. The work in question is the well-known study of obedience conducted by Milgram (1965), already referred to at the beginning of this chapter (also see chapter 15 for a fuller discussion of this study).

The experimental scenario   The **experimental scenario** is the package in which the study is presented. In a field experiment the scenario should, of course, be one that occurs naturally, without contrivance on the experimenter's part. In laboratory settings, however, it is essential to devise a scenario for which there is a convincing and well-integrated rationale, because the situation should strike participants as realistic and involving, and the experimental manipulations and the measurement process should not 'leap out' at the subject. There is a sense in which the typical laboratory experiment is like staging a play, with the exception that the subject's lines are more or less unscripted. In the case of Milgram's study, the scenario presented to subjects was that of an investigation of the effects of punishment on learning. The subject was allocated, apparently at random, the role of 'teacher', while an accomplice of the experimenter, posing as another subject, took the role of 'learner'. The learner's ostensible task was to memorize a list of word pairs. The teacher's task was to read out the first word of each pair, see whether the learner could correctly remember the second word, and to administer a graded series of punishments, in the form of electric shocks of increasing severity, if the learner failed to recall the correct word (which he had been instructed to do from time to time). The experimental scenario was set up with a view to convincing the subject that the shocks were genuine (which they were not), and that the learner was indeed a fellow subject who was actually receiving the shocks. Thus what was actually a study of the extent to which subjects would obey the experimenter's instruction to deliver steadily increasing electric shocks was presented as a study of the effects of punishment on learning.

The independent variable   The **independent variable** is the variable that is deliberately manipulated by the experimenter. All other aspects of the experimental scenario are held constant, and the independent variable is changed in some respect with a view to assessing the consequences of this manipulation. Each change in the independent variable produces a new 'condition' of the experiment: one change yields two conditions, two changes yield three conditions, and so on. For example, in Milgram's study a key independent variable was the proximity of the 'learner' to the 'teacher'. In one condition, learner and teacher were in separate rooms, and the teacher could not hear or see the learner's reactions to the shocks; in a second condition, the teacher could hear the learner, but still could not see him; in the third condition, the teacher could both see and hear the learner's reactions; in the fourth condition, the teacher had to hold the learner's hand down on a metal plate in order for the shock to be delivered (the Touch-Proximity Condition, see plate 4.1). All other aspects of the experimental setting were held constant, so that variations in the teacher-subjects' behaviour in these four different conditions should have been attributable only to the change in proximity between teacher and learner. The adequacy of an experiment often hinges on the effectiveness of manipulations of the independent variable. By *effectiveness* we mean (1) the extent to which changes in the independent variable capture the essential qualities of the variable that is theoretically expected to have a causal influence on behaviour; and (2) the size of the changes that are introduced. For example, in Milgram's study, we should consider how well the four proximity conditions capture the notion of proximity. What is being manipulated, quite clearly, is *physical* proximity (rather than, say, psychological proximity); as long as this is what the experimenter intends to manipulate, all well and good. We should also consider whether the changes between the four conditions are sufficiently large to have an effect. In this particular case, it is difficult to see how the proximity variable could have been manipulated more powerfully, but an investigator who adopts weaker manipulations runs the risk of failing to find the predicted effects simply because the variations across levels of the independent variable are too subtle to have any impact.

Another important point in this context is that subjects should be **randomly allocated** to different experimental conditions. Failure to adhere to this stipulation interferes with one's ability to draw causal inferences from the results. For example, in the four conditions of Milgram's study described above, it was found that the number of shocks teacher-subjects were prepared to administer steadily declined as the proximity between teacher and learner

PLATE 4.1   General arrangement for Touch-Proximity Condition and obedient subject in Touch-Proximity Condition in Milgram's (1963) study. (Stills from 1965 film *Obedience* © Stanley Milgram as reproduced in *Obedience to Authority* by Stanley Milgram courtesy of Tavistock Publications)

increased. This appears to show that obedience to the experimenter's instructions diminished as the learner's suffering became more salient to the teacher. Such an inference could *not* be drawn if there were grounds for thinking that the type of subject recruited for the four conditions differed in some systematic way. If, for example, there was any possibility that subjects in the high-proximity conditions were less 'punitive' in their attitudes or personalities than subjects in other conditions, this would be a plausible alternative explanation for the findings.

The dependent variable   Assessing the impact of an independent variable requires the experimenter to measure some feature of the subject's behaviour or internal state. This measured variable is known as the **dependent variable**, so called because systematic changes in this measured variable should depend upon the impact of the independent variable. In the Milgram study, the dependent variable was the number of shocks in a 30-step sequence that the teacher was prepared to deliver by throwing switches corresponding to each shock level. A key question to ask of any dependent variable is the extent to which it is a good measure of the underlying theoretical variable. For example, is the willingness to deliver what appear to be increasingly strong shocks to another person a good measure of 'destructive obedience'? In addition to this question of the 'fit' between a theoretical variable and the measured or dependent variable, the most important issue involved in designing dependent variables is what type of measure to use. This is a matter that will be discussed in some detail later in this chapter.

The follow-up   The follow-up is the phase of data collection that takes place after the independent variable has been introduced and the dependent variable has been measured. Typically, the follow-up takes the form of a post-experimental enquiry (usually in the form of an interview or questionnaire), followed by debriefing. The prime objectives of the **post-experimental enquiry** are (1) to check the effectiveness of the experimental manipulations, by measuring subjects' perceptions of those features of the experimental scenario that are relevant to that manipulation; and (2) to establish whether the subject has suffered any ill-effects as a result of his or her participation in the experiment. In Milgram's study particular attention was paid to the latter point, in view of the stressfulness of the experimental procedure and the serious way in which subjects were deceived. An example of a post-experimental enquiry designed to check the effectiveness of experimental manipulations is that used by Parkinson and Manstead (1981). Their experiment was intended to assess the effects of paying attention to or ignoring sounds that purportedly represented the subject's heartbeat; one of the questions in the post-experimental questionnaire asked subjects to rate the amount of attention they had paid to these sounds. For the manipulation to be deemed effective, subjects in the 'attend' condition should have made higher ratings than subjects in the 'ignore' condition – which they did. **Debriefing** the subject refers to the process of informing the subject as fully as possible about the nature and purpose of the experiment, and the role their particular participation played in the study as a whole. Although this process is a good idea in any context, it is particularly important wherever the subject has been deceived about the purpose of the experiment and/or about some aspects of the experimental procedure. In Milgram's study, for example, care was taken to assure subjects that the 'shocks' they had administered were in fact bogus, and that the learner had not been harmed in any way. Ideally, the debriefing process should leave subjects happy with their role in the experiment and with as much self-respect as they had on entering the laboratory.

Experimental designs

We have already seen that it is important (1) that experimenters keep all theoretically irrelevant features of the experimental setting constant across conditions, manipulating just the key independent variable, and (2) that subjects are allocated randomly to the different conditions of an experiment. Failure to achieve these goals hinders the researcher's ability to draw the inference that observed differences in the dependent variable across conditions result from changes in the independent variable. We shall now examine more closely the question of designing experiments in such a way that alternative inferences are ruled out.

Consider first a design for a study that may *appear* to be an experiment but cannot truly be described as an experimental design. This is the so-called **one-shot case study**. Following Cook and Campbell (1979), we shall use the symbol X to stand for a manipulation (i.e. of the independent variable) and the symbol O to stand for observation (i.e. the dependent variable). In these terms the one-shot design looks like this:

$$X \qquad O$$

$$\xrightarrow{\hspace{3cm}}$$
$$\text{time}$$

To take a concrete example, imagine that an educational researcher wanted to know the effect of a new teaching method on learning. The researcher takes a class of students, introduces the new method (X), and measures the students' recall of the taught material (O). What conclusions can be drawn from such a design? Strictly speaking, the answer is none; the point is that there is nothing with which O can be compared, so the researcher cannot infer whether the observed recall is good, poor or indifferent.

A simple extension of the one-shot design provides the minimum requirements for a true experimental design, and is known as the **post-test only control group design**. Let R stand for random assignment of subjects to conditions, and X and O stand for manipulation and observation, as before. This design looks like this:

$$\begin{matrix} R & X & O1 \\ R & & O2 \end{matrix}$$

$$\xrightarrow{\hspace{3cm}}$$
$$\text{time}$$

Compared with the one-shot design, there are two important modifications. First, there are two conditions. In one the subjects are exposed to the manipulation (this is usually referred to as the experimental condition, and subjects in this condition are known as the *experimental group*), and possible effects of the manipulation are measured. In the other no manipulation is introduced (this is usually referred to as the control condition, and subjects in this condition are known as the **control group**, but these subjects are also measured on the same dependent variable and at the same time point as the experimental group. Now the observation made in the experimental condition (O1) *can* be compared with something, namely the observation made in the control condition (O2). The second important modification is that in this design subjects are randomly allocated to the two conditions, ruling out the possibility that differences between O1 and O2 are due to differences between the two groups of subjects that were present before X was implemented. It follows that if O1 and O2 differ markedly, it is reasonable to infer that this difference is caused by X.

Although the post-test only control group design is one of the more commonly used experimental designs in social psychology, there are several other more sophisticated and complex designs, each representing a more complete attempt to rule out the possibility that observed differences between conditions result from something other than the manipulation of the independent variable (see Cook and Campbell, 1979 for a full discussion). The prime object of experimental design, then, is to enhance the validity of the researcher's inference that differences in the dependent variable result from changes in the independent variable.

Finally, it is worth noting that although using a control group is a basic step that enables the researcher to infer that a given manipulation has a measurable effect, in practice researchers sometimes dispense with the use of a control group in which subjects are not exposed to any manipulation, and instead use two or more conditions which vary with respect to the size or strength of the manipulation to which subjects are exposed. An example of this is the Milgram experiment referred to above, in which the proximity of the learner to the teacher was progressively increased across four experimental conditions. Comparing the amount of obedience observed in these conditions permitted Milgram to draw inferences about the effect of proximity on obedience. The underlying point, then, is that the use of sound experimental designs enables the researcher to *compare* observations made under different conditions, and thereby to draw inferences about causal relationships.

Threats to validity in experimental research

Good experimental research maximizes each of three types of validity: internal validity, construct validity and external validity.

Internal validity   This is promoted by the use of a sound experimental design. Internal validity refers to the validity of the conclusion that an observed relationship between independent and dependent variables reflects a *causal* relationship. We have already seen that the use of a control group greatly enhances internal validity, but even if one uses a control group there remain many potential threats to internal validity (Cook and Campbell, 1979 list 13!). Among these is the possibility that the groups being compared differ with respect to more than the independent variable of interest.

For example, assume for one moment that in the experiment described previously Milgram had used a different experimenter for each of the four conditions, such that experimenter 1 ran all subjects in one condition, experimenter 2 ran all subjects in the next condition, and so on. Although it might seem sensible to divide the work of running the conditions among different experimenters, to do so in this way poses a major threat to the **internal validity** of the experiment. This is because the four conditions would no longer differ *solely* in terms of the physical proximity of the 'victim'; they would also differ in that each would be conducted by a different experimenter. Thus the differing amounts of obedience observed in the four conditions *might* reflect the causal influence of the physical proximity independent variable, *or* the influence of the different experimenters (or, indeed, some combination of these two factors). The problem is that the physical proximity variable would be **confounded** with a second variable, namely experimenter identity. It is impossible to disentangle the effects of confounded variables.

Construct validity   Even when we are confident that the relationship between X and O is a causal one, in the sense that internal validity is high, we need to consider carefully the nature of the constructs involved in this relationship. **Construct validity** refers to the validity of the assumption that independent or dependent variables adequately capture the variables (or 'constructs') they are supposed to represent.

With regard to the construct validity of independent variables, the issue is whether the experimental manipulation really operationalizes the intended theoretical construct. For example, in a well-known experiment Aronson and Mills (1959) found that subjects who underwent a severe initiation in order to join what turned out to be a tedious discussion group subsequently reported greater liking for that group than did subjects who underwent a milder initiation. This was interpreted as evidence in support of a prediction derived from dissonance theory (see chapter 8). According to dissonance theory, the knowledge that one has suffered in order to attain a goal is inconsistent with the knowledge that the goal turns out to be worthless, thereby generating cognitive dissonance. To reduce this uncomfortable state of dissonance, it is argued, the individual re-evaluates the goal more positively. Gerard and Mathewson (1966) pointed out that Aronson and Carlsmith's findings are in fact open to a variety of interpretations, all of which accept that the initiation manipulation used by Aronson and Carlsmith was responsible for the observed differences in liking for the discussion group, but assert that this effect resulted from something other than the differing amounts of dissonance supposedly experienced by the two groups of subjects. Accordingly, Gerard and Mathewson conducted a modified replication of the original experiment, effectively ruling out these alternative interpretations.

Even if the researcher has cause to feel satisfied with the construct validity of the independent variable, there remains the question of whether the measured variables actually assess what they were intended to assess. As we shall see below, devising a measure to capture the essence of a social-psychological construct is by no means straightforward. There are three main types of threat to the construct validity of dependent variables in social-psychological experimentation: social desirability, demand characteristics and experimenter expectancy.

Social desirability is a term used to describe the fact that subjects are usually keen to be seen in a positive light, and may therefore be loath to provide honest reports of fears, anxieties, feelings of hostility or prejudice, or any other quality which they think would be regarded negatively. Equally, subjects may 'censor' some of their behaviours so as to avoid being evaluated negatively. To the extent that a researcher's measures are contaminated by social desirability effects, they will obviously be failing to assess the theoretical construct of interest. The most obvious means of reducing social desirability effects is to make the measurement process as unobtrusive as possible, on the premise that if subjects do not know what it is that is being measured, they will be unable to modify their behaviour.

Demand characteristics are cues in the experimental setting which convey to the subject the nature of the experimenter's hypothesis. The point here is that individuals who know that they are being studied will often be curious about what the experimenter is looking at and what types of responses are expected. Subjects may then attempt to provide the expected responses in order to please the experimenter. When behaviour is enacted with the intention of fulfilling the experimenter's hypotheses, it is said to be a response to the demand characteristics of the experiment. Orne (1962, 1969) has conducted a great deal of research into demand characteristics, and has suggested various methods of pinpointing the role they play in any given experimental situation. For example, he advocates the use of in-depth post-experimental enquiry in the form of an interview, preferably conducted by someone other than the experimenter, the object of which is to elicit from the subject what he or she believed to be the aim of the experiment, and the extent to which this belief affected behaviour in the experiment. Clearly, researchers should do all they can to minimize the operation of demand characteristics, for example by using unobtrusive measures, or by telling subjects that the purpose of the experiment cannot be revealed until the end of the study and that in the meantime it is important that they do *not* attempt to guess the hypothesis. A **cover story** which leads subjects to believe that the purpose of the study is something other than the real purpose is a widely used means of lessening the impact of demand characteristics. However, an unconvincing cover story can create more problems than it solves, raising doubts in the mind of the subject that otherwise may not have arisen.

Experimenter expectancy refers to the experimenter's own hypothesis or expectations about the outcome of the research. This expectancy can unintentionally influence the experimenter's behaviour towards subjects in such a way as to enhance the likelihood that they will confirm his or her hypothesis. Rosenthal (1966) called this type of influence the **experimenter expectancy effect**. The processes mediating experimenter expectancy effects are complex, but non-verbal communication is centrally involved. The extent to which experimenter expectancy can influence a phenomenon may be assessed by using several experimenters and manipulating their expectations about the experimental outcome. An obvious strategy for reducing these effects is to keep experimenters 'blind' to the hypothesis under test; other possibilities include minimizing the interaction between experimenter and subject, and automating the experiment as far as possible. The goal in each case is to reduce the opportunity for the experimenter to communicate his or her expectancies.

External validity   Even if the experimenter manages to circumvent all the above threats to internal and external validity, an important question concerning validity remains: to what extent can the causal relationship between X and O be generalized beyond the particular circumstances of the experiment? **External validity** refers to the generalizability of an observed relationship beyond the specific circumstances in which it was observed by the researcher. One important feature of the experimental circumstances, of course, is the type of person who participates in the experiment. In many cases subjects volunteer their participation, and to establish external validity it is important to consider whether results obtained using volunteers can be generalized to other populations. There is a good deal of research on differences between volunteers and non-volunteers in psychological studies (see Rosenthal and Rosnow, 1975 for a review; and Cowles and Davis, 1987 for a recent study). The general conclusion is that there *are* systematic personality differences between volunteers and non-volunteers. More importantly, in studies such as the one reported by Horowitz (1969) it has been found that the effects of some manipulations used in attitude change research were actually *opposite* for volunteers and non-volunteers. Such findings are explained in terms of volunteers' supposedly greater sensitivity to and willingness to comply with demand characteristics. The external validity of studies based only on volunteers' behaviour is therefore open to question, and the solution to this problem is to use a 'captive' population, preferably in a field setting.

Data Collection Techniques

Whichever research strategy is adopted by an investigator, he or she will need to measure one or more variables. In correlational designs, the researcher has to measure each of the variables that are expected to correlate. In experimental designs, the researcher needs to measure the dependent variable. In either case, the investigator is confronted with the task of translating a conceptual variable (for example, aggression or attraction) into a measurable variable (for example, willingness to harm someone, or willingness to help someone). The researcher's initial goal, then, is to specify what it is that he or she wants to record in order to represent the conceptual variable in a meaningful way. For example, is willingness to deliver a painful shock to another person, expressed behaviourally, a *representative* index of aggression as conceptualized by the investigator, or would it be better to adopt another index, such as the number of verbal insults directed at the person? In social-psychological research the investigator typically chooses to record a variable using either observational measures or self-report measures.

Observational measures

If the object of one's research is to collect information about social *behaviour*, an obvious means of doing so is by observation. Many behaviours that are of interest to social psychologists are detectable without the assistance of sophisticated equipment and are enacted in public settings, which makes them suitable for observation. Although observational methods vary in kind, as we shall see, from the relatively informal and unstructured to the highly formal and structured, the object in each case is the same: to abstract from the complex flux of social behaviour those actions that are of potential significance to the research question, and to record each instance of such actions over some period (Weick, 1985).

Sometimes the nature of the research setting or topic dictates that observation is conducted in a relatively informal and unstructured manner, with the researcher posing as a member of the group being observed. A classic example of research employing this method is Festinger, Riecken and Schachter's (1956) study of the consequences of blatant disconfirmation of strongly held beliefs. The investigators identified a religious sect which predicted that the northern hemisphere would be destroyed by flood on a certain date. By joining that sect, members of the research team were able to observe what happened when the predicted events failed to materialize. Under such circumstances, observation clearly has to be covert and informal: if other sect members suspected that the researchers were not *bona fide* believers, the opportunity for observation would be removed. This type of observation is known as **participant observation**, for the obvious reason that the observer participates in the activities of the group that is being observed.

Rather more formal methods of observation can be used when it is possible to record actions relevant to the research question without disrupting the occurrence of the behaviour. An example is Carey's (1978) series of studies investigating the hypothesis that when one pedestrian approaches another on the street, a rule of 'civil inattention' applies, whereby each looks at the other up to the point where they are approximately eight feet apart, after which their gaze is averted. This hypothesis was first advanced by Goffman (1963), on the basis of informal observation. Carey's purpose was to verify, using more formal methods, the existence of this rule, and to establish parameters such as the distance between pedestrians when gaze is first averted. He covertly photographed pairs of pedestrians as they approached and passed each other on a street, taking the photographs from upper storeys of buildings overlooking the street. The resulting still photographs were then coded for variables such as distance between the pair, whether their heads and eyelids were level or lowered, and whether gaze direction was towards or away from the approaching person.

The two examples cited above have in common the fact that the targets of the researchers' observations were unaware that they were being observed. Although such failure to inform persons of their involuntary participation in a research project may raise tricky ethical questions, it does overcome a problem peculiar to any research that uses humans as subjects, namely the tendency for the measurement process itself to have an impact on subjects' behaviour. It is well established that the simple knowledge that one is being observed can influence behaviour enacted in front of observers. The best known instance of such an effect is a study of worker productivity conducted at the Hawthorne plant of the Western Electric Company (Roethlisberger and Dickson, 1939), where it was found that merely observing workers raised their motivation and thereby increased productivity. Although this was not the first instance of researchers being aware that observation can itself influence the behaviour being observed, instances of such influence have come to be known as **Hawthorne effects**. Awareness of this problem has led many researchers to develop unobtrusive methods of observing and measuring behaviour. An entertaining and very useful sourcebook of methods of unobtrusive measurement has been compiled by Webb et al. (1981).

The most formal type of observational method is one in which the researcher uses a category system for scoring social behaviour. A well-known example of such a system is Bales's (1950b) **interaction process analysis (IPA)**, developed to study interaction in small social groups. IPA consists of the 12 categories shown in figure 4.2. The observer's task in using this system is to concentrate on the verbal interaction taking place between members of a group, and to place individual statements or 'thought units' into one of the 12 categories, noting at the same time who made the statement and to whom it was directed. Such a system should be simple enough for codings to be made in real time, general enough to be applicable to most types of group, and yet specific enough to tap important facets of verbal interaction. The IPA system is a fairly successful one, judged by these criteria, but some of its limitations are apparent if one remembers that non-verbal behaviour (widely acknowledged to be an important feature of interaction – see chapter 9) is almost totally ignored.

Observational methods of data collection have two prime advantages over the self-report methods we shall consider below: first, they can often be made unobtrusively; second, even where the subject knows that his or her behaviour is being observed, enacting the behaviour is typically quite engrossing, with the result that subjects have less opportunity to modify their behaviour than they would when completing a questionnaire. Nevertheless, there are some types of behaviour that are either impossible to observe directly (because they took place in the past) or difficult to observe directly (because they are normally enacted in private). Moreover, social psychologists are often interested in measuring people's *perceptions, cognitions* or *evaluations*, none of which can be directly assessed simply through observation. For these reasons, researchers often make use of self-report measures.

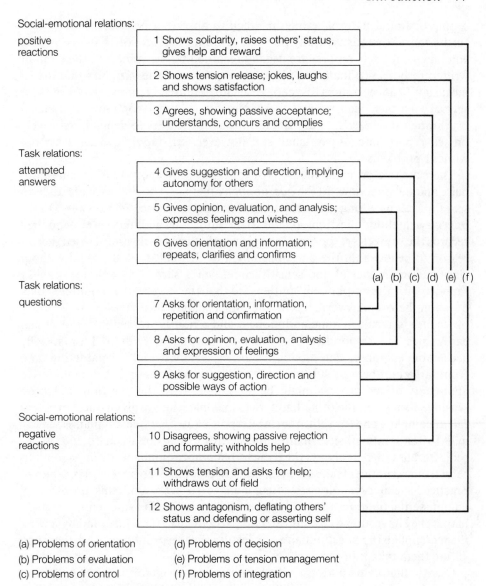

Social-emotional relations:

positive reactions

Task relations:

attempted answers

Task relations:

questions

Social-emotional relations:

negative reactions

1 Shows solidarity, raises others' status, gives help and reward

2 Shows tension release; jokes, laughs and shows satisfaction

3 Agrees, showing passive acceptance; understands, concurs and complies

4 Gives suggestion and direction, implying autonomy for others

5 Gives opinion, evaluation, and analysis; expresses feelings and wishes

6 Gives orientation and information; repeats, clarifies and confirms

(a) (b) (c) (d) (e) (f)

7 Asks for orientation, information, repetition and confirmation

8 Asks for opinion, evaluation, analysis and expression of feelings

9 Asks for suggestion, direction and possible ways of action

10 Disagrees, showing passive rejection and formality; withholds help

11 Shows tension and asks for help; withdraws out of field

12 Shows antagonism, deflating others' status and defending or asserting self

(a) Problems of orientation   (d) Problems of decision
(b) Problems of evaluation   (e) Problems of tension management
(c) Problems of control   (f) Problems of integration

FIGURE 4.2   Categories of socio-emotional (directed at friendship and emotional needs) and task-related (directed at achieving concrete problem-solving) interactions in small groups (Bales, 1950b)

Self-report measures

The essential feature of data collection using self-report measures is that questions about the subject's beliefs, attitudes, behaviour or whatever are put directly to the subject. His or her responses constitute self-report data. Self-report measurement is usually quicker, cheaper and easier to use than observational measurement. The researcher does not have to contrive a laboratory setting or find a natural setting in which to observe a behavioural response; furthermore, there is typically no need to train observers or to use recording equipment, for self-reports are usually recorded by the subject in the form of written responses. Finally, as noted above, some of the variables that are of most significance to social psychologists are not directly observable. For these several reasons, self-report measurement is very common in social-psychological research, and it is not unusual for studies to depend exclusively on self-report data. As we shall see, however, self-report measures are not without problems.

There are two principal methods of collecting self-report data: the questionnaire and the interview. In the *questionnaire* method, the subjects are handed a set of questions, along with instructions on how to record their answers. In the *interview* method, questions are put to the subject by an interviewer, who then records the subject's responses. Interviewing is particularly useful when there is reason to believe that the questions might be difficult to understand without clarification. A tactful and sensitive interviewer should be able to establish rapport with the respondent and ensure that the latter fully comprehends a question before answering. On the other hand, interviewing is a costly procedure in terms of time and money, and a poorly trained interviewer can easily bias the respondent's answers by hinting at a desired or socially acceptable response. Questionnaires are especially useful for gathering data from large numbers of subjects with minimal expense, and the comparative anonymity of the process might be preferable when the questions touch on sensitive issues. On the other hand, many people who are given questionnaires fail to complete and/or return them. Response rates for questionnaires sent by mail to randomly selected names and addresses vary between 10 and 50 per cent. Because there is always the danger that non-respondents differ systematically from respondents in some respect, low response rates are undesirable. In practice, social psychologists often manage to get round this problem by administering their questionnaires to subjects who are in some sense 'captive', in that they have already volunteered to participate in the study, and by having them complete the questionnaire in a lecture theatre or laboratory rather than letting them take it home.

Questionnaires are undoubtedly the most widely used form of data collection in social-psychological research. Some idea of the richness and variety of data collected exclusively by means of questionnaires can be gained by consulting the study reported by Folkman and Lazarus (1985). These investigators used questionnaire techniques to study how people appraised a stressful event (a university examination), what emotions they experienced as the event approached and passed, and how they coped with the stress induced by the event. It is difficult to envisage how Folkman and Lazarus could have conducted such a study without using questionnaires. It is certainly possible to measure some psycho-physiological indices of stress, such as heart rate, before, during and after exposure to a noxious stimulus such as an electric shock; but one cannot assume that the short-term stress induced by shock in a laboratory is comparable with the longer-term stress induced by 'natural' events such as examinations, ill health, divorce or bereavement. Furthermore, the individual's appraisals, emotions and coping strategies could not be assessed satisfactorily without the use of self-report measures.

Devising a good questionnaire or interview schedule is a harder task than one might imagine. As with any psychological measure, the goal is to produce questions that are **reliable**, in that they would evoke the same response from a given individual if he or she were tested more than once under similar circumstances, and **valid**, in that they measure exactly what the researcher intends them to measure. Although there are many potential sources of unreliability in the construction of questionnaires, the most serious threat to question reliability is *ambiguity*: if a question is ambiguous, a given respondent might well interpret it differently on different occasions and therefore give different answers. The most serious threat to question validity is failure on the part of the investigator to have *specific objectives* for each question: the hazier the intent of the researcher in posing a particular question, the greater are the chances that it will fail to elicit information relevant to his or her objectives. Because it is difficult to envisage all the potential pitfalls in questionnaire construction, there is no substitute for pilot work in which prototypes of the final questionnaire are administered to groups of subjects whose answers and comments provide a basis for revision. Constructing an entirely fresh questionnaire can therefore be a time-consuming and painstaking process. Fortunately, there are collections of previously developed and pre-tested questionnaires, such as those edited by Shaw and Wright (1967) and Robinson and Shaver (1969). It is worth checking these sources before setting out to construct an original questionnaire. If no suitable questionnaire already exists, the researcher should consult texts on questionnaire design such as Oppenheim (1966) and Payne (1951) before devising a fresh questionnaire.

As we have seen, self-report measures have several advantages; what are the drawbacks? Chief among these is the fact that it is not possible to collect self-report data completely unobtrusively: subjects are always aware that they are under investigation, and may modify their responses as a result of this awareness. In particular, there is ample opportunity for the respondent's answers to be influenced by motivational factors, such as social desirability. To the extent that these motivations bias the subject's responses, the self-report measure will provide a distorted reflection of his or her beliefs, behaviours, or whatever. There is no simple solution to this problem, although there are some steps that can be taken which together should reduce the scale of the problem. First, it is worth emphasizing to subjects whenever possible that their responses are anonymous. Second, it is worth stressing the point that there are no right or wrong answers. Third, it is often possible to increase subjects' motivation to respond truthfully by treating them as research accomplices rather than 'guinea-pigs'.

Choosing a measure

As we have seen, both types of measure considered here have certain advantages and disadvantages. Although there are no hard-and-fast rules for choosing one type of measure rather than the other, there are two points that should be borne in mind when judging the appropriateness of a dependent measure. First, the two types of measure can be used in conjunction with each other in many types of research. Second, the two types of measure differ in terms of the type of information they yield. Let us consider each of these points more closely.

Assume that you wish to study interpersonal attraction. Under laboratory or field conditions you introduce two people, previously unknown to each other, and ask them to get to know each other in the course of a 15 minute discussion. If you want to measure how much these two like each other at the end of the session, you could simply depend on self-report measures, such as responses to questions about how much each person liked the other, would be prepared to work with the other, and so on. You could also use observational measures: unobtrusively video recording the interaction would permit you to measure various aspects of behaviour, both verbal (e.g. the extent to which the two persons discovered mutual interests or shared attitudes) and non-verbal (e.g. the amount of smiling or direct looking at the other person).

Consider the advantages of using both types of measure. First, the observational data provide one type of check on the validity of the self-report data, and vice versa. Just as questionnaire data can be distorted by the respondents' motivations, so too can observers' perceptions be distorted by the nature of the coding system they are using. If both kinds of data point to the same conclusion, this would enhance confidence in their validity. A second, potentially more important, advantage is that while self-reported attraction can be said to be an *outcome* of the interaction, observational measures provide an insight into the *processes* that might mediate that outcome. Researchers would typically be interested in finding out *why* people did or did not like each other; examining the behaviours that occurred during the interaction might shed some light on this.

In summary, using more than one type of measure is often helpful to the researcher. If observational and self-report measures of the same conceptual variable point to the same conclusion, this enhances confidence in that conclusion. Furthermore, self-report measures often assess the outcome of a process; by using observational measures as well, the researcher may gain insight into the process responsible for that outcome.

Problems with Experimentation

It is widely assume that the experimental method provides the 'royal road' to causal inference (cf. Aronson, Brewer and Carlsmith, 1985). In fact causal inference from the results of experiments is more problematic than many commentators allow.

One problem concerns what Gergen (1978) has called the *cultural embeddedness* of social events, by which he means that 'few stimulus events considered independently have the capacity to elicit predictable social behavior' (p. 509). It follows that, even in the most tightly controlled laboratory experimental demonstration that the manipulation of independent variable X has a causal impact on dependent variable O, the circumstances in which X was manipulated may play a key role in producing the observed effects on O. The inference that 'X causes O' may therefore only be true under particular circumstances. As Gergen puts it: 'What passes for knowledge within the discipline may thus rest on an immense number of unstated assumptions and obscured conditions' (1978, p. 511).

A related problem, also articulated by Gergen, is that although the experimental method purportedly allows us to trace the causal sequence from antecedent conditions to the behaviour of interest, its capacity to do so depends on the assumption that external events are related in a one-to-one fashion with particular states or processes in the individual. Gergen argues; 'In dealing with human beings in a social setting it is virtually impossible to manipulate any variable in isolation of all the others. Even the most elemental variations in an independent variable have the capacity to elicit a host of intervening reactions' (1978, p. 515). The result is that what one experimenter believes to be a demonstration of the effect of X on O via the mediating process Z, another will prefer to explain in terms of an alternative mediating process. Social psychology abounds with such debates between rival accounts for findings (see Greenwald, 1975b; Ostrom, 1977; Tetlock and Levi, 1982; Tetlock and Manstead, 1985), and some have come to the view that experimentation is not a suitable means of settling such between-theory disputes.

Yet another inferential problem confronting the experimental researcher in social psychology also stems from the fact that social behaviour is culturally embedded. In every culture there are norms that define the boundaries of appropriate social behaviour in particular settings, with the result that most individuals behave similarly in such settings. Such behaviour is best regarded as the product of that culture's conventions or rules, rather than intraindividual psychological processes. Difficulties arise when researchers examine social behaviour in experimental settings. These settings are not free from the operation of cultural norms; indeed, there are grounds for thinking that laboratory experiments may promote the occurrence of behaviours that are guided by norms (Semin and Manstead, 1979). Inferential difficulties arise when behaviour in such settings is interpreted exclusively in terms of hypothetical internal processes. For example, it might be argued that cultural norms prescribe that one does not question the instructions of someone running a scientific experiment, and that when one is asked to deliver an increasingly strong series of shocks to another person, apparently in the interests of scientific research, one should do so. That people are willing to do so, even when the shocks are strong enough to produce fatal results, is by no means uninteresting; but whether it reveals something about the psychological processes mediating obedience to authority is another matter. In short, it is important to avoid the temptation to formulate causal laws about psychological processes where there are grounds for thinking that the phenomena being 'explained' have their origins in cultural convention (cf. Brandstaetter, 1982; Semin, 1986; Smedslund, 1985).

One final and related problem worth mentioning in this context is that although the ostensible goal of social-psychological experimentation is the accumulation of scientific knowledge, in the form of laws or principles of social behaviour that are valid across time, there is some reason to doubt whether experimentation (or, indeed, any other method) is capable of generating evidence that could be the basis of such laws. To understand why this is the case in social sciences but not in natural sciences, we have to take account of the fact that the relationship between researcher and the object of the research is radically different in the two types of science. The testing of theories in the natural sciences is concerned with the analysis and explanation of the *object world*, a world that does not engage in the construction and interpretation of the meaning of its own activity. This contrasts sharply with the objects of investigation in social sciences: being people, these 'objects' do of course attribute meaning and significance to their actions. Social psychology cannot therefore be neatly distinguished from what it studies; lay persons and social psychologists alike are concerned with understanding and interpreting their social environments. Lay persons are able to acquire social-psychological knowledge and use it to modify their actions in a way that atoms, elements and particles cannot. As Giddens (1982) puts it: 'The fact that the "findings" of the social sciences can be taken up by those to whose behaviour they refer is not a phenomenon that can, or should be, marginalized, but it is integral to their very nature. . . . Human beings . . . are not merely inert objects of knowledge, but agents able to – and prone to – incorporate theory and research within their own action' (pp. 14–16). One implication of this is that social-psychological theories should not be regarded as embodying 'laws' that will hold good across time: if learning about a social-psychological theory can lead individuals to modify the very behaviour that the theory purports to explain, it is clear that the theory has only limited temporal validity. Gergen (1973, 1978) has been the most persuasive advocate of this sobering view, although his arguments have been challenged by Schlenker (1974) and by Semin and Manstead (1983, chapter 5).

What are the implications of these problems for the status of experimentation in social-psychological research? It should be noted that even stern critics of the experimental approach do not advocate the abandonment of experimentation. For example, Gergen acknowledges that experiments will continue to play an important role in the explication of the relationship between biological processes (such as physiological arousal) and social behaviour; that studies such as the Milgram experiment are useful for raising consciousness about the insidious nature of social influence; that experiments can increase the impact of theories by providing vivid demonstrations of conditions under which a theory does make successful predictions; and that experimentation can be useful to evaluate social reforms, such as the effectiveness of measures designed to conserve energy. Thus the debate about the utility of experimentation revolves around the types of inference that can reasonably be made on the basis of experimental evidence, with 'traditionalists' such as Aronson, Brewer and Carlsmith (1985) sticking to the view that experimentation provides a firm basis on which to build knowledge, and critics such as Gergen questioning this assumption.

Summary and Conclusion

Methods are procedures followed by researchers in gathering information that helps them to answer research questions. Methodology is the term used to refer to all aspects of the implementation of these methods.

The type of method used by a given researcher will depend to a large extent on the kind of question he or she is addressing. We distinguished between three basic types of research – descriptive, correlational and experimental – and we noted that social-psychological research is typically either correlational or experimental.

In describing methods in more detail, we drew a distinction between research strategies and data collection techniques. Eight research strategies were described: field studies, field experiments, laboratory experiments, experimental simulations, sample surveys, judgement studies, formal theorizing and computer simulations. The principal ways in which these strategies differ are in terms of (1) their sensitivity to the context in which the data are collected; and (2) their obtrusiveness in implementation.

Experimentation (i.e. field experiments, laboratory experiments, experimental simulations) was singled out for more detailed discussion, in view of its dominance as a research strategy in social psychology during the last three decades. The main features of experimentation were identified as: the experimental scenario; the independent variable; the dependent variable; and the follow-up.

A true experimental design is one that enables the researcher to infer that changes in the independent variable produce changes in the dependent variable. Such a design must therefore incorporate more than one condition, allowing the researcher to compare observations made under different conditions. The minimal true experimental design is the post-test only control group design, in which subjects are randomly allocated to one of two conditions, only one of which involves being exposed to the manipulation.

Drawing strong inferences from social-psychological research depends on three types of validity: internal, construct and external. We identified confounding as a threat to internal validity; social desirability effects, demand characteristics and experimenter effects as threats to construct validity; and volunteer/non-volunteer differences as a threat to external validity.

We identified two principal methods of collecting data in social-psychological research: observational measurement and self-report measurement. Observational measures have the advantage of being less susceptible to social desirability effects, and can be made completely unobtrusive. On the other hand, they cannot directly tap covert cognitive phenomena such as causal attributions (see chapter 6). Here the researcher must rely on self-report measures, although the advantages of using both types of measure in conjunction should not be overlooked.

Finally, we noted that some social psychologists have questioned the utility of conventional methods, and of laboratory experiments in particular. The cultural embeddedness of social behaviour, the fact that social behaviour is determined by multiple factors, the difficulty of discriminating between normative and psychological causation, and the ability of humans to modify their behaviour in the light of social-psychological theories, were singled out as grounds for questioning the notion that experimentation will result in cumulative knowledge of the laws governing social behaviour.

Glossary Terms

Computer simulation	Hypothesis
Confounding	Independent variable
Construct validity	Interaction process analysis (IPA)
Control group	Internal validity
Cover story	Judgement task
Debriefing	Laboratory experiment
Demand characteristics	Obtrusive measures
Dependent variable	One-shot case study
Experiment	Participant observation
Experimental scenario	Post-experimental enquiry
Experimental simulation	Post-test only control group design
Experimenter effects	Random allocation
External validity	Reliability
Field experiment	Sample survey
Field studies	Unobtrusive measures
Formal theory	Validity
Hawthorne effect	

Further Reading

Bickman, L. and Henchy, T. (eds) (1972) *Beyond the Laboratory: field research in social psychology*. New York: McGraw-Hill. A useful, if somewhat dated, compendium of papers describing field experiments, many of them now regarded as 'classics'.

Cannell, C. F. and Kahn, R. L. (1968) Interviewing. In G. Lindzey and E. Aronson (eds), *Handbook of Social Psychology*, 2nd edn, Reading, Mass.: Addison-Wesley. A clear overview of what to do (and what not to do) when conducting interviews in the course of research.

Cook, T. D. and Campbell, D. T. (1979) *Quasi-Experimentation: design and analysis issues for field experimentation*. Chicago: Rand McNally. An authoritative account of how to minimize threats to validity by careful research design.

Diener, E. and Crandall, R. (1978) *Ethics in Social and Behavioral Research*. Chicago: Chicago University Press. A balanced view of the many ethical issues that can arise when conducting social scientific research.

Gergen, K. J. (1978) Experimentation in social psychology: a reappraisal. *European Journal of Social Psychology*, 8, 507–27. A thought-provoking analysis by one of the leading critics of the use of experimentation in social psychology.

Jones, R. A. (1985) *Research Methods in the Social and Behavioral Sciences*. Sunderland, Mass.: Sinauer. This is an unusual book; it presents the whole gamut of methods used by social scientists in an intelligent, informative and entertaining way. Highly recommended.

Lindzey, G. and Aronson, E. (eds) (1985) *Handbook of Social Psychology* (vol. 1), 3rd edn, New York: Random House. The most recent edition of this essential handbook, containing contributions on laboratory experimentation (chapter 8), observational methods (chapter 11), survey methods (chapter 12) and attitude measurement (chapter 10).

PART II

Construction of the Social World

5 Social Cognition

JACQUES-PHILIPPE LEYENS and JEAN-PAUL CODOL

Introduction

Suppose someone gave you a sheet of paper containing the following instructions: 'Here is a list of personality traits of an imaginary person called X. Take note of them. We shall ask you later who X is.' Obedient and ready to contribute to the cause of science, you read through the list of characteristics and find out that X is 'intelligent, skilful, industrious, warm, determined, practical and cautious'. If you are like the subjects used by Solomon Asch (1946, p. 263), who designed this ingenious research method, you would have no trouble concluding that X is a person 'who believes certain things to be right, wants others to see his point, would be sincere in an argument and would like to see his point won'. Moreover, most of you would agree that X is generous. In other words, we need only very little information to get an *impression of others*, for that impression to be *shared* by all the members of a community, and for everyone to be convinced that it is the *right* impression.

Asch also showed that even something insignificantly small is enough to change that impression quite radically. For example, if the word 'warm' is replaced by the word 'cold' in the above list of personality traits, the person being described is no longer considered as generous and sincere, but rather as a calculating, merciless social climber.

According to Asch's research, however, certain personality traits were more important than others in determining the impression we form of others. For instance, the opposition 'polite versus blunt' does not have the same effect as 'warm versus cold' in the preceding list. The latter traits are called **central traits** because they organize our impression and give it stability and meaning. Asch also discovered that one's final evaluation of a personality is determined by the order in which the traits are presented: the first traits on the list carry more weight **(primacy effect)** than the last **(recency effect)**. He interpreted this as the

For their comments on an earlier draft of this chapter, we would like to thank Luciano Arcuri, Jean-Léon Beauvois, Miles Hewstone, Amélie Mummendey and Jorge Vala.

progressive cognitive organization of the traits. For the everyday psychologist (Beauvois, 1984), it is evident that in the sequence 'friendly and ambitious', ambitious means doing the best one can to reach one's goals, whereas in the sequence 'calculating and ambitious', ambitious means unscrupulous. We shall again refer to Asch's important work later in this chapter.

Let us now look at another problem that has always fascinated psychologists: *the perception of others*. Asch's research showed us that it is extremely easy to get an overall impression of someone else with only a little information about his presumed personality. Now just how possible is it to draw the same conclusions by simply seeing the other person? This is a fascinating problem, and, of course, it would be very useful to be able to judge people by the way they look. Since the turn of the century, psychologists have been conducting studies aimed at finding out if we are capable of correctly perceiving certain characteristics of others, if and why certain people perceive better than others, and if and why certain personality traits are apprehended better than others. Asked to summarize past research on the subject for the 1954 edition of the *Handbook of Social Psychology*, Bruner and Tagiuri came to the conclusion that we are not able to judge others correctly (although see Funder, 1987, for a different conclusion). They attempted to explain this failure by saying that we are bad judges but that the errors we make are both shared by everyone and consistent. According to Bruner and Tagiuri, these errors result from the fact that, in a given culture, people's perception of others is based not on what others are 'really' like, but on their **implicit personality theories** regarding human beings (Leyens, 1983; Schneider, 1973). This is why many people think, for example, that bulging eyes are a sign of extroversion, that intellectuals have larger than average skulls, and that thick lips mean gluttony. Such beliefs are so well rooted, despite contradictory evidence, that they have been called *illusory correlations* just as we speak of perceptual illusions (Chapman and Chapman, 1967, 1969; Hamilton, 1979). This explanation, given in terms of implicit theories, led to changes in related research. Since then, studies no longer deal with the perception of others as an 'objective process' but study the beliefs upon which our perception of others is based, whether correct or incorrect.

A third tradition used in social-psychological research was that developed by Fritz Heider who, like Solomon Asch, emigrated to the United States. Again like Asch, Heider was influenced by Gestalt psychology and attempted to apply it to the field of interpersonal relationships. The publication of his book in 1958, *The Psychology of Interpersonal Relations*, marked a new era in social psychology. Like any respectable Gestaltist, Heider was interested in perception, and wondered whether it would be possible to apply the principles of physical object perception to the perception of human interaction. It was not the vision specialist he wanted to study, but the ordinary person who strives to interact properly with his or her fellows. In other words, the task Heider set out to accomplish was to account for *common-sense psychology*, to explain how we interpret our own and other people's behaviour and how we *attribute* personality inclinations and intentions to ourselves and others.

Thus social psychologists have long been aware of the fact that people do not just receive external information; they also process it and become the architects of their own social environment (Markus and Zajonc, 1985).

Cognition

The classic studies on the formation of impressions, the perception of others and attribution theory, together with the prodigious development of experimental cognitive psychology, are the foundation of what has been called 'social cognition'.

We first explain cognition, and discuss the contribution of cognitive psychology. We then go on to define the field of social cognition, to show that all cognition has a social origin, to illustrate the content of social cognition and to reveal that it is socially shared. Finally we present different approaches to the lay person as a social cognizer.

The meaning of cognition

Each of us is continuously subjected to large quantities of highly varied information: some of it comes directly from our senses, some from memory, and some, whether conveyed by language or not, from relating to other individuals or groups.

Cognition refers to the set of activities through which all this information is processed by a psychic system: how it receives, selects, transforms and organizes the information; how it constructs representations of reality and builds knowledge. Many phenomena are involved in this processing: perception, memory, thought elaboration and language are only some of them. These phenomena are so tightly interwoven that they interact continuously and are determined by each other.

From processed information results *knowledge*. Knowledge allows us to understand, to adapt to, and to act upon our environment. Cognition has essentially a regulatory and adaptive function. Identifying and recognizing the many objects in the environment, and attributing a value and a meaning to them, are some of the fundamental activities at the heart of all cognitive processes.

For some authors (e.g. Festinger, 1957), the term 'cognition' sometimes designates less the information processing than the contents of the psychic system. In that sense, cognition is synonymous with opinion, belief and attitude. The contemporary usage of the term, however, affords as much importance to the process as to the content.

When we speak of an object, this has to be understood in its primary and broadest sense. An *object* is anything exterior to the organism which affects the senses, regardless of its complexity. A light source and a fashion are objects, just like a tool or a person. Of course, even though such objects are very different from each other, the laws of cognition apply in all cases. These processes must be considered as general processes and it is thus not surprising that social cognition is, first and foremost, a matter of cognition.

Categorization

It has long been known through studies on the psychology of perception that individuals only record part of the signals provided by their environment. Our ability to process information is in fact very limited when compared with the complexity of the information we are exposed to. We therefore devise all sorts of strategies to reduce the processing tasks that are too difficult. Information intake is thus subject to the laws and processes that deform perception, functioning for instance by selection, rigidity and simplification.

It is important for any organism to be able to *identify* the world's objects, to give them a *meaningful structure* and, by doing so, to avoid having to question what he or she has previously learned. Confronted with a new object, the individual *compares* it with other objects he or she already knows and whose characteristics are stored in memory. The first time people see a blue jay they may not know what kind of bird it is, they probably do not know to what family of birds it belongs, but they *can* identify it as a bird. They have learned that birds have feathers and wings, that they fly and sing. It is true that not all birds have feathers, that they do not all fly and sing, and that there are other animals with wings that are not birds. But that does not matter. Such is our image of birds, and having this image enables even the very young apartment dweller to know that a flight of crows is a flight of crows and not a manifestation of the devil.

This simplifying but meaningful correspondence between the new and the acquired is set up during the **categorization** process. In the simplest sense, a *category* is a set of objects that have in common one or more *characteristics*. It should be emphasized here that these characteristics do not necessarily represent intrinsic qualities or objective properties of the objects in question. All sorts of reasons may be the basis for grouping objects together, such as that the environment often presents them together (most canaries are yellow), that they are used when performing the same function (a fork, a pan and a hotplate do not objectively have many physical features in common), or that a cause-and-effect relationship is perceived between them (Michotte, 1946). The notion of *common* characteristic should thus be considered here in a very broad sense: any reason for which a psychic system groups some objects together is a common characteristic of those objects.

Among these objects, the one we call the **prototype** is the one considered to best define or represent the category. The extent to which an object is considered as typical of a given category, called its *degree of typicality*, thus depends on how close it comes to being like the prototype (Cantor and Mischel, 1979; Rosch, 1978). In our culture, for example, a cow is generally considered as more typical of the mammal category than the whale or the bat, although both are also mammals.

It is easy to see that categories vary in *complexity*. For example, it has been verified that we have a much more elaborate conception of the individuals belonging to our own group than to other groups. That difference in complexity has consequences for our judgements of ingroup and outgroup members (Linville, 1982; Marques, Yzerbyt and Leyens, 1987; see chapter 16). Moreover, the categories we use are not *strictly independent* of each other. Since a category pertains to the properties of partially different objects, it in fact implicitly refers to the set of these objects, and thus to the categories that pertain to the objects' other properties (Billig, 1985). Last of all, categories are generally not neutral for the individual. Based on their own personal experience, or under the influence of social standards, individuals value certain characteristics of objects and thus relate them to *behaviour patterns*; for instance, because I hate a given race I am careful not to tolerate any of its potential representatives in my environment (Tajfel, 1969b).

Schemata

Categorization is only possible because people live in a physical and social environment that they perceive as relatively stable. It is because objects possess more or less invariable characteristics that the individual is able to identify them. This *object constancy* is linked to the *coherence* of the categorization system and is manifested in various ways. Shape constancy is the best known example. We recognize a familiar object whether we see it from far away or close up, from the front or the side – in other words, regardless of the shape it projects on our retina. It is the environment's relative permanency that allows us to use generalization processes.

Based on past personal or social experiences involving a given object, each of us tends to generalize in time and in space about its characteristics and properties. Generalization in turn affects the subsequent information filtering, integration and organization processes concerning these objects. This generalization and its outcome are usually called a **schema** (see Fiske and Taylor, 1984).

Cognitive schemata thus organize the representations that we make of a given aspect of the environment. We shall discuss several examples of these throughout this chapter.

Before going on to the field of social cognition itself, let us re-emphasize the following: whether the objects in question are persons or not, and whether the categories are social categories or not, makes no difference to the processes we have just described. Indeed, all social categories are initially cognitive categories.

The Field of Social Cognition

Definition

Just what does 'social cognition' mean? The question is assuredly fashionable, as measured by the quantity of books on the topic (e.g. Arcuri, 1985; Beauvois,

1984; Eiser, 1980; Fiske and Taylor, 1984; Leyens, 1983; Nisbett and Ross, 1980; Wyer and Srull, 1984). The least one could say is that the study of social cognition concerns the perception of people and ourselves as well as the 'naive' theories we entertain to justify those perceptions. Not only do we think about ourselves and others, but we think about our thinking. Very often, this kind of study is influenced by analyses provided by cognitive theory and method.

We are told that research on social cognition is highly influenced by experimental cognitive psychology; if we agree that cognition stems essentially from individual processes, then what is 'social' about social cognition apart from its object? Perhaps studies of social cognition are nothing more than particular applications of cognitive psychology (Neisser, 1980)? We are well aware of the desire of social psychologists in general, and European psychologists in particular, to stress the peculiarity of social psychology (Israel and Tajfel, 1972; Taylor and Brown, 1979; Tajfel, 1984). Does the current enthusiasm for studies in social cognition support or, on the contrary, undermine this peculiarity?

In this chapter, we defend the idea that cognition may be qualified as social in three ways. First, it has a social *origin*, being created or reinforced through social interaction. Second, and in a more obvious way, it has a social *object* since it deals with the cognition of that which is social. Third, it is *socially shared*, being common to different members in a given society or group (Lukes, 1973b; other meanings of social cognition are given by McGuire, 1986).

The social origin of cognition

There is clear evidence for the link between cognitive activity and socialization processes (see chapter 3). The largely social origin of cognition can also be observed by the effect that cultural and social factors have on information integration and transformation processes. A single example should suffice to illustrate how social values placed on objects as well as people's social origins, affect cognition. In a country where the monetary value and size of coins are correlated, try the following example. Ask poor and rich children to guess the size of some valuable coins. The chances are that the poor children will estimate the coins to be bigger than the rich children. This probable result does not mean that poor children have worse vision than rich children; when cardboard discs are used instead of coins the two groups are not different. That, in any case, is what Bruner and Goodman (1947) found in a well-known study. The difference observed here is due to the social origin of the subjects and to the value they attribute to coins (see also Tajfel, 1969a, 1981).

The content of social cognition

The ideas and concepts used in the study of social cognition have been applied to many social objects: oneself (Zavalloni, 1971; Markus and Sentis, 1982), others (Tagiuri and Petrullo, 1958), imaginary persons (Anderson, 1981), interpersonal relationships (Flament, 1982), groups (Tajfel, 1981) and memory for social information (Hastie, 1981). We will mention here just three fields of research: cognition about persons, interpersonal relationships and stereotyping. Others will be illustrated later in this chapter, and still others will be discussed in related chapters of this book.

The cognition of people There have been studies focused on *oneself* (e.g. L'Ecuyer, 1978; Wegner and Vallacher, 1980) or on *others*, considering these persons either independently of each other or by comparison (Codol, 1975; Festinger, 1954; Lemaine, 1975). In this field the concept of *personal identity* became a central theme, integrating much of the research (Codol, 1982, 1984b).

This type of approach may be illustrated by a multitude of studies, including those on the perception of similarities between oneself and others. The social-psychological literature offers a great number of examples showing how we tend to consider other people as belonging to the same category as ourselves, although we do not perceive ourselves as belonging to the same category as others. We often feel that others resemble us, whereas we do not feel we resemble others (Codol, 1986). In Hardoin and Codol's (1984) study, for example, subjects were to carry out successively two free description tasks: one self-description and one description of a target person. Results showed that when subjects described themselves first, they used the same type of traits to describe the other person as they had used to describe themselves. When they described the other person first, however, they used different traits for themselves than those they had used for that other person.

Social cognition and interpersonal relationships Research in this field has been conducted following two different traditions (see also chapter 10). In Moreno's (1934) perspective, researchers attempt to find how each member of a real group perceives his or her own interpersonal relationships with other members of the group – who (he thinks) likes him, who (she feels) rejects her, whom she likes, whom he rejects, and so on.

Studies based on Heider's (1958) **balance theory**, however, attempt to reveal the existence of biases in the perception of interpersonal relationships. This method usually consists of asking subjects on a questionnaire to predict all the interpersonal relationships that would exist between members of an imaginary group of people when a few of these relationships are known. Most of these studies were focused on friendship relationships or on hierarchical relationships. The studies revealed a number of cognitive biases in perception (Flament, 1982). Let us illustrate the most well known of them: the bias towards balance. In figure 5.1a we have represented some of the friendship relations between three persons P, O and X. As you can see, P likes O and O likes X. In your opinion, what is the relation between P and X? Does P like X or does P dislike X? Now consider figure 5.1b; again, what is the relation between P and X? If you are biased towards balance, in both cases your answer should have been: P likes X. It is consistent with the balance bias to like the friends of our friends and the enemies of our enemies (but see also chapter 2). An easy way

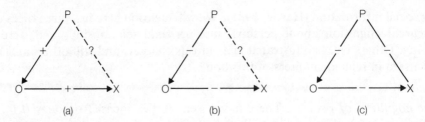

FIGURE 5.1   Structural balance in a triadic situation

to determine whether a triad is balanced or not is to multiply the signs (+ or –) of the relations; if the product is + , then the triadic situation is considered balanced. Thus figure 5.1c represents an unbalanced situation. (Remember that $+ \times + = +$; $+ \times - = - \times + = -$; and $- \times - = +$.)

The approaches of Moreno and Heider are complementary. In the first approach, the perception of the interpersonal relationships is realistic, and is dependent on all the aspects of the group situation experienced by the subjects. In the second approach, the perception involved is that of the subjects' overall *expectations* concerning the interpersonal relationships – expectations which themselves are a function both of what the subjects have experienced personally during group activity and of the ideal characteristics they attribute to it through cultural prejudices or habits.

Stereotyping   Stereotyping is a third domain of importance for the social content of cognition. Social **stereotypes** can be defined as the implicit theories of personality that a group of people share about their own group or about another group. Two features of this definition are important: that the theories are *shared* by a community of individuals, and that the theories are about the personality traits held by a *whole* group of people. For instance, 'they are all hard-working'; 'we are all bright' (note from this example that social stereotypes are not necessarily negative).

The concept of stereotype is relatively new in the dictionary of social psychologists (Lippman, 1922). Originally, researchers strove to find adequate methods to assess stereotypes about different ethnic groups (Katz and Braly, 1933). How, for example, do American students consider at a given time Germans, French, British, Swedes, Indians, Japanese and fictitious 'Wallonians' (Hartley, 1946)? The explanations for the existence of those stereotypes were either *psychodynamic* (by stereotyping we defend ourselves against a latent anxiety) or *socio-cultural* (in a given culture stereotypes are transmitted from one generation to the next).

In 1969 Tajfel published an important article, which gave the field a fresh impetus. Tajfel proposed that stereotypes can be viewed as special cases of categorization, with an accentuation of similarities within groups and of differences between groups. The title of the paper, 'Cognitive aspects of prejudice', may nevertheless be misleading. Tajfel not only focused on the cognitive dimensions of stereotypes but also insisted on their evaluative weight; for a racist, the colour of the skin probably has a different value than the height of the body (Tajfel, 1981).

This contribution by Tajfel has not always been acknowledged as it ought to be; more recent research has concentrated mainly on the cognitive aspects of stereotypes, treating them as any other kind of judgement, be it about a social or a non-social entity. In a very well-known series of studies by Hamilton (1979) and colleagues, for example, it has been shown that people tend to exaggerate the importance of rare characteristics among minority groups (an effect called **illusory correlation**). In other words, 1/3 is considered bigger than 6/18 or 9/27. Given the ever-increasing body of research in the area of stereotypes, we refer the reader to a recent review (e.g. Hamilton and Trolier, 1986).

Shared social cognitions

We do not all construct the same knowledge at the same time, and we do not all form the same opinion about another person. This everyday experience illustrates how cognition does not depend essentially on the material or 'objective' characteristics of objects. Rather, cognition is the *mental reconstruction* of that which is real, by individuals, based on their past experience and their needs, desires and intentions. Since there are no two individuals on earth who are not different in some way, their cognitions cannot be strictly identical.

It is obvious, however, that because of the social life we lead, which involves many forms of communication and influence, much information (and hence many meanings) is collectively shared by sets of individuals, groups or societies. As a great number of studies have shown, our perception is determined by the ecological context in which we exist. Our religious beliefs, political and social ideologies, ideas about right and wrong, and even scientific theories are for the most part defined by the social contexts in which they develop (Deconchy, 1984).

A now classic study conducted by Schachter and Singer (1962) will illustrate how the social context even determines how persons interpret their own sensations. Pretending to study the effects of a vitamin on vision, experimenters gave their subjects an injection of adrenaline, which is known to cause heart palpitations, increased heart rate and reddening of the face. The subjects were told to wait for a certain period during which the drug, 'Suproxin', was supposed to be taking effect. One group of subjects were told that Suproxin has the same side effects as adrenaline. Another group of subjects were led to believe that the drug's side effects were headaches and itching. The third group of subjects were not given any information about the drug's effects.

During the waiting period, each subject was put with another person who had supposedly received a similar injection. This person was in fact an accomplice, who showed signs of euphoria in half of the cases and of irritation in the other half.

Schachter and Singer found that the two groups that had not received the correct information decoded and interpreted their own sensations through the behavior of the other person. Like him, they became euphoric or irritated.

Thus, despite the objectivity of the symptoms following the injection, difficulty in defining their own state of discomfort led them to perceive and manifest the symptoms of the other person.

We can see how social cognition here is socially shared cognition. This problem has especially interested certain European authors, and in particular the French-speaking ones, who have conducted theoretical analyses and empirical studies on the notion of **social representation**. Their approaches to social representation explicitly characterize it as social in that its content and its operating laws depend strictly on interindividual processes. With the initial thrust of a book by Moscovici (1961), an ambitious theory has developed over the past two decades concerning social representation. It attempts to incorporate many psychological and social aspects of social cognition. The notion of social representation is a direct heir of Durkheim's (1898) concept of collective representation. According to Lukes (1973b, p. 7), a representation was collective for Durkheim in at least three senses: 'in its origins . . . in its reference or object . . . [and] in being common to the members of a society or group'. These are precisely the terms we used earlier to qualify cognition as *social*.

Moscovici replaced 'collective' by 'social' to emphasize the link with social psychology rather than sociology. Moreover, his view of social representations is more dynamic than Durkheim's; he saw them as created and re-created by individuals in interaction with each other, as for example in the course of conversation (Moscovici, 1985a). Moscovici has defined social representations as follows:

> By social representations we mean a set of concepts, statements and explanations originating in daily life in the course of inter-individual communications. They are the equivalent, in our society, of the myths and belief systems in traditional societies; they might even be said to be the contemporary version of common sense. (Moscovici, 1981a, p. 181)

There are many other definitions of social representations (Di Giacomo, 1985; Doise, 1986); this has led some authors (Leyens, 1983; Potter and Litton, 1985) to think that it is a heuristic notion rather than a concept. Instead of reviewing subtle differences and refinements in the various definitions, as well as the vast array of objects whose social representations have been studied, we will give simply an idea of the functions and processes assumed to operate in social representations.

Few of us could define exactly what are nuclear physics, biochemistry, the sociology of science or ethology. However, this absence of precise knowledge does not prevent most of us from discussing these matters. Indeed, we have categorized some information about these sciences, and the resulting simplicity, shared by the community, allows us to communicate about them. These are precisely the two main functions of social representations: to help the individual to master and make sense of the world and to facilitate communication. Thus, in a sense, the study of social representations is the study of the transformation from knowledge to common sense (Moscovici and Hewstone, 1983). Put yet another way, the theory of social representations 'explains how the strange and the unfamiliar become, in time, the familiar' (Farr and Moscovici, 1984, ix; see also Moscovici, 1982).

To realize these two functions of social representations, the adherents of this notion claim that people use two main processes: anchoring and objectifying. As stated by Jodelet (1984), people need to *anchor* new ideas into a pre-existing system. Yet this is not enough. The abstract must be made concrete, almost visual, by the process of *objectifying*. Recently, Moscovici and Hewstone (1983) suggested two routes that this process can take: personification and figuration.

As shown by Moscovici (1961), people have simple (and often wrong) ideas about psychoanalysis but they know the name of Freud – and that name is linked to complexes. We also probably know almost nothing about the theory of relativity, but it is sufficient to remember the name of Einstein. This is personification in the sense that theories or ideas are linked to a particular name which represents them. When we think and speak of psychoanalysis, we usually see a three-floor building. The first floor – the id – is messy. The second – the ego – is where you receive people. In the third there is a mysterious person – the super-ego – somewhat like your father or teacher, who gives you orders and blames you because you have not yet put the first floor in order. This is figuration, as is the visualization of the relativity equation $E = mc^2$. All this 'knowledge' is enough not to remain silent during conversation at a party, which is a good proof that cognitions can be socially shared.

In this perspective, the theory of social representation is an attempt at unifying problems located at the crossroads between psychology and other social sciences. But this does not rule out either a psychological or a cognitive approach to the study of social representation. Indeed, *each* individual at a given time integrates and modifies the social forms of the cultures and groups of which he is a part, to the point where, regardless of the many mediations of social representation (institutions, powers, laws, mass media etc.), it is always individuals who convey and express the social representations in the end. Individual conduct can thus be considered as a reflection of social representations; this makes observation and interviewing of individuals a perfectly legitimate approach to studying them.

The generation and communication processes of social representation, however, can only be studied in relationships between groups and individuals. The cognitive mechanisms for the apprehension and reconstruction of reality by individuals are obviously also important. From this standpoint, laboratory experimentation has also proved to be useful in understanding social representation phenomena (cf. Abric, 1984; Codol, 1984b).

Five Approaches to the Person as a Social Cognizer

Now that we have explained social cognition and stressed the social nature of its origins and content, we review the different conceptions of the lay person as a social cognizer that psychologists have used. For historical as well as illustrative reasons, we distinguish five different approaches.

The consistent or rationalizing person

A first approach refers to a number of proposals based upon the idea that inconsistency between cognitions raises an unpleasant psychological tension which has to be reduced by a search for consistency (see also chapter 7). This inconsistency has received several labels: cognitive imbalance (Heider, 1958), asymmetry (Newcomb, 1953), incongruence (Osgood and Tannenbaum, 1955) and dissonance (Festinger, 1957).

Let us briefly illustrate the most influential theory in the approach, namely cognitive dissonance theory. There is cognitive *dissonance* between two cognitions if, considering the two alone, the obverse of one would follow from the other. For example, I smoke and I know that smoking promotes cancer. The most radical way to eliminate dissonance would be to stop smoking. Unfortunately there are other ways to reduce the tension. Since there is no causal relationship between smoking and cancer, it may well be that only smokers with a certain kind of personality get cancer, and obviously I do not have that personality; moreover, I know very old persons who have smoked all their lives; I also prefer to die joyful at the age of 90 than peevish and bored at the age of 100!

With this example it may be clear that the search for consistency very often means rationalizing. As will be seen in the next approach, this view of individuals as rationalizing persons has been progressively abandoned.

The naive psychologist

As we said above, Heider (1958) set out to try to understand the naive psychology of the lay person, and in particular how lay people search for the cause or causes of a given effect. This topic is dealt with in the next chapter.

Let us go back to Asch (1946) and his studies on forming impressions. As we stated earlier, Asch gave his subjects a list of personality traits that were supposed to characterize an imaginary person. The subjects quickly formed an impression of the person and could easily decide what additional characteristics that person had. An orthodox Gestaltist, Asch believed that the traits had an effect on each other, combining to form the whole that made up the overall impression. Later, from a standpoint similar to that of Gestalt theory, Bruner and Tagiuri (1954) supported the idea that both general impressions *and* inferences made concerning additional traits were most certainly due to the implicit theories of personality held by subjects. The important idea here is that different authors all consider their subjects as naive theoreticians of personality, of knowledge about others and of knowledge about themselves, with pre-conceived ideas, be they right or wrong, about how personality traits are distributed in the population and linked to each other (Rosenberg and Sedlack, 1972).

In this conception, the naive psychologist is a rationalist rather than an empiricist. He is a disciple of Descartes or of Kant rather than of Hume. He has a theory in mind, and it is by using this theory that he makes decisions about the real world, especially with regard to behaviour: if we feel that a person is warm rather than cold we may apply different theories, but our behaviour with respect to that person will also be different (Kelley, 1950).

The data-processing trainee

Asch's work and his interpretations were questioned and debated (see Jaspars, 1982). The most unremitting critic was Anderson (1981), one of Hume's disciples, who (we might say) feels that the real world takes precedence over the represented world (Marques, 1986) and over theories (Landman and Manis, 1983). Anderson emphasizes the personality traits he presents to his subjects, rather than the theories the subjects possess about those traits.

In Anderson's way of thinking, for example, the primacy effect (i.e. the strong effect of the first traits on the list) is due not to a continuous organization of the traits but to the lowering of the subjects' attention level. He believes the subjects invest all their interest in the initial adjectives presented to them, paying less and less attention as they read down the list. Owing to their unfavourable position in the list, the final traits cannot influence the subjects, unless the experimenter can somehow keep the subjects' attention throughout the task (Anderson and Hubert, 1963).

Anderson does not interpret the warm–cold, polite–blunt experiment as Asch did. According to him, the final answer given is the result not of a general impression or an implicit theory of personality but of the 'algebraic linear integration of the weighted evaluations of ratings' attributed to the various traits.

We have now come to the conception of the person as a data processor. Knowing that you have certainly never considered the impression you have of someone as being the result of the 'algebraic linear integration of the weighted evaluations of ratings' of the information available to you, let us explain this further. In each culture, personality traits can be rated positively or negatively. For example, 'nice' would more likely be given a more positive rating than 'orderly', whereas 'disorderly' would probably be given a less negative rating than 'aggressive'. Anderson has determined the different ratings of personality traits in the American culture; these data are very important to him since, in his mind, the final evaluation of a person is a function of the ratings of each of the known traits of that person. All we need to know now is how these ratings are integrated: by simple addition, by averaging, or by some other method.

We might imagine, for example, that the final impression we have of a person is a function of the sum of all the points attributed to the various characteristics of the person (*additive* model) or is a function of the average of

TABLE 5.1   Adding versus averaging in the integration of impressions

Attributes (A) (no. N)	No weight	Weighted: friendship	Weighted: fashion model
Diana			
Spontaneous	3	3 × 10	3 × 1
Funny	3	3 × 10	3 × 1
Beautiful	3	3 × 1	3 × 10
Sum *A*	9	63	36
Average *A/N*	3	21	12
Margaret			
Attentive	8	8 × 10	8 × 1
Ugly	−1	−1 × 1	−1 × 10
Sum *A*	7	79	−2
Average *A/N*	3.5	39.5	−1

those points (*averaging* model). If we know that Diana is spontaneous (+ 3), funny (+ 3) and beautiful (+ 3), and that Margaret is attentive (+ 8) and ugly (– 1), then Diana would 'win' using the addition model (3 + 3 + 3 = 9, which is greater than 8 – 1 = 7). However, Margaret would win using the averaging model (7/2 is greater than 9/3) (see table 5.1). The ratings for each trait are not the same in all contexts either. If it is a friend we are evaluating, then beauty is not very important and is weighted 1, but spontaneity, attentiveness and humour are weighted 10; whereas if it is a fashion model we want to hire, then beauty is weighted 10 and the other three traits only 1.

According to Anderson (in a version we deliberately simplify) the best model is one that accounts for the weighted averages. In the friendship situation, then, Margaret would win; her score of 39.5 ((8×10 – $1 \times 1)/2 = 79/2$) is greater than Diana's score of 21 ((3×10 + 3×10 + $3 \times 1)/3 = 63/3$). Diana, however, would have an advantage as a fashion model, where her score of 12 ((3×1 + 3×1 + $3 \times 10)/3 = 36/3$) is greater than Margaret's score of – 1 ((8×1 – $1 \times 10)/2 = – 2/2$) (see table 5.1). Although Anderson's model is the most important in the present literature, we agree with Eiser's (1980) criticism of the impression formation literature: that very little attempt is made to present subjects with the kind of information which they would be likely to receive about real people in real life. Although assumed to reflect 'lay conceptions of personality', subjects' ratings might reflect little more, in many instances, than their appreciation of conventional linguistic usage (Leyens, Aspeel and Marques, 1987).

Now let us examine another approach to the person as data processor which involves a concept known as *program schemes*, the **script**. According to Schank and Abelson (1977), a script is a coherent sequence of events that an individual expects and that involves him or her either as a participant or as an observer. The script's basic element is the *frame*, a picture accompanied by a comment. Several frames forming a unit – the story – make up the script. In film-making terms, we might say that the script is an overused scenario: we know that Jean Gabin is difficult to get along with but is kind-hearted; that he will be the subject of the amorous assaults of his much younger partner, who usually has somewhat loose morals; that he will sit on her bed but will not lie down on it. Although monotonous in the movies, such scripts are eminently useful in daily life. It is these categories of events that enable us to respond to large chunks of information without too much effort and, if the script is highly refined, without even being aware of it. In doing so, we are ready for other information.

The most convincing experimental demonstration of the fact that we act automatically according to scripts was provided by Langer, Blank and Chanowitz (1978). These authors based their study on the idea that whenever an activity is repeated frequently, it becomes a script, and that we remain sensitive to the structure of that script while no longer paying attention to its semantic content. When confronted with such a script, we act without having to think very much. If on the other hand the structure is not typical of what we are expecting, the semantic content regains importance. Take the example of the script of a request, which has a three-part structure: an apology, the object of the request, and its justification. Langer, Blank and Chanowitz (1978) used a situation in which a confederate comes along and interrupts someone who is photocopying a series of documents. The requester would be much less successful if he said, 'Excuse me. I have five pages. May I use the Xerox machine?', than if he said, 'Excuse me. I have five pages. May I use the Xerox machine, because I have to make copies?' The semantic content of the two requests is absolutely identical, since what else would a photocopier be used for than photocopying? In the second case, however, the structure of the script is maintained, and one could bet on it that most people acceding to the request probably did not hear its exact content. Indeed, and as can be seen from figure 5.2, the second requester with the appropriate structure and the meaningless content received as much help as the third person using an appropriate

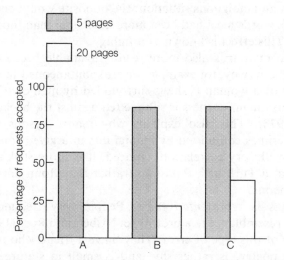

FIGURE 5.2 Percentage of subjects who accept the request as a function of the effort involved and the structure of the request. A: inadequate structure. B: adequate structure but inadequate content. C: adequate structure and adequate content (Langer et al., 1978)

structure and a meaningful content: 'Excuse me. I have five pages. May I use the Xerox machine, because I'm in a rush?' Of course, people will not process information so automatically in all situations. For instance, the same authors showed that when the request was more important – 20 pages rather than five – people did indeed pay attention to the content.

Research like Anderson's on impression information, as well as research on scripts, illustrates two ways in which social cognition psychologists have viewed lay persons as data processors. On the one hand, they are data manipulators who construct their programs as they go. On the other hand, they are sub-routine managers, although that does not mean they will not make mistakes.

Lay persons, data processors as they may be, can make mistakes; and in fact that is what actually characterizes them. Based on the criteria used by social cognition psychologists, lay persons make a tremendous number of blunders. Our intention is not to review systematically all the different errors mentioned in the literature. We shall discuss only a few here; some of the others will be discussed in chapter 6.

The cognitive miser

If it is true that we make many errors in our perception of the social world, then it becomes essential that we find out what principles cause us to be so deficient. These principles have currently been grouped together under the name of **heuristics** or biases in information processing (Tversky and Kahneman, 1978).

One of these biases is thought to be due to the *availability* of certain information in memory. It appears that whenever we have to evaluate a social situation, we give priority to the characteristics that are most readily available. Thus if the word 'hostile' is more accessible to us than the word 'nice' because we have come across it recently in various forms, then we would be more likely to use it in interpreting an ambiguous situation; the opposite would occur in the same situation if the word 'nice' had been more accessible than 'hostile' (Srull and Wyer, 1980). This effect is known as **priming**.

Certain information is also more readily available because it stands out more. This explains why, for example, we are spontaneously more apt to notice the behaviour of a woman if she is surrounded by men or of a man among several women; the uniqueness is silhouetted against the background (Taylor and Fiske, 1978). This also explains why many persons exaggerate the frequency of crimes committed by immigrants in a given country (and is an example of an illusory correlation). Indeed, it is more striking to read in a newspaper that a Turk or a Pakistani (rather than John or Andrew X) has murdered someone.

Another bias is *representativeness*. People very frequently base their judgement on resemblance to a prototype. Nisbett and Ross (1980) gave a very good example of this type of error. They 'have a friend who is professor. He likes to write poetry, is rather shy, and is small in stature. Which of the following is his field: (a) Chinese studies or (b) psychology?' The answer is that he is a psychologist, but we would not be even slightly surprised if you had considered him to be a Sinologist. Indeed, writing poetry and being shy and small in stature seem to fit better the profile of a Sinologist than of a psychologist. This is to forget that Sinologists are few in number and that, Nisbett and Ross both being psychologists, they are much more likely to have a mutual friend who is a psychologist than a specialist in Chinese studies.

In other words, people are often more sensitive to subjectively perceived like-nesses than to objective data, just as we are really convinced that the clothes make the man. Participants in a study were told that 30 engineers and 70 lawyers (or 70 engineers and 30 lawyers) had been interviewed and had taken personality tests. The subjects were given descriptions, made with the data gathered, of some of these lawyers and engineers and were asked to determine the probability that the described person was an engineer (Kahneman and Tversky, 1973).

Here is one of the descriptions given to the subjects: 'Dick is a 30-year-old man. He is married with no children. A man of high ability and high motivation, he promises to be quite successful in his field. He is well liked by his colleagues. What is the probability that Dick is an engineer?' Now since we are aware of the representativeness bias, we also know that the subjects' answers should take the proportion of engineers in the source population into account (0.7 or 0.3, depending on the case). Indeed, the person's age, marital status, intelligence, and the fact that his colleagues appreciate him are in no way indicative of his profession. Yet the subjects in both conditions of this experiment estimated that Dick had a 50 per cent chance of being an engineer. In other words, they seem to ignore the given proportions (or base rates) of lawyers and engineers; because the character sketch is representative of neither profession, they answer 50 per cent.

Although we are not very sensitive to statistics, or to other people's experience, we are extremely easy to convince with one simple, concrete and vividly described case. One of our students was well aware of this error. He was a union representative and told us: 'Whenever I present my statistics on unemployment to a group, and someone says something like "I know a woman who is a physician's wife and who is on welfare because of unemployment", I know right then and there that I might as well put the statistics away, that they won't be useful there.' (See also Bar-Hillel, 1980; Borgida and Brekke, 1981; Kassin, 1979b).

A third bias is known as *anchoring*, and refers to our difficulty in modifying our beliefs in the light of new information that contradicts those beliefs. A study conducted by Ross, Lepper and Hubbard (1975) is a perfect illustration of this type of bias. In their experiment, subjects received a series of 25 cards, each containing two notes supposedly written by persons having committed suicide. One of the notes was supposed to be true, the other false. The subjects' task was to distinguish the true notes from the false ones. As each person gave an answer to a card, he received feedback from the experimenter. This feedback was randomly distributed so as to lead the subjects to believe that they ranked as average, much better than average or much worse than average depending on which experimental group they belonged to. After the

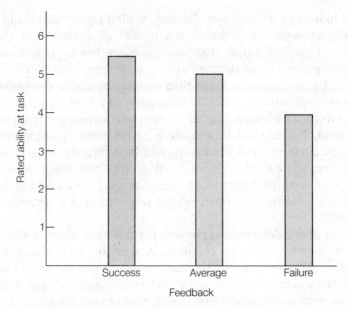

FIGURE 5.3   Subjects' post-debriefing perceptions of their ability. Subjective rating scales ranged from 1 (low ability relative to average student) to 7 (high ability) (Ross et al., 1975)

discrimination task was finished, they were debriefed and told that the feedback was in no way based on their actual ability to judge, but had been arbitrarily assigned. The subjects then received a questionnaire, supposedly aimed at interpreting additional data, on which they were asked to give their own personal evaluation of their real ability at the task they had just performed. Despite the fact that the initial evaluations had been arbitrarily assigned, subjects who had been rated high continued to consider themselves as superior to those who had obtained an average evaluation. The same was true for those who had received low scores, who continued to consider themselves as inferior (see figure 5.3). The primacy effect, described earlier in the context of impressions, can be seen as another example of the anchoring bias.

Let us look now at *accentuation* theory which, although it appeared prior to the cognitive miser era, is highly relevant to it. Given that categories refer to objects that we judge as either similar or equivalent according to a certain number of criteria, then we should tend to emphasize the similarities between objects that belong to the same category and exaggerate the differences between objects belonging to different categories. A now classic experiment conducted by Tajfel and Wilkes (1963) illustrates this phenomenon perfectly. A series of vertical lines is presented one by one to three groups of subjects. The lines are all different in height. Subjects are asked to estimate their height as correctly as possible. For one group of subjects, the four tallest lines (1–4) are labelled A and the four shortest (5–8) are labelled B. A second group of subjects sees the same set of lines, but without labels. For the third group, the lines are labelled arbitrarily, that is, without reference to their actual height. The hypothesis that differences between categories are exaggerated is definitely confirmed here. Subjects exposed to categorial labelling (the same letter for the four tallest lines, another letter for the four shortest lines) estimate a greater difference in height between the lines labelled A and B than do the other two groups. This estimated difference is also greater than the actual difference, and is exaggerated the most for the lines closest in height to the adjacent category. For example, see the shortest line in the 'long' category and the longest line in the 'short' category, i.e. the difference between lines 4 and 5 for subjects shown the classified series (see figure 5.4: note that the vertical axis gives deviations from actual differences).

The second hypothesis, which deals with the minimization of the differences within a given category, is only partially supported. Subjects in the group with categorial labelling tend to judge the lines in the same category as equivalent, although this result is not statistically significant (see also Arcuri, 1982; Capozza and Nanni, 1986). Work since Tajfel's research has also reinforced the initial hypotheses using more 'social' materials. Wilder and Allen (1978), for example, showed that when we are assigned to a group with whose members we are not very well acquainted, we would rather obtain information that emphazises how we are similar to other members of that group and how we are different from members of other groups. Wilder's research also demonstrates that we would be likely to believe that participants in a discussion share the same opinions if they belong to the same group, and do not have the same opinions if they belong to different groups.

The cognitive-affective human being

All of the research presented here as part of the fourth approach illustrates how

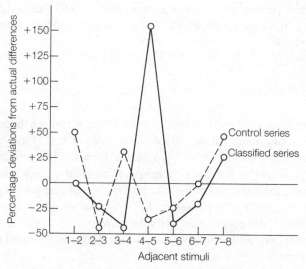

FIGURE 5.4   Comparison of actual and apparent differences between adjacent lines, for 'control series' and 'classified series' subjects (Tajfel, 1981)

the 'cognitive miser' often blunders and falls foul of logic. This might not be as important as it seems at first. After all, in everyday interaction, logic is less important than 'psychologic'. When statistics recommend you buy car Y and you choose to go along with just one friend's recommendation and buy car Z, you are certainly not being reasonable – but you keep a friend (Leyens, 1983; Miller and Cantor, 1982).

Here we see the emotional-motivational side of social life, an aspect that seems to have been ignored by the cognitive emphasis. Are we experiencing the emergence of a new era in social cognition? 'Feeling and thinking: preferences need no inferences': that was the title of a seminal article written in 1980 by Zajonc, who was reacting against the omnipresence of cognition in social psychology and against the complete removal of feeling and motivation from this type of research. His argument was like that of Pascal, who said: 'The heart has its reasons that reason does not know.' At about the same time, Neisser (1980), the father of today's cognitive psychology, developed the same reasoning. According to this author, the desire to explain everything in cognitive terms is nothing more than an intellectual exercise, and everyone knows that, for everyday mortals, intellectual exercises are not an essential activity (this opinion is shared by Kruglanski, 1980; Kruglanski and Ajzen, 1983).

Emotions also make their reappearance elsewhere in the field of social knowledge (Clark and Fiske, 1982). It has been shown, for example, that people remember something better if the recall takes place when the person is in the same mood (happy, sad) as when he or she learned the item in question (Bower, 1981). After having heard that their favourite football team has just won a game, people will also judge certain elements of their life totally unrelated to football as more satisfying (Schwartz et al., 1987). This affects behaviour. Individuals in a very good mood, for example, are more likely to help others than people in an average or neutral mood (see chapter 11); the former are also more apt to converse with a stranger than the latter (Clark and Isen, 1982).

Summary and Conclusion

In a very general way, cognition refers to all those activities through which a psychic system organizes information into knowledge. This construction cannot, however, be summarized by a set of formal operations carried out without reference to the person's social-psychological experience. Opinions, attitudes, values, feelings, emotions, the attribution of meaning, all play a role at every stage of cognitive processes: in information selection, transformation and organization. Moreover, the units of information themselves are most often of social origin, and the knowledge that is built up is linked to an individual's social experience.

Throughout this chapter we have pointed out how, at different times in the history of social psychology, researchers have given priority to one of the facets of the social knowledge acquisition process: motivation which induces error, the naive search to validate a construction of reality, systematic information processing, and so on. What each of these preferences entails is a different conception of the *person* faced with a social object. This is precisely what certain authors criticize (Moscovici, 1982). According to them, rather than the link between one person and a social object, it is the link between *people* and the social object that should be investigated.

As legitimate as this preoccupation may be, it is nevertheless *each individual* that appropriates, and thus transforms the social knowledge of the groups and cultures to which he or she belongs. Thus, the question is neither the social nature of cognition, nor the expression of this social nature in individual behaviour, but rather its content and the mechanisms upon which it is based.

As far as its content is concerned, cognition may be qualified as social if the objects to which it pertains are themselves social objects. As far as processes of social knowledge – elaboration and communication – are concerned, they can be revealed not only through the highly complex study of the relationships both between groups and between individuals, but also through the more strictly cognitive study of the mechanisms of apprehension and reconstruction of reality by individual persons.

In this chapter, we have attempted to give you an overview of social cognition by showing how the social world is a construction. It is this same idea that will be developed, from other angles, in the next three chapters of this book.

Glossary Terms

Balance theory	Priming
Categorization	Prototype
Central trait	Recency effect
Cognition	Schema
Heuristics	Script
Illusory correlation	Social representations
Implicit personality theories	Stereotype
Primacy effect	

Further Reading

Farr, R. and Moscovici, S. (eds) (1984) *Social Representations*. Cambridge: Cambridge University Press. The first English monograph on the concept of social representations, presenting a fair balance of theoretical analyses, field work and laboratory experiments.

Fiske, S. T. and Taylor, S. E. (1984) *Social Cognition*. New York: Random House. In a single volume, this is probably the most complete compendium on contemporary social cognition. Chapters cover topics such as theories of attribution, psychological control, social schemata, attention and person memory.

Hastorf, A. H. and Isen, A. M. (eds) (1982) *Cognitive Social Psychology*. New York: Elsevier. Aimed at a somewhat sophisticated audience, this volume focuses on two areas of concern: the interaction between personality, social variables and cognitive functioning, and applications of cognitive social psychology (e.g. to legal processes, organizations and medicine).

Nisbett, R. E. and Ross, L. (1980) *Human Inference: strategies and shortcomings in social judgment*. Englewood Cliffs, NJ: Prentice-Hall. This book is a 'must' for any student of social cognition (graduate or upper undergraduate level). With style and striking examples, the authors report where, how and why we make so many erroneous inferences in our social judgements.

Schneider, D. J., Hastorf, A. H. and Ellsworth, P. C. (1980) *Person Perception*. Reading, Mass.: Addison-Wesley. This is an excellent and easy-to-read introduction to the field of person perception. All the traditional topics are clearly and rigorously presented.

Tajfel, H. (1981) *Human Groups and Social Categories: studies in social psychology*. Cambridge; Cambridge University Press. Whether viewed as intellectual autobiography or simply as essays in contemporary social psychology, this book offers a valuable summary of a unique approach to social categorization and intergroup relations.

Wyer, R. S. and Srull, T. (eds) (1984) *Handbook of Social Cognition* (3 vols). Hillsdale, NJ: Erlbaum. An authoritative and up-to-date compendium of research and theorizing on social cognition.

6 Attribution Theory and Social Explanations

MILES HEWSTONE
and CHARLES ANTAKI

Introduction

We begin this chapter with a key study which illustrates the phenomenon we shall be looking at and provides a point of reference to which we return several times. In this study, Duncan (1976) examined the perception and explanation of intraracial and interracial violence by asking subjects (white American college students) to look at a videotaped interaction of an increasingly violent argument in which, finally, one participant pushed the other. Duncan varied the race (black/white) of both the potential 'protagonist' and the 'victim' of the push shown on the videotape.

Viewers were first asked to *describe* what they saw, using categories such as 'playing around' and 'violent behaviour'. The results were striking. When the videotape contained a black protagonist (and no matter what race the victim was), over 70 per cent of the subjects chose 'violent behaviour' as the appropriate category. But, when the roles were reversed, and the protagonist was white, only 13 per cent of the subjects labelled the act in this manner (see figure 6.1a).

Duncan then went a stage further in his experiment. He asked his subjects to *explain* the observed behaviour. Again the results showed a clear effect for race of protagonist. When the protagonist was black, subjects said that the violent behaviour was due to personal characteristics of the harm-doer; when the protagonist was white, on the other hand, subjects 'explained away' the behaviour in terms of the situation (see figure 6.1b).

Three points emerge from this compelling illustration of how people explain social behaviour. First, descriptions of the 'same' event can vary. Second, explanations can vary too, and can show up important individual and social

The authors are grateful to Michael Bond, Klaus Fiedler, Frank Fincham, Garth Fletcher, John Harvey, Denis Hilton, Tony Manstead and Wolfgang Stroebe for their helpful comments on an earlier version.

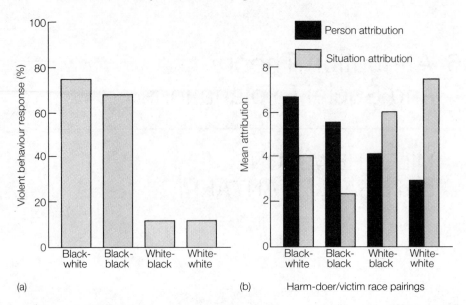

FIGURE 6.1   Description and attribution of intraracial and interracial behaviour (based on Duncan, 1976)

differences. Third, experiments can be set up to trace the ways that people make judgements of cause concerning observable social events.

In this chapter we are concerned with people's everyday, common-sense explanations for social events. We will deal, first, with the three main attribution theories – theories about the way people *attribute* behaviour to discrete causes. We will then consider some of the most interesting questions provoked by, and the research relating to, four central questions: the what, when, how and why of social explanations.

Theories of Causal Attribution

The naive analysis of action

What do people do when trying to explain the ebb and flow of social life around them? Heider (1958) treated the lay person as a *naive scientist*, linking observable behaviour to unobservable causes. We will highlight here what was perhaps Heider's major contribution to attribution theory – the division of potential sources of action into personal (or internal) and environmental (or external) types (see Heider, 1958, p. 82). According to Heider, the job of the perceiver is to decide whether a given action is due to something within the person who is performing it (e.g. ability, effort, intention), or to something outside the person (e.g. the difficulty of the task, or luck). Recall that Duncan's (1976) study, like hundreds of others, borrowed this distinction from Heider. Understanding which set of factors should be used to interpret the behaviour of another person will, according to Heider, make the perceiver's world more predictable, and give a sense of control. Heider's (1944, 1958) insights provided the blueprint for succeeding theories which we will now consider.

Correspondent inference theory

According to **correspondent inference** theory (Jones and Davis, 1965; Jones and McGillis, 1976) the goal of the attribution process is to *infer* that observed behaviour and the intention that produced it *correspond* to some underlying stable quality in the person. There are two major stages in the process of inferring personal dispositions: the attribution of intention, and the attribution of dispositions.

Attribution of intention   The perceiver's first problem is to decide which effects of an observed action, if any, were intended by the actor. If we see a black person reel backwards after being pushed by a white person, do we infer that the aggressor's behaviour was deliberate? Following Jones and Davis, to infer that any of the effects of the action were intended, the perceiver must believe that the actor *knew* the consequences of his action, and that he had the *ability* (e.g. the physical strength) to perform the action. According to the theory, the perceiver processes information backwards from effects, through action, to inferences about knowledge and ability (see figure 6.2, which is to be read from right to left).

Attribution of dispositions   The perceiver can begin this stage of the attribution process by comparing the consequences of chosen and non-chosen actions. The **non-common effects principle** is used: a perceiver makes a correspondent inference when the chosen action has a few relatively unique or non-common consequences. For example, pushing someone backwards may be seen as distinct from other possible actions (politely disagreeing, or shouting at someone) in having the consequence of physically hurting someone. The *fewer* such non-common effects there are, the *more* confident inferences about personal dispositions will be (Ajzen and Holmes, 1976; Newtson, 1974).

Also relevant are the perceiver's beliefs about what other people would do in the same situation (*social desirability*). Correspondent inferences are stronger when the consequences of the chosen behaviour are socially undesirable

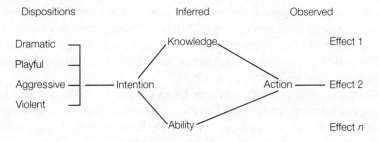

FIGURE 6.2   Attribution of dispositions from observed actions (based on Jones and Davis, 1965, p. 222)

(starting a fight in the laboratory will probably have undesirable consequences for the aggressor, leading the perceiver to conclude that the observed behaviour does indeed correspond to the disposition 'violent'). Jones and McGillis (1976) have modified this aspect of the theory to argue that only behaviours that *disconfirm expectancies* are truly informative about the actor. When people say what is expected of them in a particular situation, or while playing a particular role, then we learn little about them (see Jones, Davis and Gergen, 1961). The perceiver's expectancies may be based on prior information about the specific actor or target (*target based*), or on the target's membership of a particular class, category or social group (*category based*).

Motivational issues   So far we have considered only rather neutral explanations for the behaviour of others. Personal involvement in the other's actions is also included in Jones and Davis's model. First, the **hedonic relevance** of an action refers to the positive and negative effects of an actor's choice for the perceiver. The *more* hedonically relevant the action is to the perceiver, the *more likely* she or he is to make a correspondent inference (Jones and de Charms, 1957) and to make an *extreme* (positive or negative) judgement of another person (Chaikin and Cooper, 1973). Second, the variable of **personalism** is introduced to distinguish between cases where an actor's behaviour has general (positive or negative) relevance, and those where the behaviour is directed towards the perceiver. For example, evaluations of another person are even more extreme, especially in a negative direction, if we feel that their behaviour was aimed at us personally.

Critical issues relating to correspondent inference theory   Although experimental studies have, as indicated, yielded some support for the theory, we need to note three limitations.

1 It argues that attribution of intention must precede a dispositional inference. But there are dispositions that are defined in terms of *unintentional* behaviours, e.g. carelessness, clumsiness and forgetfulness (Eiser, 1983). For this reason, the theory is applicable only to *actions*, which have some element of choice, and not to *occurrences*, which may be involuntary (see Kruglanski, 1975).
2 How accurately does the theory describe the way people actually make attributions? Do perceivers typically pay much attention to non-chosen behaviours and their consequences? In fact, there is evidence that social perceivers attend to occurrences, not 'non-occurrences' (e.g. Nisbett and Ross, 1980), and that they tend thereafter to seek out further instances of the *same* behaviour (Snyder and Swann, 1978).
3 While behaviour that disconfirms expectancies is obviously informative, surely expectancy-confirming behaviour can also be so (see Apfelbaum and Herzlich, 1970–1: Deschamps, 1973–4). Duncan's (1976) theoretical analysis argues that violent behaviour was *expected* of black protagonists, yet he still reported stronger person attribution for black than white actors, presumably because their behaviour fitted the stereotype.

Correspondent inference theory has proved most useful as a 'rational baseline model' (Jones and McGillis, 1976, p. 404) against which actual attributions could be compared. As such, it provides a firm basis for further theorizing, which has led to a systematic analysis of biases in *how* people make causal attributions. We will consider this development later.

Covariation and configuration

The next addition to the variety of approaches that became known as attribution theory was Kelley's model of the process of ascribing causes. Kelley's (1967, 1973) attribution theory begins with the question of what information is used to arrive at a causal attribution. He outlines two different cases, which depend on the amount of information available to the perceiver. In the first case the perceiver has information from multiple sources and can perceive the *covariation* of an observed effect and its possible causes. For example, if you invite someone to supper and they refuse, how do you explain this? If you know that the same person has turned down several of your friends, but that you do not usually get rejected, you will be more likely to attribute this rejection to the person rather than yourself. In the second case, the perceiver is faced with a single observation and must take account of the *configuration* of factors that are plausible causes of the observed effect. For example, if you see a car knock down a pedestrian, you cannot normally ask about the number of previous accidents involving either driver or pedestrian. You have to take note of such factors as a wet road surface, whether the driver was drunk, and so on. We deal with both covariation and configuration in turn.

Attributions based on multiple observations: covariation   Where the perceiver has information from multiple sources, Kelley (1967, 1973) suggests that a **covariation principle** is used: an effect is attributed to a condition that is present when the effect is present, and absent when the effect is absent. The *effect* is what you are trying to explain (e.g. why you failed your driving test). The three candidate *conditions*, according to Kelley, are the *entity* (the test), the *person* (you) and the *circumstances* (e.g. the traffic conditions in which you took the test). Kelley based his model on a statistical technique, the analysis of variance (ANOVA), which examines changes in a dependent variable (the effect) by varying independent variables (the conditions) (see chapter 4). We can return to Duncan's (1976) study to illustrate further.

To ask whether the behaviour generalizes across persons, we would have to ask if other protagonists also push around the same entity (because *he* is small, or obnoxious, perhaps?). This variation over persons would yield *consensus* information – which might be based on other people in general, or on other people belonging to a specific social group. To ask whether the behaviour generalizes across entities, we would have to ask if the protagonist behaves similarly towards other entities (because he is a bully, perhaps?). This variation over entities would yield *distinctiveness* information. Finally, to ask whether the behaviour generalizes across circumstances, we would have to ask if the protagonist has behaved similarly towards the same victim in different circumstances (i.e. in different situations, or at different times). This variation over circumstances would yield *consistency* information.

Following Kelley's covariation principle, if only this protagonist (Tom) pushes around this victim (Dick); if Tom pushes around other people; and if he has pushed around Dick in the past; then we would conclude that the effect is caused by something about Tom. If we assume that each type of information could be given a high or low value, then this pattern of information would correspond to low consensus, low distinctiveness and high consistency (LLH). Two other patterns have received attention in the literature – those leading to entity and circumstance attribution (Orvis, Cunningham and Kelley, 1975). McArthur (1972) was the first to test Kelley's ANOVA model. She reported that subjects provided with varying patterns of consensus, distinctiveness and consistency made causal attributions in the way predicted by the covariation principle (see table 6.1). However, later conceptual analysis modified Kelley's model considerably and, in fact, showed that his pattern of information for circumstance attribution was incorrect. As Hewstone and Jaspars (1987) show, the LHL pattern implies a person × entity × circumstance attribution. Let us consider, briefly, a number of limitations of this research and its theoretical rationale.

Critical issues relating to the covariation principle
1 We should note, first, some limitations of the covariation principle as a basis for inferring causality. This principle actually allows causal relationships that are spurious; as statistics books remind us, correlation does not necessarily imply causation. Nor does causation necessarily imply correlation; for example, we all know that sexual intercourse is the cause of pregnancy, but the two are not, in fact, highly correlated (Einhorn and Hogarth, 1986).
2 Moving on to more psychological criticisms: in the type of experiment used to collect the relevant data (e.g. McArthur, 1972), subjects are provided with 'prepackaged' covariation information which, under normal circumstances, they might neither seek out, nor use.

TABLE 6.1   The covariation principle: hypothesized patterns of information leading to person, entity and circumstance attributions

| Causal attribution | Pattern of information | | | Example: 'Tom pushes Dick' |
	Consensus	Distinctiveness	Consistency	
Person	Low	Low	High	Only Tom pushes Dick; Tom pushes other people; Tom has pushed Dick in the past
Entity	High	High	High	Other people push Dick; Tom pushes no one else; Tom has pushed Dick in the past
Circumstance	Low	High	Low	Only Tom pushes Dick; Tom pushes no one else; Tom has not pushed Dick in the past

3 This limitation is made more serious by the fact that people may not be very skilled at assessing covariation between events (Alloy and Tabachnik, 1984).
4 Although subjects' attributions may appear *as if* they used the covariation principle, their actual information processing may be completely different from that set out by Kelley (Hewstone and Jaspars, 1987). Just because people's attributions seem to fit the ANOVA framework, this does not mean that they are doing anything like that in their heads. Can you? Most of us find it hard enough with a calculator, or even a computer. We will return later to the interesting question of the cognitive processes involved in causal attribution.

Attributions based on a single observation: configuration Of course, another drawback of the covariation model is that it requires multiple observations, yielding consensus, distinctiveness and consistency information. Yet the subject in Duncan's (1976) study, for example, does not have that information; nor do we when making most of our everyday attributions. Kelley (1972) acknowledged that the ANOVA model was 'idealized' and that there were many occasions on which the perceiver lacks the information, time or motivation to examine multiple observations. In these cases of incomplete data, attributions are made using **causal schemata**. These schemata are ready-made beliefs, preconceptions and even theories, built up from experience, about how certain kinds of causes interact to produce a specific kind of effect A perceiver can interpret information by comparing it, and integrating it, with a schema (see chapter 5).

One of the simplest causal schemata is the multiple sufficient cause (MSC) schema (Kelley, 1972). According to this schema, any of several causes (e.g. problems at home, poor school environment or lack of effort) acting individually can produce the same effect (e.g. examination failure). Kelley also put forward a number of attributional principles that accompany the causal schemata. The MSC schema is associated with the **discounting principle**: given that different causes can produce the same effect, the role of a given cause in producing the effect is *discounted* if other plausible causes are present. Thus a child whose parent died recently may have an examination failure attributed to this cause rather than to lack of effort. Kelley (1972) also proposed an **augmentation principle**: the role of a given cause is *augmented* (increased) if an effect occurs in the presence of an inhibitory cause. Thus a student from a poor background who succeeds in an examination may have her performance attributed more to effort and ability than would a student from a middle-class home.

The augmentation principle applies to both the MSC and to the more complex multiple necessary cause (MNC) schema (Kelley, 1972). According to the MNC schema, several causes must operate together to produce the effect. Kelley hypothesized that this schema would be invoked to account for unusual or extreme effects (Cunningham and Kelley, 1975).

According to Kelley (1972) there are many other kinds of causal schema available to the lay person, and they are important for three main reasons: (1) they help the perceiver to make attributions when information is incomplete; (2) they are general conceptions about causes and effects which may apply across content areas; (3) they provide the perceiver with a 'causal shorthand' for carrying out complex inferences quickly and easily (Fiske and Taylor, 1984).

Critical issues relating to causal schemata   Notwithstanding the apparent advantages of causal schemata, there are still issues which require theoretical and empirical attention. Following Fiedler (1982), two issues are central:

1 The existence and functioning of causal schemata, while intuitively plausible, have not yet been successfully demonstrated. Fiedler criticizes some of the research for being artificial, and for having a built-in device for finding a causal schema in any kind of attribution by the subject. Thus different responses are seen as evidence of the use of different kinds of schemata. But how do we know that a schema was used at all? All we can say, at present, is that people act *as if* they use schemata, but this model is nonetheless useful.
2 We seem to have lost sight of the importance of schema *content*. Following Bartlett's (1932) original sense of the term, and more recent work (e.g. Fiske and Taylor, 1984; and chapter 5), a schema represents organized knowledge based on cultural experience and not just an abstract relation between cause and effect. If we think again of Duncan's (1976) study, his white subjects seem to have possessed a schema that stereotyped the black protagonist as 'given to violence'. It was that schema, and its content, which dominated their causal attributions.

Covariation and configuration: an integration   In spite of the critical issues raised by our discussion, both covariation and configuration notions are central to attribution research. There has been extended discussion of whether attributions are 'data driven' (by covariation) or 'theory driven' (by configuration). This is one of the most fascinating issues in attribution theory, and both concepts are important. In fact, there is an interaction between data and expectations, with preconceptions influencing not only how, but what, data are processed (Alloy and Tabachnik, 1984).

Theories of causal attribution: a summary   The three theories outlined above – Heider, Jones and Davis, and Kelley – are generally considered the major contributions in the field. They converge on the following general themes: mediation between stimulus and response; active and constructive causal interpretation; and the perspective of the naive scientist or lay person. Most importantly, all share a concern with common-sense explanations and answers to the question 'why?' Based on the rich, descriptive work of Heider (1958), the theories of Jones and Davis (1965) and Kelley (1973) ambitiously attempted to formalize the rules people might be using to make causal attributions. They answered many questions, and raised a great deal more, about the nature of common-sense explanations, when and how they are made, and the functions they serve. The remainder of this chapter deals with these questions.

What Are Common-Sense Explanations?

There are many sorts of explanations – including historical, scientific and common-sense explanations. In this section we consider the nature of common-sense explanations and how to measure them, beginning with causal attributions and then moving on to consider other types of explanation. We shall see that, for attribution theory, there is one prime classification: an attribution can be *internal* or *external*. You will recall that, in Duncan's experiment, the respondent could indicate how much the 'shove' was due to personal characteristics of the harm-doer, and how much it was due to the features of the situation he found himself in. That is a clear example of an internal–external pair of attributions. After describing important issues to do with this influential classification, we shall turn our attention to explanations that cannot be fitted into its useful but rather specialized range.

Internal versus external attributions

Since Heider's (1958) work, there has been a great emphasis on the distinction between internal and external attributions. This distinction has intuitive appeal. Yet it is not quite so clear-cut as it first appears.

Can internal and external attributions be distinguished?   A central problem is that statements which seem to imply external attributions can be rephrased as statements implying internal attributions (and vice versa: Ross, 1977). This problem is particularly evident where researchers have attempted to code attributions from a free-response format. Nisbett et al. (1973, study 2) asked subjects to write brief paragraphs describing why they had chosen their college degree subject. A statement was coded as internal if it 'referred in any way to the person doing the choosing' (p. 158). Thus 'I want to make a lot of money' was coded as internal, while 'Chemistry is a high-paying field' was coded as external. An obvious criticism of this method is that the two types of statements contain similar information and in fact imply one another.

If researchers have problems in distinguishing internal and external attributions, then so too do their subjects. Some researchers have reported that many of their subjects failed to understand the distinction, and/or did not find it meaningful (Taylor and Koivumaki, 1976). It is then not surprising that the reliability and validity of such attribution measures is now challenged, not assumed.

What is the relation between internal and external attributions?   Heider proposed an inverse relation between personal and situational causality. The more the person is seen as causing the action, the less the environment will be perceived as causal (and vice versa). According to this conceptual view, measures of personal and situational attribution should be negatively correlated. However, several studies have reported positive or only slightly negative correlations (e.g. Taylor and Koivumaki, 1976) between attributions to the person and attributions to the situation when rated on separate scales. For this reason, separate measures of personal and situational attribution should always be used, and results based on a single bipolar scale should be treated with caution. It should also be noted that people are more likely to employ combinations of both internal and external attributions under certain conditions, such as when explaining extreme events (Kelley, 1973) or complex interpersonal events such as marital interaction (Bradbury and Fincham, in press) or when attributional accuracy is seen as important (Kassin and Hochreich, 1977).

Is the internal–external distinction fundamental?   In view of the problems noted above, it is legitimate to ask whether the internal–external distinction is really the most important distinguishing feature of causes. On the one hand, it has been noted that legal, philosophical and moral reasoning depend on just this kind of distinction (Totman, 1982b), although more subtly expressed. In court cases, guilt can hinge on proving that the defendant was or was not fully in control of his or her actions; to do that, the prosecution has to convince the jury that the defendant knew what he or she was doing, intended to do it, could have done otherwise, and was not temporarily insane. In other words, the barrister has to persuade the jury to make a strong, subtle and damning internal attribution.

On the other hand, the internal–external distinction may be seen as the simplistic core of attribution theory's rather limited notion of causality (Shaver, 1981b). It is limited, first, in that it is rather static. Many events can be traced backwards through a chain of proximal and distal antecedent causes (Brickman, Ryan and Wortman, 1975) and we must ask about the temporal structure of explanations. For example, why did a woman die? Because a policeman shot her; because she surprised the policeman; or because her brain was deprived of oxygen? Following the legal philosophers Hart and Honoré (1959), there are rational limits to the pursuit of causal connections backwards and forwards in time; we must ask questions such as where perceivers stop their causal analysis, and not only whether it centres on internal or external causes. So far, we know that people do not trace causes through voluntary human actions performed by some adults, which were intended to bring about the outcome which in fact occurred (see Fincham and Shultz, 1981).

Attribution theory's notion of causality is also limited in the sense that it overlooks the variety of different forms of explanation. We should not assume that causal attributions (whether internal or external) are fundamental dimensions of explanation, relevant to all situations; or that they exhaust the possibilities of ordinary language explanation. We now consider this extended perspective in more detail.

Is ordinary explanation causal?

Description   Before one even gets to an explicit 'explanation' of something, the way that it has been *described* can say an awful lot about what it means. Take this example from a daily newspaper:

What happened at the Libyan Embassy yesterday was bloody and barbaric because the people involved are bloody and barbaric. (*Daily Mirror*, 18 April 1984)

Calling the event 'bloody and barbaric' predisposes the listener to believe that the explanation is likely to be of the bloody and barbaric sort. This is very much what happened in Duncan's experiment with which we started this chapter. The same action performed by a white and a black man was called different things: when the 'protagonist' was a black man, it was more likely to be described as 'violent'. And, of course, if something is described as violent, then its cause is likely to be something aggressive and antisocial.

This kind of explanation, which Antaki and Fielding (1981) call *descriptive*, is actually very pervasive in ordinary life. On many occasions, someone will say something to you that implies a 'why' question without actually stating one; and, in reply, you might give an answer which explains by describing events or a state of affairs. Suppose Jane and John go on holiday and find themselves in a large, quiet and ornately decorated building. A group of men are prostrate in front of another man who, raised on a dais, is reading aloud. John turns to Jane and asks 'What's going on?', to which she replies brusquely 'We're in a mosque.'

Descriptions can be enough in their own right to halt the march of questions. They have the power to summarize a whole state of affairs which explains what is going on in a way that a simple cause cannot. Attribution theory has only very recently given much prominence to the power of description (Howard and Levinson, 1985), and there certainly is a link to be forged between the description of an event and the cause that then follows. On the other hand, we should also want to remind ourselves that the description *per se* can be as powerful and as conversation stopping – perhaps more so – as any cause.

Excuses and justifications   Suppose the description has been agreed between questioner and explainer, but an explanation is still required. Is the next step a cause? Not necessarily. Explanations can fulfil many functions, and the language of 'causes' is appropriate to some but not all of them. The causal language is very appropriate for what Antaki and Fielding (1981) call explanations of *agency*. An agency explanation would be wanted if, say, someone was neutrally curious about a broken window and asked what had caused it. All that would be required would be an account of what agency had brought about the breaking of the window; one could say that the wind had caused it, or the thinness of the glass, or the fact that a brick had been thrown at it by a passer-by. An account of *propriety*, on the other hand, will not be so neutrally motivated. If the person asking was the person to whom the window belonged, and you were standing close by with a guilty look on your face, what would be at issue is not merely the cause of the breakage but whether it was excusable or justifiable. Here a causal language is not the whole story, and a wide literature on the attribution of responsibility is relevant (see Fincham and Jaspars, 1980).

To illustrate the point, let us return to the example of John and Jane in the mosque. John, still not quite aware of what is going on, decides that he feels too hot and strips off his shirt. A supplicant breaks off from his worship to remonstrate, and Jane bundles John apologetically out of the mosque. In the café, she says 'What did you do a stupid thing like that for?' Being called upon to give an account of propriety, John realizes that the purely causal reply 'I was hot' is one unlikely to do him much good in the circumstances. Instead he says 'Well, how was I to know that they're so prudish?' Going on the attack is one form of explanation, as it makes John's behaviour seem quite reasonable, and turns the spotlight on the alleged oddness of the very people he offended.

Semin and Manstead (1983) have collected together a catalogue of ways there are of justifying and excusing; as may be seen from table 6.2, it is a rich and intriguing collection. At the heart of the catalogue is the distinction, made by Scott and Lyman (1968), between excuses and justifications. A *justification* usually admits that the person actually did something (e.g. 'Yes, I shot her, but she was about to blow up the building'). An *excuse*, on the other hand, tries to persuade you that the person could not be held responsible for actually doing what they did (e.g. 'I didn't actually shoot her; the gun went off accidentally'). A closely related distinction has been made by Buss (1978) between reasons and causes. *Reasons* are something you have when you do something voluntary and intentional (like shooting someone who is about to blow you up), while *causes* (like the gun going off accidentally) bring about something involuntary. As you read this chapter, there will probably be occasions on which you will think to yourself that the kind of explanations being talked about are as likely to be descriptive or justificatory as they are 'purely' causal. One particular place where that is likely to happen will be in the 'why' section, when we discuss why people might choose to explain things in particular ways.

When Do People Give Explanations?

It has been claimed that the emphasis on attribution processes in recent social psychology is exaggerated (Manis, 1977), and that most of the time people are not consciously seeking explanations or actively engaged in processing new information. In Langer's (1978) terms, much ostensibly thoughtful action is, in fact, 'mindless' (see chapter 5). Such views have led to the critical question:

TABLE 6.2 Examples of excuses and justifications

Excuses
Denial of intent, e.g. 'I did not intend to produce these results.'
Denial of volition, e.g. 'I did not want to perform this act.'
Denial of agency, e.g. 'I did not actually carry out the act.'
Appeal to mitigating circumstances, e.g. 'I am not entirely to blame.'
Justifications
Claim that effect has been misrepresented, e.g. 'No harm done.'
Appeal to principle of retribution, e.g. 'They deserved it.'
Social comparison, e.g. 'Others do the same.'
Appeal to higher authority, e.g. 'I did it for my country.'

Source: based on Semin and Manstead (1983, pp. 91–2)

under what conditions do we attempt to explain why an act has occurred? We shall answer the question in two parts: first, by considering the factors that instigate causal attributions; and second, by examining interpersonal aspects of explanations.

The instigation of causal attributions

In answer to the view that causal thoughts might be something *elicited* by procedures, rather than *emitted* by subjects, the strongest evidence for 'spontaneous' causal thinking has been provided by Weiner (1985a). He considered three types of study where normal (verbal) behaviour could be observed and coded:

1 Coding of written materials. For example, Lau and Russell (1980) analysed for content the attributions in the sports pages of newspapers and found, as one would predict, that unexpected outcomes elicited a greater number of attempts at explanation than did expected results.
2 Subjects' 'think-aloud' responses during or after task engagement, and their reported thoughts. In an interesting applied study, Carroll and Wiener (1982) collected verbal protocols from parole decision-makers as they examined actual case-history material. It was found that parole officers searched for the cause of the crime, primarily to determine the risk of the criminal to society.
3 Causal search inferred from cognitive processes. For example, Pyszczynski and Greenberg (1981) found that attribution-relevant information was most sought when prior expectations were disconfirmed, while Hastie (1984) reported that an incongruent act was more likely to *elicit* an explanation as a sentence completion than was a congruent act.

Weiner (1985a) concluded that there are two key factors in eliciting attributions: unexpected (versus expected) events, and non-attainment (versus attainment) of a goal. The importance of unexpected events is consistent with the theories of both Jones and Davis (1965) and Kelley (1967). Jones and Davis proposed that individuals were more likely to make correspondent inferences if an outcome was rare, while for Kelley lack of consensus led to a person attribution. This finding also fits with the idea that when performing familiar activities people rely on well-learned 'scripts' and that scripted actions do not require explanations (Lalljee and Abelson, 1983). In attaching such importance to unexpected events, psychologists also agree with some philosophical analyses (e.g. Hart and Honoré, 1959; Mackie, 1974). Both emphasize the significance of deviation from a normal course of events as a condition for causal reasoning and the identification of causes (Einhorn and Hogarth, 1986; Jaspars, Hewstone and Fincham, 1983).

Non-attainment of a goal (loss, defeat or failure) is also a general triggering event for attributions. Thus when someone fails a task (typically an academic achievement task), she or he is more likely to engage in attributional reasoning to explain this outcome than a success. As we will see later, performing poorly on an ability-linked performance task is potentially threatening to an actor's self-esteem and therefore elicits a special sort of explanation.

From Weiner's (1985a) review we can conclude that attributional thinking is important in everyday life, and that we know which events need explanations. An additional condition that elicits attributions has also been noted (Hastie, 1984) – the dependence of the perceiver on others for positive or negative outcomes. Thus a number of studies have reported the effect of *anticipated future interaction* on attribution (e.g. Berscheid et al., 1976). Berscheid et al. found that males and females who were about to 'go on a date' with a stranger were more likely to engage in attributional reasoning about the stranger's disposition than were subjects who did not anticipate such interaction. This finding reminds us that in everyday life we do normally have interaction goals (Jones and Thibaut, 1958) which influence not only when we make attributions, but also what type of attribution we give.

Researchers have only recently turned their attention to the explanations that are exchanged in everyday life. A recent study by Antaki and Naji (1987) looked at the tea-time and dinner-party conversations of a sample of middle-class British people. They found that the most common thing that was brought up for explanation was some long-standing state of affairs – like, say, the lack of women dentists, the peculiarity of the teaching arrangements in a local school, and so on. Antaki and Naji suggest that people want to bring up that kind of event for explanation because of an important interactional goal of conversation: accounting for the sensibleness of what one is saying. Often one states a 'fact' which needs to be bolstered by some supporting evidence, and explanations can serve that function.

This kind of observation raises the question of the relationship between the explainer and the audience, the interpersonal context in which explanations are given (Lalljee, 1981). What does the speaker assume the audience wants to know? What is their relationship? What conversational conventions are relevant? These issues all fall under the rubric of 'pragmatics', to which we now turn.

The pragmatics of explanations

The study of **pragmatics** tells us about the way in which talk accomplishes a great deal of social 'work'. The idea is that any utterance has a force and a set of implications far more extensive than its face value would suggest. For example, if you ask your tutor why she will not accept a hopelessly late essay, she might reply 'The head of department's office is down the corridor.' She has got across the message that she is not responsible; that you must take it to a higher court; and that she wants nothing to do with it or you.

In explanations, as in other utterances, the pragmatics of what is going on can tell us a great deal about the relationship between the questioner and the explainer. Your tutor could only succeed in making all those messages plain if she knew that you and she shared some important pieces of social knowledge.

Conversationalists each make use of the shared knowledge they know the other person has. That means that explanations can proceed much more economically than they would do if everything had to be spelled out in slow and tedious detail. The complexity of pragmatics can only be hinted at here (see, for example, Levinson 1983 for an extensive introduction). But, as social psychologists become more aware of language in social interaction, this area of linguistics is likely to become an important growth point in the study of explanations.

How Do People Make Attributions?

Errors and biases in the attribution process

Classic models of the attribution process, as we saw earlier, tended to view the perceiver as a fairly rational person. Kelley's (1967) ANOVA model was actually given the status of a **normative model** which indicated how perceivers *should* make accurate causal attributions (using consensus, consistency and distinctiveness according to the covariation principle). In practice, empirical evidence showed that perceivers do not act like scientists and follow such detailed and formal models. Rather, they make attributions quickly, using much less information and showing clear tendencies for certain sorts of explanation. We need, then, to consider more *descriptive* models of the attribution process.

Are we justified in referring to such tendencies as errors or biases? In fact, the term *error* should be reserved for deviations from a normative model (Fiske and Taylor, 1984) or departures from some accepted criterion of validity (Kruglanski and Ajzen, 1983). Such models or criteria are, however, rarely available for attribution research. For this reason the term *bias* should be used, although we will still use terms such as error and fallacy where the original, if insulting, label has stuck. A bias occurs if the social perceiver systematically distorts (e.g. over- or underuses) some otherwise correct procedure (Fiske and Taylor, 1984). As we will see, such biases seem to provide a better descriptive analysis of causal attribution than do complex normative models.

The fundamental attribution error   This term refers to the tendency to overemphasize dispositions and to underemphasize situational influences as causes of behaviour (Ross, 1977). This bald assertion has usually been reduced to the prediction that person attribution will be stronger than situational attribution. This effect is illustrated in an experiment by Jones and Harris (1967). In this study, subjects (Americans) were presented with short written speeches either for (unexpected behaviour) or against (expected behaviour) the Castro government in Cuba. Some targets were said to have chosen which side to support (choice condition), while others were said to have been required to take their position (no-choice condition). Observers then rated what they felt was each target person's true attitude towards Castro. The most important, and unexpected, finding was that *even in the no-choice condition*, subjects tended to

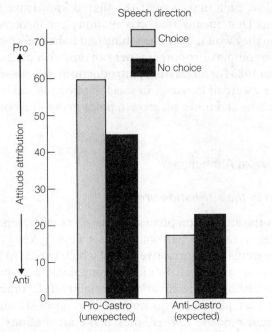

FIGURE 6.3   Attitude attribution as a function of speech direction and freedom of choice (Jones and Harris, 1967, experiment 1)

attribute attitudes in line with the speech (see figure 6.3). They seemed to attach too little weight to the situation (the no-choice instructions) and too much weight to the person. As further evidence for this same kind of effect, consider the consistent failure of perceivers to make adequate allowance for the effects of social roles on behaviour. Ross, Amabile and Steinmetz (1977) randomly assigned subjects in a 'quiz game' to the roles of questioner and contestant, with the former told to set difficult questions for the latter. Both contestants and observers overlooked the advantages conferred by the role of questioner (i.e. choosing difficult questions from *their* areas of expertise) and rated the questioner much more knowledgeable than the actor.

What causes the **fundamental attribution error**? One explanation is that the actor's behaviour is often more *salient* than the situation. As Heider (1944) noted, actor and act form a 'causal unit'; the perceiver focuses on the other person, not the situation, and he or she comes to be overrated as causally important. A second explanation is in terms of a *societal norm* for internality, so that internal attributions are viewed more favourably than external attributions (Jellison and Green, 1981). Viewed from the perspective of social representations (see chapter 5), a general 'dispositionalist theory' may be imposed on us all as we grow up in societies that emphasize individualism (Moscovici and Hewstone, 1983), and may be culturally prescribed in our language (Brown and Fish, 1982). Both these general explanations may be supported by a variety of cognitive mechanisms, based on the framework of cognitive heuristics (see Sherman and Corty, 1984; see also chapter 5). If the actor's behaviour is salient, then actor-linked causes will be highly 'available' and may assume prominence in explanations over time (Moore et al. 1979). Or since people's implicit theories give too much weight to dispositional causes of behaviour, then dispositional causes will be seen as 'representative' in explaining behaviour. Attributions can also be seen as strongly 'anchored' to person attribution, with insufficient adjustment for situational causality (Jones, 1979).

How fundamental is the fundamental attribution error (see Harvey and McGlynn, 1982; Harvey, Town and Yarkin, 1981; Reeder, 1982)? Despite its name, there are circumstances under which people will overattribute another person's behaviour to situational factors: most notably, when behaviour is inconsistent with prior expectations (Kulik, 1983), and when attention is focused on situational factors that could have produced a person's behaviour (Ajzen, Dalton and Blyth, 1979; Quattrone, 1982). In view of the fact that the bias is far from universal, and the criteria for accuracy are lacking, we should probably start looking for a more modest label for this nonetheless important effect.

Actor–observer differences   In a bold statement, Jones and Nisbett proposed that 'there is a pervasive tendency for actors to attribute their actions to situational requirements, whereas observers tend to attribute the same actions to stable personal dispositions' (1972, p. 80). Watson (1982) has provided a comprehensive review of these **actor–observer differences**. He prefers the terms *self* and *other*, rather than actor and observer, because in many studies there is not, in fact, one person acting while another observes. Following Watson, we note that there *is* an effect, but that it is confined to self–other differences in situational attribution: self-attributions to situations are higher than other-attributions to situations. Thus, for example, we attribute our own shyness in tutorials more to the situation than we do for other students.

Why does this self–other effect occur? There are a number of possible explanations (see Monson and Snyder, 1977). We will look at explanations in terms of two general ideas – how much information people have, and what they look at.

1   *Information level*   Could it be that self–other attribution differences arise from the greater amount of information available to the self-raters? We should, after all, know more about our own past behaviour, and its variability across situations, than we know about the behaviour of others. However, contrary to this suggestion, other-attributions did *not* become more similar to self-attributions as familiarity with a person increased (Nisbett et al., 1973, study 3) and there is little support for this explanation.

2   *Perceptual focus*   An ingenious experiment by Storms (1973) followed up the most fundamental difference between self and other: the fact that they have, quite literally, different 'points of view'. Storms set up a getting-acquainted conversation involving two strangers, A and B, each watched by one observer, and each filmed by one video camera (see figure 6.4). He

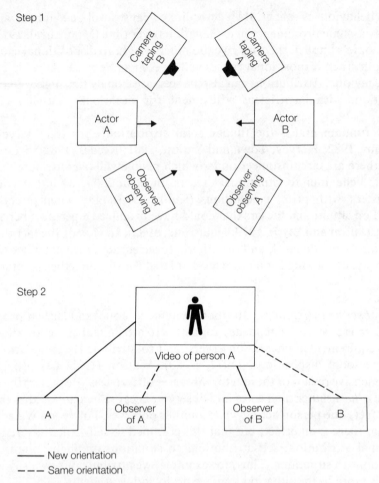

FIGURE 6.4   Testing the perceptual explanation for the actor–observer effect (Fiske and Taylor, 1984, p. 78; based on Storms, 1973)

hypothesized that it should be possible to change the way actors and observers interpret behaviour by changing their visual orientations: actors who see themselves should make more dispositional attributions about their own behaviour; and observers who see another aspect of the actor's situation should become more situational in attributing the actor's behaviour. Storms compared three orientation conditions: *no video* (control); *same orientation* (video used simply to repeat the subject's original orientation); and *new orientation* (video used to reverse the orientation of actors and observers).

The results are shown in figure 6.5 (the same-orientation results were identical to those for the no-video condition and are not shown). The most interesting finding was the predicted reversal of actors' and observers' attributions when subjects were shown a new orientation: actors' attributions became *less* situational, and observers' became *more* situational. Note, however, that in all conditions person attribution was very high (another example of the funda-

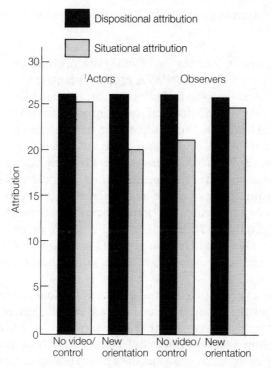

FIGURE 6.5   Actor–observer attributions as a function of orientation (Storms, 1973)

mental attribution error), and that the no-video/control conditions failed to show a difference in favour of situation attribution for actors (just as Watson, 1982 reported).

Unfortunately, some of Storms's findings have not been replicated. It seems that the participant in the centre of the visual field (person A to the observer of A, person B to the observer of B) *is* rated as more causally important, but that this weighting does not always have a clear effect on dispositional and situational attributions (Taylor et al., 1979). However **salience** effects on the weighting of dispositional and situational attributions have been found in other studies. Duval and Wicklund (1973, study 2) found that subjects who could see themselves in a mirror assigned more responsibility to themselves than did controls. The same conceptual point was made by McArthur and Post (1977). Observers watched a conversation in which one conversant was made salient (e.g. by being illuminated with a bright light), while the other was non-salient (dim light). Observers rated the salient conversant's behaviour as more dispositionally, and less situationally, caused.

The psychology of the processes that cause self–other differences in attribution is fascinating (see Farr and Anderson, 1983), and their identification is of obvious significance to our everyday understanding of each other's actions. For example, self–other attribution differences have been shown to vary as a function of marital distress (Fincham, Beach and Baucom, 1987). At present, this self-other difference is perhaps best understood in terms of the role of perceptual salience.

The underutilization of consensus   Consensus information, as we saw in our discussion of Kelley's (1967) ANOVA model, is central to attribution theory. However, consensus seems to be far less important than information about the individual (consistency and distinctiveness information). Why?

Kassin (1979a) has argued for a distinction between two types of consensus. *Explicit* consensus (as in Kelley's sense) refers to how a given sample of others actually *do* behave; *implicit* consensus refers to the perceiver's beliefs about what others *would* do if they were present. Implicit consensus may be based on the assumption that others behave as the perceiver does (the **false consensus bias**: Ross, Greene and House, 1977); on beliefs about the actor (target- or category-based expectations: Jones and McGillis, 1976); or on beliefs about the situation (Jones, Davis and Gergen, 1961). One reason why explicit consensus may be under-used, even ignored, is that it contradicts (or adds nothing to) implicit consensus.

By comparing a variety of experimental manipulations, researchers have also specified some of the conditions under which explicit consensus is used. For example, when subjects are told that the sample on which the consensus is based is a random sample (Wells and Harvey, 1977) or that it consists of members of the same social group as the actor (Hewstone and Jaspars, 1983), then consensus is used.

The tendency to underuse consensus information when making causal attributions is consistent with an effect reported in the social judgement literature – people's tendency to ignore base rates (the **base rate fallacy**: Kahneman and Tversky, 1973; see also chapter 5). However, in both areas it is important to emphasize, as we have seen, that perceivers sometimes, but not always, underuse consensus information (Borgida and Brekke, 1981).

Self-serving biases   In our treatment of actor–observer differences we excluded research dealing with attributions for success and failure. Why? Because there is another attribution bias whereby people are more likely to attribute their successes to internal dispositions, such as abilities, whereas they attribute failures to situational causes, such as high task difficulty. Taking credit for success and avoiding the blame for failure is something that most of us do at least some of the time. This **self-serving bias** is well established, but a controversy continues over whether it should be explained in terms of cognitive (information–processing) or motivational (need-serving) terms:

1 Is it a *cognitive* bias? There are, in fact, two biases at issue here – a self-enhancing bias (taking credit for success) and a self-protecting bias (denying responsibility for failure). Miller and Ross (1975) claimed support only for the self-enhancing bias, and they argued that it could be explained by cognitive factors. For example, if people intend and expect to succeed, and if behaviour can be seen as due to their efforts (whereas failure occurs *despite*

their efforts), then it may be perfectly reasonable to accept more responsibility for success than failure.

2 Is it a *motivational* bias? The cognitive explanations have been challenged, and other researchers have concentrated on the following three motives: (a) to enhance or protect self-esteem; (b) to present a favourable impression to others; (c) to maintain a sense of control over the environment (Bradley, 1978; Miller and Ross, 1975).

Researchers have tried to distinguish the cognitive and motivational explanations, but they have encountered a number of problems. It has been claimed that the cognitive explanations actually contain motivational aspects (Zuckerman, 1979), and that the cognitive research programme is so flexible that it can generate the predictions of virtually any motivational theory (Tetlock and Levi, 1982). In addition, motivational factors can have an effect on, and possibly via, information processing. For the present it appears impossible to choose between the cognitive and motivational perspectives. Both are surely correct: 'People are both rational and rationalizers' (Ross and Fletcher, 1985, p. 105).

Group-serving biases   The self-serving bias has also been extended to the study of intragroup and intergroup relations. Thus members of successful groups assume more responsibility for the group's performance than do members of a group that failed (e.g. Schlenker and Miller, 1977), while success and especially failure by members of the 'ingroup' and 'outgroup' may receive quite different explanations. Hewstone, Jaspars and Lalljee (1982) reported that schoolboys from a private school attributed the failure of an ingroup member more to lack of effort than they did that of a boy from a state school (his failure was attributed to lack of ability). We would call this an example of *intergroup attribution*: an individual attributes the behaviour of another person not simply to individual characteristics or intentions, but to characteristics and intentions associated with the group to which the other belongs (Hewstone and Jaspars, 1982, 1984). Such a simple process would act to preserve and protect stereotypes of the ingroup ('we are intelligent') and the outgroup ('they are stupid').

But there is more to group-serving biases in attribution than a mere extension of self-serving biases in the explanation of success and failure. Attributions made for a whole variety of behaviours performed by, and social conditions characteristic of, ingroup and outgroup members are often *ethnocentric* (see chapter 16), in the sense that members of a particular group favour members of their own group rather than members of outgroups (see Hewstone and Ward, 1985). Our empirical and theoretical understanding of these phenomena has largely been gained in recent years. It is now clear that intergroup attributions may serve specific functions for members of majority and minority groups, may be used to justify existing intergroup divisions, and may play a role in the development, maintenance and reduction of intergroup conflict (Hewstone, 1988). Ultimately, intergroup attributions may even form the basis of ideologies that ascribe group differences to genetic characteristics (Pettigrew, 1979) or attribute societal problems to a 'conspiracy' by a small but easily identifiable outgroup such as witches, Jews, Jesuits, Freemasons or Marxists (see Poliakov, 1980). Studied in such ways, intergroup attributions provide a compelling picture of some of the social functions served by so-called errors and biases. This is a point we return to below, after first looking in more detail at cognitive aspects of attribution.

The process of causal attribution

Having looked at some of the most prominent attribution biases, it does seem that causal attribution may often be a rapid process based on limited information processing. This view has gained ground as some researchers have moved from a view of the perceiver as 'naive scientist' to one of the perceiver as a 'cognitive miser' – a limited-capacity information processor (Fiske and Taylor, 1984). We will consider some of the relevant perceptual and cognitive processes, and how we might build process models of attribution.

Perceptual processes: salience   Taylor and Fiske (1978) have integrated evidence from a number of studies to propose that many perceivers seek a 'single, sufficient and salient' explanation for behaviour, and that causal attributions are often shaped by highly salient stimuli (a claim prefigured by Heider, 1944 and Michotte, 1946). Taylor and Fiske's overall hypothesis is that attention determines what information is salient, and that perceptually salient information is overrepresented in subsequent causal explanations. For example, a 'solo' black person in a small group of otherwise white people should be salient to observers and also perceived as disproportionately causal in the group's performance (Taylor et al., 1978). Taylor and Fiske (1978) call these attributions 'top of the head' phenomena, because they are spontaneous, relatively thought-free responses. But is the attribution process always purely perceptual? In fact, there is a role for cognitive processes too, at least some of the time.

Cognitive processes: heuristics   Cognitive **heuristics** (Tversky and Kahneman, 1974) – short cuts or rules of thumb for simplifying inferential tasks – may also guide attributions, as we noted in our discussion of the fundamental attribution error. The salience of an instance is clearly related to its *availability*. Any manipulation that focuses the perceiver's attention on a potential cause may render that cause more available, and thus more likely to be given as an explanation (Nisbett and Ross, 1980). The salient and available cause depends, of course, on the background and on how the information is presented. It might be a 'solo' person's race (as in Taylor et al., 1978), or even the subject (rather than the object) of a sentence (Pryor and Kriss, 1977). The *representativeness* heuristic may also influence attributions, and is less obviously based on perceptual factors. Nisbett and Ross (1980) give a number of illustrations, such as cases where an individual looks for causes whose principal features match those of the effect. Much prescientific medicine was dominated by this kind of thinking and some anthropological cases are fascinating (Shweder,

1977). For example, people of the Azande culture believed that the burned skull of the red bush-monkey was an effective treatment for epilepsy; the jerky movements of that monkey resemble the convulsions of an epileptic fit (Evans-Pritchard, 1937).

Process models   Whether based on perceptual and/or cognitive processes, attributions may often be 'automatic' rather than 'controlled' (Shiffrin and Schneider, 1977), until and unless the issues have more important consequences (e.g. Chaiken, 1980; see also chapter 8). As social psychologists have become more interested in how much, and how, social information is processed, so too there has been a growth of interest in, and use of, process models. A **process model** is, simply, the description of everything that goes on in the subject's head from start to finish of an experimental task (Taylor and Fiske, 1981). It is a statement of the presumed stages through which information is processed, such as *encoding, storage, retrieval, recall* and *attribution*. Process analysis provides methodological precision; we can specify the stages in social information processing and at what stage a given effect occurs.

There exists a variety of sophisticated ways of examining attributions (and other social cognitions), all of which are attempts to sidestep a major methodological problem – the fact that we can never tap directly what is going on in the heads of our research subjects. Borrowing from cognitive psychology, social psychologists have begun to use measures such as visual attention, information search, memory and response time. For example, Smith and Miller (1979) used response time in an interesting test of Kelley's ANOVA model. They reported that subjects took the shortest time (11.07 s) for what had been thought to be the most complex response (attributing an effect to 'something about the person, stimulus *and* circumstance'); and the longest time (13.64 s) for what had seemed a 'simple' response (e.g. 'something about the person'). This result led Smith and Miller to conclude that subjects were actually using a different ('subtractive') process from the one suggested by Kelley. Another example of research into the attribution process comes from work on memory. Anderson has uncovered the strong degree to which people's explanations cause their beliefs to persevere in spite of evidence to the contrary (e.g. Anderson, 1983). Fiske and Taylor (1984) attribute this to the powerful effect of explanatory schemas, which hamper the accommodation of new information.

There are advantages and disadvantages to process analysis, which Taylor and Fiske (1981) honestly appraise. The central rationale for process analysis is the belief that the same processes may well operate over a wide range of stimuli (e.g. Kruglanski, 1979). However, the social cognition approach has its limits. First, rules of inference are not always constant across different dispositions (Reeder and Brewer, 1979). Second, to overlook the content of explanations is to ignore the richness and complexity of social life (e.g. Darley and Goethals, 1980). We should also be cautious in generalizing; mini-experiments and cognitive measures may not tell us anything about thinking and behaviour outside the laboratory.

Why Do People Make Attributions – and What Are the Consequences?

We have seen that an attribution is a belief you might hold about the cause of an event. So far the kinds of events we have concentrated on have been other people's actions. But what of the explanations you might have for your own actions and states of affairs? In asking *why* people hold such beliefs, we want to emphasize the *functions* they fulfil, such as maintaining our self-esteem or claiming a certain control over our environment. We saw, earlier in the chapter, that a great deal of attention has been given to the logical structure of attributions and to a model of the cold, rational 'lay scientist'. But the founders of attribution theory had a rather warmer picture of attributions than this might imply. Theory has swung back towards appreciating people's 'hot' cognitions, and there are a number of areas of research which take up the threads of motivation that were present in the theories of Heider and his early followers.

It was recognized early on that the motivation to *control* one's world was a strong force in making one seek explanations. Forsyth (1980) has refined this notion by distinguishing between explanations and prediction: an attribution can fulfil both functions by helping us understand what has gone before and giving us reasonable grounds for guessing what will happen in the future. This powerful motivation helps us understand why, for example, some parents blame themselves when their children fall seriously ill; taking responsibility may seem a better sign of control than the alternative of uncertainty.

People may also make attributions to enhance their *self-esteem*. They can use attributions to protect their achievements and to deny their faults (as we saw earlier). There is a strong intuitive appeal to this motivational theory of attribution-making, and an extensive literature has grown up around it (see for example Weary, 1981). A related view is that people use their attributions in a more public way, as a form of *self-presentation* or *impression management* (Tedeschi and Riess, 1981). The idea is that they can actively seek approval from others by publicly taking credit for good things and avoiding blame for bad ones; in a sense, it is the self-esteem motivation transferred to the social stage.

While motivational forces can act on explanations, so too do attributions influence motivation. These effects can be seen in work on the relationship between attributions and distressing events in one's life. In the next sections we shall look closely at two important theories.

Attributions and motivation

Suppose that you have just taken a class test in statistics. You discover that you have failed – in fact, that you have failed badly. Obviously, how that makes you feel will depend on your perception of the *cause* of the failure. If you say 'I just can't understand anything to do with numbers', then you will feel rather bad. You would feel less bad if you could blithely say something like 'The lecturer – who doesn't like me anyway – is a swine when it comes to marking.'

Not only will you *feel* differently in the two different cases, but you will probably *behave* differently the next time the test comes around. In the first case you would probably be apprehensive, since your ineptitude at statistics will not have cleared up; in the second case you might be more confident, especially if a new lecturer has taken over the course and will be marking the scripts.

This idea is at the centre of Weiner's (1979, 1986) ambitious theory of the role of attributions in motivation. Any cause, according to Weiner, can fall somewhere on three dimensions: internality/externality (which we have discussed above), stability/instability (how transient or long-lasting the cause is) and controllability/uncontrollability (how much the cause is under someone's direction). These three dimensions combine to form eight possible permutations of causes. Table 6.3 shows examples of each type (for example, an internal, unstable and uncontrollable cause would be something like being ill on the day of the examination). It is the first two dimensions that are really important for self-attributions in Weiner's theory. According to Weiner, where the cause falls on the internal/external axis affects your self-esteem. For example, attributing success to one's own efforts is good for one's pride. Where the cause falls on the stability/instability dimension affects your expectations that things will change: for example, attributing failure to one's innate ability does not encourage any expectation that things will get any better.

What kind of evidence does Weiner have for these propositions? The evidence comes mainly from two sources: laboratory paper-and-pencil experiments, and work with pupils in classrooms. The laboratory experiments themselves fall into two kinds. In the more oblique kind, respondents have to *imagine* themselves or someone else reacting to success or failure. A typical experiment of this type would give the respondent one of a number of attributions for the result (bad luck, hard work and so on), then ask the respondent to guess how the person would feel. The researchers then make a link between the reported feelings and the attributions that they had manipulated. For example, Weiner, Russell and Lerman (1978) followed exactly this procedure to conclude that internal attributions for success made people feel happier. Note, of course, that this is based on the respondent's guess at how the person in the story would feel – rather an indirect way of testing the theory.

The more direct way of testing the theoretical predictions in the laboratory is to make the respondents themselves actually take part in some kind of test and see what relationship there is between attributions, performance and feelings. An example of this kind of study is a simple experiment by Weiner, Nierenberg and Goldstein (1976). Respondents were given a series of trials at making patterns with building blocks. Before going on to the next trial in the series, they were told how they had done (in fact, it was set up so that the respondent always succeeded at the task) and asked (on rating scales) to say why; then they had to estimate how likely they were to do well on the next trial. The results showed that those who rated their success as being due to stable things like 'I'm always good at these kind of tasks' were more confident about how well they would do on the next trial than were those who attributed it to unstable things like 'I tried hard.' This finding supported the notion that the important link

TABLE 6.3 Examples of perceived causes for academic and social failure

	Motivational domain	
Dimension classification	Achievement	Social
Internal-stable-uncontrollable	Low aptitude	Physically unattractive
Internal-stable-controllable	Never studies	Always unkempt
Internal-unstable-uncontrollable	Sick on the day of the exam	Coughing when making the request
Internal-unstable-controllable	Did not study for this particular test	Did not call sufficiently in advance
External-stable-uncontrollable	School has hard requirements	Religious restrictions
External-stable controllable	Instructor is biased	Rejector always prefers to study at night
External-unstable-uncontrollable	Bad luck	Rejector must stay with sick mother that evening
External-unstable-controllable	Friends failed to help	That night the rejector wants to watch television

Source: Weiner (1986, p. 294)

with expectation was the stability of the perceived cause, not its internality, since there was no relationship between the internality of the respondents' causes and how they thought they were going to do on the next trial.

There is a good deal of such laboratory work supporting the theory. Of perhaps more interest is the work with school pupils, where there is great potential in remedial work. Dweck (1975) identified pupils she saw as needing help – they were the ones who would not take personal responsibility for how they did in class – and gave them a training regime. This consisted of getting them to do a series of small tasks which had some failures deliberately built in. After each failure the hapless pupil was told, in no uncertain terms, 'that means you should have tried harder' (p. 679). The pupils actually seemed to respond to this and to persist at tasks which previously they would have given up. The aim of such research, although its success is currently debated (Fincham, in press), is to change pupils' attributions by instruction and training, and thereby affect their persistence at the task. Such classroom experiments are comparatively rare in tests of Weiner's theory. This is largely, we imagine, because experiments are much more difficult to arrange in the classroom than in the laboratory. In the laboratory, the experimenter has reasonable control over who does what, when, and with what result. In the classroom, this is not always possible.

Since Weiner's (1979) formulation of his model, much work in the laboratory (if rather less in the field) has been carried out. While the framework is clearly a persuasive and productive one, we need to note something which is significant in the light of what we have said so far about the nature of attributions and the role of language. The problem is in trying to fit people's actual explanations to Weiner's theory. As soon as researchers tried to compartmentalize the causes pupils spontaneously gave, they found that the neat $2 \times 2 \times 2$ pigeonholes of the internal, stable and controllable dimensions were far from perfect accommodation for the subtlety of natural language.

This is well illustrated in an experiment by Krantz and Rude (1984). They asked respondents to put the four 'classic' causes (ability, effort, task difficulty and luck) on either side of three dimensions (internal or external, stable or unstable, controllable or uncontrollable). But they found that it was remarkably rare for respondents to get it 'right'. Examples of spectacularly 'wrong' categorizations included task difficulty (a clear external attribution in the model) being put down as internal. Just under half of the respondents put ability (a clear stable cause in the model) down as unstable. Thus, as Weiner himself has noted, the classification of causes can vary across perceivers and situations.

In addition to the problem of classifying attributions, a very significant and far-reaching feature is that Weiner's theory privileges *perceived* causality over *actual* causality. According to the model, what is important is not what caused your failure but what you *think* caused it. This theme is very prominent in the second of the two applied theories we shall be looking at.

Attributions and depression

Depression has many definitions, but all theorists would agree that it is a serious, debilitating condition far removed from the ordinary 'blues' that we all suffer from time to time. Its causes are still a matter of controversy, as is its treatment. Recently, however, attribution theorists have claimed that one sub-type of depression is produced, at least in part, by the attributions that people make for events in their lives. The current, cognitive version (Peterson and Seligman, 1984) of the most influential theory in the area (Abramson, Seligman and Teasdale's 1978 theory of **learned helplessness**) is as follows. Certain people believe that their outcomes are independent of their actions; this belief is associated with a predisposition to explain events by attributing them to internal, stable and global causes ('global' means that the cause is believed to operate on a large number of things, not just one). If people with this kind of **attributional style** experience a bad event, then they will believe it is caused by them, that the cause is long-lasting, and that the cause will make other things bad too; this makes them depressed. Matters are made even worse by the fact that people in depressed mood states are more likely to search for explanations than are people in happy or satisfied states (see Abele, 1985).

There is no doubt that there is something intuitively appealing about this idea. What of the empirical evidence? Most studies tend to be correla-tional – looking to see whether a person's depression is positively related to how internal, stable and global their attributions are. A survey by Sweeney, Anderson and Bailey (1986) of over a hundred such studies (of very variable quality, it must be said), involving nearly 15,000 respondents, comes to a reasonably confident conclusion that the correlations are reliable, even though the actual *size* of the correlations is not large. The overall mean correlation between a composite of the internality, stability and globality of people's attributions, and their depression scores, is about $+0.3$. But, as Sweeney, Anderson and Bailey point out, this is as good as, if not better than, the typical size of correlational effects in the personality/clinical area.

The correlational evidence, then, is supportive. However, we need to think carefully about what it means. After all, as recent commentators have stressed, the theory seems really to be a *prospective* one, making the prediction that someone who has the attributional style will become depressed only after a negative event (Brewin, 1985; Coyne and Gotlib, 1983). Correlations between attributions and depression at the same time are actually not informative about the causal sequence claimed by this prospective account. Brewin notes that the strong, causal sequence interpretation of Abramson, Seligman and Teasdale's (1978) theory corresponds to what he calls the 'vulnerability' model: the style makes you teeter on the brink, but you need a bad event actually to push you over the cliff (see figure 6.6). The best tests of this interpretation of the model need to be prospective, catching people before they are likely to be exposed to a stressful or aversive event. There are actually very few of these studies, since prospective research designs are notoriously costly and difficult to set up.

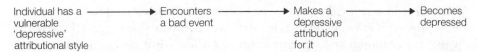

FIGURE 6.6   The 'vulnerability' model of attributions in depression (based on Brewin, 1985, p. 300)

In fact, according to Brewin, there are a number of models of the role of attributions in depression, each of which would be consistent with a finding of a simple positive correlation between attributions and depression. This is not necessarily because each is correct; rather, it is at least partly because the actual designs that researchers have used have been rather too simple to decide between them. Each model would predict that a person's depression and attributions should be at least associated, so that if one changed the other should change too. The large survey of correlations reported by Sweeney, Anderson and Bailey (1986) provides the kind of evidence that each model could invoke. Brewin is cautious about his conclusions, but is willing to say at least that attributions do have considerable predictive value and might well have some part to play in the process of recovery from, and coping with, depression.

The general idea of the role of attributions in depression is, as we noted at the beginning of this section, similar to the theme of Weiner's theory of attributions in motivation. The two kinds of thinking share problems as well as their undoubted plausibility, and we outlined some of them in our section on Weiner. In spite of these problems, the theories remain fertile and applicable. The range of use is very wide – from understanding close relationships (e.g. Fincham 1985) to maintaining behaviour change (Sonne and Janoff, 1982); and from treating 'helpless' children (Dweck, 1975) to giving attributional style therapy to depressed adults (Layden, 1982). Not all of these applications depend on a close reading of the motivation or the depression theories. Rather, they use the insight that the way people explain their world influences the way they feel and act.

Summary and Conclusion

We have covered a great deal of ground in this chapter, and the reader is entitled to ask us this: what, in a few words, has attribution theory told us about ordinary explanation? Our answer is that it has given us four headings under which to ask questions about explanation and, under each heading, has given us some positive things to say.

What explanations are   is the most wide ranging of the headings. Attribution theory is perhaps unnecessarily devoted to the distinction between internal and external causes, since we have seen that explanations are more than attributions, let alone more than internal and external ones. Nevertheless practice among researchers is changing, and more elaborate and sensitive measures are being taken of explanation; this can only be a positive sign.

When people give explanations has been comparatively under-researched, but is proving a growing field. What data we have available suggest that asking 'why?' is a common and pervasive part of ordinary life, and that attributions are likely to be embedded in the way we construct the world to ourselves and others.

How explanations are made is the jewel in attribution theory's crown. If cognitive social psychology has a place in the study of ordinary explanations, this is surely its prime spot; this chapter has described a wide range of ingenious ways of testing the cognitive processes through which attributions are mediated.

Why explanations are made, and what their consequences are is the humane face of attribution theory. The emphasis is on showing how various forms of human distress can be mediated by the way people explain the cause of events to themselves. The weight of evidence strongly implicates attributions somewhere in the aetiological and the treatment process, though as yet no one is quite sure where. If attribution theory has identified a way of helping people change, then that is a very strong entry on the plus side of the register.

Glossary Terms

Actor-observer difference	Hedonic relevance
Attributional style	Heuristics
Augmentation principle	Learned helplessness
Base rate fallacy	Non-common effects principle
Causal schemata	Normative model
Correspondent inference	Personalism
Covariation principle	Pragmatics
Discounting principle	Process model
False consensus bias	Salience
Fundamental attribution	Self-serving bias
error	

Further Reading

Antaki, C. and Brewin, C. (eds) (1982) *Attributions and Psychological Change: applications of attributional theories to clinical and educational practice.* London: Academic Press. A wide-ranging treatment of the many ways in which attributional ideas have been applied.

Fiske, S. T. and Taylor, S. E. (1984) *Social Cognition*. New York: Random House. A clear and thorough treatment of the whole field; see especially chapters 2–4 on attribution theory and 10 on research in social cognition.

Harvey, J. H., Ickes, W. J. and Kidd, R. F. (eds) (1976, 1978, 1981) *New Directions in*

Attribution Research (vols 1–3). Hillsdale, NJ: Erlbaum. Collections of chapters, many of which are cited in the text, which cover the breadth of the field.

Heider, E. (1944) Social perception and phenomenal causality. *Psychological Review*, 51, 358–74. A short exposition of Heider's rich ideas, and a more accessible source than his 1958 monograph.

Hewstone, M. (ed.) (1983) *Attribution Theory: social and functional extensions.* Oxford: Basil Blackwell. A collection of European perspectives, aimed at 'socializing' attribution theory and emphasizing 'why' certain explanations are given.

Jones, E. E. (1979) The rocky road from acts to dispositions. *American Psychologist*, 34, 107–17. Essential reading for correspondent inference theory; an updated and more readable source than Jones and Davis (1965).

Kelley, H. H. (1973) The processes of causal attribution. *American Psychologist*, 28, 107–28. Clear, succinct treatment of both covariation and configuration concepts.

Ross, M. and Fletcher, G. J. O. (1985). Attribution and social perception. In G. Lindzey and E. Aronson (eds), *Handbook of Social Psychology* (vol. 2), 3rd edn, New York: Random House. An authoritative recent review.

7 Attitudes I: Structure, Measurement and Functions

DAGMAR STAHLBERG
and DIETER FREY

Introduction

The concept of **attitude** 'is probably the most distinctive and indispensable . . . in contemporary American social psychology' (Allport, 1954, p. 43). That this is true not only for American social psychology or the mid-1950s is evidenced by the current literature dealing with the attitude theme (see the regular reviews in *Annual Review of Psychology*; for example Chaiken and Stangor, 1987).

Why is the concept of attitude so popular in social psychology? Psychology's aim is to study behaviour, and attitudes are supposed to influence behaviour. Social attitudes, therefore serve as indicators or predictors of behaviour. Furthermore, to change attitudes is seen as a meaningful starting point for modifying behaviour, not only in social-psychological research but also in everyday life, as the following examples may show:

1 Politicians try to evoke positive attitudes and opinions concerning themselves as well as their political programmes in order to be (re-)elected or to realize such programmes.
2 Carefully conceptualized commercials are delivered to potential product consumers to convince them of the merits of a new chocolate, a new detergent or a certain car model, so turning potential consumers into real ones.
3 Your partner wants to know whether you like Greece or her feminist friends, or whether you despise the dish-washing, in order to predict your behaviour: for example, whether you will readily accompany her on a journey to Greece; whether you will enjoy an evening with her feminist friends; or whether you will always quarrel about which of you is to do the dish-washing.
4 Negative social attitudes (e.g. prejudices) towards certain groups (like

migrant workers, homosexuals etc.) can lead to behavioural discrimination (for example, refusing to employ members of certain social groups).

As can be seen from these examples, the concept of social attitudes has a dominant role to play in a social-psychological model of behaviour. Thus there is ample reason for analysing this concept in more detail. First we explain what social attitudes are, i.e. how they are defined and what different conceptions of attitudes exist. Then we turn to the question: 'How are attitudes measured?' Finally, we discuss the different functions of attitudes and the relationship between attitudes and behaviour.

The Attitude Construct: Definitions and Conceptual Distinctions

The term 'social attitude' was introduced in social psychology by Thomas and Znaniecki (1918), in order to explain behavioural differences in everyday life between Polish farmers in Poland and the USA. Since then, many different definitions for the increasingly popular concept of attitudes have been proposed.

One of the most general definitions is that of Rosenberg and Hovland (1960, p. 3): attitudes are 'predispositions to respond to some class of stimuli with certain classes of response'. These classes of responses are specified as affective (concerning evaluative feelings of liking and disliking), cognitive (concerning beliefs, opinions, and ideas about the attitude object), and conative/behavioural (concerning behavioural intentions or action tendencies). This so-called **three-component model** of attitudes, which is far more a model of attitude structure than a simple definition, is presented in figure 7.1. An attitude in this model is regarded as a hypothetical construct that intervenes between observable, antecedent stimuli and subsequent behaviour.

Contrary to this multicomponent view of attitudes, other authors have proposed attitude conceptualizations that stress the evaluative character of attitudes as their most important or even sole component: 'the term *attitude* should be used to refer to a general, enduring positive or negative feeling about some person, object, or issue' (Petty and Cacioppo, 1981, p. 7; see also Fishbein and Ajzen, 1975). These sorts of definitions are labelled *unidimensional* because they focus on only one attitude component. As a consequence of this restriction, supporters of this model distinguish the attitude concept from the concept of beliefs on the one hand and from behavioural intention or overt action on the other (cf. Fishbein and Ajzen, 1975).

The term **belief** is reserved for the opinions held about the attitude object or – in other words – for the information, knowledge or thoughts someone has about the attitude object (for example: 'Karl thinks that his old car is still a reliable one'). *Attitudes*, then, stand for the emotions, which are connected with the attitude object, that is, its positive or negative evaluation (for example: 'Karl likes his old car'). **Behavioural intentions**, finally, describe some sort of predisposition to a certain kind of attitude-relevant action, i.e. the readiness to

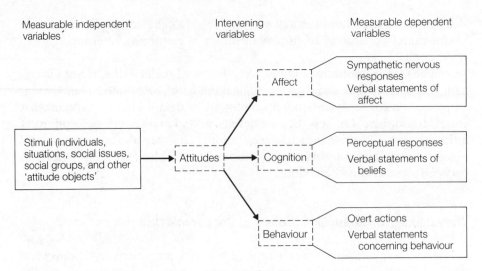

FIGURE 7.1   Three-component view of attitude (Rosenberg and Hovland, 1960)

behave towards a certain attitude object in a special way (for example, 'Karl decides not to buy a new car'). This readiness for behaviour does not necessarily imply that the *behaviour* will actually be shown. Intended behaviour will not ensue when, for example, it conflicts with social norms or with the individual's expectations of what an adequate or acceptable behaviour should be (see later for the guiding of behaviour). These four conceptual distinctions – beliefs, attitudes, behavioural intention and behaviour – are organized by Fishbein (1963, 1967) and Fishbein and Ajzen (1975) into a conceptual framework for the study of attitudes and behaviours. As far as this model describes the structure of attitudes, that is the link between beliefs and attitudes, it is presented here; the whole model will be discussed later when we analyse the relationship between attitudes and behaviour.

The **expectancy-value model** of attitudes, developed by Fishbein (1963, 1967), describes the relationship between beliefs and attitudes as follows. A person's attitude toward the attitude object (for example, 'nuclear power plants') is a function of the *value* of attributes associated with the object (for example, 'threatening the future of mankind' or 'inevitable technical instruments to guarantee energy supply') and the *expectancy*, i.e. the subjective probability that the attitude object is indeed characterized by these attributes. An attitude is predicted by multiplying the value and expectancy components associated with each attribute, and summing these products:

$$A_O = \sum_{i=1}^{n} b_i e_i$$

where A_O is the attitude towards some object O; b_i is belief i about O (i.e. the subjective probability that O is related to attribute i); e_i is the evaluation of attribute i; and n is the number of beliefs. This model of attitude structure has been empirically tested in a number of studies by Fishbein as well as other colleagues (cf. Fishbein, 1963; Fishbein and Coombs, 1974; Jaccard and Davidson, 1972).

Although there are other conceptions of attitudes to be found in the literature, the unidimensional and three-component models have received the most attention. An obvious question remains: 'Which of the two positions can be supported by the data?' The three-component model claims that the three defined components described above should be moderately correlated, thus appearing separate but not completely unrelated. Studies in which the correlational structure of the different components has been analysed have yielded contradictory results. Some authors came to the conclusion that the three-component theory found no empirical support, because factor-analytical approaches (methods to analyse basic dimensions in correlational data) were not able to justify the three components: they are often too highly correlated to be conceptually differentiated (see, e.g., Hormuth, 1979; McGuire, 1969, 1985). Support for the three-component model of attitudes was reported by Kothandapani (1971). He succeeded in showing that all three attitude components were highly correlated with themselves when measured with different kinds of scales, but very lowly correlated with the other two components (for contradictory results see Ostrom, 1969). Recent analyses of attitudinal structures using more refined statistical methods (cf. Bagozzi and Burnkraut, 1979, 1985; Dillon and Kumar, 1985) reached equally contradictory conclusions. In an overview of these research findings Chaiken and Stangor (1987) concluded that a definitive judgement of the three- versus one-dimensional issue seems premature at present.

Moreover, Breckler (1984) assumed that attitude dimensionality may vary with the kind of attitudinal object studied. This notion is also supported by the work of Schlegel (1975) and Schlegel and DiTecco (1982). They showed that attitudinal structures can be conveyed in a single affective response, as Fishbein and Ajzen (1975) postulate, when relevant beliefs about the attitude object are simple, their number is small, and they do not contradict each other. However, if beliefs are numerous, complicated and at least partly contradictory – for example, if a person has intense personal experiences with the attitude objects (in this study, the use of marijuana) – a simple evaluative response will fall short of representing the whole attitude structure.

Empirical evidence in support of unidimensional or multidimensional attitude models thus far must be considered contradictory. In practical research, however, operationalizations of attitudes following the unidimensional concept are mostly preferred, for they can be measured more simply (cf. for example Dawes and Smith, 1985; Silberer, 1983). Moreover, most standard attitude scales are based on a unidimensional attitude concept, as the next section will show.

Attitude Measurements

It is obvious that the abstract concept of an attitude cannot be measured directly. Therefore it is necessary to find adequate indicators of an attitude. Most methods of attitude measurement are based on the assumption that attitudes can be measured by the opinions or beliefs of persons about the attitude objects (e.g. Thurstone, 1931; Likert, 1932). Other methods try to assess the evaluative character of an attitude more directly. Nearly all methods are based on the unidimensional conceptualization of attitudes. For further classification, direct and indirect methods of measurement can be differentiated. With a direct measurement the subject is asked directly about his or her attitudes or opinions; that is, subjects are to give some sort of self-descriptions. All the classical approaches to attitude measurement (which we will examine below) belong to these techniques. With indirect techniques, one tries to measure attitudes without the person holding this attitude being aware of the measurement procedure. The advantage of the latter techniques is that they are less susceptible to social desirability or self-presentational motives. In the following, the most important direct and indirect procedures for attitude measurement will be discussed.

Classic approaches to attitude measurement

Thurstone's equal appearing interval scale   In 1928 Thurstone published his now famous paper with the optimistic title 'Attitudes can be measured'. He proposed different judgement techniques, which should make it possible to attain more or less quantified measures of attitudes. The most famous of these techniques, which is even identified by some authors as the 'Thurstone scale', is the **equal appearing intervals scale**; this allows for quantitative measures of attitudes.

The different steps of constructing an equal appearing intervals scale can be described as follows:

1 *Obtaining the item pool*   First, about 100 attitude statements (opinions) about the attitude object in question have to be collected. These statements should be short, unambiguous and relevant in terms of the attitude object. They have to represent the whole attitude continuum, i.e. there have to be opinions characteristic of attitudes from the extreme positive to the extreme negative. These statements can be based on the investigator's intuition, experts' opinions or literature studies.

2 *Evaluation of the statements*   A number of subjects (around 100 or even more), representative of the population of those subjects whose attitudes are to be assessed later on, evaluate all items in the pool on an 11-point rating scale. This scale indicates the amount of favourableness (or unfavourableness) towards the attitude object implied by a certain item (1 will represent as unfavourable as possible and 11 as favourable as possible towards the atti-

tude object). The judges are asked to rate each opinion on an equal interval basis, i.e. to keep in mind that the distances between the 11 categories are always the same from one category to the next.

3 *Calculation of the scale value* The arithmetic mean or the median of all category values which are attributed by the different judges to one item produces the scale value of this item.

4 *Item selection* For the selection of the 20 or 30 items which are finally chosen to form the scale, three criteria must be considered.

  (a) The items should cover the whole attitude continuum and be at equal distances.

  (b) According to the *ambiguity* criterion, all items with high interjudgement variance should be excluded.

  (c) Finally, according to the *irrelevance* criterion, all items which do not differentiate between persons with more or less positive attitudes should be excluded, because they are irrelevant to the attitude object in question.

In the final scale, items with different calculated scale values appear in random order. Subjects whose attitudes are to be measured are asked to check every statement with which they agree. The attitude score obtained then is the mean scale value for all endorsed statements.

The Thurstone scale of equal appearing intervals was, at its time of development, a revolutionary instrument, for it gave investigators techniques for measuring the important construct of an attitude. Nevertheless, this sort of scale is rarely used in contemporary research for at least three important reasons:

1 The quality of the Thurstone scale as an interval scale has been doubted. Stroebe (1980) argues that it has only the quality of rank-order scales (ordinal scaling). Indeed, the assumption that the judges can perceive the categories as being equally distant is not testable.

2 People cannot evaluate the favourableness of attitude statements towards the attitude object objectively, i.e. independently of their own opinions. For example it was found that with increasingly extreme judges' attitudes, the categorization of items in the extreme categories equally increased (cf. Eiser and Stroebe, 1972; Sherif and Hovland, 1961).

3 The construction of a Thurstone scale is very time-consuming and/or expensive, especially for investigators who only want to construct an attitude scale to operationalize one simple variable out of many others. Therefore it will not be very economical to occupy and pay about 100 judges, or even more, in order to construct one simple 20-item scale. Other scales, like the Likert scale described below, may therefore meet economical requirements much better.

Semantic differential The problem with the type of scale discussed so far is that for each new attitude object a new scale has to be constructed. The **semantic differential**, which was developed by Osgood, Suci and Tannenbaum

(1957), offers the possibility of measuring different attitudes with a unique scale.

In developing the semantic differential Osgood and his coworkers confronted their subjects with certain concepts, such as father, politics, self etc. Subjects were then asked to rate each concept on different bipolar rating scales, the endpoints of which were opposite adjectives like 'pleasant/unpleasant', 'hard/soft', and so on. Using factor analysis, Osgood, Suci and Tannenbaum identified three basic dimensions on which concepts could be described. These factors were interpreted as evaluation, potency and activity. The researchers – following a unidimensional attitude concept – assumed that the pairs of adjectives showing high loadings on the evaluation factor (high correlations with the factor) are appropriate for describing a person's attitude to the object in question. Table 7.1 shows an example of a semantic differential attitude scale which uses some of the adjective pairs found in former studies to have high loadings on the evaluative factor. The resulting attitude, then, is obtained by summing the scores from each rating scale, which normally vary between $+3$ and -3.

According to Osgood, Suci and Tannenbaum (1957), attitude scores obtained by a semantic differential measure are supposed to be parametrically scaled, i.e. there are equal distances between scale points. The reliability of the scale is, according to Robinson and Shaver (1969), comparable with that of the Thurstone and Likert scales. The main advantage of the semantic differential is its easy applicability towards different attitude objects. However, this point is also a danger: because of the high degree of abstraction of this instrument, it can be less appropriate for describing behaviourally relevant attitudes. Another – probably more severe problem – is that the factorial structure of a given semantic differential scale varies considerably with the type of the actual concept being rated. This implies that the main advantage of the semantic differential – its universal applicability – cannot be taken for granted.

Likert scale   One of the most popular standard attitude scales has been developed by Likert (1932). The great popularity of the **Likert scale** is due mostly to its low cost. Compared, for example, with the rather complicated scale proposed by Thurstone, Likert scales can be much more easily developed.

A Likert scale is constructed as follows:

1 As with the Thurstone scale, the first step in constructing a Likert scale consists of the collection of a great number of items (about 100) relevant to the attitude that should be measured. These items should clearly express positive

TABLE 7.1   Examples of evaluative ratings used in semantic differential scales

Good	$+3$,	$+2$,	$+1$,	0,	-1,	-2,	-3	Bad
Pleasant	$+3$,	$+2$,	$+1$,	0,	-1,	-2,	-3	Unpleasant
Worthful	$+3$,	$+2$,	$+1$,	0,	-1,	-2,	-3	Worthless
Clean	$+3$,	$+2$,	$+1$,	0,	-1,	-2,	-3	Dirty
Friendly	$+3$,	$+2$,	$+1$,	0,	-1,	-2,	-3	Unfriendly

TABLE 7.2 An example of a possible Likert scale item to measure attitudes towards nuclear power plants

'I believe that nuclear power plants are one of the great dangers of industrial societies':

+ 2	Strongly agree
+ 1	Moderately agree
0	Neutral or undecided
− 1	Moderately disagree
− 2	Strongly disagree

or negative beliefs or feelings about the attitude object in question. The decision as to whether a specific item reflects positive or negative attitudes or is neutral towards the attitude object and, therefore, has to be eliminated, is made by the investigator. Therefore Likert scales can be constructed without the help of the many judges necessary when constructing a Thurstone scale.

2 In the next step a large sample of people representative of the population whose attitudes are later to be assessed is asked to answer the collected items on a five-point rating scale. An example of such a possible item to measure attitudes towards nuclear power plants is shown in table 7.2. For each item a score between + 2 (favourable towards the attitude object) and − 2 (unfavourable towards the attitude object) is obtained.

3 In the third step a preliminary attitude score is completed by summing subjects' responses to the different items. To ensure that all items reflect the single attitude in question, an item analysis is performed. This means that each item is intercorrelated with the whole item score. Because only items which are highly intercorrelated with this attitude score could be regarded as indicative of the underlying attitude, all items that do not fulfil this requirement are eliminated in the final scale. Such a final scale then meets Likert's criterion of *internal consistency* (high correlations of each single item with the summed score).

4 The final attitude score again is obtained by summing the responses towards those items left in the scale.

Taken together, Likert scales are very popular in psychological research. One problem of these scales, however, can be seen in the fact that they do not strictly fulfil the requirements of equal interval scales (see Petty and Cacioppo, 1981; Stroebe, 1980). Nevertheless, in research practice they are often used as if they do fulfil these assumptions. Another problem can be seen in the ambiguity of moderate attitude scores in particular, for they could follow from general moderate responses to all items as well as from very inconsistent response patterns (see, e.g., Shaver, 1981a; and see also Stosberg, 1980 for a critique of the underlying additivity).

The one-item rating scale Very often a one-item rating scale is used to measure attitudes. This simple method is not as reliable as the more complicated techniques described above. However, it is sufficient for many representative studies such as opinion surveys and polls. The investigators formulate a single question from which they think a direct estimation of the attitude is possible. This question is then connected with a multi-point rating scale: for example, 'How satisfied are you with your life?' (very satisfied (= 7) to not at all satisfied (= 1)).

General problems of these scales All measures which are based on self-descriptions start from the assumption that the person who responds is able and motivated to disclose his or her true attitudes. However, there is a lot of evidence that there are tendencies to attitude misrepresentation, e.g. tendencies to give socially desirable answers. Because self-evaluation data can be easily falsified, or are susceptible to impression management motives, other instruments have been developed to assess attitudes (see next section). Also problematic is the assumption of the more or less explicitly tested unidimensionality of the scales discussed above, which conflicts with at least one important attitude conceptualization: the three-component model. Multidimensional measurement procedures, on the other hand, are very seldom used.

Another problem can be seen in the reactivity of the attitude measurement procedure itself. For certain attitude objects, people sometimes do not possess any explicitly or clearly formulated attitudes. However, in being asked to make statements about these attitude objects, they are urged to express a certain well-defined position. Sometimes, therefore, the process of attitude measurement itself will develop attitudes which would not otherwise have been formulated. These spontaneous attitudes may be very unstable, and therefore rather bad predictors of behaviour. Again, some of the techniques of non-direct attitude measurements mentioned below do not share these problems.

Other sorts of attitude measurements

Physiological measurements It is a well-known fact that emotional reactions are combined with physiological reactions (skin response, pulse rate, dilation of the pupils etc.). Therefore it makes sense to look at physiological reactions in order to find more objective attitude indicators.

The most important objective indicator of attitudes has been the **galvanic skin response** (GSR). The GSR measures the electrical resistance of the skin, which changes when people are emotionally aroused. Hence the GSR allows the researcher to assess a subject's emotional response towards an attitude object. For example, in an experiment by Porier and Lott (1967), black and white experimenters touched their white subjects coincidentally with their hand. The stronger the subjects' prejudices were (which was measured before by a questionnaire), the more the subjects' galvanic skin response changed when being touched by the black experimenter relative to being touched by the white experimenter. As can be seen from this example, the main problem with psycho-physiological indicators of attitudes like the GSR and the pupillary response (cf. Petty and Cacioppo, 1981) is that these measures assess the intensity of emotional responses but not their direction. Furthermore, the measures are influenced by many other features of the attitude stimulus presented (e.g. its novelty and its unexpectedness: cf. Sokolov, 1963).

An objective attitude indicator that was supposed to be a possible measure of the quality of attitude (its positiveness/negativeness) is the facial electro-myogram (EMG). Schwartz et al. (1976) showed that with positive affective states, certain face muscles are activated more strongly and others less strongly than with negative affective states. Cacioppo and Petty (1979) corroborated the usability of this instrument in an experiment concerning reactions to persuasive communications which were pro-attitudinal or contra-attitudinal for the subjects. It could be shown that the EMG could depict whether subjects listened to a pro- or contra-attitudinal communication. Petty and Cacioppo (1981) therefore concluded that the EMG measure is sensitive to different qualities (positive or negative) of an affect or emotion, but they doubted whether the instrument can also be successfully used to assess the intensity of an emotional reaction.

Physiological measures of attitudes are not very often used in practice. One reason may be the above-mentioned insensitivity of most of the instruments towards the quality of an attitudinal response. Another important reason, however, is the necessity of using technical devices, which are not easily applied in field settings.

Behaviour observation and non-reactive measurements These methods derive attitude measures from open, observable behaviour patterns. In most behaviour observation the subjects know that they are being observed. However, in non-reactive measurement the subjects are observed without their knowledge; or, even more indirectly, some of their behaviour patterns are analysed. These sorts of attitudinal measures are called behaviour indicators (Petty and Cacioppo, 1981), observation techniques (Calder and Ross, 1976), and distortion immunized methods or unobtrusive measures (Stroebe, 1980). (For a more detailed overview see Kidder and Campbell, 1970; Selltiz, Wrightsman and Cook 1976.) Some examples of these techniques are described as follows:

Marlowe, Frager and Nuttall (1965) deduced their subjects' attitudes towards 'coloreds' by their willingness to show 'colored' students around the Harvard University campus. Campbell, Kruskal and Wallace (1966) drew their conclusions about the same attitudes from the seating arrangement in college classes, i.e. by observing the distance at which black and white students sat apart from each other. Further indicators of attraction include eye contact (Argyle, 1983) and body posture (Mehrabian, 1968).

A good example of cleverly planned inconspicuous observation is that in Milgram, Mann and Harter's (1965) **lost letter technique**. To measure the political attitudes of citizens in different parts of a city, the researchers lost pos-tage-paid letters which were addressed to organizations whose ideology was made evident by their names, for example the Communist Student Organiza-tion, UNICEF etc. According to the rate at which the letters came back to a certain organization (all letters actually ended up in post office boxes rented by the researchers), a conclusion was drawn as to the popularity of each organization and thus the corresponding ideology of particular parts of the city.

Finally, the **bogus pipeline** method has to be mentioned (Jones and Sigall, 1971). Jones and Sigall report that with this technique one can disclose apparently embarrassing attitudes that would otherwise not be admitted. Following the bogus pipeline procedure, subjects are connected via electrodes to an apparatus that can allegedly predict exactly their attitudes concerning given objects by means of physiological measurements (a sort of a lie detector). The subjects can convince themselves beforehand of the accuracy of the apparatus by thinking about certain attitude objects when (supposedly) being connected to the apparatus. Subjects are then asked some attitudinal questions and requested to answer them sometimes correctly, i.e. according to their real attitudes, and sometimes incorrectly, i.e. contrary to their real attitudes. They are then shown that the apparatus was able to decide whether they gave the correct response or whether they cheated. In reality, the apparatus's responses were manipulated by the experimenter, who could not be seen by the subject and who knew the correct response pattern from a pre-test which subjects had filled out beforehand. When the subjects were convinced of the apparatus's capacity always to detect their real attitudes, those attitude questions were asked that were of real interest to the investigator. Based on the assumption that no one likes to be surpassed by a machine when giving information concerning their own attitudes, truthful information – even with embarrassing or unpleasant questions – is expected.

Although interesting findings using the bogus pipeline procedure have been documented in the literature (for an overview of this method see Brackwede, 1980), the method seems unsuitable for frequent use because it is very expensive. Moreover, it only works with uninformed persons as subjects; the more the apparatus is used, the more popular and well known it will become, and knowledge of the absence of its supposed capabilities will spread. There are, of course, also ethical issues involved in the crude misleading of the subjects.

Let us summarize the advantages and problems of the non-reactive measurements discussed. The most unobtrusive measurement procedures perhaps do not run as much risk of conscious distortions as self-description methods; however, this is often only so at the cost of enormous ambiguities of interpretation (i.e. questionable validity of the attained measures) and ethical problems. It is also difficult to determine what these objective indicators mean exactly with respect to an opinion (attitude), and they are often determined by motives or situational constraints other than attitudes. Furthermore, from a theoretical point of view the connection between attitudes and behaviour is still unclear (see below); it is therefore still questionable whether behavioural indicators can characterize an attitude or whether attitudes (according to their definitions) should or could only be measured by evaluative self-descriptive responses towards the attitude object.

Functions of Attitudes

Why do people have attitudes? Put less functionally, what are the consequences of holding attitudes? This question – and especially the motivational roots of attitudes – has been addressed by Katz (1967), Smith, Bruner and White (1956), and McGuire (1969) in their **functional attitude theories**. Four main functional bases of attitudes have been proposed, which are mainly motivational in nature.

Motivational functions

Ego-defensive functions   Katz (1967) starts from a psychoanalytical background using concepts of defence mechanisms like rationalization or projection to describe this attitudinal function. Attitudes in this function can, for example, protect someone from negative feelings towards the self or one's own group by allowing projections of these feelings towards other persons, such as minority groups. Persons who are threatened by feelings of dissatisfaction with their own marriage could manage these feelings by projecting them on to divorced people, that is, by expressing rather negative feelings towards this group of people.

The value-expressive self-realizing function   Katz (1967) assumed that people have a need to express attitudes that reflect their own central values or components of the self-concept. For instance, it could give you great satisfaction to express your opposition to laws imposing capital punishment when you deeply believe in the value of human rights. This kind of attitude expression is directed mainly towards confirming the validity of one's own self-concept and less at impressing others. The latter, nevertheless, is another important function of attitudinal expressions.

The instrumental, adjustive or utilitarian function   Attitudes help people to reach desired goals, like rewards, or to avoid undesirable goals, like punishment. More concretely for example, most people – not only social psychologists – know that similarity often breeds liking. Therefore it may be functional to adopt similar attitudes to someone whom it is desirable to win as a friend.

Knowledge or economy functions   Attitudes also serve functions of organizing or structuring an otherwise chaotic world. The intention to deal specifically with every detail of our (social) environment will probably result in a complete information overload. Attitudes allow us to categorize incoming information like new experiences along established evaluative dimensions and can help to simplify and understand the complex world in which we live. For example, if you like the work of a certain student very much, you will expect him to pass his examinations quite successfully. Your attitude, then, tells you what to expect in this situation.

This knowledge or economy function of attitudes is important. It will be analysed in more detail in the following section, which addresses the question of whether attitudes guide information processing.

Attitudes guiding information processing

Do attitudes guide information processing? To answer this question we have to look at at least three different components of information processing:

1   The active search for attitudinally relevant information.
2   The *encoding* of the information, i.e. perceptual and judgemental processes.
3   The retrieval of such information from memory.

To do this, however, it will be necessary to discuss the empirical findings as well as the theoretical assumptions of different theoretical positions, which all contribute more or less to our knowledge concerning the above question.

Active search for attitude-relevant information   **Dissonance theory** (Festinger, 1957) has proved the most successful theory for making explicit predictions about selective exposure to attitude-relevant information. In general, dissonance theory predicts that people are motivated to expose themselves to (attitude-) consonant information and to avoid (attitude-) dissonant information in order to stabilize a decision (or an existing attitude), and in such a manner to maintain cognitive consonance or avoid cognitive dissonance. For example, if someone really likes smoking cigarettes she is expected to avoid information that stresses negative consequences thereof, such as cancer and other health problems. On the other hand, she would probably enjoy hearing that very famous people also like smoking or that smoking prevents people from gaining too much weight. Smoking cigarettes and knowing that smoking causes cancer can be dissonant cognitions, because if smoking causes health problems it may follow that smoking has to be prevented. Therefore, in order not to create tension or dissonance, attitude-dissonant cognitions are avoided and consonant cognitions are selectively sought out.

This **selective exposure** hypothesis was investigated in an experiment by Frey and Rosch (1984). Subjects had to evaluate the ability of a manager; specifically, they had to decide on the basis of a written description of the manager's competence whether his working contract should be prolonged or not. This judgement had to be expressed either in a 'reversibility' or in a 'non-reversibility' condition. Subjects in the first condition were told that they could reverse their judgement later in the experimental session. Subjects in the 'non-reversibility' condition, on the other hand, were explicitly instructed that they had to make final judgements about the ability of the manager, which could not be corrected.

After expressing their judgements, subjects were given the opportunity to receive additional information about the manager. The descriptions were phrased in such a way that it was evident whether they were positive or negative

TABLE 7.3 Information seeking as a function of information/judgement consistency and judgement reversibility

| Judgement | Total[a] | Information chosen[b] | | Difference |
		Judgement consonant	Judgement dissonant	
Reversible	5.20	2.70	2.50	+0.20
Irreversible	4.84	3.19	1.65	+1.54

[a]The score could vary from 0 to 10 items of information.
[b]The score for each kind of information could vary between 0 and 5.
Source: Frey and Rosch (1984)

(e.g. 'Mr Miller did a good job and therefore his contract should be extended'; 'There are much more competent managers than Mr Miller and therefore his contract should not be extended'). Of the ten descriptions (five positive and five negative), the subjects could select as many as they wanted. The results of the experiment clearly supported the selective exposure hypothesis, as as can be seen in table 7.3.

In both experimental conditions judgement-consonant information was preferred over judgement-dissonant information (as can be seen from the positive difference scores in table 7.3). Moreover, when judgements had been announced as irreversible the selective exposure effect was stronger than when subjects expected their judgements to be reversible. The latter finding stresses the fact that there must be a certain amount of commitment to one's judgement, decision or attitude in order to produce strong selective exposure effects. When, on the contrary, a person is not committed to his or her attitude, the latter can be reversed easily and therefore can not be expected to evoke a significant selective exposure effect.

Selective exposure effects have been clearly demonstrated in a research programme by Frey (1986). This research also specifies under what conditions people do not show selective exposure effects but, on the contrary, selectively look out for dissonant information. Subjects tend to expose themselves to dissonant information when (1) their cognitive system (i.e. their attitude) is relatively strong, so that they will be able either to integrate or to argue against this kind of information; or when (2) the cognitive system is relatively weak, so that it seems better to the individual in the long run to change it and render it consonant with the existing, perhaps overwhelming, dissonant information. Imagine, for example, that a politician whom you really like has supported political decisions that you think are clearly wrong, or that he has been convicted of telling lies concerning important political facts. If this negative information is overwhelming, it seems better to reverse your attitude towards this political candidate in order to avoid future dissonance.

Perception of attitude-relevant information   We have seen that people often try to avoid attitude-dissonant information. In daily life, however, this sort of information often cannot be easily avoided. But again attitudes exert influence on information processing, this time by biasing the perception and also the evaluation of the attitude-relevant information. Fazio and Williams (1986) documented that people selectively process information about the qualities of attitude objects. They analysed attitudes towards presidential candidates in the 1984 US presidential elections. Later they correlated these attitudes with a measure of perception of the presidential candidates Reagan and Mondale, taken after television debates of the candidates. It was shown that the favourableness of the attitudes was significantly correlated with the perception of the candidates' performances ('Reagan was much more impressive' or 'Mondale was much more impressive'). Subjects with positive attitudes towards Reagan tended to find him more impressive than Mondale, whereas the opposite occurred for subjects favouring Mondale.

This finding – which is not very surprising – is in accordance with different social-psychological theories. Again, **cognitive consistency theories** have to be mentioned. They are among the most influential approaches in social psychology. The principle of consistency was introduced into social psychology by Heider (1944, 1946), as we saw in chapter 5. All consistency theories assume that persons strive to have their own cognitions (beliefs, attitudes, perceptions of own behaviour) organized in a tension-free, i.e. non-contradictory, way. When persons perceive that some of their attitudes are contradictory, they will be in a state of cognitive imbalance. This state is unpleasant and produces tension. Therefore the person will be motivated to bring the cognitions concerned into a consistent and tension-free relationship by changing one or all of these cognitions.

Apart from consistency theories, however, other social-psychological theories exist which assume that attitudes will guide the perception and evaluation of attitude-relevant information. Social judgement theories like the assimilation-contrast theory (Sherif and Hovland, 1961; Sherif and Sherif, 1967), adaptation-level theory (Helson, 1964), the variable-perspective theory (Upshaw, 1969) and accentuation theory (Eiser and Stroebe, 1972) also postulate that our attitudes will influence our perception and/or judgement of attitude-relevant information, especially attitudinal positions occupied by other people. Sherif and Hovland (1961), for example, assume that our own attitude serves the function of a judgemental anchor in comparison with which all other possible attitude positions are judged. More concretely, it is expected that other attitude positions that are relatively close to one's own position on the attitude continuum will be perceived as resembling one's own attitude even more than they actually do (assimilation) and will be evaluated very positively (as being fair and objective). Attitudinal positions, on the other hand, which are rather discrepant to one's own should be displaced away from one's own position and evaluated as being unfair and propagandistic. These distortions in perception and biased evaluations have been demonstrated by, for example, Hovland and Sherif (1952). They showed that white subjects with pro-'Negro' attitudes and 'Negro' subjects displaced attitude statements that were unfavourable towards 'Negroes' away from their own attitudinal positions. They judged these statements as more anti-'Negro' than did an 'average' white subject control group (for a critical discussion of this and other comparable studies, see Eiser and Stroebe, 1972).

To complete our discussion of the question of whether attitudes do influence information processing, *schemata* conceptions of attitudes have to be mentioned (see also chapters 5 and 6). In cognitive social psychology it is assumed that social information is not passively received and stored in memory, but is selectively encoded and actively organized in cognitive memory structures which are generally called schemata (Markus, 1977).

Research on schemata in social psychology has shown that social schemata guide the encoding of social stimuli as well as the retrieval of information stored in memory (for an overview of schemata research in social psychology see, for example, Fiske and Taylor, 1984; Schwarz, 1985). Different authors argue that attitudes can be conceptualized as schemata (e.g. Judd and Kulik, 1980; Lingle and Ostrom, 1981). They have reinterpreted the selective attention or retention effects hypothesized by cognitive dissonance theory by the assumption of attitudinal schemata effects. More concretely, Judd and Kulik (1980) assume that attitudes as schemata induce selective processing of attitude-relevant information in a bipolar manner; that is, they facilitate the encoding and retention of both attitude-consistent and attitude-contradicting behaviour and impede the processing of attitude-neutral or irrelevant information.

These authors demonstrated with their own experimental data that attitude statements (for example, regarding women's rights or capital punishment) that are strongly agreed or disagreed with generate quicker ratings on the agree/disagree dimension and on a pro/anti dimension, controlling for the fact that statements rated extremely on the pro/anti dimension were also processed more quickly. These results were in line with the assumption of schematic attitudinal effects on information processing. Further support for the schematic view can be found regarding the retrieval of attitudinally relevant information from memory.

Recall of attitude-relevant information   As early as 1932, it was assumed that attitudes guide the retrieval of information that is stored in memory. Levine and Murphy (1943) assumed that information that supports social attitudes is better remembered than that contradicting such attitudes. Empirical research conducted to test this hypothesis regularly exposes subjects to information that is either consistent or inconsistent with their attitudes, and after some time asks them to reproduce as much of the information as they can. The results of these studies can be summarized as follows.

The findings are quite inconsistent. Whereas different studies can be cited which at least partly failed to verify the hypothesis of attitudinal guidance of the retrieval process, other (mostly – but not only – early) experiments are more supportive (e.g. Jones and Aneshansel, 1956; Ross, McFarland and Fletcher, 1981). Ross, McFarland and Fletcher for example, demonstrated that attitudes exert directive influences on individuals' recall of their past behaviour concerning toothbrushing. The authors first changed or stabilized their subjects' attitudes towards the benefits of frequent toothbrushing. Afterwards, measures of attitude and behaviour recall (how often, for example, subjects brushed their teeth in the preceding two weeks) were recorded. Results showed that, for example, subjects who heard the message derogating frequent toothbrushing reported significantly more negative attitudes towards toothbrushing and at the same time remembered less frequent toothbrushing than subjects who were exposed to the message favouring frequent toothbrushing. Ross, McFarland and Fletcher therefore concluded that attitudes in this case served as retrieval cues that led to the salience of attitude-consistent behaviour or the reconstructing of actions in the light of the attitude. In an overview of relevant studies Roberts (1985) comes to the conclusion that the empirical data taken together demonstrate a 'reliable but modest relationship between opinion and recall' (pp. 236–7).

A theoretical model which integrates many of the inconsistent empirical results is the above-mentioned concept of *bipolar* attitudinal effects proposed by Judd and Kulik (1980). In their research, they demonstrated that attitudes indeed facilitate recall of attitude statements that were strongly *agreed* or *disagreed* with, compared with statements that elicit more moderate responses on the agreement scale (see also Hymes, 1986; Lingle and Ostrom, 1981).

Attitudes Guiding Behaviour

We have seen that attitudes influence information processing. Now we turn to the equally important question of whether they also guide behavioural decisions. One of the most frequently described studies in the literature addressing the question of the attitude–behaviour relationship is that of La Piere (1934). In the early 1930s, La Piere travelled with a Chinese couple throughout the USA. At the beginning of this journey, La Piere himself was quite suspicious of whether or not the three travellers would be accepted in hotels and restaurants, owing to the widespread anti-Asian prejudices at that time. However, to his surprise, service was refused to him and the Chinese couple in only one out of over 200 establishments. Six months after this unexpectedly positive experience, La Piere wrote a letter to all the hotels and restaurants he had visited during the journey, and asked them whether they would 'accept members of the Chinese race as guests in their establishments'. In line with the assumed prejudices, but contradicting the actual behaviour, 92 per cent of the responding hotels and restaurants answered with a clear negative reply. In the following years, this finding of La Piere has often been cited as evidence for a missing correlation between attitudes and other verbal responses on the one hand and overt behaviour on the other hand. Together with other studies (Ajzen and Fishbein, 1970; Corey, 1937) that also failed to find a strong relationship between attitudes and behaviour, La Piere's findings led to a rather pessimistic view about predicting behaviour from attitudes (see, e.g., Wicker, 1969).

This pessimistic view, however, is not supported by all studies observing the attitude–behaviour relationship (e.g. Fishbein and Coombs, 1974; Newton and Newton, 1950; see also as an overview Ajzen and Fishbein, 1977). In summing up, all these empirical data show that the question 'Are attitudes and behaviour correlated?' is not a very fruitful one, because it turned out to be too global or undifferentiated. Therefore, some authors in the late 1960s started to ask new questions like: 'When are attitudes and behaviour correlated?'; 'What factors affect the size of the correlation when and if it is found?'; and 'By which processes do attitudes influence behaviour?' (Zanna and Fazio, 1982).

In the following, some of these factors which qualify the attitude–behaviour relationship will be discussed.

Methodological factors

A large attitude–behaviour correlation cannot be expected when the reliability or validity of the attitude measures is already quite low (for an extensive critique of the operationalization of attitudes and behaviour in the studies testing the attitude–behaviour relationship see, for example, Meinefeld, 1977). One of the most frequently addressed methodological criticisms of attitude and behaviour measurement is that of the low correspondence of both measures in terms of their specificity. Ajzen and Fishbein (1977) pointed out that both attitudes and behaviour can be characterized by considering four different elements:

1 The *action* element (what behaviour is to be performed: for example, voting behaviour, helping someone or buying something)
2 The *target* element (at what target the behaviour is to be directed: for example, a certain political candidate, a close friend or a new product)
3 The *context* element (in which context the behaviour is to be performed: for example, in a totalitarian or democratic political system, publicly or privately, and with a full or empty wallet)
4 The *time* component (at what time the behaviour is to be performed: for example, in spring 1986, at once or during the next two years).

Many studies failed to ensure a close correspondence between the specificity of the attitude and behaviour measures concerning the four elements just mentioned. For example, the attitude measure has often been taken in a very global way, specifying only one (mostly the target element) or two of the above elements: for example, 'Do you like a certain political candidate or not?' The behaviour measure, on the other hand, has often been a very specific one (characterized along all four dimensions above): for example, 'Voting for Margaret Thatcher in the 1987 British general election'.

A close relationship, following Ajzen and Fishbein's argument, can only be found when both measures correspond in their degree of specificity. In their review of studies addressing the attitude–behaviour relationship, Ajzen and Fishbein (1977) found strong support for this notion: substantial correlations between attitudes and behaviour had only been found when both measures showed high correspondence. Davidson and Jaccard (1979) performed a more direct test of the correspondence hypothesis by analysing women's attitudes and behaviour (use of birth control pills during a two-year period). A general measure of attitude towards birth control turned out not to be substantially related to the behaviour measured ($r = +0.08$), but when the attitude measure became more specific this correlation increased (up to a correlation of + 0.57 for the attitude towards using birth control pills during the next two years).

At this point, however, it is necessary to mention that Ajzen and Fishbein's (1977) argument does not imply that global attitudes (for example, only specified in terms of a certain target) are useless in predicting behaviour. As long as the behaviour is conceptualized in a comparably global way, there can be a quite substantial relationship between global attitudes and behavioural acts. For example, there may be high correlations between global attitudes towards energy conservation and a behavioural measure which is composed of different behaviours in different contexts, like preferring to ride a bicycle instead of driving with a car for short distances, lowering the average room temperature etc. (multiple acts), and/or a repeated observation of behavioural acts (preferring the bicycle in different seasons etc.: see for example Fishbein and Ajzen, 1974; Liska, 1978; Weigel and Newman, 1976).

Special characteristics of the attitude

As mentioned before, some authors conceptualize attitudes as possessing affective, cognitive and conative components (e.g. Rosenberg and Hovland, 1960). However, most research on attitudes and behaviour has reduced attitudes to their affective component. This reduction of the attitude concept has been motivated economically, because evaluative statements are easily measured, e.g. by a Likert scale. Moreover, in cases where the affective component gives quite a good summary of the whole complex attitude (where, for example, the cognitive and affective components are consistent with each other), measures of only the affective component may be sufficiently good predictors of the behaviour. But sometimes cognitive and affective components can be inconsistent. According to Rosenberg (1968), attitudes which have a low affective–cognitive consistency are relatively unstable over time. This instability is mediated by the following process: when persons become conscious of the inconsistency of their attitude components they will be motivated to change one or both components in order to re-establish affective–cognitive consistency. Research by Rosenberg (1968) supports the assumption that the affective–cognitive consistency of an attitude correlates with its stability and resistance to attitude change. It seems reasonable to anticipate that attitudes characterized by affective–cognitive consistency and therefore stability will have greater validity as predictors of subsequent behaviour. In research by Norman (1975), the relationship between attitude and behaviour was investigated with subjects who were differentiated according to the high or low affective–cognitive consistency of their attitudes. In three experiments the relationship between the measured affective component and the investigated behaviour was higher for subjects whose attitudes showed affective–cognitive consistency than for those who had attitudes low in affective–cognitive consistency.

Findings of Bagozzi and Burnkraut (1979) also show that affective reactions to an attitude object do not always represent the complete cognitive content concerning the attitude object. A single affective response alone cannot always adequately represent the universe of beliefs related to a given attitude object. If the latter is the case, for example, because the attitude is very complex and differentiated, one can assume that behaviour will be better predicted when, in addition to the affective attitudinal response, the complex belief system of a person regarding the attitude object (cognitive component) is also considered. That is, it is better to take the whole structure of an attitude into account.

Schlegel (1975) assumed that the more direct experience subjects had with an attitude object, the more hierarchical and complex the organization of their attitude structure should be and the less the structure could be illustrated by a single affective factor. This hypothesis was confirmed in his research on attitudes towards the consumption of marijuana. Based on these research findings, Schlegel and DiTecco (1982) were able to show that for attitudes which were not based on direct experience (again with marijuana consumption) an affective response measure gives a sufficiently good summary of the whole attitude structure. Behaviour prediction in this case can be based entirely on those affective components; further measurement of cognitive structures did not improve the behaviour prediction substantially. With attitudes based on direct experiences, the picture changes. Predictions of behaviour (marijuana use) simply on the basis of affective responses towards this attitude object were not very successful, but could be substantially improved by introducing the variables of the cognitive structure of the attitude, i.e. beliefs about the attitude object.

The question of whether attitudes based or not based on a direct experience with the attitude object are better predictors of behaviour is also addressed in a research programme by Fazio and Zanna (1981). To begin with, there exists a contradiction between the findings of Schlegel and DiTecco (1982) and the research programme of Fazio and Zanna (1981) concerning the effects of direct experience on the attitude – behaviour relationship. Schlegel and DiTecco argue that the behavioural repertoire of persons who have had direct experience with an attitude object is greater. Therefore, the knowledge about this attitude object is greater and the attitude structures are more complex. These complex attitude structures cannot be integrated into a single affective attitude judgement, and therefore the latter is only a poor predictor of behaviour. On the other hand, Fazio and Zanna (1981) postulate that attitudes that are acquired by direct experience have a higher clarity (can be better discriminated against possible other attitude positions) and a greater stability over time, and people are more strongly convinced by those attitudes. Attitudes that are based on direct experiences are, therefore, more easily *available* and produce a stronger attitude–behaviour relationship.

In an extensive research programme, Fazio and his colleagues (see, e.g., Fazio and Zanna, 1981) demonstrated that direct experiences with an attitude object strongly affect the relationship between attitudes and behaviour. For example, Regan and Fazio (1977) analysed students' attitudes and behaviours which were directed towards the severity of and possible solutions to a housing shortage on the campus. They showed that behaviour could be more accurately predicted on the basis of attitudes when the attitudes were acquired by direct experience of the housing shortage. These findings were supported in more experimentally controlled studies (Regan and Fazio, 1977), and it was shown that the higher availability of attitudes based on direct experience (owing to their clarity, stability over time etc. as mentioned above) was responsible for their greater potential to predict behaviour (see Fazio et al., 1982).

The contradiction between the results and theoretical reasoning of Schlegel and DiTecco (1982) on the one hand, and Fazio and his colleagues on the other, can be resolved by assuming some curvilinear relationship. In the first stages of direct experiences, attitudes based on more direct experiences are better predictors of behaviour (owing to the mediating mechanisms like better availability postulated by Fazio et al., 1982). With increasing direct experience, however, attitude structure becomes more and more complex and, finally, cannot be sufficiently integrated into one single affective response. From then on, more direct experience will result in a decrease in behavioural predictability on the basis of the affective component of an attitude. Nevertheless, as shown by Schlegel and DiTecco (1982), this decline in behavioural predictability can be fully compensated when a cognitive attitudinal measure is added. Then, indeed, attitudes based on direct experiences remained better predictors of behaviour than other attitudes.

Situational factors

Of course, attitudes will be weak predictors of behaviour when the situational constraints are so strong that no individual behaviour is possible. One of the most frequently discussed situational constraints is that of a strong social norm in the specific situation: an attitudinally relevant behaviour has to be performed. Fishbein and Ajzen (1975) proposed a model of attitudes and behaviour which incorporates the component of social norms as a major factor. This model, called the **theory of reasoned action**, is presented in figure 7.2, and has to be regarded as the most influential and popular model of the attitude–behaviour relationship. Fishbein and Ajzen assume – as shown in figure 7.2 – that the immediate determinant of behaviour is a person's intention to perform (or not perform) this behaviour. Behavioural intention, then, is first determined by the person's positive or negative evaluation of performing this behaviour, or in other words the *attitude towards the behaviour* (the determinants of the attitude component have been discussed earlier in this chapter). The second determinant of behavioural intention is called the *subjective norm* (the person's judgement of the likelihood that relevant others, like friends, the partner etc. would expect her to show the behaviour to be predicted). Again, the subjective norm component is determined by two factors: *normative beliefs* (what relevant others expect the person to do) and the person's *motivation to comply* with these expectations.

These central concepts of the theory of reasoned action and their organization are summarized in figure 7.2. To give an example, Fishbein and Ajzen's model predicts that persons will engage in energy conservation when they

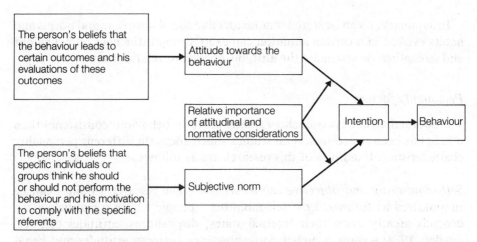

Arrows indicate the direction of influence

FIGURE 7.2   Factors determining a person's behaviour: theory of reasoned action (Ajzen and Fishbein, 1980)

believe (1) that conserving energy has a strong probability of resulting in positive consequences like guaranteeing the energy supply for future generations or of preventing negative consequences like environmental damage (the attitude component); and (2) that their friends, family and colleagues at work expect them to conserve energy and they are motivated to comply with this expectation (the subjective norm component).

The predictions of the theory of reasoned action have been tested in many empirical studies and have received considerable empirical support (see Ajzen, 1982). The Work of Fishbein and Ajzen also stimulated research which led to findings that are not perfectly consistent with this model, showing that other factors besides attitudes and social norms influence behaviour. For example, Bentler and Speckart (1979; 1981) showed that habits exert a direct influence on behaviour which was not mediated – as postulated by the model of reasoned action – by social norms or attitudes (for other findings not in line with the model of Fishbein and Ajzen see Kantola, Syme and Campbell, 1982; Manstead, Profitt and Smart, 1983).

A recent extension of the Fishbein and Ajzen model has been proposed by Ajzen and Madden (1986) by incorporating perceived control over behavioural achievement as a further determinant of behavioural intention as well as behaviour itself. Behavioural control was conceptualized as a person's expectancy of potential events that are supposed to conflict with the intended behaviour (e.g. the fact that the person might break her leg or be under extreme time pressure could conflict with her intention to conserve energy by riding the bicycle). Ajzen and Madden (1986) confirmed their own hypothesis that the incorporation of the 'behavioural control' component allows for a more accurate prediction of behaviour like students' class attendance and course achievement compared with the original version of the theory of reasoned action.

In summary, it can be stated that factors like social norms, moral norms and habits evoked in a certain situation can exert strong influences on behaviour and strengthen or attenuate the attitude–behaviour relationship.

Personality factors

The notion that some people show greater attitude–behaviour consistency than others has been tested in several studies which focus on different personality characteristics. Examples of this research are as follows.

Self-monitoring and objective self-awareness   The research findings can be summarized as follows. Low self-monitors – people whose social behaviour depends greatly upon their internal states, dispositions, attitudes etc. (cf. Snyder, 1974) – show a higher correspondence between attitudes and behaviour than do high self-monitors. High self-monitors are primarily oriented to situational cues or the potential reactions of their interaction partners when making behavioural decisions. Their behaviour does not reflect internal states such as emotions or attitudes and varies greatly across situations. This higher attitude–behaviour correspondence of low self-monitors could be partly due to their preference for situations in which existing attitudes can be openly expressed and therefore easily translated into action (Snyder and Kendzierski, 1982b).

A higher attitude–behaviour correlation has also been reported for persons who are highly 'objectively self-aware' (cf. for example Carver, 1975; Gibbons, 1978). Self-awareness can be both a trait or a state variable (Duval and Wicklund, 1972; Wicklund, 1975). The attention of a person who is highly self-aware (by trait or owing to certain situational cues) is primarily focused on the self, that is, on own feelings, emotions, norms, attitudes and other internal states, whereas the attention of a person low in self-awareness is directed at other people, the personal or impersonal environment.

Self-consistency   According to Bem and Allen (1974), one can argue that only for those persons who define themselves as relatively self-consistent over different situations does a high correlation between attitudes and behaviour exist. For those subjects who define themselves as relatively inconsistent, there exists a relatively low correlation between attitude and behaviour. Zanna, Olson and Fazio (1980) presented support for this hypothesis that behavioural consistency in the past leads to higher attitude–behaviour covariation than past behavioural variability.

Summary and Conclusion

In this chapter the structure, measurement and functions of attitudes have been discussed. Research interest in all of these topics – including the relationship between attitudes and behaviour – has been strongly renewed in recent years following the decline of interest in the late 1960s and 1970s. Moreover, enough compelling future perspectives exist to ensure the persistence of this 'come-back' of theorizing and empirical work for some years to come.

Glossary Terms

Attitude	Likert scale
Behavioural intention	Lost letter technique
Belief	Selective exposure
Bogus pipeline	Semantic differential
Cognitive consistency	Theory of reasoned action
theories	Three-component model of
Dissonance theory	attitudes
Equal appearing intervals	
scale	
Expectancy-value models	
Functional attitude	
theories	
Galvanic skin response	

Further Reading

Chaiken, S. and Stangor, C. (1987) Attitudes and attitude change. *Annual Review of Psychology*, 38, 575–630. An update of the research developments in the area of atti-tudes can be found in the reviews appearing every three years in the *Annual Review of Psychology*.

Dawes, R. M. and Smith, T. L. (1985) Attitude and opinion measurement. In G. Lindzey and E. Aronson (eds), *Handbook of Social Psychology* (vol. 1), New York: Random House, 509–66. This handbook article gives a detailed overview of the most important classical approaches to opinion and attitude measurement. Examples of different approaches are presented and their reliability and validity are discussed.

Fazio, R. H. and Zanna, M. P. (1981) Direct experience and attitude–behavior consis-tency. In L. Berkowitz (ed.), *Advances in Experimental Social Psychology* (vol. 14), New York: Academic Press, 161–202. An interesting research programme (of labora-tory and field studies) which deals with the effect of direct experience with an attitude object on attitude–behaviour consistency.

Fishbein, M. and Ajzen, I. (1975) *Belief, attitude, intention, and behavior*. Reading, Mass: Addison-Wesley. This book gives a detailed introduction to one of the most popular theoretical models concerning the attitude–behaviour relationship: the theory of reasoned action. Other important attitude theories and relevant empirical findings are also discussed.

Frey, D. (1986) Recent research on selective exposure to information. In L. Berkowitz (ed.), *Advances in Experimental Social Psychology* (vol. 19), New York: Academic Press, 41–80. Hypotheses concerning selective exposure to information derived from dissonance theory are presented and discussed in the light of relevant research findings.

Roberts, J. V. (1985) The attitude–memory relationship after 40 years: a meta-analysis of the literature. *Basic and Applied Social Psychology*, 6, 221–41. This paper presents an analysis of the available research on the selective recall hypothesis, i.e. tries to give an answer to the question of whether attitudes selectively guide the recall of attitude-relevant information.

Schlegel, R. P. and DiTecco, D. (1982) Attitudinal structures and the attitude–behavior relation. In M. P. Zanna, E. T. Higgins and C. P. Herman (eds), *Consistency in Social Behavior: the Ontario symposium* (vol. 2), Hillsdale, NJ: Erlbaum, 17–49. This article presents a fascinating analysis of attitude structures, stressing the fact that the complexity of attitudes has to be taken into account when behaviour is to be predicted.

8 Attitudes II: Strategies of Attitude Change

WOLFGANG STROEBE
and KLAUS JONAS

Introduction

The notion of using social-psychological knowledge to change attitudes and to influence behaviour conjures up visions of advertising executives planning mass media campaigns to sell cars, refrigerators or margarine. However, although advertising is the prototypical application of attitude change research, the use of persuasive appeals is only one of three strategies to influence attitudes, beliefs and behaviour that will be discussed in this chapter.

A second strategy involves direct exposure to the attitude object. For example, when introducing a new brand of margarine or laundry detergent, the manufacturer might try to attract potential customers by sending out free samples, in the hope that customers will try these samples and develop a positive attitude towards the product on the basis of this experience. Thus, while in the case of advertisements potential customers would form their attitude on the basis of socially mediated experience (i.e. the information about the product provided by the manufacturer), the free samples would allow them to base their attitude on the information gained from direct experience with the product.

Instead of relying on the uncertain effects of advertisements or of direct experience, powerful agencies (e.g. parents, governments) may decide to influence behaviour by changing the rewards and costs associated with alternative courses of action. Since this third strategy involves influencing behaviour through changing the incentives associated with this behaviour, it will be referred to as incentive-induced behaviour change. We do not want to imply, however, that incentives influence behaviour without affecting relevant beliefs or attitudes.

The authors are very grateful for the helpful comments on an earlier version of this chapter by Icek Ajzen, Alice Eagly, Mary Gergen, Miles Hewstone and Margaret Stroebe.

Governments tend to use influence strategies based on changes in incentive structure whenever they anticipate that mere persuasion may not be successful in changing behaviour. For example, when catalytic converters were introduced in West Germany to purify car exhaust fumes, the government feared that, despite the powerful environmental arguments in favour of catalytic converters, the majority of car-loving Germans would be unwilling to spend money on a gadget that was very expensive, frequently led to a reduction in engine power, and made them dependent on unleaded petrol (which is hard to obtain when travelling in other parts of Europe). Thus, rather than trying persuasion, they changed the structure of the incentives connected with catalytic converters by introducing tax relief for cars with converters and by setting the price of unleaded petrol below that of leaded petrol.

Instead of using these positive incentives, which proved to be very effective, the government could have used legal sanctions (i.e. negative incentives) to achieve the same purpose. For example, when Swedish drivers could not be persuaded to use their seat-belts, the government introduced a law that made seat-belt use compulsory for front seat passengers in private cars. This increased the frequency of seat-belt use from 30 to 85 per cent within a few months (Fhanér and Hane, 1979). In the context of this chapter, we are interested in strategies of influencing behaviour through changing the incentive structure, mainly because of the potential impact of such incentive-induced behaviour change on related attitudes.

This chapter focuses on principles of attitude formation and change. We first discuss attitude change due to the impact of direct experience with the attitude object, and next deal with attitude change through socially mediated experiences (e.g. modelling, persuasion). We then consider the effect of incentive-induced behaviour change on related attitudes. In the final section the relative effectiveness of these methods as strategies of attitude and behaviour change is evaluated.

The Attitudinal Effects of Direct Experience

A minimal situation through which direct experience affects attitudes is one of **mere exposure**, in which a stimulus is merely made accessible to the individual's perception. It is difficult, however, to recognize the attitudinal effects of mere exposure in everyday life, because these effects are usually submerged under the more powerful impact of information about the positive or negative characteristics of a stimulus that we gain from more extended experience. In addition, our attitude towards some object may be determined not only by the characteristics of the object itself but also by the positivity or negativity of the context in which we are exposed to a stimulus.

Direct experience as mere exposure

Two decades ago Zajonc (1968a) published an important paper in which he argued that 'mere repeated exposure of the individual to a stimulus is a sufficient condition for the enhancement of his attitude towards it' (1968a, p. 1). Empirical support for the mere exposure hypothesis comes from studies on the relationship between word frequency and liking for a word. Thus Johnson, Thomson and Frincke (1960) reported correlations of 0.63, 0.40 and 0.38 between the frequency of a set of words in samples of published materials (Thorndike and Lorge, 1944) and the rating they received on a good–bad scale. Similarly, Zajonc (1968a) found that the desirability ratings of the 555 personality-descriptive traits published by Anderson (1968) correlated 0.83 with the frequency of these words.

Although suggestive, such correlational evidence provides only circumstantial support for the mere exposure hypothesis because other explanations seem equally plausible. For example, liking for a stimulus might increase the probability that it will appear or be discussed. To rule out these alternatives, Zajonc (1968a) conducted an experiment in which he manipulated the frequency of exposure experimentally, using nonsense words as stimulus material. In an experiment that ostensibly dealt with 'pronouncing foreign words', 12 seven-letter 'Turkish' words were shown at six different exposure frequencies. After the exposure training, subjects were asked to guess what these 'Turkish adjectives' meant. They were told that it would suffice if they indicated on a seven-point good–bad scale whether each word meant something good or something bad. Consistent with expectations, ratings of goodness increased with frequency of exposure (see figure 8.1). These findings were widely replicated, at least for fairly complex stimuli (for reviews see Harrison, 1977; Vanbeselaere, 1983).

How can one explain these findings? Harrison (1968, 1977) suggested an interpretation in terms of response competition, which is based on an early theory of curiosity (Berlyne, 1954). According to this conception, most novel stimuli are composed of elements which the organism has encountered before in other stimuli – those with which different cognitive or behavioural responses are associated. Therefore, a novel stimulus will elicit several responses, some of which are incompatible. This response competition is experienced as an aversive state. Subsequent exposure to the stimulus will result in some response tendencies being strengthened and others weakened or even suppressed. This reduction of the aversion and tension associated with the response competition accounts for the increase in liking with increased exposure to the novel stimulus. Once the response competition has been eliminated, further exposure should not result in increased liking for a stimulus.

Even though there is considerable empirical support for the mediating role of response competition (see Harrison, 1977), the problem with this theory, as with most explanations of the mere exposure effect (Grush, 1979), is that it implicitly includes stimulus recognition as a necessary condition for obtaining the exposure effect on liking. Thus an individual must correctly identify the stimulus in order to have access to past associations (i.e. the competing response tendencies) that have been linked to it (Wilson, 1979). The explanation of the exposure-liking effect in terms of response competition is thus inconsistent

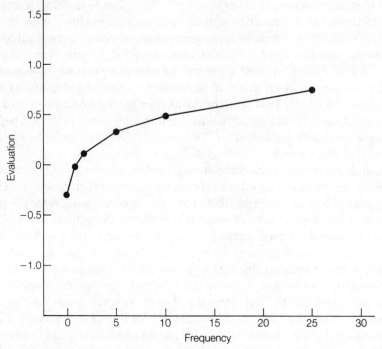

FIGURE 8.1   Relation between frequency of mere exposure and attitude (data from Zajonc, 1968a; figure based on Fishbein and Ajzen, 1975)

with findings that demonstrate that exposure can lead to liking for a stimulus even when people are unaware of having been exposed to it (e.g. Moreland and Zajonc, 1977; Wilson, 1979).

Direct experience as a source of information

Whenever exposure to a stimulus extends beyond the minimal conditions of mere exposure, the information gained about the characteristics of the object or person will become a powerful determinant of our attitude. However, this information will only result in attitude change if it is discrepant with the expectations held about the object beforehand. For example, in a study of the impact of student exchange on attitudes towards the host country, Stroebe, Lenkert and Jonas (1988) found that American students who had lived for a year in Germany did not differ from students who had just arrived in that country in the positivity of the traits they attributed to the Germans. Things were different for students who had spent a year in France. They attributed fewer positive and more negative traits to the French than students who had been there for only a short time. Apparently the students who had gone to Germany had found the Germans to be pretty much as expected, while sojourners in France were disappointed in their expectations. In line with this, there was marked deterioration in attitudes towards the French but only a slight change in attitudes towards the Germans.

These findings are consistent with other research on student exchange which typically reports some deterioration of the sojourners' attitudes towards their host nations (cf. Klineberg and Hull, 1979). It has to be remembered, however, that exchange students initially hold relatively positive attitudes towards their hosts and that the deterioration is mostly a depolarization: attitudes are still positive but less extreme. Spending money on student exchange programmes may therefore still prove to be a worthwhile investment of governmental funds. After all, at the end of the exchange experience, these students have more information about the host nation along more dimensions. Thus, any piece of stereotype-incongruent information to which they might be exposed in future will be confronted by a great deal of congruent information stored in memory. As a consequence, these students should be more resistant to stereotype-incongruent propaganda aimed at creating a negative view of this nation than they would have been without the exchange experience (e.g. Crocker, Fiske and Taylor, 1984).

Classical conditioning: the attitudinal impact of the context of experience

Why was there a slight deterioration in attitudes towards the Germans with no detectable change in beliefs about the Germans? One possibility is that the belief change responsible for the attitude change was not detected by the measures employed. It is also plausible, however, that there is some aspect of the exchange situation that changed the sojourners' affective reactions without influencing their beliefs. Living in a strange and unfamiliar country is a stressful experience that can lead to numerous somatic complaints such as stomach upsets, headache and sweating, which are well-known somatic symptoms of stress (Brislin, 1981). Extended stress is an aversive experience and it is possible that the negative feeling due to the stress became associated with the host nation through a process of **classical conditioning**. Through classical conditioning, some neutral stimulus initially incapable of eliciting a particular response gradually acquires the ability to do so through repeated association with a stimulus that already evoked this response.

The well-known example of such an initially neutral stimulus is the tone which Pavlov's dogs heard before receiving food. After these two stimuli had been paired for several trials, the tone began to evoke salivation, a response previously only elicited by the food. It is likely that this tone not only became the elicitor of a salivating response but also acquired a positive evaluation. Thus, if one could have asked the dogs to rate this sound on a number of semantic differentials before and after it had been paired with the food stimuli, it is likely that ratings would have improved over the trials. This is at least what one could infer from the findings of experiments on classical conditioning of attitudes (e.g. Berkowitz and Knurek, 1969; Staats and Staats, 1958; Zanna, Kiesler and Pilkonis, 1970).

Instead of food or electric shocks, Staats and Staats (1958) used words that elicited positive affect (e.g. gift, sacred, happy) or negative affect (e.g. bitter, ugly, failure) as unconditioned stimuli. These words were presented auditorily immediately after the visual presentation of the name of a nationality, in what was ostensibly an experiment testing whether subjects could separately learn verbal stimuli presented in the two different ways. For half the subjects (American college students) Dutch was consistently paired with positive and Swedish with negative adjectives, while the pairing was reversed for the other half. Other nationality names were always paired with neutral words. When the target nationalities were later rated on semantic differentials, the nationality that had been paired with positive words elicited a more positive rating than the nationality that had been paired with negative words.

That attitudes acquired through classical conditioning can affect behaviour was demonstrated by Berkowitz and Knurek (1969) who used the procedure of Staats and Staats (1958) to condition negative attitudes to a critical name. When subjects, in what was ostensibly a second experiment, were engaged in a discussion with two fellow students, one of whom had the critical name, they generally acted in a more unfriendly manner towards the negatively named person than to the discussion partner who had a neutral name.

It is important to note that Staats and Staats *do not* assume that the attitude towards the target nationalities changed because the association of positive (or negative) adjectives with a nationality name led to a change in the traits attributed to these people. According to classical conditioning, the change in evaluation is due to the fact that the positive evaluative reaction initially evoked by the adjectives has now also been passed on to the nationality name by mere association. Such processes could play an important role in the formation of ethnic and national attitudes.

The viability of this interpretation has been challenged by other researchers (e.g. Insko and Oakes, 1966; Page, 1969), who argued that subjects had recognized the systematic relationship between the adjective and the nationality names and were merely responding to demand characteristics by telling the experimenter what they thought he or she wanted to hear. While this may be a plausible explanation of the findings of Staats and Staats (1958), it seems more difficult to attribute the findings of Berkowitz and Knurek (1969) to demand characteristics.

Summary and conclusions

In this section we have discussed three mechanisms through which direct experience affects attitudes. Mere exposure to an object increases liking, an effect that has been explained in terms of the reduction of response competition. Since each successive exposure leads to successively smaller increments in liking, the role of mere exposure as a determinant of attitude is limited to novel stimulus materials. Direct experience beyond mere exposure provides the organism with information about the attributes of a given stimulus. Thus our attitudes towards the food we eat, the cars we drive and the many other tangible objects that form our environment are largely based on direct experience.

The findings of research on classical conditioning suggest that our attitudes may unwittingly be coloured by the context in which an object has been experienced. This process is quite functional when the relationship between stimulus and context is a stable one. Thus it is healthy to develop an aversion to certain types of alcohol because their taste has been associated with terrible hangovers in the past. It is less desirable, however, when children develop negative attitudes towards members of other nationalities or races because the significant people around them make negative remarks or show their distaste whenever certain outsiders are encountered or when their name is mentioned.

Although the distinction between direct experience and socially mediated experience (e.g. communications) as sources of attitude formation and change has proved to be empirically fruitful, it should also be acknowledged that this distinction is problematic on theoretical grounds. Since the meaning of even the most direct experiences depends to some extent on social construction (Averill, 1982), the distinction between a direct experience and one that is socially mediated is difficult to draw. For example, although most of us will consider the fall-out from the atomic disaster at Chernobyl a direct experience with nuclear power, our reactions were really determined by mass media rather than by direct experience. European governments differed widely in their assessment of the health risk. While in Germany vegetables grown outside during this period were declared unsafe for consumption and destroyed, and children in many towns were not allowed to play in sandpits because the sand was thought to be radioactive, no such restrictions were put on the French just across the border. Such differences may account for the fact that Chernobyl had a dramatic impact on attitudes towards atomic power stations in Germany but not in France.

The Impact of Socially Mediated Experience

To paraphrase one of Bandura's (1986) favourite sayings, if all attitudes had to be acquired through direct experience, attitude formation would be an exceedingly laborious, even hazardous endeavour. Fortunately, all learning phenomena resulting from direct experience can also occur vicariously, either by observing other people's behaviour and its consequences for them (modelling) or by having consequences of potential courses of action described in persuasive communications.

Modelling: forming attitudes from observing the consequences of other people's behaviour

Modelling refers to learning from observing others. Although social learning theorists like Bandura (1986) are mainly interested in the processes that mediate the observational learning of behaviour sequences, Bandura acknowledges that modelling influences can strengthen or weaken inhibitions over behaviour that individuals have previously learned. For example, exposure to models performing feared activities without any harmful effects reduces fears and creates favourable changes in attitudes (e.g. Bandura, 1977). However, since social learning theorists are interested in attitudes only as motivators of behaviour, their analyses do not contribute a great deal to our understanding of the cognitive processes that mediate attitude formation and change. Nevertheless, much of the theorizing about the impact on the observer's behaviour of the positive or negative consequences that models experience is readily translated into attitude theories. For example, according to expectancy-value theories (e.g. Fishbein and Ajzen, 1975, 1981a), the observation that an aggressive act that one expected to be punished for is in fact rewarded in a given social setting should lead to a change in one's attitudes towards performing this act in such a setting. Such changes in attitudes would be assumed to mediate the changes in observers' behaviour typically reported in modelling studies (cf. Bandura, 1977).

Modelling is widely used in advertising as a strategy of attitude and behaviour change. When famous stars from the world of film and sport appear in TV spots, using a particular brand of soap or shaving lotion, the viewers' attitudes toward the product might improve for several reasons. Some of the positive glow induced in a fan by seeing the star might 'rub off' through processes of classical conditioning. Viewers might also adopt the product because they feel that if it is good enough for the star it should be good enough for them. Finally, some viewers might adopt the product because they want to be like the admired star in evey possible respect, and buying the products he or she uses is one way to achieve this goal. Kelman (1961) has referred to the latter process as attitude change through identification. He sees the acceptance of influence through identification as a way of establishing or maintaining the desired relationship to the other and the self-definition that is anchored in this relationship.

Persuasive communications

Persuasive appeals are a more direct strategy of social influence than modelling. Rather than leaving it to individuals to draw their own conclusions from observing the behaviour of a model and its consequences, **persuasive communications** advocate a position and typically present one or more arguments designed to support it. Experimental studies of **persuasion** frequently use counter-attitudinal communications (i.e. messages which advocate a position that would normally be rejected by the recipient). Theories of persuasion account for attitude change by describing the processes or variables that mediate the impact of communications on attitudes and beliefs (Eagly and Chaiken, 1984).

A process model of persuasion   The information processing paradigm proposed by McGuire (1969, 1985) provides a useful framework for thinking about the cognitive processes involved in attitude change. In this **process model of persuasion**, the persuasive impact of a message is held to be the product of at least five steps: (1) attention, (2) comprehension, (3) yielding, (4) retention

PLATE 8.1   Gaining people's attention is the first stage of persuasion

and (5) behaviour (see figure 8.2). For example, the ultimate objective of a speech given by a political candidate on TV before an election is to get the members of the audience to vote for his or her party. In terms of McGuire's framework, the candidate's first problem is to reach the audience. If viewers use this opportunity of a break between programmes to fetch a drink (failure to attend), the appeal will not result in attitude change. However, even if viewers attend to the communication, it will have little impact if they do not understand the arguments because they are too complex (failure to comprehend) or if they

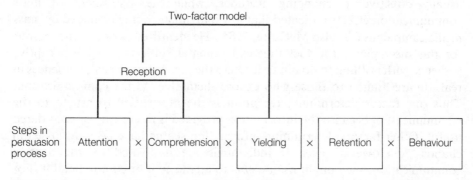

FIGURE 8.2   The information-processing paradigm of McGuire

do not accept the communicator's conclusions (failure to yield). But even if the candidate managed to persuade the audience, this will be of no use if viewers change their attitudes again before election day or if extreme weather conditions keep them away from the ballot box (failure to act).

There are two important implications of this conception. The first is that the 'receiver must go through each of these steps if the communication is to have an ultimate persuasive impact, and each step depends on the occurrence of the preceding step' (McGuire, 1969, p. 173). Thus the process of persuasion is like a hurdle race. The probability of each successive step is proportional to the joint probability of the occurrence of all previous steps. Since it is unlikely that the probability of any given step approaches unity, McGuire's model explains why it is often difficult to induce behaviour change through information campaigns.

The second implication emphasized by McGuire (1969) is that the effect of a communication on attitude change can best be understood by analysing the impact of the relevant characteristics of the communication on each of these steps. In social-psychological studies of persuasion, the impact of a communication is typically assessed immediately following exposure to the message. Thus our analysis is restricted to the first three steps of the chain. Furthermore, since attention and comprehension have usually been combined into a single step of reception of the message content to simplify measurement, McGuire's model can be reduced to a **two-factor model of persuasion**. This states that the probability of a communication resulting in attitude and opinion change is the joint product of the probability of reception and acceptance (**yielding**). This two-factor model has been widely used as a framework for research on persuasion (see Eagly and Chaiken, 1984), since the impact of most variables relevant to communication research can be analysed in terms of its effects on reception and/or acceptance. However, the model lacks specific theoretical principles that would allow one to predict the factors that affect reception and acceptance and to understand the processes which mediate these relationships. We will therefore next discuss the determinants of reception and acceptance.

1   *Determinants of reception*   In a classic paper Hovland (1959) addressed the puzzling question of why researchers working in the laboratory were usually effective in changing attitudes, while the assessment of mass communication effects indicated that few individuals were persuaded by mass media campaigns (see also McGuire, 1985). He identified as one of the reasons for this discrepancy the fact that experimental subjects provide a captive audience with nothing to do but to listen to the persuasive appeal; audiences in real life are limited to those who expose themselves to the communication. Thus one factor determining **reception** is the *motivation* to attend to the communication because the information provided is interesting or considered useful. Other factors determining information search have been discussed in chapter 7. However, even if individuals are motivated to attend to a communication, they might not *be able* to attend to it or comprehend it. For example, if we switch our car radio on to listen to a talk on the safety of nuclear

power stations, we may not be able to understand it because of poor reception, because of difficult road conditions, because the other passengers in the car talk too loudly, or because we do not know enough physics to understand the arguments.

2 *Determinants of acceptance* When people receive a communication and are faced with the decision whether to accept or reject the position it advocates, they will try to form an opinion of its validity. This assessment may be arrived at by two different routes or modes of information processing. According to what has been called the **central route to persuasion** (Petty and Cacioppo, 1986a, 1986b), recipients spend considerable time and effort on a critical evaluation of the message content. They scrutinize the message, they try to remember what they already know about the issue and then relate this knowledge to the arguments contained in the message. However, sometimes recipients may be unwilling or unable to engage in this extensive process of message evaluation. Rather than processing argumentation, they might base their decision to accept the message on some peripheral aspect such as the source's credibility or other non-content cues. This has been called **heuristic processing** by Chaiken (1980; see also Eagly and Chaiken, 1984). According to the heuristic model, people often use simple schemas or decision rules (i.e. cognitive heuristics) to assess the validity of an argumentation and to decide whether they are willing to accept it. For example, with regard to communicator expertise, people may have learned from previous experience that statements by experts tend to be more veridical than statements by non-experts. They may therefore apply the rule 'statements by experts can be trusted' in response to indications that the communicator is an expert (Eagly and Chaiken, 1984). Or they may have learned to trust people they like and, on finding a communicator likeable, they will apply the 'liking-agreement' heuristic such as 'people agree with people they like' or 'people I like usually have correct opinions on an issue' (Eagly and Chaiken, 1984).

According to Petty and Cacioppo (1981, 1986a, 1986b), heuristic processing involves one of the strategies that form the **peripheral route to persuasion**. The peripheral route subsumes those persuasion processes that are not based on issue-relevant thinking (e.g. classical conditioning, identification). Attitude change induced via the peripheral route is likely to be less enduring and less predictive of subsequent behaviour than attitude change induced by the central route (Petty and Cacioppo, 1986a, 1986b).

Petty and Cacioppo use the term **elaboration** to denote the extent to which a person thinks about the issue-relevant arguments contained in a message. At one end of the elaboration continuum message recipients use strategies that characterize the peripheral route to persuasion. At the other end, they engage in a great deal of argument evaluation and issue-relevant thinking (central route to persuasion). The probability that a recipient will critically evaluate the arguments contained in a message (i.e. the elaboration likelihood) is determined by both motivation and ability. Motivation is important because such elaboration requires time and energy. Ability is important because a certain amount of intelligence, specific knowledge or time is needed to appraise the validity of arguments contained in a message.

The **elaboration likelihood model** (ELM) developed by Petty and Cacioppo (1986a, 1986b) is a theory of the factors that determine the acceptance of a communication. The model assumes that the magnitude and direction of attitude change obtained by a given message will depend on the recipient-generated thoughts that are elicited by a communication. To the extent that a communication elicits predominantly favourable thoughts (e.g. because of high argument quality), persuasion is enhanced. To the extent that the message evokes predominantly negative thoughts, persuasion is inhibited or could even result in a 'boomerang effect' (negative change). Furthermore, since recipients are assumed to process the information more or less extensively, persuasion will be a function of the amount of message-relevant thinking as well as its favourability. For messages that elicit favourable thoughts, increased elaboration should increase persuasion. In contrast, for messages that mainly elicit negative thoughts, increased processing should reduce persuasion. For example, if a message consists of arguments that are logical, well structured and convincing, persuasive impact will be the greater the more recipients are motivated and able to think about these arguments. On the other hand, if a message consists of arguments that are weak and specious, persuasion should be greater if people are unable or unmotivated to scrutinize the message content.

Testing models of persuasion: some empirical findings   The probabilities of both reception and acceptance are assumed to depend on motivational and ability factors. Researchers have therefore tested derivations from the two-factor model and from the ELM by varying or manipulating subjects' relevant ability and/or motivation. In the following, we will present some of the findings of this research.

1   *The impact of ability on reception and acceptance*   One strategy to assess the impact of differential ability on reception and acceptance has been to study the relationship between intelligence and persuasion. According to McGuire (1969) intelligence has opposite effects upon the two processes that mediate persuasion. Higher levels of intelligence should lead to better comprehension of the message content. However, recipients with higher intelligence should also be better able to refute the arguments contained in a message. Thus intelligence should be positively related to reception and negatively related to acceptance.

These predictions were tested by Eagly and Warren (1976) who exposed high-school students representing different levels of verbal intelligence to two persuasive messages which either did or did not contain a set of complex supporting arguments. Messages without supportive arguments simply stated a recommendation (e.g. 'The use of penicillin should be eliminated'). With argument-supported messages a short introduction stating the recommendation was followed by a set of persuasive arguments. These arguments were complex and unlikely to be understood by persons of lesser verbal intelligence. But, if understood, they did offer convincing support for the recommendation given. Based on the two-factor model of McGuire (1969), Eagly and Warren made the following predictions. Since intelligent students should comprehend the complex arguments better than unintelligent students, there should be a positive relationship between intelligence and attitude change for the argument-supported communications. For unsupported messages, on the other hand, attitude change should be purely a function of subjects' willingness to accept a message. Therefore, a negative relationship between intelligence and attitude change would be expected for these conditions. The findings of this study lent strong support to these predictions.

The manipulation of **distraction** has been used as a strategy to exert experimental control over subjects' ability to process information. Suppose somebody who is exposed to a counter-attitudinal message is being distracted by having to perform an irrelevant activity or by experiencing sensory stimulation irrelevant to the message (e.g. listening to a radio-transmitted speech which is heavily masked by static). Will the distraction increase or decrease the persuasive effects of the message? Since a pioneering experiment conducted by Festinger and Maccoby (1964), these issues have been controversial in the literature on persuasion (cf. Baron, Baron and Miller, 1973; Petty and Brock, 1981). The controversy focused on the divergent findings from several experiments. For example, Festinger and Maccoby (1964) and Osterhouse and Brock (1970) found that persuasion increased under distraction conditions, whereas Haaland and Venkatesan (1968) observed the opposite relationship. Finally, Romer (1979) reported persuasion to first increase and then decrease with increasing distraction.

The two-factor model enables us to account for all of these findings, if (following Wyer, 1974) one makes the additional assumption that the probability of acceptance is negatively related to the probability that recipients devalue the communication through counter-arguments. According to this modified version of the two-factor model, low to medium levels of distraction should facilitate attitude change because these moderate levels of distraction should reduce the tendency to counter-argue while not seriously impairing attention and comprehension. However, if distraction is increased beyond this level, it should begin to interfere with reception and thus result in a decrease in persuasion. This latter prediction is consistent with the results of Haaland and Venkatesan (1968) and Romer (1979). These authors report that decreasing persuasion was indeed accompanied by a decrease in reception (measured by message recall).

According to the ELM the impact of distraction should also depend on the dominant cognitive response elicited by a communication. For communications that stimulate mainly counter-arguing, distraction should lead to enhanced persuasion by interfering with the counter-arguing process. But if the dominant response to a communication is agreeing or favourable cognitive responses, distraction should inhibit these favourable responses and thus lead to lowered acceptance.

To test this more general formulation, Petty, Wells and Brock (1976) conducted two experiments in which distraction was manipulated by having subjects record visual stimuli while listening to a message. The degree of distraction was varied by the frequency with which the stimuli flashed on a screen. The favourability of recipients' cognitive responses was manipulated by using either strong arguments (low counter-arguability) or weak arguments (high counter-arguability).

The results of both experiments supported the predictions derived from the ELM. Increases in distraction enhanced persuasion for the message versions which were readily counter-arguable, but reduced persuasion for the versions that were difficult to refute (see figure 8.3). Additional support for the assumption that both the increase and the decrease in persuasion was due to thought disruption comes from subjects' retrospective reports on their thoughts while listening to the communication. The distraction manipulation seems to have inhibited the number of counter-arguments for the version that was easy to counter-argue and reduced the number of favourable thoughts for the version that was difficult to counter-argue.

What other factors mediate distraction effects in counter-attitudinal messages? The one essential condition for distraction to affect persuasion seems to be that a message elicits counter-argumentation. A message may not elicit counter-arguments when: (1) it is uninteresting and thus no (or only a small amount of) attention is given to the message; (2) the communicator is of low credibility, and thus there is no need to scrutinize the message; (3) the topic is not involving, i.e. is of low interest to the recipient; and (4) the focus of attention is directed at the distraction, not at the message (Baron, Baron and Miller, 1973; Petty and Brock, 1981).

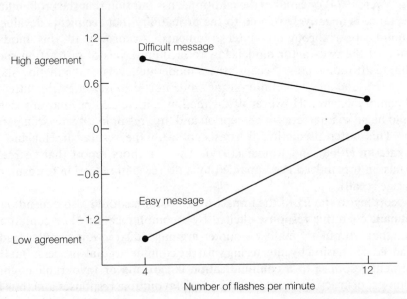

FIGURE 8.3   Mean attitude scores in relation to message and level of distraction (Petty, Wells and Brock, 1976, experiment 2)

2 *The impact of motivation on reception and acceptance* The impact of motivational factors on reception has mainly been studied in the context of Festinger's (1957) 'selective exposure' hypothesis, according to which people seek out information that reinforces their previous beliefs (see Freedman and Sears, 1965; Frey, 1986). This research is discussed in chapter 7 and will not be covered here.

The influence of motivation on acceptance has been assessed in experiments which manipulated the effect of personal involvement of recipients on the outcome of their decision to accept a message. Only under high involvement should recipients of a communication be motivated to assess the validity of the position advocated, by critically evaluating the arguments contained in the message. With low involvement, when the issue of the communication is of little relevance, the recipient should rely on peripheral cues to evaluate the validity of the position advocated by the communicator.

These predictions were tested in an experiment by Petty, Cacioppo and Goldman (1981) who exposed college students to an attitude-discrepant communication (advocating the institution of senior comprehensive exams). This communication, on a topic of which American college students have a great deal of knowledge, contained either strong or weak arguments and was attributed to a source of either high expertise (the Carnegie Commission on Higher Education) or low expertise (a class at a local high school). Subjects' involvement was manipulated by informing them that the changes advocated in this message either were going to be instituted the following year and would thus affect the subjects themselves (high involvement), or would take effect only in ten years' time (low involvement). Petty, Cacioppo and Goldman (1981) predicted that argument quality should have a stronger effect on subjects of high rather than low involvement. Source credibility, on the other hand, a peripheral cue, should result in more attitude change with low rather than high involvement. Thus when subjects believed that the changes would affect their own fate, they should be motivated to scrutinize the arguments and to engage in issue-relevant thinking. With them, argument quality would be a major factor in persuasion. Students who believed that these changes would only be instituted long after they had left the university would not be motivated to think a great deal about the communication. They would assess the validity of the advocated position by using heuristic rules such as 'the experts will know best.' The results strongly supported these predictions (see figure 8.4). Similar findings were reported by Chaiken (1980).

What makes arguments persuasive? The expectancy-value approach Suppose conditions are favourable for processing along the central route (i.e. motivation and ability are high). Which factors determine the persuasive impact of the arguments, i.e. which are the antecedent conditions for a *positive* cognitive response under these conditions? The ELM does not allow any predictions about this aspect. Therefore the predictive power of the ELM could be increased by incorporating into the model a theory of the determinants of argument quality. The expectancy-value approach (introduced in chapter 7; cf.

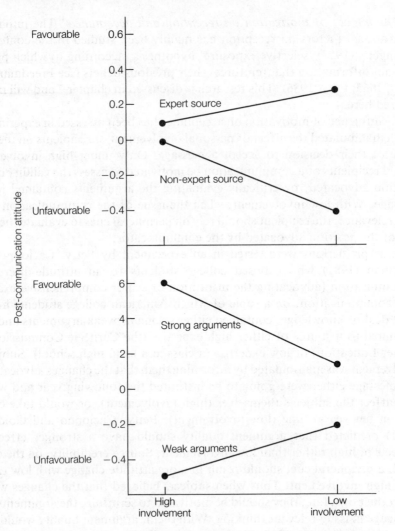

FIGURE 8.4   Top panel: interactive effect of involvement and source expertise on post-communication attitudes. Bottom panel: interactive effect of involvement and argument quality on post-communication attitudes (Petty, Cacioppo and Goldman, 1981)

Fishbein and Ajzen 1975; 1981a; Rogers, 1975, 1983) seems suited to play this role. Common to all **expectancy-value models** is the assumption that human actions are mediated mainly by two types of cognitions: (1) subjective probabilities, and (2) evaluations of action outcomes. According to this approach, individuals will choose from various alternative courses of action that action most likely to lead to positive consequences or avoid negative consequences. To change attitudes through persuasion, communicators should therefore attempt to change the relevant subjective probabilities or values.

The area of **fear appeals** will be used to illustrate the application of expectancy-value theory to persuasion. The label 'fear appeal' derives from the assumption that the impact of communications designed to motivate people to change behaviour that is deleterious to their health (e.g. heavy smoking, failure to be vaccinated) is mediated by the amount of fear they induce in the recipient (Hovland, Janis and Kelley, 1953; Janis, 1967). Leventhal's research (see Leventhal, 1970), though, strongly suggests that the cognitive impact of a fear appeal may be more important than its affective results.

Based on Leventhal's work, Rogers (1975) proposed his **protection motivation theory**. This expectancy-value conception assumes that in order to persuade recipients to change a specific health-related behaviour they must be induced to realize that (1) the severity (i.e. the negative consequences) and (2) the probability of the respective illness or condition are higher than they thought before, and that (3) the recommendation made in the communication constitutes an effective remedy against these dangerous consequences. Consequently, according to Rogers, the communicator has to select and present the message content in order to maximize these cognitions. For example, to persuade people to quit smoking, it has to be pointed out that (1) smoking leads to cancer and myocardial infarction, (2) smoking is associated with a considerable increase in the risk of contracting these illnesses, and (3) if they quit smoking now, their risk of suffering these consequences will approach that of non-smokers within a few years.

In a revision of his theory, Rogers (1983) introduced additional factors. According to the revised model, an appeal should also (4) address the psychological and financial costs of the recommendation and (5) attend to the recipients' self-efficacy (Bandura, 1982), i.e. their subjective probability that they will be able successfully to carry out the recommendation. For example, obese recipients should be given clear, detailed instructions concerning weight reduction that avoid unrealistic demands. This should increase the recipients' faith in successfully carrying out the recommendations.

Rogers and his colleagues conducted several experiments (e.g. Rogers, 1985; Maddux and Rogers, 1983; Rogers and Mewborn, 1976). Taken together these studies provide strong support for the conviction that indeed all of these factors mediate health-related behaviour, although the assumptions made by Rogers (1975) about the combination of these factors were not supported by the results of these studies. In the original version, protection motivation theory hypothesized that the severity of the consequences, the probability of contracting the illness and the effectiveness of the recommendation would combine multiplicatively. Although it is plausible that a health recommendation would have little impact when one of these components approached a value of zero (e.g. if there was no probability of contracting an illness, or if the recommended cure was absolutely ineffective) this combinatorial rule has been consistently rejected. Jonas (1987) has recently demonstrated that one reason why subjects do not combine the various components multiplicatively is that the multiplicative combination requires demanding cognitive operations that possibly exceed subjects' abilities (e.g. converting different dimensions to a common scale).

Summary and conclusions

If one accepts that individuals choose those courses of action that are most likely to lead to valued consequences or avoid negative consequences, then attitude and behaviour change should typically be the result of changes in the subjective probability that associate a given action with a set of consequences and of changes in the evaluation of these consequences. Thus, from observing the behaviour of a model and the consequences of this behaviour, individuals may learn that the behaviour in question leads to a number of consequences they had not previously associated with it. For example, if a boy sees his friend being caught and seriously punished for stealing cherries in the neighbour's garden, he might revise his estimate of both the risk of getting caught in such activities and the unpleasantness of the potential consequences of such behaviour.

Persuasive appeals are a more direct form of social influence. Instead of leaving individuals to draw their own conclusions, a position is advocated and supported by arguments. According to McGuire's (1969) two-factor model, the probability that a communication will result in attitude change under the usual experimental conditions is the product of the probability that the communication will be received and that it will be accepted. We discussed some of the factors that determine the probability of reception and presented the elaboration likelihood model (Petty and Cacioppo, 1986a, 1986b), a theory that has greatly increased our understanding of the factors that determine acceptance. However, although the ELM identifies perceived argument quality as one of the major factors that affect the acceptance of a communication when the recipient is both motivated and able critically to evaluate the arguments, it does not specify the factors that make an argument persuasive. We therefore used expectancy-value theory to derive predictions about the determinants of argument impact. When individuals are either unable or unmotivated to assess argument quality, they often engage in 'heuristic processing' (Chaiken, 1980) and rely on simple decision rules to decide on the acceptability of a communication.

The Attitudinal Impact of Incentive-Induced Behaviour Change

Powerful institutions often influence behaviour through incentives, social norms or legal sanctions rather than relying on the uncertain effects of persuasion. According to the expectancy-value model developed by Fishbein and Ajzen (1975, 1981a; see also chapter 7), any change in behaviour induced by changes in the incentive structure is assumed to be mediated by changes in individual beliefs about the consequences of this behaviour and in attitudes towards performing this behaviour. Thus the tax relief introduced in Germany to encourage people to install catalytic converters is likely to influence individuals' beliefs about the consequences of installing these converters (i.e. exemption from automobile tax for several years). While these tax benefits should also improve attitudes towards *installing* catalytic converters, they will have little direct impact on attitudes towards the converters themselves. Thus, people might install catalytic converters to receive the tax benefits even though they deplore the loss of engine power or the dependence on unleaded fuel. The following sections will be concerned with the attitudinal *consequences* of incentive-induced behaviour change and will focus on the impact of such induced behaviour change (i.e. compliance) on attitudes related to the behaviour.

An important consideration in discussing the attitudinal impact of compliance is whether the induced behaviour is consistent or inconsistent with existing attitudes. For example, if a law were to be introduced to force people to jog daily, compliance with this law would induce **counter-attitudinal behaviour** in individuals who are opposed to physical exercise, but **pro-attitudinal behaviour** in health fanatics who jog every day and enjoy it. It is plausible that one of the important variables determining the consequences of compliance is whether the induced behaviour is counter-attitudinal or pro-attitudinal. But as we will see later, there are other important factors to modify the attitudinal impact of compliance.

Counter-attitudinal behaviour and attitude change

What happens to a person's private opinion if he or she is forced to do or say something contrary to that opinion? This was the opening question of a report on a now classic experiment by Festinger and Carlsmith (1959). Since this issue has been discussed in the context of **dissonance theory**, it will first be necessary to describe this theory before providing an answer to the question.

An analysis in terms of dissonance theory   Whenever an individual chooses between alternative courses of action, there is some information (dissonant cognitions) that would have justified a different decision. For example, if John attends class on a beautiful day, the knowledge that he is missing a lot of fun at the swimming pool is a dissonant cognition, whereas the knowledge that he is increasing his chances of getting a good grade would constitute a consonant cognition. Having these dissonant cognitions leads to an aversive emotional state called *dissonance* (see also chapter 7). The magnitude of the dissonance (and thus the motivation to reduce it) depends on the number and/or the importance of the dissonant cognitions. Thus, if John knows that this would have been his last chance to spend an afternoon with his girlfriend before she leaves town, his dissonance will be greater than if he is just missing a swim and a bit of sun. There are various strategies available to John to reduce his dissonance. For example, he could increase the perceived importance of the consonant cognitions by persuading himself that the material covered this afternoon was not only vital for the examination but was also really fascinating. He could also reduce the importance of the dissonant cognitions by telling himself that it would not really have been any fun at the pool.

Applied to the question posed earlier, when a person is induced by monetary incentives or by the threat of negative sanctions to say or do something which runs counter to his or her firm convictions, the monetary incentive or the legal sanction are consonant cognitions because they justify the chosen action. For example, a businessman who files an incorrect tax return to gain a tax benefit (or to avoid paying a fine) will feel that gaining the benefit (or avoiding the fine) justifies his behaviour. Obviously, this justification will be greater if the benefit gained (or the fine avoided) was large rather than small. Thus, if an individual behaves counter-attitudinally to gain some benefit (or to avoid a penalty), dissonance will be greater if the benefit (or the penalty) is small rather than large.

Festinger and Carlsmith (1959) tested these predictions by having subjects first perform two dull motor tasks. After subjects had worked on these task for an hour, they were asked under some pretext whether they would be willing to tell the next subject that the experimental task was rather interesting. Subjects were offered either $20 or $1 for telling the lie.

How do subjects feel after they have actually told another (confederate) subject that the experiment was interesting? According to dissonance theory, their feelings should depend on the amount of money they had been paid. Subjects in the $20 condition should feel very little dissonance, because earning this type of money should amply justify deviating somewhat from the truth. Subjects who had earned only $1 should feel a great deal of dissonance, since the money did not really justify telling a lie. One way to reduce dissonance is for subjects to persuade themselves that the experimental task had in fact been quite enjoyable. Consistent with these predictions, Festinger and Carlsmith found that subjects in the $1 condition reported a more favourable attitude towards the experimental task than subjects who had been paid $20.

Festinger and Carlsmith intuitively built two features into their experimental situation which, though not specified in the original version of the theory, turned out to be essential for dissonance arousal. First, since the experimenter's request was not ostensibly part of the experiment, subjects were free to refuse the request and thus experienced high freedom of choice. Second, since the (confederate) subject indicated that she had intended not to participate in the experiment until the subject told her that the experiment was interesting, the subject's behaviour led to negative consequences (i.e. it misled the student and made him or her participate in a very dull experiment).

The importance of freedom of choice for dissonance arousal was later demonstrated by Linder, Cooper and Jones (1967), who reasoned that if subjects believed that by signing up for the experiment they had committed themselves to comply with any demand made during the experimental session, they would feel that they had no choice but to perform the counter-attitudinal behaviour requested by the experimenter. Under these conditions, the counter-attitudinal behaviour should not arouse dissonance. Instead, being offered a reward (e.g. money) for behaving counter-attitudinally should act as a reinforcement and attitude change would be expected. Linder, Cooper and Jones conducted two experiments in which they manipulated freedom of choice in addition to magnitude of reward. In line with their expectation, the dissonance-predicted inverse relationship (i.e. less change with high than with low incen-

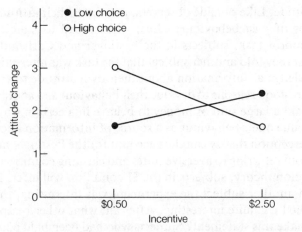

FIGURE 8.5   Mean attitudes towards the essay topic under different choice and incentive conditions (based on Linder, Cooper and Jones, 1967, experiment 1)

tive) was only found under conditions of high choice. When subjects were given little choice of refusing to perform the counter-attitudinal task, more attitude change was observed when the incentive was high rather than low (figure 8.5).

The importance of negative consequences of counter-attitudinal behaviour for the arousal of dissonance was first demonstrated by Nel, Helmreich and Aronson (1969) and later by Cooper and Worchel (1970). Cooper and Worchel (1970) replicated the Festinger and Carlsmith (1959) experiment, adding conditions in which the confederate subject was apparently not persuaded by the real subject. Consistent with predictions, the inverse relationship between size of incentive and attitude change could only be observed in the conditions with negative consequences. In the conditions where the confederate was not convinced and thus evaded the dull experience, size of incentive had no effect on attitude change.

Thus the answer to the question about the relationship between compliance and attitude change posed at the beginning of this section is not a simple one (see also Nutin, 1975). Persons who are induced to behave counter-attitudinally may change their attitudes, but the magnitude of change will depend on their freedom of choice, the size of the incentive and on the consequences of the behaviour. For individuals who felt free to refuse the counter-attitudinal task, most attitude change will result when the incentive was minimal and the behaviour led to negative consequences. With little freedom of choice, on the other hand, more attitude change will result if large rather than small incentives are offered for compliance.

An analysis in terms of self-perception theory   The dissonance interpretation of attitude change following counter-attitudinal behaviour was soon challenged by **self-perception theory** (Bem, 1965, 1972). This theory assumes that since internal cues are often weak, ambiguous or uninterpretable, people are frequently in the same situation as outside observers when asked to indicate their own attitude. Like outside observers, they infer their attitudes from relevant instances of past behaviour. Thus, when asked to state their attitude towards the motor task, subjects in the Festinger and Carlsmith experiment remember that they told another subject that the task was interesting. They will use this knowledge as information about their own attitude towards the task, unless there are good reasons to devalue their behaviour as a source of information. Being paid a large sum of money to behave in a certain way is one good reason to devalue one's behaviour as a source of information about one's attitudes. Self-perception theory can thus account for the Festinger and Carlsmith findings without referring to aversive states and clashing cognitions. According to self-perception theory, subjects in the $1 condition will infer, from the fact that they told another subject the experiment was interesting, that they *must* have found the task quite interesting. After all, what other reason could they have had to make this statement? Subjects who had been paid $20 on the other hand, will attribute their behaviour to the money and will thus not use it to infer their attitude towards the experimental task. They will therefore indicate a less favourable attitude towards the task than subjects in the $1 condition.

To demonstrate the viability of his position, Bem (1965) replicated the findings of dissonance experiments in 'interpersonal replications' of forced compliance experiments. In these replications, the different experimental conditions are described to subjects who then have to infer the attitude of an individual who complied with the experimenter's demand. These observers are usually quite able to replicate the findings of the original studies (e.g. Bem, 1965; Calder, Ross and Insko, 1973). However, such studies can only show that subjects could have inferred their attitudes from their own behaviour; they cannot prove that subjects actually *did* go through such an inference process.

With two theories as different as dissonance and self-perception theory, a decision about their relative validity should be easy. However, since the two theories differ only in their assumptions about the processes that mediate attitude change, it turned out to be rather difficult to devise some 'crucial experiment'. Such an experiment was finally conducted by Zanna and Cooper (1974), who used **misattribution** processes to demonstrate the presence of an aversive state. Subjects were given a placebo pill (a pill which has no effect) and were told either that this pill had no effect (placebo instructions) or that it would lead to some aversive feeling of tension. Then subjects wrote a counter-attitudinal essay under high- or low-choice conditions. According to dissonance theory, writing a counter-attitudinal essay under high choice should lead to aversive tension, which subjects would normally attribute to the writing of the essay. However, subjects who had been led to believe that the pill would cause an aversive tension should misattribute the tension to the pill. Thus there should be attitude change only under high choice and with placebo instructions. According to self-perception theory, giving the pill should not affect attitude change. The results supported dissonance predictions (see figure 8.6). These findings were replicated in later studies (e.g. Cooper, Zanna and Taves, 1978; Higgins, Rhodewalt and Zanna, 1979; Pittman, 1975). More recently, Croyle and

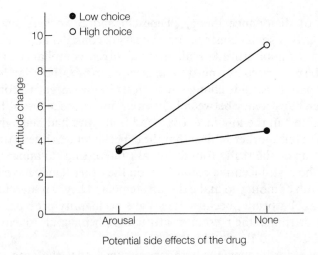

FIGURE 8.6   Mean attitudes towards the essay topic under different conditions of choice and misattribution (based on Zanna and Cooper, 1974)

Cooper (1983) managed to demonstrate such arousal differences directly through physiological recording.

The controversy was finally resolved by suggesting that the two theories should be regarded as complementary formulations with each theory being applicable to its own specialized domain. Fazio, Zanna and Cooper (1977) argued that self-perception theory accurately characterizes attitude change in the context of attitude-congruent behaviour, while dissonance theory explains attitude change in the context of counter-attitudinal behaviour. An *attitude-congruent position* is defined as any position that is still acceptable to an individual, even though it may be discrepant from his or her actual attitude. For example, people who believe that all atomic power stations should be closed down immediately would probably find the position that no new nuclear reactors should be built and the existing ones phased out within a period of ten years also acceptable, while they would find the argument that we need more atomic power stations to ensure future energy needs completely unacceptable. Thus, arguing the former position would be attitude congruent while arguing the latter would be counter-attitudinal. Again using misattribution processes as an indicator of the presence of dissonance, Fazio, Zanna and Cooper (1977) could show that attitude change due to counter-attitudinal behaviour was mediated by dissonance while attitude change due to pro-attitudinal behaviour was not.

An analysis in terms of impression management   In recent years **impression management theory** (Schlenker, 1982; Tedeschi and Rosenfeld, 1981; Tedeschi, Schlenker and Bonoma, 1971) posed the major challenge to the dissonance interpretations of forced compliance research. Impression management refers to the behavioural strategies that people use to create the social images or identities they desire (Tetlock and Manstead, 1985). Inverting a basic assumption of dissonance theory, Tedeschi and coworkers suggested that individuals have a social concern for appearing consistent to others. Thus, a subject's mark on an attitude scale after a forced compliance experiment is assumed to be motivated by a need for *appearing to be* rather than *being* consistent. The apparent attitude change of subjects in low-incentive conditions is a tactic to feign consistency between behaviour and subsequent attitude expression. The subject in the low-incentive condition, who had been given insufficient reason to tell another subject that the experiment was interesting, will now pretend that he or she really found the task interesting, to appear consistent. Subjects in the high-incentive condition, on the other hand, have been paid a reasonable sum of money to make their statement. They can therefore honestly report their real attitude, because they have no identity problem: the experimenter can attribute their counter-attitudinal behaviour to environmental factors (Tedeschi and Rosenfeld, 1981).

Since impression management theory assumes that the apparent attitude change in the low-incentive condition has been feigned for the benefit of the experimenter, counter-attitudinal behaviour must be public for a manifestation of attitude change to occur. More specifically, the theory implies that subjects must believe that the experimenter is able to connect them to both their counter-attitudinal behaviour and their marks on the attitude scale.

It is difficult to test these assumptions because, in this type of deception experiment, one never knows what subjects really believe. For example, in the Festinger and Carlsmith experiment, the attitude measure was taken by an interviewer who was ostensibly a representative of the psychology department and had no direct connection with the experimenter. Thus, the fact that there was attitude change in their low-incentive condition would tend to disconfirm impression management theory. But can we be sure that subjects really accepted this story? It is conceivable that subjects suspected that the experimenters would come to know their ratings (as in fact they did). Similar objections were raised against the findings of Hoyt, Henly and Collins (1972), who obtained attitude change from subjects even though their counter-attitudinal essays had not been signed. Thus Gaes, Kalle and Tedeschi (1978) speculated that subjects may have felt that they could have been identified by their seats or through their handwriting. However, as Cooper and Fazio (1984) commented, with 'such tortuous logic, it is very difficult indeed to accept any reasonable test that would support the notion that only feigned attitudes are involved in the induced-compliance paradigm' (p. 251).

The use of the **bogus pipeline** (see chapter 7; Jones and Sigall, 1971) therefore presents a more promising approach to pitting the two theories against each other. If the attitude change observed in forced compliance experiments was only due to a need for self-presentation, then no attitude change should occur when the bogus pipeline is used to measure attitudes. The bogus pipeline procedure was developed by Jones and Sigall (1971) to establish in subjects the belief that their 'real' attitudes can be monitored by an apparatus more sensitive than a lie detector. Since feigning consistency would make no sense under these conditions, there should be no attitude change in the low-incentive condition, when subjects expect that their attitude will be assessed through the bogus pipe-line. In a series of studies which compared the bogus pipeline procedure with normal attitude assessment, Tedeschi and his collaborators (Gaes, Kalle and Tedeschi, 1978; Riess, Kalle and Tedeschi, 1981) generated evidence that supported the impression management position.

The failure of these studies to find attitude change with the bogus pipeline is not necessarily inconsistent with dissonance theory. The bogus pipeline equip-ment might have functioned as the environmental equivalent of the arousal-evoking pills in the arousal attribution studies described earlier. Thus Stults, Messé and Kerr (1984) recently demonstrated that subjects who were attached to a bogus pipeline exhibited attitude change if given the opportunity to get accustomed to the equipment, but showed no attitude change if no habituation experience was provided. Since the opportunity to get accustomed to the bogus pipeline equipment should make the attribution of arousal to the equipment less plausible, these findings tend to support the misattribution interpretation of these bogus pipeline experiments.

After a thorough evaluation of the evidence from studies pitting impression management against dissonance theory, Tetlock and Manstead (1985) con-cluded that neither side emerged as a clear winner. They further argued that impression management and dissonance theory should be viewed not as mutually exclusive but as complementary. Thus, instead of searching for crucial experiments, researchers should examine the conditions under which concerns for self-presentation or internal consistency are likely to become dominant.

Pro-attitudinal behaviour and attitude change

In discussing the attitudinal consequences of pro-attitudinal behaviour one should distinguish between two groups of people, namely those who practise what they believe and those who do not. To return to the example of jogging, it is not only the joggers who hold a favourable attitude. There are also many 'would-be joggers', who are very much in favour of physical exercise but are too comfort-loving to act on their beliefs. Both groups would probably show a similar attitude towards jogging on an attitude scale, and yet our hypothetical jogging law would have somewhat different consequences for the two groups.

The case of the 'would be joggers' needs little elaboration. It is an example of beliefs and attitudes being confronted with direct experience, and we refer the reader to our discussion of the effects of direct experience at the beginning of this chapter. The case of the jogging addicts, on the other hand, is much more intriguing. Common sense would lead us to expect little attitude change here. After all, these people have been jogging for years and making this activity compulsory should not affect them. However, research on the effects of extrin-sic incentives on intrinsic motivation and performance has demonstrated that performance of an intrinsically enjoyable task will decrease once people have been given some reward for performing that task (Deci, 1975; Lepper and Greene, 1978).

One of the early investigations of this hypothesis was conducted by Lepper, Greene and Nisbett (1973), who introduced an attractive drawing activity during the free-play time of nursery school children. After the baseline interest of children had been observed during free play, children who showed an initial intrinsic interest in the activity were chosen as subjects and asked to perform the activity under one of three conditions. In the 'expected award' condition, children were promised a reward for the performance. In the 'unexpected award' condition, children were unexpectedly given a reward afterwards. In the 'no award' condition, children were neither promised nor given a reward. Two weeks later, the material was again provided in the classroom and the interest in the activity was unobtrusively observed. As predicted by the authors, 'expected award' subjects showed a significant decrease in interest in the activity from the baseline to post-experimental observation, whereas subjects in the 'no award' or 'unexpected award' conditions showed no significant change in overall interest. Similar findings were reported in a set of studies conducted by Deci (1971, 1972) with adult subjects, who were either paid or not paid to work on puzzle tasks that they had found intrinsically interesting.

Lepper, Greene and Nisbett (1973) interpreted these findings in terms of self-perception theory. To the extent that the extrinsic incentives are sufficiently salient, the individual will attribute his or her behaviour to these compelling extrinsic contingencies rather than to an intrinsic interest in the task. After having been rewarded for performing a task, subjects would be less likely to consider the activity interesting in itself. Thus an expected and contingent reward leads to a shift in subject's self-perceived motivation from intrinsic to extrinsic. An activity that was originally approached as an 'end in itself' is now seen as a 'means to an end' (Kruglanski, 1975). Lepper, Greene and Nisbett (1973) called this interpretation the **over-justification** hypothesis.

These findings have intriguing implications for the impact of the introduction of monetary incentives on attitudes towards activities which are already consistent with an individual's attitudes. It is not quite clear, however, whether the threat of legal sanctions will have the same impact as a monetary incentive in this case. After all, individuals have to see their own behaviour as under the control of the external incentive for the over-justification effect to occur. At least with pro-attitudinal behaviour, legal sanctions seem to be somehow less salient than monetary incentives. Thus, although most of us will neither steal nor murder, we will be unlikely to attribute our abstention to the threat of legal sanctions.

Summary and conclusion

In our discussion of the attitudinal consequences of compliance, we distinguished between counter-attitudinal and pro-attitudinal behaviour. When individuals are induced to behave counter-attitudinally, the magnitude of attitude change will depend on their freedom of choice, the magnitude of the incentive offered for the behaviour and the negativity of the consequences of the behaviour. With high choice and negative consequences, more attitude change will result when the incentive is small rather than large. When individuals feel little freedom of choice, there will be more change with large rather than small rewards.

These findings were discussed in terms of three theories. According to dissonance theory, counter-attitudinal behaviour produces dissonance, an aversive tension which individuals reduce by making their attitudes more consistent with their behaviour. Since counter-attitudinal behaviour that can be justified because of low freedom of choice and high incentives should result in less dissonance than behaviour that cannot be so justified, dissonance theory is consistent with the pattern of findings reported above.

Both self-perception theory and impression management theory offer alternative interpretations to that of dissonance theory. According to self-perception theory, individuals infer their own attitude from their past behaviour, unless there are obvious non-attitudinal causes for their actions (e.g. high incentives, low freedom of choice). According to impression management theory, on the other hand, a subject's mark on the attitude scale in a forced compliance experiment is assumed to be feigned in order to manage the impression that one is giving to the experimenter. The apparent attitude change of subjects in low-incentive conditions is a tactic to feign consistency between behaviour and subsequent attitude expression. After decades of attempts to pit these theories against each other, a consensus seems to have emerged (e.g. Fazio, Zanna and Cooper, 1977; Tetlock and Manstead, 1985) that they should be regarded as complementary rather than mutually exclusive formulations. Thus, instead of attempting to conduct 'crucial' experiments, researchers have begun to develop and explore possible conceptual frameworks that would integrate the psychological processes described by these theories (e.g. Schlenker, 1982).

Strategies of Change: an Evaluation of Their Relative Effectiveness

Since people are rarely interested in attitude change as an end in itself but as a means to changing behaviour, influencing behaviour through monetary incentives or legal sanctions would seem to be the most effective of the strategies discussed in this chapter. And indeed, there is evidence to support this notion. For example, after campaigns that pointed at the great safety advantage of using seat-belts were rather unsuccessful in Germany and Sweden, both countries introduced laws that made seat-belt use compulsory. Within a few months, the frequency of seat-belt use increased considerably. Furthermore, an assessment of attitudes of a sample of Swedish car users before and after the introduction of the law indicated that the law had brought about more positive opinions regarding seat-belt use, at least in those who complied (Fhanér and Hane, 1979). In view of the overwhelming success of strategies of direct influence, one wonders why people still bother with persuasion.

There are actually a number of considerations to be taken into account. The most obvious is lack of power. Only governments have the power to enact laws, and even they are constrained in the use of this power. For example, although the behavioural factors contributing to coronary risk (e.g. smoking, eating fatty food, overuse of alcohol) are well known, governments rely on persuasion rather than legal action to change behaviour. A law that would forbid tobacco or alcohol consumption would be unpopular enough to lead to a change in power with the next election. Furthermore, most governments recognize that changing behaviour by persuading people rather than forcing or bribing them is more consistent with present-day ideals of self-determination and democracy.

An additional constraint on strategies of influence based on the use of monetary incentives or legal sanctions is that these strategies can only be used for behaviour that can be monitored. Thus, while efficient for publicly identifiable behaviour such as seat-belt use, speeding or the use of catalyzers, positive or negative incentives are difficult to apply if the behaviour that one wishes to influence is difficult to monitor objectively. For example, in the area of race relations, governments can eliminate some of the objective and observable instances of discrimination (e.g. by introducing quotas for employment of members of racial minorities) but they cannot force people to be nice to members of outgroups, to invite them to their homes or to let their children marry one of them. This is one of the reasons why the American Supreme Court mandated the end of segregated schooling. Since they could not outlaw prejudice, they attempted to reduce it by increasing interracial contact.

A further disadvantage which is inherent in the use of legal sanctions to induce behaviour changes is that once behaviour is under the control of some extrinsic incentive, it will be not only necessary to continually monitor the behaviour but also difficult if not impossible to return to internal control. Thus speed limits become ineffective unless they are continually monitored and seen to be monitored. And even though laws like the one making seat-belt use compulsory seem to result in attitude change, one wonders what would happen if such laws became revoked. Extending notions of self-perception theory, one would expect that individuals would now attribute their past behaviour to the law. They would therefore be likely to change their behaviour if the laws were to be changed.

Thus the great advantage of influencing behaviour through persuasion is that the behaviour remains under intrinsic control and thus does not need any monitoring. Furthermore, at least for attitude change brought about by the 'central route', the change should be fairly persistent. And yet, if behaviour change is deemed important, such considerations may often be outweighed by the greater effectiveness of direct strategies.

In conclusion it should be pointed out, however, that changing the incentive structure or using persuasive appeals should not be seen as competing strategies of attitude and behaviour change. On the contrary, since changes in the incentive structure are unlikely to affect behaviour, unless people are made aware that monetary inducements or legal sanctions have been introduced to encourage a given behaviour, governments typically rely on mass media campaigns to inform the population of these changes.

Glossary Terms

Bogus pipeline	Misattribution
Central route to persuasion	Modelling
Classical conditioning	Over-justification
Counter-attitudinal behaviour	Peripheral route to persuasion
Dissonance theory	Persuasion
Distraction	Persuasive communications
Elaboration	Pro-attitudinal behaviour
Elaboration likelihood model	Process model of persuasion
(ELM)	Protection motivation theory
Expectancy-value models	Reception
Fear appeals	Self-perception theory
Heuristic processing	Two-factor model of persuasion
Impression management theory	Yielding
Mere exposure	

Further Reading

Cooper, J. and Fazio, R. H. (1984) A new look at dissonance theory. In L. Berkowitz (ed.), *Advances in Experimental Social Psychology* (vol. 17), Orlando, Fla.: Academic Press. An up-to-date account of research on dissonance theory.

Eagly, A. H. and Chaiken, S. (1984) Cognitive theories of persuasion. In L. Berkowitz (Ed.), *Advances in Experimental Social Psychology* (vol. 17), Orlando, Fla.: Academic Press. An excellent, higher-level review and evaluation of cognitive theories of persuasion.

Festinger, L. and Carlsmith, J. M. (1959) Cognitive consequences of forced compliance. *Journal of Abnormal and Social Psychology*, 58, 203–10. This is perhaps one of the best known studies ever conducted in social psychology. It is one of the few classic experiments which would still be publishable under present-day methodological standards.

Lepper, M. R. and Greene, D. (eds) (1978) *The Hidden Costs of Reward: new perspectives on the psychology of human motivation*. Hillsdale, NJ: Erlbaum. This edited book reviews most of the classic research and theorizing on the over-justification effect.

Petty, R. E and Cacioppo, J. T. (1986) *Communication and Persuasion: central and peripheral routes to attitude change*. New York. Springer. This book describes the elaboration likelihood model and summarizes the research which was conducted to test this model.

Tedeschi, J. T. and Rosenfeld, P. (1981) Impression management theory and the forced compliance situation. In J. T. Tedeschi (ed.), *Impression Management Theory and Social Psychological Research*, New York: Academic Press. A summary of the research conducted to test the impression management interpretation of forced compliance research.

Zajonc, R. B. (1968) Attitudinal effects of mere exposure. *Journal of Personality and Social Psychology Monograph Supplement*, 9 (2, part 2), 1–27. This is the original paper in which Zajonc presented the evidence for the mere exposure effect.

PART III

Communication and Social Interaction

PART III

Communication and Social
Interaction

9 Interpersonal Communication

JOHN M. WIEMANN and HOWARD GILES

Introduction

Communication between us is essential for a whole host of reasons, including access to and free exchange of information, the open discussion of ideas and proper negotiations of arguments and conflict, the provision of emotional support in times of stress, and so on. Nowadays, many different modes of communication are available to us in the pursuit of these goals, and often the choice between them for delivering a particular kind of message is a strategic one (Furnham, 1986). Undeniably, a lack of satisfying and quality communication can have serious implications for our psychological well-being and physical health, with chronic loneliness leading to depression, alcoholism and drug abuse (Peplau and Perlman, 1982). Moreover, one of the few agreed causes of marital discontent and divorce is a breakdown in communication between spouses, sometimes resulting in severe clinical conditions, negative consequences for the couple's social networks, and lowered productivity at work (see Fitzpatrick, 1984; Kitson, Babri and Roach, 1985).

Communication: its characteristics

Communication itself can be a most effective way of easing psychological suffering such as for those who have cancer or have been recently bereaved (Dunkel-Shetter and Wortman, 1982; Lehman, Ellard and Wortman, 1986). Yet many of the victim's close contacts find themselves unwilling or unable to provide effective communication, perhaps owing to ill-managed cues from the afflicted themselves. Indeed, both ageing and death itself have also been shown to have been accelerated by a lack of communicative opportunities (e.g. Blazer, 1982).

The authors would like to express their appreciation to the editors, and especially to Miles Hewstone, for their comments on an earlier draft of this chapter. Work on this chapter was begun while the first author was a Fullbright Senior Research Scholar in the Centre for Communication and Social Relations, University of Bristol.

The focus of this chapter is on the way verbal and non-verbal behaviour function in the service of interpersonal communicative goals. The communication discipline has a long tradition. Its first treatise – Aristotle's *Rhetoric* (1932 edn) – was concerned with public persuasion in the service of democratic government; indeed, it is still in use today as a text. Interestingly, social psychology's first major involvement with communicative needs also arose out of real, practical matters (Hovland, Janis and Kelley, 1953), namely, the Allies' concerns about the influence of German propaganda during the Second World War and their desire to sharpen their own persuasive line.

Communication is, of course, much more than 'attitude change', the continuing importance of which is well documented in chapter 8. And although there are a multitude of competing definitions of communication (Dance and Larson, 1976), we would rather emphasize two characteristics which distinguish it from mere behaviour. First, in order for elements of a message to be encoded, the producer must be operating at *some level* of consciousness and therefore with *some degree* of intentionality (Blakar, 1979; MacKay, 1972; von Cranach and Vine, 1973). Admittedly, people typically do not think much about greeting friends on the street; they just do it. Yet such routines were, at some point, consciously learned, practised and stored in memory for retrieval. Hence, in this case, only a very low level of consciousness and intentionality are necessary.

A second characteristic of communication is that it is a *process* in the sense that it is a system requiring more than one actor in an ongoing series of events. Here we focus attention on *interaction* rather than thinking or talking to oneself, on a set of *shared* symbols, and on the *dyad* as the basic unit of analysis which has a past (memory), present and (potential) future. Crucially, the *pattern* of participants' behaviour is arguably more important than outcomes measured at some specified point in time. For example, who got his or her way ultimately is less important to the future prospects of a marriage than precisely *how* the couple came to their decision (Krueger, 1982; Watzlawick, Beavin and Jackson, 1967).

Unfortunately, research strategies for studying communication in this way still lag behind our understanding of the phenomenon, although they have changed over the years. Earlier, scholars tended to classify communicative behaviour by the 'channel' in which information was conveyed. The simplest distinction was – and for some still is – between verbal content (language) and everything else (non-verbal behaviour), including body movements (**kinesics**) and voice qualities and intonation (**paralinguistics** and **prosodics**). Traditionally, such work focused on a single channel, e.g. the eyes, with other aspects of the message either controlled for or ignored. More recently, the distinction between verbal and non-verbal communication has become blurred (Wiener et al., 1972) with the realization that 'utterances' (verbal *and* non-verbal) emerge developmentally from the same central processing unit (Bates, 1979; Kendon, 1983); consequentially, more multi channel work has emerged.

We do not find the verbal/non-verbal dichotomy particularly useful either for our research or for the summary we are undertaking here. For instance, the

manner in which a person self-discloses some past tragic event can only be interpreted adequately if we are aware of the whole array of extra-contextual factors
simultaneously operating, including gestures, previous discourse and vocal
quality. Otherwise we cannot decide (or guess) whether the revelation was
meant as cry for help, a request for sympathy, an indication that the discloser
had transcended the trauma, or what. For us then, a *functional* approach to
communication more fully captures the complexity of the literature as well as
the experiences of ordinary communicators who send, receive, process and
negotiate intricate messages with each other. After all, communicators are
attempting not only to transmit information but also to craft (and continually
reshape) their messages in such a manner as to create and maintain (usually) a
positive esteem. Communication then can be a multifunctional 'game' (see also
Kraut and Higgins, 1984), sometimes highly emotionally charged, at other
times tactically ingenious, often quite unsuccessful.

Although we doubt whether it was seen as such by the investigators involved
at the time, we turn now to one of the earliest *functional* studies which was conducted by Argyle and Dean (1965). Although it has since been criticized (e.g.
Patterson, 1984), it is perhaps the most widely cited in the social psychology of
communication and has been an important stimulus for recent theoretical
thinking (Street and Cappella, 1985).

Eye contact, distance and affiliation

Argyle and Dean recognized that eye contact (i.e. the meeting of two people's
gaze or their looking into each other's eyes) serves many functions such as
gathering information and controlling intimacy. Conversational intimacy can
be communicated in a number of ways, such as talking about personal issues,
standing very close and being amenable to touch, smiling and, of course, eye
contact. These authors concluded that the amount of eye contact in any given
conversation is the product of a variety of approach and avoidance forces. The
former include the need for feedback and affiliative and domination desires,
while the latter include fear of being seen or revealing some inner state, the
avoidance of information about the other's responses, and the like. Using
Miller's (1944) conflict theory, Argyle and Dean reasoned that these
approach–avoidance forces work to produce a *desirable* level of intimacy by
means of the communicational resources one has to hand; in other words, an
'equilibrium' is engineered that is appropriate to the context, developing
relationship and message. Hence, if one increases intimacy by means of one
communicational element (e.g. stand a little closer), then the system will be
adjusted so as to compensate by means of other elements (e.g. reduce eye gaze).

These researchers conducted a series of experiments to test aspects of this
model dealing with eye contact and physical proximity. Before running the
main experiment, they had to determine the distance that constitutes the equilibrium point for conversation 'for local subjects and conditions'; as frequent
travellers will appreciate, this varies dramatically from culture to culture.
Argyle and Dean accomplished this by having 12 subjects (six adults and six

children) approach (a) a man whose eyes were open on one occasion but (b) closed on another, and (c) a life-size photo of the same person. The results were consistent with their theorizing: subjects stood closest to the photo (26.3 in), next to the actual person with eyes shut (30.8 in), and farthest away from him with eyes open (37.1 in). This final distance was interpreted as the equilibrium point for conversation during eye contact in this kind of setting.

The study proper employed 24 subjects (half of each sex) who were asked to discuss with a confederate researcher (either a man or woman) a card depicting an ambiguous scene and to make up a story about it. Subjects sat across the corner of a table from the confederate at distances of 2, 6 and 10 ft. The table was placed in a laboratory so that observers behind a one-way mirror could record the frequency and duration of glances into the confederate's eyes. Since the confederate was briefed to gaze steadily at the subject, his or her glances brought the pair into eye contact.

Three main results emerged (see figure 9.1). First, and as predicted by the so-called equilibrium hypothesis, eye contact decreased as proximity increased for all four combinations of subjects and confederates according to sex. Moreover, as distance increased, glances became longer. Second, there was a significant interaction between sex of subject and sex of confederate, with much less eye

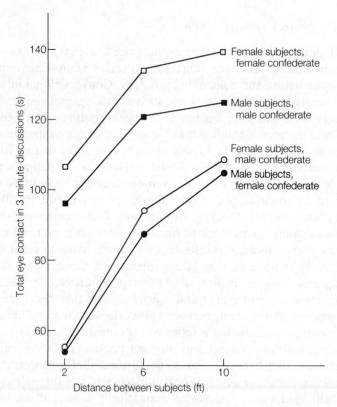

FIGURE 9.1   Relation between eye contact and distance for different combinations of subjects and confederates (Argyle and Dean, 1965, p. 300)

contact and shorter glances in mixed-sex dyads; these differences were most pronounced at 2 ft. Third, subjects in the 2 ft conditions showed 'signs of tension' even with reduced eye contact. This was probably because other forces (e.g. politeness) prevented them from reducing eye contact to zero in order to restore equilibrium. Hence the authors point to some qualification of their model, but the results clearly support the equilibrium hypothesis.

A Functional Approach to Communication

Argyle and Dean's study calls attention to the fact that any single communicative behaviour can serve a variety of functions and, by implication, the function is more interesting than the behaviour *per se*. More importantly, they illustrated that these functions are served by clusters of behaviours used in concert. By *function* we mean the inevitable, natural and unavoidable consequence of communicative behaviour. Neither purpose nor intention is implied, although these may be present (Dance and Larson, 1976). In other words, to say that communication has a control function means that every message contains information about the distribution of control between or among the people conversing (or, at least, about the message sender's desired distribution of control). This characteristic of communication has been called **meta-communication**, referring to the fact that messages have both relational-level and content-level meaning (Watzlawick, Beavin and Jackson, 1967), with the former providing guidance about how the content is to be taken or how it is to be understood. A sarcastic tone of voice, of course, indicates that the positive content of an utterance should not be understood as such.

We are discussing here *general* rather than contextually bounded functions. As the term implies, these are relevant trans-situationally and usually subsume more context-specific functions. For example, telling your lover to bring you a beer functions to get the other to perform a service for you *now*; this is a context-bound function. Yet at a more general level, you are asserting that you have the right to make such requests and expect them to be carried out. You are then, by your discourse, expressing your view of the control you have in the relationship; it is this kind of general function in which we are most interested here.

There is substantial agreement in the literature that there are two primary functions of communication; determination of (1) the distribution of **communicative control** in a relationship, and (2) the level of **affiliative messages** which will characterize it. Other functions have been identified (see Robinson, 1972; Wiemann and Kelly, 1981), for example the expression of empathy or task orientation; yet, whilst important these seem subordinate to control and affiliation.

Control

Control: its features   Control has long been considered an important, if not the most important, construct in social science and communication studies (Berger, 1985; Blakar, 1979). Depending on the specific interests of researchers, when power is used it is (theoretically at least) used up, whereas control is ongoing and is distributed (but not necessarily evenly) in relationships. We use 'control' here because it has come to mean the actualization of power or the outcome of an influence attempt, whilst power more commonly refers to the potential of an individual or social group to influence, control or coerce (cf. Foa and Foa, 1972; Wheeless, Barraclough and Stewart, 1983). More specifically, control is the constellation of constraints people place on one another by what they say and how they structure conversation, which in turn limits the options available to participants (Wiemann, 1985). To the extent that one can limit what another can do next and still be seen as acting in an appropriate, logical, coherent and sane manner, that person has control over the other(s).

Such control can be approximately mutual or it can be distributed asymmetrically as, for example, in parent–child communication, and if expectations are in line with the apparent control distribution then relational satisfaction will ensue. But since control distribution is seldom a topic of conversation – and indeed it might be a taboo – it is necessary that the negotiation referred to above takes place metacommunicatively (Wiemann, 1985). This is accomplished through manipulations of various linguistic choices, non-verbal behaviours and conversational structures (see Fowler et al., 1979; and see below) by (1) making control 'moves' or 'bids' which are responded to by one's partner, and (2) responding to the partner's moves which may be accepting or challenging the bid(s) just made.

This negotiation is usually casual in dyads where a low level of intimacy is anticipated, but it increases in intensity and seriousness in relationships where stability, high intimacy and dependency are anticipated or desired. Hence, we might expect a couple to pay more (non-conscious, perhaps) attention to control issues when they move from a casual to an exclusive dating contract. (In realtionships where institutional authority specifies control relationships, as for example in the military, then of course little negotiation is needed.) It may well be then that moves and counter-moves eventually lead to the establishment of an equilibrium for control distribution in much the same manner Argyle and Dean claim exists with regard to intimacy. Further, it is likely that communicators seek optimal control distribution rather than maximal control (or dominance) for one or the other. Partners, in other words, tend to give up some control (either across the spectrum of mutual activities or in specific contexts) in order to satisfy the other's desire to control, and/or to take control in order to satisfy their partner's desire to be submissive.

Control: communication correlates   Control moves can be constructed from a variety of discrete behaviours, including talking more than one's own partner, talking less but self-protectively questioning more, formal terms of address and pronoun usage (e.g. *tu* versus *vous* in French), staring, and exhibiting a relaxed posture (e.g. arms akimbo, reclining or backward leaning posture, open legs etc.) (see Argyle, 1975; Brown and Gilman, 1960; Mehrabian, 1972). Control appears a major factor in a short dyadic encounter which can sometimes be of crucial importance, for example, in the doctor–patient consultation. Here 'good' communication is obviously vital for effective health care, as the physican must be able to develop rapport with patients and draw them out in order to gain as much information as possible to provide appropriate diagnosis and treatment. In order to do this, a doctor's best bid would seem to be to encourage patients to open up by being a good listener, allowing them the ideal empathic context in which to express themselves. However, findings from American research (see table 9.1) present a rather contrasting profile of doctor–patient communication. The conversational *imbalance* displayed runs the risk of a physican 'not getting to the bottom' of the problem by not letting patients frame it in their terms, or allowing them their own interpretations of events.

One of the major control features mentioned in table 9.1, *interruptions*, has received widespread empirical attention in other social contexts, given that it is an integral element of the turn-taking system (Duncan and Fiske, 1977; Wiemann and Knapp, 1975). For instance, examining sex differences, Zimmermann and West (1975) report that in mixed-gender dyads men interrupt women more than vice versa; in fact, 98 per cent of the interruptions were male initiated. They concluded that this behaviour is one of many indicators of unequal control distribution in society which favour males (see Markel, Long and Saine, 1976; Smith, 1985). Other such indicants include the frequent use by women of *intensifiers* ('so', 'very', 'really'), *hedges* ('sort of', 'kind of', 'well', 'you know'), *polite forms*, *intonations* (using a rising pattern in declarative statements), and *tag questions* ('This is an interesting area, *isn't it?*') (Lakoff, 1975; but for a counter-view see Brouwer, Gerritsen and DeHaan, 1979). However, the supposition that women use this so-called 'powerless speech style' has been questioned in several studies which show, for instance, that interruptions (at least on some occasions) can serve predominantly positive functions (e.g. expressing support, showing interest) and that women interrupt as much as, if not more than, men (Dindia, 1987; Kennedy and Camden, 1983; Wiemann et al., 1987). Hence, while it would be an error to conclude that interruptions and similar conversational devices are never used as indices of control distribution, it would be an error of equal magnitude to see them only in that light.

However, use of this powerless speech is not in any case confined to females, or even necessarily related to gender (Brouwer, Gerritsen and DeHaan, 1979; Lamb, 1981; Leet-Pellegrini, 1980), but seems to correspond generally with

TABLE 9.1 A socio-linguistic profile of conversational imbalance in medical consultations

1 Doctor does most of the talking.
2 Doctor initiates 99 per cent of the utterances.
3 Patient poses only 9 per cent of questions raised.
4 Doctor keeps asking further questions before patient has answered last one.
5 Doctor interrupts patient more (except when doctor is female).
6 Doctor determines agenda and topic shifts.
7 Doctor determines encounter's termination.

Sources: after Fisher and Todd (1983); West (1984)

low-status speakers as shown by Lind and O'Barr (1979) in their research on courtroom language. They found that law students reacted less favourably to witnesses' attractiveness and credibility, not to mention their advocated position, when they spoke to a supposed lawyer with linguistic intensifiers, hedges and rising intonation than when they did not incorporate these features into their testimony. Interestingly, Scherer (1979) showed that 'the voice of social influence' varies cross-nationally. In a role-playing study in the United States and West Germany, he found that individuals who were consensually agreed to be the most influential in various decision-making groups adopted different conversational styles in the two countries.

Control features: their social meanings   This last study also highlights the issue that the social meaning of differing speech styles has considerable significance for person perception and impression management (Giles and Powesland, 1975). Features such as the diversity of one's vocabulary, a fast speech rate and a prestigious accent can have a very positive effect on a person's perceived control (Bradac and Wisegarver, 1984). Studies all over the world have shown that a standard accent not only conveys impressions of status and perceived competence (Ball, Gallois and Callan, in press; Stewart, Ryan and Giles, 1985), and from a very early age, but also has profound effects on others' tendency to cooperate with such speakers. For example, Giles and Farrar (1979) used an authentic bidialectal interviewer to ask housewives to complete a three-item, open-ended questionnaire on the economic situation; half were approached with the request in a standard British accent, the others in a non-standard but local regional accent. The respondents produced 32, 44 and 77 per cent more words to the standard-accented interviewer on the three questions respectively than when she invited their cooperation with the same non-verbal manner in her non-standard accent. Moreover, with regard to job suitability, a series of studies on employment interviews (see for example table 9.2) has

TABLE 9.2   Perceived job suitability and accent usage

Job	Perceived job status[a]	Prestige accent[b]	Non-standard accent[b]
Industrial plant cleaner	1.44	−	+
Production assembler	3.00	−	+
Industrial mechanic	3.55	−	+
Foreman	4.36	=	=
Personnel manager	5.79	+	−
Accounts manager	6.07	+	−
Production control manager	6.31	+	−

[a]As rated by an independent sample of subjects (1 = low status; 7 = high status).
[b]+ indicates prestige accented speaker significantly more suitable than non-standard; − indicates the opposite; and = indicates no perceived difference.
Source: after Giles, Wilson and Conway (1981)

shown that a standard-accented speaker induces far more favourable reactions for higher-status occupations than the same person producing the very same message in a non-standard accent (see Kalin, 1982). Similar kinds of findings have also emerged with regard to a speaker's, and more particularly a child's, perceived educational potential (see Edwards and Giles, 1984). Of course, *how* something is said has to be gauged against other interactional features such as the content of the message (Giles and Johnson, 1986). Yet it is remarkable just how powerful vocal features can be, even when other contextual information such as speakers' socio-economic backgrounds, visual cues and quality of achievements are examined simultaneously (e.g. Elwell, Brown and Rutter, 1984; Giles and Sassoon, 1983; Seligman, Lambert and Tucker, 1972). Indeed, the same discourse from a speaker can be interpreted in widely different but schema-consistent ways. For instance, selected findings from a recent study showed that some of the very same statements made by an audio-taped speaker talking at length about his car were attributed to his being pompous, arrogant and egocentric when young and with a standard accent, but to his being narrow-minded, obsessed with the past, and out of phase with the present when elderly and with a non-standard accent (Giles et al., in press).

Control features: their dynamic nature   The above findings notwithstanding, we should not conceive of language features as static givens. Often they can be socially constructed owing to changing environmental conditions. An illustration of this process is provided by findings from Thakerar and Giles (1981). They asked subjects to listen to a tape recording of a student talking about an intellectual task he had just completed. They were then requested to rate him along a number of personality attributes and speech dimensions. This a control group duly did, but there were two other experimental conditions. Just before rating, the experimental subjects were provided with additional information. One group (high status) were told that the student had done well thus far in his undergraduate studies, whereas the other (low status) that he had done poorly. As figure 9.2 shows, subjects reconstructed their perceptions of his speech in a manner stereotypically consistent with his supposed social characteristics. In the next phase of the experiment, subjects were asked to listen once again to the taped extract and rerate the speaker, just in case they wished to change their minds after a second hearing; instructions were provided such that they were not compelled to modify. Rather than the two experimental groups realigning their speech perceptions in accord with the control groups, these subjects actually *polarized* their ratings.

Individuals can variously perceive the general status of language patterns around them given the prevailing social climate and their group identities. For instance, Young, Giles and Pierson (1986) found that before the Sino-British Treaty (which gave political sovereignty over Hong Kong to the People's Republic of China in 1997) was signed, Cantonese students perceived the Chinese language to possess a lower status in government services, the mass media, schools and religious contexts than English. However, after signing, the Chinese language was perceived to assume the higher-status position on these dimensions, whilst the status of English had correspondingly declined. As the

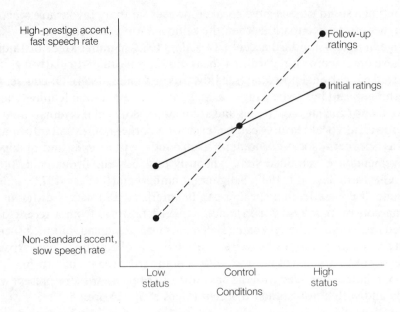

FIGURE 9.2   The perception of speech characteristics as a function of speaker's competence (based on Thakerar and Giles, 1981)

authors pointed out, since the social fabric of Hong Kong had changed little between the first and the second data collection, these findings can be seen as a reflection of the weakened position of Westerners through the process of socio-political negotiation.

Control: communicative management   Such studies have implications at the *behavioural* level too. It is a well-established finding that people have beliefs about the social meanings of various language features appropriate for certain settings (Brown and Fraser, 1979). Hence, we tend to speak more prestigiously and in a grammatically more sophisticated way in more formal situations (Labov, 1966). Indeed, in certain bi- and multilingual settings *diglossia* operates, wherein people use the high-status language or dialect for rather public settings (e.g. education, media) and the lower-status or vernacular for more private ones (e.g. in the home, neighbourhood: Fishman, 1972). But besides these prescribed norms we can, of course, modify our communicative styles so as to achieve the desired impression we wish to make at that moment. We can, therefore, linguistically shape our perceived identities in the ears of others and thereby attempt to control the kinds of attributions they make about us (see Baumeister, 1982; Giles and Street, 1985; Weary and Arkin, 1981). The extent to which we can succeed as linguistic chameleons is a complex issue, as we often hypercorrect our speech and 'leak' contradictory (Noller, 1982) and/or 'giveaway' information by means of other modalities and features (DePaulo, Stone and Lassiter, 1985). Nevertheless, our communicative performances in search of social control (Tedeschi, Lindskold and Rosenfeld, 1985) are fashioned to some extent by the perceived features of our interactants.

This is neatly demonstrated by a series of studies by Caporeal, Lukaszewski and Culbertson (1983) on the institutionalized elderly in California. They found that certain nurses would use a kind of 'baby talk' to their elderly patients, irrespective of the latter's functional autonomy. Needless to say, those elderly who had been thus categorized resented such 'put-downs'. In a series of recent British studies, we also found such 'over-accommodative' behaviour directed at the *non*-institutionalized elderly as well as to other socially stigmatized groups (e.g. the visually handicapped) (Coupland, Coupland, Giles and Henwood, 1988; see also Jones et al., 1984; DePaulo and Coleman, 1986). It appears that young people's tendency to fashion their communicative behaviour not to where the elderly actually are, but to where they *stereotype them to be*, might sometimes be in part a function of their need to induce dependency in their elders (Ryan et al., 1986). In other words, it is a resource for establishing social control.

Whatever the function of such over-accommodations for varying people, the net effect can be one of reducing the social control of those who are recipients of it (cf. Rodin and Langer, 1980). Furthermore, it is our contention that when sufficient people in differing settings address an elderly person in a communicative style, evoking images that they 'are past it', there comes a time when even the most resilient will begin to take on the characteristics they believe to be elderly. Therefore language can trigger a response of talking, looking, thinking and feeling older and in due course may be a long-term constituent element in the social construction of death.

Summary We have in this section provided a flavour of the many ways differents aspects of communicative behaviour can be used for social control interactively, and in contexts which have significant implications for our health, wealth and stealth. We should, however, emphasize the point that while we have distinguished conceptually between context and communication, there is no such fine dividing line in most of social reality. Very often our language patterns are those which principally define what a situation *is*, for example as formal, tense and emotional (see Forgas, 1983; Giles and Hewstone, 1982; Giles and Wiemann, 1987). Indeed, those in control – be they parents, media programmers, teachers, politicians or whoever – can (consciously or non-consciously) act as linguistic machiavellians to the extent that their (even supposedly objective and descriptive) communicative choices can dictate to us our understanding of social events and objects (Blakar, 1979; Eiser, 1975).

Affiliation

Affiliation: its features As alluded to above, communicative control and interactive affect are interdependent forces; mutuality does not necessarily imply relational satisfaction, any more than asymmetry inevitably implies antipathy. Indeed, whereas the social meaning conveyed by a non-prestige accent is unfavourable in many formal contexts, it has on the other hand far more positive connotations with respect to social attractiveness and integrity (Giles and

Powesland, 1975). In other words, a stereotyped picture of a standard accented speaker often exists as an educated, competent and ambitious person, yet one who is interpersonally cold and untrustworthy. And it is to this latter constellation of attributes that we now turn, in terms of our second fundamental communication function – affiliation, or the love–hate dimension of communication relationships.

Affiliation is similar and related to intimacy (e.g. Argyle and Dean, 1965) but, we believe, is a more precise term. Affiliation is concerned with expressed affect (positive *and* negative), while intimacy refers primarily to knowledge about another that is of a personal nature. Intimacy is frequently displayed by the use of affiliative behaviours, of course. Further, intimacy is almost always used in conjunction with positive (approach–approach) relationships.

The negative side of the affiliation continuum is important if we wish to understand the maintenance of unsatisfactory, unhappy, even hostile relationships and the decline of those which once prospered. Interestingly, there has been an overwhelming bias to study only the positive communicative patterns and to examine strategies which enhance 'appropriate', 'open', 'honest', truthful', 'effective', 'efficient' and 'successful' exchanges (Grice, 1975; Habermas, 1979; Higgins, 1980; but see for example Duck, 1982 and Duck and Gilmour, 1981 for the beginning of a return to this situation). Messages which lead to and maintain negative relationships are treated typically as somewhat psychopathological. Clearly, there are many relationships which are characterized by ongoing hostility, deception or antagonism where abnormal behaviour (in the clinical sense) is not manifest, and we will examine these later. Further, it is our contention that problematic talk, communicative dilemmas and outright miscommunication are regular features of social interaction – as much between *friends* as between strangers or enemies (Coupland, Giles and Wiemann, in press).

Affiliation: its positive aspects   Affiliation is expressed by increased proximity (closer than situationally normative), other-directed gaze, eye contact, touching, open posture, intimate topics, self-disclosures, and the offer of general support for the presented self-concept of one's partner (e.g. Altman and Taylor, 1973; J. K. Burgoon, 1983; Cushmann and Cahn, 1985). Interestingly, research has shown that people can decode the social meanings of these cues in others' non-verbal displays (Forgas, 1978). For instance, how many times have you made (probably accurate) guesses about the relational status of a couple in a bar or restaurant (e.g. whether they are on a first or second date versus whether they have been married for a long time), and also guessed which of them is the more 'into' the relationship based on communicative cues? Doubtless we use others' language behaviours and monitor our own in ongoing interaction in order to display our desired level of affiliation.

Of course affiliative expression is a varied and complex process. Alberts (1986), in an analysis of the conversational features accompanying the development of heterosexual relationships in certain romantic novels, found that the initiation of them was characterized (somewhat counter-intuitively) by teasing, anger and conflict. A particular feature discovered here was 'face-threatening' acts, as illustrated by this example of a man and woman meeting. The man's opening bid is:

> Business or pleasure? No don't tell me, let me guess. For you business only. You hate to fly and you don't look like you've had a day's pleasure in your life.

A feature of such (fictional anyway) initial exchanges, which lead to relational involvement, is counter-banter or the use of reciprocal face-threatening acts. Hence, the woman retorted in this particular case:

> I don't talk to strange men. Especially rude, conceited men with corny come-ons who dress like refugees from the sixties and look old enough to know better.

Alberts argues that this kind of discourse raises arousal levels which generate attributions and may possibly lead to potential romanticism. We conjecture that it is the *counter* that is of crucial importance here. In other words, it could be the sequential negotiation, or proliferation, of face-threatening acts that *really* make the interaction special; after all, this is a deviation from a conversational norm. Whatever, Alberts (1986) is fascinating reading in terms of how we construct our discourse ingeniously to intensify the development of romantic encounters (see however Ulrich, 1986 for a critique of generalizing ordinary language use from literature).

Affiliation: its management Interlocutors may desire different levels of affiliation, and this has to be negotiated (albeit a not particularly romantic view) in much the same way as was control. Indeed, a man who desires more affiliation than his date appears willing to give will have to work to keep the expression of his affiliation within tolerable limits for her; he will have to accept those limits (temporarily, at least, and possibly while attempting to modify them) or terminate the relationship.

This process is quite complex, as, like control, people seldom discuss affiliation issues until a point of imminent change or crisis has been reached (Baxter and Wilmot, 1985). (When was the last time you ended a conversation with someone you had just met in a lecture by saying, 'Let's be friends'?) The working out or negotiation of affiliation level takes place over time and is guided by cultural expectations of how fast relationships should progress (e.g. prolonged courtship in some cultures, injunctions such as 'no kissing on the first date' in others) and are sometimes mediated by instrumental purposes far removed from affiliation (as romantic involvements in spy trials often attest).

We would like to suggest that the negotiation process can be modelled by using Argyle and Dean's equilibrium hypothesis, with only slight modification. Assume that each person's equilibrium point for affiliation in a specific budding relationship is the point at which he/she begins the negotiation of how much affiliation (affection) will be displayed in the relationship. This initial negotiation will lead to an implicitly agreed upon affiliation level which will optimize the desires of each party. That is, they will arrive at a level that allows each to be satisfied as much as possible given the other's desired level of affiliation. While the equilibrium point for the relationship could theoretically range anywhere between the desired affiliation level of the two participants, we speculate that it is most likely to approximate the level of the *least* affiliative partner.

Attempts to increase or decrease the affiliation level are based on the desire by one partner to have the relational level most closely approximate his or her desired level. Since some subset of the possible 'intimacy' behaviours is likely to be used to propose increased affiliation (e.g. attempt to hold date's hand while maintaining other related behaviours at current level), one's partner (the 'target' if you like) can accept the bid, attempt to maintain the current level of affiliation, or even lower that level. Most difficult for a partner is to decline the bid for increased affiliation without rejecting the bidder outright. Argyle and Dean's framework suggests that this might be accomplished by accepting one affiliation gesture, but reducing affiliation communicated in another channel so that total expressed affiliation does not change (e.g. allows hand to be held, but reduces intimacy of topic or reduces partner-directed gaze).

When an intimacy level is consistently expressed by both partners, stability reigns and communication between them feels and seems 'natural' and 'normal'. Atypical behaviour, especially if it is frequent and persistent, is taken as an attempt to reopen the negotiation process, which frequently occurs prior to one partner actually verbalizing his or her feelings. In other words, one acts out 'I love you' before saying it in order to make sure that the pronouncement will be greeted with the desired response and to minimize the risk of rejection (e.g. to have partner say 'I love you too' rather than yawn or laugh).

Affiliation: its communicative development   Which combination of affiliative behaviours will be seen as 'normal' will depend on the nature of the rela-

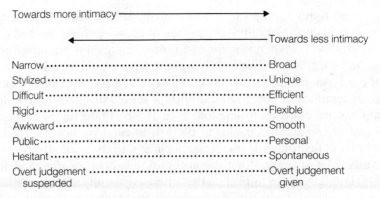

FIGURE 9.3   General dimensions of communication associated with relationship development (Knapp, 1983)

tionship (e.g. parent–child, lecturer–student) and the level of affiliation achieved. Knapp (1983) proposed eight dimensions along which communicative behaviours so vary (see Figure 9.3). He pointed out that behaviour along each dimension will move toward greater affiliation until an 'optimal level' is reached. At that point it will stabilize, but fluctuations (sometimes sizeable) will occur from time to time on one or several of the dimensions.

Knapp (1984) developed a communication model of relational development and deterioration composed of ten 'interaction stages', as depicted in figure 9.4. His premise is that movement from stranger to intimate is both accomplished and characterized by specific types of communication strategies. Movement is generally systematic and sequential, but it can be either forward or backward; and while it can occur within stages, it is always to a new 'place'. The model is depicted as a staircase, with 'terminating' as the bottom step and 'bonding' as the top. At any step, the relationship can be stabilized. For example, a relationship can reach the experimenting stage where partners are learning

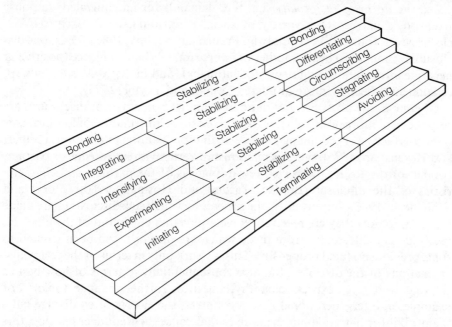

FIGURE 9.4 Staircase model of interaction stages (Knapp, 1984)

about each other and the 'fit' between them ('Do you like to sail? So do I!'), but may not progress beyond that. Such encounters can be happy and satisfying because the partners do not wish to increase the affiliation level. According to this model, a relationship that was at one time stabilized at the experimenting stage of interaction and then began to deteriorate would move laterally to stagnating – the negative side of this level of affiliation.

The notion that relational decline is simply the reverse of its development has been criticized by Baxter (1984, 1985) and Duck (1982). Indeed, Baxter (1983) presents data supporting her claim that breakup differs from buildup because of shared knowledge and the mutual history of the partners. But the import of

Knapp's model for our purposes is that it associates types of messages, or more generally communication strategies, with the level of affiliation characteristic of a relationship at any given time. And while Knapp sees a variety of verbal and non-verbal communicative behaviours (see e.g. Knapp, Ellis and Williams, 1980) contributing to maintenance or change, **self-disclosure** is clearly the most potent strategy available (Altman and Taylor, 1973; with respect to marital communication see Gottman and Levenson, in press).

Self-disclosure and positive affiliation Self-disclosure is the voluntary making available of information about one's self that would not ordinarily be accessible to the other at that moment. It typically consists of information verbally revealed by one person to another, but can also be information that one allows the other to learn, for example, by spending time with the other or permitting the other into a private place. It serves to escalate a relationship towards positive affiliation because of the operation of what Gouldner (1960) called the *norm of reciprocity* (i.e. the 'demand' for an equivalent response from one's partner to a variety of social behaviours, particularly self-disclosures: see Jourard, 1971; Ludwig, Franco and Malloy, 1986). Thus, one disclosure is thought to beget another of approximately equal valence (positive or negative information) and depth (of intimacy), and in this way, step by step, relationships become more intimate (Altman and Taylor, 1973).

Of course, the process is not quite this simple. Some type of disclosures are responded to more positively than others. Positive information of low intimacy is most effective in producing positive affiliation in initial interactions (Gilbert and Horenstein, 1975), but this relationship varies with knowledge or partner, content of disclosure, perceived rewardingness of the partner, and characteristics of the discloser (Bradac, Tardey and Hosman, 1980; Gilbert and Whiteneck, 1976). Importantly, the *process* by which self-disclosures are made is crucial to how they are received. Revelations that come 'out of the blue' are received very differently from those which are or which can be attributed to some previously stated propensity. This is so not only in terms of the recipients' evaluations of the discloser, but also consequentially in terms of how best to respond next (e.g. express empathy, question further, change topic). For example, in intergenerational first encounters, the elderly often divulge quite 'painful' information about themselves that cause their younger interlocutors some communicational difficulties (Coupland, Coupland, Giles and Wiemann, 1988; also Gilbert, 1977). People do vary in terms of their criteria for deciding when and how to disclose (Petronio, Martin and Littlefield, 1984) as well as the ability to induce their partners to 'open up' (Miller, Berg and Archer, 1983).

Further, valence and level of self-disclosure are judged appropriate in the context of the current state of the relationship. A potential relational partner would predictably be 'put off' by too intimate disclosures in an initial interaction because they also put great demand on the partner to reveal intimate information about him or herself. Indeed, Berger (1979; see also Berger and Calabrese, 1975) suggested that self-disclosure is often the next phase after biographical exchange of non-intimate information in pursuit of social knowledge about the other. Similarly, intimate positive revelations early on are usually seen as 'coming on too strong' or bragging, and thus deter relational development (Knapp, 1984). Self-disclosure is then a powerful tool in the affiliation negotiation process (Altman and Taylor, 1973).

Lies and deception: dangers to affiliation? In pursuit of affiliative goals, people also lie about their aspirations, intentions and credentials, as well as their group's capabilities, attributes and potential (see Bradac, Friedman and Giles, 1986; Ekman, 1985). They also evade difficult questions and keep secrets, although sometimes, of course, they must tell the truth. We as hearers often second-guess the lies, evasions and secrets of others (Hewes et al., 1985). As we have argued elsewhere, communication can sometimes be complex and exhausting work as we attempt to 'pull the wool over the ears of others' while debugging their messages at one and the same time (Giles and Wiemann, 1987).

Not all 'non-truths' are, of course, maliciously motivated. Camden, Motley and Wilson (1984) have provided a list of the types of social motivations underlying 'white lies' (see table 9.3). They collected their data by means of 'interpersonal communication diaries' in which respondents were asked to record instances over a couple of weeks when they believed *they* had been told white lies. To us, and despite the fact that these motives exude a sense of creating, maintaining or repairing a positive self-esteem, they nonetheless appear too 'socially agreeable'. Surely, many of us can recount instances when we or others have deceived or lied so as to be, for example, *tactless*, or have tried to create *instability* in a particular relationship (see Baxter, 1985)? Indeed Ragan and Hopper (1984), after an analysis of the way lovers are seen to *exit* from their relationships in novels, show that one partner often uses a 'suspension of the let-it-pass rule' (e.g. 'What do you mean by that? I haven't a clue as to what you're getting at!') so as to underscore strategically the apparent lack of mutual understanding that now exists between them. In other words, people can use communication subtly so as to achieve negative affiliation levels, and paradoxically, (as these authors claim) it takes coordination to accomplish 'consensus about dissensus'.

TABLE 9.3 Motives for 'white lies'

1   *Tact* to save the listener embarrassment: e.g. 'What a pretty skirt' (when it is ill-fitting)
2   *Relational stability* when the speaker wishes to avoid conflict: e.g. agreeing with listener's valued beliefs on the Falklands in order to maintain the friendship
3   *Psychological compensation* in order to present a favourable social image: e.g. 'Sorry, I can't join you tonight. I have so many other colleagues I've arranged to see already' (when you will be bored and alone all night!)

4   *Power deference* in order to avoid being made dependent on a controlling other:
     e.g. 'Sorry, I can't come to your office right now.
     There is an important scholar on the other line ringing from Venezuela' (when there's not)

Source: based on Camden, Motley and Wilson (1984)

Negative affiliation: personal versus social identities   But why did these kinds of more negative motives not surface in the Camden study? One answer may lie in the particular methodology used. Informants were asked to uncover *others'* lies to them personally, some of which may have escaped them entirely, and others of which may have produced misattributions. An equally plausible, if not more significant, answer might rest in the fact that the student diaries were 'interpersonal' and did not reflect the full range of self-presentation strategies, and attributions of these strategies. Following on from Tajfel and Turner (1979), much of our social lives is spent in *intergroup* encounters (which may be dyadic) between individuals from different socio-economic classes, age groups, occupational categories and so forth (see chapter 16). In such encounters our social group identities can be of supreme importance, and we then use language to create, maintain or bolster our sense of distinctive and valued ingroup identity (Giles, 1979). In other words, we communicate with each other not always as individuals with unique temperaments and personalities, but some-times as undifferentiated representatives of social groups (Giles and Johnson, 1981). Under these circumstances, it would seem that tactless lies and deception which 'put down' linguistically an outgroup and/or elevate an ingroup are rational choices for maintaining a favourable group identity. Much then of what is supposedly interpersonal communication is actually *intergroup* (Gudykunst, 1986). In this regard, group membership is not always self-evident; it is often a creative process in which linguistic 'work' must be done and group membership be displayed (Louw-Potgieter and Giles, in press). Moreover, intergroup communication can of course involve multiple cate-gories, as shown in Ting-Toomey's (1986) analysis of conflict between black male and white female interactants.

But given that communication features (e.g. dialect, jargon, slang, body movements) are very often valued dimensions of group identity, the desire for positive differentiation is likely to manifest itself along communicative dimen-sions (Giles, 1977). A compelling illustration of this, termed *ethnic affirma-tion*, is provided empirically by Yang and Bond (1980). They found that when 'forcing' Chinese bilingual students to complete a value survey in English rather than in Cantonese, respondents compensated for this by becoming more Chinese in their values in the former than in the latter condition.

When relations between social groups are cooperatively stable and inter-group stereotypes are complementarily positive (D. M. Taylor, 1981), then Gudykunst and Kim's (1984) so-called 'communicative distance of sensitivity' will obtain when dyadic interaction involves the two categories. Herein, speakers may attempt some form of **speech accommodation** to each other (Giles, 1984) in a manner not unlike that reported by Mulac et al. (1983) where males and females attenuated their distinctive linguistic styles from intra- to intergender encounters (see also Hogg, 1985). However, as relations between social categories become more conflictual, communicative patterns may be mediated by socio-linguistic stereotypes in an increasingly negative affiliative manner. Hence, Lukens's (1979) so-called communicative distances of 'indifference', 'avoidance' and 'disparagement' would be reflected in *speech* *divergence* (e.g. the accentuation of a Welsh speaker's accent, or even a shift into the Welsh language itself, when talking with an English person: see Bourhis and Giles, 1977), *behavioural confirmation* (e.g. the communicative tactic of inducing people, perhaps by asking 'impossible' questions, to act in a stereotype-consistent manner: see Word, Zanna and Cooper, 1974) and *verbal derogations* (or ethnophaulisms), respectively. Furthermore, we can add the 'distance of aggression' to this list to take into account situations where verbally aggressive acts are superseded by their physical counterparts (Hewstone and Giles, 1986).

Of course, the achievement of negative affiliation in dyads need not be so consciously fashioned in all cases. For instance, Schaap and Buunk (in press) have shown that a feature of unhappy married couples is the inability of husbands to recognize discontent or negative affect in their wives. As a consequence the latter feel neglected, misunderstood and uncared for, thereby prompting them into a verbalized expression of this unfortunate state of affairs. In turn husbands withdraw emotionally, inducing wives to get them involved again (Watzlawick, Beavin and Jackson, 1967). Such a destructive communication cycle is naturally enough the breeding ground of relational malcontent (Noller and Fitzpatrick, in press).

Summary   In this section we have shown how communication can serve affiliative functions at the relational (including both interpersonal and intergroup) level. Communication can be used craftily in building up relationships through patterns of appropriate self-disclosure. It is also an effective mechanism for maintaining harmony. Gottman (1982) argued that an important feature of happily marrieds is the ability of one partner to defuse communicationally negative affect once it has been expressed by the spouse. Whilst we have observed that communication functions in pursuit of positive and negative affiliation, we should emphasize that the latter need not always be psychologically debilitating as, for example, in its capacity to sustain group identity. Furthermore, it is possible that the communication of negative affiliation has actually very positive outcomes under certain circumstances.

The Goal: Communicative Competence

Throughout this chapter, we have presented an analysis of interpersonal communication from a functional perspective. These functions are general in that they are inevitable by-products of every message exchange. They are the vehicles people use to define, change and stabilize relationships. Our analysis illustrates how people get things done through communication; and how communication not only reflects our social world, but builds upon it and helps determine it (Giles and Wiemann, 1987). By focusing on relationships, we have attempted to call attention to the fact that the work of communication is a *joint* activity. But it is also important to keep in mind that individuals are separate from the several relationships and groups in which they are simultaneously involved. What is good for one relationship may have a negative impact on another or on the individual apart from relational considerations. People face the general communication problem of balancing competing demands for affiliation, and to control and to be controlled in a variety of relationships with finite interpersonal resources. They must use these resources to relate with their environment, including other people, by both adapting to the environment and attempting to adapt it to them. How do we understand and explain the success and failure of individuals as they attempt to cope with this difficult problem?

A theory of *communicative competence* (Wiemann, 1971; Wiemann and Kelly, 1981; Wiemann and Bradac, in press a, b) offers a framework for examining effective interpersonal communication. The position we adopt is *relational* and pragmatic. It is relational in that the primary level of analysis is that of interactants in relationships. Indeed, when we listen to a couple conversing we can form judgements not only about the individuals separately involved but also about the communicational style and language features used by them *as a pair* (Giles and Fitzpatrick, 1984). Our position is also pragmatic in that what communicators actually do and how they do it is the focus of analysis. Hence, communicative competence here is defined as the appropriate pragmatic use of social knowledge and social skill in the context of a relationship (Wiemann and Kelly, 1981).

This definition implies several characteristics of communicative competence. First, behaviour must be appropriate to the context in which it is displayed, the primary context usually (but not always) being the relationship of those present. In this latter respect, Giles and Fitzpatrick (1984) argued that a speaker could effect 'couple talk' even when separate from his or her partner. Here, couple identity can mediate individual linguistic choices through 'we'-related topics, references to 'our' activities, and an 'us' focus manifesting expressedly shared attitudes and couple (rather than self-) disclosures. Second, communicative competence for us means that both knowledge of communication rules and the skills to implement that knowledge are necessary for the ongoing achievement of a competent relationship.

Finally, a third feature of communicative competence is that it is in the relationship, not the individuals. Thus, we refer to *relationships* as competent – and *individuals* as socially skilled. This conceptualization challenges the 'disease' metaphor of interpersonal behaviour implied in much social science literature, wherein a person below some skill threshold is seen as inadequate (incompetent) and therefore not a particularly desirable relational partner. While a number of skills may enhance one's opportunity to enter into competent relationships (see for example Check, Perlman and Malamuth, 1985), it does not guarantee them. (Even the best, most skilled communicators have negative relational experiences.) Neither does a repertoire of relatively few skills preclude successful relationships. (Even the most unskilled interpersonal bumblers find people with whom they are congruent and form happy relationships.) Communicative competence does not refer to approaching perfection or achieving excellence. Rather, we feel communicative competence is doing well enough to preserve a relationship with a desired definition (Wiemann and

Bradac, in press b). In other words, it is being able to avoid relational traps and pitfalls and to repair damage when avoidance tactics fail.

Thus we have a model of interpersonal communicative competence that directs our scrutiny to individuals, with varying levels of communication-relevant knowledge and skill, interacting in the context of relationships which they create or achieve by their ongoing communication. Communication outcomes can only be fully understood at the *relational* level (whether between or among individuals or groups) and in terms of patterns of interlocking behaviours which serve to define the relationship as a specific type of system.

The primary dimensions along which competence is assessed by both participants and observers are control and affiliation levels. A relationship is seen as competent to the extent that the individuals who compose it are either (1) sufficiently satisfied with the control and affiliation definition they jointly create to maintain it, or (2) when dissatisfied, able and willing to work toward redefinition or termination of it. Individuals negotiate relational definitions by employing a variety of communication strategies and tactics along the lines suggested throughout this chapter. There is no implication that there are universal 'good' or 'moral' relational definitions that all should work towards in order to be considered competent. Note that under specification 1 above a long-term, hostile 'enemies' relationship is competent if both parties are satisfied with that relational definition and both are sufficiently attracted to it to remain in the relationship.

Summary and Conclusion

Our intent has been to highlight the *social dimension* of interpersonal communication in the main by discussing its relational character *within* the dyad and between groups. However, we should also be aware of the complementary need to look from *without*, in the sense that communication is embedded not only within a complex web of social networks (Duck and Miell, 1984; Milardo, 1982) but also in the wider milieu of various societal forces.

In this vein, Dryden and Giles (1986) focused their attention on doctor–patient communication which, as we saw from table 9.1, has tended to be a rather one-sided interview. These authors argued that the success of any current attempts to transform the consultation towards a more patient-centred negotiation (Tate, 1983) would be severely restricted if health-related images created in society were not congruent. They pointed out that the conversational imbalance existing in doctor–patient communication actually is in line with media portrayals of doctor–patient interactions. Added to this is the complementary image of the physician as someone who is high status, successful, and an omnipotent curer (that is, high in perceived control) whilst also honest, to be trusted, and kind-hearted (that is, high in positive affiliation). It would not be surprising to find physicians reluctant to alter this situation. Such social representations (see chapter 5) make it difficult to modify both physicians' communication strategies on the one hand and patients' on the other. Thus we need to invoke research not only in interpersonal but also in mass media communication (Hawkins, Wiemann and Pingree, in press).

Yet, with this in mind, it is surprising that mainstream social psychology has not embraced communication phenomena and processes more enthusiastically, given (1) the discipline's heavy focus upon language issues in its early days (Farr, 1980a); (2) current media pleas for people to get down and discuss their problems; (3) the crucial roles of communication in 'life and death' issues as outlined at the outset of this chapter; and (4) the fact that much of our social behaviour is manifest linguistically. Communication research does at last appear to be moving from the periphery to the core of the subject. Indeed, recent analyses of dissonance (M. Burgoon, 1983), equity (Winterhoff-Spurk, Hermann and Weinrich, 1985) and attribution (Antaki, 1981) all point to the inevitable fact that social-psychological processes cannot be fully understood without paying attention to communication. After all, as Blakar (1985) and others have argued, individuals, organizations and societies would not function without interpersonal communication.

Glossary Terms

Affiliative messages	Metacommunication
Communication	Paralinguistics
Communicative competence	Prosodics
Communicative control	Self-disclosure
Kinesics	Speech accommodation

Further Reading

Berger, C. R. and Bradac, J. J. (1982) *Language and Social Knowledge*. London: Edward Arnold. This is a comprehensive, readable summary of social science literature on the role that language plays in initiating, maintaining and terminating social relationships.

Giles, H. and Powesland, P. F. (1975) *Speech Style and Social Evaluation*. London: Academic Press. An integrative overview of how speech style influences the judgements we make about other people.

Knapp, M. L. (1984) *Interpersonal Communication and Human Relationships*. Boston: Allyn and Bacon. An introduction to the role interpersonal communication plays in social relationships, integrating a variety of communication and social-psychological perspectives into a coherent view of day-to-day experience.

Knapp, M. L. and Miller, G. R. (eds) (1985) *The Handbook of Interpersonal Communication*. Beverly Hills: Sage. An invaluable sourcebook for those with particular interests in certain communication phenomena and processes and/or for those students requiring an in-depth knowledge of the area.

McLaughlin, M. L. (1984) *Conversation: how talk is organized*. Beverly Hills: Sage. A well-written, comprehensive synthesis of various approaches to analysing and understanding conversation as a communicative event.

Noller, P. and Fitzpatrick, M.A. (eds) (1988) *Marital Interaction*. Clevedon: Multi-lingual Matters. A theoretically integrated volume of empirical research concerned with communication in marriage.

Watzlawick, P., Beavin, J. and Jackson, D. D. (1967) *Pragmatics of Human Communication*. New York: Norton. This is one of the most influential books on interpersonal communication available, presenting a pragmatic analysis of communication.

Wiemann, J. M. and Harrison, R. P. (eds) (1983) *Nonverbal Interaction*. Newbury Park, Calif.: Sage. A collection of research reviews and summaries of several central concepts of non-verbal communication.

10 Social Relationships

MICHAEL ARGYLE

Introduction

Most social behaviour takes place between people who are in some kind of personal relationship – couples, friends, kin, workmates, neighbours – or in a professional relationship such as that between doctor and patient. Most people who seek help or training for their social behaviour want help with their relationships.

Social psychology until recently dealt with friendship and interpersonal attraction, while sociologists studied marriage and the family, and developmental psychologists were concerned with parents and children. 'Social relationships' has now emerged as a more unified field. It is primarily a branch of social psychology, with its own journals, conferences and handbooks. While a large part of the work in the subject has been carried out in the USA, much of the initiative for integrating and developing the field has come from Britain (e.g. Duck, 1982, 1984; Duck and Gilmour, 1981; Hinde, 1979) and the main journal is British – the *Journal of Social and Personal Relationships*.

The research methods which have been used are a little different from those in other branches of social psychology, though the same principles are involved (see chapter 4). The measurement of aspects of relationships can be achieved by objective or subjective methods. Behavioural data have the advantage of greater objectivity, but are usually limited to small and atypical samples of behaviour. For example, sequences of interaction between married couples, together with physiological measures, have been recorded in the laboratory (Gottman, 1979). Observations have been made of children in playgrounds or in school and between mothers and children, but the problem of sampling remains. A valuable objective technique is setting couples a communication task, such as sending messages where the words are ambiguous, to indicate which meaning is intended (Noller, 1984). An important innovation was the use

I am indebted to David Clarke, Steve Duck, Robert Hinde and the editors for their comments on this chapter.

of diary methods, which provide reports by subjects of all interactions over a period (Wheeler, Reis and Nezlek, 1983). Another way is to telephone subjects on successive days, or to 'bleep' them to fill in self-report scales. However, most research on relationships has used questionnaires, rating scales, or other self-report devices, usually combined with **factor analysis** or similar procedures. These have been used to assess satisfaction with relationships, conflict, closeness, emotions, conceptions of relationships, rules and reported activities. Self-report methods are the only way of finding out about most of these things, but are open to the familiar sources of bias. For example, more couples claim to be very happily married than seems likely in view of the high divorce rate.

A number of different research designs have been used. Laboratory and field experiments were used in the earlier interpersonal attraction research, to study the effects of similarity, proximity, reinforcement, physical attractiveness and so on (Duck, 1973). Byrne (1971) showed subjects the supposed attitudes of target persons, manipulating the similarity to their own. However, since psychologists became interested in relationships closer than the very early stages of friendship and love, experiments have been abandoned – though other kinds of laboratory research are still done, for example comparing interaction in happy and disturbed marriages. Relationship research for some time has used statistical comparisons of various kinds, either comparing groups or making internal statistical analyses. These have been used for example to study the formation and decline of relationships, and to analyse the causal factors involved; to investigate the role of personality variables, e.g. similarity; to study the effects of relationships on health and other aspects of well-being; and to compare the features of different relationships, like work, marriage and friendship. There are considerable problems in unravelling the direction of causation in this kind of research, and increasing use is made of designs in which data are collected at different points of time, such as **path analysis**.

Theories of Relationships

As with other areas in social psychology, more than one level of theory is needed, from biology to sociology, and no one theory is sufficient to explain the phenomena.

Biological

Insects and other lower animals have completely unlearned sets of relationships, which ensure survival of the group: it is necessary to mate, rear infants, cooperate in groups, and establish leadership hierarchies. In higher mammals, such as non-human primates, early experience plays a role, and those reared in isolation form much weaker relationships. In humans such innate factors play an important though diminished part, for example in producing gender differences in relationships (see chapter 2). An important application of evolutionary theories to relationships (**socio-biology**) has been the suggestion that parental, sibling and other kin relationships acquire their special strength from a biological urge to help the genes survive, and hence to look after those with shared genes (Alexander, 1979). Research on kidney donors shows that indeed people will do this for close kin, though not quite at the predicted rates – 86 per cent for children, 67 per cent for parents, and 50 per cent for siblings (Fellner and Marshall, 1981). Social institutions, like the family, are perpetuated because they provide for satisfaction of biological needs and survival of the species, but they can take a variety of forms.

Reinforcement and need satisfaction

Many experiments on interpersonal attraction have shown that people like others who are rewarding in some way, or even people who are present when the experimenter gives rewards (Clore, 1977). There is no agreed list of social motivations which can act as rewards, but these have been shown to include love or attraction, sex, respect or status, information including validation of opinions, tangible help, money or goods (Foa and Foa, 1975b). However, these 'social needs' do not operate in quite the same way as biological ones; for example deprivation does not always increase their strength (Hinde, 1979). Reinforcement has definite limits as a source of relationships:

1 Kinship bonds do not decay much with time, and have not been shown to depend on reinforcement (Hill, 1970).
2 In close relationships there is concern for the other, and it may be rewarding to see the other person rewarded.
3 There may be a concern for equity of rewards as well as for own outcomes (Kelley and Thibaut, 1978).

Exchange theories

These theories are further developments of reinforcement theory. They offer an economic model of relationships: it is supposed that each person tries to maximize his or her rewards and minimize the costs, and is attracted to a relationship accordingly (Chadwick-Jones, 1976). Reciprocity of rewards is expected. The Thibaut and Kelley version (1959) proposed the construction of payoff matrices (see chapter 13), showing the payoffs for each person resulting from each combination of their possible social acts. The couple become inter-dependent, since each person's outcomes depend on the joint behaviour of both. Thibaut and Kelley argued that people will stay in a relationship only if the payoff is greater than that which had been received in past relationships or could be obtained in alternative relationships available. One person can have power in the sense of being able to control another's outcomes, or via this to control his behaviour. This theory has led mainly to very artificial experiments, using techniques like the prisoner's dilemma game. Research on real-life relationships has been hampered by the difficulty of scaling rewards, but the

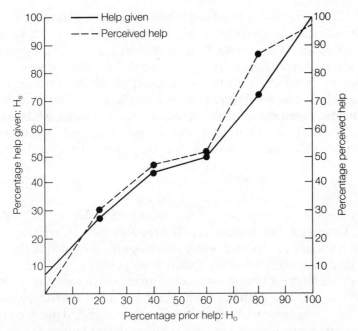

FIGURE 10.1 Amount of reciprocated help and degree of perceived help as a function of degree of prior help (Wilke and Lanzetta, 1970)

theory has nevertheless inspired a lot of research into marriage and other relationships (Burgess and Huston, 1979). A less artificial experiment was carried out by Wilke and Lanzetta (1970). Subjects played a business game, so that subjects believed that they had been helped in different percentages of the trials in the first part; later when the other needed help this was reciprocated at nearly the same rate at which help had been received (see figure 10.1).

However, reciprocity does not always occur. O' Connell (1984) studied 108 people who had been helped in building a house: 69 per cent gave no reciprocation to friends and 74 per cent gave no reciprocation to kin. On the other hand, people are reluctant to ask for help which cannot be reciprocated; those who are unable to return help suffer a loss of self-esteem.

A common criticism of **social exchange theory** is that in many relationships people do not appear to be trying to maximize their gains at the expense of others. We have seen that socio-biologists have suggested that concern for close kin depends on quite different processes. Clark and Mills (1979) argued that in close or 'communal' relationships positive acts such as gifts should not be linked to any reciprocity so that they can be seen as altruistic signs of love. It is only unhappily married couples who think in terms of exchange of rewards (Murstein, MacDonald and Cerreto, 1977). Later developments of exchange theory have taken account of altruistic and empathic concern for the other by accepting that some weighting of the payoffs of the other is common (Kelley and Thibaut, 1978). A serious problem with experimental games in this tradition is that moves are made independently and simultaneously, i.e. without interaction. Later versions of exchange theory recognize that there is a sequential pattern of interaction in relationships, that the payoffs arise from this, and that it is in this way that the pair become interdependent (Kelley et al., 1983).

The analysis of relationships from the 'social skill' point of view is similar: interactors try to achieve a pattern of interaction which meets their various needs, and which also synchronizes in such respects as intimacy, dominance, emotional tone, speed and the detailed sequence of social acts, while also taking account of the other's point of view. People with inadequate social skills have difficulty in establishing and maintaining relationships (Argyle, 1969, 1983).

Equity and fairness

Exchange theories usually include a concern with fairness in some way. Hatfield, Utne and Traupmann (1979) proposed that in relationships and groups people want to receive rewards which are proportional to their inputs; the latter could include hard work, ability, beauty, kindness and so on. If there is inequity people will be discontented and more likely to leave the relationship. These authors obtained evidence from recently married American couples for the hypothesis that those with equal benefit will be satisfied most, overbenefit second, underbenefit lowest. Hatfield, Utne and Traupmann (1979) asked a random sample of newly-weds to report on their marital happiness, and also to rate how far they felt that they were receiving too much or too little in relation to what they put into the marriage. It can be seen that those who thought they were underbenefiting were less happy, but so (to a lesser extent) were those who were overbenefiting (figure 10.2).

Equity theory has received quite a lot of support from American studies of dating and married couples, though it seems to work better for females than for males, as can be seen in figure 10.2. Murstein, MacDonald and Cerreto (1977), however, found that concern with exchange or equity is negatively correlated with marital adjustment. And Lujansky and Mikula (1983) in Austria found no effects of equity at all on either strength or duration of romantic relationships. It is possible that there are cultural differences here. During the 1970s European students, in experimental games, preferred an *equal* distribution of rewards, while American students preferred *equity* – a constant ratio of rewards to inputs (Gergen, Morse and Gergen, 1980). As with exchange theory a more general objection is that in close relationships people do not think in terms of rewards or costs at all – until they start to be dissatisfied with the relationship.

Cognitive theories

These theories are concerned with how one person interprets the behaviour of another, or how he or she combines different features of the situation to make a judgement (see chapter 5). Balance theory, and other consistency theories, were concerned with liking as a function of, for example, consistency between P's and O's opinions or beliefs – though the effects of similarity can be explained

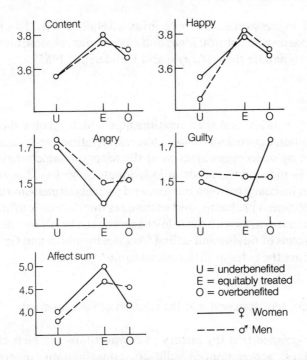

FIGURE 10.2   The affect variables of contented, happy, angry and guilty and the Austin total mood measure as a function of the perceived equity–inequity in the marriage (Hatfield, Utne and Traupmann, 1979)

in other ways (Berscheid, 1985). The most influential cognitive theory in recent research has been attribution theory (see chapter 6). It has been found that when couples are in conflict they tend to blame each other, and to attribute the other's behaviour to personal characteristics like selfishness (Orvis, Kelley and Butler, 1976). After the breakdown of a marriage people spend a lot of time thinking about it, to work out an explanation, partly to protect themselves from acknowledgement of failure (Harvey et al., 1982).

Effects of socialization and culture

Like all other aspects of social behaviour, relationships are affected by socialization via imitation, modelling and the rest. In addition attachment to parents and siblings is probably established during an early sensitive period, and these attachments are found to be necessary for later close attachments. The formation of this powerful affectional bond is important for parent–child relationships, and probably also for siblings and marriage; it does not appear to be based on reinforcement (Bowlby, 1969). Another effect of socialization is that the behaviour of lovers mimics that between mothers and infants. The reason that women form closer attachments than men to friends and kin may be that mothers form closer and more protective bonds with daughters. Females are more emotionally expressive than males, and there is evidence that mothers discourage such expressiveness in male infants (Hall, 1984). The family is the medium for passing on cultural ideas and rules about relationships, and teaching the skills to handle them (Argyle and Henderson, 1985).

Social systems

A number of theories deal with relationships which involve more than two people – families, networks or whole cultures. Relationship systems have often been analysed by sociologists in terms of the functions which they are believed to serve, i.e. in meeting the needs of individuals or society, for example rules which prevent intimacy between doctors and patients. Rules can be regarded as solutions to common problems, and sometimes there are only a limited number of logical alternatives, as with the rule of keeping to the left (or the right) of the road, and systems of buying and selling (Argyle, Furnham and Graham, 1981). We shall discuss the rules of different relationships later.

The Formation, Maintenance and Dissolution of Relationships

It has been suggested that the history of relationships can be usefully divided into five stages: acquaintance, build-up, consolidation, deterioration and ending (Levinger, 1983). This pattern fits friendship and love; kin, neighbours and workmates are different, though they too may go through phases of build-up and deterioration. We will deal with the processes involved in acquaintance and build-up first.

Acquaintance

Physical attractiveness   This can be measured by averaging ratings of judges on seven-point scales. Attractive students have more dates: physical attractiveness correlates 0.61 with frequency of dates for females, 0.25 for males (Berscheid et al., 1971), and affects friendship choices as well. Interestingly, although one might think that physical attractiveness operates primarily at an early stage of relationships (as a kind of filter: see Stroebe et al., 1971), there is ample evidence that the correlation in levels of physical attractiveness is higher for married than for dating couples (Murstein and Christy, 1976). Attractive girls have been found to receive higher grades in American university classes (Singer, 1964), and to be judged less guilty in simulated trials. They are more likely to be offered jobs, and to be given help. Part of the explanation lies in the 'physical attractiveness stereotype' – the widely held belief that attractive people are also warm, kind, interesting, strong, sociable and altruistic (Dion, Berscheid and Walster, 1972). The basic process may be that attractive people seem to be in good health, and so perhaps are seen as biologically sound.

Frequency of interaction   It is necessary to meet the other person, typically at work, in the neighbourhood or at a club. Physical proximity and frequency of interaction have been found to lead to choice of friends, as was found by Festinger, Schachter and Back (1950) in a student housing estate. However, frequent interaction can also produce more disliking for a minority, i.e. relationships are more polarized (Warr, 1965). And proximity does not make many neighbours into friends, probably because they are not similar enough in age, status or outlook.

Similarity   In friendship and love we prefer people who are similar to ourselves in certain respects. Field experiments have shown that people with similar attitudes, beliefs and values are more likely to become friends. Lea and Duck (1982) found that friends are particularly likely to share values which are important to them, and which are also uncommon.

We prefer people with similar interests, and who are of similar age and social background. However, in the field of personality, similarity has no effect; most people like those who are attractive, rewarding etc. It was believed for a time that the possession of complementary needs or traits was a source of friendship, e.g. dominant–submissive, but this has not been confirmed (Kelley et al., 1983).

There are several possible explanations for the effects of similarity. Similarity of values gives social support for one's views, or can be interpreted in terms of balance theory. Similarity of other kinds makes for easier and more rewarding interaction (Berscheid, 1985).

The importance of frequency of interaction and similarity explains why most friends are chosen from work or from leisure settings, like sports, church and other organizations.

Reinforcement   There is no doubt that reinforcement leads to liking; the more important question is whether this is the only process involved. Jennings (1950) found that the popular girls in a reformatory were the ones who helped and protected others, encouraged and cheered them up, made them feel accepted and wanted, and were concerned with the feelings and needs of others. Later experiments have shown that experimental confederates who agree, or smile, are liked more than those who disagree or frown. Evidence of liking by such non-verbal signals as smiling and looking is particularly effective (Argyle, 1988). So is a shift from a negative to a positive attitude – the 'gain–loss' effect. These findings have been incorporated successfully into social skills training, for example increasing rewardingness in marital therapy, and teaching positive non-verbal signals to social isolates (Argyle, 1983).

Build-up and consolidation

The growth of involvement   As a relationship deepens, two people see more of each other, do and talk about more personal things together, and become increasingly committed to the relationship. The frequency of interaction may increase, by dint of having lunch twice a week, playing squash, sharing accommodation, going on holidays together. The conversation changes by both talking more and about more intimate matters at a deeper level of **self-disclosure** (Jourard, 1971). The latter involves risk and trusting the other to keep confidences; it is normally reciprocated. However, self-disclosure is done with care and strategically. Miell (1984) found that close friends disclosed more than acquaintances on certain topics like their own personality. Argyle, Trimboli and Forgas (in press) found interesting peaks and troughs, e.g. students told parents a lot about money and success, but very little about sex or love.

There is a growth of *commitment*, the intention to continue the relationship. Rusbult (1980) postulated that commitment depends on the amount of time, effort, money or other resources which have been put into a relationship, including shared property and children. It has been found that commitment is affected more by 'investment' (in all these senses) than by rewards (Lund, 1985). For exchange theory commitment depends on such matters as the committing of irretrievable resources, the comparative rewards and costs of alternative relationships, and the costs of the changeover (Kelley et al., 1983). It has been found that outcomes in relation to alternatives, but not equity, predicted commitment in dating (Michaels, Acock and Edwards, 1986). Hinde (1979) suggested that commitment also depends on public pledges such as the marriage ceremony, and private pledges of friendship. A further source of commitment is a shared social network. This is probably one reason for the stability of arranged marriages; the two families are already linked in the network.

Trajectories   Relationships increase in strength, on such variables as frequency of interaction, self-disclosure, sexual intimacy (in some cases), positive affect, and perceived probability of marriage. Trajectories vary in shape: they may level off at a fairly non-intimate level, which would be expected for many work relationships or with neighbours, for example. **Cluster analysis** has been used to classify these trajectories into different shapes. Huston et al. (1981) found four different trajectories from love to marriage, as shown in figure 10.3. Sometimes there are stepwise increases in the path of love – with first sexual intercourse, engagement, marriage, or just the decision to meet once a week, for example.

Decline and breakdown

Many relationships diminish in closeness, and many dissolve entirely. Decline follows the trajectory of growth in reverse: reduced frequency of contact, affection, self-disclosure and so on.

In all relationships there is some degree of conflict. Decline of relationships is due to an increase in conflict in relation to rewards, or the availability of more attractive alternatives. Different strategies of disengagement are used. Older people use more indirect strategies such as gradual withdrawal, while younger people often use direct confrontation. They use more or less deception to avoid embarrassing or hurting the other (Baxter, 1985).

Disengagement varies with the type of relationship. Work relationships may

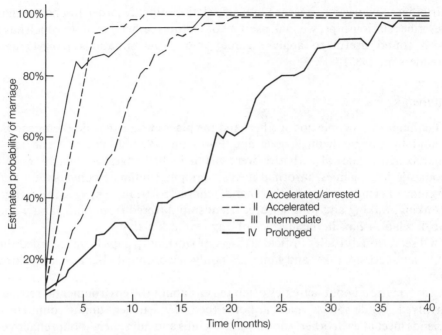

FIGURE 10.3   Four different trajectories to marriage (Huston et al., 1981)

decline or become hostile, but the relationship is often maintained. The same applies to kin, though the frequency of contact may decline. Friendships often decline and dissolve, though friendships formed at school and college can be very longlasting. The main cause of decline here is geographical separation; another is the breaking of friendship rules, of rewardingness, keeping confidence, standing up for each other, and being jealous of other relationships (Argyle and Henderson, 1984).

Couples who have love affairs or live together often break up (perhaps at the end of the college year) because they are bored with the relationship, or have different interests or background (Hill, Rubin and Peplau, 1976). The breakup of marriage is extremely distressing, often resulting in depression and other forms of illness. As we shall see there is usually a high level of conflict in marriage, and a couple may not have the skills for resolving conflicts peacefully. Typical problems are money, unfaithfulness, in-laws and drink. Minor irritations escalate, and blame is attributed to the other. There is often a precipitating event, such as violence, drunkenness or infidelity. This is followed by a period of separation, which may become permanent (Argyle and Henderson, 1985).

The Components of Relationships

So far this chapter has taken a fairly one-dimensional view of relationships, as if they were all degrees of friendship and love. We shall see that there are great differences between different kinds of relationships. In order to analyse and describe relationships, we shall use a set of features rather like those which have been found useful to analyse games and social situations (Argyle and Henderson, 1985).

Activities

The things that people do together, and the places where they do them, can be found by asking them. Argyle and Furnham (1982) found that the most characteristic marital activities were being in bed together, watching TV, domestic jobs, games, informal meals, shopping, intimate conversation and arguing. Friends, on the other hand, characteristically engaged in eating, drinking, talking and joint leisure; friendship differed from both family and work relationships in the absence of any real task activity.

Observational studies in field settings of working groups have recorded the amount of gossip, jokes and games, not only in workbreaks but also in working time.

Information about activities often tells us about the environmental settings involved. While spouses meet at home (bed, TV, kitchen, dining room etc.), friends meet at each other's homes and in clubs and pubs, neighbours chat over the garden fence, and so on.

Goals and conflicts

The motivational basis of relationships can be explored by analysing the goals and satisfactions achieved, and the conflicts. For example in marriage there is a lot of satisfaction and there are a lot of rows; these are two partly independent dimensions of marital satisfaction (Snyder and Regis, 1982). Argyle and Furnham (1983) asked subjects to rate their degree of satisfaction with a number of relationships on 15 satisfaction scales. Factor analysis of these scales produced three orthogonal factors.

I   Material and instrumental help
II   Social and emotional support
III Common interests

The average scores for each relationship on these three dimensions of satisfaction are shown in figure 10.4. It can be seen that the spouse is the greatest source of satisfaction, especially for factor I.

The amount of conflict or negative affect in a relationship is fairly independent of the level of positive satisfaction. Argyle and Furnham (1983) found that the spouse is the greatest source of both satisfaction and conflict; the work superior, on the other hand, is typically a major source of conflict but a low source of reward. Neighbours are low on both.

Overall satisfaction is a joint product of rewards and conflicts. In one study it was found that marital satisfaction could be predicted from frequency of

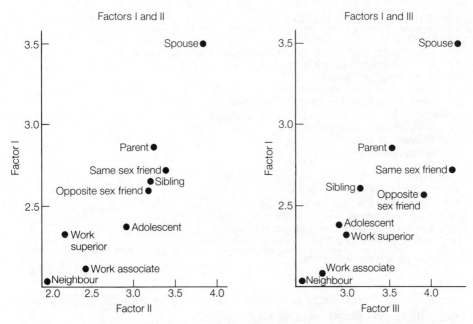

FIGURE 10.4   Relationships plotted on the satisfaction dimensions. Factor I: material and instrumental help. Factor II: social and emotional support. Factor III: common interests (Argyle and Furnham, 1983)

intercourse minus frequency of rows (defined as one partner storming out of the room) (Howard and Dawes, 1976).

Rules

Spouses, children, neighbours and people in professional relationships are ruled by laws; those in work relations are ruled by contracts. In addition there are many widely endorsed but informal rules – behaviour which it is believed ought or ought not to be performed in each relationship. Argyle, Henderson and Furnham (1985) carried out pilot interviews to obtain a pool of informal rules; there were 33 rules which might apply to any relationship, and up to 12 more for each of 22 relationships. Samples of 60 adult subjects rated the importance of each rule for each relationship. For each there were a number of rules which it was agreed were important. Some rules were very general and applied to nearly all relationships, e.g. 'should respect the other's privacy', and 'should keep confidences'. There was a major division between the rules for family, friends and other close relationships and those for neighbours, workmates and other less close relationships. Rules for the first group emphasized maintaining intimacy; those in the second group emphasized avoiding it.

In order to test whether these rules were of any importance in practice we studied a sample of broken friendships. It was found that the lapse of friendship was attributed in many cases to the breaking of certain rules, especially rules of rewardingness and rules about relations with third parties, e.g. not

TABLE 10.1   Rules and friendship

Exchange
13   Seek to repay debts, favours or compliments, no matter how small
17   Share news of success with the other
20   Show emotional support
25   Volunteer help in time of need
27   Strive to make him/her happy while in each other's company
Intimacy
24   Trust and confide in each other
Coordination
18   Respect privacy
21   Don't nag
Third party
10   Don't criticize other in public
11   Stand up for the other person in their absence
12   Keep confidences
23   Be tolerant of each other's friends
26   Don't be jealous or critical of other relationships

Source: Argyle and Henderson (1984)

being jealous, and keeping confidences. The rules for friendship in Britain fell into the clusters shown in table 10.1.

The study was replicated in Hong Kong, Italy and Japan, and a number of predictions were confirmed. For example in the East there was more endorsement for rules of obedience to superiors, for avoiding loss of face, for preserving harmony in groups, and for restraining emotional expression (Argyle et al., 1986).

Jealousy commonly ensues when the other partner in a heterosexual relationship becomes involved with a third party. Some people are more jealous than others, e.g. those with low self-esteem. Jealousy is greater when dependency is high, when the third party is disliked, and if the situation is attributed to deficiencies in the original relationship (Bringle and Buunk, 1985).

Skills

How to establish, maintain, and arrive at successful outcomes in relationships is partly described by the kind of rules which have just been considered. As with sport there is more to it than following the rules; skill at performance is needed too. For example to establish a new relationship like friendship involves the successful negotiation of several stages. The skills needed include gradual and reciprocated self-disclosure, arranging special occasions for meetings, and being sufficiently rewarding to the other. In order to maintain a relationship it is necessary both to keep up the level of rewards, and to avoid or deal with the common sources of conflict. In marriage, where there is a great deal of conflict, skill is needed at negotiating points of disagreement, and in diverting interaction sequences which have led to conflict in the past. In work relationships it is found that certain styles of handling people result in greater productivity, or other indices of effectiveness. The most successful supervisors of working groups for example are those who use initiating structure, consideration and the democratic-persuasive style (see chapter 14).

There are various forms of social skills training (SST) for relationships. Traditional SST often includes training in making friends, or performing better in work relationships (Argyle, 1983). There are several kinds of marital therapy, such as the American behavioural marital therapy with its emphasis on increasing rewards, clearer communication and negotiating contracts (Jacobson and Margolin, 1979). Training for relationships could well include several other components: (1) learning improved interactional skills, including verbal and non-verbal communication, and handling interaction sequences like negotiating disagreements; (2) learning the facts of life about relationships and correcting mistaken ideas; and (3) learning the informal rules of relationships (Argyle and Henderson, 1985).

Concepts and beliefs

A number of investigators have studied ideas about relationships; for example, they have asked people to rate the properties of friendship. There is convergence in finding the following properties; authenticity, affection, confiding, help, trust, companionship, self-respect and conflict (Davis and Todd, 1982). Love, on the other hand, is characterized by needing the other, caring for the other, and possessiveness (Rubin, 1973). It is possible to study the perceived similarities and differences between relationships. Wish, Deutsch and Kaplan (1976) found four perceived dimensions by using **multidimensional scaling**: equal versus unequal; cooperative and friendly versus competitive and hostile; socio-emotional and informal versus task oriented and formal; and superficial versus intense. The first two dimensions are shown in figure 10.5. This is quite strong evidence that there is more than one dimension, i.e. that of closeness, to relationships.

The ideas that people have of relationships are partly due to the mass media, and many investigations have been made of how relationships are represented or misrepresented in TV soap operas and advertisements (Livingstone, in press).

Socially inadequate and isolated adolescents have been found to have concepts of friendship like those of young children – focusing on benefits to self but lacking the ideas of commitment and loyalty (La Gaipa and Wood, 1981).

Power and roles

By power is meant the capacity to influence another's behaviour, and it can be assessed by observation or self-reports. In many relationships there are power differences; these are institutionalized as part of certain relationships, e.g. superiors and subordinates at work, and parents and children. The sources of power are the ability to reward or to punish, the possession of valued characteristics, the possession of expertise and the possession of skills of social influence – the use of skilled verbal utterances and the appropriate non-verbal signals (Argyle, 1983). However, in family studies little correlation has been found between influence over decisions and features of interaction like talking time or interruptions.

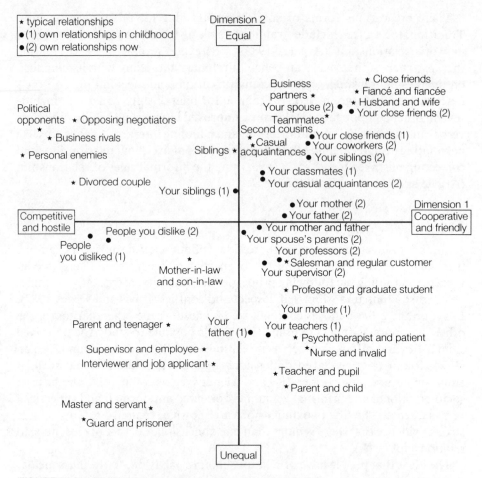

FIGURE 10.5   The first two dimensions of relationships (Wish, Deutsch and Kaplan, 1976)

For a long time, and in most cultures, wives had an 'expressive' and nurturant role inside the home, while husbands had an 'instrumental' role in finding food, earning money, building houses and dealing with the world outside. Pressure from women is causing these roles to change in three ways: more women have jobs, and sometimes have better jobs than their husbands; they have more equal power; and they do less of the housework than before, though they still do most of it.

Power relations between parents and their children keep changing as the children grow up (Huston, 1983). There are other role relationships defining the nature of different kin relations, for example, on dimensions other than power, in defining the relationships between siblings, cousins, in-laws and others (Argyle and Henderson, 1985).

The Distinctive Properties of Some Relationships

Marriage

This is the most intimate relationship, and on all indices of closeness there is a large gap between marriage and other relationships. Spouses do a great deal together: they cooperate over running the home and rearing children, in joint leisure, intimate talk, help and sex. As a result there is a high level of satisfaction; there is also a high level of conflict, but overall the benefits to health and happiness are very great. There is a high level of investment of time and money (in joint property and children), leading to a high level of commitment, and to distress in marital breakdown. However, marital satisfaction varies a lot with stage in the family life cycle; it is quite low when the children are very young, and even lower when they are adolescents (figure 10.6).

There are different ways of being married, and a well-based typology is that by Fitzpatrick (1984). This distinguished between 'traditionals', who have a lot of sharing and companionship; 'independents', who have a lot of companionship but believe in individual freedom and have most conflicts; and 'separates', who avoid conflict by having less companionship.

Friendship

Friendship differs from marriage primarily in being less close; there is usually no sex and no cohabitation. There is another difference: friends spend their time together eating, drinking, talking and in joint leisure, and there is little or no work or joint responsibility. Friends choose each other because they have shared interests and enjoy each other's company. They are a source of a great deal of fun and joy, but a smaller source of serious help. Bleeping studies (see the first section of the chapter) show that people experience the greatest level of joy when with friends (Larson, 1984). While friendship is with individuals, friends are part of larger networks which have to be handled with skill. Friendship is the most important relationship for young people before they are married. Friendships can lapse without much formality or distress, and often do.

Workmates

People are brought together by the working organization, but the relationship may strengthen and develop into friendship or deteriorate into hostility. Work relationships are stronger if the work brings people together physically, if they are cooperating on a joint task, if they have equal status, if they share a wage incentive, and if one helps the other. Work relationships are weaker if the reverse of these conditions operates, e.g. if one is inspecting the other's work, or if they are on opposite sides in some way. Often work relations are much more complex than this, and contain both positive and negative elements.

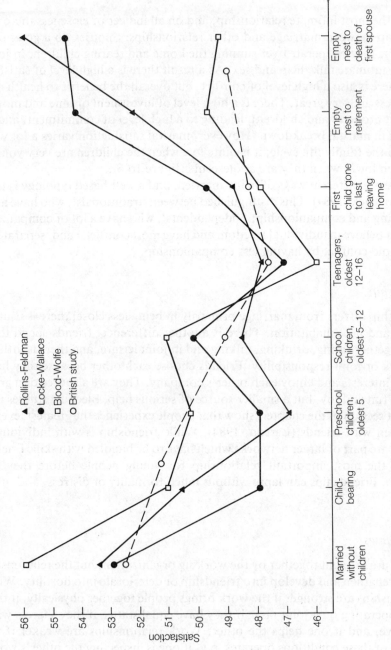

FIGURE 10.6 Marital satisfaction at different stages of family life: results of four studies (Walker, 1977)

Some studies have found that work relationships are weak and superficial compared with friendship or kin. For example, Kayser, Schwinger and Cohen (1984) found that in work relationships people expect to receive money and goods, while in love and friendship they expect to receive affection and esteem (figure 10.7). However, working relationships can often lead to friendship, and many friendships are drawn from work. People at work develop informal relationships, especially over coffee, lunch or other breaks, with a lot of gossip, jokes, games and other fun. The cooperative relationships so formed may feed back into cooperation over the work proper, and into friendship outside (Homans, 1950).

Kin

The main kin outside the nuclear family are parents, grown-up children, and siblings. These relationships are similar in intimacy to friends, but are otherwise totally different. There is a strong positive bond, which hardly changes with time. It may be based on selfish gene processes, or early attachment, or both. Frequency of contact, shared interests and proximity are usually much less than for friends (except for some working-class people who live near their kin). There is little shared leisure, but more help with money, shopping, baby-sitting, and on occasions of serious need; there are regular meetings, just to be together and share the family news, especially at Christmas and other anniversaries.

The Effects of Relationships

One reason for the growth of interest in relationships is the finding that relationships often produce great benefits for happiness and for mental and physical health – though they can also cause distress.

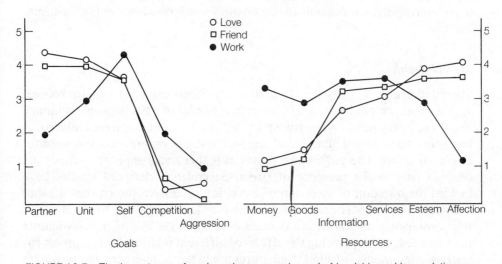

FIGURE 10.7   The importance of goals and resources in work, friendship and love relationships (Kayser, Schwinger and Cohen, 1984)

TABLE 10.2   Happiness of the married, single and divorced

	Percentage 'very happy'	
	Men	Women
Married	35.0	41.5
Single	18.5	25.5
Divorced	18.5	15.5

Source: Veroff, Douvan and Kulka (1981)

Happiness

There are many findings to the effect that those who are married, have friends and so on are happier. There is more limited evidence about the direction of causation: gaining a relationship is joyful, losing one is distressing, and experimental encouragement to strengthen them has positive effects (Reich and Zautra, 1981). Marriage provides the greatest satisfaction, as we saw earlier (figure 10.4). Married people are happier than the unmarried of the same age, especially for men, and especially when the partners have a close relationship (see table 10.2). Friendship is an independent source of happiness, especially for the young and old, and is a major source of positive moods.

In every case the quality of the relationship is important. However, the process involved is less clear. It is not known whether these benefits are due to the innate power of smiles and gazes to activate the pleasure centres, or to the benefits of self-esteem, the need to be loved, a need for companionship, or some other process. Other sources of satisfaction include material help, information and advice, which may come from spouse, kin, friends, work superiors or others. Another source of satisfaction is doing things together – playing games, working together, sharing domestic life together. It seems likely that it is the regularity and predictability of contact between, for example, spouses, kin and close friends, which makes these relationships particularly satisfying; it is possible to rely on the rewards obtained for the indefinite future.

Mental health

Mental ill health is partly the effect of stress. Stress can have a major source, such as work, or can be caused by the minor hassles of daily life such as money problems, noisy neighbours, transport difficulties and adolescent children. It has often been found that social support reduces or prevents the harmful effects of stress. The *buffering* hypothesis is that social support produces its benefits only in the presence of stress. Several well-designed studies have tackled the question of direction of causation, and have shown that the link between social support and mental health is at least partly due to the effect of relationships on mental health (Cohen and Wills, 1985). Other investigators have succeeded in separating the effects of different relationships. Support for the buffering model is found if measures are taken of interpersonal resources which would be available in the event of stress. Social support also has direct effects, regardless of stress, if measures are made of integration into a social network (Cohen and Wills, 1985).

Hobfoll (1986) in Israel has found that there are a number of conditions under which social support has negative effects: after a long period of support (source gets tired), after an abortion (best forgotten), and for wives of servicemen (rumours of wars add to anxiety). However, under many other conditions the combination of social support and high self-esteem predicted the most favourable outcomes for mental health.

American studies have found large differences between the single and the married in rates of mental disorder (Gove, 1979). In a recent investigation in London, O'Connor and Brown (1984) found that 70 per cent of women with a 'true, very close relationship' were free of affective disorder, compared with 43 per cent of those who did not have such a relationship. The classic study by Brown and Harris (1978) showed the buffer effect of having a close confidant. They studied 458 women in south London, 114 of them psychiatric patients, and obtained careful measures of their degree of depression, experience of stressful *life events* during the past year, and the amount of social support received. Table 10.3 shows that 41 per cent of women who had experienced stressful life events and who did not have a supportive husband became depressed, compared with only 10 per cent of those who did.

Loss of a social relationship is a major source of stress. The rates of unhappiness, depression and other forms of mental disorder are very high for the divorced, separated and bereaved; if there is a sex difference here, it is men who suffer more (Stroebe and Stroebe, 1983).

Friends too contribute to mental health, and both close friends and social networks have been shown to be important. Relationships at work are important since work can be a major source of stress, and support from workmates can be an effective way of dealing with work difficulties.

Individuals with insufficient social support feel *lonely*. De Jong-Gierveld and Kamphuis (1985) studied the subjective meaning of this term, and developed a unitary 11-item scale to measure the cognitions and feelings involved. Loneliness is due partly to social isolation, partly to wanting more social contacts than can be found, and partly to an insufficient degree of self-disclosure through keeping to impersonal topics of conversation (Peplau and Perlman 1982).

There are several ways in which social support might relieve distress:

1 There may be an immediate effect on the self system, increasing self-esteem and self-confidence.

TABLE 10.3   Depression as a function of stress and social support

	Percentage depressed		
	High support	*Mid support*	*Low support*
Had stressful life event	10	26	41
No such events	1	3	4

Source: Brown and Harris (1978)

2 There could be a direct impact on emotions, whereby social interaction generates some degree of positive affect, and thus suppresses depression and anxiety.
3 External stresses may be perceived as less stressful, in the knowledge that support and help are available, so that problems can be dealt with.
   If a relationship is a fairly long-standing one, it could be expected that these benefits could be relied upon.

Physical health

Bodily health, recovery from operations, and length of life have all been found to be affected by the quality of supportive relationships. In a famous study in California, 6900 adults were followed up over a nine-year period. Altogether 8 per cent of them died during this period. Within each age group those with the weakest social attachments were more likely to have died. An index based on marriage, friends and other links was devised. In each age group, individuals who were 'most connected' in their social relationships had lower mortality rates than those who were 'least connected'. This was most obvious for males aged 50–59 at the beginning of the study: 9.6 per cent of the closely connected died, compared with 30.8 per cent of the least connected, as figure 10.8 shows.

Marriage has been shown to have a particularly strong effect. Lynch (1977) collected large-scale medical statistics which showed that single, divorced or widowed individuals are much more likely to die from a number of kinds of illness than married people of the same age; the illnesses included tuberculosis, pneumonia, cirrhosis of the liver, various cancers, diabetes, stroke and coronary. The effects are stronger for men, probably because wives provide more social support than do husbands.

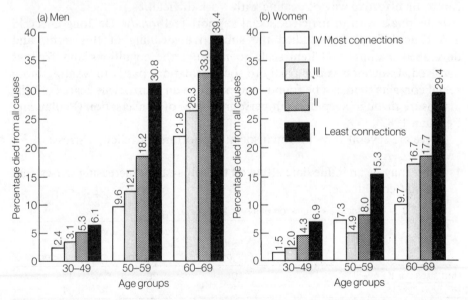

FIGURE 10.8   Social networks and mortality (Berkman and Syme, 1979)

One way in which stress is bad for health is by impairing the immune system, the natural defence against disease. There is a lot of empirical evidence to show that people are more likely to catch colds, flu or other infectious diseases if they are under stress or have recently experienced stressful life events (Jemmott and Locke, 1984). Those concerned are more susceptible to whatever germs are about. Social support can restore the immune system, through its power to replace negative emotions like anxiety and depression and their accompanying bodily states by positive emotions.

A second way in which relationships may affect health is through the adoption of better health practices. It is found for example that people who live alone drink and smoke more (House, 1980). Some of the illnesses to which the single are more prone than the married reflect this – tuberculosis, pneumonia and cirrhosis of the liver. Those who have good relationships are able to cope with stress by seeking help and social support.

Relationships can be supportive in a number of ways – by providing a close confidant, integrating into a social network, giving positive reactions and hence confidence, or providing help or information.

Effects of Culture and History

There are variations in the character of each relationship between cultures, and in the course of history. A man may have several wives or a concubine; there has been a historical shift towards one wife, greater equality of roles, and recently towards shorter duration of marriage. Choice of partner through romantic love is the norm in the Western world; elsewhere arranged marriages are more common. Historical changes can reveal the origins of some of these differences. The rise of the nuclear family has been linked to the requirements of industrialization. The changing roles of husbands and wives are due to pressures from women for more equal rights, and the emergence of romantic love was partly due to popular films and literature (Argyle and Henderson, 1985).

Third World families are much more extensive, i.e. more relatives are recognized and live together, and kinship is the dominant type of relationship. The ecology may be a factor: the importance of kinship for working-class people in Europe is probably because they have low geographical mobility and so tend to live near their kin.

In a number of Third World cultures there are varieties of formal friendship, such as blood brothers, whereby friends are made into a kind of pseudo kin. Work relationships are different in Japan, for example, where supervisory relations are more formal and hierarchical, and groups are closer and demand more conformity.

Summary and Conclusion

The most effective research method is the statistical field study, preferably with objective measures, and with sophisticated designs to uncover the direction of causation. The main theory behind relationship research has been exchange theory, but it is necessary to take account of biological, cognitive and historical processes as well.

Much research has been concerned with the formation and later development of relationships. At early stages appearance, frequency of interaction, similarity and reinforcement are important. Later stages involve the development of commitment, for example via disclosure and investment of resources. Finally there may be decline and dissolution.

Relationships can be analysed in terms of their main components: activities, sources of satisfaction, rules, skills required, concepts and beliefs, and power. The main relationships of marriage, friendship, workmates and kin are quite different in these terms, and different theories are needed to account for them.

Relationships have profound effects for happiness, and for both mental and physical health. Marriage has the greatest positive effects, especially for men. Relationships have been shown to buffer the effects of stress in various ways. The loss or absence of relationships, on the other hand, is a major source of stress, ill-health and mortality.

Social psychology is important for the study of relationships, since it has enabled us to understand them at a more detailed level of analysis (than sociology, for example), it has found the skills needed to establish and maintain them, and it has enabled us to study the detailed benefits which relationships can bring. The study of relationships has been important for social psychology too: it has helped us to extend our concepts from those developed for simpler phenomena, to develop new research methods adequate to relationships, and to build up an extended picture of human social behaviour.

Glossary Terms

Cluster analysis	Path analysis
Equity theory	Self-disclosure
Factor analysis	Social exchange theory
Multidimensional scaling	Socio-biology

Further Reading

Argyle, M. and Henderson, M. (1985) *The Anatomy of Relationships*. London: Penguin. A readable overview, emphasizing the importance of rules in relationships.

Berscheid, E. (1985) Interpersonal attraction. In G. Lindzey and E. Aronson (eds), *Handbook of Social Psychology*, 3rd edn, Hillsdale, NJ: Erlbaum. An up-to-date and readable overview by one of the founders of the field of interpersonal attraction.

Duck, S. and Gilmour, R. (eds) (1981–4) *Personal Relationships* (5 vols). London: Academic Press. These five volumes contain original contributions from many major international researchers in the area of interpersonal relationships. The volumes give a state-of-the-art overview on issues of relationship formation, maintenance and dissolution.

Kelley, H.H., Berscheid, E., Christensen, A., Harvey, J.H., Huston, T.L., Levinger, G., McLintock, E., Peplau, L.A., and Peterson, D.R. (1983) *Close Relationships*. New York: Freeman. This is an important book with original contributions from most of the major American researchers in this area.

11 Prosocial Behaviour

HANS W. BIERHOFF
and RENATE KLEIN

Introduction

Today's altruist might be tomorrow's passive bystander; it all depends on the social situation. This is the message in Latané and Darley's (1969) well-known article on bystander apathy. For example, if a model acts altruistically or egoistically the chances are high that observers will do the same (Rushton, 1975). A host of additional situational variables (e.g. number of bystanders and time pressure) exert powerful influences on **altruistic behaviour**.

Before we go into detail, it is useful to give a definition of altruistic behaviour. In the following, the terms *altruism*, *prosocial behaviour* and *helping behaviour* are used interchangeably. The definition will be illustrated by some examples. In addition, we will present some results from one of our empirical studies which are related to the motives behind altruistic responses.

In general, social psychologists have suggested two different types of definitions of prosocial behaviour. Some have excluded egoistically motivated behaviour (e.g. reciprocity) and emphasized empathically motivated behaviour (e.g. termination of the victim's suffering). Others have argued that it is impractical to define altruism on the basis of an assumed motivational state because it seems to be impossible to decide in each individual case whether the behaviour was empathically motivated or not. In line with the second approach, Bierhoff (1980) has specified two conditions that define prosocial responses: (1) the *intention to benefit* another person, and (2) *freedom of choice* (e.g. lack of professional obligations).

Examples of Prosocial Behaviour

The parable of the Good Samaritan is an excellent example of altruistic behaviour. While the altruistic behaviour of the Samaritan was not observed by

We thank Miles Hewstone, Siegfried Sporer and Wolfgang Stroebe for their helpful comments.

bystanders, other forms of altruism do take place in public. Consider, for example, the emergency aid for Africa organized by Bob Geldorf, or 'ferry aid' as an answer to the ferry disaster in Zeebrugge. These modern examples of altruism make it clear that altruistic responses need not be without personal gain. For example, pop stars like Tina Turner or Paul McCartney might gain an advantage by sacrificing time and money for people in need because by acting altruistically they might promote their records. In addition, many people admire them for their unselfishness. This might add to the recognition these pop stars receive in public. Altruistic behaviour is not necessarily unselfish behaviour. In many cases rewards – subtle or obvious – accrue.

Prosocial behaviour is determined considerably by rewards and costs. This is not to deny that truly selfless altruists live among us, who act altruistically without taking the (negative) consequences into account. In fact, such interventions are most likely in emergency situations which demand immediate action. For example, when an aeroplane crashed into the Potomac near Washington National Airport, TV cameras showed that a bystander jumped into the river and saved one of the survivors although the water was very cold and frostbite was the consequence of this heroic deed.

A central question of research on altruism is related to the motives underlying altruistic responses. Research on altruism has found a number of altruistic motives (e.g. moral obligation, empathy, reciprocity, self-esteem enhancement, and recognition).

In an empirical study we tried to learn something about the motives for prosocial behaviour following traffic accidents (Bierhoff, Klein and Kramp, 1987). The content analysis of answers in response to five written accident-scenarios which were described to our respondents showed that self-esteem enhancement and moral obligation were the most often mentioned motives for altruistic behaviour on behalf of traffic victims. In addition, motives like empathy and reciprocity were also frequently mentioned.

It is especially interesting to consider the results for the motives which impede altruistic responses. The factors mentioned (e.g. stress, danger, time and material losses) can nearly all be subsumed under the category *costs of helping*. Therefore people tend to think that the anticipation of negative consequences reduces altruism. This is especially true for loss of time, which was the most often mentioned reason for not helping. Other frequently mentioned inhibiting factors are danger, stress and lack of competence.

Empirical results indicate that each of these factors reduces altruistic responses. Loss of time is a good example because it illustrates the inhibiting influence of negative consequences on altruism. The assumption that loss of time reduces altruism is plausible because a basic rule of our daily life is that 'time is money'. In many real-life situations people are in a hurry. Waiting is a frustrating experience. Therefore, the willingness to sacrifice time for a person in need can be understood as generosity (Levine, 1987).

Darley and Batson (1973) conducted an experiment which fits nicely into this framework. Their subjects were students in a theological seminary. While some of the students were instructed to think about professional problems, others

PLATES 11.1 AND 11.2   What are the motives underlying responses such as those shown in the photographs above, and are volunteers and professionals both altruistic?

were asked to think about the parable of the Good Samaritan. While thinking about their respective topic, students were sent to another building. As they left, the experimenter indicated that they would be either late ('Oh, you're late; they were expecting you a few minutes ago'), on time ('The assistant is ready for you, so please go right over') or early ('If you have to wait over there, it shouldn't be long').

On their way, students met a 'victim' who ostensibly had fallen to the floor. The percentage of subjects who offered help constituted the dependent variable of the study. The results are summarized in figure 11.1. While the instruction to the students had a slight effect on altruism – those who were instructed to think about the parable tended to help more – the 'hurry' variable exerted a much stronger influence. In general, subjects were less helpful when they were in a hurry. This result is remarkable because the reason for the hurry was not very serious. Late arrival only meant that the assistant had to wait for a while.

This experiment shows that seemingly trivial variables can exert a profound effect on altruistic responses. The results of the Darley and Batson experiment also illustrate what levels of altruism may be expected in emergency situations where only a single bystander is involved. The 42 per cent of subjects in the neutral medium-hurry condition who helped may be more or less representative of the level of altruism which might be expected in comparable real-life situations (cf. Latané and Nida, 1981).

The general level of altruism may also be inferred from another study (Bierhoff, 1983) in which students were asked to volunteer for a reaction-time experiment. Students were informed that if they participated in the experiment without payment the money would be sent to children in need. The choice was between zero and 12 half-hour sessions. On average subjects volunteered 3.71 sessions. In a replication of this study the mean value of altruism was 4.40 sessions. In summary, these results indicate that the general level of helpfulness is higher than some pessimists might have assumed. The willingness to work 2 hours for people in need is a substantial contribution, which should be taken as an indication that people tend to be altruistic in many situations.

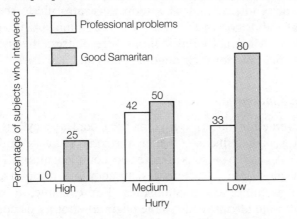

FIGURE 11.1 The effect of instruction and degree of hurry on altruistic responses in an emergency situation (based on Darley and Batson, 1973 and Greenwald, 1975a)

Patterns of Prosocial Behaviour

The interpersonal relationship between donor and recipient can be defined in different terms. Gergen and Gergen (1983) argue that donor and recipient negotiate about the meaning of their interpersonal relationship. For example, the relationship might be interpreted as a mutual exchange. On the other hand, the relationship might be understood as a long-lasting dependency of the help recipient. Therefore, the social construction of the altruistic relationship – the subjective beliefs and viewpoints of the donor and the recipient – has important consequences for the development of the relationship. If the altruistic act is defined as an instance of a mutual exchange, the help recipients might infer that they are equal friends. If, on the other hand, the altruistic act is defined as evidence for the dependency of help recipients, they might infer that they are weak and passive persons.

The broad scope of helping episodes and the different meanings of the altruistic act can be more easily understood within the framework of social interdependence. For example, a social relationship may be interpreted as a symmetric or as an asymmetric system (Jones and Gerard, 1967). Bierhoff (1984) has applied this framework to altruistic behaviour. The resulting four patterns of altruistic relationships indicate the formal structures of donor–recipient relationships, and are now described.

Pseudo-contingency

Consider the following requests: 'Excuse me, I wonder if you could tell me how to get to the King's Arms?'; 'Excuse me, I wonder if you could give me 40 pence?' Such requests elicit substantial amounts of altruistic responses (84 and 34 per cent helping, respectively; Darley and Latané, 1970).

Because the social interdependence which is caused by simple requests is superficial, Jones and Gerard (1967) coined the term 'pseudo-contingency' for this type of social interaction. This term illustrates nicely that the mutual dependency of the donor and the recipient is minimal. Although donor and recipient achieve a mutual coordination of responses, this synchronization plays only a minor role for their ongoing plans and activities.

Asymmetrical contingency

The second interaction pattern – asymmetrical contingency – is characterized by one-sided social influence. While a strong social interdependence is achieved, the roles of the persons involved are complementary. The asymmetry may be the result of power differences. In addition, normative expectations contribute to asymmetrical relationships. For example, if one person is expected to respond altruistically to the plight of another person, a one-sided interaction is rendered likely. Because the norm of social responsibility (see later) prescribes that people should help those who are dependent on their help, a normative framework can elicit an asymmetrical relationship (Schopler and Bateson, 1965).

An example will clarify this point. Two psychology students live together in the same apartment. While one of them is preparing for an important examination, he encounters great difficulties. Therefore, he asks his fellow student whether he could help him out by getting some library books for him. He adds that without this help he would have no chance of passing the examination. The fellow student might have other plans than searching for psychology books in the library. But the appeal makes it clear that the future examinee is dependent on him. As a consequence, normative constraints develop. The fellow student asks himself whether he can ignore his personal responsibility: obviously not. Because it will be difficult to deny a personal responsibility for the fate of the other who needs help urgently, the potential donor finds himself in an asymmetrical relationship which is ruled by the norm of social responsibility.

The norm of social responsibility pushes the potential donor to act altruistically (Berkowitz, 1973; Berkowitz and Daniels, 1963). The normative burden should increase proportionately with the degree of dependency which the potential help recipient displays. Therefore, normative expectations can overcome individual plans of the potential helper and coerce him or her to act altruistically.

Reactive contingency

The structure of social responses in emergencies is represented well by another type of social interaction, which was named 'reactive contingency' by Jones and Gerard (1967). Emergency situations combine the features of requirement of immediate action and unforeseeability of events (Latané and Darley, 1969). The unforeseeability of the sequence of events in emergencies implies that well-practised routines or habits are likely to be inappropriate. In addition, the helper does not have enough time to consider the balance of rewards and costs for helping and not helping or to scan his or her cognitive map of values and normative beliefs in order to recognize the fitting role prescription.

We gave an example of such an emergency situation in the introduction. The person who jumped into the icy Potomac was confronted with an unforeseeable event and had to deal with the urgency of immediate action. He was obviously overwhelmed by the emergency situation. Although Latané and Darley (1969) mention that the potential helper in such situations is in an unenviable position and wonder why anyone intervenes at all, this kind of 'impulsive' helping can be observed in many real-life emergencies.

Because of the overwhelming influence of emergency situations, the importance of individual plans and personal convictions to altruistic responses should be small compared with cues which indicate that an immediate action on behalf of the victim is necessary. Individual plans which were pursued by the helpers before they ran into the emergency lose their binding strength, while situational variables control their responses.

Mutual contingency

The fourth interaction pattern – mutual contingency – is best exemplified by the norm of reciprocity (see later). The exchange of prosocial responses develops as a reciprocal cycle of giving and receiving. In principle, the roles of donor and recipient are interchangeable. One altruistic episode in the relationship between two persons is likely to facilitate later altruistic episodes, when the person who received help during the first episode is willing to act altruistically on behalf of the other person.

The principle of reciprocity is expressed by 'tit for tat'. It is a powerful determinant of altruistic behaviour (Gouldner, 1960). The reciprocity principle encourages social relationships involving equal rights and equal duties for the interaction partners. While some theorists have *devalued* this kind of altruistic relationship as egoistically motivated behaviour, others have shown that the mutual exchange of prosocial acts supports the recipient's self-esteem, especially when the altruistic act relates to feelings of competence of the recipient. Specifically, Trivers (1971) has described reciprocal altruism (e.g. helping in time of danger, sharing food) as the result of biological evolution, while Youniss (1986) has proposed that reciprocal altruism develops in children's friendships (cf. Piaget, 1932).

Our analysis so far has been aimed at clarifying the conceptual realm, but we have not said much about the major research issues which are reflected in empirical studies on prosocial behaviour (see Bierhoff, 1987a). One research area is concerned with the importance of the 'social field' (see Rosenbaum and Blake, 1955) on the acquisition of altruistic responses. Another research area refers to the processes which underlie altruism. A third topic centres around the determinants of altruism in specific situations. A final topic of research is concerned with potential misunderstandings between donors and help recipients.

While this list of focal points is not exhaustive, it illustrates the broad scope of research on altruism. In this chapter we emphasize the influence of normative beliefs as motives which underlie altruistic responses. In addition, the reasons for misunderstandings between donors and recipients are discussed. Finally, we ask what the determinants of emergency helping are. The issue of emergency intervention illustrates the assumption that social behaviour – and especially prosocial behaviour – is strongly influenced by situational determinants (e.g. number of bystanders, clarity of the situation).

Normative Expectations

As we have seen, two norms of social behaviour carry much weight for altruistic behaviour: the norm of social responsibility and the norm of reciprocity.

The norm of social responsibility fits an interpretation of the interpersonal relationship between donor and recipient that emphasizes asymmetrical exchanges. This type of social construction of the altruistic relationship results in a one-sided dependency. In contrast, the norm of reciprocity is compatible with the view that donor and recipient occupy equal positions. The implications of these distinct types of altruistic relationships for the recipient depend on donor characteristics, recipient characteristics, and characteristics of the aid.

Norm of social responsibility

The **norm of social responsibility** prescribes that persons should help other people who are dependent on their help. Feelings of responsibility are assumed to be a positive function of the perceived dependency of the others (Berkowitz and Daniels, 1963).

To elicit the norm of social responsibility, Berkowitz and Daniels (1963) created a worker – supervisor relationship. Surprisingly enough the instructions implied that the supervisor was in the position of the dependent other. While the supervisor had the task of instructing the workers, the worker-subject had to construct paper boxes. Ostensibly the experiment was planned to develop a test of supervisory ability. It was explained by the experimenter that the supervisor's evaluation would in part depend on the worker's performance. Results indicated that subjects worked harder during a 30 minute work period for a highly dependent supervisor compared with a supervisor who was only evaluated on the basis of the quality of his written instructions.

The adherence to the norm of social responsibility depends on the awareness of the normative standard and the motivation to act in accordance with the standard (Berkowitz and Connor, 1966). Awareness of normative standard and motivation to comply are both related to situational variables.

For example, more altruistic responses are elicited when external – and not internal – factors have caused the victim's dependency (Meyer and Mulherin, 1980). This result demonstrates how attribution processes (see chapter 6) influence social behaviour. *External attributions* for the cause of the victim's dependency reduce the perceived responsibility of the victim for his or her own fate and increase the adherence to the norm of social responsibility, because the donor's awareness of the appropriateness of the normative standard is heightened and – as a result – the donor feels responsible for the mitigation of the victim's plight.

Personal norms

Normative beliefs are learnt during the socialization process. It is conceivable that the internalization of social norms differs across individuals. In an attempt to distinguish between cultural rules and individual feelings, Schwartz (1977) contrasted social norms with personal norms. Because individuals differ with respect to their social learning of cultural values and rules, each person is characterized by a unique cognitive set of individual values and normative beliefs. From her cognitive structure the individual delineates *feelings of moral obligation* in specific situations.

Moral obligations can be measured with rating scales. A typical example is: 'How much personal obligation do you feel to help other people in trouble?' (Schwartz, 1977, p 236). Schwartz argued that personal norms are constructed by individuals as self-expectations for specific actions in particular situations. Therefore, it is reasonable to expect that an individual constructs different norms in different situations and at different times. Schwartz (1978) assumed that individuals differ with respect to the stability of their norm construction process. From this reasoning the hypothesis was derived that the prediction of altruism on the basis of personal norms is more successful with persons who exhibit a stable cognitive norm structure. For these persons weak feelings of moral obligation should elicit low helpfulness and vice versa.

An example is provided by Schwartz's (1978) study. The key norm was whether people feel a moral obligation to read schoolbooks to blind children. This key norm was measured as part of a more extensive survey at two measurement points, six months and again three months before the students received an appeal for volunteers to tutor blind children.

While the surveys were ostensibly carried out by the university, the appeal was attributed to the Institute for the Blind. Results indicated that students who exhibited a small absolute change in their survey answers (high stability) were more predictable ($r = +0.47$ for the correlation between specific norm and behaviour) than students who exhibited a large absolute change ($r = -0.03$). In fact, the altruistic behaviour of the low-stability students was not predictable at all. In contrast, high-stability students were more helpful when their personal norm (measured three or six months ago) was altruistic and less helpful when their feelings of moral obligation were indifferent (no obligation to agree).

Schwartz and Howard (1981) proposed a *process model of altruism* which specifies five *successive* steps:

attention → motivation → evaluation → defence → behaviour

The process is started when a person becomes aware that others need help. The attention phase includes recognition of distress, selection of an effective altruistic action, and self-attribution of competence. The next phase is related to the construction of a personal norm and the subsequent generation of feelings of moral obligation (motivation phase). The third phase (evaluation of anticipated consequences of altruistic responses) centres around an assessment of potential costs and benefits. The expected costs include social costs (e.g. social disapproval), physical costs (e.g. pain), self-concept distress (e.g. violation of the self-image) and moral costs (which result from violating personal norms).

In the example above the recognition of the unfulfilled needs of blind children is the first part of the attention phase. Next, the question whether effective actions to remove the problems are available and whether the potential helper feels competent to execute these actions (e.g. reading to blind children) is considered. If the answer is affirmative feelings of moral obligation are generated in the motivation phase. The potential helper may feel strongly that she is obliged to help. If strong feelings of moral obligation are generated, the potential helper will consider the expected consequences of helping (e.g. how much time must be invested, how much approval is gained by acting altruistically). If the evaluation is inconclusive (e.g. pros and cons are in balance) the potential helper might be inclined to deny her personal responsibility or she might deny the seriousness of the needs of the blind children (defence phase). Only if the anticipatory evaluation yields a positive result is a decision to read to the blind children likely (behaviour phase).

The process model of altruism seems to hold some promise for a positive view of human nature. This perspective is undermined, however, by two assumptions which are closely related to the model:

1 The *defence phase* is of crucial importance to the whole model. Schwartz and Howard (1981) assume that defence processes are activated when the anticipated evaluation is undecided. In addition, the defence mechanisms are assumed to reduce the likelihood of altruistic responses. Therefore, if the defence process comes into play, altruistic responses are rendered unlikely. Denial of need, denial of effective action, denial of personal ability to intervene, and denial of personal responsibility inhibit the readiness to help in accordance with personal norms of altruism.

2 *Boomerang effects* are predicted as the result of a strong norm burden. The inhibition of personal norms by boomerang effects explains that under circumstances which – in theory – are conducive to high levels of altruism, low rates of altruistic responses were actually observed (Schwartz, 1970). Individuals who are especially inclined to act altruistically may become suspicious owing to a suspected manipulative intent of the victim. They might think that the victim exaggerates her problem or that the victim tries to exploit feelings of moral obligation by displaying cues of helplessness. Such conclusions are not unlikely because altruistic people encounter many situations in real life in which others try to exploit their altruistic motivation (Schwartz, 1977).

Although normative beliefs about altruistic behaviour seem to be a standard lesson of socialization (Bilsky, 1987), counter-normative processes should not be overlooked (see above). These norm-inhibiting processes include threats to perceived freedom of choice (Wicklund, 1974) and especially denial of responsibility (Montada, Dalbert and Schmitt, 1987). Individuals tend to act against reductions of their behavioural freedom by denying their responsibility to act altruistically. This is the process which Schwartz and Howard (1981) described as a defence mechanism against normatively prescribed actions.

Norm of reciprocity

Reciprocity is a universal principle of human behaviour (Triandis, 1978). With respect to altruism, the **norm of reciprocity** prescribes a mutual exchange of favours between donors and recipients. Today's donor is tomorrow's recipient and vice versa. The helpfulness of each person in a reciprocal relationship is a positive function of the helpfulness of the other person (Pruitt, 1968).

Gouldner (1960) proposed a general norm of prosocial reciprocity. He specified two prescriptions which define reciprocity: (1) people should assist those who have assisted them, and (2) people should not attack those who have assisted them. While the first assumption was supported by empirical results (Wilke and Lanzetta, 1970), the second assumption was refuted by experimental results (Helm, Bonoma and Tedeschi, 1972). These findings indicate that the norm of reciprocity is domain specific. The donor's rate of altruistic responses predicts later altruistic responses of the recipient, but it is a poor predictor of the suppression of later aggressive responses of the recipient directed against the donor.

Gouldner (1960) derived several hypotheses about reciprocity. For example, he suggested that the obligation to reciprocate a favour is positively related to the perceived value of the reward previously received. Furthermore, the willingness to reciprocate should be stronger when the resources of the previous donor were small.

With respect to donor's resources, Pruitt (1968) showed that low resources (e.g. $1) – compared with high resources (e.g. $4) – elicit provision of more rewards in return (given a fixed amount of prior help). In addition, more rewards were provided to another person who had sent out 20 per cent of $1 (= $0.20) than to a person who had sent out 20 per cent of $4 (= $0.80). These results justify the conclusion that the *perceived effort* of another person is of crucial importance for the magnitude of the indebtedness of the help recipient and his willingness to reciprocate the favour. Indebtedness (Greenberg, 1980) or gratitude (Tesser, Gatewood and Driver, 1968) are assumed to be the motivational factors which mediate reciprocity of altruism.

Acquisition of normative beliefs

One source of normative beliefs is the socialization process, which includes the internalization of social norms (e.g. the norm of social responsibility, the norm of reciprocity). In addition, models in the social field can transmit appropriate situational norms. Bandura (1971) described one function of social models as the facilitation of performance by informing the observer which existing behaviour patterns are appropriate in the given social situation.

One of the major research issues mentioned above referred to the social field as a determinant of altruistic responses. In 1955, Rosenbaum and Blake reported a first example of facilitation of prosocial behaviour by social models. These researchers asked students to volunteer for an experiment. In one condition these students had witnessed another student (a confederate of the experimenter) who agreed to participate. In another condition they witnessed a student who refused to participate. The results revealed that subjects in the positive condition almost unanimously helped while subjects in the negative condition almost never did.

Rosenbaum and Blake (1955) assumed that the readiness to volunteer may be influenced by the structure of the social field within which the students were asked to participate. Observation of the model's acceptance or rejection of the invitation contributed to the definition of the situation. A compliant model led to the inference that it was appropriate to participate in the experiment, while a refusing model transmitted the message that it was inappropriate to accept the invitation.

This indicates that normative beliefs about altruistic behaviour arise out of social interactions and the norms which emerge in the social field. Situational norms emerge from a *shared interpretation* of an event. Norms of altruism may be established with minimal effort by introducing a social model (cf. Snyder and Kendzierski, 1982a). This transmission of the shared meaning of an event by social models contributes also to the socialization process (Rice and Grusec, 1975).

Impulsive Helping and Emergencies

Everyday episodes usually follow well-rehearsed scripts (Langer, Blank and Chanowitz, 1978). Emergencies are among those situations which require deviations from scripted performances. Latané and Darley (1969) described five characteristics which distinguish emergencies: dangerous situations; rareness of the events; few commonalities with other events; unforeseeability of the events; and requirement of instant action. These characteristics render it highly unlikely that normative beliefs (e.g. 'women and children first') determine the willingness to intervene. In addition, the high time pressure reduces the cognitive guidance of actions.

Numerous studies indicate that the willingness to intervene is higher when a bystander is alone than when she is in the company of other bystanders (Latané and Nida, 1981). In one of the first experiments which showed this effect (Latané and Rodin, 1969) students overheard that a woman who worked next door in her office climbed on a chair, fell on the floor and moaned. In one condition the student was alone; 70 per cent of such students intervened. In a second condition another student (a confederate of the experimenter) was present, who was instructed to be passive; only 7 per cent of students intervened in this passive-confederate condition. In a third condition two strangers were present during the accident. Although two persons could intervene in this case, in only 40 per cent of dyads did at least one student intervene (see figure 11.2). In this condition the *individual* likelihood of intervention can be calculated as 22.5 per cent. Details of this calculation are explained in Bierhoff (1980, p 148). The results of this experiment are representative of the results of later studies.

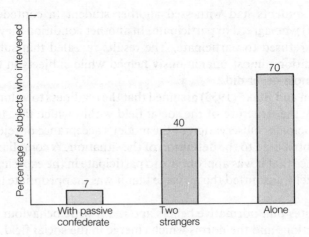

FIGURE 11.2　The effect of a second bystander on emergency intervention (based on Latané and Rodin, 1969)

The likelihood of receiving help tended to be higher in *alone* conditions than in *group* conditions.

Empirical evidence indicates that three types of social processes cause the social inhibition of altruism (Latané and Darley, 1976; Schwartz and Gottlieb, 1976):

1　A single bystander feels that the responsibility to intervene is focused on her. With other bystanders present the felt responsibility is attenuated. The **diffusion of responsibility** leads to less altruism. This effect increases with the number of bystanders (Latané, 1981); when bystanders perceived as more competent are present, the inhibition is particularly pronounced.

2　**Pluralistic ignorance** depends on the ambiguity of the emergency situation. High ambiguity elicits feelings of uncertainty in the bystander. Because each bystander hesitates and tries to work out what is going on, the bystanders are models of passivity for each other (see Rosenbaum and Blake, 1955). This social comparison process leads to the erroneous conclusion that the other bystanders interpret the event as harmless. Therefore a social definition of the situation emerges which hinders altruistic responses.

3　A third factor which presumably reduces the willingness to help is **evaluation apprehension**. The presence of the other bystanders elicits feelings of uneasiness because the other bystanders are observers of a potential intervention. These anxieties exert their inhibiting influence especially in situations in which the bystander is in doubt whether she is able to intervene successfully. But it is also possible that the process of evaluation apprehension increases the likelihood of an intervention. If a bystander believes that she is competent and able to perform very well, the presence of others is possibly an incentive for the bystander to intervene. Under these special conditions the bystander may feel that she shows her superiority and strength by intervening.

In many situations the three processes – diffusion of responsibility, pluralistic ignorance and evaluation apprehension – contribute in like manner to social inhibition. Therefore, the inhibitory influences usually reinforce each other and suppress the willingness to intervene. The combination of these inhibitory processes is illustrated by many everyday examples of bystander apathy in emergencies. The German magazine *Stern* (October 1987) reported a number of such incidents, which all resemble the well-known case of Kitty Genovese. She was murdered in 1964 in New York while 38 neighbours observed the crime. Because the whole attack lasted for more than 30 minutes the neighbours would have had enough time to intervene or to call the police. They did neither.

Successful leadership in a group of bystanders is one factor which counteracts inhibitory tendencies in groups of bystanders (Bierhoff, 1987b). Effective leaders are willing to accept responsibility. Therefore, the diffusion of responsibility effect is avoided. In addition, effective group leaders are likely to define the event as an emergency and to act as an appropriate model. As a consequence the social field is structured in a way which enhances the likelihood of responsible action. Empirical evidence shows that successful leaders cause groups to reach a higher intervention rate than less effective group leaders (Firestone, Lichtman and Colamosca, 1975). This effect crucially depends on the ability of effective group leaders to accept the responsibility for intervention and to exhibit the characteristics of helpful models.

Another technique which reduces the frequently observed social inhibition effect is based on the focusing of responsibility upon a specific person in advance (Staub, 1970). If it is announced that an observer is responsible for another person, the diffusion of responsibility effect may be reduced. These examples show how important the attribution of responsibility for an emergency is.

The Psychology of Receiving Help

The psychology of giving help and the psychology of receiving help are complementary. The recipient is influenced by motives different from those of the donor. For example, while the donor is likely to emphasize her contributions and efforts, the recipient might prefer to minimize the amount of help received.

This state of affairs is reflected in the different perspectives of donors and recipients. The recipient wants to prevent the conclusion that he was unable to master his fate. Because of the negative implications of weakness and inferiority associated with the role of a help recipient, the recipient will be inclined to define the altruistic relationship as mutual exchange.

The donor has the advantage that giving help is regarded as desirable and fair. Although she has to incur costs (e.g. time, money and effort), the positive consequences of giving help may outweigh the negative consequences. Therefore the donor is inclined to think that she has demonstrated strength and virtue.

The aid relationship comprises *four basic components* (Fisher, DePaulo and

Nadler, 1981). Donor characteristic (e.g. manipulative intent) and recipient characteristics (e.g. self-esteem) exert a modifying influence on the consequences of receiving help. In addition, aid characteristics (e.g. amount of help) and context characteristics (e.g. opportunity to reciprocate) influence feelings of indebtedness, evaluation of the donor, and self-attributions of the recipient.

These components of the aid transaction influence the magnitude of self-threat and self-support inherent in the aid for the recipient (Fisher, Nadler and Whitcher-Alagna, 1982). Negative responses of the recipient are predicted if self-threat prevails. Negative responses comprise negative feelings, negative evaluation of donor and aid, low willingness to reciprocate, and high readiness for subsequent self-help. On the other hand, positive responses are predicted if self-support prevails. Situational variables and dispositional factors exert an influence on the magnitude of self-threat and self-esteem, which in turn determines whether negative reactions or positive reactions of the recipient prevail.

Situational cues which emphasize the negative implications of receiving help (e.g. scornful comments) are especially threatening for high self-esteem recipients. In one study, self-threatening aid elicited a high degree of subsequent self-help when the recipient's self-esteem was high (DePaulo et al., 1981). In this study subjects received help which was accompanied either by a positive comment ('Good luck on the next task') or by a negative comment ('I guess this is hard for you'). High self-esteem subjects worked especially hard on a difficult task when they had received the negative message instead of the positive message. In general, receiving help is more threatening for persons with high self-esteem than for persons with low self-esteem (Nadler and Mayseless, 1983). In addition, the willingness to *seek help* depends on the self-threat associated with receiving help, and this effect is especially pronounced for high self-esteem individuals (Nadler, 1987).

These results may be interpreted as a plea for more reciprocity in altruistic relationships, especially with regard to high self-esteem recipients. Altruistic responses which are embedded in a mutual give and take may have more desirable effects than one-sided aid which offers no opportunity to repay. A warning should be added: this plea should not be understood as an argument in favour of the norm of self-sufficiency. Long-lasting discrimination against the underprivileged requires efforts to improve their fate, which include aid from professional services (e.g. social workers) and from non-professional donors. Professional and non-professional helpers may be equally successful (Wills, 1982).

The most adequate model for altruistic relationships was described by Brickman et al. (1982). These authors introduce the notion of *responsibility attribution* as a key concept. They distinguish between responsibility for the *cause* of a problem and responsibility for the *solution* to the problem. Their compensatory model relieves the target person of the responsibility for the origin of his problem but holds the help recipient responsible for the solution to his problem. According to this model, help recipients are seen as innocent victims of deprivation who are capable of profiting from temporary aid. After the elimination of the deprivation, recipients are considered to be responsible for their own future and to be competent enough to help themselves (Bierhoff, 1987c).

Summary and Conclusion

Finally, some general statements regarding the most important determinants of altruism in everyday situations are appropriate. What are the factors which presumably exert the largest effects on prosocial behaviour? Such summarizing statements should be considered with caution, but a first sketch of important determinants is useful.

Anticipated consequences – especially loss of time and danger – explain a notable amount of variation in altruism. In many everyday situations time pressure reduces the willingness to help considerably. Anticipated consequences may reduce altruism directly as a function of a cost–benefit analysis or indirectly via defence mechanisms.

A second potent factor is social models, who define altruistic responses in a given situation as appropriate or inappropriate. The phenomenon of pluralistic ignorance which was observed in emergency situations is an example of the inhibiting influence of social models on observers. In addition, social models contribute heavily to the socialization of altruism in children.

A third influence factor which seems to be very important is diffusion of responsibility. This factor decisively contributes to the inhibition of intervention in groups of bystanders. Processes of responsibility denial also contribute to defence mechanisms.

A fourth general principle is based on mutual give and take. A person who reciprocates a favour follows a normatively prescribed sequence of behaviour which corresponds with the socially shared understanding of the situation. Therefore the perceived legitimacy of such behaviour sequences is relatively high.

A fifth factor which should be mentioned in passing is the mood of the potential donor. A number of studies indicate that good mood enhances altruism compared with neutral mood (see Bierhoff, 1988, for a summary of this research).

These factors seem to be potent determinants of altruism. In addition, some authors discuss the modifying influence of an altruistic personality (especially Rushton, 1980). Individual differences in altruism may explain some additional portion of the variance above that explained by situational factors. However, in many areas the dominating influence of situational determinants of altruism should be emphasized.

Glossary Terms

Altruistic behaviour	Norm of reciprocity
Diffusion of responsibility	Norm of social responsibility
Evaluation apprehension	Pluralistic ignorance

Further Reading

Bierhoff, H. W. and Montada, L. (eds) (1987) *Altruismus: Bedingungen der Hilfs-bereitschaft*. Göttingen: Hogrefe. A collection of empirical studies and theoretical contributions with special emphasis on the motives of altruistic behaviour.

Piliavin, J.A., Dovidio, J.F., Gaertner, S.L. and Clark, R.D. (1981) *Emergency Intervention*. New York: Academic Press. A monograph on emergency interventions which especially stresses the effects of arousal and expected consequences.

Rushton, J.P. and Sorrentino, R.M. (eds) (1981) *Altruism and Helping Behaviour: social, personality, and developmental perspectives*. Hillsdale, NJ: Erlbaum. Developmental theories, situational determinants and individual differences in altruism are comprehensively discussed.

Staub, E., Bar-Tal, D., Karylowski, J. and Reykowski, J. (eds) (1984) *Development and Maintenance of Prosocial Behaviour: international perspectives on positive morality*. New York: Plenum. Covers psychological approaches to social development and social determinants of prosocial behaviour. In addition, applied research on prosocial behaviour (e.g. on blood donation) is included.

Wills, T.A. (ed.) (1982) *Basic Processes in Helping Relationships*. New York: Academic Press. The helping relationship – especially in a therapeutic context – is the focus of this book. The relevance of social-psychological theories for client–clinician interactions is demonstrated.

12 Aggressive Behaviour

AMÉLIE MUMMENDEY

Introduction

In 1984 alone there were 2722 cases of actual or attempted murder or man-slaughter in West Germany; this represents four or five victims of extreme violence for every 100,000 inhabitants. The number of victims of serious and dangerous physical injury in the same year was 63,746 – about the number of inhabitants of a medium-sized town. Unfortunately, there is nothing special about West Germany in terms of such statistics; the figures for other European countries are comparable, and those for the United States even higher. Of course, these figures do not reflect the full spectrum of human aggression; everyday cases of less extreme physical or psychological injury are innumerable, and death or serious injury in the course of war are not even included in these statistics.

Thankfully, the probability that any of us will be victims or uninvolved witnesses of extreme violence is – at least in Europe – small. But we are daily witnesses of such events as mediated by the newspapers and, especially, television. The more spectacular the event, the more insistently we ask 'why?' What causes someone to insult, threaten, hit, torture or kill another person? We are particularly interested in the causes, because we hope that by identifying them we may find a means of controlling and reducing violent and aggressive behaviour.

In the course of 70 years of social-psychological research on aggression, different theories of its causes have been developed. A great number of experiments have been carried out to investigate which factors or conditions increase or limit the extent of human aggression.

In this chapter we first present some of the most influential theoretical attempts to explain aggressive behaviour: aggression as instinct; frustration and aggression; and aggression as learned behaviour. In the third section we consider the main variables that mediate aggression – such as arousal, the social construction of aggression, and norms. In the course of the chapter we

This chapter has been translated by Miles Hewstone and Claudia Hammer-Hewstone.

PLATE 12.1   Police and young people clash on the streets of West Berlin – an example of intergroup aggression

KILLER RAMBO AS I SAW HIM
BY BOY WHO SURVIVED

ARMED to the teeth . . . this is the chilling Rambo figure which confronted the victims of the Hungerford massacre.

It is drawn from the memory of Darren Gray who came face to face with Michael Ryan. Strangely, the face of hate looks nothing like pictures of Ryan.

FULL STORY PAGE FIVE

PLATE 12.2   The Hungerford massacre in Britain (reported here in *The People*) highlighted the impact of mass media models on social behaviour and its perception by others

will review a selection of the empirical research on factors which influence aggression. We will also deal with some of the problems inherent in classical aggression research – problems which in recent years have led to a number of changes in how aggression is both perceived and researched as a social-psychological problem.

Theories of Aggression

Consider the following episode, which takes place in a bar in an unidentified West German city but could just as easily have happened in many other European or North American cities. A crowd of young people are there, some sitting at tables, most crushed against the bar. Among them are a group of Turkish youths, whose parents came to West Germany as migrant workers (*Gastarbeiter*). The bar is cramped, hot and loud. Two young men, Thomas (who is German) and Özal (who is Turkish), get involved in a heated discussion. Suddenly the German springs to his feet, shouts at the Turk and punches him on the chin. The Turkish youth stumbles, smashes his head against the edge of the table and falls to the ground. Blood pours from his mouth.

For what theories can we reach to identify the causes of the young German's aggressive behaviour? We will first look more closely at the major theoretical approaches to aggression; later we will try to analyse this episode from these different theoretical perspectives.

In psychological research on aggression, there are two basic and influential positions: one sees aggression as a form of behaviour which is governed by innate instincts or drives; the other sees aggression as a form of behaviour which like other behaviour is acquired through individual experience. There is also a third, intermediate position which integrates the concepts of drive and learning – the frustration-aggression hypothesis. We shall deal with each approach in turn.

Aggression as instinct

At the beginning of this century William McDougall wrote in his *Introduction to Social Psychology* (1908) that the whole spectrum of human behaviour, including hostile and aggressive behaviour, was under the control of 18 different instincts. However, the assumption that behind hostile behaviour lies a hostile **instinct** does not help to explain the occurrence of such behaviour. One concept, namely observed behaviour, is simply replaced by another, namely the assumed basic drive. It is for this reason that such simple concepts faded quickly into the background. In the place of instinct, it was psychoanalysis on the one hand and ethology on the other that had the most influence, especially on everyday ideas about the causes of aggression.

The psychoanalytic approach   In the framework of *psychoanalysis* Freud first developed a conception of aggression as the servant of the 'pleasure principle'.

Aggression was seen as a reaction to frustration experienced in the pursuit of 'pleasure' or the satisfaction of *libido* (the sexual energy of the 'life instinct'). After 1920, with the publication of *Beyond the Pleasure Principle* and possibly influenced by his experiences during the First World War, Freud gave up this conception of aggression in favour of a *dual instinct theory*. Alongside the desire for self-preservation (the life instinct, *Eros*), Freud conceived a second instinct (the 'death instinct', *Thanatos*), a tendency towards death and a return to the state of the inorganic. The destructive energy associated with this second instinct must continuously be turned away from the individual, to the outside, in order to prevent self-destruction. Just as sexual energy is used up and tension reduced through sexual activity, Freud assumed that aggressive behaviour diverts destructive energy and also reduces tension. This leads to the idea of **catharsis** which was important for later research: hostile and aggressive tendencies can be expressed in non-destructive ways, such as biting humour or fantasy, thereby diverting destructive energy and weakening the tendency towards actual aggressive behaviour. Thus Freud viewed the primary function of an instinct as the reduction of a 'tension of needs'. The need for destruction generates tension, which is reduced by aggressive behaviour, but which builds up again during a 'rest period' without aggressive behaviour. Therefore Freud viewed human aggression as unavoidable.

This short summary of the orthodox psychoanalytic theory of aggression raises the general problem of how to test these assumptions empirically. Essential concepts such as destructive energy are so global and inexact that one can derive no precise predictions or hypotheses and then go on to test them. This approach is really only able to attempt an explanation of events or behaviour that have already taken place. Needs usually have identifiable causes and can be evoked: thus hunger arises as a need for nutrition following food deprivation. It is doubtful whether, in a similar manner, an individual would experience a greater need for aggression because deprived of the possibility to aggress against others.

For these reasons, the psychoanalytic instinct theory of aggression has no real influence on contemporary aggression research. However, independent perspectives generated from this theory have led to central concepts in empirical research on aggression. This can be seen in the case of the frustration-aggression hypothesis, which we consider later. First, we deal with an alternative approach to aggression as instinct.

The ethological approach   Some ethological, just like psychoanalytic, approaches postulate the existence of instinctive, aggressive energy. Unlike the psychoanalytic concept of drive, the ethological approach to aggression accords it a species-serving function (Lorenz, 1963). Aggression is an innate behavioural disposition arising from natural selection; like other dispositions – such as looking after the young – aggression increases the chances of survival and successful conservation of the species. Aggression ensures that members of the same species do not live too close to each other, but rather disperse over a wide territory, thus developing greater resources for future generations. Fights between rivals serve to select the strongest and healthiest leaders of a herd. Through within-species aggression, a hierarchy is established within a social unit which places the best individuals in the highest ranks. The following assumptions about the occurrence of aggressive behaviour are made: within each individual there is a potential for behaviour-specific energy (i.e. aggression), which is automatically stored up. The probability and intensity of aggressive behaviour depend on the actual strength of this potential.

For each domain of behaviour there are fixed action patterns. These action patterns are fed not through external stimuli but by an internal, central arousal potential, and they are stimulated by this behaviour-specific energy. This stimulation requires an external 'eliciting stimulus' which directs the energy outwards into fixed patterns of behaviour, such as attacking or biting a member of the same species. When energy has been used up in behaviour, the tendency for further aggressive behaviour is decreased. If, over a longer period of time, there is no effective 'eliciting stimulus', then aggression may build up to a point where it spontaneously 'explodes' without obvious external stimuli (Lorenz, 1963).

These basic assumptions were summarized in the form of a hydraulic model similar to a continuously heated steam boiler: as pressure builds up, so steam must be continuously released. If the safety valve for releasing steam is blocked, pressure buildup is too high and steam is spontaneously released.

Lorenz and Freud agree on the assumption that human aggression is unavoidable. However, Lorenz draws rather different conclusions about the possibilities for controlling violence. To avoid the spontaneous explosion of the 'steam boiler' in the form of uncontrolled aggression, he recommends the continual and controlled discharge of small amounts of energy through socially acceptable forms of aggression. Active, or even passive, participation in competitive sports is given as examples of acceptable forms of aggression.

This assumption has been criticized and refuted by many examples: well-known scenes of the fights between opposing football fans, as well as the results of empirical studies, show that sporting competitions often have the effect of escalating violence rather than controlling or weakening it (see Gabler, Schulz and Weber, 1982). In general, hydraulic models of motivation or behaviour have been rejected as mistaken analogies. Thus Hinde (1960) criticized the way in which psychological or behavioural energy was confused with physical energy; the former is a hypothetical construct, while the latter has characteristics that can actually be investigated. This mistaken analogy gives a totally false impression of the exactness of the model. Unlike the case of physical energy, there is no empirical basis to Lorenz's idea of a spontaneous buildup of aggressive energy.

Let us return to Thomas and Özal, and the question of what caused the aggressive outburst in the bar. If we take aggression as an instinct then we must assume that, at the time of his aggressive act, Thomas had built up a sufficient potential (energy) for aggressive behaviour; Özal functioned simply as a suitable 'eliciting stimulus'. This interpretation might seem at first plausible. But we are left in the dark if we look more closely and ask: why did Thomas become violent in exactly this situation; why was it Özal who elicited the aggression; and why did Thomas show exactly this form of aggressive behaviour?

Frustration and aggression

The frustration-aggression hypothesis   In 1939 five authors, the so-called Yale Group, published a book with the title *Frustration and Aggression* which initiated experimental research on aggression within social psychology (Dollard et al., 1939). For several decades their **frustration-aggression hypothesis** was the theoretical core of research in this area.

These authors rejected the concepts of a death instinct and of specific innate instincts as drives towards aggression. They leaned far more on the older ideas of Freud, but also emphasized the formulation of operational concepts and of empirically testable assumptions. Their energy model of aggression assumes that a person is motivated to act aggressively, not by innate factors, but by a drive induced by **frustration**. By frustration they mean the condition which arises when goal attainment is blocked; while aggression is action aimed at harming another organism. These two concepts are linked to the following two statements: frustration always leads to some form of aggression; and aggression is always a consequence of frustration.

Aggression is not always directed towards the cause of frustration. If, for example, this person is physically strong or socially powerful, then the frustrated individual can turn his or her aggression towards another, less dangerous person. The target of aggression can be replaced. One form of reaction can also be replaced by others. Target substitution and response substitution are forms of **displacement** of aggression. This concept, like catharsis, is borrowed from psychoanalysis: aggression, whether directed at the target or displaced, discharges the aggressive energy produced by frustration. Through this catharsis the readiness for aggression disappears.

Immediately following the publication of the Yale Group's book, the simple hypothesis concerning the causal relationship between frustration and aggression was questioned. Critics argued that frustration did not always lead to aggression, and that other reactions – such as crying, fleeing or apathy – were also observed. In addition, while frustration may lead to aggression, it is not always necessary; aggression often occurs without preceding frustration. A paid assassin, for example, often carries out his task without knowing his victim, let alone being frustrated by him.

Given these objections, the authors quite soon changed their original assumptions. Frustration was seen only as a stimulus to aggression, which took its place in an individual's hierarchy of possible response tendencies; nonetheless, aggression was seen as the *dominant* response tendency following frustration (Miller et al., 1941). Thus frustration creates a readiness for aggression, but whether this is expressed in actual behaviour depends on additional conditions.

This question of the specific stimulus conditions that bring about aggressive behaviour leads us to the work of Berkowitz, and his revision of the frustration-aggression hypothesis.

Cue-arousal theory   As an answer to the question about the causes of aggression, it is unsatisfactory to say that frustration *sometimes* does (and therefore sometimes does not) lead to aggression. This 'sometimes' must be incorporated into our theoretical assumptions, and it is exactly this that Berkowitz (1964, 1969, 1974) does. Between the concepts of frustration and aggression he inserts an intervening concept – that of appropriate environmental conditions (or *cues*) for aggression. Frustration does not immediately evoke aggression, but generates in the individual a state of emotional arousal, namely *anger*. This aroused anger generates an inner readiness for aggressive behaviour. But this behaviour will only occur if there are stimulus cues in the situation which have an aggressive meaning: that is, cues which are associated with anger-releasing conditions, or simply with anger itself. Stimuli acquire their quality of being aggressive cues through processes of **classical conditioning**; in principle, any object or person can become an aggressive cue in this way.

Thus an aggressive act has two distinct sources: the aroused anger within the harm-doer, and the cues within the situation. Berkowitz and his colleagues carried out a series of experiments to test systematically these assumptions of **cue-arousal theory** (see Berkowitz, 1974). One experiment in particular aroused considerable interest, generating extensive criticisms and both successful and unsuccessful replications of what has become known as the *weapons effect*.

According to Berkowitz, through experience certain objects become associated with aggression; these objects have a high value as aggressive cues. Weapons, especially revolvers, are a prime example. Revolvers, unlike knives or sticks, are objects which have a clear and limited function. The presence of revolvers, as objects with aggressive meaning, should then lead in general to more extreme aggression than the presence of objects with neutral connotations.

Berkowitz and LePage (1967) tested exactly this hypothesis, asking: if weapons function as aggression-arousing cues, do frustrated or angered people show more aggression in the presence of weapons than when they are absent or when only aggression-neutral objects are present? The subjects (male college students) had to perform a task, and had their performance evaluated by an experimental confederate. This evaluation consisted of a number of electric shocks, ranging from 1 (very satisfactory) to 7 (very poor). The number of shocks was independent of the actual performance, and served the purpose of generating different strengths of aroused anger. As expected, the subjects who received a higher number of shocks reported more anger than those who had only received one shock. In a second phase of the experiment, the recipients of both high levels ('angered' subjects) and low levels ('non-angered' subjects) of shock had to evaluate the performance of the confederate, also by means of giving electric shocks.

At this stage the various experimental conditions were manipulated, in terms of aggression-arousing cues. In one condition, a shotgun and a revolver were placed on a nearby table; the subjects were told that the weapons belonged to the confederate, and that they should pay no attention to them. In this way the weapons were associated with the opponent. In a second condition, the same weapons were visible, but not linked to the opponent (unassociated condition). In a third (control) condition, no objects were present. Finally, an additional control condition was arranged for the angered subjects only. Some badminton rackets – aggression-neutral objects – were placed on the nearby table.

The results are shown in figure 12.1. For non-angered subjects there was no significant effect of the aggressive cues on the number of shocks given to the confederate. For the angered subjects, in contrast, there was a clear effect: angered subjects gave more shocks in the presence versus the absence of weapons; the level of aggressive behaviour was not significantly different in the associated and unassociated weapons conditions. Finally, the angered subjects also gave more shocks in the presence of weapons than in the presence of badminton rackets.

These results support the hypothesis concerning the role of aggression-arousing cues in eliciting aggression. This weapons effect has since been replicated in naturalistic situations (Simons and Turner, 1976), using slides instead of actual weapons (Leyens and Parke, 1975), with knives (Fischer, Kelm and Rose, 1969), and with toy weapons in a study using children (Turner and Goldsmith, 1976).

Nevertheless, a number of experiments have not managed to confirm Berkowitz's assumptions, finding either no weapons effect (e.g. Turner and Simons, 1974), or an effect without first arousing anger in the experimental subjects (Fraczek, 1974; Schmidt and Schmidt-Mummendey, 1974). Thus there seems to be a weapons effect in the sense of an aggression-intensifying effect of

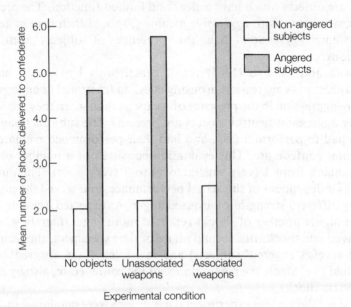

FIGURE 12.1   The 'weapons effect' (Baron, 1977 p. 165, based on Berkowitz and Le Page, 1967)

situational characteristics; but it is questionable whether this effect should be understood in Berkowitz's sense as a classically conditioned cue. One also has to take account of the perceived costs of attacking an opponent – such as punishment from a third party, or the revenge of a victim. According to some critics, the intensifying effect of aggressive cues may be rather that they signal to the individual that aggression is an appropriate form of behaviour in that situation (see Page and Scheidt, 1971).

If we apply the perspective of the frustration-aggression hypothesis, in its broadest sense, to our example of Thomas's aggressive act towards Özal, then our interpretation of what happened in the bar is somewhat different. Thomas must have been frustrated; we could imagine that he got upset about what Özal said during their discussion, perhaps he felt insulted, and then he reacted with aggression to this frustration. It is also conceivable that Thomas's anger stemmed from other things that happened, but that Özal was the most suitable target for his aggression. Likewise, we might ask about the potentially aggressive cues which transformed Thomas's anger into actual aggressive behaviour. For example, some Germans hold a stereotype of Turks as 'given to violence'. In this way Özal, as a Turk, might have been associated with violence and thus functioned as an aggressive cue for Thomas; or this cue might have signalled the appropriateness of aggression in this situation. But why did Thomas show this particular form of aggression, rather than one of the many imaginable alternatives? How did he acquire his repertoire of behavioural alternatives, and his expectations about which action would be most expedient?

The expected consequences of aggressive behaviour receive attention in the third theoretical perspective on aggression, to which we now turn. This social-learning approach deals in the most detail with the environmental conditions that lead people to acquire and maintain aggressive behaviour.

Aggression as learned behaviour

In the approaches sketched above, aggression is seen as the inevitable and necessary consequence of increased drive or energy, brought about by factors either within the person or in the external environment. A historically more recent view sees aggression rather as a specific form of social behaviour, which is acquired and maintained in the same way as any other form of social behaviour. From the perspective of learning theory, the following questions arise. How does an individual acquire aggressive forms of behaviour? Under what conditions do they become a part of the behavioural repertoire? Which factors determine whether such available forms of behaviour actually occur? Which factors are responsible for the fact that aggressive behaviour is enacted not once but repeatedly, thus becoming habitual? With regard to the relevant conditions, we have already looked, for example, at eliciting stimuli and the link between frustration and aggression. Now we turn to the question of how aggressive behaviour is acquired and maintained.

Instrumental conditioning How is aggressive behaviour acquired?

Individuals behave in order to reach desired goals. If a child really wants that gleaming, bright red fire-engine standing on the table, then he will go to the table and get it. But the situation becomes complicated if another child is playing with the toy. Somehow this other child must be made to give up the fire-engine. One possibility is direct: simply grab the toy. Different consequences can ensue from this behaviour. If this aggressive behaviour is successful (i.e. it is seen as a useful way of obtaining an attractive object), then the child will use the same means in other, comparable situations. By means of positive reinforcement, the tendency to behave aggressively will be strengthened. Indeed, it has been shown that people acquire different forms of aggressive behaviour through this process of **instrumental conditioning**. Quite different forms of positive reinforcement can be effective in this way: attractive objects like toys, money or sweets (Walters and Brown, 1963); winning social approval or increased status (Geen and Stonner, 1971); and avoiding pain (Patterson, Littman and Bricker, 1967).

Social modelling   In order to generate rewarding experiences through behaviour, the individual must know not only how to behave in this way, but also how to use the behaviour in this way. Bandura (1973) proposed that the first step towards acquiring a new form of aggressive behaviour was the process of **modelling**: individuals acquire new and more complex forms of behaviour by observing this behaviour and its consequences in other people – or models. A typical experiment on modelling was carried out by Bandura, Ross and Ross (1961, 1963), in which children observed an adult playing with some toys. This adult showed very unusual, and for the children quite new, behaviour: he marched into the playroom, hit a large inflated toy (a Bobo doll) with a rubber hammer, and then kicked and yelled at it. Children in the control condition see an adult who plays quietly with the toys. In a second phase of the experiment, the model is either rewarded by the experimenter or experiences no positive consequences. Then the children have a chance to play with the same toys. It was found that the children imitated the model's behaviour when they had seen it rewarded. The effect was found whether the model was seen in real life or only observed on video. Further, either a realistic or a comic figure could serve as a model. While many studies with children emphasized the acquisition of new forms of behaviour (see Bandura, 1977; Baron, 1977), similar studies with adults showed how a model could reduce inhibitions about behaving aggressively in a certain situation (Baron, 1971; Epstein, 1966).

Recall our example: Thomas punches Özal in the face. It does not take us long to find models for this sort of behaviour. At least in Western cultures we can hardly avoid seeing such behaviour, if not at first hand then at least through the mass media. It is not only the behaviour of the model that is observed, but the way it is anchored in a social context. The observer learns that in many cases exactly these forms of behaviour have positive consequences.

Violence on television: the impact of mass media models on aggression   Bandura and his coworkers planned their provocative Bobo-doll studies to test hypotheses about imitation which were derived from social learning theory. These results seem directly relevant to the important general question: does the presentation of violence on television encourage viewers to act aggressively? However, there are several grounds for caution in generalizing directly from Bandura's studies: the films used were not realistic TV films; the measured behaviour had little to do with realistic attacks on other people; and in real life we are unlikely to find the absolute similarity between the situation observed and the one in which the viewer later acts. For these reasons a great many studies were later conducted which bore a closer resemblance to realistic TV viewing (see Comstock, 1975 for a review).

A series of correlational studies agree that there *is* a positive association between viewing violent television programmes and behaving aggressively (e.g. McCarthy et al., 1975). Of great interest here is the *direction* of this effect. To address this question, a series of three field experiments were carried out in the United States and Belgium (Parke et al., 1977). Juvenile offenders were shown exciting films (with or without violence) five nights running in the hostels in which they lived. Trained observers coded the actual amount of violence shown by the boys in the course of a normal day. The boys who had viewed violent films showed more aggressive behaviour than those who had viewed non-violent but still exciting films. In a subsequent laboratory experiment, the same boys were given the opportunity to give electric shocks to an opponent (actually a confederate) who had provoked them. The boys who had viewed violent films also gave more electric shocks than did those who had seen non-violent films.

These findings are corroborated by the results of other field and laboratory studies. For example, Liebert and Baron (1972) showed that boys and girls (aged 5–6 and 8–9) who had previously viewed film extracts with violent scenes gave more severe punishments to a pretend opponent than did children who had viewed a film of an exciting race. These consistent results might give the impression that independent individuals are directly influenced by television. But this conclusion has been critized by Leyens, Herman and Dunand (1982), who point out that it is not independent but *interdependent* individuals who sit together in front of the television or go to the cinema. Television viewing – like almost all social behaviour – takes place in a social context. Individuals interact with one another, and talk about the films they see or want to see. They can also influence each other to behave aggressively.

Overwhelmingly, laboratory and field studies show only short-term effects of media violence on viewer's aggressive tendencies (see Leyens and Herman, 1979 for a review). To learn something about the possible long-term effects of viewing televised violence, longitudinal studies have measured both viewing habits and observed aggression at several points in time. For example, Eron et al. (1972) tested their sample at the age of eight years and then at the age of 18. The pattern of correlations obtained supported the hypothesis that relatively high aggressivity at the age of 18 was related back to relatively frequent viewing of violent films at the age of eight. Other longitudinal studies, albeit over a shorter period, report similar results (Eron and Huesmann, 1980; Huesmann, Lagerspetz and Eron, 1984; Singer and Singer, 1979). These studies are critically reviewed by Friedrich-Cofer and Huston (1986) and by Freedman (1984).

Frequent viewing of televised violence does not only have a direct impact on the viewer's readiness to behave aggressively; it also influences attitudes towards aggression. People who learn from television that conflicts are often violently resolved, and that one aggressive act tends to be followed by another, also overestimate the likelihood that they themselves will be victims of violence, are suspicious of others, and demand more state funding and harsher sentences in the fight against crime. As a rule, such attitudes are associated with a conservative outlook. But interestingly, one study showed no difference between liberals and conservatives when they were both 'heavy' consumers of television violence (Gerbner et al., 1980).

A three-year longitudinal study of children in West Germany also showed long-term effects of viewing violence on attitudes to aggression (Krebs, 1981; Krebs and Groebel, 1979). Boys and girls who preferred and watched more violent television, later judged aggressive retaliation more positively.

Summary and conclusions

The assumptions about the causes of aggressive behaviour postulated by the theories discussed in this chapter can be placed on a continuum from internal to environmental. At one extreme, the instinct theories developed by Freud and Lorenz conceive of aggressive behaviour as motivated by an aggressive instinct. Using hydraulic systems such as the steam boiler as a metaphor, these instinct theories assume that from time to time the individual has to release the aggressive energy continually produced by this instinct and behave aggressively (i.e. 'let off steam') in order to avoid damaging consequences for the organism.

Social learning theory represents the other extreme of the continuum. According to this position, aggressive behaviour, like most forms of behaviour, is learned through instrumental conditioning and/or modelling. It is thus under the control of environmental reward contingencies.

Frustration-aggression theories take an intermediate position. Like instinct theories, they conceptualize aggressive behaviour as motivated by a need to release aggressive energy. However, this aggressive energy is not automatically produced by some internal process but results from an environmental event, the frustration of some goal-directed behaviour. Since the original hypothesis that frustration is both a necessary and a sufficient cause of aggression could not be supported empirically, more recent versions of this theory abandon this assumption and attempt to specify the conditions under which frustration leads to aggression.

These theories have important implications for the social control of aggression. While the environmental control of aggressive behaviour should be difficult or even dangerous according to theories that attribute aggression to internal causes such as instincts or drives, learning theory suggests numerous strategies of aggression control.

Mediating Variables in Aggression: from Internal States to
Socio-Cultural Factors

Research into the factors which mediate aggressive behaviour initially focused
on internal states such as aversive arousal or pain. However, although frustration, anger or pain are important elicitors of aggressive behaviour, it soon
became obvious that whether individuals responded to such stimuli with
aggressive behaviour was greatly dependent on their own interpretation of the
other person's behaviour. Thus people are more likely to behave aggressively if
they interpret a given action as aggressive rather than an unintentional or even
benevolent. This discussion of social construction, social interpretation and
attribution as modifiers of aggressive behaviour will lead us, finally, into the
analysis of the role of social norms in aggression.

The role of arousal in aggression

Aversive arousal and aggression   Let us imagine that someone experiences
frustration: perhaps because despite hours of trying he cannot mend his tape-
recorder; perhaps because, as a result, his girlfriend teases him publicly about
how impractical he is. We would expect that such events raise a person's general
level of arousal, and are experienced negatively. We would also expect that,
as this aroused anger increases, so does the readiness to respond aggressively – perhaps by throwing the tape-recorder at the wall, or insulting the
girlfriend.

Thus the experience of negative arousal seems to be an important factor in
the readiness to respond aggressively. Alongside frustrations, there are many
other experiences which can heighten an individual's level of aversive arousal
and increase the probability of aggression. In particular, research has looked at
environmental influences on aggression, such as noise, crowding and heat.

Donnerstein and Wilson (1976) planned the following experiment to investigate the influence of noise on aggression. In phase one, half the male subjects
were angered by having some written work negatively evaluated by a confederate (the other subjects had the work judged positively). In phase 2, the
subjects had the opportunity to give this confederate electric shocks of varying
intensity when he made mistakes in a learning task. The strength of shock
delivered served as the measure of aggression. During this phase of the learning
task the subjects wore headphones, by means of which slightly or extremely
unpleasant levels of noise were transmitted. The results were clear, as shown in
figure 12.2: noise, as an aversive stimulus only increased aggression when the
subjects had previously been angered.

Other experiments supported these findings (Geen and O'Neal, 1969;
Konečni, 1975): noise can make people more aggressive, but only when this
aggressive behaviour (either through provocation or by watching aggressive
models on film) has become the individual's dominant response tendency, that
is, the individual was already prepared to behave aggressively.

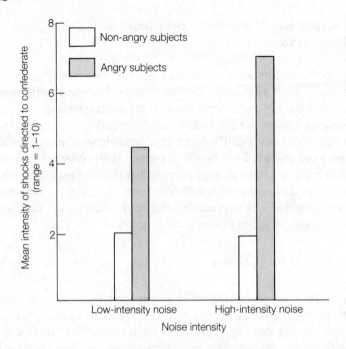

FIGURE 12.2   The effects of noise and induced anger on the intensity of electric shocks delivered (data from Donnerstein and Wilson, 1976; figure from Baron, 1977, p. 130)

Studies on the influence of crowding look, at first sight, less consistent. Correlational studies on the relation between density of housing and violent crime showed negative results (e.g. Altman, 1975). Although there was more violent crime in densely populated than less crowded residential areas (Scherer, Abeles and Fischer, 1975), this effect disappears as soon as additional variables such as income or education are controlled for. Laboratory experiments show both increased (Freedman et al., 1972) and decreased (Hutt and McGrew, 1967) effects of crowding on the extent of aggressive behaviour. Of great importance here is whether spatial density is subjectively perceived as pleasant (a disco) or unplesant (a crowded underground train) (see Stokols, 1972). When crowding interferes with what a person wants to do, then it is perceived as unpleasant. In this case aggressive tendencies can be intensified, but so too can the tendency to leave the situation (see Kruse, 1975 for a review).

Our own experience, as well as expressions like 'the long hot summer', together with some statistical analyses, support the assumption that the number and intensity of violent acts, especially in cities, increase as the temperature rises. People are negatively aroused by high temperatures. This assumption relating aggression to heat has been tested in a series of experiments. Here too it was proposed that a heat-induced state of arousal would intensify aggressive tendencies if the individual was already prepared to act aggressively owing to previous provocation. Interestingly, Baron and Bell (1975, 1976) found different results in a series of experiments. Contrary to the hypothesis, aggressive behaviour (duration and intensity of electric shocks)

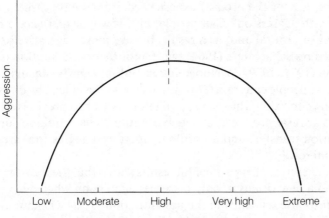

FIGURE 12.3   Curvilinear relation between negative affect and aggression (Baron, 1977, p. 146)

actually decreased, as the temperature increased from 20 to 30°C. People who had previously been provoked behaved *less* aggressively under 'heat' conditions, while people who had previously been treated in a friendly manner behaved *more* aggressively. Baron and Bell therefore proposed a curvilinear relation between temperature and aggression (see figure 12.3).

According to Baron and Bell, the influence of temperature on aggression is mediated by the level of negative affect, and not only the general arousal, that a person experiences. For people in a neutral mood, an unpleasant temperature can worsen their mood and increase aggressive tendencies; such people's readiness to behave aggressively is similar to that generated by provocation and the resulting negative affect. If unpleasant temperature brings an additional negative experience to this degree of negative affect, then maximal readiness to respond aggressively will be surpassed. Under these conditions individuals feel so bad that all they want to do is get away. Bell and Baron (1976) tested this idea experimentally. They allocated subjects to experimental conditions that were ordered in terms of aroused negative emotions. This was done using hot and cold temperatures, linked to positive or negative evaluation by a confederate. The data revealed the predicted curvilinear picture; the highest intensity of aggressive behaviour was shown by subjects who experienced mild negative affect. In conditions of both extremely positive and extremely negative affect, there was significantly less aggressive behaviour.

Non-specific arousal and excitation transfer   As provocation, heat and noise are conditions normally experienced as aversive, one would expect them to be perceived as direct sources of increased aversive arousal, which influence readiness for aggression. The extent of general physiological arousal is, however, also influenced by other activities like physical exertion, sensational news stories, thrilling spy films or erotic films. Can such non-specific sources of arousal complement the arousal experienced from sources which are clearly associated with aggression? Can people, in this way, experience a heightened general level of arousal and, as a result, behave more aggressively?

Influenced by Schachter's (1964) two-factor theory of emotion (see chapter 5), Zillmann (1971, 1979) developed his **excitation-transfer-theory**. According to this theory, people can transfer residual arousal produced by one source to a new arousing condition; that is, arousal left over from a previous situation can be added to arousal produced in a new situation. The conditions under which such excitation transfer, and accordingly increased aggression, are found are clearly of interest.

First of all, a series of experimental results shows that the transfer of residual excitation to a new situation only increases aggression when aggression is the dominant response tendency in the new situation. Thus when an individual is already primed to act aggressively, the transferred residual arousal may increase the likelihood of an aggressive response. In one experiment, Zillmann, Katcher and Milavsky (1972) induced conditions of provocation or no provocation using a confederate, and arousal by means of physical exertion or no exertion. Subjects had either to pedal on a cycling machine for 2.5 minutes, or to view a series of slides. Subsequently they had the opportunity to give the confederate electric shocks. Consistent with the hypotheses, the additional arousal only increased aggression when aggression was the dominant reaction: physical exertion only increased the level of shocks delivered by subjects who had previously been provoked.

There also seems to be a second factor that influences the conditions under which increased physiological arousal leads to more aggression – namely, how the arousal is interpreted or labelled. If, in response to a disparaging comment or an unjustified accusation, we feel our blood pressure and respiration rate increase and our face blush, we interpret this state of arousal as anger. And we see the insulting person as the cause of this anger. Arousal interpreted as anger increases the probability of an aggressive response. But the same signs of physiological arousal can also be felt in a situation where we are, quite unexpectedly, asked to deliver a short talk in front of a seminar group. Now the obvious interpretation is embarrassment or fear, and an aggressive response is less likely.

Zillmann, Johnson and Day (1974) created experimental conditions which led subjects to attribute the cause of general arousal either to a neutral or to an aggression-relevant source. It was expected that only in the latter case would the transfer of residual arousal increase aggression. Once again male subjects were provoked by a confederate, and then later had the opportunity to give him different levels of electric shock. Between these two phases, a cycling machine was pedalled for 1.5 minutes to generate an increased state of arousal. In addition a 6 minute rest period was arranged, which for one group of subjects was before, and for the other group after, the cycling exercise. Zillmann, Johnson and Day predicted that in the sequence exertion–rest–reaction, the residual arousal felt in the reaction phase would be interpreted as anger, because the rest period had provided the opportunity to recover after the

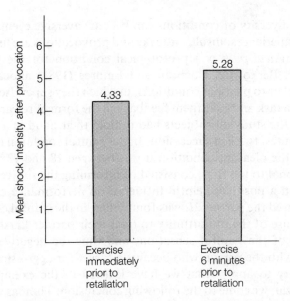

FIGURE 12.4 Arousal by physical exercise and aggression (based on data from Zillmann, Johnson and Day, 1974)

exercise. In the sequence rest–exertion–reaction, however, the arousal should be traced back to the exertion, and thus no increase in aggression was expected. The results showed exactly this pattern (see figure 12.4). We should here emphasize that there were clear differences in aggressive behaviour, although all subjects were provoked and physically aroused to the same extent.

In answer to the question of under which conditions general arousal is related to an increase in aggression, we can follow the available reviews: such an increase is to be expected when the individual lacks clear information about the causes of arousal. Given clear information, the arousal will be correctly interpreted and will have no effect on the extent or the probability of aggressive behaviour (see Rule and Nesdale, 1976; Tannenbaum and Zillmann, 1975).

Aggression as pain-elicited behaviour The theoretical position described above sees the relation between arousal and aggression as a *sequence*: the most different conditions lead to general arousal; depending on its perceived causes, this arousal is then labelled and leads to a specific emotion, such as anger. The kind of behaviour that is expected depends, in turn, on the type of emotion.

Berkowitz (1983) criticized this view and proposed an alternative theory: there is no such thing as unspecific or neutral arousal. Aversive events have a direct negative effect and lead directly to the arousal of aggression or to flight; subjective emotional experiences in the form of anger or fear may or may not accompany these forms of behaviour. Anger and aggression are, then, *parallel* and not sequential processes.

The more unpleasant the event, the greater the individual's readiness for aggression. Whether aggression is actually shown depends on situational cues.

In principle, a diversity of conditions can become aversive events, depending on individual experiences: insults, attacks and provocations are usually seen as unpleasant. *Physical pain* is a prototypical condition for the triggering of negative affect. Berkowitz, Cochran and Embree (1981) allocated subjects either to painful or to pleasant conditions, in which they supervised confederates working on a task and gave them feedback in the form of rewards of punishments. During the study all subjects had to hold their hand in a container of water for 7 minutes, twice in succession. In the painful condition the water was an icy 6°C; in the pleasant condition it was between 18 and 23°C. A second factor, orthogonal to the first, consisted of informing the subjects either that punishment had a positive, helpful influence on performance or that it disturbed and injured the partner. It was found that, in the painful condition, the subjects made use of the opportunity to treat their partner harshly. But note that the cause of the painful sensation, and thus the negative affect, had nothing to do with the person who became a target for aggression.

If we now try to apply what we have learned to the example involving Thomas and Özal, we come to the following conclusion: Thomas was probably in a state of aversive arousal, he felt angry. The surroundings of the bar – crowded, hot and noisy – probably further heightened his arousal. Thomas saw Özal's behaviour in the course of their discussion as the cause of his anger. Most likely, Özal was not the first person whom Thomas had punched on the chin. Indeed, Thomas had probably learned to react in this way.

The social construction of aggression

Frustration, anger, aggressive cues and experience with aggressive models, whether direct or channelled through the media, are clearly important conditions for the occurrence of aggressive behaviour. In our considerations thus far we have implicitly assumed a definition of aggression which without doubt defines as aggressive both Thomas's behaviour and that operationalized in experiments such as those involving the delivery of painful electric shocks. Let us compare this implicit definition of aggression with the one suggested by Baron: 'Aggression is any form of behaviour directed toward the goal of harming or injuring another living being who is motivated to avoid such treatment' (1977, p. 7). From what we know, Thomas's behaviour satisfies these implied criteria, namely intention to harm and (potential) injury to the victim. At issue here is not the kind of behaviour in itself. Almost every behaviour, even a failure to act (as in the case of giving help), can become aggression if someone judges that the actor intended to harm the victim. Conversely, cases of extreme violence need not be identified as aggression: if asked, Thomas would describe his behaviour as necessary self-defence because he felt threatened by Özal. More extremely still, members of institutions that torture other people describe their cruelty not as aggression but as a necessary means for the defence of their system and its values.

When we appraise a behaviour as aggressive, we go beyond a simple description to make an evaluation: the behaviour is bad and inappropriate, and it violates a norm; the perpetrator deserves to be punished for it. Being judged by an observer or even a participant has, then, social consequences; if a behaviour is judged to be aggressive, a negative sanction seems appropriate. If the same behaviour is judged to be morally justified, positive sanctions are even possible. Clearly, when asking about the causes of aggression, more is of interest than simply the conditions for the occurrence of that behaviour. Of even greater importance are the conditions for judging individual behaviour as 'aggressive'.

The interpretation of individual behaviour as aggressive   Blumenthal et al. (1972) carried out a large-scale study of American men's attitudes to different forms of violence. The results show clear differences between social groups. Students with negative attitudes to the police judge police behaviour during student demonstrations (e.g. assaults on students) to be violent; but the behaviour of positively perceived student demonstrators (e.g. 'sit-ins') is judged non-violent. Conversely, for people with positive attitudes to the police, the behaviour of student demonstrators was negatively evaluated: for them, sit-ins were violent acts deserving arrest, and the use of firearms by the police was supported against demonstrators who damaged property. These authors conclude that the same behaviour can be seen as necessary and good, or as abhorrent and punishable, depending on whether the precipitating action is seen as legitimate or illegitimate. Camino and Trocolli (1980; cited by Leyens and Fraczek, 1984) showed, in a similar study carried out in Brazil, that the judgement of a critical behaviour as violent was dependent on the sociopolitical beliefs of the subjects. Those who believed in a 'just world' (see Rubin and Peplau, 1975) judged the police to be less violent than those who did not share this belief.

   Alongside these large-scale studies, many experiments have also been carried out to investigate the influence of various criteria on whether a behaviour is judged to be aggressive. These studies conclude that *intention to harm*, *actual harm* and *norm violation* are the main criteria for labelling an act as aggressive (Ferguson and Rule, 1983).

Social influence and coercive power   Aggression is, then, as we have seen, not purely a descriptive but also an evaluative concept. It involves subjective judgements about the actor's intentions and whether the behaviour is normatively appropriate. Tedeschi and coworkers suggested that aggression be analysed in the following way: by separating behaviour from evaluation. When viewed in an evaluatively neutral manner, aggressive behaviour involves a special form of social influence: an individual coerces another person to do something which that person would not have done without that coercion. Aggression thus consists of the application of **coercive power**, whether in the form of threat or punishment. By means of a threat, we make clear that we want something special from someone, and that punishment will follow non-compliance. A punishment is any form of treatment that is aversive for the victim. The interesting research question is to define the conditions under which people seek to use this coercive form of influence. Tedeschi, Lindskold and Rosenfeld (1985) differentiate seven factors that increase the probability of threats and punishments in the course of a social interaction. These factors are: (1) norms of self-defence, reciprocity and distributive justice; (2) challenges to authority; (3) intense conflict over resources; (4) self-presentation and face-saving; (5) need for attention; (6) desire to control immediate behaviours of others; and (7) failure to consider future consequences. In this sense Thomas's behaviour towards Özal could be described as self-defence, and perhaps also as retaliation for some previous insult. The question of whether this form of coercive power is evaluated as *aggression* is quite independent of this description. This question has less to do with the conditions for the occurrence of the behaviour, than with the conditions under which certain behaviours are consensually *interpreted* as 'aggressive'. As we have seen, exactly the same behaviour is labelled as aggressive when perceived as illegitimate and as violating norms; but as non-aggressive when there is no norm violation.

Attribution and aggression   Actions in themselves do not contain the defining criteria mentioned above – intention to harm, actual harm and norm violation – but are actively constructed in these terms. That does not mean, however, that these perceptions happen by chance. On the contrary, everyday interactions are regulated by an impressive social consensus. Exactly here lies an important task for social psychology, namely to discover the cognitive and normative factors that influence interpretation and evaluation. Thus Rule and Ferguson (1984) ask about the conditions under which people react to aversive events *as if* they were aggressive ones. In other words, we are talking about the nature and process of causal attributions for aversive events (see chapter 6), and their influence on emotional and behavioural reactions. Rule and Ferguson highlight two aspects of these causal attributions. First, there are the factors that determine who, or what, is perceived as *responsible* for an aversive event. Second, there are the determinants of an *is–ought* discrepancy with respect to the behaviour in question; that is, a perceived discrepancy between what the actor actually did, and what he or she should have done in a given situation. In our example, we would perceive a large is–ought discrepancy if Thomas had punched Özal for no reason, e.g. in the absence of a previous insult. The discrepancy would be smaller if the action had been a *reaction* to a verbal provocation; and there would be almost no discrepancy if Thomas had merely replied with a verbal insult instead of a punch.

The is–ought discrepancy is, then, particularly important when the actor is held responsible for having caused the aversive consequences. To attribute responsibility, we must decide whether the aversive consequences were *intended* or not; if unintended, the perceiver must decide whether the consequences were, for the actor at least, *forseeable* or not. If the consequences were intended, the perceiver must decide whether the actor's motives were malevolent or not. Dependent on this decision process, the perceiver classifies the aversive consequences as accidental, forseeable, and arising from malevolent or well-meaning motives. The more aversive the consequences, and the greater the is–ought discrepancy perceived by a victim or an observer, the more angry and revengeful he or she will be. The results of various studies based on self-descriptions indicate that people become angry when they feel that they are victims of wilful and/or unjustified aversive actions performed by others (Averill, 1982; Mikula and Petri, 1987).

Norms as regulators of aggression

Perceived injustice and the norm of reciprocity   Parents typically tell their children that they should not hit, scratch or kick other children; and that if found behaving in these ways, they will be punished. But if their little son comes home in tears, claiming that someone took away his bike, or kicked him, the same parents typically tell him to stand up for himself: 'If someone kicks you, then kick them back!' A high percentage of voters throughout the world ardently support the death penalty: someone who kills, or tries to kill, another person deserves to die. Gouldner (1960) proposes that the *norm of reciprocity* ('tit for tat') is a socially shared prescription that operates in many different societies (see chapter 11). If someone thinks they are a victim of aggression then, following the reciprocity norm, they can feel justified in retaliating. Moreover, they can be sure that many other people will support this retaliation, seeing it as just and appropriate.

Experimental studies support this observation, when students watch actors on the stage. The initiator of a hostile act is perceived as aggressive, offending and behaving unfairly. An actor who physically attacks another in response to provocation is, however, judged to be acting defensively and fairly (Brown and Tedeschi, 1976).

As we have seen, certain information increases the probability that an action will be labelled as aggressive and that, as a consequence, the violence will be reciprocated or escalated. In the same way, information that weakens the attribution of responsibility or the perception of norm violation can have exactly the opposite effect on the unfolding of an interaction: the perpetrator is judged less negatively, and the tendency to retaliate is weaker. We might learn, for example, that Thomas had drunk too much alcohol, that he was tired or under stress; in other words, he was not fully in control of his actions, and he neither desired nor could have foreseen the consequences of his behaviour. Such additional information can be used to *excuse* the actor. Another possibility is that the consequences of behaviour are re-evaluated, the act being seen as justified, appropriate, unavoidable or even necessary: 'Finally, Thomas showed Özal what for! That's the way to treat people like him.' These kinds of accounts are classified as *justifications* (see chapter 6; and see Schönbach, 1985 for an alternative classification of accounts).

This information can be used deliberately, as an *account*, to influence another person or the public in how they interpret an event. Or, it might be available for witnesses to the event to choose from. In either case, this information affects how the behaviour is evaluated, and seems to reduce both the anger, and the tendency to retaliate, felt by the victim (Rule, Dyck and Nesdale, 1978; Zumkley, 1981).

Zillman and Cantor (1976) reported, for example, that excuses given *before* a provocation prevented anger from being aroused and reduced the tendency to retaliate against the provoking other. When excuses were given *after* the provocation, the victim also expressed less anger than when no mitigating information was given, but the tendency to take revenge was not reduced. In a recent study Johnson and Rule (1986) were interested in the effect of *strength* of excuse (either before or after provocation) upon the amount of, and subjective interpretations of, physiological arousal, as well as the tendency to retaliate aggressively. The results were consistent with previous findings. The strength of an excuse only had an effect when it was given *before* a provocation: a strong excuse was clearly more effective than a weak excuse in reducing both the strength of anger and the intensity of aggressive reactions to provocation. A strong excuse involved the subject's opponent explaining that he had just received a poor mark for his performance, and that this placed his career in jeopardy; a weak excuse referred only to the poor mark, not the effect this would have on a career. When these excuses were given only after the provocation, then they had no effect on anger or retribution, irrespective of their strength. Hence this information influences the subjective interpretation of arousal: if one has information that excuses someone's provocation, then this behaviour is seen as less provocative and deliberately malicious. In addition, one's own arousal is not necessarily interpreted as anger and the wish to retaliate is weaker. However, if the excuse is given only after provocation, the arousal has already been interpreted as anger, and the tendency to take revenge seems justified by usual norms.

The role of norms in intergroup aggression and collective violence   The scene is West Berlin. About 30 young people – including youths, students and former tenants – have occupied a large still-habitable house to prevent its demolition. The police, in vain having asked the squatters to leave the house, are preparing to evict them. The police break down doors, storm into the flats and try to drag the occupants out of the building. The squatters throw stones and set about the police; sympathizers on the street set cars alight, tear up the cobblestones and build barricades to prevent police reinforcements from getting through.

The people involved in this incident are behaving in ways which, as individuals, they would probably never dream of doing. Experimental studies confirm the impression gained from everyday observations: individuals in groups show much more aggressive behaviour than they do when acting as individuals (Jaffe and Yinon, 1983). The group situation seems to produce more explosive outbursts, while those involved are prepared to accept worse consequences for themselves. In the tradition of early mass psychology, associated with LeBon, Tarde and Sighele, this group influence was analysed as follows: individuals in groups or masses behave more irrationally, more impulsively and less normatively than they do as individuals (see chapters 1 and 16). A modern version of this perspective is found in work on **deindividuation** (Diener, 1980; Zimbardo, 1969). Deindividuation refers to a special individual state in which control over one's own behaviour is weakened, and there is less concern about normative standards, self-presentation and later consequences of one's behaviour. Various factors contribute towards deindividuation, such as anonymity, diffusion of responsibility, the presence of a group, and a shortened time perspective. When individuals become deindividuated – and this may be produced by a group situation – then it is predicted that usual inhibitions will be lowered, and impulsive behaviour such as violence or vandalism (see also chapter 17) become possible.

However, empirical findings do not give unconditional support to these assumptions. Thus anonymity may increase (Donnerstein et al., 1972), reduce (Baron, 1970) or have no effect on (Lange, 1971) aggression. In general, however, there is support for the idea that being in a group or crowd has a deindividuating effect on individuals; and that such individuals are less conscious of their identity, losing their usual inhibitions about aggressive behaviour.

In opposition to the basic assumptions of deindividuation theory stands *emergent-norm theory* (Turner and Killian, 1972). According to this view, conspicuously extreme forms of behaviour are more likely in group or crowd situations, *not* because individuals lose their inhibitions or care less about norms, but because new norms arise in groups, which are adhered to by all concerned and are shared in specific situations. In situations of confrontation between the police and demonstrators, norms may develop that people should defend themselves against the police. Aggressive forms of behaviour such as stone-throwing become possible not because individuals conform *less* to norms but, on the contrary, because they conform *more* to norms in this situation. Thus in group or crowd situations it is not necessarily the extent of normative control that changes but rather *the norms themselves*, to which behaviour is oriented. If the function of anonymity is to weaken the pressure to conform to norms, then from emergent-norm theory one should predict the following: under conditions of anonymity, aggressive behaviour in a group situation should be weakened *if* the situational norms demand aggression. Behaviour that conforms to norms, in this case aggressive behaviour, would then be most likely *not* when individuals were anonymous but when they were identifiable and could be called to account for norm violations (see Reicher, 1982).

Mann, Newton and Innes (1982) designed a study to decide between the competing approaches of deindividuation and emergent norms. Their results supported both theories: anonymous subjects were more aggressive, but especially when aggressive behaviour was normative, and less so when it was normatively inappropriate. Rabbie, Lodewijkx and Broeze (1985) clarified the picture a little further: their male subjects behaved more aggressively under conditions of anonymity, while female subjects were more aggressive when identifiable.

Alongside anonymity, deindividuation is also promoted by the presence of others or a group; thus more, or more intense, aggression is expected in groups than in individual situations. However, here too the experimental findings are not clear-cut. Rabbie (1982) questions the empirical basis for the assumption that groups behave more irrationally or show more violation of norms than do individuals, because only rarely have group situations been compared explicitly with individual situations. On the basis of a number of studies, Rabbie concludes that groups are *not* always more aggressive than individuals (Rabbie and Horwitz, 1982; Rabbie and Lodewijkx, 1983). It depends on which norms are dominant within a group. In particular, group members create a shared interpretation of an opponent's behaviour. Consistent with this interpretation, they react clearly more extremely towards the opponent than they do as individuals. If the group members agree that their opponents violated norms, then they influence each other to punish the opponent more severely. The dominant, normative orientation is, then, reinforced by group processes (see chapter 15). Studies by Rabbie and colleagues support this *norm-enhancement hypothesis*: groups behave more aggressively than individuals when such behaviour can be defined as legitimate and normatively appropriate. The latter conditions were satisfied by allowing subjects to see their aggression as punishment for an opponent who had previously taken advantage of them in an experimental game.

In group situations, individuals are provided with information about the appropriateness and legitimacy of possible forms of behaviour. Thus aggressive interactions seem, in both interpersonal and intergroup contexts, to be guided by the same principles. It is just not convincing to explain observable differences in interpersonal and intergroup aggression in terms of inner states and a loss of rationality. In both individual and group situations, actors seem to see their own behaviour as quite appropriate. If more extreme forms of aggression characterize group situations, then this seems due to the fact that group members mutually reinforce each other in the view that they are all behaving appropriately.

Summary and Conclusion

At the beginning of this chapter we asked what can cause a person to insult, hurt or even kill another person. Why is it that people will treat others in ways that they would certainly never wish to be treated themselves?

We have looked at a number of theoretical approaches and a variety of empirical findings in the field of aggression. We can summarize the picture as follows: Aggressive behaviour can be learned through instrumental conditioning or modelling. The readiness actually to use this behaviour arises when it is seen as a useful means to an end – terminating a situation which is physically or psychologically aversive, and for which another person is held responsible. Under these conditions, there is a good deal of evidence that the use of aggressive means is socially acceptable and normatively appropriate – provided that the aggression takes the form of reciprocal retaliation or reaction.

We have also seen that the same behaviour can be judged aggressive, or not, depending on relevant norms and how the aggressive behaviour is attributed. The same behaviour can also be judged from different *perspectives*. In particular, there are clear differences in the evaluation of identical behaviour from the perspective of harm-doer and victim. Both experimental (Mummendey, Linneweber and Löschper, 1984) and naturalistic (Felson, 1984) studies have shown that own behaviour is seen as less violent and less inappropriate.

Aggressive behaviour, whether between individuals or groups, is, like other forms of social behaviour, regulated by socially accepted and situationally relevant norms. In looking for the causes of aggression, therefore, we should not concentrate on the conditions that energize individual drives or reduce the rational control of behaviour. Rather, we should look for the conditions (at least from the actor's perspective) which make intentionally harming another person seem both situationally appropriate and justified.

Glossary Terms

Catharsis	Excitation-transfer theory
Classical conditioning	Frustration
Coercive power	Frustration-aggression
Cue-arousal theory	hypothesis
Deindividuation	Instinct
Displacement	Instrumental conditioning
	Modelling

Further Reading

Averill, J. R. (1982) *Anger and Aggression: an essay on emotion.* New York: Springer. Detailed, high-level approach to the social construction of anger.

Bandura, A. (1973) *Aggression: a social learning analysis.* Englewood Cliffs, N J: Prentice-Hall. Comprehensive treatment of the social learning approach to aggression.

Baron, R. A. (1977) *Human Aggression.* New York: Plenum. Readable, wide-ranging introductory overview.

Geen, R.G. and Donnerstein, E.I. (eds) (1983) *Aggression: Theoretical and empirical reviews.* New York: Academic Press. A two-volume work giving the current versions of the most important theories of aggression, as well as empirical research, at an advanced level.

Zillmann, D. (1979) *Hostility and Aggression.* Hillsdale, N J: Erlbaum. Lays the foundations of and critically discusses relevant theoretical positions, with an emphasis on the integration of affective and cognitive aspects of hostility and aggression.

13 Conflict and Cooperation

JANUSZ GRZELAK

Introduction

When a pedestrian rushes to help the victim of a car accident, the victim's lot depends on what the pedestrian does, but not vice versa. When the drivers of two cars join forces to clear the road of a fallen tree too heavy to be moved by one of them alone, or when two students decide to share an apartment too expensive to be rented singly, each person's well-being depends upon *both* what he or she does and what the other does. This type of mutual dependence is called social **interdependence**. Members of large groups or communities can also be interdependent. In a community suffering a fuel shortage, for example, every inhabitant has the choice either of conserving fuel resources (e.g. by keeping the thermostat low) and suffering somewhat from the cold, or of ignoring conservation and heating the house as usual, thus running the risk of freezing if everyone else in the community does the same.

At one pole of social interdependence there are situations of a full correspondence of interests (like that of the two drivers), where a line of action beneficial to one partner evidently benefits the other too, maximizing the gains of both. At the other pole we find cases where the interest of one party contradicts the interests of the other: one party stands to lose as much as the other party stands to gain. Situations like war, a boxing match, a game of poker, or rivalry between two applicants for the same job, can all be placed near this pole. No matter how much we would like to deal solely with complete correspondence of interests, the realities of life are such that at best intermediate situations predominate: typically, the parties' interests are neither the same nor completely opposite. Such would be the case if one of the two students mentioned above preferred to pay more for an apartment close to the college while the other gave priority to cheap lodgings further away.

This chapter was written as a part of my work at Warsaw University and revised during my visit to the Catholic University of Brabant (Tilburg, Netherlands). I wish to thank John Rijsman for arranging my visit and my colleagues at both universities for their help. I owe special thanks to Boguslaw A. Jankowski for his help with the English version of the chapter.

We might think of solving the problem of non-correspondent interests in a number of ways. Without offering the most preferred solution to either party, a way out could be found that would possibly satisfy both parties. This could be the students renting a moderately priced apartment together, not too far from the college. Behaviour that yields maximal *joint* profit for all the parties involved is called **cooperation**. The other solution is to choose what suits one's *own interest*, in disregard of the other's preferences (individualism). Still another way would be to choose what makes one fare *better* than the other. Behaviour that yields maximal *relative* gain is labelled **competition**.

Under what conditions, in the face of discordant interests, is a person prepared either to meet the other's interests half-way, i.e. to cooperate; or to care only for his or her own profit; or to get more than the other, i.e. to compete? In present-day psychology the issue has been most extensively studied using mathematical decision theory and in particular game theory (Von Neumann and Morgenstern, 1944). This chapter begins with a short introduction to the main tenets of this theory and a discussion of the research inspired by them. Next we go into the motivational and cognitive factors underlying behaviour in conflict situations. The chapter closes with some remarks on the relationship between conflict, social comparison and social identity.

Homo Oeconomicus? Maximizing Self-Interest

Theoretical notions and experimental paradigms

Imagine that you would like to study how people solve **conflicts of interests**. You could do it in various ways, like observing people in real-life conflicts, interviewing them about what they feel and think, or running experiments. You could not, however, ask them all the possible questions or encompass all situational factors and features of their behaviour. You would need a theory beforehand, a theory prompting you as to which of the countless factors are important and which can be neglected.

For over three decades many psychologists have adopted game theory to study conflicts of interest. In terms of this theory, any situation of interdependence can be characterized by: the number of persons involved; the number of actions (strategies) available to each person; the outcomes resulting from all possible combinations of actions; and each person's preferences over all outcomes. *Outcomes* refer here to consequences of any action that are of value (positive or negative) to a person, be it money, other material possessions, or non-material possessions such as power, status and social approval. It is assumed that every individual is a rational, selfish being in the sense that he or she maximizes his or her own interest. In other words, facing a choice between two or more actions, every party is thought to choose that action whose consequences are of the highest subjective value. Since people are interdependent, what is rational to them depends upon how their individual preferences are related to one another: whether they are conflicting, and if so to what extent and in what way. These relationships – the **interdependence structure** – define the strategic properties of the situation and determine what is one's best action in the light of the best action of others.

In principle, game theory provides a formal and normative rather than a descriptive model of decision-making. However, the image of **Homo oeconomicus** maximizing own profit is deeply rooted in Western culture, pervades much of our thinking and forms the core of not only economic but many psychological theories (Stroebe and Frey, 1982).

This relatively simple view of social interdependence has served as a basis for developing various experimental laboratory analogues of real-life situations. Some of the experiments set out to simulate a *natural conflict* scenario. For instance, in the method devised by Deutsch and Krauss (1960), the two subjects are equipped with a road chart and play the roles of truck drivers; their task is to bring a truck-load to its destination as quickly as possible. The choice is between a long route and a short route, the latter being in part a single-lane road on which they have to move in opposite directions. Choosing the shorter route presupposes a coordination of movement and hence cooperation between the players (companies named 'Acme' and 'Bolt'). Otherwise they waste time by either blocking each other or by taking the longer road (see figure 13.1).

Even though this situation simulates a distinct conflict of interest, its strategic structure (i.e. which choice is in the best interest of one or the other to make) is far from obvious. Most investigators trade vividness for precision, replacing realistic scenarios with more abstract models generally labelled

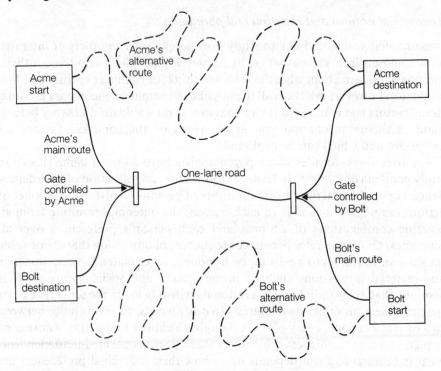

FIGURE 13.1   Road map for the trucking game (Deutsch and Krauss, 1960)

experimental games. We are particularly interested in non-negotiable **mixed-motive** (non-constant sum) games.

In experimental games the complex strategic decisions of everyday life have been represented by simple actions such as pressing a key or entering a letter to mark the given strategy; the great variety of outcomes (material, psychological and social) are reduced to a mere score or a sum of money. Despite their external dissimilarity to real-life situations, experimental games were thought to offer convenient analogies as long as they could model accurately the relations between the parties' interests. These relations can be expressed in various ways. The most frequent method is a table – or *payoff matrix* – showing the payoffs (outcomes) resulting from all possible combinations of the parties' moves.

Consider an example of a two-person situation. Suppose you are taking part in this kind of game. You are presented with two cards, one displaying the letter C, the other the letter D, and with a table like the one in game 1 in figure 13.2 known as the prisoner's dilemma game (PDG). The other person is seated behind a partition, equipped as you are and unable to communicate with you. You are told that numbers in the table represent the amounts of money which you and the other person can gain depending upon the choices both of you make. The first of the two digits in each cell of the table (the one in a circle) says

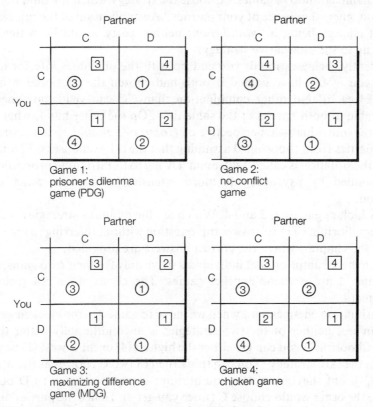

FIGURE 13.2   Examples of two-person games in matrix form (numbers in circles denote rewards for you, numbers in boxes denote rewards for partner

how much money (e.g. in pounds) you can get; the other (in a box) says how much your partner gets. If both of you opt for C, each wins £3; if your choices are different, the choice of D is rewarded with £4 and the choice of C with £1; if both of you choose D, each gets £2.

As long as both you and your partner prefer to gain as much money as possible, there should be no problem in choosing one from among the two cards. Suppose you and your partner pick D; then you win £2 instead of £1 if you had chosen C. Should you choose D and your partner choose C, you get £4 instead of £3 if you had chosen C. Thus D is the dominating strategy, being definitely superior to C irrespective of the other's choice.

This also implies that by choosing D you avoid the worst outcome, i.e. £1, which is associated with C. For this very reason, choice D satisfies one of the game-theoretical prescriptions for rational decision, the *minimax rule*. The prescription is: 'Choose the strategy for which the least attractive outcome is superior (or not inferior) to the least attractive outcomes of the other strategies.' It is a kind of safety rule: try to fend off the worst evil.

Note that your partner's situation is symmetrical; that is, the same reasoning applies to the other party in the game. Therefore the choice of D by both of you, which yields £2 for each of you, is most likely to occur. By the bilateral choice of D you both meet the second and the most important prescription of rational choice in mixed-motive games: 'Choose the strategy which it would not pay to abandon, given the choice of your partner.' An application of the rule leads to a pair of choices being in *equilibrium;* neither party would be better off by switching to the alternative strategy.

Evidently, being rational, you end up with the outcomes inferior to those which you would have gained if both had chosen the irrational strategy C (CC = £3 each)! No other combination than CC can yield outcomes more favourable to both parties at the same time. On the other hand, what reason (from the individualistic perspective of *Homo oeconomicus*) can restrain any of the parties from choosing D assuming that the other chooses C? None. This is why the situation is called a dilemma. Owing to its intriguing properties it has been studied by psychologists more extensively than any other conflict situation.

Now look at games 2, 3 and 4. Which are the minimax strategies and which are in equilibrium? Try to answer this question without referring to note 1 at the end of the chapter, where the correct answers are provided.

Given the assumption that individuals strive only for their own gains, game 2 and game 3 are both no-conflict games. The choice does not seem to be problematic.

The situation changes a lot when we move to game 4 – the chicken game. As you can see, neither of the two strategies is unconditionally better than the other. Choosing D you can get either the highest (4) or the lowest (1) payoff, so D is not the safe strategy. You can think then of two C choices as the best solution (3,3), but they are not in equilibrium: it pays to switch to D once you assume the other would choose C (since you get 4). Hence the parties' interests are not correspondent, although the conflict is much weaker than in the PDG.

Conflicts of the same structure can be represented in various forms. For instance, a frequently used form of the PDG is a decomposed PDG (Pruitt, 1967). The payoffs are split into components: the payoff table shows what portion of the payoffs each individual allocates to (l) the self and (2) the other. The number of possible decompositions is infinite, and which decomposition is used depends upon the purpose of the study. Figure 13.3 shows one of the decomposed versions of game 1. It should be read as follows. If you choose C, you award 1 to yourself (your payoff) and 2 to the partner (partner's payoff). The same refers to your partner, who is presented with an identical table: if he chooses C, he gives 1 to himself and 2 to you. The total of gains resulting from the two C choices equals 3 for each of you. Your choice of D means that you decide to give 2 to yourself and zero to the partner. This, if the partner still chooses C, yields 4 for you (2 from each of you) and 1 for the partner (what he or she allocated to him- or herself). And so on. As you can see, the sums of what each of you awards to self and to other, amount to the payoffs shown in game 1. Other games with a dominating strategy (e.g. game 2) can also be decomposed, without losing their original strategic properties.

An interdependence between more than two parties is often presented as a matrix or in a decomposed form. The normative solution of *n*-person games is the equilibrium solution (as in two-person games) as long as the involved parties cannot negotiate and form coalitions.

The growing interest in multiperson dilemmas has resulted in still another type of laboratory analogue of real conflicts. Some of these experiments simulate the exploitation of natural or man-made resources that are scarce and yet in common demand, like energy or fresh air. In the laboratory, this may be a money pool on which subjects are free to draw in successive choices; after each

		Your payoffs	Partner's payoffs
You	C	1	2
	D	2	0

		His/her payoffs	Partner's (i.e. your) payoffs
Partner	C	1	2
	D	2	0

FIGURE 13.3 A decomposition of game 1 (PDG)

draw the pool is replenished in varying degree (to simulate the regeneration of resources), but not enough to allow all subjects to harvest at maximal level. Individually, each person should readily engage in exploitative behaviour in the hope that the others proved suckers, but if everybody did the same the pool would soon be gone altogether. Thus a party's immediate interest is in conflict with the long-term joint interests of all parties (Dawes, 1980; Hardin, 1968).

The remaining part of this section will show to what extent people follow the theoretical prescription and what situational factors make them deviate from individualistic behaviour, that is, care for others' interests (for an extensive review see Colman, 1982a). Needless to say, this is more than a theoretical issue. It is of importance to all who want to know what determines the quality of social relationships – what makes them beneficial to all the persons involved.

When do people cooperate? Situational determinants

Payoffs and interdependence structure   In spite of differences in experimental procedure, in level of payoffs, or in subjects' status, experimental results have shown conclusively that cooperation in various games increases as (l) conflict between individual interest and joint interest decreases, and as (2) the departure of cooperative behaviour from the game-theoretical rules, i.e. minimax and equilibrium, decreases (e.g. Rapoport and Chammah, 1965, 1969; Guyer and Rapoport, 1972). The latter means that people tend to choose a cooperative action more often when by doing so they do not risk getting the worst of the available outcomes, and when it is not profitable for them to abandon cooperation as long as their partner does not do so. For instance, in two-person situattions the highest cooperation (some 80 per cent of choices or more) has been recorded in no-conflict games with two dominating strategies, as in game 2. In this game cooperative strategies are both minimax and in equilibrium. In games of moderate conflict in which the cooperative strategy complies with the minimax rule but does not lead to the most profitable equilibrium, as in the chicken game, cooperation declines to 50–60 per cent. A similar level most often prevails in the maximizing difference games in which cooperative strategies are in equilibrium, but they are not safer than the non-cooperative ones. However, the level of cooperation in these games sometimes goes down as low as 50 per cent, showing that a high proportion of subjects prefer relative gain to own or joint profits (McClintock and McNeel, 1967). The lowest frequency of cooperation has naturally been noted for C strategies that are neither minimax nor in equilibrium, as in the PDG (below 40 or even 30 per cent). A similar trade-off between a game's strategic properties and cooperation has also been recorded in *n*-person games (Tyszka and Grzelak, 1976).

In general, people do differentiate between various types of interdependence situations and the observed differences correspond most (but not all) of the time to the differences in the strategic properties of the situations.

It has been found that people are even more sensitive to the effects of their actions than the theory postulates. For instance, subjects pay attention not only to which strategy is the dominating one (like C in a no-conflict game or D in the PDG) but also to the difference between the profitability of alternative choices: the more the former is superior to the latter, the more often it is chosen (see Murnighan and Roth, 1983 for two-person games; and Komorita and Barth, 1985 for *n*-person situations). Moreover, even a seemingly slight change in only one of the available outcomes may lead to substantial changes in behaviour. For instance, adding only a little to the outcomes for mutual cooperation in the PDG presented in figure 13.2 (e.g. making it 3.25) may result in a high increase of cooperative choices, although the strategic logic of the game remains the same (Rapoport and Chammah, 1965).

Furthermore, the subjects' behaviour is affected by how the structure of interdependence is presented to them. In the decomposed PDG the level of cooperation was found to be higher than in the classical matrix form (Pruitt and Kimmel, 1977). The effect is especially strong in those decompositions where a major portion of the payoff comes from the partner's move, i.e. when each person can give more to the other than to himself. Such a payoff structure emphasizes each party's dependence upon the partner's generosity (Evans and Crumbaugh, 1966). Not surprisingly, compared with the standard version the decomposed PDG is marked by a quicker reciprocation of the partner's cooperative choices and a slower retaliation of non-cooperative ones (Tognoli, 1975).

Partner's strategy   In a two-person situation one's readiness to behave in a prosocial way is strongly affected by what the other party does and, in cases of repeated conflict, by the history of interaction between the two persons.

For instance, in a PDG repeated 300 times, the level of cooperation declined over the first few dozen trials but then rose again, reaching its maximum (about 65 per cent) in the second half of the trials (Radlow, 1965). There is a clear relationship between the parties' earlier experiences and their later choices. When both parties start a PDG with bilateral cooperation, the level of cooperation tends to exceed 40 per cent in subsequent games; starting with bilateral non-cooperation (DD choices) tends to lower subsequent cooperation to some 20 per cent (Terhune, 1968).

By what strategy can a party be induced to cooperate in the repeated game? A number of experiments show that a tit-for-tat strategy (i.e. reciprocating the partner's choices) has proved particularly effective when interests conflict, as in the PDG (Rapoport, 1976). The effect of the tit-for-tat strategy is understandable if one considers that in the repeated PDG, for instance, the parties have plenty of opportunity to compare the advantages of bilateral cooperation with the poor results of reciprocated rivalry.

Cooperation also depends on the absolute frequency of the partner's cooperative choices. In the PDG type of conflict, consistent cooperation by the partner (100 per cent) elicits more cooperative choices than the absolute lack of cooperation (0 per cent), whereas for the chicken type of conflict the opposite is true. The difference is understandable, since in the latter the mutual non-cooperative choices (DD) yield the lowest outcomes. However, in both cases a higher cooperation is elicited when the partner cooperates most of the time (around 80 per cent) than when he or she does it all the time. Social life brings us the same experience: being an obliging person is often interpreted as weakness. The tendency to exploit someone's unreserved cooperation, though recorded in various games, is observed more often in the chicken than in the PDG type of conflict (Sermat, 1967).

Finally, let us note that far higher cooperation is obtained if in a series of games the partner replaces his primarily individualistic choices with cooperative choices than vice versa. This effect is even stronger when the partner fails to make any cooperative move at the beginning, suddenly switches over to 100 per cent cooperation, and continues with the tit-for-tat strategy (Bixensteine and Wilson, 1963; Harford and Solomon, 1967). Thus we are more prone to cooperate with a 'reformed sinner' than with a 'lapsed saint'.

Communication and personal closeness   The effects of communication on cooperation are highly consistent. Generally speaking, the more opportunity there is to take in the partner's intentions and attitudes, the more likely are the partners to become constructively and dependably cooperative. Firm evidence for this has been offered by Wichman (1972), who had four experimental groups play PDG in different conditions: when the partners (1) could both see and hear, (2) could only hear, (3) could only see, and (4) could neither see nor hear each other. The level of cooperation fell markedly across those conditions: 87.0, 72.1, 47.7 and 40.7 per cent. Cooperation substantially rises with the extent or frequency of communication as well as with its content and trustworthiness (Deutsch, 1958; Swingle and Santi, 1972). Communication also contributes to cooperation in multiperson games (Liebrand, 1984).

This would mean that people who know each other should engage in cooperation more readily than complete strangers. The results support this claim: even a fleeting interaction with the partner has served to reduce markedly the frequency of non-cooperative choices that are aimed at protecting the party's interest (McClintock and McNeel, 1967). People behave, of course, more cooperatively towards those whom they like than towards strangers and disliked partners (Swingle and Gillis, 1968). In addition, Kranas (see Grzelak and Tyszka, 1974) in five- and six-person games of various kinds has found that subjects who liked each other tended to cooperate regardless of type of game, whereas the other subjects were influenced in their choices by type of conflict and its intensity (i.e. they responded more to the situation than to the partner).

Size of group   The observed level of cooperation varies with the number of the parties involved. In triads, the frequency of common-interest choices is lower than in dyads (Marwell and Schmitt, 1975); in seven-person groups it is lower than in triads (Hamburger, Guyer and Fox, 1975); and it is even lower in 12-person groups (Fox and Guyer, 1977). We may generalize these findings by saying that cooperation declines as the number of participants in a conflict increases, even though this applies more clearly to the PDG than to other types of situations, e.g. games of limited resources (Stroebe and Frey, 1982; Liebrand, 1984).

In the light of the findings mentioned earlier, the low cooperation often observed in the large groups is not surprising. Needless to say, in large groups and communities the fate of the individual depends on the behaviour of a multitude of other people: the individual can have only a negligible influence on the masses; communication with other participants in a conflict is almost impossible; and the participants are strangers to one another.

Summary

Experimental research on conflict of interests has shown that the tendency to solve conflicts in line with the common interest grows as the conflict between own interest and others' interest decreases; as the rewards for cooperation are increased; as the partner either cooperates too (but not unconditionally) or reciprocates the same choices; as the parties get to know each other; and as the opportunities for communication grow. Moreover, there is evidence that in some settings the partners' tendency to work for joint profit decreases as the number of persons involved increases.

Self-Interest Revisited: *Homo Oeconomicus* Socialized?

Own benefit versus other's benefit

Having reviewed the situational determinants of cooperation, we realize that people are more likely to give priority to their own interest as the costs of furthering the other's interest increase. However, exceptions to this rule are so frequent that they cannot be considered accidental. Recall the surprisingly high percentage of D choices in the maximizing difference game. Even in situations where a person cannot fail to notice the advantages of strategies that maximize his or her own interest irrespective of the partner's decisions (like the dominating non-cooperative strategy in PDG or the dominating cooperative strategy in no-conflict situations), sometimes more than 40 per cent of subjects opt for what seemingly is the less profitable strategy. Does this imply that people are often irrational, or should we rather reconsider the concept of self-interest used in the simplest psychological interpretation of game theory?

In everyday life we somehow take it for granted that, for example, a mother derives most of her joys (and anguish) from the consequences her actions have for her child rather than for herself. When it comes to money, we more easily expect people to care only about their own monetary gain. Evidently, even when money or points are at stake (as in most laboratory experiments) people may also be concerned with the other's gains or losses (Messick and McClintock, 1968). If a person opts for a consistently non-cooperative strategy in *all* the games of figure 13.2, his or her behaviour may be but need not be viewed as unreasonable. Alternatively, we might think of a different rationale: in all situations the person may be seeking to maximize the relative rather than (own) absolute gain. This interpretation makes the person's behaviour coherent and logical, for only the choice of D in all these situations can result in gaining an advantage over the partner. Similarly, choosing C in all the situations may be the most reasonable behaviour for someone who cares as much for the other's as for own benefit.

Social orientations

Concept and measurement   We may now redefine the concept of self-interest as being a function of two variables: own outcomes and other's (or others') outcomes. In a two-person setting, **social orientations** are characterized by what people want to achieve in interaction with others: to maximize only own gain (individualism), only partner's gain (altruism), joint profit (cooperation) or relative gain (competition); or yet other goals, like maximizing partner's losses (aggression), own losses (masochism) or other's predominance over own gains (martyrdom), or minimization of joint gain (sadomasochism) (for a theoretical framework see Griesinger and Livingstone, 1973; MacCrimon and Messick, 1976). In some models the number of basic orientations is reduced to but a few, for example to individualism, altruism and equality, the last being understood as the tendency to minimize an absolute difference between own and other's outcomes (Wieczorkowska, 1982).

Inferences about the type and strength of orientations are based on the subject's preferences for suitably differentiated outcome allocations to the self and to the other. A subject is typically made to reveal her preferences either by making a number of choices in decomposed games[2] (e.g. McClintock et al., 1973), by rating or ranking different allocations in terms of their attractiveness (Radzicki, 1976); or, in a set of allocation pairs, by choosing in each pair the option preferred to the other (Schulz, 1986). In each of these methods the social orientations are measured by identifying the criteria by which the subjects are guided in their choices or evaluations. If the subject consistently opts for a choice yielding maximal own profits, we conclude that he or she is guided by an individualistic criterion. Opting consistently for moves that give him or her an advantage over the partner, the subject displays a competitive orientation; and so on.

Although the studies have disclosed marked individual differences with respect to what goals people strive for, social orientations are not usually considered to be stable, trait-like individual characteristics, since they are also situation dependent. They can vary from situation to situation depending on the partner's characteristics (wealth, prestige, identity), on group norms and on other factors (Grzelak, 1982; McClintock and Van Avermaet, 1982).

Social orientations and behaviour   We may therefore expect behaviour in the same conflict situations to vary greatly, according to the subject's orientations. Take for instance an individual who values the partner's profit at least 50 per cent as much as his or her own: in this case the prisoner's dilemma (figure 13.2) turns into a dilemma-free, no-conflict situation in so far as the value of the outcomes of cooperative choices is enhanced by the partner's profit.

Many experiments consistently show the impact of social orientations on behaviour. For instance, Kuhlman and Marshello (1975) have used decomposed games to identify subjects with individualistic, cooperative and competitive orientations. These subjects were then made to play PDGs with an alleged partner who adhered to one of three strategies: 100 per cent cooperative, 100 per cent competitive, or tit for tat. Figure 13.4 shows the results. In each of the three situations the highest level of cooperation was displayed by the cooperators, the middle by the individualists, and the lowest by the competitive subjects; the difference between the two latter groups tended to disappear when the partner behaved in a competitive way.

The results of this experiment also show the possibility (mentioned earlier) of making the partner cooperate by applying frequent (or unqualified, as in this study) cooperation, or a tit-for-tat strategy. The former is most effective in relation to cooperators and the latter to individualists (see Schulz, 1986). The dependence of motivation on patterns of behaviour has likewise been demonstrated by Liebrand and Van Run (1985) in *n*-person simulated **social dilemmas** (resource games). Conducted on both American and Dutch subjects, their study revealed that in either group the most thrifty (cooperative) were the altruists, followed by the cooperators and the individualists; the competitive subjects were the least thrifty.

All in all, social orientations seem to account for much of the observed interpersonal variation in behaviour in conflict situations.

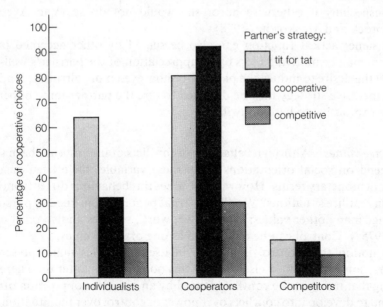

FIGURE 13.4   Cooperation and social orientations (based on Kuhlman and Marshello, 1975)

Limitations

Fairness Any interpersonal situation that involves the allocation or exchange of goods is apt to raise the question of whether or not the allocation is fair and just. The implementation of rules of fairness reduces the chances of conflict, increases hopes that the outcome may be accepted with satisfaction by both parties, and thus makes the solution of conflict easier (Mikula, 1980). So far, research on social orientations as well as on behaviour in conflict situations has mainly focused on the simplest form of equity, namely equality of outcomes: that is, on relations between the parties' gains and losses, regardless of how they are related to the parties' inputs (effort, amount and quality of work contribution, needs etc.). A few studies have already reported results showing that more attention should be paid to the fairness aspect of interdependence. For instance, fairness of outcome distribution has been found to affect people's readiness to give up their free access to the common resources in a dilemma and to make only one of the dilemma participants responsible for managing the resources: people are more ready to do this in an unfair than in fair distribution of outcomes (Rutte and Wilke, 1983). Moreover, a participant who has high control over the resources receives stronger social support from others when his advantageous position is justified by his high inputs than when such justification is not provided (Wilke et al., 1986).

Tactics At the same time, the subject's subordination to an equity norm (say, 'unto each according to his [her] merits' or 'the same to each') may be purely tactical, i.e. instrumental for him- or herself. By conforming to socially accepted rules in our behaviour we may induce the partner to follow the same rules, especially if otherwise he or she would not do so (Van Avermaet, McClintock and Moskowitz, 1978).

The same tactical function can also be served by other accepted tactics. Altruism may be motivated less by an appreciation of the partner's well-being than by the desire to induce the partner to show even more altruism. Similarly, the cooperative strategy may be designed to lure the partner into cooperation only to exploit his or her goodwill.

Exchange values Although behaviour in conflicts of interests has been shown to depend on social orientations, both these variables have been measured chiefly in monetary terms. How radically does this behaviour differ from behaviour in real-life situations? We all know that people are inclined to pursue and exchange many other values: status, love, work, services and so on (Foa and Foa, 1975a). Control can be considered as one of such values.

The notion that control is a value in itself underlies many present-day theories, some mentioned elsewhere in this book (e.g. chapter 6). There is no denying that many of the conflicts caused by an objective opposition of interests tend to develop into conflicts over power or control over the situation, each party being determined to have the final say. Such is often the case with political negotiations, commercial deals and marital strife. Does the conflict of interest disappear in this way? No; only the interests underlying the conflict tend to change.

One would therefore be well advised to exercise caution, pending further investigations, when generalizing the available research results to values other than money.

Summary

The image of self-interest displayed in this section differs markedly from the one that emerged from the previous section, where people were assumed to be concerned chiefly with their immediate profits. The fact is that people seek to make gains and, unfortunately, also to impose losses upon other people. The interpersonal differences observed in the solution of conflicts can be largely ascribed to differences in social orientations – in particular, the extent to which people are oriented towards maximizing their own profit (individualism), maximizing the partner's profit (altruism), achieving an advantage over the partner (competition), joint profit (cooperation), or equity.

Interpretations of Conflict: from Situation to Representation

Perception of interdependence and behaviour

The theories of conflict and cooperation that derive from game theory have induced investigators to search for the determinants of cooperation among situational rather than cognitive factors. The point is that human beings respond to the world as they perceive it, not to the world as it is. This commonplace observation requires a caveat: the world is perceived differently by different people, i.e. one and the same situation may assume entirely different representations in people's minds, giving rise to controversies, quarrels and conflicts. Any situation is perceived and interpreted in terms of the individual's system of schemata or scripts (see chapter 5).

Imagine yourself to be a subject in an experiment on decision-making. In the laboratory you are seated at the head of a long table. Another young person appears and is seated at the other end of the table. You have not been told yet what it is all about, and already the first doubts creep into your mind. The very placement at the two ends of a table suggests confrontation rather than cooperation. The researchers need not tell you that this is your opponent – you already know! And even if they do not inform you, the mental schema is there, likely to be filled in with such details as the line that runs across the middle of the table: for you it is the dividing line.

A study by Eiser and Bhavnani (1974) has demonstrated the role of the interpretation of the game's context: the same PDG matrix evoked far fewer cooperative choices when played as a classical experimental game or as a simulation of economic bargaining than as a simulation of international negotiations or human interactions. Whereas in the first two cases, notably in economic bargaining, an essentially competitive 'seller–buyer' script must have been activated, the latter two cases tend to be associated with actions aimed at developing positive relations and at ensuring mutual satisfaction.

The importance of the subjective representation of the task is underlined by an experiment by Abric and Vacherot (1976). As many as a quarter of the subjects playing PDG had developed its representation as an intellectual problem rather than as a conflict situation. This resulted in a marked decline in the number of those defecting choices that were made in response to the partner's defecting strategy. In another experiment, Abric (1976) had subjects play a PDG 100 times. One half of the subjects (students) were told at the beginning that they were going to play against a machine, the other half that their partner was to be a student whom they did not know. Half-way through the trials one half of each group was told that their partner would now be changed from the machine to a student, and vice versa. Figure 13.5 presents the results obtained. The highest level of cooperation was shown by those subjects who thought they were playing against a live partner ('student') all the time, the lowest level by those playing against a machine; cooperation rose dramatically in the group that changed over from the machine to the live partner. When asked to characterize their partner, the subjects who believed they were playing against a live partner described him or her as being 'subjective', responsive and flexible. The machine was described in exactly opposite terms. In actual fact, the 'partner' followed the same, tit-for-tat strategy all the time, replicating the subject's move. Thus the subjects were playing against themselves, as far as strategy goes. Nevertheless, as long as the subjects believed they were playing against one type of partner, they did not modify their initial image, especially not with respect to the partner's responsiveness. Incidentally, the partner's flexibility

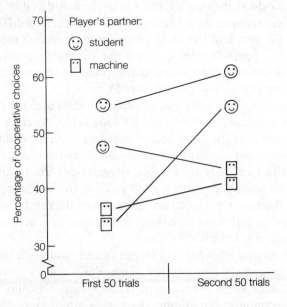

FIGURE 13.5 Cooperation and partner's representation (based on Abric, 1976)

and responsiveness has been found to raise significantly the level of cooperation (Apfelbaum, 1974).

These findings all demonstrate that a person's image of the situation, of the goal, and especially of the partner and type of relationship involved, strongly affects his or her behaviour.

Kelley and Thibaut (1978) have incorporated cognitive processes into their theory of social interdependence. The starting point of their analysis is a (hypothetical) 'given matrix', based on the subject's evaluations of the possible outcomes of her own and her partner's actions, viewed solely in terms of own needs and aspirations. The subject's knowledge or conjectures concerning her partner's evaluations and possible actions, the attractiveness of the pending interaction and so on are all factors that serve to transform the given matrix into the 'effective matrix'. The latter matrix becomes the basis for the subject's behaviour. Suppose you have the choice between two films, which you can watch either alone or with a partner you like. You may find it more rewarding to watch any of the films together with that partner than to separate from him or her. For as long as you do not know your partner's tastes, you are bound to rate watching the more attractive of the two films higher than seeing the other film together. This distinction may disappear or become reversed once you realize that your partner definitely prefers the other film. That would be an example of the transformation of a given matrix into an effective one. Other types of transformation may consist of modifications that would allow us to imagine the course of interaction over time and the changes effected through a suitable coordination of our own and the partner's actions. Whereas some transformations may be seen as a mere re-evaluation of the kind described in the previous section, in this case the transformation takes place as a result of information referring to the partner (the theory is summarized in Kelley, 1979).

Perception of interdependence and social orientations

Do we know what we want to know? Roaming about a strange city, a hungry tourist is particularly sensitive to all signs that would allow her to locate a restaurant. Could the same apply to a person whose particular social motivation makes her sensitive to every kind of information instrumental for this motivation?

A study by Eiser and Tajfel (1972) has shown that in a situation of interdependence (resembling a game situation), cooperatively motivated subjects were more concerned with obtaining information about a partner's motivation than were competitively motivated subjects. In initially ill-defined game situations, individualists were found to inquire more eagerly for their own payoffs, altruists for their partner's payoffs, and equity-oriented subjects for both own and the partner's payoffs, than subjects scoring low on each of these dimensions. When asked to recall the payoffs listed in the PDG matrix which subjects had seen 10 minutes earlier, as many as 37 per cent of them reproduced the matrix in such a distorted fashion that the game ceased to be a PDG. The most drastic changes were made by equity-oriented subjects: they tended to reduce the difference between their own and the partner's payoffs for the DC and CD choices, i.e. where they were in fact the greatest (Grzelak, 1981).

Social orientations and expectations about others   We know that, in general, cooperation is one of the basic dimensions on which people perceive various interpersonal relations (Wish, Deutsch and Kaplan, 1976). Should the selectivity of perception described above result in individual differences as far as the generalized image of other people and their motivations is concerned? For instance, Liebrand et al. (1986) have found that individualists tend to interpret others' cooperative and competitive behaviour in terms of power (as 'weak' or 'strong'), whereas cooperators see it in terms of moral evaluations ('bad' or 'good').

The issue of crucial importance is perception of others' motivation. Attribution of motivation and intention enables us to foresee how others might act and how their actions could be met. The relationship between one's own social orientation and the perceived orientations of others has been studied extensively, giving rise to a controversy over the question: is there a fundamental tendency to attribute one's own orientation to others? (This is known as egocentric attribution or as the false consensus phenomenon: see chapter 6.)

In one of the earliest studies of this question, Kelley and Stahelski (1970a, 1970b) discovered that people identified by them as competitively oriented were particularly prone to attribute their own motivation to others, whereas cooperators tended to attribute a competitive as well as a cooperative motivation to others. The cooperators were also more flexible and responsive than the former. These findings have inspired the 'triangle hypothesis', which contradicts egocentric attribution: competitively oriented people perceive the world as if it were restricted to their own kind, whereas cooperatively oriented people perceive the entire spectrum of social motives, being capable of adapting to different types of partner. A telling illustration of the triangle effect has been provided by Kuhlman and Marshello (1975) in a study which we described earlier. As shown in figure 13.4, competitively oriented people behave much more competitively than do either individualists or cooperators: moreover, they persist in this behaviour regardless of their partners' behaviour, whereas the others tend to modify their behaviour in response to changes in partner behaviour. The results reported by Maki and McClintock (1983) suggest that both individualists and cooperators are better aware of the heterogeneity of human motives and are more readily able to identify such motives than are altruists and competitors.

On the other hand, in the study by Dawes, McTavish and Shaklee (1977) subjects were four times as likely to attribute their own motivation to others as they were to attribute a different motivation. Similar results have been obtained in many other studies (e.g. Codol, 1976; Messé and Sivacek, 1979). So there seems to be firm evidence in support of the notion of egocentric attribution as well.

How can we account for these discrepant findings? The answer is not clear yet. Evidently, besides one's own orientation, there are many other factors that possibly affect expectations about the partner(s). Some of them may stem from perceived properties of conflict, like perceived strength of the incentives for others either to cooperate or to compete, or number of available strategies and their distinctiveness (Miller and Holmes, 1975). It could also be a result of compromise between the tendency to conform to social pressure and positively to differentiate the self from the others (Codol, 1976). It would not be unreasonable to assume that all these factors are at work with varying force; hence the results vary from situation to situation. All in all, it would seem that the influence of one's own social orientation on the attribution of intention to others diminishes as the situational cues become more differentiated and explicit.

Summary

Cooperation is contingent not only on the properties of the situation and the social orientations of those involved in the conflict but also on the subjective interpretations of the situation. The way people behave in a conflict is thus crucially affected by the available social knowledge as much as by the current processing of incoming information from which emerges the subjective representation of the situation. The record of past experiences shapes our judgement of how cooperative people are. This judgement, as well as the information on which it is based, depends on our own social orientation. However, there are two divergent streams of observations: (1) that we perceive others as sharing our intentions; and (2) that competitors perceive others to be alike, whereas cooperators are able to perceive the full heterogeneity of social intentions.

From Sophisticated Thinking to Habitual Reactions

Even if people have been found to perceive the world in very individual ways, differing vastly from those predicted by theorists, the notion of a rational *Homo oeconomicus* can be upheld by stating that human beings are rational within the framework of their individual visions of the world. However, what happens then is that the notions of *rational* and *oeconomicus* are being modified – at the expense of their precision and hence usefulness – to accommodate evidence which would otherwise be inconsistent. In this and the next section we briefly discuss some of these facts, pointing out that cooperation is governed by more than just one set of rules. More questions will be raised than answered. But the limits of our knowledge are set not only by what we know but also by what questions we know to ask.

Deliberate decision-making

An individual as conceived by decision theory is a predominantly calculating being who thinks numerically to maximize his or her own interest. There is plenty of well-founded evidence to show that actual human thinking very often consists in using various heuristics instead of logical or probabilistic rules of thinking (see chapter 5). Thus even in situations where cooperation is due to deliberate decision-making, 'deliberate' need not imply the use of the logic of game theory. To illustrate: if a married couple is in conflict about how to spend their leisure time, we should not expect either partner to consider all possible configurations of own and other's choices, estimate the satisfaction ensuing for each of them, and eventually make a decision from some abstract matrix. A simple, rather frequent approach is to reduce the problem to just a few options, which might be described as picking up from the hypothetical matrix some of its elements that appear to be most plausible on account of either the anticipated (dis)satisfaction or their availability in view of the past record. This approach is certainly practised in multiperson situations where the structure of the conflict cannot be easily surveyed. Sometimes it might be due simply to the limited capacity of the human mind (Simon, 1976).

Another question is about how the numerical language devised by decision theorists and employed in descriptions of conflicts of interest corresponds to the internal language in which we express our subjective representations of a real conflict. The popular experimental game paradigm relies on verbal instructions and numbers, invoking chiefly numerical thinking more typical of economic exchange than of everyday interpersonal situations. What if our behaviour in a real-life conflict is governed not only by deliberate thinking but also by vivid imagination? The sight of my partner who, previously hunched and dejected, now looks up and radiates in response to my behaviour, may reinforce my altruism more effectively than even the highest number in the payoff matrix.

Learning rules: win/stay, lose/change

There is a great deal of support for the notion that cooperation is based on cognitive processes. Doise and Mugny (1984) have been able to show that progress in cooperation is contingent upon the development of cognition, the intellectual ability to grasp mentally the participants in an interaction, and the ability to coordinate one's behaviour with that of others (see also chapter 3). However, the cooperative behaviour observed in some situations may be attributed to the most basic mechanism of learning by reward and punishment. Studies have revealed the reinforcing effect of previous experience on people's behaviour in a conflict situation (e.g. Rapoport and Chammah, 1965 in two-person games; Czwartosz, 1976 in three-person games). The most spectacular demonstration of the simplest kind of learning has been provided with the studies of a 'minimal social situation'.

In an ingenious experiment, Sidowski, Wyckoff and Tabory (1956) placed two subjects in a setting which prevented them from either seeing each other or even suspecting each other's existence. Each subject was asked to press one of two keys, L or R, either to gain a maximal score (+) or to avoid electric shock (–). The rewards and punishments were arranged as shown in figure 13.6, but the subjects had no knowledge of this matrix. Note that for each party the outcome is determined by the other party, not by the subject himself. After a series of trials and errors the subjects had learned to coordinate their moves,

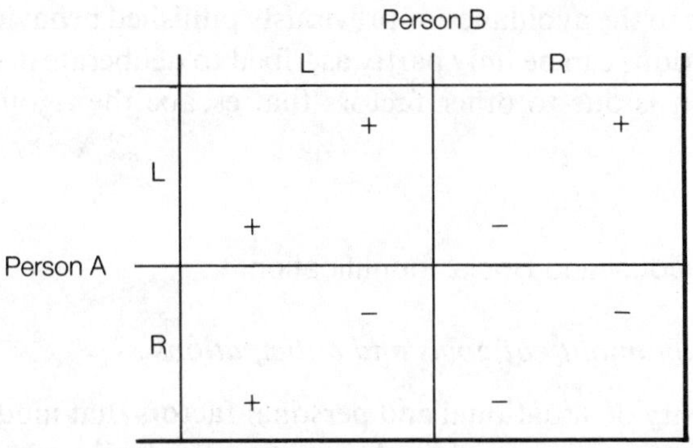

Person B

FIGURE 13.6   Minimal social situation (Sidowski, Wyckoff and Tabory, 1956)

giving preference to LL. In effect, they had learned to cooperate through mutual rewards in a situation that cannot be described as social!

Naturally, the frequency of cooperation rose steeply to 96 per cent when the subjects were informed of the involvement of another person and the mutual interdependence of choices, even though they continued to be ignorant of the exact nature of the relationship (Kelley et al., 1962). Thus, one can learn to cooperate without being aware of the relationship between own interest and other's interest, and hence without deliberate decision-making, provided the behaviour that results in joint profit is rewarding for the individual alone. This may well be a model of numerous social situations involving a coordination of interests. In real life the huge number of interdependencies linking us to other people is clearly beyond our grasp; distinct conflicts of interest crop up only in isolated cases.

Finally, we should mention *habitual* reactions of either the cooperative or the competitive kind. Is it not true that we press our foot against the accelerator when being overtaken by a smaller car? This may well be based on earlier experience: nice weather, a good road straight ahead, and the reassuring sound of a powerful engine – those are the elements of a familiar script of racing. And even though in reference to conflict and cooperation such habitual reactions seem out of place, their role should not be underestimated. Not infrequently an abrupt response gives rise to a prolonged conflict. The overbearing manner of a newcomer to the job may activate an old schema of an excessively competitive person, leading one to a defensive reaction, long before one comes to realize that the other's manners merely serve to hide his shyness and insecurity.

Summary

At the root of (non-)cooperative behaviour lies not only conscious information processing, but also non-conscious learning which, in turn, is the source of habitual reactions. Our conscious information processing is based on rules as well as heuristics, together with imaginative thinking. A considerable portion of our (non-)cooperative behaviour consists of responses which were acquired earlier, or is due to the avoidance of previously punished behaviour. Behaviour in conflict situations can be only partly ascribed to deliberate decision-making; much more of it is due to other factors that escape the rigours of decision theory.

Me or We? Individual and Social Identification

Mutual trust: community of goals and anticipations

The great diversity of situational and personal factors that modify the willingness to cooperate causes us to look for more general social-psychological mechanisms, in an effort to increase the cohesiveness and intelligibility of our notions. An early intuition resulted in the view that a mutually beneficial solution to a conflict presupposes mutual trust between the parties (Deutsch, 1973). This intuition also underlies Pruitt and Kimmel's (1977) goal expectation theory.

According to this theory, cooperation in PDG-like situations develops only if both parties reject short-term gain in favour of a long-term perspective. That is, the two partners must realize that the essence of their interdependence is of a kind that makes it unprofitable to exploit the partner's willingness to cooperate, ensuring lasting effects only through mutual cooperation as a solution to the conflict. The facilitative effect of many of the factors discussed so far is connected precisely with the gradual emergence of a joint long-term goal. This interpretation explains why cooperation increases with the continuation of the game, and how it succeeds the frustrating experience of mutual non-cooperation (notably in the case of the tit-for-tat strategy, when the reciprocation of C demonstrates the advantages of mutual cooperation). It also accounts for why cooperation increases in decomposed games, where maximum profit for one party results from the moves of the other party (which underlines the advantages of mutual giving); why communication is so beneficial; and so on.

Another condition of mutual cooperation, besides the mutual goal, is the expectation that the partner is willing to persist in cooperation in the given situation. Such an expectation is promoted by some of the factors mentioned earlier (e.g. communication) and, further, by an awareness of the partner's cooperative record and the realization that cooperation should be rewarding in view of the situational incentives and pressures.

Evidently, maximal cooperation can be achieved when cooperation becomes a mutual, coveted goal and at the same time appears highly probable from what the player knows about his or her partner. All in all, goal expectation theory, while integrating convincingly our knowledge about the prisoner's dilemma, carries many notions that seem applicable to other types of conflict.

Social comparison and social categorization processes

The two extremes of the cooperation–competition continuum can be aptly interpreted in the framework of social comparison theories as well as in terms of theories of social categorization (see also chapter 16).

According to Rijsman (1983), individuals compare their attitudes, achievements and abilities with those of others, in order to distinguish themselves from others and to establish an identity. Three component processes are involved in this: attribution, comparison and validation. The other person becomes a separate entity by attributing to him or her certain things or events on the basis of available cues, such as bodily characteristics, possessions, group membership and actions. Comparing themselves with others, individuals are bound to discover the similarities as well as the distinctions that make them unique persons. A compromise between these conflicting tendencies is found by defining the self on subjectively important dimensions as similar to others – and yet moderately superior (see chapter 5). Finally, individuals ascertain the validity of their self-image by comparing themselves with others and by making sure that others' responses to them and other objects confirm this image.

Competition in conditions of conflict of interests may thus be viewed as a particular implementation of what Rijsman called the social competition motive. This applies singularly to the laboratory conflict, where in the absence of a social context there is only one area in which players may compare themselves to, and demonstrate their superiority over, the partner: by obtaining higher payoffs than the other. The importance of competition as an outcome of social comparisons has been demonstrated in a series of experiments conducted by Poppe (1980). Others' intentions were found to be perceived chiefly on the dimension of competition, rather than cooperation, individualism or altruism. In a game situation in which alternative cues differentiating the self from the other were unavailable, subjects tried to win a moderate (rather than maximal) advantage over the partner in order to demonstrate their moderate superiority. If a game were started with an advantage of 6 points, the advantaged person accepted having his or her superiority reduced by one half, but certainly not to nil.

The tendency to compete with a given partner should therefore decrease (and the willingness to cooperate increase) once the person's differentiation is based on comparing himself or herself with people other than those sharing interdependence. Such a possibility is given in multiperson conflicts, especially of the intergroup type. Here the self is defined not only by differentiating the self from every other partner but also by establishing the similarity of the self to the members of one's own group, that is, by distinguishing 'we' from 'them' (Tajfel, 1978c; Turner and Oakes, 1986). The problem of categorization and intergroup relationships is discussed at length in chapter 16. Here let us mention only that the problem of interpersonal cooperation is strongly linked with the issue of intergroup competition, as the formation of the 'we' category involves an identification with one's own group and thus may become a major stimulus to cooperation within the group. A study by Brewer (1979) has shown that individuals perceive members of their own group as more trustworthy, honest and cooperative than members of the other group. Moreover, it was found that making the subjects aware of their group identity promotes cooperative behaviour in dealing with the dilemma of limited resources, even in the absence of any information that would imply an intergroup competition (Kramer and Brewer, 1986).

Therefore there are grounds for expecting that the number and strength of real-life conflicts can be substantially reduced when the participants are willing and able to find any cues, any reason to think of the other(s) as belonging to the same category, sharing the same fate, and thus being true partners rather than opponents.

Summary

In situations involving deliberate behaviour, cooperation is promoted by personal values and circumstances that make us realize that in the long run the only sensible solution to a conflict is mutual cooperation, and confidence that the partner will reciprocate our cooperation. One of the principal determinants of cooperation is the process of self-identification through a comparison with others. In two-person conflicts individuals seek to distinguish themselves from the other by gaining an advantage (competition). In a multiperson setting our self-identity can likewise be established by recognizing our similarity to others, which entails cooperation with members of our group and competition with members of the other group.

Summary and Conclusion

There are many social situations in which individuals face a conflict between their own and another person's (or persons') interests. Solving the conflict in a way beneficial not only to self but also to others – i.e. the level of cooperation – depends upon the extent to which an individual's cooperative behaviour has been rewarded in the past, the strategic and social characteristics of the conflict, an individual's value orientation, and his or her perception of the situation and of the other parties to the conflict.

The level of cooperation increases as the strength of conflict diminishes, as the costs of cooperation decline, as the partner either also cooperates or reciprocates the same behaviour, as the opportunities for communication and for reducing interpersonal distance grow and, very often, as the number of parties to the conflict increase.

There are great interpersonal differences in people's value (social) orientations, in what they seek to achieve in interaction with others: to maximize own profit or partner's profit, to gain an advantage over the partner, joint profit, equality of gains, or other goals. The more individuals care about the other's gain, the more often they choose a cooperative solution to the conflict. Social orientations also influence perception of conflict and attributions of intent with regard to other parties to the conflict. Some studies show that people expect others to share their own intentions. Other studies show that this is so in the case of competitively but not cooperatively oriented individuals; the latter are able to perceive the full range of social motivations.

In sum, cooperation is promoted by all the situational and individual factors which facilitate awareness of the profitability of cooperation in the long run and provide a basis for building expectations that others will cooperate as well.

Notes

1 The minimax strategies in games 2 and 4 are C. In game 3 both (!) strategies are equally safe (or rather unsafe, since they both may result in the lowest outcome: 1). In games 2 and 3 a pair of CC strategies is in equilibrium, whereas game 4 has two pairs of strategies in equilibrium: one, more profitable to you, is C for the partner, and D for you (CD); the other, D for the partner and C for you (DC), is better for the partner.

2 The partner is a hypothetical person to the subject, and no information about his or her choices is provided, in order to make the subject's own choices independent of the partner's choices.

Glossary Terms

Competition	Interdependence (payoff)
Conflict (of interests)	structure
Cooperation	Mixed-motive game (conflict)
Experimental games	Social dilemma
Homo oeconomicus	Social orientations
Interdependence	

Further Reading

Colman, A. E. (ed.) (1982) *Cooperation and Competition in Humans and Animals.* New York: Van Nostrand Reinhold, chapters 1, 2, 5, 9 and 11. Reviews of research on various forms of conflict of interest and ways of conflict resolution in animals and humans; includes biological, decision-making and anthropological perspectives.

Hamburger, H. (1979) *Games as Models of Social Phenomena.* San Francisco: Freeman, chapters 1–7, 9 and 10. An introduction to game theory and experimental games as laboratory models of conflicts of interests.

Kelley, H. H. (1979) *Personal Relationships: their structures and processes.* Hillsdale, NJ: Erlbaum. A presentation of a non-game approach to social interdependence, the theory and its application to close interpersonal relationships.

McClintock, C. G. and Van Avermaet, E. F. (1982) Social values and rules of fairness. In V. J. Derlega and J. L. Grzelak (eds), *Co-operation and Helping Behaviour: theory and research*, New York: Academic Press. Conceptualization of social orientations; their measurement and relationship to equity principles.

Maki, J. and McClintock, C. G. (1983) The accuracy of social value prediction: actor and observer influences. *Journal of Personality and Social Psychology*, 45, 829–38. An example of an experimental study on the relationship between an observer's own social orientation and the perceived orientations of actors.

Messick, D. M. and Brewer, R. M. (1983) Solving social dilemmas. A review. In L. Wheeler and P. Shaver (eds), *Review of Personality and Social Psychology* (vol. 4), Beverly Hills: Sage. A review of the main conceptualizations of and empirical studies on social dilemmas.

Stroebe, W. and Frey, B. S. (1982) Self-interest and collective action: the economics and psychology of public goods. *British Journal of Social Psychology*, 21, 121–37. A discussion of the model of *Homo oeconomicus* as applied to a conflict between self-interest and contribution to the provision of public goods.

PART IV

Social Groups

14 Group Performance

HENK WILKE and
AD VAN KNIPPENBERG

Introduction

A large portion of student life is spent in groups. Participation in courses, workgroups and tutorials involves group activities. Group activities also play a large role in other stages of life. Most of us are brought up in families; classroom and club experiences are very often coloured by interaction with other people. Having a profession quite often implies working with others. For these groups the common denominator is interaction and this interaction is assumed to give rise to certain outcomes for each of its group members. In their turn these outcomes motivate persons to join and to stay within a group.

Several kinds of outcomes may be distinguished. Take a workgroup, for example. One may want to join a workgroup because one's friend is already a member of it, i.e. outcomes derived from interpersonal attraction are involved. Another good reason for joining or remaining within a workgroup is that the outcomes of the group at large coincide with one's personal outcomes, i.e. group performance is to the benefit of individual group members. This is the case when interaction within the workgroup helps someone to pass his or her final examination. Also interaction in itself, i.e. as a process, may be perceived as rewarding. These outcomes are involved if one wants to get to know other persons or if one enjoys interacting with other people. Lastly, external outcomes may also be at stake. For example, a student may join a specific workgroup because being a member of it enhances one's status on the campus or because this membership makes a good impression on faculty.

Thus, we may be attracted towards a group for several reasons: because of the people who are in it; because the group task is important to us; because we like interacting; and because an external agent rewards us. Needless to say, these reasons may act in combination.

In this chapter we will mainly focus on task performance of individuals and groups, and we are only indirectly concerned with incidental outcomes which may be provided by other participants, or which may be experienced during the process itself.

Determinants of Productivity

What determines the actual performance of an individual or group? Consider the following problem.

A man bought a horse for $60 and sold it for $70. Then he bought it back for $80 and again sold it for $90. How much money did he make in the business?

According to Steiner (1972) the way an individual or a group performs a task depends primarily on two elements, namely task demands and human resources. In this section we will turn to these two elements and indicate how they are related to potential and actual performance.

Task demands   are the resources required to perform a task. In order to solve the horse-trading problem one has to split the problem into two negotiations, namely one in which $70 are compared with $60 and another one in which $90 are compared with $80. One has to realize that in both instances a gain of $10 is made and that the gains sum to $20.

Human resources   include all relevant knowledge, abilities, skills or tools possessed by the individual or group attempting to solve the problem. In the case of the horse-trading problem, the individual or group may or may not possess the needed analytical and computational resources to meet the task demands. Thus, task demands specify the kinds and amounts of resources that are needed, whereas the human resources specify whether the individual or the group possesses these resources.

Potential productivity   of an individual or a group refers to the extent to which the available human resources suffice to meet the task demands. When an individual or group potentially possesses all necessary skills to solve the horse-trading problem, then this individual or group has a greater potential productivity than a group or an individual lacking some of the human resources to meet the task demands.

Actual productivity   Suppose now we have an individual of a high potential productivity, because she possesses the necessary human resources to meet the task requirements. Does this guarantee a high actual performance? From daily life we may observe that a high potential productivity may not always be attained. In our example an individual may be able to distinguish between two negotiations. However, the positions of seller and buyer may be mistaken: one may end up with a wrong answer; one may make some unexpected computational errors; or one may make the right computations but nervously write down a wrong answer. In these cases actual productivity – actual performance – fails to equal potential productivity: one possesses the human resources needed to perform the task, but something in the *process*, consisting of the actual steps taken by an individual when confronted with the task, may go wrong.

The above reasoning suggests the following relation between actual perform-ance, potential performance and process losses (see also Steiner, 1972):

actual performance = potential performance – process losses

Not only intrapersonal but also interpersonal processes may affect actual performance and may keep a group below its potential performance. Thomas and Fink (1961) allowed college students one minute to solve the horse-trading problem. Thereafter they formed groups of two to five members and asked them to discuss the same problem, and it was explicitly stated that this discussion did not have to lead to consensus. In spite of these instructions the results indicated that most groups actually reached consensus. When in these groups the majority of its members initially had the wrong solution, the final consensus tended to be incorrect, suggesting that consensus involves a process loss for groups having a majority of participants who initially failed to achieve the right solution.

A main weakness of consensus is that it tends to neglect minority opinions. Research done by Maier and Solem (1952) demonstrates how this process loss may be overcome. In their research subjects individually had to come to a solution for the horse-trading problem. Thereafter they were randomly allocated to groups. In half of these groups procedural instructions to a leader were given: the leader had to refrain from expressing his or her own judgement, and his or her function was merely to guard the discussion time. In the other half of the groups the leader was instructed to stimulate active participation of all members. It appeared that incorrect group solutions did occur more frequently in procedural leadership groups than in participatory leadership groups, suggesting that by encouragement of uniform participation process losses may be avoided. When procedural instructions were given, single individuals who had already achieved the correct solution were sometimes persuaded to accept the wrong solution, i.e. a process loss occurred.

This chapter deals with a class of phenomena having to do with *group performance* in a broad sense. We start out with the problem of the effect of the presence of others on individual task performance. Next we discuss group productivity of small interacting groups. Finally, the relatively more complex problems of the development of group structure and the effects of variations in group structure on the task performance will be analysed.

Task Performance in the Presence of Others

How the presence of others affects an individual's task performance was one of the earliest research interests in social psychology. As early as 1897 Triplett observed that cyclists rode faster when racing together than when racing alone.

In the years that followed, numerous experiments were carried out in which the effect of the presence of others was investigated on a wide variety of tasks. Some studies showed performance improvement as a result of the presence of others, i.e. **social facilitation**; others showed performance impairment, i.e. **social inhibition**. Probably because of a lack of theoretical progress, the interest in *social facilitation and inhibition* (SFI) research suddenly dropped in the late 1930s. The issue was neglected until Zajonc (1965) published an article which represented a major theoretical breakthrough in understanding social facilitation and inhibition phenomena. Zajonc's work inspired social psychologists to resume the study of the effects of the presence of others on task performance, and since then social facilitation and inhibition has constituted a lively research area in social psychology once again.

Early social facilitation and inhibition studies

SFI is traditionally studied in two broad categories of social situations: audience presence and co-action. The first type of study deals with the question of how the *presence* of a passive audience influences individual performance. **Co-action** studies focus on the question of how the presence of someone else performing the same task affects an individual's task performance. In both research areas, the results seemed contradictory. For instance Travis (1925) found that, when working in front of an audience compared with working alone, well-trained subjects clearly improved their performance on a pursuit-rotor task. An opposite audience effect was shown by Pessin (1933). He found that subjects needed fewer trials to learn a list of nonsense syllables when practising alone than when facing an audience. When, however, subjects were later asked to recall the list of syllables, their performance was better with than without an audience. Similar patterns of results were found in co-action studies. Sometimes co-action seemed to facilitate performance (e.g. Triplett, 1898), particularly the quantitative aspects of performance, while in other studies the quality of performance was impaired in co-action settings (e.g. Gates and Allee, 1933).

Zajonc's explanation of ambiguous SFI results

In his classic article, Zajonc (1965) noted a distinct regularity in SFI research which so far had been only tacitly understood. Furthermore, Zajonc proposed a set of ideas which could account for the observed results.

Zajonc suggested that the presence of others led to improved performance (social facilitation) if subjects worked on easy, well-learned tasks. However, the presence of others led to impaired performance (social inhibition) if subjects were engaged in difficult tasks which were not (yet) well learned. This simple distinction between easy and difficult tasks could account for many seemingly conflicting results of audience as well as co-action studies. It explains for instance the results of Triplett (1898), Travis (1925), Pessin (1933) and Gates and Allee (1933) mentioned above.

Zajonc not only observed these regularities but also proposed a theoretical explanation. Zajonc's crucial suggestion is that audiences enhance the emission of dominant responses. A **dominant response** is described as the response which prevails, i.e. which takes precedence in a subject's response repertoire in a given stimulus situation. In easy tasks, Zajonc argues, the correct responses are dominant, and therefore audiences facilitate performance on easy tasks, e.g. pedalling a bicycle. However, in complex tasks (like reasoning or learning) the wrong answers tend to be dominant, and therefore audiences give rise to performance deterioration on such difficult tasks.

Why do audiences elicit dominant responses? According to Zajonc, audiences create arousal in subjects, i.e. enhance their general drive level or activation level. In Zajonc's view, the mere physical presence of others suffices to induce arousal in the subjects. As an innate response, the presence of others leads to some sort of preparedness, a readiness to respond to whatever unexpected action the other might undertake (Zajonc, 1980b). Furthermore, according to Zajonc, enhanced drive or arousal leads to an increased emission of dominant responses, a notion Zajonc derives from Hull-Spence drive theory (see Spence, 1956; Zajonc and Nieuwenhuysen, 1964).

In figure 14.1 Zajonc's explanation of SFI phenomena is presented schematically. According to Zajonc, the presence of others (conspecifics) leads to an increased arousal or drive level which, in turn, elicits an enhanced emission of dominant responses. Since dominant responses tend to be correct in easy tasks, performance on easy tasks will be facilitated. Performance on difficult tasks, where dominant responses tend to be incorrect, will be impaired.

Zajonc's explanation seemed to account for many of the observed effects in the SFI literature. Furthermore, his article inspired social psychologists to disagree with him. In subsequent literature, alternative explanations were suggested for the relationships between presence of others and arousal and between arousal and task performance, and in fact some entirely different models were proposed. A brief outline of some of these alternatives is presented below.

Alternative explanations of SFI

Cottrell (1968, 1972) was among the first to criticize Zajonc's approach. He suggested an alternative explanation for the connection between presence of others and arousal. In Cottrell's view, increased arousal constitutes a learned response to the presence of others, and not an innate one. Subjects tend to be aroused by audiences because they have learned to associate the presence of

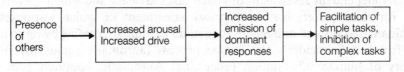

FIGURE 14.1   Zajonc's (1965, 1980b) model of SFI phenomena

others with performance evaluation which, in turn, is linked to positive or negative outcomes. Thus audiences produce 'evaluation apprehension' which enhances drive (or arousal). Mere physical presence of others is not sufficient to elicit arousal and the concomitant increased emission of dominant responses.

Several experiments yielded support for Cottrell's view (e.g. Henchy and Glass, 1968; Paulus and Murdoch, 1971). The former experiment may serve as an example. Henchy and Glass assigned subjects to one of four conditions: 'alone'; 'expert together' (i.e. task performance in the presence of two others, explicitly introduced as experts); 'non-expert together' (i.e. task performance in the presence of two non-experts); and 'alone recorded' (in which the subject performed the task alone, but was filmed for later evaluation by experts). As predicted by Cottrell's approach, facilitation of dominant (well-learned) responses only occurred in the expert-together and in the alone-recorded conditions, while task performance in the non-expert-together condition was similar to that in the alone condition. These results thus seem to demonstrate that some concern for being evaluated is necessary for the enhanced emission of dominant responses.

Another explanation of why audiences are arousing was suggested by Sanders, Baron and Moore (1978; see also Sanders, 1981). In their view, the simple physical presence of others serves as a distracting stimulus (e.g. because of noises or gestures, anticipated approving or disapproving reactions, the tendency to make social comparisons). The presence of others leads to increased drive because it brings about a 'response conflict between attending to the task at hand and attending to the distracting stimuli' (Sanders, 1981, p. 233). Two distinct effects of the presence of others on task performance may then be noted. First, distraction as such always leads to impairment of performance, on both complex and simple tasks, because attending to the distracting stimuli (the audience) subtracts from attention to the task. Secondly, the drive increment, evoked by the distraction–response conflict, facilitates performance on simple tasks and hinders performance on complex tasks, because (as in Zajonc's view) increased drive results in enhanced emission of dominant responses. Thus the presence of others (always) inhibits performance on complex tasks, and facilitates performance on simple tasks only when the positive effect of drive increment outweighs the negative effect of distraction.

While the theoretical alternatives put forward by Cottrell and Sanders mainly pertain to why the presence of others elicits arousal in individuals, Manstead and Semin's (1980) approach focuses on the information-processing aspects of the explanation of SFI phenomena. In Zajonc's theory, the distinction between simple and complex tasks plays a central role. This distinction, however, appears to be an uneasy one, because there is no solid theoretical basis for an independent assessment of which tasks are easy and which are difficult (or, for that matter, for the *a priori* assessment of which responses are dominant). Manstead and Semin suggest an elegant alternative by referring to Shiffrin and Schneider's (1977) two process (automatic versus controlled) theory of human information processing. Automatic, routinely processed tasks tend to be characterized by suboptimal performance. The presence of an evaluative audience leads subjects to devote more attention to the progress of the automatic task sequences, which generally results in improved performance. In more complex tasks, i.e. tasks which require cognitively controlled processing, the presence of an evaluative audience tends to impair performance, because the audience places further attentional demands upon the individual, which subtract from the already demanding task requirements. This explanation of SFI phenomena substantially modifies Zajonc's model in that it avoids the somewhat strained assumption of arousal-induced emission of dominant responses by introducing more advanced information-processing views on activation level and on (competitive) allocation of attention.

A cognitive-motivational model of group influences on individual performance

The social facilitation literature in the past decades presents a wide range of views and theories, the most influential of which have been described in the previous section. This area of research would benefit from a more comprehensive theoretical model which incorporates the most valuable ideas of the approaches outlined above. Such an integrative model has recently been proposed by Paulus (1983). A slightly modified version of this model is described in some detail as follows.

In Paulus's model three steps can be distinguished:

1 Presence of others generally increases (but sometimes decreases) the potential social consequences of an individual's performance.
2 Variations in social consequences affect the individual's psychological processes.
3 These psychological processes do have specific effects on individual task performance.

Our adapted version of Paulus's model is schematically represented in figure 14.2. Step by step, we shall describe the propositions put forward by Paulus (1983).

In terms of the model, presence of others generally implies that the *social consequences* of performing well or poorly are enhanced. In this respect, Paulus adopts the viewpoint of Cottrell (1968) who suggested that the presence of others is associated with performance evaluation which, in turn, is linked to positive or negative outcomes. According to Paulus, in some co-action settings (e.g. being a member of a rope-pulling team) social consequences of individual performances may be reduced because success or failure of the group cannot easily be attributed to one particular individual (see also the next section). However, the typical audience situation entails increased focusing on the individual's performance and, hence, social consequences will be enhanced. Therefore, in the model presented in figure 14.2, decreased social consequences are not included.

Paulus made a distinction between negative and positive social

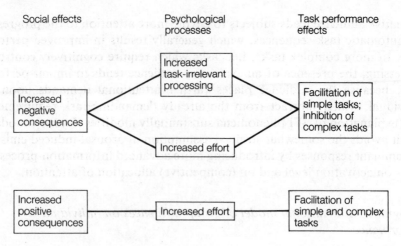

FIGURE 14.2   A cognitive-motivational model of SFI effects (based on Paulus, 1983)

consequences. *Negative consequences* are associated with the prospect of failing, i.e. with the possibility that the individual's accomplishments do not meet the standards set by the audience. Negative consequences are, for instance, embarrassment, disapproval and contempt. Conversely, the prospect of success in the presence of others may enhance potential *positive* consequences, e.g. approval or admiration.

As can be seen in figure 14.2 , increased negative consequences affect the individual's psychological processes. First, negative consequences give rise to increased *task-irrelevant processing*. In the definition of Paulus, task-irrelevant processing is described as focusing attention on factors other than the task at hand. For example, the individual may begin to worry about whether he or she will be able to perform well or may start looking for signs of disapproval. This concept of task-irrelevant processing is quite similar to the distraction effect posited by Sanders, Baron and Moore (1978; see also Sanders, 1981). Second, negative consequences elicit increased effort. Negative consequences enhance the motivation to perform well because the costs of failing are increased. Third, in the model proposed by Paulus, arousal is introduced as a separate effect of increased negative consequences. As a slight modification of Paulus's model, we suggest that arousal is a psychological state that tends to accompany task-irrelevant processing, e.g. arousal is associated with the subject's worrying about failing and subsequent negative evaluations. In fact, in the original model, arousal always coincides with task-irrelevant processing. Therefore we have not included arousal in our version of the model.

What is the combined effect of increased task-irrelevant processing and increased effort on performance of simple tasks? Paulus suggests that performance on simple tasks will be facilitated. When an individual is working alone on a simple, routine task, performance tends to be suboptimal because of low expenditure of effort (see Kahneman, 1973; see also Manstead and Semin,

1980). In such situations individuals may not try very hard because simple tasks are generally not very challenging or inspiring. When others watch, the potential negative consequences of poor performance are enhanced and therefore effort increases, which facilitates performance. Although the model predicts that task-irrelevant processing also increases, this need not hinder performance on easy tasks because the task does not require the individual's full attention.

On complex tasks, however, the combined effect of increased task-irrelevant processing and increased effort is inhibition of task performance. Working alone on a complex task, e.g. solving a difficult problem, already requires considerable effort from the individual. Presence of others may lead to enhanced effort, but the performance gains resulting from this will generally be less high than in the case of simple tasks. Furthermore, increased task-irrelevant processing is much more harmful for complex tasks than for simple tasks since a complex task demands the individual's undivided attention, and, therefore, any attention paid to non-task factors (e.g. worrying) leads to poorer task performance (see Manstead and Semin, 1980). Thus the net result of increased task-irrelevant processing and increased effort is impairment of performance on complex tasks.

An example may illustrate the latter process. Consider a boy of average intelligence who, sitting alone in his room, tries to solve the horse-trading problem. As there is little time pressure, he can carefully select the appropriate steps to solve the problem. He takes his time and, in a few minutes, he comes up with the correct solution. Now consider the same boy trying to solve the horse-trading problem while his older brother, known to make sarcastic remarks about his younger brother's incompetence, looks over his shoulder. The boy increases his effort. But, since he is worried that he will be criticized for working too slowly, he nervously picks the wrong numbers and finally reaches the wrong solution; his preoccupation with being negatively evaluated (task-irrelevant processing) has impaired his performance.

Presence of others may also increase the positive consequences of individual task performance. A successful performance may elicit approval from others, increased liking or material rewards. According to the model, increased positive consequences lead to increased effort, simply because there is more at stake. Trying harder results in facilitation of performance on both simple and complex tasks. Suboptimal performances on simple tasks are easily improved by working harder. And even for complex tasks the additional effort induced by potential positive outcomes is expected to lead to a performance increment. An example of the latter is the situation in which a highly skilled piano player gives a musical performance in the presence of others. Increased potential positive outcomes (applause, admiration) would motivate the player to play better than he or she would when playing alone.

Paulus's model provides an elegant explanation for many social facilitation and inhibition phenomena. The model is an eclectic one, because it contains many important theoretical notions of scholars in the field (Cottrell, 1968; Manstead and Semin, 1980; Sanders, Baron and Moore, 1978). What Paulus's model amounts to is that the net result of task-irrelevant processing and increased effort is decisively different for simple and complex tasks. Since the effect of task-irrelevant processing on simple tasks is generally negligible, while the performance may strongly benefit from increased effort, the presence of others tends to facilitate performance on simple tasks. Conversely, task-irrelevant processing may be quite damaging to performance on complex tasks, which will generally not be compensated by the effect of increased effort. Therefore the presence of others tends to inhibit performance on complex tasks.

Performance in Interacting Groups

Having described how individual performance may be influenced by the presence of others, we now take one step further and pose the question of how interacting groups do perform. Steiner (1972, 1976) has convincingly argued that this question can only be answered if the nature of the task involved is taken into account. In order to make predictions about group performance he developed a clever classification of tasks, which is based on the three questions in table 14.1.

Steiner's classification of tasks

The first question – 'Can the task be broken down into subcomponents, or is the division of the task inappropriate?' – compares divisible and unitary tasks. Reading a page of a book is essentially a one-person job; having two persons read alternate lines would serve no purpose. Thus reading a page or solving an arithmetic problem are *unitary* tasks; splitting up a unitary task makes little sense. *Divisible* tasks, however, can be broken down into subtasks and assigned to different people. Playing a football game, building a house and planting a garden are tasks which can be broken down into subtasks. Thus for unitary tasks mutual assistance is impractical, whereas for divisible tasks a certain division of labour is feasible. In this view, pulling a rope is a unitary task. To be sure, Steiner remarks that it can be conceived of as involving a number of subtasks such as grasping a rope, bracing one's feet, contracting one's biceps etc., but all phases have to be performed by a single individual. Several people may pull on the same rope but when this occurs, Steiner maintains, we have an instance of parallel performance rather than a division of labour.

The second question – 'Which is more important: quantity produced or quality of performance?' – compares maximizing and optimizing tasks. When tasks entail doing as much as possible of something, or doing it as rapidly as possible, then we call this a maximizing task. For example, if an individual or group is requested to exert a maximum force on the rope or if a group of mountaineers is asked to ascend a cliff as rapidly as possible, we call this a maximizing task, since the criterion of success is to complete the task in a maximum way. In contrast, optimizing tasks have as their criterion to produce some specific preferred outcome. When individuals or groups are asked to exert a

TABLE 14.1 A summary of Steiner's typology of tasks

Question	Answer	Task type	Examples
Can the task be broken down into subcomponents, or is division of the task inappropriate?	Subtasks can be identified	Divisible	Playing a football game, building a house, preparing a six-course meal
	No subtasks exist	Unitary	Pulling on a rope, reading a book, solving a mathematics problem
Which is more important: quantity produced or quality of performance?	Quantity	Maximizing	Generating many ideas, lifting the greatest weight, scoring the most runs
	Quality	Optimizing	Generating the best idea, getting the right answer, solving a mathematics problem
How are individual inputs related to the group's product?	Individual inputs are added together	Additive	Pulling a rope, stuffing envelopes, shovelling snow
	Group product is average of individual judgements	Compensatory	Averaging individuals' estimates of the number of beans in a jar, weight of an object, room temperature
	Group selects product from pool of individual members' judgements	Disjunctive	Questions involving 'yes–no, either–or' answers, such as mathematics problems, puzzles, and choices between options
	All group members contribute to the product	Conjunctive	Climbing a mountain, eating a meal, relay races, soldiers marching in file
	Group can decide how individual inputs relate to group product	Discretionary	Deciding to shovel snow together, opting to vote on the best answer to a mathematics problem, letting leader answer question

Sources: Steiner (1972, 1976); adapted from Forsyth (1983)

force of exactly 100 pounds we speak of an optimizing task, since success is determined by the extent to which the specific criterion of 100 pounds will be approximated.

The third question – 'How are individual inputs related to the group's product?' – gives rise to five possible answers:

1 *Additive tasks* permit that the contributions of various members are summed. For example, when several people shovel snow from the pathway, each performs the same acts while taking care to stay clear of one's closest coworkers. In this case group task performance can be expressed as the total surface cleared of snow.
2 *Compensatory tasks* require a group decision from the average of individual members' solutions. Group members' estimates of the temperature of the room, the number of beans in a jar, or the number of cars in a parking lot may be averaged in a group so that overestimations are pitted against under-estimations and finally the right answer may be achieved.
3 *Disjunctive tasks* require that the group selects one specific judgement from the pool of individual members' judgements. The horse-trading problem dealt with earlier is a disjunctive task, since in a group several judgements may arise and one answer has to be selected.
4 *Conjunctive tasks* require that all group members act in unison. The speed at which a group of mountain climbers can ascend a cliff is determined by the slowest member.
5 *Discretionary tasks* are tasks which leave it to the group how the task will be performed. For example, the group's decision on the temperature of the room can be made in several ways. One person, the leader, may decide and the other group members are bound by this decision. Some but not all members may come to an agreement. The final group judgement may also be the average of all individual members' judgements. Thus discretionary tasks are involved when the group has the freedom of choice to select its own decisional procedures.

Predicting group productivity

Steiner's ingenious classification has two attractive properties. First, with the help of this classification many tasks can be classified. Three examples may demonstrate this. A tug-of-war contest involves a task that is unitary, maximizing and additive. Assembling a car is divisible, optimizing and conjunctive. Solving the aforementioned horse-trading problem is a unitary, optimizing and disjunctive task.

Second, Steiner's classification of tasks allows us to make predictions about group performance. In the following we will show how group performance for a specific task is dependent on the group members' resources to deal with the task. This approach is in agreement with what we tried to demonstrate in the introduction to this chapter, where we stated that group productivity is equal to potential productivity minus process losses. The different classes of tasks demand different sorts of resources: skills, abilities and tools. If group members possess these human resources, the task demands are met and the task may be fulfilled successfully. If, in contrast, the group does not possess those necessary resources, group failure may be observed. In the following we will demonstrate the predictive value of Steiner's classification as for additive, compensatory, disjunctive and conjunctive tasks.

Additive tasks   For additive tasks the individual contributions are added together, and therefore it is not surprising that it has been established that the more persons in the group, the better the group performance. Especially for unitary tasks such as pulling a rope and clapping after a concert, the old saying 'many hands make light work' applies. Steiner (1976) remarks that the recipe for group success is rather simple: each group member should do as much as he or she can while maintaining the necessary coordination with the other group members. However, although this recipe is simple, adhering to it may not be.

This fact was acknowledged by Ringelmann, who carried out his research between 1882 and 1887 (see Kravitz and Martin, 1986). Ringelmann was a professor of agricultural engineering at the French National Institute of Agronomy, who investigated the relative efficiency of work furnished by horses, oxen, men and machines in various agricultural applications. He had young men pull a rope, either alone or in groups of two, three or eight members. He measured the momentary force exerted by means of a recording dynamometer. When subjects worked alone, they pulled with an average force of 63 kilograms. But two men did not pull with a force of 126 kilograms, three with a force of 189 kilograms, and so on. The two-person group had an average pull of only 118 kilograms (for a loss of 8 kilograms); three-person groups pulled with an average of 160 kilograms (for a loss of 29 kilograms); and the eight-person group exerted a force of 256 kilograms below its potential. Thus the production loss per subject increases with group size. This inverse relationship between the number of people in the group and individual performance is termed the *Ringelmann effect*.

Why do individuals reduce their performance when group size increases? Ringelmann explains this result in terms of *coordination losses*. According to Steiner (1972, 1976) group productivity is not equal to potential productivity, because losses owing to faulty processes must be taken into account.

Stroebe and Frey (1982) point out that the production losses of the Ringelmann group may be ascribed to at least two sorts of losses:

1   *Motivation losses*, i.e. the tendency to let the others do the work, while taking advantage of the fact that one's own contribution is not identifiable and that one shares in the total group product, which makes it profitable to each of the group members to withhold their own contribution. Incidentally, this type of motivation loss is also at the root of many public choice problems. For example, for each of us it is most attractive to let others pay

the taxes or to let others take care of the environment, because while doing so one profits in two ways: one withholds one's contributions to the public good, and one profits from the public good (e.g. the welfare state and the clean air) when it is provided. In the area of public goods this motivation loss is dubbed the **free-rider effect**. Each individual is faced with a **social dilemma**: it is in any one person's interest not to contribute to a public good, but if nobody contributes one is worse off than if all had contributed.

2 *Coordination losses*, e.g. group members might not have pulled in the same direction or, when they did, they might not have exerted their potential force at the same moment.

Extending Steiner's original approximation of group performance (see the introduction to this chapter) we are now in a position to become more specific:

$$\frac{\text{group}}{\text{productivity}} = \frac{\text{potential}}{\text{productivity}} - \frac{\text{motivation}}{\text{losses}} - \frac{\text{coordination}}{\text{losses}}$$

And indeed, from results of subsequent experimental studies (e.g. Ingham et al., 1974) in which researchers tried to distinguish the two kinds of productivity losses, it appears that, as well as coordination losses, motivation losses play an important role in rope-pulling groups.

Production losses have also been demonstrated with other tasks such as shouting, pumping air and brainstorming (see Jackson and Harkins, 1985). In a study on **social loafing** Latané, Williams and Harkins (1979) requested subjects to cheer or clap as loudly as they could and recorded their performance (in dynes/cm^2). It appeared that the production loss for two-person groups was 29 per cent, for four-person groups 49 per cent, and for six-person groups 60 per cent. In a second experiment they tried to disentangle production loss into two components, namely motivation and coordination losses. Subjects were asked to participate in a shouting task and the cheering was again measured by a sound-level meter. Each subject was asked to shout by himself or herself, in actual groups of two or six, and in pseudo groups of two or six.

The results are depicted in figure 14.3. The dashed line along the top represents potential productivity to be expected if no coordination and motivation losses occur. The dark area at the bottom shows the obtained productivity per person in actual groups. Group productivity is obviously lower than the potential productivity, and this decrease can be considered as representing the sum of the losses due to coordination and motivation losses. Figure 14.3 also shows the productivity of pseudo groups. In this condition subjects were led to believe that others shouted with them, but actually they were shouting alone, thus preventing coordination losses. By inference, motivation losses can now be estimated. The lightly shaded area in figure 14.3 represents motivation losses (reduced effort). The area representing coordination losses is inferred by subtracting the productivity of pseudo groups in which only motivational losses were incurred from the productivity of actual groups which did incur both coordination as well as motivational losses. These results demonstrate that half

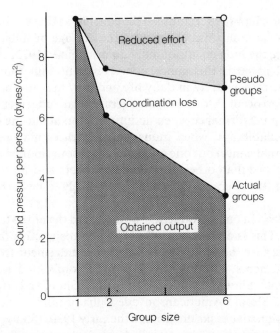

FIGURE 14.3 Intensity of sound produced per person when cheering in actual or pseudo groups of 1, 2 and 6, as a result of reduced effort and faulty coordination of group efforts, experiment 2 (based on Latané, Williams and Harkins, 1979)

of the productivity losses may be ascribed to motivation and the other half to coordination losses. This suggests that actual productivity in real groups is equal to potential productivity of group members minus coordination and motivational losses.

The subsequent question is how these losses may be prevented. Recent research (e.g. Harkins and Jackson, 1985) suggests that when participants have the idea that their contribution can be evaluated through comparison with the contributions of others, the Ringelmann effect disappears, i.e. group productivity is then equal to potential productivity of group members.

In sum, for additive tasks group performance is equal to potential performance of group members minus process losses. Two kinds of process losses seem to be involved, namely losses due to faulty coordination and losses due to decreased motivation. The Ringelmann effect, i.e. the fact that rope-pulling group members do not live up to their performance potential, is due to these two types of losses.

Compensatory tasks For compensatory tasks the group product is the average of individual judgements. In a series of early studies (Gordon, 1924; Knight, 1921) individuals were asked to make private estimates of the temperature of a room, the number of beans in a jar and the number of buckshot in a bottle. It appeared that the statistical average of the many judgements came closer to the correct judgement than the judgements rendered by most of the individuals. Also Shaw (1981) comes to the conclusion that the bulk of evidence indicates that – for compensatory tasks – the average of judgements is more accurate than are the judgements of individuals. Steiner (1972, 1976), however, is more critical towards this conclusion. He points out that 'statisticized' groups do occur rather rarely in daily life and they may not be recognized as such when they do occur. Moreover, the average of all judgements only leads to a superior group performance when no information about the competence of members is available and when individual prejudices may be presumed to generate errors that cancel out one another. When some individual judgements have more influence than others or if some members abstain from expressing their judgement, the average judgement is less likely to be correct.

Disjunctive tasks   In our introduction we discussed the horse-trading problem in some detail. This is a unitary, optimizing and disjunctive task. It is a disjunctive task because the group has to select one judgement from the pool of individual judgements. Groups are very often confronted with disjunctive tasks, for example: Should a student pass or fail? Should a certain investment be made or not? Should Americans invade Cuba or not?

Interest in disjunctive tasks did arise in the early 1930s (Shaw, 1932). Besides the horse-trading problem, the so-called missionary/cannibal problem was quite often employed. This disjunctive task has the following content:

> Three missionaries and three cannibals are on one side of the river, and want to cross to the other side by means of a boat that can only hold two persons at a time. All the missionaries but only one cannibal can row. For safety reasons, the missionaries must never be outnumbered by the cannibals, under any circumstances or at any time, except when no missionaries are present at all. The question is: how many crossings will be necessary to transport the six people across the river?

The obvious answer is 13 crossings. Shaw (1932) observed that overall groups outperformed individuals. These results were explained by referring to the enhanced opportunity of groups to correct errors and to reject incorrect suggestions.

Later on successful and failing groups were compared more closely. Another explanation was then proposed: the so-called *truth-wins* rule. This rule says that if there is one group member who proposes the correct answer then it is likely that the group will succeed. This explanation did not always hold either. For some problems the truth-wins rule does apply, e.g. for the cannibal/missionary problem. However for others, e.g. for the horse-trading problem, it appeared quite often that having one successful member was no guarantee for group success.

This result was explained by pointing out that the missionary/cannibal problem has a very appealing solution – it has *eureka* appeal – while other tasks have a less obvious solution. The consequence is that if in an *eureka* task group one member has the correct solution the other group members more or less automatically adhere to this solution, which is not the case for problems which do not have such an obvious and insightful solution. For non-*eureka* tasks it can easily occur that a correct solution by one member will not be supported by the other group members or that a group member with a wrong solution dominates the solution process.

Thomas and Fink (1961) described a three-step model which appears to encompass the critical aspects of group success as for disjunctive tasks:

1 *Potential performance*   Do group members possess the necessary resources to solve the problem?
2 *Motivation*   Do group members, possessing the correct solution, actually propose this solution?
3 *Coordination*   Do correct solutions elicit support more often than incorrect solutions?

In the same vein, Steiner (1972; see also our introduction) summarizes the findings as follows. For disjunctive tasks a group's potential productivity is determined by the resources of its most competent member. However, even when there is a very competent member, process losses may prohibit the group from producing the correct solution. This is the case when the most competent member does not employ his or her resources or when other group members do not adhere to his or her solution. The latter seems to be very likely, (1) when the most competent member has a low status in the group and (2) when the most competent member is not confident enough either to express his or her solution or to persuade the other group members.

Conjunctive tasks   For conjunctive tasks it is necessary that all members contribute to the task. For tasks like climbing a mountain and soldiers marching in file the criterion is that all group members make the proper response. When conjunctive tasks are unitary it has been observed that each member must contribute lest the group fails (Steiner, 1972), i.e. group process depends on the competence of the least proficient member. Because the chance of having an incompetent member increases with group size, it is logical that as the number of group members increases the group productivity will diminish. In daily life, however, many conjunctive tasks are divisible; subtasks are then allocated to individual members. For example, climbing a mountain can be divided into several subtasks like rope leader and followers, where the followers are connected with a rope to the rope leader who takes the lead. If the most able climber performs the most difficult subtask, i.e. when she is made rope leader, and when the easiest subtasks are performed by the less able climbers, the group productivity is higher than the potential productivity of the least able group member. In sum, performance of unitary conjunctive tasks depends on the least able group member. However, for divisible conjunctive tasks the group performance can be made higher than the potential productivity of the least able group member, if the abilities of the group members coincide with the difficulty of the specific subtasks involved.

TABLE 14.2   Group performance of groups working on various types of tasks

Task	Group productivity	Description
Additive	Better than best	Group out-performs the best individual member
Compensatory	Better than most	Group out-performs a substantial number of group members
Disjunctive (*eureka*)	Equal to the best	Group performance matches the performance of the best member
Disjunctive (non-*eureka*)	Less than the best	Group performance can match that of the best member, but often falls short
Conjunctive (unitary)	Equal to the worst	Group performance matches the performance of the worst member
Conjunctive (divisible with matching)	Better than the worst	If subtasks are properly matched to ability of members, group performance can reach high levels

Sources: Steiner (1972, 1976); Forsyth (1983)

Conclusions

From the foregoing, two conclusions may be drawn. First, Steiner's classification allows us to make a set of predictions for the tasks under consideration. In table 14.2 these predictions are summarized. Second, the basic idea that group productivity is equal to the extent to which group members succeed in meeting the demands of the tasks minus eventual process losses appears to offer a deeper understanding of the nature of the tasks. Moreover, it has been suggested that process losses may be specifically ascribed to motivation and coordination losses.

Group Structure

In the preceding sections we explained how group members' resources may meet task demands. Most of the tasks we dealt with were unitary tasks – tasks which cannot be broken down into subtasks. In the present section we extend our analysis of group behaviour by describing behaviour of groups for tasks which can only be solved when the overall task is divided into several subtasks, and in which the subtasks are assigned to different group members, i.e. we are dealing with divisible group tasks. An example is playing a soccer game. Several subtasks, like defence and attack, may be distinguished and assigned to specific soccer players. However, a soccer team cannot easily win a match when the subtasks are not well integrated into a convincing overall conception of how the soccer team as a whole should perform its overall task.

Group structure pertains both to the differentiating elements as well as to integrating mechanisms. The elements are persons and positions, while the *integrating mechanisms* are communication, attraction, status, control and roles (see Collins and Raven, 1968). Before we go into more detail about the ways those elements of social structure are interconnected, we will give an example of how a group structure may develop over time.

Development of structure

Whyte (1948) illustrates the development of structure in his well-known story of Tom Jones's restaurant. Tom Jones starts his restaurant with two employees. There is almost no division of labour; all three cook, serve and wash dishes. After some success, Jones is able to hire new personnel and divides the labour into service employees, kitchen employees and dish washers. Coordination is done by Tom Jones himself. The relationships remain close and personal: the formal control is low. After further expansion Tom Jones introduces supervisors for service, food production and dish washers. Also a checker is introduced. This person has to total bills for his waiters and to see that food is served in a correct style and in the right portion. With increasing numbers of customers, Jones cannot be personally in touch with his customers any more and contact with his employees becomes formal. He supervises the organization from a distance.

The foregoing story illustrates the development of structure within a restaurant setting. In the initial phases, all employees perform more or less the same job. Through informal communication among the three of them, mutual adjustments can take place so that the total job may be done. Important for this implicit adjustment is that personal relations are good, i.e. mutual attraction should be high. There is no formal control. Being part of the group, Jones can minutely follow and correct the course of affairs. Although there is almost no division of labour it is clear that Jones is in charge. He fulfils the leadership role and his position is evaluated as higher than those of his coworkers. In the final stage of the restaurant a division of labour has taken place. A formal network of supervisors and workers has evolved while Jones supervises the organization as a whole.

This structure, once established, is largely independent of the persons who occupy the various positions. Each participant – boss, supervisors, cooks and waiters – plays his **role**, and the behaviour of each is determined by certain rules, standards of conduct or norms which specify acceptable behaviours. Moreover, an organizational structure develops and is subsequently maintained, because the role behaviours are under control: the boss controls the supervisors, and the supervisors control the waiters, dish washers and kitchen personnel.

It may be assumed that these positions are evaluated differently by personnel and customers. Presumably Jones has a higher status than the supervisors, while the position of a supervisor is evaluated more highly than that of a waiter.

These status differences, i.e. evaluations of positions in the group, may reinforce the established structure of the group. The structure has emerged and is maintained by communication. By communication, positions and roles are defined and assigned to certain persons. Moreover, communication enables the organization to maintain and change the pattern of roles and norms.

Lastly, attraction among group members may strengthen or weaken the informal **cohesion** of the group. In sum, this example demonstrates how the elements of group structure (persons and positions) are integrated by roles, norms, status, control, attraction and communication.

In the following we will deal with the formation of status, with roles, norms and communication networks. For the other integrating mechanisms the reader is referred to chapters 10, 13 and 15.

Status

A classic example of how **status** differences may arise in the laboratory is offered by an observation study done by Bales (1950a), who created problem-solving groups of unacquainted persons. The interactions within three- to six-person groups were observed by means of Bales's **interaction process analysis (IPA)** (table 14.3). This observation system specifies four broad behavioural categories, namely positive and negative socio-emotional behaviours, task behaviours and behaviours referring to exchange of information. As one may see from the left-hand side of table 14.3, task behaviour refers to all activities which aim at task completion, whereas socio-emotional behaviour is directed towards interpersonal relations.

Task and socio-emotional specialists   Bales and Slater (1955) trained their assistants to observe the behaviour of groups. These observers became practised at listening to a group discussion, breaking the verbal content into the 'smallest meaningful units' that can be distinguished (Bales, 1950a), and then classifying these units into categories.

From the studies of Bales and Slater (1955) it appeared that group members vary widely in their scores concerning these behavioural categories. Moreover this study suggests two kinds of leaders within a group – a sociol-emotional

TABLE 14.3   Bales's observation system scores for socio-emotional and task leaders

Bales's IPA categories	Socio-emotional specialists		Task specialists	
	Initiates	Receives	Initiates	Receives
Socio-emotional behaviour (positive)				
1 Shows solidarity	x	x		
2 Shows tension release	x	x		
3 Agrees	x			x
Task behaviour				
4 Gives suggestion		x	x	
5 Gives opinion		x	x	
6 Gives orientation		x	x	
Information exchange				
7 Asks for orientation	x			x
8 Asks for opinion	x			x
9 Asks for suggestion	x	x		x
Socio-emotional behaviour (negative)				
10 Disagrees			x	x
11 Shows tension	x			x
12 Shows antagonism			x	x

Sources: after Bales (1950a); Bales and Slater (1955)

and a task leader. The right-hand side of table 14.3 suggests that socio-emotional leaders initiate more often than any other group member for positive socio-emotional behaviours (categories 1 to 3) and information exchange (categories 7 to 9), while they receive most information (categories 4 to 6). In contrast, a task leader initiates task behaviour more frequently than any other group member. Moreover, other group members address this person quite often as for information exchange (categories 7 to 9) and they also express negative emotional behaviour towards this task specialist (categories 10 to 12).

Bales and Slater (1955) indicate that these two kinds of specialists arise quite often in discussion groups. The two functions – task and socio-emotional expertise – are rarely fulfilled by one and the same person. They give two reasons for groups having two leaders. First, the same person rarely has the ability to fulfil both functions. Second, as one may see from the right of table 14.3, a task leader arouses considerable hostility, i.e. very often other group members express negative socio-emotional behaviour towards the task leader (categories 10 to 12).

Burke (1967, 1974) has since reported evidence that the two functions may be performed by a single person during a one-hour discussion meeting, provided that members of the group are convinced from the outset that good task performance, rather than harmonious interpersonal relationships, is the ultimate aim. Under these circumstances disharmonious group tensions may be kept at a minimum or, if they do arise, may be tolerated more easily by group members.

Additional questionnaire data collected by Bales and Slater (1955) indicated that the socio-emotional specialist was liked more than any other group member, while the task specialist was perceived as the group member who contributed most to task achievement.

The latter findings demonstrate that status differences in groups do appear. However, the question is how do these status differences arise in groups of which the members were previously unacquainted with one another?

Emergence of status Expectation-states theory (Berger, Rosenholtz and Zelditch, 1980) assumes that in Bales's study *a priori* status expectations were involved. Status differences are likely to emerge in groups that are working on a cooperative task, such as the problem-solving groups of Bales and Slater (1955).

Because the group hopes it can successfully complete its task, the group members become aware of the possibility that some members possess superior skills and abilities that will favour goal attainment. This is then the beginning of the status-organizing process. One tries to identify those individuals who are expected to contribute most to goal attainment. These group members are addressed more often and are encouraged to take more initiatives. Moreover, other group members are most likely to comply with their influence attempts. The theory also points out which characteristics may give rise to status differentials. Specific status characteristics refer to the abilities and skills which are of direct relevance to goal attainment, e.g. mathematical abilities when the task makes an appeal to this ability. In the absence of specific status information, groups may still develop expectations by considering diffuse status characteristics – any quality of the person one may think of relevance to goal attainment. Sex, age, wealth, ethnicity and status in other groups may serve as diffuse status characteristics if group members associate these qualities with goal attainment.

Empirical support for expectation-states theory has been found by Berger, Rosenholtz and Zelditch (1980) and others. For example, Greenstein and Knottnerus (1980) observed that a person having a greater ability was more influential than a person with a lower ability; Torrance (1954) reported that in crews working on the horse-trading problem a person higher in military rank was able to exert more influence than persons lower in rank; Ofshe and Lee (1980) found that someone who showed more assertiveness was more influential then someone who was less assertive in his behaviour; Ridgeway (1978) found that a person who showed the strongest group orientation was more able to influence other group members than another person who apparently pursued his own self-interest.

A summary of these findings may be found in figure 14.4. This figure demonstrates why in initially leaderless groups, like those investigated by Bales and Slater (1955), a group structure may come into existence. By matching each person with the subtasks that one is most qualified to perform, group structure does arise. Because some qualifications give rise to higher expectations of successful task contribution than others, status and influence differentiation in groups do occur. That status differences do not always lead to a better group performance appears from the study by Torrance (1954), who employed pilots, navigators and gunners as subjects. The group discussion data indicate that of the pilots who had reached the correct answer before group discussion, one-tenth failed to persuade their associates to accept it, while one-fifth of the navigators and one-third of the gunners failed to do so. Thus a correct solution is more likely to prevail when it is offered by a high-status person than when it is offered by someone having a lower status. However, Torrance's results suggest that this also holds for higher-status members who advocate the wrong solution, i.e. high-status members appear to be more successful in persuading the other group members to accept the wrong solution than are low-status members. Thus a high-status person who is on the wrong track is a bigger obstacle for group success than an equally mistaken low-status person.

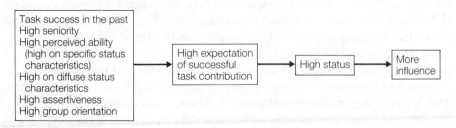

FIGURE 14.4   Characteristics which give rise to high status and more influence (based on Veen and Wilke, 1984)

The leadership role

One of the most salient distinctions of roles is that of leader and followers. A leader guides the group and facilitates the group's behaviour, while the followers are likely to accept the suggestions of the leader. The followers expect the leader to lead the group to group achievement. The leadership role is a position that may be occupied by any of the group members. Why is it then that a certain person becomes the leader? In the following we will deal with several answers, namely: (1) the leader is born to leadership; (2) a leader should exhibit certain behaviours; (3) a leader should exhibit certain behaviours in specific situations (see also Smith and Fritz, 1987).

The great man theory of leadership What are the characteristics of a successful leader? Until 1950 this so-called *trait approach* was very popular. Reviewing studies in which characteristics of leaders were compared with those of non-leaders, Stogdill (1948) found that leaders are more intelligent, have more education, are more inclined to take on responsibilities, are more active and have a higher socio-economic status.

He concluded that the trait approach yields interesting data, but that dependency on situational factors seems to be of major importance in determining who will become leader.

The behaviour approach Another approach to leadership focuses on the behaviours of leaders. Several methods of investigation were used to establish how leaders do behave. In the previous section we have already seen that Bales and Slater (1955), employing observation methods (Bales's interaction process analysis: Bales, 1950a), discovered that leaders score higher than their followers as for task and socio-emotional activities. Consequently two kinds of leaders can be distinguished: the best-liked person or *socio-emotional leader*, who takes care of harmonious group atmosphere, and the best-idea person or the *task leader*, who more than any other follower contributes to task achievement.

The questionnaire method has been employed in the Ohio State University leadership studies. The following steps were taken. First, researchers developed a list of nine key types of behaviour that seem to characterize military and organizational leaders. Second, a questionnaire was constructed and submitted to subordinates in all kinds of organizational settings, asking them to rate leaders. Third, correlations between these ratings were calculated and these correlations were compared via factor analysis – a method used to trace salient patterns of correlations. Two factors explained 83 per cent of the variations in the followers' evaluation of their leaders (Halpin and Winer, 1952): these factors were consideration and initiating structure. *Consideration* refers to the degree to which the leader responds to group members in a warm and friendly fashion and involves mutual trust, openness and willingness to explain decisions. *Initiating structure* is defined as the degree to which the leader organizes, directs and defines the group's structure and goals, regulates group behaviour, monitors communication and reduces goal ambiguities (Halpin and Winer, 1952; Lord, 1977).

Other questionnaire studies have also revealed two broad categories of leader behaviour. Most notable are the investigations performed at Michigan. Likert (1967) employed similar steps to those taken in the Ohio State University leadership studies. His results also revealed two factors, namely *employee centred* and *production centred* behaviour; these seem to match the aforementioned factors, i.e. consideration and initiating structure, respectively.

Thus in a group there seems to be a need for two kinds of leadership styles, each having its own impact on group productivity. Steiner (1976, p. 418) summarizes these findings as follows:

actual productivity = potential productivity – unrealized productivity

In his view, task leaders bolster the group's potential productivity. They take care that as many of the social resources as possible of the group are mobilized. Socio-emotional leaders serve to minimize unrealized productivity. They prevent the accumulation of tensions that might undermine harmonious group relations, which may be detrimental to actual group productivity.

At present, the behavioural approach does not seem to be popular any more. The main reason is that observational studies (e.g. Lord, 1977) quite often found little support for the consideration factor. In an observational investigation Couch and Carter (1952) reported a low correlation between ratings of leadership and the consideration factor. They even found that consideration and initiating structure together explained less variation than a third factor, *individual prominence*, which refers to the leader taking the leadership role by proposing himself or herself as leader.

From these studies it may be concluded that the results of questionnaire studies do partially contradict findings collected with the help of observational methods. Ilgen and Fujji (1976) have pointed out that the main weakness of questionnaire studies is that researchers ask respondents for desirable conceptions about their leaders, instead of for realistic ones. Observational studies, on the other hand, are performed by trained outsiders who are less sensitive to such a biasing.

In sum, research using the behavioural approach has clearly demonstrated that leaders take care of task success: observational studies indicate that, more than their followers, leaders contribute to the task process; while questionnaire results indicate that leaders should behave in a task-oriented way. A second factor – consideration or socio-emotional behaviour – receives less support: questionnaire results indicate that respondents appreciate it if their leader favours a harmonious group atmosphere; while results collected by means of observational methods indicate relatively less support for this factor. Individual prominence – the leader should be assertive and stand out in his or her group – is possibly a much more important behaviour of leaders.

Situational demands for leadership The example of Jones's restaurant demonstrates that in the beginning Jones's leadership was rather implicit, but became more explicit as his restaurant increased in size and complexity. Many groups start in a leaderless way. Committees and clubs quite often start as leaderless groups, and the leadership role emerges later. The question to consider is: when does a group require the instalment of an explicit leader?

As is suggested by the example of Jones's restaurant, the size of the group is an important reason to introduce explicit leadership. Large groups seem to have a greater need for explicit leadership than small groups. This appears from a study of Hemphill (1961). He compared the behaviours of large-group leaders with those of small-group leaders. He observed that large groups rely more often on a leader to make rules clear, keep members informed and make group decisions. In his review of situational factors affecting the need for leadership, Hemphill (1961) suggested that other factors also facilitate the emergence of explicit leaders in groups, namely the *nature of the task* and the *availability* of a group member who has experience in the leadership role. He specified the following task circumstances promoting the emergence of a leader:

1 Groups must have the feeling that task success is possible.
2 Group members must attach a great value to task success.
3 The task itself requires coordination and communication.

These task requirements are clearly involved in so-called social dilemmas (see Dawes, 1980). Social dilemmas are task structures in which it is in anybody's interest to behave selfishly. It is a dilemma because, if everyone makes a selfish choice, each person is worse off than when everyone has made a collective choice. We have already met this dilemma in the context of the free rider. All group members are inclined to keep their task expenditure at a minimum; however, when all group members do so, the group as a whole fails.

Other illustrations can also be given. For example, every student in a hall of residence is inclined to heat his or her room to a maximum, because it is known that the price of heating is to be shared anyway; however, if all students behave likewise, the collective bill may be extremely high. Dawes (1980) refers to societal problems such as overpopulation, energy depletion and pollution as social dilemmas. Recently, Rutte and Wilke (1984) considered the question of under what circumstances group members will opt for a leader in a social dilemma. Two factors appeared to be of relevance: (1) when the group failed to maintain the collective resource, and (2) when large differences in outcomes between group members emerged. Under these circumstances the group was more inclined to install a leader in the future than when the leaderless group did succeed and distributed the outcomes equally. The first factor refers to task success: if *task success* is *in danger* one opts for a leader. The second factor pertains to equity: when the outcomes are *inequitably allocated*, group members prefer a leader who takes decisions on behalf of all group members (see also chapter 13).

Three additional results seem to be of importance. First, Rutte and Wilke (1985) investigated subjects' preferences for other decision structures as well, to wit: unanimity, large majority, small majority, and each for himself or herself. It appeared that over all conditions of the experiment the preference for a leader was lower than for any other decision structure, suggesting that group members have a strong reluctance to opt for a leader, who takes away their own decisional freedom. Second, when asked which group member they would like to choose as a leader, most subjects were likely to prefer themselves, indicating that holding such a powerful position is very attractive, and that being powerless is a demotivating factor. Third, when elected leader, subjects took care of group success and allocated the outcomes in a fair way (Steiner, 1972, 1976).

These findings may be related to Steiner's ideas about group productivity, i.e.

$$\text{group productivity} = \text{potential productivity} - \text{motivational losses} - \text{coordination losses}$$

The instalment of a leader is a means to increase the coordination of group efforts, which obviously reduces coordination losses. In turn, improved coordination may motivate group members to contribute to group success. However, motivational losses may still play a role. The loss of subordinates' freedom to take decisions may induce them to minimize their efforts, and to leave it to the leader to take care of group productivity.

By implication, the results of the experiment by Rutte and Wilke (1985) suggest that group members in a leaderless group have no need to install a leader if the group acts successfully without a leader and when the outcomes of the group performance are allocated in a fair way, indicating that in some groups coordination by a leader is considered superfluous (see also Kerr and Jermier, 1978).

Table 14.4 shows that when a group is composed of competent group members (characteristic 1) who have a great need for independence (2) and a sense of professional identity (3), then task-oriented leadership is unnecessary. It may be assumed that without the intervention of a task leader the group is able to mobilize sufficient potential productivity to coordinate its efforts and to motivate its members. In addition, the properties of the task may make a leader superfluous. When the task itself automatically controls the behaviour of the group members, e.g. in an assembly line, then a task or coordinating leader is not necessary (characteristics 5–7 in table 14.4). In that case there is more need for relationship-oriented leadership which keeps the group members' motivation at a satisfactory level. Lastly, the type of organization also dictates whether a task leader is necessary. When the organization is highly formalized (characteristics 9–11) then task leadership is unnecessary, because leadership has been built into formal rules. In that case there is a greater need for a relationship-oriented leadership, which humanizes the rigid organizational environment.

TABLE 14.4 Substitutes for leadership

Characteristic	Will tend to neutralize	
	Relationship-oriented leadership	Task-oriented leadership
Of the group member		
1 Ability, experience, training, knowledge		x
2 Need for independence	x	x
3 'Professional' orientation	x	x
4 Indifference toward group rewards	x	x
Of the task		
5 Unambiguous and routine		x
6 Methodologically invariant		x
7 Provides its own feedback concerning accomplishment		x
8 Intrinsically satisfying	x	
Of the organization		
9 Formalization (explicit plans, goals and areas of responsibility)		x
10 Inflexibility (rigid, unbending rules and procedures)		x
11 Highly specified and active advisory and staff functions		x
12 Closely knit, cohesive workgroups	x	x
13 Organizational rewards not within leader's control	x	x
14 Spatial distance between superior and subordinate	x	x

Source: Kerr and Jermier (1978)

Table 14.4 also makes clear that when group members are indifferent towards organizational rewards (characteristic 4), when the groups are very cohesive (12) and when the leader has neither the means (13) nor the faculties (14) to motivate his subordinates, both relationship- and task-oriented leadership seem to be inadequate.

In sum, these findings suggest that there is a greater need for leadership as groups increase in size. In large groups coordination and motivation of group members may become a problem, which may be solved by the instalment of a leader. Two other circumstances seem to lead to the introduction of a leader, namely endangered task success and an unfair allocation of outcomes over group members. By implication, these data suggest that leadership is unlikely when a leaderless group achieves task success and when the group outcomes are allocated in a fair way. Other circumstances, referring to the persons involved, the task and the type of organization, also indicate when having a leader is ineffective. In the following section we will explain Fiedler's approach, which offers an explicit model of leader effectiveness.

Contingency of behaviour and situation   According to Fiedler (1978) studies of leadership have failed to acknowledge that the effect of the behaviour of the leader is contingent on characteristics of the situation involved. His so-called contingency model assumes that group productivity can only be predicted when one knows both the leader's style and his or her situational control; that is, the specific leadership style and the situational control together determine a leader's effectiveness.

Leadership style refers to the extent to which a leader is either relationship or task motivated and is based on the leader's ratings of the **least preferred coworker (LPC)**. The *high-LPC-leader* or *relationship motivated* leader perceives this coworker in a relatively favourable manner, i.e. even the *least* preferred coworker is perceived quite favourably. This type of leader derives major satisfaction from successful interpersonal relationships. The *low-LPC-leader* or *task-motivated leader* rates his or her least preferred coworker in a very unfavourable way and is described as a person who derives most satisfaction from task performance.

As well as the leadership style, *situational control* is of importance. A leader's situational control refers to the degree to which the leader feels secure and confident that the task may be accomplished. The leader's situational control is dependent on the degree to which (1) the leader–member relations are conceived as supportive, loyal and reliable; (2) the task is structured, because the task contains clear-cut goals and detailed methods of solution; and (3) the leader is in a position to supervise his or her workers and to reward or punish his or her subordinates.

According to Fiedler, leadership style and situational control determine leadership effectiveness as measured by group performance, i.e. one has to know the interaction of leadership style and situational control to be able to predict the effectiveness of the leader. Figure 14.5 summarizes the results of numerous investigations (see Fiedler and Potter, 1983; Chemers, 1983). The effectiveness of relationship-oriented (high-LPC) leaders is represented by the solid line, and that of task-motivated (low-LPC) leaders by the dashed line. We observe that task-motivated leaders perform best in situations of high and low control, whereas relationship-oriented leaders are most effective in moderate control situations.

Referring to more than 100 investigations, Fiedler and Potter (1983) claim that Fiedler's contingency theory is widely supported by empirical results. Yet the model possesses certain limitations. First, a theoretical problem is the exact meaning of the LPC instrument (Schriesheim and Kerr, 1977), suggesting that no satisfactory interpretation of LPC scores exists. Hosking (1981) has pointed out that not knowing the meaning of LPC scores implies not knowing why these measures should be expected to correlate with group performance. Second, there are numerous methodological problems associated with Fiedler's contingency model, including: (1) the group atmosphere scale – a scale meant to measure leader–member relations – is not independent of the leader, yet the leader's situational favourableness is conceptualized as an independent dimension; (2) quite often LPC scores were obtained from persons who did not actually perform the leadership function; (3) LPC scores correlate with group performance, suggesting that LPC is not an independent variable; (4) LPC scores are unstable over time. Third, several investigators (see e.g. Hosking, 1981) suggest that the weight of evidence does not support Fiedler's model.

Thus the literature shows that Fiedler's contingency model is rather controversial. However, opponents (e.g. Hosking, 1981) as well as supporters (e.g. Chemers, 1983) are of the opinion that considerably more work remains to be done.

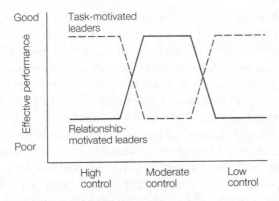

FIGURE 14.5 Situational control and performance of leaders (Fiedler and Potter, 1983)

Norms

Every group develops certain standards of conduct – **norms** – which regulate the interaction among group members. For example, in Tom Jones's restaurant certain rules came into being which specified acceptable behaviours in the interaction between the boss, cooks and waiters. Quite often these rules of behaviour are rather *implicit*, and one becomes aware of them only when they are broken. This was demonstrated by Garfinkel (1967), who asked students to act at home as if they were a boarder. For 15 minutes students had to be polite and speak formally and only when spoken to. It appeared that the reactions from the students' family members were rather negative. The students reported 'accounts of astonishment, bewilderment, shock, embarrassment and anger, with charges by various family members that the student was mean, inconsiderate, selfish, nasty or impolite' (Garfinkel, 1967, p. 47). By deviating from the expected behaviour of a proper son or daughter, students had discovered the hidden rules within their family.

Rules of behaviour may also be rather *explicit* and laid down in formal rules. When, in student's residence, informal rules do not suffice to provide regular meals or a clean kitchen, one may decide to draft formal regulations with punishments for contraventions.

In the following we will sketch how implicit and explicit group norms affect the behaviour of groups. The question is: what constitutes a normal production level for a group? In answering this question we will focus on how in groups a certain standard comes into being and how these standards are maintained during subsequent interaction. By way of a summarizing statement we will argue that these norms or standards promote the survival of any group, because group norms help a group to accomplish its goals and to maintain itself as a group.

Development of norms Suppose you and two other people are forming an investors' club. One of the questions which arises is: how much gain on the invested capital may be considered normal, i.e. a standard worth achieving? The work of Sherif (1935) – to be described in more detail in chapter

15 – demonstrates that group members tend to converge towards a common norm, which is the average of the *a priori* individual judgements. This suggests that an investors' club will be likely to reach a common standard of gains which is equal to the average of the individual preferences beforehand. This co-called *convergence* or *funnel* pattern in norm formation (but see also chapter 15) is a widely established phenomenon. For example, Hoekstra and Wilke (1972) analysed wage recommendations made by managers who first had to make recommendations on an individual basis and thereafter in groups consisting of five to seven managers. They observed that for the 432 managers who participated (see Bass, 1965) the mean of individual recommendations was equal to the average of group recommendations. From this study two other results are noteworthy. First, it appeared that the managers took into account the specific characteristics (notably performance) and circumstances of the employees for whom they had to make wage recommendations. These differences between the employees concerned resulted in differential wage recommendations. Second, in this cross-cultural study it was established that the national origin of the managers played an important role: (groups of) managers from Belgium, the US and Holland were less generous in their wage recommendations than (groups of) managers from Great Britain, Greece, Spain and Italy. These results make it plausible that groups having to make decisions converge towards a common norm, and that circumstances such as the experiences of group members and their analysis of the problem at hand determine to a large extent the establishment of the specific standard. Thus, group norms may vary as a consequence of the information available to the group members.

How norms may be changed as a consequence of feedback about the success and failure of the actual group performance has been investigated by Zander (1971), who asked group members to perform a ball-propelling task. This task requires that all group members stand in a simple file, grasp a long pole and swing it in unison so that the end of the shaft strikes a wooden ball and rolls it down an extended channel. The ball stops next to one of several numbers painted on the side of the channel, providing a score for that shot. Five shots make a trial, and the group may achieve up to 50 points on each trial. Zander observed that the group's aspired norm (agreed upon by the group members) tends to be close to the immediately preceding score. If the performance improves, the aspired group performance goes up. Zander also detected that aspired levels of group productivity changed more after an improvement than after a deterioration of group performance, i.e. production norms are raised more often when the performance increases than they are lowered when the performance decreases. Zander also showed that norm formation is dependent on previous success and failure of the group: norms change more easily after success than after failure of the group.

Maintenance of group norms   Norms about an acceptable production level are rather resistant to change. In the pioneering research of Roethlisberger and Dickson (1939) at the Western Electric Company, it was observed that the workers in a 'bank wiring' section consistently produced below their capacities and below the goals set by the management. Results of interviews showed that older workers adhered to the norm of a limited production, because they saw this norm as essential for group survival, e.g. fairness and job tenure. The results of this study also showed how workers who tried to perform above the informal work norm were discouraged. These 'rate busters' were exposed to sanctions in the form of 'binging' (hitting the arm of the rate buster to indicate disapproval and to disrupt work) and psychological isolation in the group (by not talking to the violator).

The use of communication to affect the behaviour of norm violators has been demonstrated by Schachter (1951), who asked groups to decide on what should be done with a delinquency case. In each experimental group, confederates of the experimenter performed three different roles: (1) the mode, who accommodated to the average judgement; (2) the slider, who initially adopted an extreme position but moved toward the group norm during the discussion; and (3) the deviate, who chose and maintained an extreme position throughout the discussion. The results indicated that initially the group discussion was primarily directed towards the two persons with a deviating point of view, the slider and the deviant. After it became apparent that the deviant would not change, the influence attempts subsided. The group eventually excluded the deviant from discussion by not asking her questions and by ignoring her contributions.

That norms are highly resistant to change has also been demonstrated by Coch and French (1948). They found that workers in the Harwood Manufacturing Corporation showed a strong resistance to a change in the methods of doing their jobs. This resistance expressed itself by grievances about the piece rates that went with the new methods, high turnover, low efficiency, restriction of output and marked aggression against management. By varying the degree of participation, Coch and French did a field experiment. In a no-participation group, workers were merely notified about the introduction of the new work methods, which were said to be no more difficult than the former methods. This group improved little and resistance developed almost immediately after the change occurred. Marked expressions of aggression against management occurred, such as conflict with the methods engineer, expression of hostility against the supervisor, deliberate restriction of production, and lack of cooperation with the supervisor. In the participation group, workers participated in the decisions necessary to carry out the work transfer. In this condition the workers raised their production rates, and the other measures also showed that the participation groups responded in a favourable way to the induced change. In sum, the results of the Coch and French study show that group norms are very difficult to change. However, when rather persuasive techniques are introduced, this resistance to the change of group norms may be weakened and a certain openness to new standards may be realized.

Functions of group norms   In the previous paragraphs we have indicated that group norms are developed and maintained. In this perspective, norms are coordinating devices (see Steiner, 1972) that contribute to the survival of groups. This proposition which has been elaborated by Cartwright and Zander (1968) in dealing with the functions of group standards or norms. They distinguish four functions, which we will explain in the following:

1 *Group locomotion*   Norms help groups to accomplish their goals. If an executive committee is to make workable plans, it is necessary that members of the committee believe in the same policy for the organization.

2 *Group maintenance*   Norms help groups to maintain themselves as a group. For example, the requirement that members regularly attend meetings or wholeheartedly support the party platform serves to ensure that the group will continue to exist as an entity.

3 *Social reality*   Quite often there is no objective reality. Norms help the group to create and maintain a commonly shared frame of reference, which serves as a social reality. For example, a curriculum committee of psychologists having to decide upon minimum requirements for graduation in psychology has to face questions like what type of work graduates face, what skills they need, how much practical experience is necessary, and how much statistics they need. Shared agreement about these matters creates a certain standard of conduct, which is necessary to design a comprehensive plan.

4 *Defining relationships to social surroundings*   Norms help group members to define their relationships to social surroundings, such as other groups, organizations, institutions and other components of the society. The aforementioned curriculum committee, for example, needs to define the relationship of psychologists to other social scientists, to other educational programmes, to research, to industrial and mental health organizations and to the society at large, without which the designing of a programme is insufficient.

Communication networks

Elements – people and positions – of the group structure may also be linked by **communication networks**, which may be considered to be coordination devices. In the following we describe several kinds of communication networks, and ask which leads to better group performance and group motivation.

Group performance   In many organizations all communications have to go through formal channels, while other organizations are less restrictive and permit anyone to communicate freely with anyone else.

Leavitt (1951) asked whether communication patterns in groups affect their efficiency. In his experiments subjects were seated around a circular table separated by vertical partitions. Slots, which could be opened and closed by the experimenter, allowed the subjects to pass certain messages to certain other

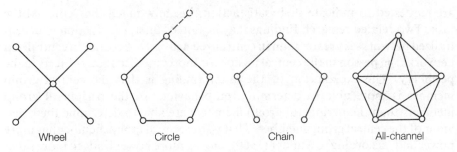

FIGURE 14.6   Some communication networks (based on Leavitt, 1951)

group members. Figure 14.6 shows a number of communication networks. The networks become increasingly centralized from right to left. The wheel is most centralized since any group member in the periphery must send messages through the single central person. In contrast, in the all-channel network no one controls the distribution of messages and any person may communicate with any other person without having to rely on someone else.

Employing rather simple tasks, which required merely the gathering of information, Leavitt (1951) found that wheels were more efficient than circles, Shaw (1964), however, using more complex tasks which required mathematical operations, found the reverse: circles appeared to be more efficient than wheels. In an experiment in which complex tasks were employed he demonstrated that for the first in a series of problems, circle groups were indeed superior to the more centralized wheel groups. However, for the fifth problem wheels were superior to circles. Thus, after some time more centralized networks perform better on complex tasks than less centralized networks (see also Mackenzie, 1976).

Steiner's ideas (Steiner 1972, 1976) suggest that both simple and complex tasks require coordination. Groups on simple tasks merely have to gather information. This is also necessary for complex tasks. However, groups performing complex tasks also have to perform rather complex operations upon this information. Thus complex tasks are relatively more discretionary than simple tasks, i.e. complex tasks leave it more to the group how to perform the task. Because of the rather undiscretionary nature of the simple task, simple task groups immediately profit from the introduction of a coordinating, centralized network of relations. For complex task groups these coordination advantages only begin to pay off after a while, since initially the group has to pay attention to the complex operations of the task itself. It is even possible that initially the introduction of a centralized network may impair group productivity, because of the high coordination losses involved. Being confronted with the double task of how to solve a problem and how to organize the group may be too heavy a task. However, as soon as these groups have discovered the operations necessary to perform the task, complex task groups may also profit from the advantages that a centralized network offers.

Group motivation   In many network studies (see Shaw, 1981, p. 154) subjects are requested to indicate their satisfaction, i.e. how much they enjoyed the task. Two related research findings may be noted. First, satisfaction in decentralized networks is greater than in centralized networks. Second, in centralized networks the person in the central position is more satisfied than subjects in the periphery. The explanation of the latter finding is that the central group member is more able to determine the behaviour of the peripheral group members than the peripheral group members are able to determine the behaviour of the central group member. That is, the central group member has more power and, according to Mulder (1960), having more power leads to more satisfaction. In decentralized networks subjects have equal power and the satisfaction of the members is greater than the satisfaction of peripheral group members in the centralized network. As a consequence of sheer numbers, the total satisfaction or group morale in decentralized networks is greater than in centralized networks. These findings suggest that in the long run having a centralized network reduces coordination losses. Simultaneously, however, the danger of increased motivation loss arises.

Summary and Conclusion

This chapter has provided a tour through the area of group performance. We were influenced mainly by Steiner's view that actual performance is equal to potential productivity minus process losses. We looked at group performance from two perspectives.

From the perspective of an individual as a social being, we indicated how individual task performance is affected by the presence of others. Process losses appear to have two components. First, the presence of others evokes task-irrelevant processing – which may be viewed as *intrapersonal* coordination loss. Second, the presence of others increases effort; in other words, motivation losses are smaller than when individuals work alone. The combined effect of these two processes is that the presence of others facilitates performance on simple tasks and inhibits performance on complex tasks.

Subsequently, from the perspective of the group we considered how freely interacting group members perform a task. There we established that process losses imply again the same two components, but now on an *interpersonal* level, i.e. interpersonal coordination and interpersonal motivation losses which may facilitate or inhibit group performance.

In the last part of the chapter we dealt with group structure. We indicated how and why group structure develops over time, and that two critical group functions operate, i.e. task and socio-emotional leadership. We suggested that leaders in successful groups are able to reduce coordination and motivation losses. However, having a leader as such may enhance motivational losses, and in some circumstances the instalment of a leader is therefore neither preferred by regular group members nor necessary, given the characteristics of group members and the task and type of organization. Subsequently we argued that norms are essential for any group to accomplish its goals and to maintain itself as a group. Lastly, we elucidated how Steiner's model of group performance may be applied to explain productivity and satisfaction in so-called communication networks. As for group performance in the long run, centralized networks are superior. However, although coordination losses may be minimized, enhanced motivation losses may be incurred.

Glossary Terms

Co-action	Norms
Cohesion	Role
Communication network	Social dilemma
Dominant response	Social facilitation
Free-rider effect	Social inhibition
Interaction process analysis (IPA)	Social loafing
	Status
Least preferred coworker (LPC)	

Further Reading

Cartwright, P. and Zander, A. (1968) *Group Dynamics: research and theory*, 3rd edn. New York: Harper & Row. This volume of collected papers presents much of the classic seminal research and thinking in the area of group dynamics. The introductory chapters provide excellent summaries of the basic ideas.

Forsyth, D. (1983) *An Introduction to Group Dynamics*. Monterey, Calif.: Brooks/Cole. A well-written, up-to-date and comprehensive introduction to group dynamics.

Katz, D. and Kahn, R. L. (1978) *The Social Psychology of Organizations*, 2nd edn. New York: Wiley. A broad theoretical view on how groups work in organizations.

Paulus, P. B. (1983) *Basic Group Processes*. New York: Springer. A collection of sophisticated reviews on group dynamics.

Shaw, M. E. (1981) *Group Dynamics: the social psychology of small group behavior*, 3rd edn. New York: McGraw-Hill. A comprehensive introduction to the field of group dynamics. The conclusions are summarized by means of hypotheses.

Steiner, I. (1972) *Group Processes and Productivity*. New York: Academic Press. An original treatment of factors affecting group performance.

Zander, A. (1977) *Groups at Work*. San Francisco: Jossey-Bass. Sophisticated yet accessible treatment of how groups operate. Emphasis is on group aspirations.

15 Social Influence in Small Groups

EDDY VAN AVERMAET

Introduction

Imagine you are one of a group of seven people who represent the student body at departmental meetings. The forthcoming meeting will discuss and take a vote on a proposed change in the curriculum: several applied courses are to be dropped and replaced by more theoretically oriented subjects. Before the meeting the student representatives get together to try to reach a common position on the issue. You have given the issue a lot of thought and you favour the departmental proposal. At the student meeting you then learn that some people share your view but that others do not. You try to convince them of your viewpoint and they try to convince you. What will be the outcome? Most likely you will reply: it all depends on the circumstances! In giving that reply you concur with social psychologists, who for many years now have been systematically studying the factors that determine social influence in small groups.

Broadly speaking the study of social influence coincides with social psychology itself, because the entire field deals with the influence of social factors on behaviour. Typically, however, the concept of social influence is given a more restricted meaning: *social influence* refers to a change in the judgements, opinions and attitudes of an individual as a result of being exposed to the judgements, opinions and attitudes of other individuals (de Montmollin, 1977). With this restricted definition in mind the present chapter will introduce you to some of the more important phenomena that have been studied concerning social influence.

The first topic is conformity or majority influence. Do individuals change their opinions when they learn that the majority of the members of a group to which they belong hold a different opinion? Do they perhaps only give in overtly and maintain their own conviction in private, or does majority influence really change people's minds? Under which conditions do individuals manage to resist majority influence? Next we turn our attention to the reverse phenomenon, namely innovation or minority influence. Can a minority in a group bring about changes in the opinions of a majority? Which characteristics should a minority have in order to produce an effect? When does minority influence fail? Do minorities exert their influence through the same mechanisms as majorities? Do they have more or less influence? Is there only a difference in quantity of influence, or do majorities and minorities produce qualitatively different effects?

The third and fourth sections will deal respectively with the phenomena of group polarization and obedience. Group polarization refers to the fact that, under certain conditions, the outcome of a group discussion is more extreme than the initial average position of the individual group members. We will look into some of the theories and experiments that have been developed to account for this most remarkable phenomenon. Finally, we will pay attention to a special case of social influence: when and why will individuals, merely at the persistent request of an authority, carry out orders which they themselves consider unethical and which they are, in principle, unwilling to execute?

Because this chapter is only intended as an introduction to the field of social influence, we will necessarily have to be somewhat superficial and definitively selective in the treatment of both theory and research. Undoubtedly valuable contributions will be left out, and we therefore wish to encourage the active student to look also at some of the excellent books and papers referred to at the end of this chapter.

Conformity or Majority Influence

Sherif and the autokinetic effect

In an early social influence experiment Muzafer Sherif (1935) placed subjects alone or in groups of two or three in a completely darkened room. At a distance of about 5 metres a single and small stationary light was presented to them. As you may already have experienced yourself, in the absence of reference points a stationary light appears to move rather erratically in all directions. This perceptual illusion is known as the **autokinetic effect**.Sherif asked his subjects to give an oral estimate of the extent of movement of the light, obviously without informing them of the autokinetic effect. Half of the subjects made their first 100 judgements alone. On three subsequent days they went through three more sets of trials, but this time in groups of two or three. For the other half of the subjects the procedure was reversed. They underwent the three group sessions first and ended with a session alone. Subjects who first made their judgements alone developed rather quickly a standard estimate (a personal norm) around which their judgements fluctuated. This personal norm was stable, but it varied highly between individuals. In the group phases of the experiment, which brought together people with different personal norms, subjects' judgements converged towards a more or less common position – a group norm. With the reverse procedure this group norm developed in the first session and it persisted in the later session alone.

This famous experiment shows that, where confronted with an unstructured and ambiguous stimulus, people nevertheless develop a stable internal frame of reference against which to judge the stimulus. However, as soon as they are confronted with the different judgements of others they quickly abandon this frame of reference so as to adjust it to that of others. On the other hand, a frame of reference formed in the presence of others continues to affect a person's judgements when the source of influence is no longer present. In the introduction, conformity was described as a change in an individuals's judgement in the direction of the judgements expressed by the majority of the members of a group to which the individual belongs. Strictly speaking Sherif's study is not a **conformity** or **majority influence** experiment because he merely brought together two or three people who held different opinions. To turn it into a conformity study one would have to replace all the subjects but one by confederates who unanimously agree upon a particular judgement. Jacobs and Campbell (1961) did just that and in addition, after every 30 judgements, they replaced a confederate by a naive subject until the whole group was made up of naive subjects. Their results indicated that the majority had a significant effect on the subjects' judgements, even after they had gradually been removed from the situation.

Up to this point you may not be too surprised. After all, it is normal and even adaptive that people are influenced by or conform to the judgements of others when the judgemental stimulus is ambiguous or when they feel uncertain about their own judgement. But would you also conform to the judgements of others when they appear to be patently wrong, when their judgements are completely at odds with what your senses and physical reality tell you? Would social reality prevail, or would you call them as you see them?

The surprise of Solomon Asch

The question raised above constituted the starting point of a series of famous conformity experiments conducted by Solomon Asch in the early 1950s (Asch, 1951, 1956). In his first study Asch invited seven students to participate in an experiment on visual discrimination. Their task was simple enough: 18 times they would have to decide which of three comparison lines was equal in length to a standard line. On each trial one comparison line was in effect equal in length to the standard line, but the other two were different (for an example, see figure 15.1). On some trials these were both longer or shorter, or one was longer and the other shorter. Also, trials differed in terms of the extent to which the two incorrect lines were different from the standard line. All in all the task was apparently very easy, as is shown by the fact that in a control group of 37 subjects, who made their judgements in isolation, 35 people did not make a single error, one person made one error and one person made two errors. Hence, summing over subjects and trials, a negligible 0.7 per cent errors were made in the control condition. In the experimental condition the subjects, who were seated in a semicircle, were requested to give their judgements aloud, in the order in which they were seated, from position 1 to position 7. Actually there was only one real subject, seated in position 6. All the others were confederates of the experimenter and, on each trial, they unanimously gave a

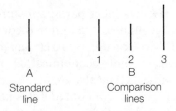

FIGURE 15.1   An example of the stimuli presented in Asch's experiment

predetermined answer. On six 'neutral' trials (the first two trials, and four other trials distributed over the remaining set) the confederates gave correct answers. On the other 12 'critical' trials they unanimously agreed on an incorrect line. The neutral trials, particularly the first two, were added to avoid suspicion on the part of the real subject and to avoid an attribution of poor vision as the cause of the responses of the confederates. It should be pointed out that, throughout the experiment, both the experimenter and the confederates acted in a rather impersonal and formal manner, not showing any surprise or negative reaction to the answers given. As a matter of fact, as you might expect, only the real subjects showed various signs of non-neutral behaviour.

The results reveal the tremendous impact of an 'obviously' incorrect but unanimous majority on the judgements of a lone subject. In comparison with the control condition, which you will remember yielded only 0.7 per cent errors, the experimental subjects made almost 37 per cent errors. Not every subject made that many errors, but it is instructive to observe that out of Asch's 123 subjects only about 25 per cent did not make a single error (compared with 95 per cent in the control condition), another 28 per cent gave eight or more (out of 12) incorrect answers, and the remaining subjects made between one and seven mistakes. From a methodological point of view, it is important to grasp clearly the distinction between percentage of errors and percentage of influenced subjects. Students (and even textbooks) sometimes confuse the two measures by asserting that 37 per cent errors means that 37 per cent of the subjects were influenced. The above distinction is also important from an inter-pretational viewpoint, because just by itself the error percentage presents only an incomplete picture of the amount of influence exerted (it says nothing about the distribution of this influence).

Essentially similar results have been obtained on numerous occasions, using different subject populations and different judgemental tasks. For those who might feel that the Asch effect reflects only the conformist attitude of a specific time in history or of a specific culture and is therefore a thing of the past, more recent replications of the Asch study in Belgium (Doms and Van Avermaet, 1982) and in The Netherlands (Vlaander and Van Rooijen, 1985) have obtained essentially comparable results (but see Perrin and Spencer, 1980 for a negative finding). Asch's experiment, with its astonishing results, provided the ground-work for a rich tradition of theoretical speculations and empirical studies, directed at determining the boundaries of the phenomenon, the conditions under which conformity increases and decreases, and whether conformity is only public or also private. The next paragraphs present a selection of this research against the background of the major theoretical perspective within which it can be situated. Most of this research has made use of a paradigm, modelled after Asch's, but far more economical. Using the so-called 'Crutch-field' technique (1955), subjects typically are placed in separate cubicles where they see the responses of (simulated) confederates appear electronically on a panel. The savings in time and confederates are great, but some of the realism of the original Asch procedure is lost in the process.

Why people conform: normative and informational influence

When people have to express a judgement about some aspect of reality in the presence of others they have two major concerns: they want to be right, and they want to make a good impression on the others. To determine what is right, individuals have two sources of information: what their senses and physical reality indicate, and what others say. Throughout life individuals have learned to appreciate the value of both sources of information. On numerous occasions they have experienced the adaptive value of founding their judgements and behaviours on their own view of reality. On the other hand, a lot of what they have learned about reality is based on information provided by others, and in their experience relying on others' judgements has proved adaptive as well. Moreover, in most instances both their own judgements and those of others have coincided, providing people with a stable view of their environment. The conformity situation, however, opposes these two sources of information and confronts the individual with the conflict of choosing between two – in principle – reliable bases of information. If, in this perspective, the individual conforms, he is said to have undergone **informational influence**: he yields to others because he trusts their judgement more than his own. There is, however, also another reason why a person might yield to group pressure. Because we are dependent on others for the satisfaction of a variety of needs, it is important that we maximize their liking for us. To the extent that disagreeing with others can be anticipated to lead to dislike or even outward rejection, and that agreeing will lead to more positive evaluations and continued group member-ship, people are induced to conform to others' judgements for normative reasons. Hence, conformity caused by the desire to be liked and by the aversion to being disliked is due to **normative influence**.

Informational and normative influence (Deutsch and Gerard, 1955) are then the major general mechanisms through which groups have an impact on their members. Of course, the relative weight of these two mechanisms varies from situation to situation. In some instances, people will conform more because of the information others provide, whereas in others they will conform mainly for normative reasons. Moreover – and this is an equally important distinc-tion – normative and informational influence processes can be expected to produce effects at different levels. If a person conforms mainly because of what others will think of her, she will change her overt behaviour while privately maintaining her prior conviction; but if she trusts the information provided by others she will in addition also change her private opinion. Hence a distinction should be made between public conformity or **compliance** and private conformity or **conversion**. As a matter of fact, researchers in this field have used public and private response modes in conformity settings as a means of assessing whether normative or informational influence is the more important change mechanism. Results of these experiments have shown that, at least as far as the original Asch experiment is concerned, normative influence is more important than informational influence. This can be inferred from the observation that public responses are far more influenced by the group's judgement than are responses given in private (for a review see Allen, 1965).

In a more general sense, and through the manipulation of various characteristics of the influence situation, social psychologists have attempted to collect evidence for the theoretical proposition that conformity will increase or decrease as a function of the amount of informational and/or normative dependence of an individual on the group.

Normative and informational influence: experimental evidence

Beginning with normative influence, Endler (1965) showed that direct reinforcement for conforming responses leads to an increment in conformity. Deutsch and Gerard (1955) increased the interdependence of the group members by promising a reward (tickets to a Broadway play) to the five groups that would make the fewest errors of judgement. Setting this goal for the group, which clearly made the members very dependent on each other for obtaining a desired effect, produced twice as much conformity as a baseline condition. Thibaut and Strickland (1956) described the setting as a test of cooperative ability and told the subjects that groups would be compared on this dimension. Subjects in this condition of competition between groups conformed more than subjects for whom accuracy of individual judgement was emphasized. As a final example of the role of normative influence, Dittes and Kelley (1956) varied the subjects' status within the group. They observed more conformity in subjects of medium status than in subjects of either very low or very high status. High-status subjects can afford to deviate; low-status subjects have nothing to lose (they may not even care about the group); but medium-status subjects have most to gain by conforming and most to lose by not conforming.

Turning to the role of informational influence, it has been shown that the subject's perceived competence at the judgement task relative to others, as well as his self-confidence, determine the amount of conformity (e.g. Mausner, 1954). Di Vesta (1959) showed that more conformity obtained on later trials if the early trials contained many neutral trials (where the majority gives correct answers), because under these conditions the subject is more likely to attribute competence to the other group members. Task difficulty or stimulus ambiguity is another variable which, through the informational mechanism, influences conformity. These factors contribute to more uncertainty in a person and to a heavier reliance on the unanimous judgements of others (e.g. Asch, 1952; Crutchfield, 1955).

The size of the majority is yet another example of a relevant variable in this context. Asch (1951) ran groups in which the size of the 'majority' varied from one to 16. One person had no effect, but two persons already produced 13 per cent errors. With three confederates the conformity effect reached its full strength with 33 per cent errors. The addition of even more confederates did not lead to further increments in conformity. Later studies by Gerard, Wilhelmy and Conolley (1968) and by Latané and Wolf (1981) have questioned this conclusion and suggest that adding more members to the majority will in effect lead to more conformity but with diminishing increments per added member. On the other hand, the degree of perceived independence of the influence sources is also important. Adding more members to the majority will only lead to more influence if the majority members are perceived as independent judges and not as sheep following the others or as members of a group who have arrived jointly at a judgement. Wilder (1977) showed that two independent groups of two people have more impact than four people who present their judgements as a group, and three groups of two have more effect than two groups of three, who in turn yield more conformity than one group of six. Clearly, independent sources of information are more reliable than a single aggregated information source.

Finally, a fascinating series of studies, excellently summarized by Allen (1975), has looked at the effects of replacing one of the confederates by another person who deviates from the majority position. When Asch gave the subject a supporter in the form of a confederate who answered before the subject and who gave correct answers on all trials, the conformity of the real subject dropped dramatically to a mere 5.5 per cent. In trying to find out whether the reduced conformity was caused by the break in the unanimity of the majority or by the fact that the subject now had a social supporter (for his own private opinion), Asch added a condition in which the confederate deviated from the majority but gave an even more incorrect answer than they did. Hence the majority was not unanimous, but the subject received no social support either. The results showed that the extreme dissenter was nearly as effective in reducing conformity as was the social supporter. Breaking the unanimity would therefore appear to be crucial but, as Allen and Levine (1968, 1969) later showed, this conclusion only holds with respect to unambiguous stimulus situations as in Asch's experiments. With opinion statements only a genuine social supporter will lead to reduced conformity.

The role of social support is further demonstrated in studies where the subject has a partner for the first part of the experiment, who then ceases to respond owing to an alleged breakdown in the equipment (Allen and Bragg, 1965), or who then leaves the room (Allen and Wilder, 1972). Even under these non-responding-partner or absent-partner conditions people continue to resist influence, at least as long as they are assured that the partner responded in the same setting (under pressure) as they do. Merely knowing that another person thinks as you do is not sufficient! Also, when a subject is originally given a partner who then deserts him by switching to the incorrect majority responses, he will not maintain his prior 'independence'. Rather he will conform as if he had never had a partner (Asch, 1955).

Although the social support effects can also partially be interpreted in terms of normative influence, it is instructive to look at them from an informational point of view. Looking at the desertion effect first, it is understandable that a person, upon learning that someone whose judgements he trusts (because they coincide with his own) changes sides, will be strongly influenced by that person's behaviour. 'Here is an intelligent person changing his position; I'd better do as he does because he can be relied on!' In a similar vein the other social support effects would tend to indicate that the subject's refusal to conform is caused by the fact that, as Allen puts it, the social supporter provides him with an independent assessment of reality, which is sufficient to outweigh the potential informational value of the majority's responses. This interpretation is strongly supported by the data of an experiment by Allen and Levine (1971). Here too the subject was given a supporter, but in one of their two support conditions the social support was invalid. The supporter, although giving correct answers, could not possibly be perceived as a valid source of information because the subject knew that he had extremely poor vision (as was evident from a pre-experimental eye examination and from his eyeglasses with thick lenses). The results, shown in figure 15.2, indicate that, although invalid social support is sufficient to reduce the amount of conformity significantly

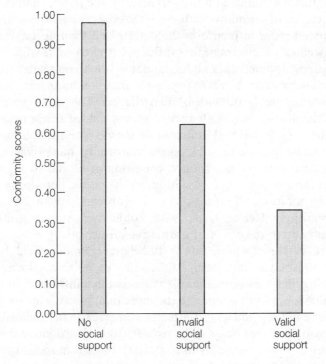

FIGURE 15.2 Conformity in the absence and the presence of social support (based on Allen and Levine, 1971)

compared with a unanimous majority condition, the valid social supporter has much more impact. The lesson to be learned from all these studies is obvious: if you are afraid of being influenced by a group (at least publicly – and that is often what counts!), make sure you bring a partner along, and preferably one you can count on to stick by your position!

The joint effects of normative and informational influence

As was briefly suggested earlier, in most situations normative and informational factors both play a role in determining the amount of conformity. The studies reviewed above focused on one or the other, because they wanted to illuminate their unique effects. A recent study by Insko et al. (1983) looked at their joint effects. In this study the subjects, in groups of six, had to judge whether a colour, shown on a slide, was more similar to another colour shown to the left or to another colour shown to the right. On the criticial trials four confederates who answered before the subject and another who answered last gave responses which deviated from those given by most subjects in a control condition where they were alone. Two variables were manipulated: the subject had to respond publicly or privately, and the experimenter could or could not determine which response was more correct. In the 'determined' condition the experimenter referred to an apparatus through which he could accurately measure which response was more correct; in the 'undetermined' condition this was said to be impossible. Insko anticipated more influence in the public than in the private condition because of normative influence (the concern with being liked), and he also anticipated more influence in the determined than in the undetermined condition because of informational influence (the concern with being right). The latter prediction becomes understandable when you realize that not only will you try harder to be correct in the determined condition but you have every reason to assume that the others too will try harder. The results were completely in line with the predictions. Both manipulations yielded a clear main effect and no interaction. As figure 15.3 indicates, in the determined and undetermined conditions public responding led to more conformity than private responding, and at the same time the determined condition produced stronger influence effects than the undetermined condition, in the public but also in the private condition. In addition, all means differed significantly from the no-influence control condition. Hence, even with 'objective' stimuli, informational influence can add to the effect of normative influence!

In concluding, literally hundreds of studies have demonstrated the impact of a majority on isolated individuals, although – as we saw – the addition of a person sharing their viewpoint makes them resist that influence. But is resisting the only behavioural option open to the individual (and his or her supporter)? Can he or she not try actively to attempt to persuade the majority that they might be wrong and that he or she is right? Just look around and you will say 'yes'. However, it was not really until the late 1960s that social psychologists, mainly under the impetus of the French psychologist Serge Moscovici, began

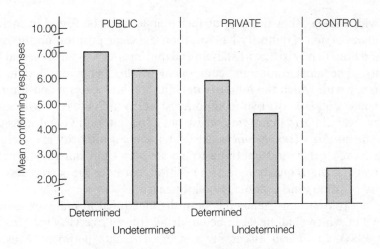

FIGURE 15.3   Mean conformity data on ten critical trials (data from Insko et al., 1983)

seriously to study the conditions under which a minority can do more than merely resist and itself become an active source of influence.

Innovation or Minority Influence

The power of a consistent minority

In 'Twelve Angry Men', a brilliant film by Sidney Lumet, twelve jurors have to decide over the guilt or innocence of a young man charged with the murder of his father. At the outset of the deliberation all but one are convinced of the youth's guilt. Does the lone juror (Henry Fonda) yield to the unanimous majority? No! Does he only passively resist their influence attempts? No! Instead he actively attempts to persuade the others of the correctness of his own position, standing firm, committed, self-confident and unwavering. One by one the other jurors change sides, until in the end they all agree that the accused is not guilty. History and present-day social life provide ample examples of this same phenomenon: Galileo, Freud, new forms of art, the growing impact of the ecological movement, and the women's movement are but a few examples.

In his book *Social Influence and Social Change* Moscovici (1976) argues that most instances of **minority influence** or **innovation** cannot be accounted for by the mechanisms which traditionally have been proposed to explain majority influence. Indeed, if you think of it, minorities do not have a lot going for them: they are few in number; they often do not have normative control over the majority; at first they are more often ridiculed than taken seriously; they are perceived as 'dummies' and 'weirdoes'. In other words, they do not seem to have access to the informational and normative means of control, explicitly or implicitly available to a majority. How can they then have influence?

Moscovici answers that the core of their impact is to be found in their own *behavioural style*. A minority has to propose a clear position on the issue at hand and hold firmly to it, withstanding all the time the pressures exerted by the majority. The most important component of this behavioural style is *the consistency* with which the minority defends and advocates its position. This consistency consists of two components: intra-individual consistency or stability over time (*diachronic* consistency) and interindividual consistency within the minority (*synchronic* consistency). Only if minority members agree amongst each other and continue to do so over time can they expect the majority to begin to question its own position, consider the correctness of the minority position, and eventually be influenced.

The key role of consistency has been demonstrated in many experiments, only two of which shall be described in detail (for an overview see Maass and Clark, 1984). In what is essentially a reversed Asch experiment, Moscovici, Lage and Naffrechoux (1969) had subjects participate in a study on colour perception in groups of six. Subjects first underwent a test for colour blindness. Upon passing this test they were then shown 36 slides, all clearly blue and differing only in intensity. Their task was simply to judge the colour of the slides by naming *aloud* a simple colour. Two of the subjects, seated in the first and second position, or in the first and fourth position, were actually confederates of the experimenter. In the consistent condition they answered 'green' on all trials, which made them diachronically as well as synchronically consistent. In the inconsistent condition they answered 'green' 24 times and 'blue' 12 times. The experiment also contained a control condition, where the groups were made up of six naive subjects. As figure 15.4 shows, in the control

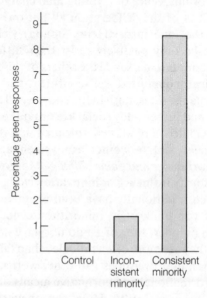

FIGURE 15.4   Percentage green responses given by majority subjects in the experiment by Moscovici, Lage and Naffrechoux (1969)

condition only 0.25 per cent green responses were given, revealing the obvious-
ness of the correct response. Out of 22 naive subjects only one person gave two
green responses. In the inconsistent minority condition 1.25 per cent responses
were green, only slightly and insignificantly more than in the control condition.
In the consistent minority condition, however, green responses were made 8.42
per cent of the time, which is significantly more than in either of the other two
conditions. In terms of the number of subjects who said green, 32 per cent of
the people gave at least one green response. This should not be taken to imply
that the overall effect was a consequence of isolated individuals who were each
influenced independently by the minority. On the contrary, the effect was the
result of a change of the responses within the respective groups, as can be
inferred from Moscovici's observation that there were really two categories of
groups: those in which nobody was influenced, and those in which several
people were influenced. It should also be noted that the minority's seating
position made no difference.

This experiment clearly shows that a consistent minority can have a distinct
effect on the public judgements of the members of a majority group. Before
proceeding it is instructive to compare Moscovici's setting with that of Asch. In
the Asch study one subject is opposed by a consistent majority of six; in
Moscovici's experiment a group of four naive subjects stands against a consistent minority of only two confederates. In Asch's study the conflict confronting the subjects is induced by the majority; in Moscovici's experiment a
similar conflict is induced by a minority. Although the minority does not have
'the numbers', their consistent behavioural style makes them influential – at
least after a while, when the majority subjects begin to observe that the
minority maintains its position in spite of their opposition. It is indeed a typical
observation that, in contrast to conformity studies, the minority effect only
begins to show after a certain period (Nemeth, 1982). The impression of
potential correctness of the minority position is further advanced when
majority members notice that one or more of their own group members begin
to answer like the minority – a finding reminiscent of what happens in a conformity setting when a social supporter of the subject deserts to the majority.
The picture that begins to unfold then is that a consistent minority sets in
motion a variety of intra- and interpersonal processes in the majority which
ultimately result in influence.

Before discussing these processes, however, let us look at a second experiment which demonstrates that consistency need not necessarily take the form of
repetition of the same response, but can also be expressed through a clear
pattern in the responses of the minority. Nemeth, Swedlund and Kanki (1974)
essentially replicated Moscovici's earlier experiment, but they added two
conditions in which the confederates said 'green' on half of the trials and
'green-blue' on the other half. In a random condition the green and green-blue
responses were randomly distributed over the trials, but in a correlated
condition the confederates said green to the brighter slides and green-blue to
the dimmer slides (or vice versa). In the latter condition the confederates were
definitively not repetitive in their answers, yet they were consistent in that their

responses were patterned after a characteristic of the stimulus (its brightness). The results showed that, compared to a no-influence control condition, the random condition had no effect. The correlated condition, on the other hand, produced almost 21 per cent influenced responses. Interestingly, and in contrast to Moscovici's findings, a repetitive and consistent 'green' minority did not significantly affect the subject's responses. Nemeth gives an interesting clue as to why this happened. Her subjects were allowed to respond with all the colours that they saw in the slides, whereas Moscovici's subjects could only respond with a single colour. If a minority does not show any flexibility in its behaviour (when the context allows for it) it has no effect in spite of its consistency, because under these circumstances it also tends to be perceived as rigid and unrealistic.

Nemeth's experiment again shows that consistency is a necessary condition for minority influence, but at the same time it indicates that whether or not this consistency leads to effective influence depends on how it is interpreted by the majority subjects. The image one forms of the minority and the nature of the attributional processes activated jointly by the minority's behavioural style, by the context in which they emit these behaviours, and by the behavioural reactions of the members of one's own group, appear crucial mediating variables in determining the minority's ultimate effect on the judgements of a subject.

Why and when consistency leads to influence: an attributional account

In their very perceptive analysis of the minority influence literature, Maass and Clark (1984) start with the plausible assumption that majority members, upon confronting a minority position, will ask themselves: 'Why do they respond as they do?' Their unexpected behaviour sets in motion an attributional search for the causes of their behaviour. By applying Kelley's (1967) *covariation* principle (see chapter 6) one should expect a person attribution, because we are dealing with a configuration of low consensus and high consistency over time (distinctiveness information is usually absent). Research does indeed support this reasoning, because consistent minorities tend to be perceived as certain and confident. This attribution is further enhanced when one observers that the minority maintains its position in spite of the opposition from the majority group. If the social pressure emanating from the majority is conceived as an inhibitory cause, the *augmentation* principle (Kelley, 1973) indeed dictates an even stronger person attribution. This attribution should lead majority members to take the minority position seriously, induce them perhaps to start looking at reality from their perspective and – as a result – to be influenced. Things are more complicated, however, because an attribution of confidence and certainty does not necessarily lead to an inference of competence. A person can be perceived as certain and confident, but if this confidence is viewed as an expression of dogmatism, craziness or some other idiosyncratic characteristic of the minority, no influence should obtain. Generally speaking, and in terms of Kelley's *discounting* principle, in the presence of other plausible causes, consistent behaviour of a minority should be less likely to have much impact. As a matter of fact, it can be postulated that majority members would first look for such alternative interpretations – in view of the unexpected nature of the minority's behaviour – and only take their position seriously after these alternative interpretations have been ruled out.

Experiments are consistent with the above line of thought. Mugny and Papastamou have conducted a variety of studies in which they show that a consistent minority, which behaves in a very rigid, extreme and dogmatic manner (e.g. through the use of slogans), is less influential than an equally consistent minority whose negotiation style is more flexible (Mugny, 1982). Similarly, if through instructions the majority members' attention is focused on the minority's psychological characteristics rather than only on their position, the minority produces less influence (Mugny and Papastamou, 1980). Idiosyncratic attributions are also more likely if the minority consists of only one person (Moscovici and Lage, 1976) unless that person shows other behaviours that can counter such attribution (e.g. Nemeth and Wachtler, 1974). Also, if the minority appears to have something to gain from the position it takes, self-interest becomes a plausible alternative cause of their behaviour (Maass, Clark and Haberkorn, 1982).

The impact of the minority will of course also depend on the strength of the prior conviction of the majority members and on the certainty and confidence they attribute to each other. Paicheler (1976, 1977) showed that a minority defending a position in line with the *Zeitgeist* (the direction in which social norms are changing) had more impact than a minority opposing it. If (owing to the *Zeitgeist*) majority members have already become uncertain with respect to their opinions, then a consistent minority which explicitly defends the new norm provides a clear anchor toward which to move. Moscovici's observation (reported earlier) that the minority effect is often a group effect (nobody moves or everybody moves) suggests that as the perceived confidence in one's own group decreases, the minority gains in impact. This so-called *snowball effect* was nicely demonstrated by Kiesler and Pallak (1975). After learning an initial distribution of opinions on a discussion topic (with two people deviating strongly from six others), subjects were later informed that one majority member had either moved even further away from the minority (reactionary condition), or moved towards the minority (compromise condition), or completely defected to the minority (defection condition). Compared with a control condition, where the distribution of opinions remained identical, and with the reactionary condition, the compromise condition produced more and the defection condition yielded most influence. Conversely, if majority members stick to their guns and display the same certainty and confidence as the minority, minority influence disappears. As Doms (1983) and Doms and Van Avermaet (1985) have shown, when a subject can enjoy the consistent refusal of fellow majority members to give in, the minority effect disappears completely. Even when he can observe the majority's behaviour only temporarily before being confronted alone by the minority opposition, he resists their influence to a sizeable degree.

The global picture that emerges is that consistency is definitely a necessary condition for minority influence but it is by no means sufficient. Other components of the minority's behaviour as well as the behavioural reactions of other majority members can either promote or reduce the likelihood of the attributions necessary for minority influence.

Majority and minority influence: compliance and conversion

At this point you might raise the important question: at which level does this influence occur? Perhaps under certain conditions a minority may not lead to public influence (because of normative pressures from the majority), but it could still be influential at a more latent, private level. In our discussion of majority influence we argued that in a conformity setting the normative pressures lead to public influence and that informational pressures lead to public and private influence, but do not forget that in this setting all others are opposed to the subject. In the minority setting, on the other hand, the subject has to deal with two groups – the opposing minority and his own majority group. It is plausible to assume that the minority has less normative control over the subject than does a majority. As a matter of fact, research shows that minorities are strongly disliked (Moscovici and Lage, 1976). For this reason one might expect minorities to have less public influence on a subject, at least when other resisting majority members are also present. But how about private influence? Could it be that a minority has a more profound impact on one's private opinion than does a majority, whose answers one might simply accept because 'if so many people agree, they must be right and I must be wrong' without really having given a lot of thought to the issue at hand?

Precisely these thoughts have led Moscovici (1980, 1985b) to formulate some very striking propositions about the differences in process and effect between majority and minority influence. These propositions have generated a lot of research and quite a bit of controversy, because other researchers have emphasized the similarities between the two influence modalities (Latané and Wolf, 1981; Tanford and Penrod, 1984). The question itself is fascinating and yet very complicated, and we can therefore only present you with an introduction to it (for an excellent discussion see Maass and Clark, 1984). Before doing so, it is perhaps helpful to keep in mind that Moscovici essentially deals with the contrast between a situation in which a unanimous majority confronts a single person and a situation where a minority group stands against a majority group. You should be careful not to generalize from this situation to all conceivable minority-majority interaction settings, where the impact of intra- and interpersonal processes and the direct versus indirect effects of minorities and majorities might be different.

Moscovici proposes that the majority, in the conformity paradigm, activates a *social comparison process* in which the subject compares his response with that of others, 'concentrates all his attention on what others say, so as to fit in with their opinions and judgements' (1980, p. 214) without giving a lot of attention or thought to the issue itself. Add to that the role of the normative pressures exerted by the majority, and only public compliance in their presence is expected. Any private effects would be short-lived because once the person, freed from the presence of the majority, again focuses on the issue at hand, he will return to his prior opinions.

In contrast a minority will evoke a *validation process* – cognitive activity aimed at understanding why the minority consistently holds on to its position. Attention will be focused on the object, and in the process the subject – to some extent without even being aware of it – may begin to look at the object as the minority does and become privately (or latently) converted to its position. The majority's normative pressures (at least if they overtly resist) will however prevent this effect from being shown publicly. Therefore, relatively speaking, minorities will lead to conversion (without compliance) and majorities will lead to compliance (without conversion).

To test this theory, various kinds of experiments have been designed. As an example we will describe one ingenious and provocative experiment conducted by Moscovici and Personnaz (1980). Subjects participating in pairs were first shown a series of five blue slides. In private they wrote down the colour of the slide as well as the colour of the after-image of the slide (on a rating scale going from 1 = yellow to 9 = purple). The after-image is what one sees on a white screen after having fixed on a colour for a while, and it is the complementary colour of the original one. The after-image of blue is yellow-orange, and the after-image of green is red-purple. Next, subjects were informed that their colour response was shared by 81.8 per cent (or by only 18.2 per cent) of the people who had previously participated. The other 18.2 per cent (or 81.8 per cent) had judged the slides green. During the next phase (15 trials) the colour responses had to be given publicly, but no judgements of the colour of the after-image were asked for. The first subject to respond, a confederate, always said green. In view of the information received prior to this phase, the real subject perceived this green response as a minority or a majority response. The third phase (15 trials) was again private, the confederate and the subject writing down both the colour of the slide and the rating of the after-image. The experiment concluded with a fourth phase in which the subject answered again in private, but in the absence of the confederate. Moscovici felt that if the influence source had brought about a real change in the perception of the subject this ought to result in a shift of the judged colour of the after-image towards the complementary colour of green (the higher end of the response scale), even though there had never been a direct influence attempt by the confederate with respect to this judgement. The results, shown in figure 15.5, indicate that compared with a no-influence control condition the majority source produced no changes in this judgement, whereas the minority source did.

Using a somewhat different methodology – a spectrometer on which subjects had to adjust the colour so that it matched the slide and the after-image they had previously seen – Personnaz (1981) replicated this differential effect of a majority and a minority influence source. A direct replication of the minority effect of Moscovici and Personnaz by Doms and Van Avermaet

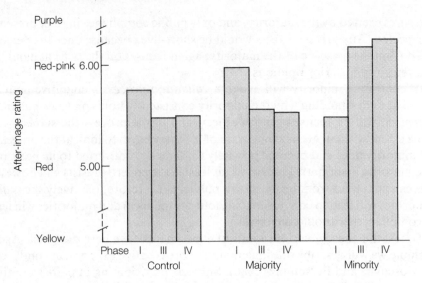

FIGURE 15.5   Judgements of the colour of the after-image during each of the phases of Moscovici and Personnaz's experiment (data from Moscovici, 1980)

(1980) also succeeded, but Sorrentino, King and Leo (1980) failed in their attempt. Moreover, Doms and Van Avermaet observed the after-image effect not only in the minority but also in the majority condition. They argue that under certain conditions majorities too may be capable of focusing the subject's attention on the stimulus and can induce private change.

Rather than argue over the reliability or the robustness of the effect in this specific experiment (there are many other relevant experiments), we would agree with Moscovici that, in the typical real-life contexts in which majorities and minorities exert their influence, there is probably a privileged relationship between minorities and private change on the one hand and majority and public change on the other hand. Owing to the conditions under which minorities usually have to try to exert influence they can at first expect just private change, and only later public change (see earlier for the snowball effect). Majorities, on the other hand, can immediately count on public influence; eventually, when they are perceived as credible and/or have caused the person really to think about an issue from their perspective, they will also produce private change. But the very fact that majorities and minorities usually operate under different context conditions makes perhaps premature the theoretical proposal that ties the observed differences exclusively to the nature of the influence source itself (Doms and Van Avermaet, 1985). A number of fundamental questions remain therefore to be answered more directly by future research. Do minorities always generate more cognitive activity than majorities? Does cognitive activity necessarily take the form of focusing on the issue, or will it sometimes take the form of focusing only on the source? Even when the former is the case, will it necessarily lead to a change towards the source? When and why do each of these events occur?

Another interesting perspective on the comparison between majority and minority influence is offered by Latané and Wolf (1981). In contrast to Moscovici they view influence as a unitary process regardless of its source. Social influence, or social impact as they call it, is a multiplicative function of the strength (power, expertise), immediacy (proximity in space and time) and size (number) of the influence source. This implies that the effect of any one of these variables will be greater as the value of another variable increases. Regarding the effect of size, the variable of most interest to them, they postulate a power function, with each additional influence source having less impact than the previous one. Fifty people have more impact than five people, but adding one extra person will make less of a difference in the first case than in the second. This principle of marginally decreasing impact is expressed through the equation

$$\text{impact} = sN^t$$

where s is a scaling constant which reflects the impact of a single source, t is an exponent with a value of less than one, and N is the number of influence sources (people). This implies that impact increases as some power of the size of the influence source. Against this background it is already understandable why Latané and Wolf expect minorities to have less impact than majorities. In addition, in the case where an individual stands with others as the object of social influence, the source's impact will be divided over the target members. Each target will experience less impact than when it is alone. As the size of the target group increases, the source's impact on each target member will decrease. There are therefore two major reasons why minorities are less powerful than majorities as influence sources: they have smaller numbers, and their impact is divided (diffused) over more targets. Latané and Wolf cite a lot of research consistent with their major predictions as well as with other implications of their theory. In a meta-analysis of the data of many studies Tanford and Penrod (1984), who recently proposed a refinement of Latané's social impact theory, reached basically similar conclusions.

An interesting characteristic of Latané and Wolf's model is that it clearly views social influence as a mutual and reciprocal process, and it should therefore stimulate research in which both minorities *and* majorities can be active sources of influence. As you may have noticed, in most studies either the majority or the minority is essentially a group of frozen confederates. A lot could be gained by paying more attention, not only theoretically but also empirically, to reciprocal influence effects. On the other hand, as Maass and Clark (1984) have remarked, the social impact models (and the studies cited in their support) deal mainly with public influence and have little to say about the processes through which the antecedent factors of strength, immediacy and size operate. It is precisely to process and to level of influence that Moscovici's model speaks the most.

In concluding, viewed in a broad societal context, one could perhaps argue that social change does owe more to minority influence than to majority influence. Rarely do we find ourselves in an Asch setting (as a matter of fact we avoid it); most likely we are part of the majority, feeling at ease with our ways of thinking about reality and looking at reality as most others do. It takes an active minority to unsettle this equilibrium and really to make us think about why we act as we do: 'Du choc des opinions jaillit la vérité' ('Out of the clash of opinions springs the truth': after the French poet Colardeau, 1732–76)! As Nemeth has recently suggested (1986), the effect of minority influence may not always be a change in the direction of that minority, but it will at least force us to look at things from a different angle, to take on a different and more creative perspective, and perhaps lead us to inherently better solutions of the problems confronting us.

Decision-Making in Groups

Group polarization

Consider again the hypothetical student meeting we mentioned earlier at the beginning of the chapter. Suppose that at the outset all the student representatives are opposed to the departmental proposal, but with a certain amount of variation as to the extremity of their opposition. In an attempt to reach a consensual position they engage in a discussion, each student presenting her own arguments and reacting to those of others. If you guess that the decision will be resolved through a compromise around the average of the initial individual positions, you are probably wrong. In situations of this sort people tend to converge on a position which is more extreme than this average.

Like yourself, for some time social psychologists too held the belief that groups would be less extreme, more moderate and more cautious than individuals. But in 1961 Stoner, a graduate student, ran an experiment – since then followed by more than 300 – that proved the opposite. He presented his subjects in groups of four or five with a choice dilemma questionnaire. This questionnaire, developed further by Kogan and Wallach (1964), measures a person's tendency towards risk-taking. It consists of 12 items, each of which describes the dilemma confronting a protagonist, who has to choose between an alternative high in probability of success but low in value and another much more attractive path of action but with a lower probability of success. The subject, acting as imaginary adviser to the protagonist, has to indicate the minimum probability of success under which he would recommend the latter, risky alternative. In Stoner's experiment subjects first filled out the questionnaire in private (pre-consensus), then discussed each item amongst themselves and tried to reach a consensus (consensus), and finally again wrote down an individual judgement (post-consensus). Stoner observed that the achieved consensus and the average of the post-consensus individual judgements favoured a riskier decision than would be expected on the basis of the average of the pre-discussion individual judgements.

Stoner's observation of this **risky shift** immediately led social psychologists to attempt to replicate and explain the phenomenon. Pretty soon it became obvious that the shift was not always towards more risk, because in a number of cases the shift was in the opposite, 'cautious' direction. Moreover, in 1969 Moscovici and Zavalloni very nicely demonstrated that the decisional shift following a group discussion also obtained with a totally different judgemental dimension. Using Stoner's original procedure they had French high-school students first write down in private their attitudes towards President De Gaulle (or towards North Americans) by indicating the extent of their agreement with statements such as: 'De Gaulle is too old to carry out successfully his difficult political job' (or 'American economic aid is always used to exert political pressure'). Next, as a group, they had to reach a consensus on each item; and finally they made another private attitude rating. With this totally different dimension they observed a shift comparable with Stoner's: as a result of the discussion, subjects became more extreme in their attitudes. As figure 15.6 shows, the attitude towards De Gaulle, which was slightly positive before the discussion, became more positive after the group discussion; this change was maintained during the post-discussion private measurement. The attitude towards the Americans shows a similar polarization pattern but in the negative direction; the original slightly negative attitude became more negative after the discussion.

The phenomenon at hand is therefore much more general than originally assumed. On any judgemental dimension groups tend to shift in the direction of the pole which they already, on the average, favour initially. Hence, **group polarization** refers to an enhancement of an initially dominant position due to group discussion (Myers, 1982). An excellent summary by Lamm and Myers (1978) documents this phenomenon in a wide variety of contexts: stereotypes, interpersonal impressions, gambling behaviour, prosocial and antisocial behaviour, negotiations, jury decisions, group counselling and religious social support systems.

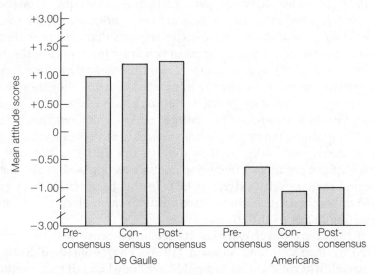

FIGURE 15.6   Polarization of attitudes towards De Gaulle and towards the Americans (data from Moscovici and Zavalloni, 1969)

Explaining group polarization: normative and informational influence

As it became apparent that there was more to group polarization than a shift towards risk, many of the early theories proposed to explain the phenomenon had to be dropped, for the simple reason that they could explain only the risky shift and none (or too few) of the other instances of polarization. In the search for more general explanations, two have attracted most attention. These explanations are very similar to those proposed earlier as underlying the conformity effect.

The *normative* or *social comparison* point of view departs from Festinger's theory of social comparison (1954), which holds that because of a need to evaluate one's own opinions (and abilities) people will compare their opinions with those of others. Furthermore, because people want to have a positive self-image and also want to be perceived positively by others, this comparison process will be biased in the direction of viewing oneself as 'better' or 'more correct' (i.e. closer to the norm) than others. The implication of this theory is therefore that when, during the group discussion, you discover that others hold opinions more in the direction of the valued alternative, you will yourself become more extreme in order to differentiate yourself positively from the others. Indirect support for this explanation is found in studies indicating that people indeed think that they are closer to the normative position than others (Codol, 1975), but at the same time they admire views that are even more extreme than theirs, in the valued direction of course (Jellison and Davis, 1973). Direct support would be obtained if one could show that merely knowing the others' position on an issue, without having heard any of their arguments, would be sufficient to produce a polarization effect. Some experiments have in fact supported that prediction (e.g. Myers, 1978; Sanders and Baron, 1977), but others have not, particularly those that tried to test the social comparison hypothesis against the informational influence hypothesis.

The *informational influence* perspective suggests that the group discussion generates a number of arguments, most of which are in support of the position already favoured by the group members. To the extent that these arguments coincide with those you have already considered yourself, they should already serve to strengthen your own position. But the group is also likely to produce arguments you had not thought of before, making your reaction even more extreme. The group polarization phenomenon basically becomes then a process of mutual *persuasion*, whereby the extent of the shift is a function of the proportion of the arguments favouring one side as opposed to another, their cogency and their novelty (Myers, 1982). In this perspective the arguments presented rather than the communicated positions themselves would constitute the instigating factor of the effect.

One of the many clever experiments set up to prove just this point was conducted by Burnstein and Vinokur (1973). They wanted to create a discussion situation in which subjects would have knowledge of their mutual positions but would not be able to provide strong persuasive arguments, and contrast it with a condition where subjects would not know each other's position and yet strong arguments would be presented. To achieve this goal subjects in one condition all had to argue against their own position, and they knew this of each other. Subjects in this condition could therefore infer each other's position, but they would not be exposed to strong arguments. In general people are indeed relatively poor at generating a sizeable number of good arguments against their own opinion. In this condition social comparison theory would predict a shift but the persuasion hypothesis would not. In a second condition all subjects in fact had to argue for their own position, but they were left uncertain as to whether the other group members argued for or against their own position. The social comparison hypothesis predicts no shift in this latter condition because subjects did not know each other's true position. The persuasion hypothesis, on the other hand, does predict a shift because of the greater number and quality of arguments to be expected. The results of the experiment provided more support for the persuasion hypothesis. Still, a little thought on your part might suggest that you could use the quality of the arguments presented by others to make inferences about their own true position. If this reasoning holds, social comparison theory too would predict a clearer shift in the second condition. In view of this consideration and of other experimental evidence (e.g. Myers, Wojcicki and Aardema, 1977), the most adequate conclusion appears to be that normative and informational factors operate jointly to produce group polarization (Isenberg, 1986). Moreover, as Meertens (1980) has clearly shown, group discussions entail a wealth of group dynamic processes, not yet covered by either of the proposed theories, which should be taken into account before we will fully understand why and when group decisions will be more polarized than individual decisions.

Groupthink: an extreme example of group polarization

In view of the frequency with which, in reality, decisions are made by groups composed of like-minded participants (councils, committees, juries, governments), the research on group polarization has far-reaching implications. The processes involved may indeed lead such groups to advocate decisions which are incorrect, unwise or in the worst case disastrous.

Irving Janis (Janis and Mann, 1977; Janis, 1972) has described a number of instances of political and military decision-making which provide dramatic illustrations of the utmost stupidity shown by groups in spite of the superior 'intelligence' of their members. The Bay of Pigs invasion in 1961 is perhaps the best known example. President Kennedy and a small group of advisers decided to send a relatively small group of Cuban exiles to invade the Cuban coast with the support of the American air force. Everything went wrong, and within a matter of days the invaders were killed or captured. How, as a group, could Kennedy and his advisers have been so stupid, as they later admitted themselves?

Janis, who undertook a most careful analysis of all the available documents in this and other similar cases, speculates that they became the victims of an extreme form of group polarization, which he calls **groupthink**. Groupthink obtains when the decision process of a highly cohesive group of like-minded people becomes so overwhelmed by consensus seeking that their apprehension of reality is undermined. As Janis contends, this process is encouraged when a number of conditions are fulfilled: when the decision group is highly cohesive; when it is isolated from alternative sources of information; and when its leader clearly favours a particular option. Against the background of these antecedent conditions the group discussions that evolve are likely to be characterized by an illusion of one's own invulnerability, and by attempts at mutually rationalizing actions which are in line with the proposed option while at the same time ignoring or discounting inconsistent information. These processes occur both at the intraindividual (self-censorship) and at the interindividual level (conformity pressures). Even though some members of such groups may at one time or another have their private reservations about the proposals made, they are not likely to express them overtly. The ultimate outcome of these processes is a decision endorsed by all, but far removed from what might be expected if rational and balanced information-seeking and information-providing processes had operated.

Although Janis's analysis is more penetrating than our brief presentation can show, the above material should be sufficient for you to grasp the essentials of the phenomenon – and to suggest some cures for groupthink. How should the leader behave? What would you think of a devil's advocate in the group? Which benefits can be gained by having the group members write down their personal thoughts and arguments independently and individually?

Obeying Immoral Orders: the Social Influence of an Authority

Milgram's obedience experiment

The various social influence phenomena described in the previous sections have a number of characteristics in common. The most important of these are that influence sources and targets typically have equal status; the pressure exerted by the influence source is more implicit than explicit; and the source makes no attempt at directly controlling or sanctioning the resistance that targets of influence attempts might eventually show. For example, in Asch's experiments all the subjects were students, the majority only very implicitly exerted pressure by merely stating an opinion that was different from the subject's, and the subject's responses never led to any explicit negative reactions on the part of the majority. An entirely different influence context is created when an influence source has high status, explicitly orders a person to emit a behaviour which he or she spontaneously would not emit or would even have strong feelings against, and continuously monitors whether the person indeed carries out the orders given. Precisely this setting was created in a famous and at the same time notorious series of studies on **obedience** carried out by Stanley Milgram and dramatically pictured in his best-selling book *Obedience to Authority* (Milgram, 1974). The essential components of Milgram's basic experiment as well as some of its variants have already been introduced in chapter 4. For the sake of clarity and vividness in the context of this chapter, however, a more integrated and detailed presentation of these studies is necessary.

Through a newspaper advertisement Milgram recruited volunteers to participate, for a payment of $4, in a study on learning and memory. The participants in the experiment were aged between 20 and 50, and they represented almost the entire range of professional levels. Upon arriving at the laboratory the subject was met by the experimenter, actually a biology teacher in his early thirties, and another 'subject', a confederate of the experimenter who in fact was a sympathetic middle-aged accountant. The experimenter explained that the study dealt with the effects of punishment on learning, and that one of the subjects would be the teacher and the other the learner. Lots were drawn and the subject would be the teacher. Teacher and learner were taken to an adjacent room where the learner was strapped into a chair and electrodes were fixed to his wrists – because the punishment to be applied was electric shock. The experimenter explained that the shocks could be extremely painful, but they would cause no permanent damage.

Next the teacher was taken to his own room, where he received his orders. The learning task was a paired associates task; each time the learner gave an incorrect answer the teacher had to punish him with an electric shock, beginning at 15 volts (V) and increasing the shock intensity by 15 V with every new mistake. To this end the teacher had to use a shock generator with a row of 30 pushbuttons, each marked by the appropriate intensity (from 15 V to 450 V). Several verbal labels gave the subject a clear sense of the meaning of successive groups of shock levels: the labels went from slight shock (to 60 V), through moderate shock (to 120 V), strong shock (to 180 V) and very strong shock (to 240 V), to intense shock (to 300 V), extreme intensity shock (to 360 V) and 'danger: severe shock' (to 420 V). The two final shock levels were marked 'XXX'. Various additional features of the shock generator gave the apparatus a distinctly 'real' appearance. Moreover, to demonstrate the reality of the shocks the teacher himself received a sample shock of 45 V.

The learning task could then begin. As you probably suspect, the confederate made numerous errors, thereby 'forcing' the subject to administer increasingly stronger shocks. Each time the subject hesitated or refused, the experimenter prodded him to go on through means of at most four graded orders: 'Please continue'; 'The experiment requires that you continue'; 'It is absolutely essential that you continue'; 'You have no other choice, you must go on.' The experiment was terminated when, in spite of the experimenter's prods, the subject refused to continue, or when he had administered three shocks of the highest intensity. Before presenting the results we should add that the subject was not only exposed to the explicit influence attempt by the experimenter; he also confronted an increasingly explicit appeal by the learner. Whereas at first the subject could hear the victim only react with a minor grunt (from 75 V to 105 V), at 120 V he began to shout that the shocks became very painful. Further in the sequence he started screaming in agony; he shouted to be let out and that he could not stand the pain. From a given point on he refused to

Shock generator used in the experiments. Fifteen of the thirty switches have already been depressed.

Learner is strapped into his chair and electrodes are attached to his wrist. Electrode paste is applied by the experimenter. Learner provides answers by depressing switches that light up numbers on an answer box.

Subject receives sample shock from the generator.

Subject breaks off experiment. On right, event recorder wired into generator automatically records switches used by the subject.

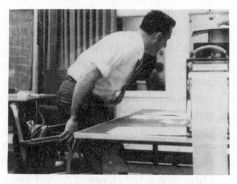

PLATE 15.1 Milgram's obedience experiment (copyright 1965 by Stanley Milgram. From the film *Obedience*, distributed by the New York University Film Division and the Pennsylvania State University, PCR. All photographs taken at the Yale Interaction Laboratory, Yale University, during the course of the experiments)

provide more answers – but the subject still had to shock because 'no answer is an incorrect answer'.

How did Milgram's subjects, faced with the conflict between the pressures emanating from the authority, from the victim and from their own inner self, react in this situation? Very much to his own surprise, Milgram observed that 62.5 percent of his subjects continued to administer shocks to the highest level. The average maximum shock level was 368 V. The authority of 'the man of science', who never threatened with any sanctions let alone held a gun to the subject's head, was sufficient to override the inner (conscience) and outer (the victim's cries) forces that could have made the subject disobey. This is a frightening perspective. Were Milgram's subjects perhaps 'evil' people? All the evidence speaks against it. For one thing, the subjects' behaviour during the experiment clearly testifies to the strong conflict they experienced: they were extremely tense and nervous, they perspired, bit their lips and clenched their fists. Moreover, a control condition in which subjects were allowed to choose any shock levels they themselves considered appropriate showed that only two out of 40 people exceeded the 150 V level and 28 never even went beyond 75 V. Clearly Milgram's subjects were not sadists; they apparently were caused to behave the way they did by the powerful role of situational factors. In variations of his basic experiment Milgram has looked at the difference a number of these situational factors make. Some of these variations, as they relate to characteristics of the authority, the closeness of the victim and the behaviour of the subject's peers, are briefly summarized in the next paragraphs.

Situational determinants of obedience

The physical (and emotional) proximity of the victim was manipulated by means of four different conditions. In a first condition the victim heavily pounded on the wall separating his room from the teacher's; in the second he was heard crying and shouting (as described earlier). In two other conditions the subject and the victim were actually in the same room. In one of these the subject not only heard but also saw the victim. In the final condition the subject had to hold the victim's hand on a shock plate. The obedience rates corresponding to these four conditions of increasing contact are shown in figure 15.7. Maximal obedience went from a high of 65 per cent of the subjects to a low (?) of 30 per cent. Data such as these should invite you to speculate about the differences between traditional and modern warfare in terms of the differential resistance they would induce towards disobeying military orders.

The authority of the experimenter and the amount of control he had was varied in a number of ways. When he was absent from the subject's room and gave his orders over the telephone, maximal obedience dropped to 21 per cent (a number of subjects said over the phone that they were giving higher shocks than they in fact did!). When the experiment was carried out in a less scientific and prestigious environment – a rundown office building rather than Yale University, where the original study took place – obedience did not drop significantly. The fact that the authority patently violated a promise made to the

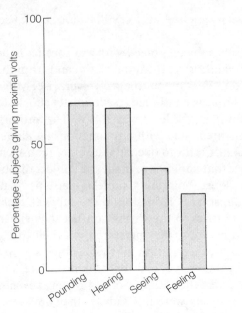

FIGURE 15.7   Obedience as a function of physical proximity (data from Milgram, 1974)

learner did not reduce obedience greatly either. In one of the experimental variations the learner, who had said earlier that he had a heart condition, only agreed to the experiment 'on the condition that you let me out when I say so'. From the tenth shock on (150 V) he in effect demanded that the experiment be stopped, but the experimenter ignored him and insisted that the subject had to go on. The percentage of subjects showing maximal obedience in this frightening setting was reduced by only 10 per cent compared with a baseline condition. A final relevant variation is one in which the experimenter, before having instructed the subject to increase the shock level with every new mistake by the learner, had to leave the room. He carried over his authority to a second subject present, who at first would only have to register the learner's reaction times. This second subject then came up with the idea of increasing the shock level with every error and, throughout the learning session, he insisted that the teacher applied his rules. The results speak for themselves. Only (?) 20 per cent of the subjects obeyed the equal-status authority to the end. In addition, when a subject refused and the 'authority' decided that he would administer the shocks himself, a number of subjects physically attacked the 'torturer' or pulled out the plug of the shock generator. Such heroism was unfortunately never shown when the authority was 'the man of science in his white coat'!

In a final pair of experimental variations presented here, Milgram investigated the role of peer pressure. In the first there were three coteachers, the subject and two confederates. The first confederate presented the task, the second registered the learner's responses, and the subject administered the shocks. At 150 V the first confederate refused to continue and took a seat away from the shock generator. At 210 V the second confederate refused. The effect

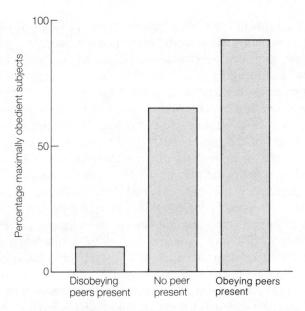

FIGURE 15.8   Obedience as a function of peer behaviour (data from Milgram, 1974)

of their behaviour on the subject was dramatic: only 10 per cent were maximally obedient (see figure 15.8). Rather than interpreting this result to mean that, with peers present, a person will listen to the voice of his conscience, it is probably more parsimonious to state that their 'independence' towards the authority influence source is caused by their 'dependence' on another influence source. The latter's impact is great, particularly when you realize that they only influenced the subject implicitly, through their behaviour. They never said anything to the subject! The subject's dependence on the behaviour of his peers (rather than on his conscience) was clearly demonstrated in a reversal of the above condition. If the subject, who administered the learning task, was accompanied by a coteacher, who gave the shocks, 92 per cent of the subjects participated in the experiment to the end. Of course, they did not have to give the shocks themselves; but what kept them from protesting as the confederates had done in the prior condition? In view of the fact that peer behaviour can produce either 10 per cent or 92 per cent obedience, the powerful role of inter-personal rather than intrapersonal factors is distinctly revealed. Again these experiments should make you think of real-life examples whereby you protest or do not protest against acts of violence, merely as a function of what others do.

What would you have done?

While reading the above paragraphs you probably constantly said to yourself: 'I would not have obeyed!' For your comfort, that is how most people react upon hearing a description of the Milgram experiments. Milgram himself and others (e.g. Bierbrauer, 1979) asked people from all walks of life, including psychiatrists, how many people would obey the experimenter. Invariably, they all expected low obedience rates (with a maximal average shock of 130 V). Only with a very vivid and lengthy re-enactment of the experiment could Bierbrauer get Stanford students to expect an average maximal shock of 260 V, which is still an underestimation of what real subjects did. One explanation for the difference between what we think we and others will do and what we in effect do is to be found in the *fundamental attribution error* (see chapter 6) – a tendency to underestimate the role of situational factors and to overestimate the impact of personality factors. In the Milgram situation the latter do not make a lot of difference: his analyses revealed only minor differences between men and women, between people holding different professions or between those scoring differently on personality inventories. Moreover, replications of Milgram's study in different countries and cultures have demonstrated the generality of the effect (e.g. Mantell, 1971; Meeus and Raaijmakers, 1986; Shanab and Yahya, 1978).

In concluding, experiments such as these raise serious ethical concerns – and they should. Does the scientific benefit and the moral lesson learned from them outweigh the costs and the potential harm to participating subjects? Regardless of your answer to this question, however, ask yourself if your ethical concerns would be as great if these studies had shown that people actually disobey the immoral orders given them by an experimenter.

Summary and Conclusion

This chapter has introduced you to various aspects and forms of social influence in small groups. It is perhaps appropriate to conclude with some critical thoughts.

First, we started out by giving both a broader and a more restricted definition of social influence. After having read this chapter you may begin to wonder whether the more restricted definition is really more useful. Strictly speaking the obedience phenomenon studied by Milgram, for instance, does not fall under this definition, although nobody will doubt that this is a clear instance of social influence. To some extent the definition given is perhaps more a reflection of the typical research paradigms used in this area than of the broader phenomenon itself. If you think of the impact others' behaviour has on a person's prosocial or antisocial behaviour (chapters 11 and 12), or if you think of attitude change as it results from exposure to a persuasive message (chapter 8), is there really a fundamental reason to treat these as an entirely different category of phenomena? Would it not be better in the end simply to *define* social influence as the effect of one person's (or several persons') behaviour on another person's behaviour and to analyse *theoretically* all social influence phenomena from this common and more parsimonious perspective (Nuttin, 1986)?

Second, throughout this chapter we may have given the impression that social influence phenomena are the result of deliberate decisions made by people who know and admit that they have been influenced by the social forces acting upon them. You should know however that, with the interesting exception of Milgram's subjects who gladly and openly admit that they acted as they did because of the experimenter's request, conformity and minority studies show exactly the opposite. Here subjects frequently categorically deny to the experimenter (and to themselves) that their responses are in any way affected by what others say. In Milgram's experiment with two disobeying confederates, subjects did not attribute their independence to the example set by the behaviour of their peers. This should not necessarily be taken to imply that the information-processing accounts presented in several paragraphs of this chapter are invalid, but at the very least these processes do not necessarily operate at a conscious level. Carried to its extreme some people might even conclude that, in the final analysis, behaviour comes first and thought follows after!

Although these final critical remarks, as well as the imperfections of some of the 'little' experiments conducted in social-psychological laboratories, may leave you with some doubts and questions, the different lines of research sketched in this chapter offer valuable perspectives towards understanding both everyday and major historical as well as contemporary events. The My Lai massacre in Vietnam, the mass suicide by the followers of the Reverend Jim Jones, the Baghwan movement, the impact of Lech Walesa and Solidarity in Poland, and the recent peaceful revolution in the Philippines are but a few examples of major events in which social influence in one form or another played a key role. At the same time, and perhaps less notably so, social influence is an essential ingredient of our everyday social life: what determines which line of clothing we wear, what guides us in our choice of vacation spots, which films do we see? In the final analysis, can you think of any behaviour, thought or feeling which would not be at least partly the result of social influence processes?

Glossary Terms

Autokinetic effect	Innovation
Compliance	Majority influence
Conformity	Minority influence
Conversion	Normative Influence
Group polarization	Obedience
Groupthink	Risky Shift
Informational influence	

Further Reading

Allen, V. L. (1965) Situational factors in conformity. In L. Berkowitz (ed.), *Advances in Experimental Social Psychology* (vol. 2), New York: Academic Press. A very good and critical summary of all the studies on conformity and its determinants, with special attention to the issue of public versus private change.

Allen, V. L. (1975) Social support for nonconformity. In L. Berkowitz (ed.), *Advances in Experimental Social Psychology* (vol. 8), New York: Academic Press. A detailed account of theory and research with respect to the factors leading to a reduction in conformity to a majority.

Asch, S. E. (1956) Studies of independence and conformity: a minority of one against a unanimous majority. *Psychological Monographs*, 70 (9, whole No. 416). This text presents Asch's own account of his famous conformity experiments. The best way to learn about these studies is to read them first hand.

Janis, I. L. (1972) *Victims of Groupthink*. Boston: Houghton Mifflin. This book contains Janis's theory of groupthink, amply illustrated with case materials.

Lamm, H. and Myers, D. G. (1978) Group-induced polarization of attitudes and behavior. In L. Berkowitz (ed.), *Advances in Experimental Social Psychology* (vol. 11), New York: Academic Press. A well-written overview of experimental and field studies on the phenomenon of group polarization.

Maass, A. and Clark, R. D. III (1984) Hidden impact of minorities: fifteen years of minority influence research. *Psychological Bulletin*, 95, 428–50. A densely written, exhaustive and integrative overview of research on minority influence and its relation to majority influence.

Milgram, S. (1974) *Obedience to Authority: an experimental view*. New York: Harper and Row, London: Tavistock. Milgram's own dramatic, best-selling story of his many experiments on obedience to authority.

Moscovici, S. (1980) Toward a theory of conversion behavior. In L. Berkowitz (ed.), *Advances in Experimental Social Psychology* (vol. 13), New York: Academic Press. A presentation of Moscovici's propositions with respect to the relationship between influence source (majority or minority) and level of effect (compliance or conversion), supplemented by an overview of relevant experimental studies.

16 Intergroup Relations

RUPERT BROWN

Introduction

84 ARRESTS IN MINERS' PICKET BATTLE
Stones, wooden fencing spars, a shovel and a bucket were among missiles hurled at police in riot gear who held back as many as 7000 pickets trying to stop the movement of coking coal from Orgreave to the British Steel works at Scunthorpe, Lincolnshire. . . . Violence broke out again when the lorries returned, and pickets scattered across a field as a posse of mounted police pursued them, followed by officers carrying riot shields. (An incident from the 1984–5 British coal strike as reported in *The Times*, 30 May 1984)

41 SOCCER FANS DIE IN STAMPEDE AT EURO CUP FINAL
At least 41 soccer fans died and more than 150 were seriously injured when a six foot concrete wall topped with fencing collapsed at the front of terracing 45 minutes before the scheduled start of last night's European Cup Final in Brussels between Liverpool and Juventus of Turin. . . . The disaster occurred when the wall at one end of the stadium gave way during a stampede by Italian spectators after they were charged by a section of the Liverpool crowd. (The Heysel stadium tragedy in 1985 as reported in *The Times*, 30 May 1985)

Even the most casual peruser of newspapers cannot help but notice headlines such as these which frequently appear on our breakfast tables. The events referred to – exactly a year apart in two European countries – are both instances of **intergroup behaviour**: that is, actions by members of one group towards members of another group. It happens that the incidents chosen involved social conflicts of one kind or another, but the definition of intergroup behaviour is by no means restricted to these. Many instances of intergroup cooperation and solidarity can be observed in everyday life, even if newspaper editors usually seem to give them somewhat less prominence. Common examples would include acts of solidarity by members of one trade

The author would like to thank Miles Hewstone and Patricia Warren for their helpful comments on an earlier version of this chapter.

PLATE 16.1   War on the picket lines: Yorkshire's Orgreave coking plant

PLATE 16.2   Football carnage in Brussels

union towards their colleagues in another union in dispute with their employer (during the British coal strike referred to in the first newspaper report, French rail workers and dockers refused to handle coal destined for British power stations), or alliances between community groups or political parties to achieve some common goal.

At first glance, these phenomena seem far removed from the social psychologist's usual province. Surely the explanation for incidents like these, involving as they do such large numbers of people, lies in an understanding and analysis of the historical, political or economic factors at work in each context? This is unarguable. Nevertheless, it must also be recognized that in the last analysis intergroup behaviour does still involve actions of individuals. It was individual policemen who rode their horses at the striking miners at Orgreave. It was individual football fans who were involved in that tragic stampede in Heysel stadium. Thus, however important socio-structural forces undoubtedly were on each of these occasions, it is still important to know how these forces were perceived by, reacted to and reshaped by the individuals concerned. This, then, brings intergroup relations squarely into the psychologist's domain and justifies their place as the subject of a chapter in this textbook of social psychology.

This chapter will consider some of the ways intergroup behaviour can be understood from the social-psychological perspective. It begins by briefly examining some popular notions of intergroup conflict and prejudice which attempt to explain them either as the result of some deep-rooted 'herd instinct' or as the expression of some particular personality type. As will be shown, these ideas are rather limited in their application. A much more fruitful approach is to see intergroup behaviour as a response to real or imagined group interests, and this is the subject of the second section. Here, the causes of competition and cooperation between groups are seen as principally lying in the conflictual or compatible nature of the groups' goals. The third section takes up a question which arises out of the second: namely, does group membership in and of itself give rise to discriminatory behaviour? As we shall see there are good grounds for thinking that it does; this leads naturally to the fourth section, where the link between group membership and social identity processes is explained. A central idea which emerges out of this is the importance for the individuals of being able to see their group as positively distinct from other groups. For those who belong to groups which are consensually derogated this can sometimes be difficult. In the fifth section, therefore, some of the responses of subordinate group members to their 'inferior' position are examined.

Popular Notions of Intergroup Conflict and Prejudice

The group as a dehumanizing force

When events occur like those with which this chapter began, it is not long before someone suggests that those involved somehow got 'carried away by the mob' and were led into acts of violence by forces outside their control. This popular explanation of intergroup aggression stems from one of the earliest social-psychological theories of group behaviour, that proposed by LeBon (1895). According to LeBon, the anonymity, contagion and suggestibility which he saw as being endemic to crowds caused people to lose their rationality and identity, creating instead a *group mind* (see chapter 1). Under the influence of this collective mentality, and freed from normal social constraints, people's destructive instincts are released, resulting in wanton violence and irrational behaviour. For LeBon, then, the events at Orgreave and Brussels would be instances of this 'decline into barbarity', similar to those which he claimed to have observed in the Paris Commune of 1871.

Although some of LeBon's ideas have now largely been discredited – particularly the concept of group mind – his speculations about the effects of anonymity in the group have proved influential for subsequent attempts to explain collective behaviour. The most well-known of these is Zimbardo's (1969) theory of *deindividuation* (see chapter 12). According to Zimbardo, being in a large group provides people with a cloak of anonymity and diffuses personal responsibility for the consequences of one's actions. This is thought to lead to a loss of identity and a reduced concern for social evaluation. The resulting behaviour is then 'irrational' and 'regressive' because it is not under the 'usual' social and personal controls. Although Zimbardo does allow that this disinhibited behaviour might take prosocial forms (e.g. Zimbardo, 1969, p. 300), the main thrust of his theory is to suggest that people's behaviour will degenerate in group settings (see also chapter 12). In support of this theory it has been found that small groups in the laboratory may show greater aggression than individuals, particularly when their members are made anonymous by wearing clothes and hoods which disguise their identity (Yaffe and Yinon, 1979; Zimbardo, 1969).

Despite this supportive evidence there are two reasons for believing that this one-sided emphasis on the negative consequences of group membership (e.g. identity loss and antisocial behaviour) is misplaced. First, there are several studies which have revealed that the anonymity provided by a group can lead to *less* and not more antisocial behaviour (Diener, 1976; Johnson and Downing, 1979). Johnson and Downing, for instance, found that making people anonymous by asking them to wear a nurse-like gown led to a decline in aggression, whereas donning robes which resembled Ku Klux Klan outfits had the opposite effect. Whether people's actions become prosocial or antisocial in the group thus seems to depend not on anonymity but on the norms prevailing in the situation. Second, people's behaviour in groups may not, in fact, be as unreasonable and uncontrolled as Zimbardo and others have suggested. For example, in the US urban riots of the 1960s the looting and violence was not completely wanton but showed clear signs of selectivity (Fogelson, 1971). Similar observations were made by Reicher (1984) in his study of a civil disturbance involving the police and a (mainly black) community in Bristol, England. Although the incident was certainly violent – several people were injured and police cars were destroyed – Reicher noted that there were several features of it which did not easily fit the LeBon-Zimbardo theory. The crowd's behaviour, despite its violence, was actually rather controlled. It was aimed at specific targets (e.g. the police) and avoided others (e.g. local shops and houses). Furthermore, it was geographically confined to a small area in the heart of the community. If people had simply been responding to deep-rooted antisocial instincts, why did they not chase the police far beyond the immediate neighbourhood and spread the violence at random? Also, those taking part in the 'riot', far from losing their identities, seemed quite unanimous in a new sense of pride in their community engendered by their activities.

The conclusion seems clear. People in groups are not invariably disposed to unreasoning and violent acts. How they will behave seems to depend very much on the immediate situational cues and, most importantly, on the norms prevailing in the group at the time. As we shall see in a later section, those norms are largely determined in turn by the respective goals of the group involved.

Prejudice as personality type

More common than the outright manifestations of intergroup conflict which we have been concerned with until now are various forms of **prejudice** – that is, the holding of derogatory attitudes about the members of a social group (racism, jingoism, sexism and so on). Intergroup attitudes such as these are very commonly associated with – both as precursors to and consequences of – the kinds of violent encounters described earlier. The question is: where do these prejudiced attitudes originate? (See also chapter 3.)

One view which has enjoyed considerable currency both within and outside psychology is that prejudice is primarily a personality problem. The theory which did most to popularize this idea within social psychology was that proposed by Adorno et al. (1950). Their starting hypothesis was that an individual's political and social attitudes formed a coherent pattern and that this pattern was 'an expression of deep-lying trends in personality' (Adorno et al., 1950, p. 1). Working from a Freudian perspective, they believed that most people's personality development involved the repression and redirection of various instinctive needs by the constraints of social existence. The parents, of course, were considered to be the main agents of this socialization process, and in 'normal' development they usually struck a healthy balance between discipline and allowing the child self-expression. The problem with the bigot, argued Adorno et al., was that this balance was upset by the parents adopting an excessively harsh disciplinary regime and by being overanxious about the child's conformity to social mores. The effect of this, they believed, was that the child's natural aggression towards the parents (an inevitable consequence of being subjected to constraints) was displaced on to alternative targets because of the fear of the consequences for displaying it directly. The likely choice of targets would be those seen as weaker or inferior to oneself – for example, members of deviant groups or ethnic minorities. The end result, therefore, was someone overdeferential towards authority figures (since these symbolize the parents) and overtly hostile towards non-ingroup members – the so-called 'authoritarian personality'.

In the postwar era this theory stimulated a massive research effort into the nature and origins of racial prejudice. Adorno et al. themselves developed a personality inventory – the F-scale – which was designed to distinguish between those with potentially Fascist (or racist) tendencies and those with more 'democratic' leanings. By a combination of psychometric, projective and clinical methods they were able to show that high-scoring adults on this F-scale did seem to have had rather different childhoods and to have more dogmatic and conservative attitudes than low scorers. Others proposed alternative scales which purported to measure slightly different orientations, but which shared the same underlying premise linking personality types to social attitudes, and had the same objective of quantifying individual differences in the expression of these attitudes (e.g. Eysenck, 1954; Rokeach, 1948). In the 1950s these approaches attracted both firm adherents and trenchant critics, with the F-scale itself coming under the closest scrutiny (Brown, 1965; Christie and Jahoda, 1954). The various controversies need not detain us here. However, it is important to note the limitations of this kind of 'individual differences' perspective (see also Billig, 1976 for a more extended critique). First, by locating prejudice in the dynamics of the individual personality, they tend to neglect *socio-cultural factors* which are often much more powerful determinants. Pettigrew (1958) demonstrated this clearly in his cross-cultural study of prejudice in South Africa and the United States. Not surprisingly, he found that white South Africans showed very high levels of anti-black prejudice, as did respondents from the southern United States. However, he also found that they did not appear to have particularly high levels of authoritarianism as measured by the F-scale. In other words, in terms of personality type they were rather similar to 'normal' populations, despite their overtly racist attitudes. With these and other findings Pettigrew argued convincingly that the origin of this racism lay much more in the prevailing societal norms in which his respondents lived than in any personality dysfunction. A second problem, closely related to the first, is the inability of the personality approach to explain the widespread *uniformity* of prejudice in certain societies or subgroups within societies. If prejudice is to be explained via individual *differences* amongst people, how can it then be manifested in a whole population or at least in a vast majority? In prewar Nazi Germany – and in many other places since – consistently racist attitudes and behaviour were shown by hundreds of thousands of people who must have differed on most other psychological characteristics. A third problem concerns the *historical specificity* of prejudice. At the same time that uniformities of attitude are difficult to explain with the personality approach, it is equally hard for it to account for the sudden rises and falls of prejudice. Again, the example of Germany springs to mind. The growth of anti-semitism in the Hitler era took place over the space of a decade or so – much too short a time for a whole generation of German families to have adopted new forms of child-rearing practices giving rise to authoritarian and prejudiced children. An even more dramatic example is provided by attitudes of Americans towards the Japanese which underwent a rapid change after the bombing of Pearl Harbor. And, just to complete the picture, after the war the

US and Japan became close economic and political allies with considerable cultural and tourist traffic between them. Examples such as these strongly suggest that the attitudes held by members of different groups towards each other have more to do with the objective relations between the groups – relations of political conflict or alliance, economic interdependence and so on – than with the familial relations in which they grew up.

Interpersonal versus group behaviour

In attempting to explain intergroup behaviour by means of variations in personal types, the personality approach makes the assumption that people's behaviour in group settings is essentially similar to their behaviour in all other situations. Thus, whether we are alone, or interacting with one or two other close friends, or participating in some event involving a group which is important to us, our behaviour is still seen to be mainly determined by the make-up of our personalities. In making this assumption of a similarity between individual, interpersonal and group situations, the personality approach is not alone in social psychology. For example, several theories of social relations propose that people are attracted to one another according to the degree of similarity in their social attitudes (e.g. Byrne, 1971; Festinger, 1954; Newcomb, 1961; see chapter 10), and at least some of these theories have suggested that the same may be true for attraction between members of different groups (e.g. Pettigrew, 1971; Rokeach, 1960). The proposed causal factor is different – a relationship of attitudinal similarity rather than individual personality type – but the basic hypothesis of a behavioural isomorphism between all social settings is the same.

There are, however, a number of difficulties with this hypothesis. First, such a hypothesis cannot easily account for the widespread uniformity of behaviour which is so typical of situations where groups are psychologically salient. This is particularly problematic for any personality type explanations, as we saw in the previous section, but also presents problems for theories of interpersonal relationships since, in many intergroup situations, people may simply be unaware of all the relations between themselves and outgroup members. As Brown and Turner (1981, p. 45) wrote: 'One football fan will taunt another, particularly if they are wearing different coloured scarves, quite oblivious of the many personal attributes that they may or may not have in common.' A second, and closely related, problem concerns situations where several hundred members of different groups are involved – like the two incidents described at the start of this chapter. Here, the number of different possible interpersonal relationships between the protagonists must have been enormous, and yet the behaviour was observably predictable and uniform. Finally, people's behaviour, besides being more uniform in group settings, is also often qualitatively different. For example, in experimental situations involving the distribution of rewards, groups appear to be more competitive than individuals under the same conditions (e.g. Dustin and Davis, 1970; Wilson and Kayatani, 1968; see chapter 13). In research on bargaining it has been found that two individuals negotiating do not follow the same pattern as in exchanges between two groups or group representatives (Stephenson, 1978). Similarly, the effects of attitudinal similarity, which at the interpersonal level nearly always seem to promote attraction (Byrne, 1971), are more complex at the intergroup level since both attraction *and* repulsion can result under the appropriate conditions (Brown, 1984a).

It was considerations like these which led Tajfel (1978b) to suggest that it is important to distinguish between interpersonal and intergroup behaviour and, consequently, to argue that theories addressing problems at the one level might not easily be extrapolated to explain phenomena at the other. For Tajfel, *interpersonal behaviour* meant acting *as an individual* with some idiosyncratic characteristics and a unique set of personal relationships with others (e.g. J. Smith of certain physical appearance, intelligence and personality, and with various friendships and animosities with a number of individuals). *Intergroup behaviour*, on the other hand, meant acting *as a group member* (e.g. behaving as a *police officer*, or as a *Liverpool supporter*). In the first case the various social categories one belongs to are less important than the constellation of individual and interpersonal dynamics. In the second case the reverse is true; *who* one is as a person is much less important than the uniform you are wearing or the colour of the scarf around your neck.

What Tajfel proposed, therefore, was that any sequence of social behaviour could be depicted as falling somewhere along a *continuum* defined by the two extremes of interpersonal and intergroup behaviour. Quite where it fell would depend, he thought, on three factors. The first was the clarity with which different social categories could be identified. Where social divisions like black and white, man and woman, are clearly discernible, this will tend to locate the behaviour towards the intergroup end. Where the category differences are less clear or less relevant, the behaviour is more likely to be interpersonal. The second was the extent to which the behaviour or attitudes within each group was variable or uniform. Interpersonal behaviour will show the normal range of individual differences; when groups are salient, people's behaviour becomes much more similar. The factor was how far one person's treatment of or attitude towards others is idiosyncratic or uniform and predictable. In our interpersonal dealings we negotiate a variety of ways of responding to those we know; intergroup encounters, on the other hand, tend to be marked by stereotyped perceptions and behaviours.

It is worth noting that these three criteria do not just distinguish interpersonal behaviour from *intergroup* behaviour. Turner (1982) pointed out that behaviour within the group (*intragroup* behaviour) is also often marked by an awareness of category boundaries, uniformity of behaviour and stereotypical perceptions. For this reason, Brown and Turner (1981) proposed that the continuum which Tajfel (1978b) had identified should be extended and relabelled as the **interpersonal-group continuum** (see table 16.1). This demarcation is very similar to a distinction which Asch (1952) had made some years previously in writing of the individual and the group as 'the two permanent poles of all social processes' (Asch, 1952, p. 251).

TABLE 16.1 The interpersonal–group continuum

Factor	Interpersonal ◄————► Group	
Presence of two or more social categories?	Obscured or not relevant	Clearly visible and salient
Uniformity of behaviour and attitudes within one group?	Low	High
Stereotyped or uniform treatment of other group members?	Low	High

In practice, of course, any particular social episode will fall somewhere between the extremes on each of the three criteria and so will contain both interpersonal and group elements. However, in many situations the predominance of one or the other level will be clear with, as Tajfel suggested, the corresponding implications for the kind of theoretical analysis we should adopt. In particular, this means that theories of intergroup behaviour must focus their attention on variables concerning people's social relations as group members, and not as individual persons. In the remainder of this chapter some examples of such genuinely intergroup theories will be considered.

Intergroup Behaviour as a Response to Real or Imagined Group Interests

Instead of regarding intergroup conflict as the result of some primitive herd instinct, or prejudice as a problem associated with a particular personality type, it may be more useful to view them as the 'normal' responses of ordinary people to the intergroup situation confronting them. One feature of these situations which seems to be particularly important is the nature of the respective goals of the groups concerned: are the goals *incompatible*, so that what one group is seeking will be at the expense of another; or are they *concordant*, so that both groups are working towards the same objective and may even need each other for its attainment? An example of the former case would be the relationship between workers and their employers in a capitalist economy where one party's wages are at the expense of the other's profits. The miners' strike referred to earlier was a classic instance of such an industrial conflict. An example of concordant goals would be when minority political parties form coalitions to achieve political power (e.g. the Communist and Socialist parties in France in the early 1980s).

The idea that goal relationships like these could be important determinants of people's behaviour towards members of their own and other groups crops up frequently within the social sciences (Campbell, 1965). Within social psychology the best known proponent of this approach is Sherif (1966). At the heart of Sherif's theory is the proposition that group members' intergroup attitudes and behaviour will tend to reflect the objective interests of their group *vis-à-vis* other groups. Where these interests conflict then their group's cause is more likely to be furthered by a competitive orientation towards the rival group, which is often easily extended to include prejudiced attitudes and even overtly hostile behaviour. At the same time the success of the **ingroup** in achieving the goal is likely to be furthered by very positive attitudes towards other ingroup members, thereby engendering high morale and cohesion. Where, on the other hand, the groups' interests coincide then it is more functional for the group members to adopt a cooperative and friendly attitude towards the **outgroup**. If this is reciprocated then a positive joint outcome is more probable.

Sherif's summer-camp studies

To demonstrate the validity of this perspective Sherif, together with his colleagues, conducted three field experiments which have become classics in the literature (Sherif and Sherif, 1953; Sherif, White and Harvey, 1955; Sherif et al., 1961). Although these experiments differed slightly from one another they are similar enough in conception and outcome for us to be able to consider them together. They were longitudinal (lasting some three weeks) and were designed to show systematic changes in behaviour as a result of changing intergroup relations. The full design included three stages: group formation, intergroup conflict and conflict reduction.[1] To effect this design, Sherif and his colleagues arranged for the experiments to be conducted in the context of a boys' summer camp. In fact, as far as those participating in the experiments were concerned, that is exactly what it was, since all the activities were exactly the kinds of things which went on in American summer camps in the 1950s (and probably still do!). The difference was, of course, that (unknown to the boys) the adults running the camp were all trained researchers making careful observations of all that went on. The boys themselves – all white, middle class and aged around 12 years – had all been carefully screened before being invited to the camp, and only those who seemed to be psychologically well adjusted and from stable homes were accepted. In addition, none of the boys knew each other before coming to the camp. Although this was a highly select and unrepresentative sample it did ensure that any behaviour they subsequently exhibited could not be attributed to a prior history of social or psychological deprivation, or to pre-existing personal relationships between the boys.

Group formation   In the first stage of experiments the large group of 22 to 24 children was split up into the two experimental groups of the study. Care was taken to match these two groups as carefully as possible. In the first two experiments, in addition to matching on various physical and psychological characteristics, it was also arranged to have the majority of each boy's best friends in the *outgroup* (these friendships had formed in the first few days of the camp). In the third experiment the boys never actually met each other prior to the groups being formed, and were initially camped some distance from each other and unaware of the other group's presence. For some days the children engaged in various activities in these groups without, however, having much to do with the other group. Very quickly, the groups developed an internal structure and evolved mini-cultures of their own with their own group symbols and names, and norms of appropriate behaviour. Although the other group did not figure much in their thinking, it is interesting to note that in the first two experiments the observers did record some instances of comparisons between the groups; in these comparisons 'the edge was given to one's own group' (Sherif, 1966, p. 80). Furthermore, in the third study, where the groups did not know of each other's existence at this stage, on being informed of the presence of the other group several boys spontaneously suggested to the camp authorities that the other group be challenged to some sporting contest. As we shall see, it is significant that these expressions of ingroup favouritism occurred *before* the intergroup conflict phase of the experiment had actually been introduced.

Intergroup competition   The second stage then began. It was announced to the boys that a series of intergroup contests would take place (e.g. softball, tug-of-war etc.). The overall winner of these contests would receive a cup and each member of this successful group would be given a gleaming new penknife – just the kind of prize every 12-year-old boy covets. The losers would receive nothing. In this way, an objective conflict of interest was introduced between the groups. In technical terms, they had moved from being independent of one another to being negatively *interdependent*: what one group gained the other lost. With the advent of this conflict stage the boys' behaviour changed dramatically. Whereas in the first stage the two groups had coexisted more or less peaceably, they were now transformed into two hostile factions, never losing an opportunity to deride the outgroup and, in some instances, physically attack it. In a variety of micro-experiments, disguised as games, Sherif and his associates were able to document systematic and consistent ingroup favouritism in judgements, attitudes and sociometric preferences. Changes took place *within* the groups too. They invariably became more cohesive and the leadership structure sometimes changed, with a more aggressive boy assuming dominance. These behaviours were all the more remarkable when it is remembered that in the first two studies at least, every boy's best friends had been placed in the *other* group. How fragile those initial interpersonal relationships proved to be in the face of the changing intergroup relationship!

Conflict reduction   Having so easily generated such fierce competition, the researchers attempted to reduce the conflict by introducing a series of **superordinate goals** for the groups – that is, goals which both groups desired but which were unattainable by one group by its own efforts alone. One such superordinate goal was engineered by arranging for the camp truck to break down some miles from the camp. Since it was nearly lunchtime the children had a clear common interest in getting the truck started to return them to camp. However, the truck was too heavy to be push-started by one group on its own. Only by both groups pulling on the tug-of-war rope attached to the front bumper – the same rope which they had used in *contest* only days earlier! – could the truck be moved. After a number of scenarios like this a marked change was observed in the boys' behaviour. They became much less aggressive towards members of the other group, and on a number of quantitative indices showed a clear reduction in the amount of ingroup favouritism.

On the face of it, these experiments seemed to provide strong support for Sherif's theory. The behaviour of these ordinary well-adjusted children was shown to vary systematically with the changing intergroup relationship. The fact that both competitive and cooperative behaviour could be elicited from the same group was very problematic for the 'group mind' approach. Moreover, the changes in the boys' behaviour were too widespread and too rapid to be attributable to any enduring personality disposition. Both the popular theories considered earlier, then, were shown up as deficient by these findings. These deficiencies were underlined by later research inspired by the summer-camp experiments. In a variety of experimental and field studies it has been invariably found that groups which either adopt or have imposed on them 'win–lose' orientations show more intergroup discrimination than those with more collaborative orientations (e.g. Blake and Mouton, 1962; Brown, et al., 1986; Diab, 1970; Ryen and Kahn, 1975). Furthermore, in confirmation of Sherif's findings, increased ingroup cohesion seems regularly to result from the experience of intergroup conflict (Dion, 1979).

Another area where Sherif's ideas have been particularly influential has been where attempts have been made to reduce ethnic prejudice. The best known social policy to this end has come to be known as the *contact hypothesis*. Broadly speaking, this hypothesis suggests that contact between members of different groups, under the appropriate conditions, lessens intergroup prejudice and hostility. This idea has provided the rationale for desegregation policies in housing, employment, and education which have been partially implemented in the USA and elsewhere. Although the contact hypothesis has been proposed in several different forms over the years (e.g. Allport, 1954; Cook, 1962; Pettigrew, 1971, 1986), on one issue these theorists are all agreed: contact between groups by itself, without some cooperation over common goals, will not reduce and may even exacerbate prejudice. The evidence from studies of ethnic relations largely confirms this (Amir, 1976; Hewstone and Brown, 1986). The success of contact policies may also depend on the extend to which the participants from different groups are interacting on an interpersonal or an intergroup basis (Brown and Turner, 1981; Hewstone and Brown, 1986). If the contact is of a more interpersonal nature – i.e. people are seen as individuals and group memberships are not significant – then any change of attitude may not generalize to other members of the respective groups. Wilder (1984), for example, found that contact between members of different college groups who were seen as typical (or representative) of their group was much more efficacious than contact between atypical group members (but cf. Miller, Brewer and Edwards, 1985 for a contrary point of view).

Impressive though the support for Sherif's ideas undoubtedly is, some work in the last decade has begun to suggest some qualifications to them (see Turner, 1981a for a review). For instance, Rabbie and his colleagues have found that the actual experience of intergroup cooperation and competition may produce rather different outcomes than merely anticipating them (e.g. Rabbie and Wilkens, 1971). In general, anticipated competition and cooperation result in weaker effects on intergroup attitudes (in the same general direction as Sherif had found), provided that at least some degree of ingroup affiliation has occurred. Where that affiliation is minimal or absent, differences between anticipated competition and cooperation tend to disappear (Rabbie and deBrey, 1971). Also, the imposition of superordinate goals as a recipe for conflict reduction may not always be effective. Indeed, sometimes it may even increase antagonism towards the outgroup. Worchel, Andreoli and Folger (1977) noted that in Sherif's studies the cooperation over superordinate goals always proved successful. They showed, in contrast, that when that cooperation did not achieve its aims and had been preceded by a competitive episode, liking for the outgroup diminished. In addition, it may also be important for groups engaged in cooperative ventures to have distinctive and complementary roles to play. When this does not occur and the groups' contributions are not easily recognizable, liking for the other group decreases, perhaps because the group members are concerned for the integrity of the ingroup (Brown and Wade, 1987; Deschamps and Brown, 1983).

Mere Group Membership as a Source of Intergroup Discrimination

In the previous section we saw how important intergroup goal relationships were in shaping group members' attitudes and behaviour towards both their own group and various outgroups. However, an important question remains unanswered from all this research: does the mere fact of belonging to one group have any consequences for our attitudes towards other groups? Does being of one nationality (or religion or ethnicity or class), in and of itself, generate predictable orientations towards members from another country (religion and so on)? It is this question we address in this section.

Recall, for a moment, that curious observation in one of the summer-camp studies where the boys in one of the groups, on learning that there was another group in the vicinity, showed some signs of competitiveness towards this outgroup *before* the actual intergroup competitions had been announced by the experimenters. Just being in one group and becoming aware of a second group seemed to trigger feelings of rivalry. This was confirmed in a subsequent study by Ferguson and Kelley (1964), where it was found that two laboratory groups working alongside each other with no suggestion of any competition between them nevertheless showed clear favouritism for their own group when evaluating the two groups' products. However, in this and the earlier Sherif studies there were clearly additional factors present other than just group belongingness itself: the group members had interacted and worked with one another for one thing. What would happen if these factors were removed from the situation and one was left simply with the fact of being a member of one group and not of another?

Minimal group experiments

Rabbie and Horwitz (1969) were the first to investigate this question. Following Lewin (1948) they reasoned that the essential condition for the arousal of group feelings was the perception of some interdependence of fate amongst the group members. Accordingly, they arranged for schoolchildren who did not know each other to be divided at random into two groups of four persons. Members of the two groups were given identification badges (green or blue) and were initially seated either side of a screen so that they could see only members of their own group. In the control condition, that was the extent of their group experience. In the experimental conditions, on the other hand, the groups further experienced a 'common fate' by being given – or by being deprived of – some new transistor radios. Subsequently in all conditions the screen separating the groups was removed and each person was asked to stand up and read out some personal biographical details about himself or herself, while the other children rated him or her on a number of scales. Rabbie and Horwitz (1969) found that in the experimental conditions these impressionistic ratings were markedly affected by the person's group affiliation: ingroup members were consistently rated more favourably than outgroup members. In the control condition, however, no such ingroup bias was observed, although in a subsequent extension of the experiment (which increased the sample size) some biases were observed on two of the scales (Horwitz and Rabbie, 1982). Nevertheless, the conclusion from this experiment seemed to be that classification into a minimal group *by itself* exerted little influence on group members' judgements. Only when that classification coincided with some common experience of reward or deprivation did group-related perceptions emerge.

That conclusion proved to be premature, however. Tajfel et al., (1971) took the **minimal group paradigm** one stage further and showed that mere categorization *was* sufficient to elicit intergroup behaviour. Like Rabbie and Horwitz, they assigned schoolboys to one of two groups on a very arbitrary basis – their alleged preference for one of two abstract artists Paul Klee and Vassilij Kandinsky. However, in this experiment the children knew only which group they themselves had been assigned to; the identities of their fellow ingroup and outgroup members were kept hidden by use of code numbers. Then, under the general pretext of the experiment ('a study of decision-making'), the children were asked to allocate money to various recipients using specially prepared booklets of decision matrices (see figure 16.1 for an example).[2] The identity of the recipients on each page was unknown but their group affiliation was revealed. To eliminate self-interest as a possible motive in the allocations, the children were never able to award money to themselves directly.

The results were clear. Although they made some effort to be fair in their allocations, the children showed a persistent tendency to award more money to ingroup recipients than to those whom they believed belonged to the other group. This was true even when, in absolute terms, the ingrouper might be

Numbers are rewards for:

member 74 of Klee group	25	23	21	19	17	15	13	11	9	7	5	3	1
member 44 of Kandinsky group	19	18	17	16	15	14	13	12	11	10	9	8	7

FIGURE 16.1　A sample matrix from the Tajfel et al. (1971) minimal group experiment

worse off. For example, in the matrix shown in figure 16.1 the mean response from people in the Kandinsky group was somewhere between the [11, 12] and [13, 13] options. Notice that this choice results in the Kandinsky recipient actually receiving 6 or 7 points *less* than he might otherwise have done but, crucially, he thereby receives more than the Klee recipient. The results are rather surprising when one considers how sparse this social setting really was. The children were allocated to two meaningless groups on a flimsy criterion.[3] They never interacted with members of their own or the other group. The two groups had no current or past relationship with each other. And yet, when asked to allocate sums of money to anonymous others, the children consistently favoured ingroup members over outgroupers. Simply being assigned to a group does, after all, seem to have predictable effects on intergroup behaviour.

Intergroup discrimination in this minimal group situation has proved to be a remarkably robust phenomenon. In more than two dozen independent studies in several different countries using a wide range of experimental participants of both sexes (from young children to adults), essentially the same result has been found: the mere act of allocating people into arbitrary social categories is sufficient to elicit biased judgements and discriminatory behaviour (see Brewer, 1979; Brewer and Kramer, 1985; Tajfel, 1982a).

Despite this empirical consensus the minimal group paradigm has attracted controversy. This has focused on the interpretation of the observed data as revealing discrimination or fairness (Branthwaite, Doyle and Lightbown, 1979; Bornstein et al., 1983a; Turner, 1980, 1983a), possible demand characteristics associated with the paradigm (Gerard and Hoyt, 1974; Tajfel, 1978b), statistical treatment of the data (Aschenbrenner and Schaeffer, 1980; Brown, Tajfel and Turner, 1980), rival ways of measuring intergroup orientations (Bornstein et al., 1983a, 1983b; Turner, 1983a, 1983b, and doubts about the paradigm's external validity associated with its obviously high degree of artificiality (Aschenbrenner and Schaeffer, 1980; Brown, Tajfel and Turner, 1980).

Space does not permit a discussion of all these issues here. However, it is worth making the following observations on two of the more important issues in question. The first concerns whether or not participants in these experiments are really showing ingroup favouritism or, alternatively, are displaying behaviour better described as some form of *fairness*. It seems clear that people do show a clear propensity towards equalizing ingroup and outgroup outcomes in these situations. However, it is also true that they are nearly always more 'fair' to ingroupers than to outgroupers. In other words, although people's choices cluster around the centre or 'fair' point (e.g. [13, 13] in figure 16.1), when an ingroup member is the recipient on the top line the responses tend to be to the *left* of centre; when an outgroup member is the beneficiary on the same line the responses move to the *right* of centre. Furthermore, the evidence for this persistent bias is derived not just from particular reward allocation matrices but from a variety of other dependent measures which have also shown that ingroup members or products receive more favourable ratings than equivalent outgroup stimuli (Brewer, 1979; Brown, Tajfel and Turner, 1980). Again, this bias is seldom very extreme in its extent but it is both reliable and pervasive. Thus, as Turner (1980) suggests, the intergroup discrimination observed as a result of social categorization represents something of a compromise between ingroup favouritism and 'fairness'. In the section which follows some explanations of this compromise are considered.

The second issue concerns the *artificiality* of the minimal group paradigm, which has led some commentators to question its utility since the results may not be generalizable to the real world. (Aschenbrenner and Schaeffer, 1980). Of course, this criticism is also applicable to laboratory experiments in any discipline, not just to the particular paradigm we are concerned with here. Any attempt to control variables and obtain a measure of precision in observation inevitably involves an element of artifice. Indeed, that artificiality may be an experiment's principal virtue, since it permits the investigation of processes or combinations of processes which may not exist naturally uncontaminated with other factors (Henshel, 1980; Turner, 1981b). What these particular experiments show is that mere group membership has predictable consequences in and of itself. What implications these will then have for 'real' groups in the world outside the laboratory depends on the conjunction of these consequences and the consequences of other processes which we have already discussed (see earlier sections) and which are yet to be considered (see later). Thus, the real point of the minimal group experiments is not that they have generated a 'finding' which should then simply be extrapolated wholesale to all groups everywhere. Rather, they should be seen as a further step in discovering not just the shape of one of the pieces of the jigsaw, but how that piece interlocks with all the others.

Explanations of intergroup discrimination in minimal groups

It is one thing to establish a phenomenon: it is quite another to explain it. What underlies the apparently gratuitous discrimination in these most minimal of groups? One explanation is in terms of norms (Tajfel et al., 1971). According to this view, being made aware that one is a member of a group like 'Klee' or 'Kandinsky' might, in most of the cultures in which the experiments have been conducted, evoke associations with teams and team games. These associations might make a competitive norm highly salient. This could then lead to the unequal allocation of money between the groups in an attempt to 'win'. That this competitiveness is not full-blown might be explained by a countervailing norm of fairness – another valued attribute in Western cultures. This form of explanation is supported by the findings from a cross-cultural study which found variations in the extent of minimal group discrimination among children of European, Samoan and Maori origin (Wetherell, 1982). All three groups showed clear ingroup favouritism, although the latter two showed somewhat less than the first. These two groups showed more concern with joint outcomes. One might plausibly surmise that these results reflected the different cultural norms in the three samples (Wetherell, 1982).

Attractive though such an account may be, it has at least two shortcomings which have inhibited its widespread adoption as an explanation of intergroup discrimination (Turner, 1980). First, such a normative account needs to be able to predict in advance which of a number of norms will predominate in any particular situation. After all, there are a variety of cultural norms which might be relevant: fairness, as we have seen, is one; profit maximization – surely salient in most Western countries – is another; equity is yet another. Without some theory of norm salience we are only able to explain after the event why a particular pattern of discrimination occurred. At present such a theory does not exist, and so the so-called 'explanation' becomes little more than a redescription of the experimental findings. A second and related criticism is that normative accounts are by their nature rather too general and over-inclusive. They do not really permit one to predict the systematic variations in response to the minimal group situation which it is possible to observe even *within one culture* (Turner, 1981a). For example, introducing status or changing the nature of the recipients both have reliable effects on levels of discrimination (Brown and Deschamps, 1980–1; Commins and Lockwood, 1979).

A second explanation offers some hope of avoiding these problems; this explanation is in terms of categorization processes (e.g. Doise, 1976). Some earlier work had shown that if a non-overlapping classification is imposed on a set of physical stimuli (e.g. lines of different lengths, squares of varying area) then judgements of stimuli falling into different classes will become distorted, with the effect that perceived differences *between* the two categories become exaggerated (Tajfel and Wilkes, 1963; Marchand, 1970; see chapter 5). A similar phenomenon has been observed with more social stimuli: attitude statements which are categorized as having come from one of two sources may be seen as more different from one another than those which have not been so classified (Eiser, 1971). Doise (1976) argues that these judgemental biases are the result of a fundamental cognitive process, that of **categorical differentiation**. He suggests that in order for social categories to be useful ordering and simplifying devices it is important that they discriminate clearly between class and non-class members. Thus, the function of the differentiation process is to sharpen the distinctions between the categories – and, relatedly, to blur the differences *within* them[4] – so as to better organize and structure our mental and social worlds. If we apply this analysis to the minimal group context it suggests that the situation confronting the experimental participants is sufficiently ill defined for them to latch on to the previously meaningless categories (Klee and Kandinsky) and use them to make sense of it. Once that particular (and only) classification has been adopted the inevitable categorical differentiation occurs, and occurs in the only way possible here – by allocating different amounts to ingroup and outgroup recipients. In fact, Doise suggests that differentiation can occur at any or all of three different levels: the evaluative, the perceptual and the behavioural. The last, which is manifested in minimal group experiments, is assumed to be the most influential.

The advantage of an approach such as this is that it can make predictions about variations in differentiation or discrimination in particular contexts. Take, for example, the case where two social categories cut across one another (e.g. ethnicity and gender). The categorical differentiation model suggests that in 'criss-cross' situations like this the discrimination observed in terms of either of the original categories will be reduced because the simultaneous processes of between-category differentiation and within-category assimilation effectively cancel one another out (see figure 16.2). Deschamps and Doise (1978) and Deschamps (1977) have found evidence of such reduced differentiation when categories (both real and artificial) are crossed. Similarly, Arcuri (1982) found that memory errors in the recall of a social episode were affected by the presence and arrangement of two different categorizations in a way which supported the categorical differentiation model. Note, however, that if the two crossing categories result in a double ingroup in juxtaposition with a double outgroup (e.g. in figure 16.2, black men versus white women), then there is evidence that this results in enhanced rather than reduced differentiation (Brown and Turner, 1979).

Closely related to these categorization processes are a number of other phenomena which are worth mentioning briefly (see chapter 5 for a fuller

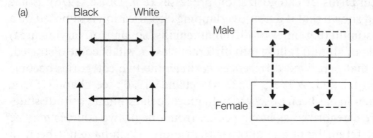

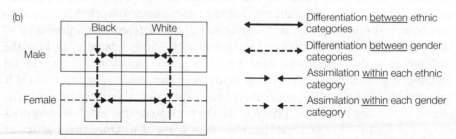

FIGURE 16.2 Effects of criss-cross categorizations according to the categorical differentiation model: (a) simple categorization (b) crossed categorizations

discussion). One is the phenomenon of *stereotyping* – that is, the attribution to all members of a category of various traits and characteristics that make up the **stereotype**. Stereotyping acts as a kind of mental short cut, so that the perception of a person as belonging to a particular category (e.g. men) carries with it the inference that that person is likely to be dominant, task oriented, aggressive, rational and so on (Ashmore, 1981). Precisely because stereotypes are short cuts, they sometimes lead us to make quite incorrect inferences. For example, in our perceptions or memories of confusing or complex situations we will often fall back on stereotypes to fill in the gaps in our minds. Hamilton and Rose (1980) found that people's recall of a number of slides depicting various occupational groups (e.g. stewardess, salesman) associated with different traits (e.g. attractive, talkative) was reliably influenced by common stereotypes of these occupations. Thus, although in the slides which were actually presented there were just as many 'attractive stewardesses' as 'attractive salesmen', subjects erroneously remembered more of the former than the latter. Hamilton (1981) called this illusory correlation, since subjects falsely perceived a correlation between the occupational categories and certain traits when in fact there was none. (See also Rothbart, 1981 and S. E. Taylor, 1981 for other cognitive biases associated with stereotypes.) Another phenomenon associated with categorization is an enhanced perception of homogeneity within groups: members of the same group are seen as very similar to one another. As noted earlier, this accompanies the accentuation of differences *between* categories. What is interesting about this perception of homogeneity is that it appears not to be a symmetrical process: outgroups are usually seen as more homogeneous than ingroups (Quattrone and Jones, 1980). 'They' are all the same, but 'we' are distinguishable from one another, it seems. Although this effect has been reported several times, it is possible that it is limited to majority groups' perceptions of minorities. When a *minority* is viewing the majority, or another minority, it is the *ingroup* which is seen as more homogeneous (Simon and Brown, 1987).

The categorization model offers a simple and powerful explanation of minimal intergroup discrimination in terms of a cognitive process which has been shown to be operative in a number of other domains (e.g. Bartlett, 1932; Bruner, Goodnow and Austin, 1956; Piaget, 1942). Despite these advantages, however, there is one important limitation to such an explanation: it cannot readily account for the asymmetry which is such a pervasive feature of intergroup differentiation. In other words, why does the ingroup (and not the outgroup) come off best in intergroup perceptions, judgements and resource allocations? The categorization approach can account for the fact that groups are made more distinctive from one another, but it cannot explain why that distinctiveness is so often valued positively for the ingroup and negatively for the outgroup. To understand what underlies that *positive* distinctiveness we need a new concept, that of social identity.

Group Membership and Social Identity

Who am I? Who are we?

Segmenting the world into a manageable number of categories does not just help us to simplify and make sense of it; it also serves one other very important function – to define who we are. Not only do we classify others as members of this or that group, but we also locate *ourselves* in relation to those same groups. Our sense of identity, in other words, is closely bound up with our various group memberships. As a simple demonstration of this, readers may just ask themselves the following question: 'Who am I?' Analysis of people's answers to that question (repeated a number of times) usually reveals several (if not the majority) of the self-descriptions referring to group affiliations either explicitly (e.g. 'I am a member of the Juventus supporters' club') or implicitly through reference to the occupation of social roles (e.g. 'I am a miner'), to gender (e.g. 'I am a woman') or to nationality (e.g. 'I am German') (Kuhn and McPartland, 1954).

This idea that **social identity** derives from group membership has a long history (e.g. Mead, 1934), but it was not until quite recently that it was realized that social identity processes might have implications for intergroup behaviour (Tajfel, 1978b; Tajfel and Turner, 1979). This can happen if we assume, with Tajfel and Turner (1979), that by and large people prefer to have a positive self-concept rather than a negative one. Since part of our self-concept (or identity) is defined in terms of group affiliations, it follows that there will also be a preference to view those ingroups positively rather than negatively. But how do we arrive at such an evaluation? Tajfel and Turner (1979) extend Festinger's (1954) social comparison theory and suggest that our group evaluations are essentially relative in nature; we assess our own group's worth or prestige by comparing it with other groups. The outcome of these intergroup comparisons is critical for us because indirectly it contributes to our own self-esteem. If our own group can be perceived as clearly superior on some dimension of value (like skill or sociability) then we too can bask in that reflected glory (see also Cialdini et al., 1976 for an illustration of this phenomenon amongst college football supporters). Because of our presumed need for a positive self-concept, it follows that there will be a bias in these comparisons to look for ways in which the ingroup can, indeed, be distinguished favourably from outgroups. Tajfel calls this 'the establishment of positive distinctiveness' (Tajfel, 1978b, p. 83).[5]

How can this theory – social identity theory, as it is known – help to explain the persistent tendency for people to display intergroup discrimination, even in as barren a context as the minimal group paradigm? Consider again the situation facing the experimental subjects. They have been allocated to one of two equally meaningless groups. Indeed, so meaningless are they that there is literally nothing to differentiate them except the group labels and the fact that they themselves are in one group and not the other. They are referred to by code numbers, thus leading to feelings of anonymity. Given this anonymity the only possible source of identity, primitive though it may be, is their ingroup. However, that group is initially indistinguishable from the other group and hence, according to the theory, contributes little positive to its members' self-esteem. Accordingly, the pressures of distinctiveness come into play and the members of both groups seek to differentiate their own group positively from the other by the only means which the experimenters have provided – by allocating more money to fellow ingroupers than to outgroupers. Recall, also, that they will often do this even at the cost of some absolute gain to the ingroup (the maximizing difference strategy).

This presumed link between intergroup discrimination and self-esteem was demonstrated by Oakes and Turner (1980). They found that subjects in a minimal group experiment who were not given the usual opportunity to make intergroup reward allocations showed lower self-esteem than those who were. In a follow-up experiment Lemyre and Smith (1985) confirmed this result and established that it was indeed the opportunity to display *intergroup* discrimination which *elevated* self-esteem. Control subjects who, although having been categorized, could only distribute rewards between two ingroupers or two outgroupers, or who could not distribute rewards at all, showed lower self-esteem than those able to make *intergroup* decisions.

Social identity theory, then, seems to provide a plausible account of people's readiness to favour these most minimal of ingroups. But its applicability is not limited to these rather contrived experimental situations; part of its attraction has been its ability to make sense of a wide range of phenomena in naturalistic contexts. We shall describe just three examples; for others see Tajfel (1982b) and Brown (1984b).

Wage differentials

The first example is the well-known tendency for groups of workers in indus-trialized countries to be concerned about the size of wage relativities *vis-à-vis* other groups of workers. This was particularly prevalent in the British engineering industry in the 1970s but, historically, examples of disputes centring on differentials go back at least as far as the early nineteenth century. What is interesting about these industrial conflicts is that they may have little 'realistic' basis in the sense that there is rarely an explicit conflict of interest between the groups concerned. Often, indeed, the workers may have different employers and may work in a completely different industry. The other important aspect of differentials disputes is – as the words imply – that they are about the *difference* between groups rather than about their levels of wages in absolute terms. These two points were borne out very clearly in a study of an aircraft engineering factory by Brown (1978). He showed, using matrices adapted from the minimal group laboratory, that shop stewards from one department in the factory would be prepared to sacrifice as much as £2 per week in absolute terms in order to increase their differential over another group to £1. An example of one of these matrices is shown in figure 16.3. When presented with this array of wage relativities, members of the toolroom were

Wages for toolroom group	£69.30	£68.80	£68.30	£67.80	£67.30
Wages for production and development groups	£70.30	£69.30	£68.30	£67.30	£66.30

FIGURE 16.3   A matrix used to measure intergroup differentiation in wage comparisons (Brown, 1978)

virtually unanimous in choosing the extreme right-hand box. That this inter-group differentiation cut across the group's 'real' interests was confirmed in another part of the study, where the same stewards were asked to respond to a hypothetical superordinate goals scenario involving factory-wide redundancies. Only a minority of those interviewed responded to this scenario by proposing cooperative strategies involving other groups. These findings seemed much more explicable by social identity theory than the Sherif theory we described earlier.

Ethnolinguistic groups

As a second illustration of social identity processes, we turn to the attempts by various ethnic and national groups to maintain the integrity of their language (Giles, 1977). Examples abound. Just in Europe one thinks immediately of the Flemings and Walloons in Belgium, the Catalans in Spain, the Bretons in France, and the Welsh in Britain. In all these cases we see attempts by groups to make themselves distinctive from other groups in one of the most fundamental ways of all – language. Language is fundamental in two ways. First, our membership of ethnic/national groups is intimately connected with language or dialect use. It is part of our cultural heritage, and indeed may even be a defining attribute for group membership. In other words, our social identities may be directly expressed through language. But language is important to inter-group relations in another way: it is also the prime means of communication with outgroups. Depending on the language, dialect or accent we choose to use we can communicate more or less effectively with members of the outgroup; we can attempt to integrate or cut ourselves off. So language is both an expression of and a mediator of intergroup behaviour. These considerations have led Giles and his colleagues to explain the behaviour of ethnolinguistic groups in terms of social identity processes (Giles and Johnson, 1981). Giles has suggested that, where identity is threatened, efforts to establish distinctiveness may take the form of linguistic divergence; two experimental studies have found exactly that (Bourhis and Giles, 1977; Bourhis et al., 1978). Both were set in the context of a language laboratory, and in both some language students were confronted with a speaker who threatened their linguistic identities. Clear evidence of language divergence by the students was found, either by broadening their accent or by switching languages altogether. This differentiation is particularly significant since, as some of Giles's earlier work had established, in most inter*personal* contexts people tend to converge in their language use (Giles and Powesland,

1975). That in intergroup contexts the opposite can happen is further evidence that different (identity) processes may be at work (see also chapter 9).

Occupational groups

As a third example we consider another occupational group, namely nurses – people who are more usually associated with caring and self-sacrifice than with group favouritism and animosity. Indeed, this cooperative ethos is enshrined in some codes of nursing ethics (e.g. UKCC, 1984). And yet there is evidence that nurses, too, are quite ready to display ingroup bias, particularly in relation to their nursing colleagues. For example, in Skevington's (1981) study of a British hospital it was found that higher-status registered nurses considered themselves as generally superior on a wide range of task-related attributes (e.g. intelligence, confidence, responsibility), whilst the lower-status enrolled nurses regarded themselves (and were regarded) as superior on more socio-emotional dimensions (e.g. cheerful, thoughtful). A similar pheno-menon was observed by van Knippenberg and van Oers (1984) in their study of academic and psychiatric nurses in the Netherlands. Like Skevington, they found clear evidence of ingroup bias on attributes specific to each group – e.g. theoretical insight versus interpersonal relations. Although there was some agreement between the groups as to their respective merits on these attributes, van Knippenberg and van Oers convincingly showed that the concession that an outgroup might be superior on one set of dimensions was considerably outweighed by the claim to *ingroup* superiority on another set. The degree of positive differentiation favouring the ingroup on the latter dimensions was generally twice as high as the amount of negative differentiation on the other attributes. In both of these studies the source of the intergroup differentiation seemed traceable to efforts by the nurses to maintain their professional identity. However, a study by Oaker and Brown (1986) of relations between specialist nurses (e.g. intensive care, operating theatre staff) and general nurses on the wards raised some questions about this interpretation. Whilst finding clear evidence of ingroup favouritism – both groups regarded their own group as friendlier than the other – and some evidence of discord between the groups, Oaker and Brown failed to establish a positive correlation between that ingroup bias and strength of ingroup identification. In fact, quite contrary to what social identity theory would predict, the observed association was *negative*. There is thus some doubt about the exact nature of the presumed link between intergroup differentiation and social identity.

These doubts are reinforced by two further studies in which the predicted positive association between identification and differentiation was examined in some detail (Brown and Williams, 1984; Brown et al., 1986). Both were carried out in industrial settings – one a bakery, the other a paper mill. In both studies the ingroups of interest were the respondents' own workgroup, and the outgroups were other workgroups in the factory and the management. On a variety of indices, clear positive differentiation was observed. The identi-fication with the ingroup was also predominantly positive. And yet, within each group, the relationship between the strength of this identification and the indices of differentiation was very variable, ranging in different groups from positive (as predicted), through non-existent, to negative. A much more powerful and reliable predictor of intergroup differentiation in both studies was perceived conflict with the outgroup – a finding more in keeping with the Sherif approach we considered earlier.

How may these findings be understood? One possibility is that the notion of social identity as merely a cognitive self-definition or a sense of belongingness to a group is too narrow. Perhaps we need to think of group memberships not just as contributors to self-concept and self-esteem, as proposed by social identity theory, but also as providing a variety of social interpretations or ideologies for the individual. For instance, membership of a trade union could have a number of meanings (self-interest, political, moral), all of which could result in an equally strong sense of attachment or identification. But the kind of intergroup attitudes and behaviour displayed to any given outgroup (management, say) will depend crucially on which of these meanings predominates in the individual or group (Brown et al., 1986).

Subordinate Status, Intergroup Comparisons and Social Unrest

The three examples chosen to illustrate social identity processes all had one other feature in common, a feature characteristic of nearly all real-world intergroup relationships: they all featured groups of unequal status. The three groups in the aircraft engine factory formed a clear hierarchy among themselves and, of course, all enjoyed much less power and status than their employers (Brown, 1978). Minority group languages or dialects are nearly always devalued by the dominant linguistic group (Giles and Powesland, 1975). In each of the nursing studies there was an identifiable 'inferior' group. These are just three (fairly mild) instances of status disparity. To list the numerous other examples of inequality and oppression around the world would take up the rest of this chapter, if not the book. Instead, let us consider what the consequences are of belonging to a group of subordinate status.

At first glance these seem negative. Members of such groups will frequently discover that they have lower wages (if they have a job at all), poorer housing, fewer educational qualifications, and are consensually regarded as being inferior on a whole host of criteria. Thus not only are they worse off in a direct material sense, but psychologically too they may well be disadvantaged. If identity is indeed maintained through intergroup comparisons, as social identity theory suggests, then the outcome of the available comparisons is unremittingly negative for their self-esteem.

Leaving the group

One reaction to this state of affairs is simply to try to leave the group, as Tajfel (1978b) has suggested. Examples of members of 'inferior' groups distancing themselves physically or psychologically from their group are not hard to find. In their classic studies of ethnic identification Clark and Clark (1947) found that black children in the USA showed identification with and preference for the dominant white group – a finding replicated with minority groups in other countries (e.g. Milner, 1983; Morland, 1969; Vaughan, 1964). Disidentification with the ingroup is by no means a phenomenon restricted to children, as Lewin (1948) noted of American Jews who attempt to 'pass' into Gentile society. However, this is not a universal or necessary consequence, as is revealed by studies in different historical contexts which failed to find such misidentification (Hraba and Grant, 1970; Vaughan, 1978). We return to this point shortly.

Social comparisons

Nevertheless, such individualistic strategies may not always be possible, especially if the group boundaries are relatively fixed as is the case with many ethnic and religious groups. In cases like these, Tajfel and Turner (1979) suggest that a number of other avenues may be pursued. One is to restrict the comparisons made to other similar or subordinate status groups so that the outcome of these comparisons is then more favourable to the ingroup. Such was the case in Brown's (1978) factory study mentioned above, where the workers' concern was over differentials amongst themselves rather than with the much larger difference between themselves and management. In another context, Rosenberg and Simmons (1972) found self-esteem to be higher amongst blacks making comparisons with other blacks than in those who compared themselves with whites. Another strategy is to sidestep the main dimensions of comparison (on which the subordinate group is regarded as inferior) and either invent new dimensions or change the value of those existing dimensions. Thus, Lemaine (1966) found that in a children's camp those groups whose hut constructions seemed poorer than others found new attributes to emphasize (e.g. the hut's garden). Similarly, the lifestyle of subcultural groups like the 'punks' of the 1980s or the 'hippies' of the 1970s is characterized by a complete negation of the dominant society's values in fashion, music and morality. Still a third route is to confront directly the dominant group's superiority by agitating for social and economic change. Such were the goals of the black movement in the USA in the 1960s and the revolution in Spain in 1937, and such are currently the demands of feminist groups in many industrialized societies. These different strategies – the individualistic and the three collective – are summarized in table 16.2.

Cognitive alternatives

Which of these tactics will be chosen may well depend on the prevailing social climate. If it is such that no real alternatives to the status quo may be conceived then the first two options seem more likely; without some sense that the power relations are not immutable, it is difficult for subordinate groups openly to

TABLE 16.2 Responses to a negative social identity

	Individualistic strategy	Collective strategies	
		Change standing of one's group in society	
	(1)	(2)	(3)
Aim	Change one's personal standing in society		
Method	Leave the group, e.g. blacks attempting to 'pass' as whites	Restrict comparisons to other subordinate groups, e.g. concern by workers over worker–worker wage differences; neglect of worker–employer disparities	Change the dimensions of comparison, e.g. adoption of new cultural and musical forms by 'punks' in Britain	Direct confrontation with dominant group, e.g. demands for social change by feminists in industrialized countries
Possible outcomes	Some individuals may benefit, but many unable to; position of groups unchanged	Some changes may occur among subordinate groups; major status differences between groups unchanged	May create climate for change if new dimensions achieve social recognition	May lead to change if society is unstable and dominant group's position is under challenge from other directions

challenge the existing order (the third strategy). Tajfel and Turner (1979) have proposed that for such 'cognitive alternatives' to exist some perception of instability and illegitimacy is necessary. The system must be seen to be changing and to be based on arbitrary principles of justice. Experimental studies support this idea. Where laboratory groups coexist in stable and justifiable status relations, subordinate groups show little sign of throwing off their inferiority; if, however, the status hierarchy is implied to be flexible or unfair then the subordinate groups respond by displaying strong ingroup favouritism and hostility towards the dominant group (Brown and Ross, 1982; Caddick, 1982; Turner and Brown, 1978).

Relative deprivation

A rather similar conclusion is reached by Runciman (1966) and Gurr (1970). They argue that a key factor in generating social unrest amongst subordinate groups is a sense of relative deprivation. *Relative deprivation* arises from a perceived discrepancy between what one has and what one feels entitled to. This discrepancy can arise from comparison either with one's own group in the past (Davies, 1969) or, more often, with other groups (Runciman, 1966). Where these comparisons reveal a gap between achievements and aspirations, then people will often feel sufficiently motivated to attempt social change. This will be especially true, as Walker and Pettigrew (1984) have argued, where the comparisons are made on an intergroup basis rather than between self and others. In this they strongly endorse the importance of Runciman's (1966) distinction between 'egoistic' and 'fraternalistic' deprivation – a distinction ignored in many treatments of relative deprivation (e.g. Crosby, 1976; Gurr, 1970). The significance of relative deprivation as a factor generating unrest is supported by a number of studies. Gurr (1970) correlated the level of relative deprivation in 13 countries – as measured by people's ideal–actual discrepancies on Cantril's (1965) self-anchoring scale – with an index of societal turmoil derived from archival sources. As predicted, the correlation was positive; those samples showing the most relative deprivation tended to have more demonstrations and riots. A more direct connection between deprivation and political action was established by Vanneman and Pettigrew (1972) and Abeles (1976). Vanneman and Pettigrew found that amongst whites in the USA the holding of racist attitudes and support for conservative political candidates was related to the white respondents' feelings of relative deprivation, thus showing that relative deprivation can be experienced by dominant groups as well as by subordinate groups. Abeles (1976), on the other side of the coin, discovered that black militancy in the USA was correlated with relative deprivation and, interestingly, that levels of militancy appeared to be higher amongst blacks of higher economic and educational status – groups who objectively were less deprived (in an absolute sense) than poorer and less well-educated blacks. Finally, Guimond and Dubé-Simard (1983) found that fraternalistic, but not egoistic, relative deprivation was reliably correlated with support for Quebec nationalism in Canada. A recurring theme in all these

studies is the importance of perceived illegitimacy in generating dissatisfaction
with the status quo.

Summary and Conclusion

This chapter began with two violent intergroup encounters. In the pages which
followed various social-psychological theories were examined which have been
proffered as explanations of scenes such as these. How successful are they in
doing this? It is not difficult to see that, taken singly, not one of the approaches
can plausibly claim to have provided the whole – or even most of – the answer,
if by 'the answer' we mean being able to explain why the events happened
where, when and as they did. Mainly this lack of explanatory power has to do
with a point which was made at the outset but is worth re-emphasizing here.
Social events have historical precursors, and are often controlled by economic
and political processes far beyond the reach of any purely social-psychological
analysis. This means that, as social psychologists, we ought to be suitably
modest in our ambitions to be able to explain them.

But, even with this caveat firmly in mind, it seems that none of the
approaches by itself really provides an adequate explanation of what happened
at Orgreave or Brussels. To be sure, in both cases we have examples of what
look like mob rule in action, a display of aggressive behaviour not normally
seen in polite society. But a closer inspection revealed that this 'crowd instinct'
explanation did little justice to the rational side of group behaviour. However
distasteful we may regard what happened, we have to recognize that the
protagonists involved did actually have objectives when perpetrating their acts
of violence: these were not completely arbitrary or random. To be sure, also,
some of these protagonists were more involved in the conflict than others, and
doubtless there are some personality variables which predispose some
individuals to greater outgroup hostility than others. But when one observes
the active and simultaneous involvement of such large numbers of
people – whether outside that coking depot or in the football stadium – it
seems unlikely that everyone involved was so individually predisposed. On the
other hand, both events seemed like classic examples of 'realistic
conflicts' – the type described by Sherif. The miners and the police were
disputing the territory outside the depot and, more generally, engaged in a
political struggle over the conduct of industrial disputes. The fighting Liverpool and Juventus fans, too, could be regarded as reflecting on the terraces the
objective conflict over European football supremacy to be disputed on the
field itself. But even this analysis, useful though it is, takes for granted the
groups concerned and the psychological significance of those groups for their
members. Being a miner (or a policeman), a Juventus (or Liverpool) supporter,
was important for those involved far beyond the immediate context in which
they were so tragically participating. For many of them, their whole lives – or,
as we might say in psychological language, their whole *identities* – were
dominated by the fortunes of their group. What happened to the group

mattered to them, and they would be prepared to risk injury or imprisonment to defend it. In short, therefore, a viable social-psychological explanation of intergroup behaviour is likely to draw on more than one of the theories considered here. On their own, each has its weaknesses; taken together, their strengths provide us with, if not the end of the story, then at least a promising beginning.

Notes

1 This last stage was not included in the two earlier experiments. There were also some differences in the group formation phase which will be noted presently.
2 The following should be noted for figure 16.1:
   (a) On each page subjects must choose one box.
   (b) This is one of several different types of matrix used. It was designed to measure the tendency to *maximize the difference* (MD) between ingroup and outgroup recipients. In the experiment this matrix would be presented to each subject at least twice: once as shown, and once with the group affiliations of the two recipients reversed.
   (c) In the original experiments 1 point = 0.1 p. Given that each booklet contained some 16 pages (each with point values ranging from 1 to 29), the total amount of money which each person thought he was dispensing was not inconsiderable. In 1970 this probably amounted to about £0.50 which, at today's prices, is probably equivalent to around £3.00.
3 In a later experiment this was made still flimsier by tossing a coin to determine group membership. Similar results were found (Billig and Tajfel, 1973).
4 Actually, in the original experiments just referred to, evidence for this process of category assimilation was *not* found (Tajfel and Wilkes, 1963; Eiser, 1971). However, other experiments *have* found such evidence (e.g. Doise, Deschamps and Meyer, 1978).
5 Here again is a further parallel with Festinger's (1954) theory: Festinger suggested that ability comparisons within the group would be subject to a 'unidirectional drive upwards' (Festinger, 1954, p. 124). Note, however, that Festinger believed that the kind of intergroup comparisons we are discussing here are rarely made (p. 136).

Glossary Terms

Categorical differentiation
Ingroup
Intergroup behaviour
Interpersonal – (inter)group
   continuum
Minimal group paradigm

Outgroup
Prejudice
Social identity
Stereotype
Superordinate goal

Further Reading

Brown, R. J. (1988) *Group Processes:dynamics within and between groups*. Oxford: Basil Blackwell. A thorough overview of the field.
Doise, W. (1976) *L'articulation psychosociologique et les relations entre groupes*. Brussels: De Boeck. Also published in English as *Groups and Individuals*,

Cambridge: Cambridge University Press, 1978. A review of early intergroup relations research from the social categorization perspective.

Hamilton, D. L. (ed.) (1981) *Cognitive Processes in Stereotyping and Intergroup Behaviour*. Hillsdale, N. J.: Erlbaum. A collection of chapters emphasizing cognitive aspects of intergroup behaviour, concentrating particularly on North American Research.

Hewstone, M. and Brown, R. J. (eds) (1986) *Contact and Conflict in Intergroup Encounters*. Oxford: Basil Blackwell. A collection of chapters examining the contact hypothesis in several international contexts, and developing a new 'intergroup' approach.

Sherif, M. (1966) *Group Conflict and Cooperation: their social psychology*. London: Routledge & Kegan Paul. A concise account of Sherif's theory and a summary of his summer-camp studies.

Tajfel, H. (1981) *Human Groups and Social Categories: studies in social psychology*. Cambridge: Cambridge University Press. Contains all Tajfel's major theoretical and empirical writing, from his early research on the categorization of physical stimuli to his more recent work on social identity.

Turner, J. C. and Giles, H. (eds) (1981) *Intergroup Behaviour*. Oxford: Basil Blackwell. A collection of theoretical and review chapters covering most aspects of intergroup behaviour, mainly from a social identity perspective.

Worchel, S. and Austin, W. (eds) (1985) *Psychology of Intergroup Relations*. Chicago: Nelson Hall. A wide-ranging collection of theoretical and empirical chapters covering all aspects of intergroup behaviour.

EPILOGUE

17 Applied Social Psychology

GEOFFREY M. STEPHENSON

Introduction

Application benefits social psychology

It is in the nature of social psychology to be applicable. Many core processes studied by social psychologists – communication, bargaining, intergroup relations, persuasion and others – are institutionalized in various areas of social, organizational and political life. Hence they offer good opportunities for social psychologists to apply their knowledge and, reciprocally, for social psychology itself to be enhanced directly by study of these phenomena in real-life settings. For example, it may be that health campaigns – e.g. to induce people to give up smoking – can be improved by the application of social-psychological studies of persuasion, and in turn it may be that the relative effectiveness of different health campaigns can contribute to our theoretical understanding of attitude change (see chapter 8). To take another example, industrial negotiations are not always successful, as the strike record in many industrialized societies indicates: so will laboratory studies of bargaining indicate why things sometimes go wrong, and can an analysis of successful and unsuccessful industrial negotiations enhance our understanding of the bargaining relationship (see chapter 13)? Hospital and other patients frequently complain of failures in communication: can the social psychologist's knowledge of verbal and non-verbal communication be put to good use in that domain, and what do real-life failures in communication tell us about the processes of interpersonal communication (see chapter 9)? In London, community liaison officers have been appointed by the Metropolitan Police whose task it is, amongst other things, to improve relations between the police and the black community in London. Can social psychologists who study intergroup relations give those officers any sound advice on how to proceed? And can the officers reasonably be expected to comment on the soundness of the principles embodied in that advice (see chapter 16)? On the face of it, social psychology should be applicable. Equally, social psychologists have realized that studies of phenomena in 'the real world', far from threatening the purity of the discipline, are vital to its proper development.

Social psychology's social role

It can be argued that an important factor underlying the 'crisis' in social psychology that occurred in the late 1960s and 1970s was the feeling that experimental social psychology was not very useful. Ring (1967), in his influential indictment of experimental social psychology's 'frivolous values', argued persuasively that many studies in social psychology had no bearing on any important issues in social life. One powerful message from his article was that social psychology *should* be applicable but demonstrably was not! Experimental social psychology has changed its image since Ring's stinging attack, and certainly it is to be hoped that a reader who has arrived at this point in the book will have been impressed by the *importance* of the broad social issues which social psychologists address: obedience to authority, social and intellectual development, aggression between groups, the nature of altruism, and so on. Such issues have been topics of philosophical, educational and political debate for centuries, but can now be shown also to be amenable to scientific study. Social psychologists are potentially able to contribute a distinctive viewpoint to the analysis and discussion of important social problems and social issues. At the same time, however, social psychologists are beginning to recognize that the work of other disciplines offers a rich source of material which they can make use of. For example, social psychologists interested in attribution of responsibility may turn profitably to works of legal scholarship as a resource for their own theoretical and experimental work (Fincham and Jaspars, 1980; Lloyd-Bostock, 1984).

Whilst there is agreement about the principle of the applicability of social psychology, social psychologists differ in the role that they ascribe to application. The difference lies primarily between those who adopt what we may call a pure science model of application, and those who favour a social science model. Let us describe the two approaches in turn.

The Pure Science Model

Solving social problems

In his forthright defence of the **generalizability** of experimental social psychology, Turner (1981b) sees applied social psychology as a form of 'social engineering':

> It [applied social psychology] would not usurp politics in this role but would inevitably be subordinated to it in terms of feasible objectives – which in turn would demand that political and social goals be explicit and acceptable. Its function would be to optimize social institutions and practices by employing

specifically social psychological theory to analyse and reconstruct social arrangements to ensure the better achievement of their goals. (p. 31)

In other words, social psychology takes political and social objectives as 'givens' that it accepts uncritically. By virtue of their expertise, social psychologists may rightly criticize the *practices* by which institutions and their representatives in society attempt to implement these objectives. For example, the deterrence or, if necessary, the pursuit and punishment of those who offend against the law are objectives that are taken for granted. Social psychologists may, as social psychologists, merely advise on how *best* to deter, catch or punish: social psychologists are technical advisers.

This **pure science model** is portrayed in figure 17.1. The *practices* by which institutional goals are implemented, but not the *goals* themselves, are open to criticism by social psychologists as likely to be ineffective or inadequate in some respect. Suggested modifications may be accepted, and outcomes influenced accordingly. This is a process which occurs explicitly as a result of recommendations made by consultant social psychologists, or it may occur more gradually as knowledge accumulates in a particular domain. For example, there is considerable concern in a number of countries about the dangers of relying exclusively on eye-witness identification of a criminal suspect. Scepticism concerning the relationship between the confidence of an identification and its accuracy (it approaches zero) dates back to the work of Munsterberg (1908), but only recently has an injunction gone out in England that such evidence *should not* be relied upon when it is uncorroborated.

The pure science model in practice

This pure science model sets the *applied* social psychologist apart from those doing 'pure' or 'basic' research. It is a model to which many social psychologists would subscribe, and it is a model which does indeed underlie much research directed to the solution of specific social problems. In such research, an objective (e.g. to make anti-smoking propaganda more effective) is pursued by asking the social psychologist to suggest the appropriate strategies (e.g. to help design films which past research on attitude change suggests will be

FIGURE 17.1 Pure science model of application as contribution to effective fulfilment of institutional goals

influential for the target groups concerned). The social psychologist here acts as a consultant to groups, organizations and institutions.

There is one immediate problem with this role: the applied social psychologist must frequently accept institutional goals which reflect an inadequate understanding of the issues. Raven and Haley's (1982) study of infection control in hospitals is a good example of this. Infections acquired by patients whilst in hospital for other reasons (so-called 'nosocomial' infections, from the Greek *nosokomas* meaning hospital) are an apparently intractable problem; they are estimated to affect 1.6 million people per year in the US, of whom 15,000 will die as a result of the acquired infection. Raven and Haley were called in to improve the effectiveness of infection control personnel who had recently been appointed to 453 hospitals, and whose job it was to advise, cajole and threaten the staff of the hospitals into obedience of the rules of hygiene. As consultant social psychologists, Raven and Haley's task was merely to help implement the prescribed goal of ensuring the effectiveness of the newly appointed infection control officers.

The problem as presented to the social psychologists was one of obedience – obedience to hospital rules, and now to the requests of the infection control personnel. An equally compelling problem, they soon discovered, was that existing authority relationships within the hospital actually encouraged *disobedience*. For example, staff nurses frequently reported that they would be prepared to disobey improper orders from physicians. To give two instances, no less than 40 per cent of the 7000 or more staff nurses interviewed said they would obey a physician who told them to transfer a patient from isolation whilst that patient was still infectious, and nearly 23 per cent said they would obey an order to continue with a contaminated catheterization. Now, although a clear majority say they would refuse to obey the improper orders, recall that in the Milgram experiment on obedience (described in chapter 15) a large proportion of prospective subject 'teachers' similarly stated that they would refuse to give powerful electric shocks to a 'learner'. In practice, however, the majority of subjects *were* prepared to obey the immoral orders. The numbers of staff nurses reporting compliance – and they are high enough as it is – no doubt underestimate what would happen in practice.

Whilst existing role relationships were clearly the more important problem, Raven and Haley were obliged to direct their attention to the authority and skills of the officers appointed to improve infection control. Had the social psychologists been called in at an earlier stage, the recommended solution to the problem of decreasing nosocomial infections might well have been different, and based more on an analysis of the existing structure of role relationships within the hospital. The reader as applied social psychologist might like to consider to which social-psychological theories he or she would be inclined to turn for assistance in the analysis of this problem of nosocomial infections. There are many that spring to mind: theories of conformity, attribution, social influence, attitude change, attitude and behaviour, group performance, intergroup relations, and no doubt others. The conscientious consultant might also wish to make observations in a number of hospitals, using well-established interview and observational techniques, concerning the circumstances in which rules are broken and the understanding which the personnel have of the circumstances. It might also be thought important to consult managerial psychology colleagues, in order that theories of organizational performance, supervision and product control could be borne in mind: and the relevance of epidemiological and medical literature and background should not be overlooked. As it is, the consultant social psychologists in this instance had to work within the framework imposed by their employer.

The pure science model clearly separates the roles of pure and applied researchers. However, there is quite frequently a closer connection between theory and application than this simple statement of the pure science model immediately suggests. The next section explores this connection further.

Applications may be used to test theory

The results of applications of theory in the real world may act as interesting *tests* of the theories themselves. One of the first pieces of applied social-psychological research was carried out by Lewin and his associates in the 1940s (see Lewin, 1965). Lewin applied his theory of group action to a number of medical problems of the time, including that of persuading young mothers attending health clinics to follow the prescribed feeding instructions for their babies. He hypothesized that, because individuals act always as constituent elements in larger social systems, a decision by a group into which the individual has been incorporated would be a more powerful influence than individual instruction by an expert (see chapter 15).

Lewin compared the relative effectiveness of individual instruction for 20 to 25 minutes with the more economical practice of 'group decision'. In the latter the nutritionist discussed the issues with a small group of six mothers who, as a group, were encouraged to discuss the problem with each other and the nutritionist for the same length of time as the individual instruction took. Group decision was considerably more effective than individual instruction; some 85 per cent of the mothers followed the advice four weeks after group decision, compared with 52 per cent after individual instruction. For other food in similar experiments the results were even more dramatic. As pure experiments, these studies were deficient in many respects. For example, it is difficult to say precisely what are the differences between the two techniques, without knowing more than we are given about the content of the instructions and the discussions. Attitudes towards the nutritionist, amount of information conveyed, relationships with fellow group members, degree of commitment; all of these might have been 'critical' factors in determining the results. In fact, subsequent work suggested that making a personal decision (especially in the context of group consensus) was the principal factor inducing compliance (Pelz, 1965). The main point, however, is that the results of this piece of application were consistent with Lewin's **field theory** approach in social psychology, and gave encouragement to that viewpoint. More recently, a similar sequence of events has taken place in relation to applications of cognitive *dissonance theory* in social psychology. Totman (1976), for example, has demonstrated that giving patients the illusion of choice over the medicine they receive, even if that choice is apparent rather than real, has beneficial effects: the medicine is more effective because the individual is more committed to it. Such findings go beyond dissonance theory in that they indicate an interesting effect of mind over body, but they are consistent with the prediction from dissonance theory that individuals committed by their own choice will manifest their beliefs in the medicine to a greater extent than those who are less committed (see chapter 8).

There is an increasing tendency to exploit application in the interests of performing rigorous tests of theory in so-called 'applied' settings. This practice has the distinct advantage of ensuring that theory is relevant to situations outside the laboratory, although such research does not directly evaluate the effectiveness of changes in institutional practices and procedures. For example, a number of attempts have been made to examine the validity of Ajzen and Fishbein's (1980) theory of *reasoned action* (see chapter 7) with respect to the outcome of many different intentions, for example: voting intentions (Fishbein and Ajzen, 1981b); intentions of pregnant women to breast feed their infants (Manstead, Plevin and Smart, 1984); and intentions to give up smoking (Fishbein, 1982). The primary aim of all these studies was to test the validity of Ajzen and Fishbein's theory of reasoned action, but the results equally have implications for practice, for example, in health care. Let us examine just one instance. The results of Manstead, Plevin and Smart's (1984) study broadly but not entirely supported predictions made from the theory, but the authors also argue strongly from their results that attempts to increase the prevalence of breast feeding should focus *not* on changing perceived social norms (a key theoretical determinant of intentions) but on changing beliefs about the beneficial consequences of breast feeding in individual pregnant women: this suggestion emerges as a *by-product* of the authors' attempt to assess the validity of the theory of reasoned action. Such studies may play an important part in the revisions of theory in social psychology. There have also been a number of attempts to examine the validity of social identity theory in applied settings, with varying degrees of success (see chapter 16). This has led to modifications in the theory which enable it to account for the unpredicted findings obtained in the 'applied' laboratory of real-world problems. Any practical implications of such studies are, however, essentially fortuitous, and applied social psychology as such is not deemed to contribute to the development of the discipline. The 'real world' is regarded as an extension of the laboratory, a place where theories can be tested in somewhat less than ideal conditions.

Whilst the pure science model as described has some virtues, there are a number of drawbacks. First, by allowing others to establish the goals, it fails – as we have seen in the case of Raven and Haley's nosocomial infections – to ensure that social psychology contributes to the *analysis* of problems. Social psychologists have both a right and duty to appraise critically the performance of institutions – like medicine or law – as *social psychologists* and not just as lay critics who happen to be social psychologists. Second, by not actively seeking out problematic social issues which may serve to channel their theoretical interests – e.g. the effects of increasing divorce rate, the social impact of new technology in work organizations – social psychologists fail both to enhance society's ability to cope with change and also to exploit the existing possibilities of theoretical development which studying the impact of these changes will yield. There is, in fact, a growing number of scholars who would assign to application a much more fundamental role both in the development of theory in social psychology and in the contribution of social psychology to theory and research in other social disciplines, like law or industrial relations (Stephenson and Davis, 1986). Let us now examine the social science approach in more detail.

The Social Science Model: Addressing Social Issues

Those adopting the social science approach would argue that social psychology provides an indispensable and distinctive dimension in the understanding of society and its institutions. Social psychology's applied role is not, therefore, limited to tinkering, advising or consulting, in order that others – politicians, judges, advertising agencies and so on – may do their jobs more effectively. Rather, the social psychologist is required to work in collaboration with other social scientists in order to ensure that a more complete understanding is achieved of the character and operations of the institutions in question. We cannot, for example, appreciate the significance of criminal statistics, or of police and judicial response to offenders, without some knowledge of the social psychology of crime reporting by victims. More generally, to understand the criminal justice system, we require a social-psychological analysis of decision-making at crucial stages in the career of the criminal – from the decision to commit the crime, through the victim's decision to report, the gathering of evidence, the decision to prosecute, to the trial itself, the sentencing and beyond (cf. Konečni & Ebbeson, 1982). Of course, the system may also be viewed from sociological, legal, economic and political perspectives, but the theoretical perspective of the social psychologist is a vital ingredient.

Figure 17.2 is designed to reflect simply the essence of the **social science model**. Social psychology is portrayed as being *essentially* responsive to social

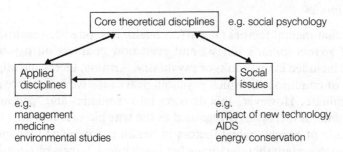

FIGURE 17.2   Social science model of application as interaction between social psychology, applied disciplines and social issues

issues, developing theories that are capable of adding a distinctive dimension to the discussion of these issues. Almost certainly this was the motivation underlying many of the major 'discoveries' in our discipline – such as the bases of intergroup prejudice and hostility (Sherif, 1966; Tajfel, 1970), compliance with illegal orders (Milgram, 1974), social comparison processes in group morale, and persuasion (Stouffer et al., 1949). It is undoubtedly the motivation underlying some current theoretical developments in social psychology in Europe, e.g. the role of minority influence in social change and social movements (see Moscovici and Nemeth, 1974). Researchers concerned with social inequalities – especially sexual inequalities – have contributed to significant advances in our theoretical understanding of the determinants of mental health (Baker-Miller and Mothner, 1981) and academic and occupational success (Kanter, 1977). Moreover, this work frequently challenges the assumptions of conventional theorizing and methodology in social psychology (Wilkinson, 1986). Theories developed in response to social issues enable social psychology to be heard in debates within applied disciplines like medicine, industrial relations and education, regarding what should be done to meet the challenge of social issues. This flow of influence from social issues to research and theory in social science through the elaboration of policy in applied fields is represented in figure 17.2, as is the reciprocal nature of the processes.

One implication of the model is that to contribute effectively the social psychologist working in these fields must become familiar with other disciplinary perspectives. The challenge this presents is increasingly being taken up, and is evident in the publication of journals (e.g. *Law and Human Behaviour*) which have a social-psychological orientation but a strongly interdisciplinary flavour, and in which social psychology helps define and contribute to the critical understanding of social issues.

Health, and the criminal justice system, have both raised issues which social psychologists have tackled with some degree of success. It is, therefore, appropriate to choose from these areas to illustrate the work that social psychologists are doing broadly within the social science framework.

Social Psychology and Health

A causal model

The view that mental factors may affect health has long been enshrined in the notion of *psychosomatic* illness, and even now chapters on psychosomatic illness are included in textbooks of psychiatry. Asthma, ulcers and migraine are examples of conditions in which psychological causative factors are presumed to predominate. However, this division into 'somatic' and 'psychosomatic' disguises what is increasingly regarded as the true picture. It is now fair to say that the role of psychological factors in health is conceived very much more broadly, to the extent that the somewhat mechanical, largely physical approach to health and illness that characterizes the medical profession looks increasingly outmoded. This transformation of outlook has taken place over the whole range of medical and psychiatric illness. For example, the medical profession in many European countries is now observing the wholesale closure of hospitals in which psychiatric patients were formerly treated (see Zani, 1987). Or again, hospitalization and 'treatment' for people with a mental handicap is now seen to have been necessitated not by illness but by society's intolerance, and as policies of **normalization** are pursued this view will increasingly prevail (e.g. Mansell et al., 1987). The 'medical model', indeed, is beginning to look equally outmoded in cases of physical illness where once it reigned supreme, and health generally is no longer regarded as a prerogative of the medical profession (Illich, 1976).

Totman (1979, 1982a) proposes that the *social functioning* of the individual is crucial to health. For example, the focus on the importance of **life events** for health, and the role of social networks in sustaining recovery from psychiatric illness, illustrate the importance of adequate interpersonal and social relationships to both physical and mental health (see chapter 10). Life events like taking a new job or moving house – which are experienced as stressful by the individuals concerned – are associated with subsequent ill health, both physical (Dohrenwend and Dohrenwend, 1974) and psychiatric (Brown and Harris, 1978). Social support and acceptance in a network of social relationships is associated with good recovery from psychiatric illness (Henderson, Byrne and Duncan-Jones, 1981; Quine, 1981). Social support from colleagues at work has beneficial effects on workers' health (Fusilier, Ganster and Mayes, 1986), and unemployment in school leavers appears markedly to increase the reported level of stress (Feather and O'Brien, 1986).

Totman (1979, 1982a) suggests that life events may have undesirable effects because they undermine the individual's ability to perform appropriately and competently. Figure 17.3 tries to portray in a simple way what Totman is trying to say. Within a given social network, people agree on what they would like individually to achieve, and they know in what way it is appropriate for them to

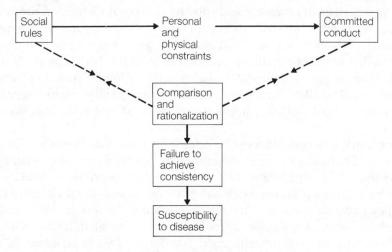

FIGURE 17.3   View of susceptibility to disease as a product of breakdown in fit between social rules and committed conduct (based on Totman, 1982a)

attain these goals. This set of knowledge Totman refers to as 'social rules'. However, various physical and personal constraints may prevent our behaving in such a cooperative and productive way, so that our *committed conduct* falls short of what we would intend. We discover this by a comparison process which leads to attempts to achieve consistency by changing the rules, distorting attributions of responsibility and so on. Too great an inconsistency leads to a breakdown in the process, and increases susceptibility to illness. Illness, on this view, is facilitated by *social* breakdown. More particularly, adequate social functioning – and subsequently good health – are undermined if (a) unrealistic standards are set by the individual, (2) the ability to rationalize inadequacies and failure is lacking, or (3) the individual is deprived of others whose performance is complementary to his or her own. What all these circumstances do is detract from the ability to collaborate effectively with others in pursuit of common goals, something which can only be achieved by consistently following rules of conduct which we share with others. Let us examine some of the circumstances in which mismatches between rules and conduct may occur, thereby creating a threat to health.

Behaviourally induced coronary heart disease

The working environment contains many potential 'stressors', that is, factors which, by causing individuals to feel under pressure, create tension, anxiety, poor performance and consequent ill health. Physical conditions, unrelenting job demands, role conflict, and intergroup conflict have all been shown to cause symptoms of stress, although it should be noted that people vary in their responsiveness to such externally induced demands (see Altman, Valenzi and Hodgetts, 1985). There is, in addition, good evidence that excessive *internally* induced demands may predispose individuals to ill health, and to coronary heart disease in particular. Friedman and Rosenman (1959) defined a coronary-prone 'type A' behaviour pattern which apparently was strongly associated with the incidence of coronary heart disease (CHD). A distinction needs to be drawn, however, between those qualities which define the type A syndrome – which are many and various – and that smaller number of qualities that appear to predict susceptibility to CHD. Matthews et al. (1977) suggest that the key coronary-prone behaviours are low frustration threshold, irritability and hostility, impatience, competitiveness and energetic voice style. Merely being hard working, achievement oriented and ambitious does not qualify.

More work has been devoted to establishing the link between behaviour patterns and coronary proneness than thought has been given to explaining the association. The significant fact about coronary-prone individuals is, according to Totman's analysis, that they are out of line with their fellows, and that they make demands on themselves which make a socially integrated life difficult to attain. They suffer chronically that sense of failure which stems from adhering to rigorous and rigid standards. This is reflected in their tendency to become physiologically aroused – with increased blood pressure, for example – in situations where their competence is called into question. For example, Glass et al. (1980) showed that competition *per se* did not raise the level of physiologically detrimental responses more amongst type A people than amongst others. What *did* produce such a difference was their partner ridiculing their poor performance.

Can those who are at odds with the world and their fellows change their orientation to life, and relax the standards and expectations by which they judge their performance? And if they do change, will this reduce the risk of CHD and associated disorders? The methodological problems of conducting research which would put this to the test are legion, and it is not surprising that so little work on intervention has been conducted. Dembroski and MacDougall (1982) suggest, however, that changes in attitudes and behaviour in type A people towards a less competitive and abrasive style are effective in reducing the risk of ill health, at least to the extent that physiological measures associated with CHD are responsive to changes in the perceived quality of social relationships.

The effects of stress on health: the example of bereavement

Many attempts have been made to correlate indices of stressful life events with illness, but for a variety of reasons the results have been inconclusive. There are, of course, methodological problems involved: not the least is the tendency for ill people to interpret events in a doleful way (see Schroeder and Costa, 1984 for an analysis of this problem).

Stroebe and Stroebe (1987a, 1987b) argue convincingly that the study of specific life events which can be unambiguously diagnosed, e.g. divorce or bereavement, overcomes most of the methodological problems associated with the more popular global methods of studying the health–stress relationship. Bereavement, by which is meant the death of a spouse, is an event which manifestly affects what we might call 'social fitness', by depriving an individual of an important role partner, and a means of social support in the individual's pursuit of social competence. If any life event might be expected to affect the social competence of individuals then bereavement is a formidable contender.

Stroebe et al. (1982) elaborate on the likely impact of bereavement from the viewpoint specifically of a social psychologist. The loss of a partner affects four main areas of social-psychological functioning, which we may define in terms of established expectations in the relationship. First, there is what the authors call a loss of 'social validation of personal judgements'. Many processes discussed in earlier chapters testify to the importance of social comparison and validation. Sherif's (1936) experiments on the development of social norms showed how fundamental is the movement towards agreement, and Festinger (1954) postulated that there is a drive towards comparison in human judgement, including those important judgements of self-worth (chapter 15). Tenets of attribution theory suggest that the loss of a partner's viewpoint would make it difficult to behave in a confidently appropriate way (chapter 6), and Schachter and Singer's (1962) socio-cognitive theory of emotion would predict confusion, uncertainty and suggestibility in the emotional life of the bereaved.

The remaining areas of loss caused by the death of a spouse, as defined by Stroebe and his colleagues (Stroebe et al. 1982), include loss of 'social and emotional support', loss of 'material and task supports' and loss of 'social protection'. The importance of *emotional* support to the developing organism emerges clearly in chapter 3, and the importance of affiliation in reducing anxiety is apparent from both human and animal studies (see chapter 2). The loss of material and task supports stems especially from role differentiation within marriage, an interesting example of which has recently been defined by Wegner, Guiliano and Hertel (1985) in the field of memory: married couples specialize in the recall of different classes of event, and are mutually inter-dependent in that cognitive area as they are in the more obvious task areas, like cleaning the home, repairing the car and changing babies' nappies.

In all these ways the social competence or what we might call 'social fitness' of the individual is undermined by the loss of a marital partner, thereby jeopardizing emotional and physical health; in consequence, especially in the first six months following bereavement, the risk of dying is heightened, particularly in men. Large-scale cross-sectional data also indicate substantial increases in the mortality ratios of widowed to married people, especially in cases where behavioural factors are paramount, such as homicide, suicide and accidents (including motor accidents), but also in those less dramatic cases which account for the larger proportion of deaths overall – coronary heart disease and strokes. As figure 17.4 shows, roughly three widowers die from strokes or heart attacks for every two married men dying from the same conditions. It should also be noted that the increase in susceptibility to heart attacks and strokes is the same for widowers as for widows, and that the greater susceptibility in men is found especially in deaths due to violence (murder and suicide) and alcoholism (as indicated by the figures for cirrhosis of the liver).

The mortality data indicated that age and sex were both significantly associated with susceptibility to illness following bereavement. Let us consider first the effect of age. Would you expect the older or younger bereaved to suffer more or less stress following bereavement? Younger people probably suffer greater problems of adjustment than older persons. Their expectations are high, set-backs are more problematic, responsibilities are high (large mortgage and young children perhaps) and the dependence upon others is correspondingly greater. However, older married couples have had longer in which to develop a collaborative, interdependent relationship. Nonetheless, one might well expect the younger bereaved to be more 'thrown' and more likely, relatively speaking, to be depressed as a result of bereavement. The results bear out this expectation, and Stroebe and Stroebe (1987b) single out the expectedness of loss and the availability of social support as the most important factors favouring the resilience of the elderly.

Men would appear to be more vulnerable than women to the impact of bereavement. That, it seems, is a more immediately understandable finding, given the known effects of sexual inequality on family life (Williams and Watson, in press). The social support provided by the partner is probably easier

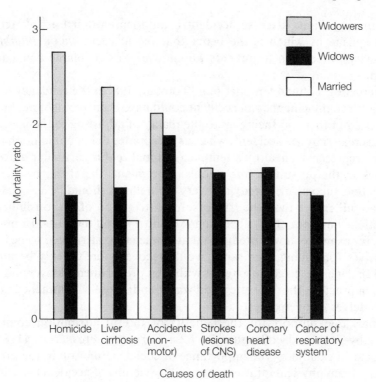

FIGURE 17.4   Mortality ratios of widowed to married for six causes of death (based on Stroebe et al., 1982)

for women to replace than for men, and women are more likely to seek it out; this fact received intriguing support from the finding of a longitudinal study, which showed that it was the *more* severely depressed men who refused an interview with the research team but the *less* severely depressed women.

Recovering from illness: an attributional analysis

It has long been known that the length of time a patient stays in hospital may be affected not only by the recovery process but by organizational and communication problems in the hospital itself (Revans, 1964). Recently, however, studies have shown that the process of recovery from physical illness itself appears to be strongly associated with the patients' understanding of their social role in the aetiology of the illness.

Accidents which result in physical injury are of particular interest in this respect. Such injuries may on occasion have been entirely beyond the ability of the individual to foresee and avoid, but in most cases of, say, injuries sustained in road accidents, games or in the home, the individual may feel that there was something he or she could have done that might have led to the avoidance of an accident or to a lessening of its impact. An 'accident' is, strictly speaking, an occurrence which was not foreseen, and certainly not intended. Nevertheless, apportioning blame after an accident is an apparently irresistible tendency, a prerequisite of which is the belief that the accident was *avoidable*. If it was unavoidable then arguments about who was to blame can hardly be started.

In terms of Totman's model (e.g. Totman, 1982a) the tendency to blame oneself, or to imagine that an accident could have been avoided, might be seen as an attempt to avoid facing up to the reality of adjusting to the new circumstances created by the accident; whereas acceptance that it could not have been avoided represents a healthy attempt to rationalize this particular unfortunate set-back in the pursuit of one's goals. One might, therefore, be inclined to predict that successful, speedy recovery from illness should be associated with the 'fateful' rather than the 'remorseful' attribution of responsibility. Such predictions have not always been made by attribution theorists. In one recent study, for example, it was predicted that women who attributed some blame to themselves for having been raped would recover more quickly because they would find it easier to come to terms with their predicament (Meyer and Taylor, 1986). In practice, the opposite trend was found: those who attached no blame to themselves recovered best.

Remarkable support for the benefits of fateful attribution comes from studies by Frey and colleagues in West Germany. Frey et al. (1985) were interested in examining the importance of social attribution in the process of recovery from physical injuries sustained by victims of accidents – principally accidents at work, road accidents, and accidents sustained at home. Injuries ranged from 'slight' to 'severe' and, of course, severity of injury strongly affected the process of recovery. Within each category of severity, however (severity having been rated independently by a doctor who was unaware of the aims of the study), response to convalescence varied systematically according to the attributions of the patients regarding *responsibility for the accident*, and also regarding *responsibility for the outcome of convalescence*. The investigation was carried out twice, the second time with a larger number of patients (Frey and Rogner, 1987) and controlling for the time of interview (within three days of hospitalization). Let us examine in detail some results from the second study, which replicated and extended the results of the first study.

In order to take into account the effects of severity of injury, all the measures of recovery or response to convalescence were adjusted so as to remove the observed influence of severity. The results showed that those patients who believed that the accident was 'highly avoidable', or that they were much to blame for it, stayed in hospital appreciably longer than those who thought the accident could not have been avoided or did not accept responsibility for it (see figure 17.5). Ratings of the healing process and subjective ratings of well-being followed the same pattern: an 'unavoidable' accident is much easier to recover from. Patients were also asked a number of questions regarding the importance of their own will in aiding convalescence and their ability to predict their recovery time: the combined index of cognitive control of convalescence indicated that those with a low degree of perceived control spent longer in hospital and felt worse.

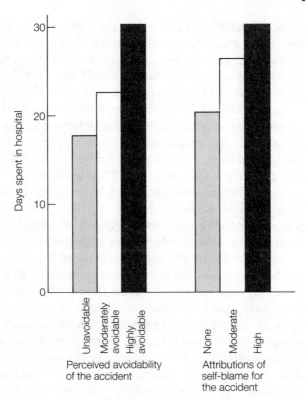

FIGURE 17.5   Days spent in hospital recovering from a road accident according to attributions of responsibility for the accident (all means adjusted to remove the contributions of
severity of injury) (Frey and Rogner, 1987)

Social psychology and health: a model of helping and coping

We have seen that social-psychological processes are important in the onset of a
range of medical disorders, and that social perceptions and attributions of
patients are very strongly related to their prospects of a speedy recovery in the
case of physical injury. At issue in all the instances we have discussed is the
competence of individuals to respond to stressful crises in a way which
maximizes their prospects of healthy psychological and physical survival. Let
us now consider an attempt to apply our knowledge to the problem of how to
assist individuals to survive unscathed.

   One reason why women face up to the challenge of bereavement better than
men, it is suggested, is because they are more likely to ask for help, and they
have more people in their social networks to whom they can turn for assistance.
Whilst asking for assistance has been little studied by social psychologists,
giving help has been a major topic of research (see chapter 11). Research has
concentrated on elucidating the characteristics of the victim who requires
assistance, the characteristics of the potential benefactor, and the situational
cues which make it more or less likely that help will be given. In addition, the

emphasis in research has been on those situations in which help is urgently required, like assisting someone who has collapsed dramatically in public.

Giving help to those who are emotionally distressed, anxious, depressed or otherwise failing to cope with the problems of life can itself be a stressful experience, leading to what has been termed 'burnout'. This concept was described by Maslach (1978) as a condition in which the professional helper (social worker, psychiatrist, clinical psychologist) feels emotionally exhausted, with little respect or sympathy for clients, and a tendency to attribute blame to the clients for their problems. Whilst social support from colleagues may alleviate the condition (see Russell et al., 1987), Maslach suggests ways in which the client's dependence on the help-giver may be reduced, by stressing the obligations of the client as well as those of the help-giver. The work on 'burnout' raises in an interesting way the whole question of what kind of help it is appropriate to give those whose ability to cope has been undermined.

Attribution of blame and responsibility have featured in the broad field of cognitive social psychology, and were considered at length by Brickman et al. (1982) in relation to the question of what is an effective help-giving strategy. They discern four current models of helping and coping in the caring professions, according to (1) attribution of responsibility to the individual client for having the *problem* in the first place, and (2) attribution of responsibility for providing a *solution* to their condition. The four models are presented in table 17.1. We are all most familiar with the *medical model* in which the 'patient' who requires 'treatment' is a passive, helpless creature who is absolved of responsibility for both the problem and the solution. The medical model has, of course, come under consistent attack in all areas of treatment, and there are some instances, for example in the treatment of the elderly, where the denial of the patient's responsibility for the solution exacerbates the very symptoms of mental and physical deterioration that treatment seeks to address. The problem of burnout for those working with clients who have psychiatric, behavioural and personality problems seems to arise from an unthinking application of the medical model's assumption of full responsibility by the 'therapist' for treatment and the outcome of treatment. In fact, the evidence that psychodynamic treatments as such are effective is slight, and there is some evidence that well-intentioned attempts at counselling over many years may be detrimental to the client (see McCord, 1978).

TABLE 17.1   Four models of helping and coping

| Attribution of responsibility to self for the problem | Attribution of responsibility to self for solution | |
	High	Low
High	Moral model (requirement = motivation)	Enlightenment model (requirement = discipline)
Low	Compensatory model (requirement = power)	Medical model (requirement = treatment)

Source: Brickman et al. (1982)

The *enlightenment model* puts the blame squarely on the shoulders of the patient, a view espoused by a minority in psychiatry (see Mowrer, 1975), and taken up by groups like Alcoholics Anonymous. Responsibility for *treatment*, however, rests with the group or organization, entry into lifetime membership of which requires conversion to a new, *prescribed* way of life (see Kinney and Leaton, 1983).

Neither the moral nor the compensatory models prescribe treatment. However, the *moral model* emphasizes personal responsibility for the problem and suggests that self-discipline is the prerequisite for recovery, a view which is summed up neatly by Glasser's (1975) observation. 'People do not act irresponsibly because they are "ill"; they are "ill" because they act irresponsibly' (p. xvi). This high moral tone is absent from the **compensatory model** which seeks not to blame patients for their condition, but rather to provide them with the necessary equipment, facilities or opportunities which they may use to deal with the problems they face at present (see also chapter 11). In many different spheres of treatment the compensatory model is coming to the fore, from 'treatment' of psychiatric 'patients' in the community, to the treatment of addictions (see Eiser, 1982). Eiser argues, for example, that smokers are able to shift responsibility for giving up smoking away from themselves, because the very concept of smoking as an 'addiction' implies the need for an externally provided 'cure'. Adhering to the concept of addiction will make the introduction of safer alternatives to smoking tobacco problematic. It encourages the idea that giving up smoking or any other drug is impossible without external intervention; this idea, as Eiser points out, will undermine the effectiveness of even the new pharmacologically based therapeutic techniques, which after all can merely *compensate* for and not cure an addiction. Doubtless Brickman's portrayal of the four models is oversimplified, but it provides a convenient coherent social-psychological framework for interventions by professionals in health and social services, and it provides a useful framework in terms of which past research and experience may be conceptualized and priorities for future work established.

Social-Psychological Issues of Criminal Justice

The decision-making sequence in criminal justice

The criminal justice system has been a particular object of study by social psychologists in the United States, in Britain, and also more recently in other European countries (e.g. Wegener, Losel and Haisch, in press). Psychologists have studied crime and criminals for a century or more, and also aspects of the legal system – like eye-witness testimony – for not much less. The concerted contribution of *social* psychologists to these areas is, however, of more recent origin. This is especially so in the field of criminology, where personality psychologists and sociologists have had the predominant influence (see Wilson and Herrnstein, 1985 for an account of the psychological contribution).

Figure 17.6 portrays the successive decisions taken by different actors as a

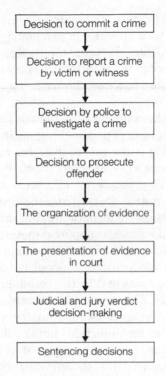

FIGURE 17.6 Decision-making stages in the process of criminal justice

'criminal' passes through the various stages of the criminal justice system, from the initial decision to commit a crime to the sentence he or she receives. In the interests of simplicity it omits a number of areas of decision-making, e.g. the decision to grant bail, and plea bargaining before prosecution for an offence. The sequence as portrayed defines broadly the main areas of criminal justice research in social psychology.

There are important questions concerning the relation between interpersonal and legal justice which have hardly been touched upon by social psychologists working within the area of interpersonal justice (for a review see Mikula, 1980), although Tajfel's (1984) perceptive discussion of public and private morality bears upon this problem. At each point in the sequence, however, there are *particular* social issues which are raised and which have been addressed by social psychologists, extensively in some areas, like jury decision-making, but hardly at all in others, such as organization of evidence by the police. Let us briefly examine some of these.

The decision-making sequence: brief review of issues and research

Decision to commit a crime   This may be viewed best, at the individual level, as a rational decision, determined by consideration of the likely benefits and costs of transgressing. Certainly much evidence shows that people are opportunistic and do not, for example, steal regardless of how difficult it is to do so without getting caught. Property marking schemes, for example, do act as a deterrent (Laycock, 1985), and expert shoplifters are highly and intelligently responsive to adverse conditions (Weaver and Carroll, 1985). Ehrlich (1982) suggests that there is a 'market' for offences, obeying economic laws of supply and demand. Not only are people directly employed as criminals, for example by drug traffickers; we are all indirectly 'employed' by the decisions of others not to protect their property, like supermarket owners who facilitate theft by permitting easy access to goods. And yet there are problems with such an analysis. For example, why should juvenile crime peak in early adolescence, and why should boys be much more criminal than girls? We shall return to these questions.

Decision to report a crime   This decision is certainly not taken by every victim of crime. In fact on average only about one-third of victims report crimes, rape rarely being reported and car theft nearly always being reported (Hough and Mayhew, 1983; Sparks, Genn and Dodd, 1977). The generally low figure raises some important social issues, given that only a small fraction – varying from one part of a country to another – of *reported* crimes are investigated and result in prosecution. Would resources be more appropriately spent on prevention than on prosecution of such a small minority? Are we justified in destroying the reputation of the one or two shoplifters who do get caught, given the vast majority who escape unnoticed and undetected? Should shops not be obliged to spend more on prevention? Social-psychological studies (e.g. Greenberg et al., 1979) have indicated some of the reasons why people may or may not report: beliefs that the police would not be able to help; discourage-ment from bystanders and friends; belief that the crime is not serious enough; and failure to feel angry enough *at the time*. An interesting sidelight from the civil law is thrown on this issue by Lloyd-Bostock's (1979) finding that victims of accidents at work tend not to attribute blame to their employers until persuaded of the feasibility of bringing a prosecution for damages.

Decision to investigate a crime   The broad question of what crimes to investigate and prosecute is beset by social and political controversy, partly because of the class bias arising from prosecution of small-scale property crime (Box, 1972). Only recently have social psychologists begun their contribution to the debate by conducting basic research on what in practice determines the police response to crime. Police discretion in Great Britain operates at different levels, from the decision of the individual officer to arrest or not, through the decision of the custody officer to accept a charge, and of a higher officer to recommend prosecution, right through to Chief Constables or Commissioners of Metropolitan Police who set priorities for their forces each year. The position has now been reached where offences are scaled on a number of dimensions (e.g. seriousness, prospects of successful detection and prosecution) and ascribed more or less police time in accordance with their priority. Grant, Grant and Toch (1982) point to the dangers of 'proactive' policing – in which police deliberately maintain a high profile in areas of high crime. Police are likely to arrest 'defiant' individuals who appear to be hostile; such arrests frequently lead to violence and subsequent charges for assault and 'resisting arrest'. Their observations show, however, that this tendency for police to generate offences was remarkably reduced during a sustained campaign to target these behaviours in one US city.

Social organization of evidence The social-psychological factor in police encounters with witnesses and suspects has not featured greatly in research. The interrogation of suspects is, however, an area that has come under a degree of scrutiny in the UK, partly as a result of a number of celebrated cases in which false confessions had been accepted by the police and subsequently the courts, and innocent people had been wrongly convicted. How could that happen? And why is it that about 50 per cent of suspects, under no obligation to say anything, nevertheless do speak when interrogated and do confess fully? Observations suggest that it is *not* necessary for police officers to offer inducements or to oppress suspects physically or psychologically in order to secure a confession (Softley, 1980). Indeed, the rule that confessions should be voluntary is generally observed. However, rather as in the Milgram experiment on obedience (see chapter 15), the *situation* induces suspects to confess. Self-esteem is low; the territory is unfamiliar; there is no accustomed social support; there is an *implicit* threat in the isolation and physical dependence on one's 'captors'; and, finally, officers are perceived to have the authority and right to require compliance (Irving, 1980; Irving and Hilgendorf, 1980). It is not surprising that false confessions *are* sometimes made, and social psychologists are now making a serious attempt to understand that phenomenon (see Gudjonsson and Clark, 1986; Irving, 1987).

Procedural justice We become accustomed to courtroom procedure from books, plays, films and television, if not from direct experience or observations. The tense, emotional drama of the **adversary system**, in which the *appearance* of truth rather than the truth itself is the uppermost consideration, is familiar even to those whose legal system is inquisitorial, as is the case in most countries in Western and Eastern Europe. Bennett and Feldman (1981) have written one of the most compelling analyses of the adversary system. They suggest that the side that tells the most *coherent* story, regardless of its truth, is the side that will win its case. Indeed, they have experimental evidence that subjects telling coherent but false stories about themselves are more readily believed than those telling less coherent but true stories! More recently, in a realistic mock jury study by Holstein (1985), it was shown that the existence of competing interpretations of the evidence (competing 'stories') in favour of the same outcome was detrimental to the achievement of that outcome as a verdict. Two stories in favour of innocence cannot be right; so one apparently must be wrong!

Eye-witness testimony No topic has prompted more research, however, than the question of the validity of eye-witness testimony, and eye-witness identification of suspects. This is germane to the more general debate about the propriety of the adversary system because, it is argued (e.g. Loftus, 1984), the results of research run counter to common sense, and juries need special guidance on the acceptability of eye-witness testimony. We shall return to this topic.

Judicial and jury decision-making Jury decision-making in particular runs eye-witness testimony a close second in terms of its popularity amongst social psychologists. Many experimental studies have been performed, examining in particular how the characteristics of the jurors – their personalities and attitudes – affect their judgements, especially in relation to characteristics of the defendants and of the victims (Dane and Wrightsman, 1982; Hans and Vidmar, 1982). There are not many firm conclusions, possibly because most of the studies have been *simulations*, in which (usually) students individually judge a hypothetical defendant on the basis of an abbreviated description of a trial provided by the experimenter. In such circumstances, quite small differences in the information provided may greatly affect judgements which, of course, are not constrained by the seriousness of an actual trial, and the social and role expectations impinging on jurors in the real courtroom and the real jury deliberation room. In real trials, as an interesting study by Kerr (1982) demonstrated, many of the factors found to be of importance in *simulations*, e.g. the ethnic similarity of jury and defendant, have no effect on verdicts, whilst other factors never studied in artificial laboratory conditions, e.g. the prosecuting lawyers' *respectfulness*, were shown to have a marked effect on verdicts (respectfulness reduces the likelihood of successful conviction).

One major question – frequently lost sight of – concerns the jury's effectiveness. Do juries make good decisions? The received wisdom, stemming from the American study by Kalven and Zeisel (1966), is that juries' verdicts largely coincide with judges' views, and that, when they err, juries err in favour of the defendant and base their decisions largely on objective evaluation of the evidence. Such a sanguine view does not bear too close scrutiny. Even accepting Kalven and Zeisel's own figures (and the study can be criticized on methodological grounds), more than 13 per cent of those defendants that the judges would acquit are convicted by American juries; another 7 per cent obtain 'hung' verdicts and are retried. The fact that these figures are together lower than those for perverse *acquittals* (20 per cent and 5 per cent respectively) is no real testimony to the good sense of jurors! Baldwin and McConville (1979), in a detailed British study which examined not only judges' but also police and lawyers' opinions of the verdicts, found a number of cases of apparently perverse decisions to acquit that startled even the prosecution lawyers and the police. There are many psychological features of groups which could account for bizarre decision-making (see chapters 14 and 15). Cliques may form within the group, and essentially irrational competitive considerations prevail. Differences in status are associated with power to influence, but not necessarily with intelligence. A dispassionate appraisal of the evidence is unlikely to occur if group tendencies towards polarization and towards consensus prevail in the early stages of discussion; and, when they prevail, processes of both minority and majority influence are unlikely to be consistently associated with truth. Nonetheless, the jury is defended as a democratic bulwark against an over-bearing state or judiciary, and undoubtedly there are famous cases where juries have established freedoms by acquitting a defendant who had offended against what the jury – and the public at large – regarded as oppressive laws. The broad political debate about the validity of jury decision-making is one that will no doubt continue.

Given that the jury system will be in existence for some time to come, it is good that social psychologists have made incisive contributions to policy debates regarding key structural and procedural variables in jury performance. For example, we may ask what effect the *size* of jury will have on the verdicts reached? Is a large jury (e.g. of 12 people) more likely to return a not guilty verdict than a smaller jury (e.g. of six people)? Or, to take a procedural variable, when cases against a defendant are *joined* (the defendant is tried simultaneously on two or more charges, say, manslaughter and criminal damage), is conviction on either more or less likely than when cases are severed (i.e. heard separately)? Or, a related question: does previous experience as a juror change attitudes towards defendants? It seems that the effects of varying jury size depend upon the *decision rule* employed. When decisions are reached by majority vote, convictions are more likely when only a few individuals initially favour a guilty verdict, and the probability of obtaining such unreliable convictions is especially pronounced in small juries (Davis et al., 1975). On the question of joined or severed trials, evidence suggests (e.g. Bordens and Horowitz, 1985) that it is to the disadvantage of defendants for trials to be joined, although this effect is mitigated if the weaker and less serious cases are dealt with first (Davis, 1984). Juror experience was also found in experiments with students to be detrimental to the defendant (Davis, 1984), a finding that has been confirmed in real-life jury verdicts. The more juries that jurors have served on previously, the more likely they are to bring in guilty verdicts (Dillehay and Nietzel, 1985).

Sentencing and punishment   These lie at the heart of the criminal justice system, but their purpose continues to be debated by lawyers, laypeople and (not least) criminals themselves. Questioned recently by a group of long-stay prisoners, visiting social psychologists were asked what 'good' it was doing to keep active, energetic people locked up uselessly in prison when they could be working productively on behalf of their families outside the prison. We fell back upon the classic justifications of punishment: general deterrence, specific deterrence, retribution, incapacitation and reform. This response did not go down well, for the prisoners' view was that for whatever reasons society might want criminals in *general* to be locked away, it was not appropriate in *their* particular case, and was serving no useful purpose. Should sentencing be tailored to the needs of individual criminals? Or should 'guidelines' give the judges little discretion to vary sentences? This is a matter of some debate

(Fitzmaurice and Pease, 1986), as is the question we shall examine in more detail later: how do judges in practice use the discretion that is available to them?

Having mapped out the field, and some of the principal issues, we now examine aspects of decision-making in just three of the areas we have outlined: the decision to commit a crime by young delinquents; the testimony of eye-witness observers of a violent crime; and the sentencing behaviour of judges. In all cases the observations of the social psychologist concerned challenge established viewpoints, expose the need for further sustained research, and indicate clearly the contribution to be made to theory in social psychology and to social policy debate.

Juvenile crime as a particular social issue

Juvenile crime has fascinated psychologists for many decades, with Burt's (1925) pioneering study of delinquent boys in London setting the trend. There are good common-sense reasons for the emphasis on youthful crime. In the first place, it preoccupies the criminal justice system in terms of the sheer numbers involved. Moreover, adult criminals have invariably been youthful criminals, so understanding juvenile crime may enable us to take measures which will terminate criminal careers before they become established. Youthful delinquency is also a distressing experience for the families concerned, and may be severely detrimental to the personal and career prospects of the individual, even though he or she does not end up as a 'career criminal'. For good social and humane reasons, then, it is important to understand why young people commit crime. Juvenile crime also presents an absorbing theoretical challenge to society and to social psychologists in particular. We may well ask why the process of socialization so spectacularly breaks down in adolescence, if indeed it does so.

Examine figure 17.7. This shows the distribution of convicted offenders by age in England and Wales for two years, 23 years apart, and it gives the picture separately for males and females. One undoubted conclusion from the figures portrayed is that the number of convicted offenders overall has increased, for whatever reasons. The pattern across time according to age and sex, however, is similar. Crime is apparently rampant in adolescence, and especially in boys in early adolescence.

Figures like these are alarming to politicians and to citizens alike. Citizens fear for their safety, and politicians view with some alarm the projections that envisage a doubling of the prison population by the turn of the century. Why is 'socialization' apparently so ineffective? And why in particular should there be so dramatic a rejection of conventional values in the early years of adolescence? Social psychology is, of course, unlikely to provide the whole story. Biological, personality and developmental psychology all have something important to say about the association of crime with both age and sex, but social psychology in particular should contribute to our understanding of why adolescents, and especially boys, choose to break the law in a given social environment.

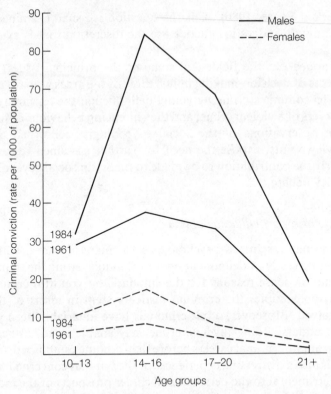

FIGURE 17.7   Number of males and females found guilty of serious offences in England and Wales in 1961 and 1984, by age (Central Statistical Office, 1986, Crown copyright)

The concept of delinquent involvement   When we ask people at large about their involvement in crime, in the context of research interviews, there is good evidence that individuals are truthful, and that what they say is consistent with what is known officially about their involvement (see Emler, 1984). Adopting this procedure, the myth of the criminal category is soon exploded. What varies is the *extent* of involvement with crime. For example, whilst few people commit armed robbery, about half admit to theft of items from a shop (Hindelang, Hirschi and Weis, 1981), and a large majority to avoidance of fares on public transport (e.g. Shapland, 1978). When a large number of criminal activities are examined, ranging from the relatively trivial to the most serious, studies of normal populations show that a range of scores is obtained whose characteristics indicate that 'delinquency involvement' is a scalable characteristic. Delinquency, in other words, can be regarded as a generalized behavioural dimension, and self-reports can be used effectively as a research tool to investigate its distribution in different groups. Use of such tests indicates that individual differences are greatest in instances of serious misconduct, and that differences are *generalized*, with only drug abuse standing out as a distinctive offence. The sex and age pattern found in official delinquency is closely replicated (Emler, 1984),

Delinquency as reputation management So why are some young teenagers, especially boys, incorrigibly delinquent and involved with fairly serious crime (and some incorrigibly good), with the majority involved in only petty delinquency to a greater or less extent? The picture that is emerging from social-psychological studies (Emler, 1984) suggests that delinquency is employed *strategically* by boys especially to establish a *reputation* amongst groups of peers. This view is consistent with the fact that convicted delinquents have been shown in longitudinal studies to have significantly rejected authority in the past, including that of parents, but especially of teachers and police (Farrington, Biron and LeBlanc, 1982). They have also been on the whole less successful at school, and come from relatively deprived backgrounds. Periods of unemployment *additionally* contribute to their involvement in serious crime (Farrington et al., 1986). The delinquent reputation may be seen as an alternative route to acceptance and prestige from the 'academic' route, and it is one that holds *some* degree of allure to all except the most diehard successful conformists: hence the prevalence of involvement in *some* degree of delinquency (Reicher and Emler, 1986).

If delinquency is employed to establish a reputation, we should expect to find that most delinquent conduct has an admiring audience. This is precisely what happens in practice. Emler, Reicher and Ross (1987), in a study of a normal population of boys and girls, found that most classes of delinquent conduct – including drugs, theft, aggression, vandalism and status offences (e.g. illegal driving) – were performed almost invariably in the company of others. More importantly the group orientation was particularly characteristic of those activities in the delinquency scale that were statistically most central to the scale, such as gross vandalism, rather than more peripheral activities like truancy. Girls, interestingly enough, were even more likely to commit crimes in groups.

Attitudes to authority are highly correlated with delinquency, a factor that statistically accounts for the difference in delinquency between boys and girls (Reicher and Emler, 1985). Precisely why the gender difference exists is not clear, but one possible explanation lies in the greater academic (or at least career) expectations that boys are subjected to and hence the greater sense of failure amongst those boys who fail to 'make it' at school. School organization certainly contributes in its own right to delinquency (Rutter and Giller, 1983), and Hargreaves (1967) documented neatly how relevant are theories of inter-group relations to the emergence of a delinquent orientation amongst members of the lower streams in a school where streaming was based on academic achievement. In line with Emler's emphasis on 'reputation management', boys who became the influential leaders were those who most blatantly rejected school values, were most disruptive in class and were most delinquent within and outside school. The *opposite* qualities led to high status in the higher streams.

Just as most children are delinquent to some extent, so are most children *non*-delinquent most of the time. It is perhaps not surprising that, given opportunities to succeed in work beyond the school environment and later still in stable sexual and family relationships, involvement in delinquency decreases, and ceases to impress the significant others in one's environment. The finding that unemployment in adulthood in itself contributes to involvement in crime should be understood in both its economic and *social* contexts (Farrington et al., 1986). Crime may be relatively more financially rewarding in periods of unemployment, but equally important it may again serve, as in adolescence, to enhance social reputation and prestige.

Eye-witness testimony

'Eye-witness testimony is unreliable' has become a well-rehearsed chant in praise of the scientific contribution of psychology to the study of legal procedure. However, neither the legal profession nor all psychologists are certain either that acceptance of eye-witness testimony is a dubious practice, or that psychologists should testify in court as expert witnesses in cases of disputed eye-witness evidence (see the debate between Egeth and McCloskey, 1984 and Wells, 1984). But is eye-witness testimony always so remiss? Do people invariably have to invent , distort, exaggerate and otherwise extend their feeble recollections in order to be able to tell a good story? The assumption that they do is evident in these words of the leading authority on the subject, who says:

> It is highly unlikely that eye-witness testimony will ever be eliminated as a form of evidence. . . . We might, then, profitably concentrate our efforts on building a research base to guide us in understanding the errors of eye-witnesses and in developing procedures that produce the least amount of error or distortion in eye-witness reports. (Loftus, 1984, p. ix)

Witnessing a murder: a cautionary case-study   The bulk of the work on which is based Loftus's gloomy premise about the errors of eye-witnesses has been carried out in laboratories, and it has concentrated on eye-witness identification of people seen under fairly innocuous conditions, or even of people seen on *films*. The circumstances in which the subjects of Yuille and Cutshall's study (1986) found themselves could hardly have been more different. Let the authors tell the story in their own words:

> The incident involved a gun shooting which occurred on a spring afternoon outside of a gun shop in full view of several witnesses. A thief had entered the gun shop, tied up the proprietor, and stolen some money and a number of guns. The store owner freed himself, picked up a revolver, and went outside to take the thief's licence number. The thief, however, had not yet entered his car and in a face-to-face encounter on the street, separated by six feet, the thief fired two shots at the store owner. After a slight pause the store owner discharged all six shots from his revolver. The thief was killed whereas the store owner recovered from serious injury. Witnesses viewed the incident from various vantage points along the street, from adjacent buildings, or from passing automobiles; and they witnessed various aspects of the incident, either prior to and including the actual shooting or after the shots were fired. (p. 292)

Twenty-one of the witnesses were interviewed by the police shortly after the event, and 13 of these agreed to take part in a subsequent research interview some four to five months later. In both sets of interviews, verbatim accounts of the incident were obtained, and follow-up questions were asked in order to clarify points of detail. In addition the researchers asked two misleading questions following Loftus's (1974) well-known procedure, e.g. asking half the witnesses had they seen 'the' broken headlight and the other half 'a' broken headlight (there was no broken headlight).

Eye-witness accuracy   The sheer volume of accurate detail produced in both the police and research interviews is truly impressive (see figure 17.8). The researchers obtained much more detail than did the police, because they were concerned with memory for details which were of no forensic interest to the police (e.g. description of the blanket covering the thief's body). Witnesses who were central to the drama gave more details than did peripheral witnesses, but the overall accuracy between the two groups did not differ, and there was virtually no correlation at all between the number of items recalled and their accuracy: more detail does not mean greater inaccuracy.

Figure 17.8 shows the average number of details obtained per witness, with

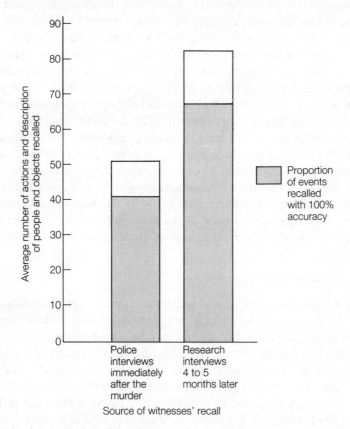

FIGURE 17.8   Accuracy of recall by witnesses of a murder (based on Yuille and Cutshall, 1986)

an indication of the number of those details which were entirely accurate. Note the high level of accuracy in both police and research interviews – a level which was maintained throughout, including memory for the *new* material which had not been disclosed to the police but which did emerge four months or so later in response to the more detailed questioning by the researchers. It may also be noted that a number of the errors some four months after the event concerned documented details like time and date of the event, and not the publicly unverifiable details of the events themselves. Many of the errors also concerned details like the number of gunshots (eight in all), which were scored very strictly for accuracy. There were, in other words, few if any *inventions*, and many of those that did occur could plausibly be put down to perceptual distortion stemming from the disadvantageous viewpoint of one or two peripheral witnesses. In further contradiction of laboratory studies, it was found that the wording of the misleading question had no effect (nor were witnesses at all misled by either question form). Moreover, reported stress at the time of the incident was negatively related to accuracy. Those witnesses who were deeply affected by the event and, for example, suffered from nightmares following it, were the most accurate of the witnesses – a result which appears to contradict the findings of a considerable body of laboratory research. Interestingly, Smith and Ellsworth (1987) have recently shown that the distorting effect of misleading questions on memory does not always occur in laboratory studies. Their work indicates that subjects are only affected by misleading questions if they believe that the questioner already knows what actually happened. When subjects believe that the questioner is ignorant of what really happened, misleading questions have no effect at all.

Of course, the Yuille and Cutshall case study by no means undermines all the evidence indicating that in other circumstances the distorting effects of reconstructive processes in memory may be much in evidence. The extreme unreliability of identification evidence is a case in point. Nevertheless, this unique study demonstrates clearly that it is not easy to ensure that laboratory studies represent 'the task, stimuli and responses in a form that captures the essence of real-world settings' as Wells and Loftus (1984, p. 7) suggest should be the case. Observations in the natural context are surely required. That is again the theme of the work reported in the final section of this chapter – on sentencing.

How complex a process is sentencing?

There are a number of reasons why we should expect great variability between different judges in their sentencing practices. In the first place their philosophies of sentencing may differ. One may be biased towards the victim and hence a relatively 'harsh' sentencer, favouring incapacitation of the offender. Another may be biased towards the offender and favour rehabilitative methods. One may see the cause of crime as moral defect and favour the principle of retribution, whereas another may perceive the need to help the individual readjust to an uncongenial society. There appear at least to be consistent differences in libertarianism amongst US judges in the Supreme

Court, which according to some researchers are related to differences in cognitive style (Tetlock, Bernzweig and Gallant, 1985). In the second place, attributional biases (see chapter 6) will operate differently in different cases. Certainly, simulation research indicates that defendants' remorsefulness, victims' suffering, defendants' attractiveness and the like, all have effects on recommended sentence which might be predicted from attributional analyses of responsibility (Dane and Wrightsman, 1982).

Third, as soon becomes apparent when talking to judges and magistrates, sentencing is *perceived* to be a highly complex process by the sentencers themselves despite individual differences in style between the judges (Tetlock, Bernzweig and Gallant, 1985). Sentences are perceived to fit the criminal, not the crime; they are 'individualized' (Hogarth, 1971), and are potentially influenced by a wide range of individual and social factors (Diamond and Herhold, 1981). The apparent complexity of the process is reflected in interview, questionnaire and simulation studies which also demonstrate that there is disagreement between studies using different methodologies on what are the important factors. Some studies emphasized the importance of family situation, for example, others employment status, prior record, or the probation officers' recommendations (Konečni and Ebbeson, 1979).

Although many factors may theoretically enter into sentencing decisions, in many legal contexts decision-makers operate within institutional constraints that place strict limits on their freedom to depart from the application of straightforward criteria. For example, Garber and Maslach (1977) found that parole hearings – which vitally affect the prisoner's interests – took a derisory 1 minute in the case of unsuccessful applicants, and a mere 2 minutes in the case of successful applicants. Questions asked by the panel merely verified a *prior* decision, so that, for example, potentially successful applicants were asked about future plans, which were duly described and 'verified' a successful outcome, whilst potentially unsuccessful applicants were asked about their current disciplinary problems within the institutions, leading predictably enough to an unimpressive whingeing performance by the prisoner which fully justified the negative outcome of his application!

The *apparent* complexity (or confusion) in the sentencing field suggested to Konečni and Ebbeson (1979, 1982) that an *archival* approach was needed, in which all the facts known to the sentencer – i.e. the judge – are examined for their association with subsequent verdicts. When this was done, in a series of 400 cases in San Diego, a very *simple* picture emerged. Judges accepted the probation officers' recommendations, subject only to a correction factor according to the offender's bail status at the court hearing (was he or she free on bail, or attending from prison). When these two factors were taken into account, only a non-significant amount of variance was left unexplained. The probation officers' recommendations themselves were determined simply by the severity of offence and the number of previous convictions, in addition to bail status. So, just three factors 'explain' the sentencing behaviour of many judges, over many cases; of those factors, two are strictly legalistic and codifiable (severity of offence and number of previous convictions), and the third represents police evaluations of the offender's 'dangerousness'.

It may well be suggested (e.g. Hood, 1962) that, between different courts or jurisdictions, different norms or tariffs may prevail for particular offences; and it will be pointed out (e.g. King, 1986) that San Diego judges may not be typical of *all* judges, and especially not of English magistrates. Social psychologists have also alleged that Konečni and Ebbeson underestimate the role which attributional factors may play in different circumstances, suggesting that judges are under considerable normative pressure to play safe when sentencing (Bray and Kerr, 1982). This may be so, but does not detract from the finding that sentencers themselves greatly underestimate the strength of situational factors, and that social psychologists may well be misled if they believe the findings from attributional simulation studies. The evidence such as we have it from these detailed archival studies is that judges by and large follow very safe traditional criteria based on the severity of offence and criminal record and the reputation of the offender, and that sentencing – contrary to belief – is not always a complex process in practice. A number of writers have in recent years expressed fears that the judicial system is dominated by liberal sentimentalists whose concern for the offender's rehabilitation makes them disinclined to mete out punishment. Robinson (1980) even asks 'Can justice survive the social sciences?' If the behaviour of San Diego judges *is* typical, we can be sure that 'justice' will survive intact.

Summary and Conclusion

These examples from the applied fields of health and of law have illustrated how social psychology can contribute a distinctive voice in debates about important social issues. The quality of an individual's social relationships may directly affect health, and the ways in which social psychologists are demonstrating this have profound implications for preventive medicine and for our understanding of the healing and therapeutic process. The examples from the legal and judicial fields have indicated in addition how important it is to the development of the discipline to employ a range of methods including, fundamentally, naturalistic observation (see chapter 4). Not only may the results of naturalistic studies *contradict* those obtained in laboratory contexts; they are needed at the very least to *complement* laboratory work, a point strongly made by Carroll and Wiener (1982) in their assessment of the usefulness of attribution theory in the study of legal processes.

The distinction has been drawn in this chapter between the pure science and social science approaches to application in social psychology. The approaches are illustrative of broad preferences and inclination in the work of different social psychologists. There is no rigid dichotomy, and in particular few social psychologists adhere rigidly to the pure science approach, developing theories independently of their importance for real-world social issues. (Of course, it would be difficult to justify the elaborate and expensive testing of truly *useless* theories, though it will be recalled that Ring, back in 1967, claimed that social psychology had plumbed the depths of triviality.) However, the pure science ethos strongly affects the methods employed by social psychologists for both good and bad. It is good for a number of reasons. It ensures social psychology's rightful and secure position in the psychological sciences, and reminds social psychologists that the issues they deal with are the concern also of colleagues who adopt contrasting perspectives, including the biological perspective (see chapter 2). It is good, too, in its reminder that *evidence* for our theories is of paramount importance. It is sometimes suggested that because our subjects may challenge our theories we should abandon the scientific enterprise and merely *debate* the issues (see chapter 4). On the contrary, our subjects' critical awareness makes the scientific demand for evidence all the more compelling.

Too strict adherence to the pure scientific model, however, would foster an elegantly irrelevant social psychology. This is most surely being countered by recognition of the fundamental role of application in social psychology. Our subjects are indeed our audience – and, rightly and inevitably, the dialogue we establish with them must inform the progress of our discipline. The social science model of application spells out the implications of that dialogue, and the evidence we have reviewed, both in this chapter and throughout the book, testifies to the growing social awareness of social psychology – an awareness which augurs well for the future.

Glossary Terms

Adversary system	Life events
Compensatory model	Normalization
Field theory	Pure science model
Generalizability	Social science model

Further Reading

Cochrane, R. (1983) *The Social Creation of Mental Illness*. London: Longman. A comprehensive account of social psychological factors in mental illness. Deals especially well with controversial topics, e.g., social class and racial differences.

Deutsch, M. and Hornstein, H. A. (eds) (1975) *Applying Social Psychology: implications for research, practice and training*. Hillsdale, NJ: Lawrence Erlbaum. Interesting historically as the first major attempt by leading social psychologists of the day to define the field of applied social psychology. Research in a number of applied areas is described and problems of consultancy discussed, as are some implications for training in social psychology.

Eiser, J. R. (ed.) (1982) *Social Psychology and Behavioural Medicine*. Chichester: Wiley. Lengthy but carefully selected collection of edited readings illustrating social psychology's contribution to the growing field of behavioural medicine.

Emler, N. (1984) Differential involvement in delinquency: toward an interpretation in terms of reputation management. In B. Maher (ed.), *Progress in Experimental Personality Research* (vol. 13), New York: Academic Press. An elaboration of the author's reputation management perspective on delinquency, compared with other perspectives.

Kerr, N. L. and Bray, R. M. (eds) (1982) *The Psychology of the Courtroom*. London: Academic Press: Contains detailed reviews of social psychological studies of courtroom procedure, eye-witness testimony, jury and judicial decision-making and methodological and policy issues.

Konečni, V. J. and Ebbeson, E. B. (eds) (1982) *The Criminal Justice System: a social-psychological analysis*. San Francisco: Freeman. The most innovatory and challenging textbook in this area of research. Attempts, not altogether successfully, to restrict its coverage to real world studies of decision-making in the criminal justice system.

Stringer, P. (ed.) (1982) *Confronting Social Issues* (2 vols). London: Academic Press. A mixed collection of articles, some of which raise in an interesting way questions of research strategy in social psychology, including some ethical issues of application.

Totman, R. (1979) *Social Causes of Illness*. New York: Pantheon. Thoughtful development of a social psychological theory of psychosomatic influences in health. An interesting attempt to integrate diverse perspectives, and containing readable reviews of unfamiliar and fringe medical territory.

Glossary

Actor–observer difference Tendency for situational attributions by the actor to be higher than those by the observer.

Adversary system The system of criminal and civil justice which prevails in Great Britain, the United States and other (mainly English speaking) countries. Under the adversary system the conduct of the trial is left to the lawyers who respectively represent the prosecution and the defence.

Affiliative messages Messages concerned with expressed affect, positive (e.g. love) *and* negative (e.g. hate).

Altruistic behaviour Positive social behaviour which is intended to benefit another person and is carried out although the actor had the choice of acting differently.

Attitude An enduring positive or negative feeling about some attitude object (some person, object or issue).

Attributional style A general way of explaining events in the world.

Augmentation principle The role of a given cause is increased if an effect occurs in the presence of an inhibitory cause.

Autokinetic effect The illusion of movement of a stationary point of light when viewed in a totally dark environment.

Balance theory Theory dealing with the organization of cognitive elements; based on the principle of consistency among elements in a relationship. Heider stated that unbalanced states produce tension, which is reduced by change in the elements (especially attitudes).

Base rate fallacy Tendency to underuse base rates (e.g. the probability of an event occurring) in favour of individuating information.

Behavioural intention A predisposition to act in certain ways towards some attitude object.

Belief Opinion held about an attitude object, i.e. the information, thought or knowledge one has about some person, object or issue.

Bogus pipeline A procedure of attitude measurement that establishes in subjects the belief that their 'real' attitudes can be monitored by an apparatus more sensitive than a lie detector.

Categorical differentiation The exaggeration of real differences between two categories.

Categorization Cognitive process which groups a set of objects that have one or more characteristics in common (associated with the tendency to emphasize similarities within and exaggerate differences between categories).

Catharsis Release of aggressive energy through the expression of aggressive responses, or through alternative forms of behaviour.

Causal schemata Abstract, content-free conceptions of the way certain kinds of causes interact to produce an effect.

Central route to persuasion A person's careful and thoughtful consideration of the arguments presented in support of a position.

Central trait A personal characteristic that strongly influences a perceiver's overall impression of someone possessing that trait (e.g. warm/cold).

Classical conditioning Through classical conditioning some neutral stimulus initially incapable of eliciting a particular response gradually acquires the ability to do so through repeated association with a stimulus that already evoked that response.

Cluster analysis Statistical procedure which finds the main grouping of measures from the correlations between them.

Co-action Two or more individuals performing the same task in each other's presence.

Co-adapted complex A group of characters which are interdependent in the sense that evolutionary change in one would have effects on others.

Coercive power The use of threats and punishments in pursuit of social power.

Cognition The activity by which information is received, selected, transformed and organized by human perceivers so as to construct representations of reality and to build knowledge.

Cognitive consistency theories Models of attitude organization (e.g. *dissonance theory*) which assume that persons strive for consistency in their cognitions (e.g. beliefs, attitudes, perceptions of own behaviour). Inconsistency is an unpleasant state which motivates individuals to establish consistency by changing cognitions to make them consistent.

Cohesion The forces that hold a group together.

Communication Message exchange between two or more participants which is characterized by the intentional, conscious (at some level of awareness) use of a mutually intelligible symbol system.

Communication network Pattern of communication channels in a (task) group.

Communicative competence The appropriate pragmatic use of social knowledge and social skill in the context of a relationship.

Communicative control   The various constraints people place on one another by what they say and how they structure conversation.

Compensatory model   The view that people who turn to members of the helping professions cope best with stressful circumstances when they are not blamed for their helplessness, but are given the skills which will enable them to accept responsibility for the course of their own improvement.

Competition   A behaviour leading to maximal relative gain: outcomes higher for a person than for the other person(s) involved in an interdependence situation.

Compliance   A change in overt (public) behaviour after exposure to others' opinion.

Computer simulation   A research strategy that involves constructing, testing and using computer programs that simulate the behaviour of a system.

Concrete operational stage   A stage in the development of cognitive ability (approximately 7–11 years) when, according to Piaget, the child is able to perform logical operations, provided that the operations involve real or easily imagined phenomena.

Conflict (of interests)   An interdependence situation in which the actors' preferences for the available outcomes are not identical (i.e. they are at least partly discordant).

Conformity (majority influence)   Social influence resulting from exposure to the opinions of the majority of one's group.

Confounding   A variable that incorporates two or more potentially separable components is a confounded variable. When an independent variable is confounded the researcher's ability to draw unambiguous causal inferences is seriously constrained.

Conservation   Understanding that a quantity (such as volume, number or weight) remains constant despite alterations in appearance (such as a change of containers, rearrangement or reshaping).

Construct validity   The validity of the assumption that independent and dependent variables adequately capture the abstract variables (constructs) they are supposed to represent.

Control group   A group of subjects who are typically not exposed to the independent variable(s) used in experimental research. Measures of the dependent variable derived from these subjects are compared with those derived from subjects who are exposed to the independent variable, providing a basis for inferring whether the independent variable determines scores on the dependent variable.

Conversion   A change in covert (private) behaviour after exposure to others' opinions; internalized change; a change in the way one structures an aspect of reality.

Cooperation   A behaviour leading to maximal joint outcomes for all the persons involved in an interdependence situation.

Correspondent inference   Perception that an actor's behaviour reflects an underlying disposition.

Counter-attitudinal behaviour   Behaviour (usually induced by monetary incentives or threats) which is inconsistent with the actor's attitudes or beliefs.

Covariation principle   An effect is attributed to a condition that is present when the effect is present, and absent when the effect is absent.

Cover story   A false but supposedly plausible explanation of the purpose of an experiment. The intention is to limit the operation of demand characteristics.

Crowd psychology   The study of the mind (cf. *group mind*) and the behaviour of masses and crowds, and of the experience of individuals in such crowds.

Cue-arousal theory   Frustration leads to aggression only in the presence of cues which, through classical conditioning, have become associated with aggression (e.g. weapons) and indicate that aggressive behaviour is situationally appropriate.

Debriefing   The practice of explaining to subjects the purpose of the experiment in which they have just participated, and answering any questions the subject may have. It is especially important to debrief subjects when the experimental procedure involved deception – in which case the debriefing should also explain why the deception was considered to be necessary.

Deindividuation   An individual state in which rational control and normative orientation are weakened, leading to a greater readiness to respond extremely and in violation of norms.

Demand characteristics   Cues that are perceived as telling subjects how they are expected to behave or respond in a research setting, i.e. cues that 'demand' a certain sort of response.

Dependent variable   The variable that is expected to change as a function of changes in the independent variable. Measured changes in the dependent variable are seen as 'dependent on' manipulated changes in the independent variable.

Dialectics   Used here to refer to the two-way causal influence between levels of social complexity.

Diffusion of responsibility   Social inhibition of helping, caused by a weakened sense of responsibility in a group of bystanders of an emergency. Each individual member of the group feels less responsibility to intervene in a group than when alone.

Discounting principle   The role of a given cause in producing an effect is decreased if other plausible causes are present.

Displacement   Replacing the target of aggression with another target, or substituting one aggressive response for another.

Dissonance theory   A consistency theory which assumes that dissonance is an aversive motivational state, which motivates individuals to reduce it. Strategies of dissonance reduction include attitude, opinion and behaviour change as well as the search for consonant or the avoidance of dissonant information.

Distraction   While listening to a persuasive communication individuals are distracted by having to perform an irrelevant activity or by experiencing sensory stimulation irrelevant to the message.

Dominant response   Response which takes precedence in a subject's response repertoire.

Elaboration   Refers to the extent to which a person thinks about the issue-relevant arguments contained in a message.

Elaboration likelihood model (ELM) A model of persuasion that assumes that the magnitude and direction of attitude change obtained by a persuasive communication will be a function of the amount of message-relevant thinking as well as its favourability. The amount of message-relevant thinking (i.e. elaboration) is determined by both motivation and ability.

Equal appearing intervals scale An attitude scale that requires the respondent's agreement or disagreement with a set of statements about the attitude object. The respondent's attitude score is the average of the scale value of the statement with which he or she agrees. These scale values are based on judges' ratings of the attitude position reflected by the attitude statements forming the scale.

Equity theory Theory of social behaviour suggesting that individuals try to establish perceived equality of the outcome: input ratios in relationships.

Evaluation apprehension The stressful experience of a person whose behaviour in achievement situations is observed by others. The experience may elicit anxiety and deterioration of performance or high levels of performance, depending on the familiarity of the task and prior exercise.

Excitation-transfer theory Sources of arousal not directly related to aggression may be added to aggression-specific arousal, thus intensifying aggressive responses.

Expectancy-value models These models assume that decisions between different courses of action are based on two types of cognitions: (1) subjective probabilities that a given action will lead to a set of expected outcomes, and (2) evaluation of action outcomes. According to this approach individuals will choose among various alternative courses of action that action which will be most likely to lead to positive consequences or avoid negative consequences.

Experiment A method in which the researcher deliberately introduces some change into a setting to examine the consequences of that change.

Experimental games Well-structured laboratory models of natural interdependence situations represented in a payoff table or matrix.

Experimental scenario The 'package' within which an experiment is presented to subjects. In field experiments it is, ideally, something that happens naturally. In laboratory experiments it is important to devise a scenario that strikes the subject as realistic and involving.

Experimental simulation A type of laboratory experiment that investigates the properties and processes of a particular sort of natural setting (e.g. a jury trial) by simulating what are thought to be its essential features in a laboratory setting.

Experimenter effects (sometimes referred to as experimenter expectancy effects) Effects unintentionally produced by the experimenter in the course of his or her interaction with the subject. These effects result from the experimenter's knowledge of the hypothesis under test, and they increase the likelihood that the subjects will behave in such a way as to confirm the hypothesis.

External validity Refers to the generalizability of research findings to settings and populations other than those involved in the research.

Factor analysis Statistical procedure which extracts the main dimensions underlying a larger number of measures from the correlation between them.

False consensus bias   Tendency to see one's own behaviour, feelings, beliefs and opinions as typical.

Fear appeals   Persuasive communications that attempt to motivate recipients to change behaviour deleterious to their health by inducing fear about the potential health hazards.

Field experiment   An experimental study (i.e. involving the manipulation of one or more independent variables) conducted in a natural ('field') setting.

Field studies   A term used to describe non-experimental research conducted in field settings. The object of such research is typically to arrive at a sophisticated description of what occurs in such settings.

Field theory   The framework adopted by Kurt Lewin and other *Gestalt* social psychologists in the 1940s and 1950s, which represented the individual as an element in a larger system of social forces.

Formal theory   A non-empirical research strategy, but typically used in conjunction with empirical strategies. A formal theory is a set of interconnected assumptions and postulates from which the theorist derives certain hypotheses or predictions about what will happen under specified circumstances. The goal of a theory is to provide an explanation for some observed phenomenon.

Free-rider effect   Strategy of leaving it to other group members to contribute to the collective product.

Frustration   An event that interferes with goal-directed behaviour; and/or the resulting individual state.

Frustration-aggression hypothesis   Aggression is always a result of frustration (see *catharsis, displacement*).

Functional attitude theories   Assume that holding a given attitude serves a number of different functions for the individuals (e.g. adjustive, ego-defensive, value-expressive, knowledge functions).

Fundamental attribution error   Tendency of perceivers to overemphasize the actor, and underemphasize the situation, as a cause of events.

Galvanic skin response (GSR)   The GSR measures the electrical resistance of the skin which changes when people are emotionally aroused. It can be used as a measure of the intensity of an individual's affective response.

Generalizability   The belief that laboratory-based experimental social psychology can be applied to real-life situations, and is thereby of practical value.

Group mind   The concept of the supra-individual nature and independence of the collective mind of a social group.

Group polarization   A change in the average position of a group, following group discussion, in the direction of the initially dominant pole.

Groupthink   A group decision process, strongly oriented towards consensus, among like-minded and cohesive individuals, resulting in one-sided and incorrect conclusions.

Hawthorne effect A term used to described the effect of subjects' awareness that they are being observed on their behaviour.

Hedonic relevance The extent to which an actor's behaviour has positive or negative consequences for the perceiver.

Hedonism (psychological) The doctrine that every activity is motivated by the desire for pleasure and the avoidance of pain.

Heritability The proportion of the variance in a character accounted for by genetic variance.

Heuristic processing Assessing the validity of a communication through reliance on heuristics, i.e. simple rules like 'statistics don't lie', 'expects can be trusted' rather than through evaluation of the arguments.

Heuristics Short cuts that reduce complex problem-solving to more simple judgemental operations; their use is generally automatic and non-reflective.

Homo oeconomicus A model in which people are seen to strive exclusively to maximize their own interests.

Hypothesis A proposed explanation for an observed relationship between events.

Illusory correlation An overestimation of the strength of a relationship between two, usually distinct, variables (e.g. 'crime' and 'immigrants'); a possible cognitive basis of stereotyping.

Implicit personality theories Assumptions that people have about how two or more traits are related, such that if a person has one of the traits, he or she is seen to have another one as well.

Impression management theory Assumes that individuals have a social concern for appearing consistent to others and may feign attitudinal responses to create the impression of consistency.

Independent variable The variable that an experimenter manipulates or modifies in order to examine the effect on one or more dependent variables.

Individualism The doctrine that emphasizes the rights, values, and interests of the individual from which all rights and values of the society have to be derived and justified (ethical and political individualism). The doctrine that all explanations of individual or social phenomena are to be rejected unless they are expressed wholly in terms of individuals (methodological individualism).

Individuo-centred approach Any approach to the study of social behaviour and social functions relying exclusively or largely on the study of individual experience and behaviour.

Informational influence Influence based on the informational value of opinions expressed by others, on what they tell a person about an aspect of reality.

Ingroup A group to which a person belongs, or thinks he or she belongs.

Innovation (minority influence) Social influence resulting from exposure to the opinions of the minority of one's group.

Instinct An innate behaviour pattern that appears in response to an appropriate 'eliciting stimulus'.

Instrumental conditioning A type of learning in which a response is followed by a reward or reinforcement, resulting in an increase in the frequency of the response.

Interaction process analysis (IPA) A formal observational measurement system devised by Bales for coding the interactions of members of small social groups. It consists of categories and procedures for coding interaction in terms of these categories.

Interdependence A situation in which outcomes of each of two or more persons depend both on what each of them does him/herself and what the other person does.

Interdependence (payoff) structure A complete set of relations between preferences of all the actors for all the available outcomes.

Intergroup behaviour Actions by members of one group towards members of another group.

Internal validity Refers to the validity of the inference that changes in the independent variable result in changes in the dependent variable.

Interpersonal–(inter)group continuum A continuous dimension of social behaviour distinguishing between actions performed as an individual and actions performed as a group member.

Judgement task A research strategy in which the investigator presents the subject with certain stimuli and asks him or her to judge these (e.g. to estimate how similar or different they are).

Kinesics The study and classification of body movements.

Laboratory experiment An experiment conducted in the contrived setting of the researcher's laboratory; the principal advantage of this strategy is the high degree of control over variables that can be exercised in such a setting.

Learned helplessness The belief that one's outcomes are independent of one's actions; attributional style of explaining negative events internally, stably and globally.

Least preferred coworker (LPC) In Fiedler's theory of leadership, individual identified by leader as 'most difficult to work with'.

Life events Changes in an individual's circumstances – like bereavement, moving house, changing a job and getting divorced – which may disrupt social functioning and lead to symptoms of stress and illness.

Likert scale An attitude scale that requires respondents to indicate the degree of their agreement or disagreement with a set of statements about the attitude object. The respondent's attitude score is the sum of his or her responses to these statements.

Lost letter technique An indirect measure of attitudes by the frequency with which apparently lost postage-paid letters addressed to political organizations are mailed by the finders.

Majority influence (conformity) Social influence resulting from exposure to the opinions of the majority of one's group.

Mental contagion   The hypothetical mechanism underlying the spread of affect and of ideas in crowds.

Mere exposure   A stimulus is merely made accessible to the individual's perception. Mere repeated exposure is a sufficient condition for the enhancement of attraction.

Metacommunication   The use of extralinguistic cues (e.g. smiling) to qualify the referential, verbal content (e.g. 'oh, I hate you').

Minimal Group Paradigm   A set of experimental procedures designed to create *ad hoc* groups on essentially arbitrary criteria with no interaction within or between them, and with no knowledge of who else belongs to each group. Once such a situation has been created people's perceptions of or reward allocations to the groups may be measured.

Minority influence (innovation)   Social influence resulting from exposure to the opinions of the minority of one's group.

Misattribution   Erroneous attribution (typically induced by the experimenter) of an emotional response to a cause that could not have been responsible for the emotional experience.

Mixed-motive game (conflict)   A conflict in which the involved parties' preferences for the available outcomes are discordant but not contradictory.

Modelling   The tendency for individuals to acquire new (and more complex) forms of behaviour by observing this behaviour, and its consequences, in real-life or symbolic models.

Moro reflex   A response of the newborn, evolutionarily related to a pattern functioning in attachment to the mother.

Multidimensional scaling   Statistical procedure which finds the dimensions which best represent a set of data where the distances between the data points are known.

Non-common effects principle   An analysis of the effects of various alternatives available to an actor; non-common or unique effects are informative.

Normalization   The principle by which people with mental handicap are regarded as being entitled to the same living conditions, services and choices as are regularly enjoyed by the majority.

Normative influence   Influence based on the need to be accepted and approved by others.

Normative model   Standard, optimally correct way of making an inference or judgement.

Norm of reciprocity   Normative belief which prescribes a mutual give and take.

Norm of social responsibility   Normative belief which prescribes that people should help others who are dependent on them.

Norms   Implicit or explicit rules specifying what one ought to do or to neglect.

Obedience   Carrying out the orders given by a person invested with authority.

Obtrusive measures   Are those which make the subject aware of the fact that his or her behaviour is being observed and recorded, and therefore carry the risk that the subject will modify his or her behaviour in the light of that awareness.

One-shot case study   A research design in which observations are made on a group after some event has occurred or some manipulation has been introduced. The problem is that there is nothing with which these observations may be compared, so one has no way of knowing whether the event or manipulation had an effect.

Outgroup   A group to which a person does not belong, or thinks he or she does not.

Over-justification   Individuals are rewarded for performing a task which they previously found interesting in itself. This over-justification decreases their liking for the task.

Paralinguistics   Those vocal characteristics of speech referred to as 'tone of voice' (e.g. pitch, loudness).

Participant observation   A method of observation in which the researcher studies the target group or community from within, making careful records of what he or she observes.

Path analysis   Calculation of causal links between variables by multiple regression to find which variables earlier in time predict later ones.

Peripheral route to persuasion   Subsumes those persuasion processes that are not based on issue-relevant thinking (e.g. classical conditioning, heuristic processing).

Personalism   The degree to which a perceiver believes that another's behaviour is directed at him or her.

Persuasion   Change in opinion, attitude or behaviour that occurs through persuasive communications.

Persuasive communications   Communications that advocate a position and typically present one or more arguments designed to support it.

Pluralistic ignorance   Erroneous conclusion of each bystander in a group of observers of an emergency that the other bystanders interpret the event as harmless.

Polygyny   The tendency of one male to mate with one or more females.

Positivism   The doctrine according to which knowledge should be based on natural phenomena and their temporal and spatial relationships as identified and verified by the methods (methodology) of empirical science.

Post-experimental enquiry   A technique advocated by Orne for detecting the operation of demand characteristics. The subject is carefully interviewed after participation in an experiment, the object being to assess perceptions of the purpose of the experiment.

Post-test only control group design   A minimal design for a true experiment. Subjects are randomly allocated to one of two groups. One group is exposed to the independent variable; another (the control group) is not. Both groups are assessed on the dependent variable, and comparison of the two groups on this measure indicates whether or not the independent variable had an effect.

Pragmatics   The study of the social relations implicit in language and language use.

Prejudice   A derogatory attitude or set of attitudes towards all or most of the members of a group.

Preoperational stage   A stage in the development of cognitive ability (approximately 2–7 years) during which the child is able to reason intuitively and represent things symbolically, but is not yet able to perform logical mental operations.

Primacy effect   The tendency for information received early to have a stronger influence than later information on one's judgements or memory about persons, objects or issues.

Priming   The finding that a *schema* is more likely to be activated if it has recently been used in the past.

Pro-attitudinal behaviour   Behaviour which is consistent with the actor's attitudes or beliefs, although it may not correspond to his or her attitudinal position.

Process model   A statement of the presumed stages through which information is processed.

Process model of persuasion   A model which states that the persuasive impact of a message is the product of at least five steps: (1) attention, (2) comprehension, (3) yielding, (4) retention and (5) action. The probability of each successive step is assumed to be proportional to the joint probability of all previous steps.

Prosodics   The melodic aspects of speech, such as intonation and stress.

Protection motivation theory   An expectancy-value theory of persuasive appeals in the health area.

Prototype   The best exemplar of a given category; an abstract representation of the attributes associated with a category, which is stored in memory and used to organize information.

Pure science model   The conception of social psychology as a theoretical discipline whose laws can be effectively applied to the problem of implementing the goals of societal institutions; this model implies that theoretical and applied social psychology are separable endeavours.

Random allocation (sometimes called random assignment)   The process of allocating subjects to groups (or conditions) in such a way that each subject has an equal chance of being assigned to each group.

Recency effect   The tendency for the most recent information received to have a stronger influence than early information on one's judgements or memory about persons, objects or issues.

Reception   Attending to a communication and comprehending the arguments contained in it.

Reliability   A measure is reliable if it yields the same result on more than one occasion.

Risky shift   The strengthening of an individual's and a group's tendency towards favouring a risky decision following group discussion.

Role   A set of behaviours associated with a position.

Salience   The distinctiveness of a stimulus relative to the context.

Sample survey   A research strategy that involves interviewing (or administering a questionnaire to) a sample of respondents who are selected so as to be representative of the population from which they are drawn.

Schema   A cognitive structure that represents organized knowledge about a given concept or stimulus, and which influences perception, memory and inference.

Script   An expected sequence of behaviours that are appropriate in a given situation.

Selective exposure   The tendency of individuals to avoid dissonant information.

Self-disclosure   Revealing personal information about oneself to another person.

Self-perception theory   Assumes that individuals infer their own attitudes from contextual cues and relevant instances of their past behaviour.

Self-serving bias   Tendency to attribute success to internal causes and failure to external causes.

Semantic differential   A method of attitude measurement which uses bipolar evaluative adjective rating scales (e.g. good–bad, kind–unkind) to assess attitudes. The respondent's score is the sum of these ratings.

Social dilemma   Payoff structure in which it is in the interest of any individual to act selfishly while it is detrimental to everyone's interests if all do so.

Social exchange theory   A general theoretical model that views relationships in terms of rewards and costs to the participants.

Social facilitation   Performance improvement resulting from the presence of others.

Social identity   A person's sense of who they are, derived from their group membership(s).

Social inhibition   Performance impairment resulting from the presence of others.

Social loafing   Phenomenon occuring when the presence of others results in a decrease of individual effort.

Social orientations   Individual's tendency to maximize a specific goal in an interdependence situation (e.g. individualistic, altruistic, cooperative and competitive orientations).

Social representations   Shared social ideas, in the form of common-sense 'theories', whose main functions are to make sense of the world and facilitate communication.

Social science model   The conception of social psychology as a theoretical discipline whose principles are derived from its distinctive contribution to the analysis of compelling social issues; this model imples that theoretical and applied social psychology cannot be effectively separated.

Socio-biology   The study of the biological basis of social behaviour.

Socio-centred approach   Any approach to the study of individual and social behaviour emphasizing the conditioning functions of the social/societal structural context.

Socio-cognitive conflict   The communication of discrepancies between the perspectives of two or more participants in a task, which promotes opportunities for the participants to become aware of deficiencies in their individual understanding.

Sociology The social science dealing with social systems/structures such as social relationships, social institutions, whole societies.

Speech accommodation The process whereby speakers modify their language behaviours to others present, e.g. towards (convergence) or away from (divergence) them.

Status Evaluation of a role by the group in which the role is contained or defined.

Stereotype A preconceived idea (or *implicit personality theory*) which the members of a group share about the characteristics of groups of people. By stereotyping we overlook individuality.

Suggestion The technique and/or process by which another person is induced to experience and behave in a given way, i.e. as determined by the suggesting agent, e.g. a hypnotist.

Superordinate goal A goal desired by two or more groups but which can only be achieved by the groups acting together, not by any single group on its own.

Theory of reasoned action Assumes that an individual's behaviour towards some attitude object is a joint function of the attitude towards this object and his or her normative beliefs (i.e. beliefs about the behaviour expected by relevant others). The impact of normative beliefs on behaviour depends on the individual's willingness to conform with these behavioural expectations.

Three-component model of attitudes Defines attitudes as hypothetical constructs that consist of affective, cognitive and behavioural components.

Two-factor model of persuasion An abbreviated version of the process model of persuasion. The two-factor version states that the probability of a communication resulting in attitude and opinion change is the joint product of the probability of reception (i.e. attending to and comprehending the communication) and yielding (accepting the position advocated).

Unobtrusive measures (also called non-reactive measures) Are measures that the subject is not aware of, and which therefore cannot influence his or her behaviour.

Utilitarianism The doctrine that the determining condition of individual and social action is the (expectation of the) usefulness of its consequences (psychological utilitarianism). The doctrine that the aim of all social action should be the greatest happiness of the greatest number (ethical utilitarianism).

Validity A measure is valid if it measures precisely what it is supposed to measure.

Völkerpsychologie (German = Psychology of peoples) An early (nineteenth- to twentieth-century) form of a historical and comparative socio-cultural psychology dealing with the cultural products (language, myth, custom etc.) resulting from social interaction.

Yielding Accepting the position advocated in a communication.

References

Abele, A. (1985) Thinking about thinking: causal, evaluative and finalistic cognitions about social situations. *European Journal of Social Psychology*, 15, 315–32.

Abeles, R. P. (1976) Relative deprivation, rising expectations and black militancy. *Journal of Social Issues*, 32, 119–37.

Abelson, R. P. (1968) Simulation of social behavior. In G. Lindzey and E. Aronson (eds), *Handbook of Social Psychology*, 2nd edn, Reading, Mass.: Addison-Wesley.

Abramson, L. Y., Seligman, M. E. and Teasdale, J. (1978) Learned helplessness in humans: critique and reformulation. *Journal of Abnormal Psychology*, 87, 49–74.

Abric, J. C. (1976) Jeux, conflits et représentations sociales. Thèse doctorat d'état, Université de Provence.

Abric, J. C. (1984) A theoretical and experimental approach to the study of social representations in a situation of interaction. In R. Farr and S. Moscovici (eds), *Social Representations*, Cambridge: Cambridge University Press.

Abric, J. C. and Vacherot, C. (1976) The effects of representations and behavior in experimental games. *European Journal of Social Psychology*, 2, 129–44.

Adorno, T. W., Frenkel-Brunswick, E., Levinson, D. J. and Sanford, R. N. (1950) *The Authoritarian Personality*. New York: Harper.

Agassi, J. (1963) *Toward a Historiography of Science*. The Hague: Mouton.

Ajzen, I. (1982) On behaving in accordance with one's attitudes. In M. P. Zanna, E. T. Higgins and C. P. Herman (eds), *Consistency in Social Behavior: the Ontario symposium* (vol. 2), Hillsdale, NJ: Erlbaum.

Ajzen, I., Dalton, C. A. and Blyth, D. P. (1979) Consistency and bias in the attribution of attitudes. *Journal of Personality and Social Psychology*, 37, 1871–6.

Ajzen, I. and Fishbein, M. (1970) The prediction of behavior from attitudinal and normative variables. *Journal of Experimental Social Psychology*, 6, 466–87.

Ajzen, I. and Fishbein, M. (1977) Attitude–behavior relations: a theoretical analysis and review of empirical research. *Psychological Bulletin*, 84, 888–918.

Ajzen, I. and Fishbein, M. (1980) *Understanding Attitudes and Predicting Social Behaviour*. Englewood Cliffs, NJ: Prentice-Hall.

Ajzen, I. and Holmes, W. H. (1976) Uniqueness of behavioural effects in causal attribution. *Journal of Personality*, 44, 98–108.

Ajzen, I. and Madden, T. J. (1986) Prediction of goal directed behavior: attitudes, intentions, and perceived behavioral control. *Journal of Experimental Social Psychology*, 22, 453–74.

Alberts, J. C. (1986) The role of couples' communications in relational development: a content analysis of courtship talk in Harlequin romance novels. *Communication Quarterly*, 34, 127–42.

Alexander, R. D. (1979) Natural selection and social exchange. In R. L. Burgess and T. L. Huston (eds), *Social Exchange in Developing Relationships*, New York: Academic Press.

Alexander, R. D. and Norman, K. M. (1979) Concealment of ovulation, parental care, and human social evolution. In N. A. Chagnon and W. Irons (eds), *Evolutionary Biology and Human Social Behaviour: an anthropological perspective*, Mass.: Duxbury.

Allen, V. L. (1965) Situational factors in conformity. In L. Berkowitz (ed.), *Advances in Experimental Social Psychology* (vol. 2), New York: Academic Press.

Allen, V. L. (1975) Social support for nonconformity. In L. Berkowitz (ed.), *Advances in Experimental Social Psychology* (vol. 8), New York: Academic Press.

Allen, V. L. and Bragg, B. W. E. (1965) The generalization of nonconformity within a homogeneous content dimension. Unpublished manuscript, cited in V. L. Allen (1975).

Allen, V. L. and Levine, J. M. (1968) Social support, dissent and conformity. *Sociometry*, 31, 138–49.

Allen, V. L. and Levine, J. M. (1969) Consensus and conformity. *Journal of Experimental Social Psychology*, 4, 389–99.

Allen, V. L. and Levine, J. M. (1971) Social support and conformity: the role of independent assessment of reality. *Journal of Experimental Social Psychology*, 7, 48–58.

Allen, V. L. and Wilder, D. A. (1972) Social support in absentia: effect of an absentee partner on conformity. Unpublished manuscript, cited in V. L. Allen (1975).

Alloy, L. B. and Tabachnik, N. (1984) Assessment of covariation by humans and animals: the joint influence of prior expectations and current situational information. *Psychological Review*, 91, 112–49.

Allport, F. H. (1924) *Social Psychology*. Boston: Houghton Mifflin.

Allport, G. W. (1935) Attitudes. In C. M. Murchison (ed.), *Handbook of Social Psychology*, Worcester, Mass.: Clark University Press.

Allport, G. W. (1954) *The Nature of Prejudice*. Reading, Mass.: Addison-Wesley.

Allport, G. W. (1968) The historical background of modern social psychology. In G. Lindzey and E. Aronson (eds), *Handbook of Social Psychology* (vol. 1), 2nd edn, Reading, Mass.: Addison-Wesley.

Altman, I. (1975) *The Environment and Social Behavior*. Monterey, Calif.: Brooks-Cole.

Altman, I. and Taylor, D. (1973) *Social Penetration: the development of interpersonal relationships*. New York: Holt, Rinehart & Winston.

Altman, S., Valenzi, E. and Hodgetts, R. M. (1985) *Organizational Behaviour: theory and practice*. London: Academic Press.

Amir, Y. (1976) The role of intergroup contact in change of prejudice and ethnic relations. In P. A. Katz (ed.), *Towards the Elimination of Racism*, New York: Pergamon.

Anderson, C. (1983) Abstract and concrete data in the perseverance of social theories. *Journal of Experimental Social Psychology*, 19, 93–108.

Anderson, N. H. (1968) Likableness ratings of 555 personality-trait words. *Journal of Personality and Social Psychology*, 9, 272–9.

Anderson, N. H. (1981) *Foundations of Information Integration Theory*. New York: Academic Press.

Anderson, N. H. and Hubert, S. (1963) Effects of concomitant verbal recall on order effects in personality impression formation. *Journal of Verbal Learning and Verbal Behavior*, 2, 379–91.

Andreyeva, G. M. and Gozman, L. J. (1981) Interpersonal relationships and social context. In S. Duck and R. Gilmour (eds), *Personal Relationships. Vol. 1: Studying Personal Relationships*, London: Academic Press.

Antaki, C. (ed.) (1981) *The Psychology of Ordinary Explanations of Social Behaviour*. London: Academic Press.

Antaki, C. and Fielding, G. (1981) Research on ordinary explanations. In C. Antaki (ed.), *The Psychology of Ordinary Explanations of Social Behaviour*. London: Academic Press.

Antaki, C. and Naji, S. (1987) Events explained in conversational 'because' statements. *British Journal of Social Psychology*, 26, 119–26.

Apfelbaum, E. (1974) On conflicts and bargaining. In L. Berkowitz (ed.), *Advances in Experimental Social Psychology* (vol. 7), New York: Academic Press.

Apfelbaum, E. and Herzlich, C. (1970–1) La théorie de l'attribution en psychologie sociale. *Bulletin de Psychologie*, 24, 961–76.

Arcuri, L. (1982) Three patterns of social categorization in attribution memory. *European Journal of Social Psychology*, 12, 271–82.

Arcuri, L. (1985) *Conoscenza Sociale e processi psicologici*. Bologna: il Mulino.

Argyle, M. (1969) *Social Interaction*. London: Methuen.

Argyle, M. (1975) *Bodily Communication*. London: Methuen.

Argyle, M. (1983) *The Psychology of Interpersonal Behaviour*. 4th edn. Harmondsworth: Penguin.

Argyle, M. (1988) *Bodily Communication*. 2nd edn. London: Methuen.

Argyle, M. and Dean, J. (1965) Eye-contact, distance and affiliation. *Sociometry*, 28, 289–304.

Argyle, M. and Furnham, A. (1982) The ecology of relationships: choice of situation as a function of relationship. *British Journal of Social Psychology*, 21, 259–62.

Argyle, M. and Furnham, A. (1983) Sources of satisfaction and conflict in long-term relationships. *Journal of Marriage and the Family*, 45, 481–93.

Argyle, M., Furnham, A. and Graham, J. A. (1981) *Social Situations*. Cambridge: Cambridge University Press.

Argyle, M. and Henderson, M. (1984) The rules of friendship. *Journal of Social and Personal Relationships*, 1, 211–37.

Argyle, M. and Henderson, M. (1985) *The Anatomy of Relationships*. London: Heinemann, Harmondsworth: Penguin.

Argyle, M., Henderson, M., Bond, M., Iizuka, Y. and Contarello, A. (1986) Cross-cultural variations in relationship rules. *International Journal of Psychology*, 21, 287–315.

Argyle, M., Henderson, M. and Furnham, A. (1985) The rules of social relationships. *British Journal of Social Psychology*, 24, 125–39.

Argyle, M., Trimboli, L. and Forgas, J. (in press) The bank manager/doctor effect: disclosure profiles in different relationships. *Journal of Social Psychology*.

Aristotle (1932 edn) *The Rhetoric of Aristotle*, [335–22 BC] (trans. L. Cooper). Englewood Cliffs, NJ: Prentice-Hall.

Aronson, E., Brewer, M. B. and Carlsmith, J. M. (1985) Experimentation in social psychology. In G. Lindzey and E. Aronson (eds), *Handbook of Social Psychology*, New York: Random House.

Aronson, E. and Mills, J. (1959) The effects of severity of initiation on liking for a group. *Journal of Abnormal and Social Psychology*, 59, 177–81.

Asch, S. E. (1946) Forming impressions of personality. *Journal of Abnormal and Social Psychology*, 41, 258–90.

Asch, S. E. (1951) Effects of group pressure on the modification and distortion of judgements. In H. Guetzkow (ed.), *Groups, Leadership and Men*, Pittsburgh: Carnegie.

Asch, S. E. (1952) *Social Psychology*. New York: Prentice-Hall.

Asch, S. E. (1955) Opinions and social pressure. *Scientific American*, 193, 31–5.

Asch, S. E. (1956) Studies of independence and conformity: a minority of one against a unanimous majority. *Psychological Monographs*, 70 (9, whole no. 416).

Aschenbrenner, K. M. and Schaeffer, R. E. (1980) Minimal group situations: comments on a mathematical model and on the research paradigm. *European Journal of Social Psychology*, 10, 389–98.

Ash, M. G. (1985) Gestalt psychology: origins in Germany and reception in the United States. In C. Buxton (ed.), *Points of View in the Modern History of Psychology*, New York: Academic Press.

Ashmore, R. D. (1981) Sex stereotypes and implicit personality theory. In D. L. Hamilton (ed.), *Cognitive Processes in Stereotyping and Intergroup Behaviour*, Hillsdale, NJ: Erlbaum.

Averill, J. R. (1982) *Anger and Aggression: an essay on emotion*. New York: Springer.

Bagozzi, R. P. and Burnkraut, R. E. (1979) Attitude organization and the attitude–behavior relationship. *Journal of Personality and Social Psychology*, 37, 913–29.

Bagozzi, R. P. and Burnkraut, R. E. (1985) Attitude organization and the attitude–behavior relation: a reply to Dillon and Kumar. *Journal of Personality and Social Psychology*, 49, 47–57.

Baker-Miller, J. B. and Mothner, E. (1981) Psychological consequences of sexual inequality. In E. Howell and M. Bayes (eds), *Women and Mental Health*, New York: Basic.

Baldwin, J. and McConville, M. (1979) *Jury Trials*. Oxford: Clarendon Press.

Bales, R. F. (1950a) *Interaction Process Analysis: a method for the study of small groups*. Reading, Mass.: Addison-Wesley.

Bales, R. F. (1950b) A set of categories for analysis of small group interaction. *American Sociological Review*, 15, 257–63.

Bales, R. F. and Slater, P. E. (1955) Role differentiation in small decision-making groups. In T. Parsons and R. F. Bales (eds), *Family, Socialization and Interaction Process*, Glencoe: Free Press.

Ball, P., Gallois, C. and Callan, V. J. (in press) Language attitudes in Australian English: a social-psychological perspective. In D. Blain and P. Collins (eds), *Studies in Australian English*, St Lucia: University of Queensland Press.

Bandura, A. (1971) Analysis of modeling processes. In A. Bandura (ed.). *Psychological Modeling*, Chicago: Aldine, 1–62.

Bandura, A. (1973) *Aggression: a social learning analysis*. Englewood Cliffs, NJ: Prentice-Hall.

Bandura, A. (1977) *Social Learning Theory*. Englewood Cliffs, NJ: Prentice-Hall.

Bandura, A. (1982) Self-efficacy mechanism in human agency. *American Psychologist*, 37, 122–47.

Bandura, A. (1986) *Social Foundations of Thought and Action*. Englewood Cliffs, NJ: Prentice-Hall.

Bandura, A., Ross, D. and Ross, S. A. (1961) Transmission of aggression through imitation of aggressive models. *Journal of Abnormal and Social Psychology*, 63, 575–82.

Bandura, A., Ross, D. and Ross, S. A. (1963) Imitation of film-mediated aggressive models. *Journal of Abnormal and Social Psychology*, 66, 3–11.

Bar-Hillel, M. (1980) The base-rate fallacy in probability judgements. *Acta Psychologica*, 44, 211–33.

Baron, R. A. (1970) Anonymity, de-individuation and aggression. Unpublished doctoral dissertation, University of Minnesota.

Baron, R. A. (1971) Exposure to an aggressive model and apparent probability of retaliation as determinants of adult aggressive behavior. *Journal of Experimental Social Psychology*, 7, 343–55.

Baron, R. A. (1977) *Human Aggression*. New York: Plenum.

Baron, R. A. and Bell, P. A. (1975) Aggression and heat: mediating effects of prior provocation and exposure to an aggressive model. *Journal of Personality and Social Psychology*, 31, 825–32.

Baron, R. A. and Bell, P. A. (1976) Aggression and heat: the influence of ambient temperature, negative affect, and a cooling drink on physical aggression. *Journal of Personality and Social Psychology*, 33, 245–55.

Baron, R. S., Baron, P. H. and Miller, N. (1973) The relation between distraction and persuasion. *Psychological Bulletin*, 80, 310–23.

Barrows, S. (1981) *Distorting Mirrors: visions of the crowd in late nineteenth century France*. New Haven: Yale University Press.

Bar-Tal, D. (1978) Attributional analysis of achievement-related behaviour. *Review of Educational Research*, 48, 259–71.

Bartlett, F. (1932) *A Study in Experimental and Social Psychology*. Cambridge: Cambridge University Press.

Bass, B. M. (1965) *A Program of Exercises in Management and Organizational Psychology*. Pittsburgh: Management Development Associates.

Bates, E. (1979) *The Emergence of Symbols*. New York: Academic Press.

Baumeister, R. F. (1982). A self-presentation view of social phenomena. *Psychological Bulletin*, 91, 3–26.

Baumrind, D. (1967) Child care practices anteceding three patterns of preschool behavior. *Genetic Psychology Monographs*, 75, 43–88.

Baxter, L. A. (1983) Relationship disengagement: an examination of the reversal hypothesis. *Western Journal of Speech Communication*, 47, 85–98.

Baxter, L. A. (1984) Trajectories of relationship disengagement. *Journal of Social and Personal Relations*, 1, 29–48.

Baxter, L. A. (1985) Accomplishing relationship disengagement. In S. Duck and D. Perlmann (eds), *Understanding Personal Relationships*, Beverly Hills: Sage.

Baxter, L. A. and Wilmot, W. M. (1985) Taboo topics in close relationships. *Journal of Social and Personal Relationships*, 2, 253–69.

Beaudichon, J. (1982) *La Communication Sociale chez l'enfant*. Paris: Presses Universitaires de France.

Beauvois, J. L. (1984) *La Psychologie Quotidienne*. Paris: Presses Universitaires de France.

Bell, P. A. and Baron, R. A. (1976) Aggression and heat: the mediating role of negative affect. *Journal of Applied Social Psychology*, 6, 18–30.

Bell, R. Q. and Harper, L. V. (1977) *Child Effects on Adults*. Hillsdale, NJ: Erlbaum.

Bem, D. J. (1965) An experimental analysis of self-persuasion. *Journal of Experimental Social Psychology*, 1, 199–218.

Bem, D. J. (1972) Self-perception theory. In L. Berkowitz (ed.), *Advances in Experi-*

mental Social Psychology (vol. 6), New York: Academic Press.

Bem, D. J. and Allen, A. (1974) On predicting some of the people some of the time: the search for cross-situational consistencies in behavior. *Psychological Review*, 81, 506–20.

Bem, D. J. and Funder, D. C. (1978) Predicting more of the people more of the time. *Psychological Review*, 85, 485–501.

Bem, S. L. (1981) Gender-schema theory: a cognitive account of sex typing. *Psychological Review*, 88, 354–64.

Bem, S. L. (1983) Gender-schema theory and its implications for child development: raising gender-aschematic children in a gender-schematic society. *Signs: Journal of Women in Culture and Society*, 8, 598–616.

Benelli, B. (1983) Effects of language acquisition on the development of children's knowledge. *Cahiers de Psychologie Cognitive*, 3, 203–21.

Bennett, W. L. and Feldman, M. S. (1981) *Reconstructing Reality in the Courtroom: justice and judgement in American culture*. New Brunswick: Rutgers University Press.

Bentler, P. M. and Speckart, G. (1979) Models of attitude–behavior relations. *Psychological Review*, 86, 452–64.

Bentler, P. M. and Speckart, G. (1981) Attitudes 'cause' behaviors: a structural equation analysis. *Journal of Personality Social Psychology*, 40, 226–38.

Berger, C. R. (1979) Beyond initial interaction: uncertainty, understanding, and the development of interpersonal relationships. In H. Giles and R. N. St Clair (eds), *Language and Social Psychology*, Oxford: Basil Blackwell.

Berger, C. R. (1985) Social power and interpersonal communication. In M. L. Knapp and G. R. Miller (eds), *Handbook of Interpersonal Communication*. Beverly Hills: Sage.

Berger, C. R. and Calabrese, R. (1975) Some explorations in initial interactions and beyond. *Human Communication Research*, 1, 99–112.

Berger, J., Fisek, M. H., Norman, R. Z. and Zelditch, M., Jr (1977) *Status Characteristics and Social Interaction*. New York: Elsevier.

Berger, J., Rosenholtz, S. J. and Zelditch, Jr (1980) Status organizing processes. In A. Inkeles, N. J. Smelser and R. Turner (eds), *Annual Review of Sociology*, Palo Alto Ca., Annual Reviews Inc.

Berkman, L. S. and Syme, S. L. (1979) Social networks, host resistance, and mortality: a nine-year follow-up study of Alameda County residents. *American Journal of Epidemiology*, 109, 186–204.

Berkowitz, L. (1964) Aggressive cues in aggressive behavior and hostility catharsis. *Psychological Review*, 71, 104–22.

Berkowitz, L. (1969) The frustration-aggression hypothesis revisited. In L. Berkowitz (ed.), *Roots of Agression*, New York: Atherton.

Berkowitz, L. (1973) Reactance and the unwillingness to help others. *Psychological Bulletin*, 79, 310–17.

Berkowitz, L. (1974) Some determinants of impulsive aggression: the role of mediated associations with reinforcements of aggression. *Psychological Review*, 81, 165–76.

Berkowitz, L. (1983) The experience of anger as a parallel process in the display of impulsive, 'angry' aggression. In R. G. Geen and E. I. Donnerstein (eds), *Aggression: theoretical and empirical reviews* (vol. 1), New York: Academic Press.

Berkowitz, L., Cochran, S. and Embree, M. (1981) Physical pain and the goal of aversively stimulated aggression. *Journal of Personality and Social Psychology*, 40, 687–700.

Berkowitz, L. and Connor, W. H. (1966) Success, failure, and social responsibility. *Journal of Personality and Social Psychology*, 4, 664–9.

Berkowitz, L. and Daniels, L. R. (1963) Responsibility and dependency. *Journal of Abnormal and Social Psychology*, 66, 429–36.

Berkowitz, L. and Knurek, D. A. (1969) Label-mediated hostility generalization. *Journal of Personality and Social Psychology*, 13, 200–6.

Berkowitz, L. and LePage, A. (1967) Weapons as aggression-eliciting stimuli. *Journal of Personality and Social Psychology*, 7, 202–7.

Berlyne, D. E. (1954) A theory of human curiosity. *British Journal of Psychology*, 45, 180–91.

Berscheid, E. (1985) Interpersonal attraction. In G. Lindzey and E. Aronson (eds), *Handbook of Social Psychology*, 3rd edn, New York: Random House.

Berscheid, E., Dion, K., Walster, E. and Walster, G. W. (1971) Physical attractiveness and dating choice: a test of the matching hypothesis. *Journal of Experimental Social Psychology*, 7, 173–89.

Berscheid, E. Graziano, W., Monson, T. and Dermer, M. (1976) Outcome dependency: attention, attribution and attraction. *Journal of Personality and Social Psychology*, 34, 978–89.

Berti, A. E. and Bombi, A. S. (1981) *Il Mondo Economico nel bambino*. Frieze: La Nuova Italia.

Berti, A. E. and Bombi, A. S. (1983) Il guadagno del negoziante: ostacoli e factitazioni all'apprendimentio di nozioni economiche in terza elementaire. *Orientamenti Pedagogici*, 30, 491–503.

Berti, A. E., Bombi, A. S. and De Beni, R. (1986) Acquiring economic notions: profit. *International Journal of Behavioural Development*, 9, 15–29.

Bickman, L. and Henchey, T. (eds) (1972) *Beyond the laboratory: field research in social psychology*. New York: McGraw-Hill.

Bierbrauer, G. (1979) Why did he do it? Attribution of obedience and the phenomenon of dispositional bias. *European Journal of Social Psychology*, 9, 67–84.

Bierhoff, H. W. (1980) *Hilfreiches Verhalten*. Darmstadt: Steinkopff.

Bierhoff, H. W. (1983) Wie hilfreich ist der Mensch? *Bild der Wissenschaft*, 12, 118–26.

Bierhoff, H. W. (1984) Altruism and patterns of social interaction. In E. Staub, D. Bar-Tal, J. Karylowski and J. Reykowski (eds), *Development and Maintenance of Prosocial Behavior*, New York: Plenum.

Bierhoff, H. W. (1987a) Donor and recipient: social development, social interaction, and evolutionary processes. *European Journal of Social Psychology*, 17, 113–30.

Bierhoff, H. W. (1987b) Helfendes Verhalten and Führung. In A. Kieser, G. Reber and R. Wunderer (eds), *Handwörterbuch der Führung*, Stuttgart: Poeschel.

Bierhoff, H. W. (1987c) Verantwortungszuschreibung und Hilfsbereitschaft. In H. W. Bierhoff and L. Montada (eds), *Altruismus: Bedingungen der Hilfsbereitschaft*, Göttingen: Hogrefe.

Bierhoff, H. W. (1988) Affect, cognition, and prosocial behaviour. In K. Fiedler and J. Forgas (eds), *Affect, Cognition, and Social Behaviour*, Toronto: Hogrefe.

Bierhoff, H. W., Klein, R. and Kramp, P. (1987) Hemmschwellen zur Hilfeleistung: Untersuchungen der Ursachen und Empfehlung von Massnahmen zum Abbau. Unpublished manuscript, Bergisch Gladbach: German Federal Agency of Traffic.

Billig, M. (1976) *Social Psychology and Intergroup Relations*. London: Academic Press.

Billig, M. (1985) Prejudice, categorization and particularization: from a perceptual to a rhetorical approach. *European Journal of Social Psychology*, 15, 79–104.

Billig, M. and Tajfel, H. (1973) Social categorization and similarity in intergroup behaviour. *European Journal of Social Psychology*, 3, 27–52.

Bilsky, W. (1987) Untersuchungen zur Rezeption prosozialer Dilemmata: Versuche angewandter Altruismusforschung. In H. W. Bierhoff and L. Montada (eds), *Altruismus: Bedingungen der Hilfsbereitschaft*, Göttingen: Hogrefe.

Binet, A. and Henri, V. (1894) De la suggestibilité naturelle chez les enfants. *Revue Philosophique*, 38, 337–47.

Bixensteine, V. E. and Wilson, K. V. (1963) Effects of level of cooperative choice by the other player on the other player choices in a prisoner's dilemma game. *Journal of Abnormal and Social Psychology*, 67, 139–47.

Blakar, R. M. (1979) Language as a means of social power. In R. Rommetveit and R. M. Blakar (eds), *Studies of Language, Thought and Verbal Communication*, London: Academic Press.

Blakar, R. M. (1985) Towards a theory of communication in terms of preconditions: a conceptual framework and some empirical explorations. In H. Giles and R. N. St Clair (eds), *Recent Advances in Language, Communication and Social Psychology*, London: Erlbaum.

Blake, R. R. and Mouton, J. S. (1962) Overevaluation of own group's product in intergroup competition. *Journal of Abnormal Social Psychology*, 64, 237–8.

Blazer, D. G. (1982) Social support and mortality in an elderly community population. *American Journal of Epidemiology*, 115, 684–94.

Blumenthal, M., Kahn, R. L., Andrews, F. M. and Head, K. B. (1972) *Justifying Violence: the attitudes of American men*. Ann Arbor: Institute for Social Research.

Blumer, H. (1946) Collective behavior. In A. M. Lee (ed.), *New Outlines of the Principles of Sociology*, New York: Barnes & Noble.

Bordens, K. S. and Horowitz, I. A. (1985) Joinder of criminal offences: a review of the legal and psychological literature. *Law and Human Behavior*, 9, 339–53.

Borgida, E. and Brekke, N. (1981) The base rate fallacy in attribution and prediction. In J. H. Harvey, W. Ickes and R. F. Kidd (eds), *New Directions in Attribution Research* (vol. 3), Hillsdale, NJ: Erlbaum.

Bornstein, G., Crum, L., Wittenbraker, J., Harring, K., Insko, C. A. and Thibaut, J. (1983a) On the measurement of social orientations in the minimal group paradigm. *European Journal of Social Psychology*, 13, 321–50.

Bornstein, G., Crum, L., Wittenbraker, J., Harring, K., Insko, C. A. and Thibaut, J. (1983b) Reply to Turner's comments. *European Journal of Social Psychology*, 13, 369–81.

Bourhis, R. Y. and Giles, H. (1977) The language of intergroup distinctiveness. In H. Giles (ed.), *Language, Ethnicity and Intergroup Relations*, London: Academic Press.

Bourhis, R. Y., Giles, H., Leyens, J.-P. and Tajfel, H. (1978) Psycholinguistic distinctiveness: language divergence in Belgium. In H. Giles and R. St Clair (eds), *Language and Social Psychology*, Oxford: Basil Blackwell.

Bovet M., Parrar-Dayan, S. and Deshusses-Addor, D. (1981) Peut-on parler de precocité et de regression dans la conservation? I: Precocité, *Archives de Psychologie*, 49, 289–303.

Bower, G. H. (1981) Emotional mood and memory. *American Psychologist*, 36, 129–48.

Bowlby, J. (1969) *Attachment and Loss. Vol. 1: Attachment*. Harmondsworth: Penguin.

Box, S. (1972) *Deviance, Reality and Society*. London: Holt, Rinehart & Winston.

Boyd, R. and Richerson, P. J. (1986) *Culture and the Evolutionary Process*. Chicago: Chicago University Press.

Brackwede, D. (1980) Das Bogus-Pipeline-Paradigma: Eine Übersicht über bisherige experimentelle Ergebnisse. *Zeitschrift für Sozialpsychologie*, 11, 56–9.

Bradac, J. J., Friedman, E. and Giles, H. (1986) A social approach to propositional communication: speakers lie to hearers. In G. McGregor (ed.), *Speaking for Hearers*, Oxford: Pergamon.

Bradac, J. J., Tardey, C. H. and Hosman, L. A. (1980) Disclosure styles and a list at their genesis. *Human Communication Research*, 6, 228–38.

Bradac, J. J. and Wisegarver, R. (1984) Ascribed status, lexical diversity and accent: determinants of perceived status, solidarity and control of speech style. *Journal of Language and Social Psychology*, 3, 239–56.

Bradbury, T. N. and Fincham, F. D. (in press) Assessing spontaneous attributions in marital interaction: methodological and conceptual considerations. *Journal of Social and Clinical Psychology*.

Bradley, C. W. (1978) Self-serving biases in the attribution process: a re-examination of the fact or fiction question. *Journal of Personality and Social Psychology*, 35, 56–71.

Brandstaetter, J. (1982) Apriorische Elemente in Psychologischeen Experimenten. *Zeitschrift fuer Sozialpsychlogie*, 13, 267–77.

Branthwaite, A., Doyle, S. and Lightbown, N. (1979) The balance between fairness and discrimination. *European Journal of Social Psychology*, 9, 149–63.

Bray, R. M. and Kerr, N. L. (1982) Methodological considerations in the study of the psychology of the courtroom. In N. L. Kerr and R. M. Bray (eds), *The Psychology of the Courtroom*, London: Academic Press.

Breckler, S. J. (1984) Empirical validation of affect, behavior, and cognition as distinct components of attitude. *Journal of Personality and Social Psychology*, 47, 1191–205.

Brewer, M. B. (1979) Ingroup bias in the minimal intergroup situation: a cognitive-motivational analysis. *Psychological Bulletin*, 86, 307–24.

Brewer, M. B. and Kramer, R. M. (1985) The psychology of intergroup attitudes and behaviour. *Annual Review of Psychology*, 36, 219–43.

Brewin, C. R. (1985) Depression and causal attributions: what is their relation? *Psychological Bulletin*, 98, 297–309.

Brickman, P., Rabinowitz, V. C., Karuza, J., Jr, Coates, D., Cohn, E. and Kidder, L. (1982) Models of helping and coping. *American Psychologist*, 37, 368–84.

Brickman, P., Ryan, K. and Wortman, C. B. (1975) Causal chains: attribution of responsibility as a function of immediate and prior causes. *Journal of Personality and Social Psychology*, 32, 1060–7.

Bringle, R. G. and Buunk, B. (1985) Jealousy and social behavior: a review of person, relationship, and situational determinants. In P. Shaver (ed.), *Self, Situations and Social Behavior, Review of Personality and Social Psychology*, 6, 241–64.

Brislin, R. W. (1981) *Cross-Cultural Encounters: face-to face interaction*. New York: Pergamon.

Brouwer, D., Gerritsen, M. and DeHaan, D. (1979) Speech differences between women and men: on the wrong track? *Language in Society*, 8, 33–50.

Brown, G. W. and Harris, T. (1978) *Social Origins of Depression*. London: Tavistock.

Brown, P. and Fraser, C. (1979) Speech as a marker of situation. In K. R. Scherer and H. Giles (eds), *Social Markers in Speech*, Cambridge: Cambridge University Press.

Brown, R. (1965) *Social Psychology*. New York: MacMillan.

Brown, R. (1980) The maintenance of conversation. In D. R. Olson (ed.), *The Social Foundations of Language and Thought*, New York: Norton.

Brown, R. (1986) *Social Psychology*. 2nd edn. London: Collier Macmillan.

Brown, R. and Fish, D. (1982) The psychological causality implicit in language. *Cognition*, 14, 237–73.

Brown, R. and Gilman, A. (1960) The pronouns of power and solidarity. In T. Sebeok (ed.), *Style in Language*, Cambridge, Mass.: MIT Press.

Brown, R. C. and Tedeschi, J. T. (1976) Determinants of perceived aggression. *Journal of Social Psychology*, 100, 77–87.

Brown, R. J. (1978) Divided we fall: an analysis of relations between sections of a factory work-force. In H. Tajfel (ed.), *Differentiation between Social Groups: studies in the social psychology of intergroup relations*, London: Academic Press.

Brown, R. J. (1984a) The role of similarity in intergroup relations. In H. Tajfel (ed.), *The Social Dimension* (vol. 2), Cambridge: Cambridge University Press.

Brown, R. J. (1984b) (ed.) *Intergroup Processes. British Journal of Social Psychology*, 23, whole no. 4.

Brown, R. J., Condor, S., Matthews, A., Wade, G. and Williams, J. A. (1986) Explaining intergroup differentiation in an industrial organization. *Journal of Occupational Psychology*, 59, 273–86.

Brown, R. J. and Deschamps, J.-C. (1980–1) Discrimination entre individus et entre groupes. *Bulletin de Psychologie*, XXXIV, 185–95.

Brown, R. J. and Ross, G. F. (1982) The battle for acceptance: an exploration into the dynamics of intergroup behaviour. In H. Tajfel (ed.), *Social Identity and Intergroup Relations*, Cambridge: Cambridge University Press.

Brown, R.J., Tajfel, H. and Turner, J. C. (1980) Minimal group situations and intergroup discrimination: comments on the paper by Aschenbrenner and Schaefer. *European Journal of Social Psychology*, 10, 399–414.

Brown, R. J. and Turner, J. C. (1979) The criss-cross categorization effect in intergroup discrimination. *British Journal of Social and Clinical Psychology*, 18, 371–83.

Brown, R. J. and Turner, J. C. (1981) Interpersonal and intergroup behaviour. In J. C. Turner and H. Giles (eds), *Intergroup Behaviour*, Oxford: Basil Blackwell.

Brown, R. J. and Wade, G. S. (1987) Superordinate goals and intergroup behaviour: the effects of role ambiguity and status on intergroup attitudes and task performance. *European Journal of Social Psychology*, 17, 131–42.

Brown, R. J. and Williams, J. A. (1984) Group identification: the same thing to all people? *Human Relations*, 37, 547–64.

Bruner, J. S. (1975) From cognition to language: a psychological perspective. *Cognition*, 3, 255–82.

Bruner, J. S. (1977) Early social interaction and language acquisition. In H. R. Schaffer (ed.), *Studies in Mother–Infant Interaction*, London: Academic Press.

Bruner, J. S. (1981) The social context of language acquisition. *Language and Communication*, 1, 155–78.

Bruner, J. S. (1983) *Child's Talk: learning to use language*. Oxford: Oxford University Press.

Bruner, J. S. and Goodman, C. D. (1947) Value and need as organizing factors in perception. *Journal of Abnormal and Social Psychology*, 42, 33–44.

Bruner, J. S., Goodnow, J. J. and Austin, G. A. (1956) *A Study of Thinking*. New York: Wiley.

Bruner, J. S. and Sherwood, V. (1981) Thought, language and interaction in infancy. In J. P. Forgas (ed.), *Social Cognition: perspectives on everyday understanding*, London: Academic Press.

Bruner, J. S. and Tagiuri, R. (1954) The perception of people. In G. Lindzey (ed.), *Handbook of Social Psychology* (vol. 2), Reading, Mass.: Addison-Wesley.

Burgess, R. L. and Huston, T. L. (eds) (1979) *Social Exchange in Developing Relationships*. New York: Academic Press.

Burgoon, J. K. (1983) Nonverbal violations of expectations. In J. M. Wiemann and R. P. Harrison (eds), *Non-Verbal Interaction*, Beverly Hills: Sage.

Burgoon, M. (1983) Argument from Aristotle to analysis of variance: a modest reinterpretation. *Journal of Language and Social Psychology*, 2, 105–22.

Burke, P. J. (1967) The development of task and social-emotional role differentiation. *Sociometry*, 30, 379–92.

Burke, P. J. (1974) Participation and leadership in small groups. *American Sociological Review*, 39, 832–42.

Burnstein, E. and Vinokur, A. (1973) Testing two classes of theories about group induced shifts in individual choice. *Journal of Experimental Social Psychology*, 9, 123–37.

Burt, C. (1925) *The Young Delinquent*. London: University of London Press.

Buss, A. H. and Plomin, R. (1984) *Temperament: early developing personality traits*. Hillsdale, NJ: Erlbaum.

Buss, A. R. (1978) Causes and reasons in attribution theory: a conceptual critique. *Journal of Personality and Social Psychology*, 36, 1311–21.

Buss, A. R. (ed.) (1979) *Psychology in Social Context*. New York: Irvington.

Butterfield, H. (1963) *The Whig Interpretation of History*. London: Bell.

Byrne, D. (1971) *The Attraction Paradigm*. New York: Academic Press.

Cacioppo, J. T. and Petty, R. E. (1979) Neuromuscular circuits in affect-laden information processing. *Pavlovian Journal of Biological Science*, 14, 177–85.

Caddick, B. (1982) Perceived illegitimacy and intergroup relations. In H. Tajfel (ed.), *Social Identity and Intergroup Relations*, Cambridge: Cambridge University Press.

Calder, B. J. and Ross, M. (1976) Attitudes: theories and issues. In J. W. Thibaut, J. T. Spence and R. C. Carlson (eds), *Contemporary Topics in Social Psychology*, Morristown, NJ: General Learning Press.

Calder, B. J., Ross, M. and Insko, C. A. (1973) Attitude change and attitude attribution: effects of incentive, choice, and consequences. *Journal of Personality and Social Psychology*, 25, 84–99.

Camaioni, L. and Laicardi, C. (1985) Early social games and the acquisition of language. *British Journal of Developmental Psychology*, 3, 31–9.

Camaioni, L., Volterra, V. and Bates, E. (1976) *La Comunicazione nel primo anno idi vita*. Roma: Boringhieri.

Camden, C., Motley, M. T. and Wilson, A. (1984) White lies in interpersonal communication: a taxonomy and preliminary investigation of social motivation. *Western Journal of Speech Communication*, 48, 309–25.

Camino, I. and Troccoli, B. (1980) Categorization of violence, the belief in a just world and political activism. Unpublished manuscript, University of Paraiba.

Campbell, D. T. (1965) Ethnocentric and other altruistic motives. In D. Levine (ed.), *Nebraska Symposium on Motivation*, Lincoln, Nebr.: University of Nebraska Press.

Campbell, D. T., Kruskal, W. and Wallace, W. (1966) Seating aggregation as an index of attitude. *Sociometry*, 29, 1–15.

Cantor, N. and Mischel, W. (1979) Prototypes in person perception. In L. Berkowitz (ed.), *Advances in Experimental Social Psychology* (vol. 12), New York: Academic Press.

Cantril, H. (1965) *The Pattern of Human Concerns*. New York: Rutgers University Press.

Caporeal, L. R., Lukaszewski, M. P. and Culbertson, G. H. (1983) Secondary baby talk: judgements by institutionalized elderly and their caregivers. *Journal of Personality and Social Psychology*, 44, 746–54.

Capozza, D. and Nanni, R. (1986) Differentiation processes for social stimuli with different degrees of category representativeness. *European Journal of Social Psychology*, 16.

Carey, M. (1978) Does civil inattention exist in pedestrian passing? *Journal of Personality and Social Psychology*, 36, 1185–93.

Carlsmith, J. M., Aronson, E. and Ellsworth, P. C. (1976) *Methods of Research in Social Psychology*. Reading, Mass.: Addison-Wesley.

Carraher, T. N., Carraher, D. W. and Schliemann, A. D. (1985) Mathematics in the streets and in schools. *British Journal of Developmental Psychology*, 3, 21–30.

Carroll, J. S. and Wiener, R. L. (1982) Cognitive social psychology in court and beyond. In A. Hastorf and A. Isen (eds), *Cognitive Social Psychology*. New York: Elsevier North-Holland.

Cartwright, D. (1979) Contemporary social psychology in historical perspective. *Social Psychology Quarterly*, 42, 82–93.

Cartwright, D. and Zander, A. (1968) Pressures to uniformity in groups. In D. Cartwright and A. Zander (eds), *Group Dynamics: research and theory*, 3rd edn, New York: Harper & Row.

Carver, C. S. (1975) Physical aggression as a function of objective self-awareness and attitudes toward punishment. *Journal of Experimental Social Psychology*, 11, 510–19.

Central Statistical Office (1986) *Key Data*. London: HMSO.

Chadwick-Jones, J. K. (1976) *Social Exchange Theory*. New York and London: Academic Press.

Chaiken, S. (1980) Heuristic versus systematic information processing and the use of source versus message cues in persuasion. *Journal of Personality and Social Psychology*, 39, 752–66.

Chaiken, S. and Stangor, C. (1987) Attitudes and attitude change. *Annual Review of Psychology*, 38, 575–630.

Chaikin, A. L. and Cooper, J. (1973) Evaluation as a function of correspondence and hedonic relevance. *Journal of Experimental Social Psychology*, 9, 257–64.

Chandler, M. J. (1982) Social cognition and social structure. In F. C. Serafica (ed.), *Social Cognitive Development in Context*, London: Methuen.

Chandler, M. J. (1985) Social structures and social cognitions. In R. A. Hinde, A.-N. Perret-Clermont and J. Stevenson-Hinde (eds), *Social Relationships and Cognitive Development*, Oxford: Oxford University Press.

Chapman, L. J. and Chapman, J. P. (1967) Genesis of popular but erroneous diagnostic observations. *Journal of Abnormal Psychology*, 72, 193–204.

Chapman, L. J. and Chapman J. P. (1969) Illusory correlation as an obstacle to the use of valid psychodiagnostic signs. *Journal of Abnormal Psychology*, 74, 271–80.

Chapman, M. (1986) The structure of exchange: Piaget's sociological theory. *Human Development*, 29, 181–94.

Check, V. P., Perlman, D. and Malamuth, N. M. (1985) Loneliness and aggressive behaviour. *Journal of Social and Personal Relationships*, 2, 243–54.

Chemers, M. M. (1983) Leadership theory and research: a systems-process integration. In P. Paulus (ed.), *Basic Group Processes*, New York: Springer.

Christie, R. and Jahoda, M. (1954) (eds), *Studies in the Scope and Method of the Authoritarian Personality*, New York: Free Press.

Cialdini, R. B., Borden, R. J., Thorne, A., Walker, M. R., Freeman, S. and Sloan, L.

R. (1976) Basking in reflected glory: three (football) field studies. *Journal of Personality and Social Psychology*, 34, 366–74.

Clark, K. B. and Clark, M. P. (1947) Racial identification and preference in Negro children. In T. M. Newcomb and E. L. Hartley (eds), *Readings in Social Psychology*, New York: Holt, Rinehart & Winston.

Clark, M. S. and Fiske, S. T. (eds) (1982) *Affect and Cognition: the 17th annual Carnegie symposium on cognition*, Hillsdale, NJ: Erlbaum.

Clark, M. S. and Isen, A. M. (1982) Toward understanding the relationship between feeling states and social behavior. In A. Hastorf and A. Isen (eds), *Cognitive Social Psychology*, New York: Elsevier North-Holland.

Clark, M. S. and Mills, J. (1979) Interpersonal attraction in exchange and communal relationships. *Journal of Personality and Social Psychology*, 37, 12–24.

Clarke, A. M. and Clarke, A. D. B. (1976) *Early Experience: myth and evidence*. London: Open Books.

Clore, G. L. (1977) Reinforcement and affect in attraction. In S. Duck (ed.), *Theory and Practice in Interpersonal Attraction*, London: Academic Press.

Coch, L. and French, J. R. R., Jr (1948) Overcoming resistance to change. *Human Relations*, 1, 512–32.

Codol, J.-P. (1975) On the so-called 'superior conformity of the self' behaviour: twenty experimental investigations. *European Journal of Social Psychology*, 5, 457–501.

Codol, J.-P. (1976) Contre l'hypothese du triangle. *Cahiers de Psychologie*, 19, 381–94.

Codol, J.-P. (1982) Differentiating and non-differentiating behavior: an approach to the sense of identity. In J.-P. Codol and J.-P. Leyens (eds), *Cognitive Analysis of Social Behavior*. The Hague: Nijhoff.

Codol, J.-P. (1984a) La perception de la similitude interpersonnelle: influence de l'appartenance catégorielle et du point de référence de la comparaison. *Année Psychologique*, 84, 43–56.

Codol, J.-P. (1984b) On the system of representations in an artificial social situation. In R. Farr and S. Moscovici (eds), *Social Representations*, Cambridge: Cambridge University Press.

Codol, J.-P. (1986) Estimation et expression de la ressemblance et de la différence entre pairs. *L'Année Psychologique*, 86, 527–50.

Cohen, S. and Wills, T. A. (1985) Stress, social support, and the buffering hypothesis. *Psychological Bulletin*, 98, 310–57.

Colley, A. (1986) Sex roles in leisure and sport. In D. J. Hargreaves and A. M. Colley (eds), *The Psychology of Sex Roles*, London: Harper & Row.

Collins, B. E. and Raven, B. H. (1968) Group structure: attraction, coalitions, communication, and power. In G. Lindzey and E. Aronson (eds), *Handbook of Social Psychology* (vol. 4), 2nd edn, Reading, Mass.: Addison-Wesley.

Colman, A. E. (1982a) *Game Theory and Experimental Games*. Oxford: Pergamon.

Colman, A. E. (ed.) (1982b) *Cooperation and Competition in Humans and Animals*. New York: Van Nostrand Reinhold.

Commins, B. and Lockwood, J. (1979) The effects of status differences, favoured treatment and equity on intergroup comparisons. *European Journal of Social Psychology*, 9, 281–9.

Comstock, G. (1975) *Television and Human Behavior: the key studies*. Santa Monica, Calif.: Rand Corporation.

Comte, A. (1853) *The positive Philosophy* (vol. 1). London: Longmans Green.

Cook, S. W. (1962) The systematic analysis of socially significant events. *Journal of Social Issues*, 18, 66–84.

Cook, T. D. and Campbell, D. T. (1979) *Quasi-Experimentation: design and analysis issues for field settings*. Chicago: Rand McNally.

Cooper, J. and Fazio, R. H. (1984) A new look at dissonance theory. In L. Berkowitz (ed.), *Advances in Experimental Social Psychology* (vol. 17), New York: Academic Press.

Cooper, J. and Worchel, S. (1970) Role of undesired consequences in arousing cognitive dissonance. *Journal of Personality and Social Psychology*, 16, 199–206.

Cooper, J., Zanna, M. P. and Taves, P. A. (1978) Arousal as a necessary condition for attitude change following induced compliance. *Journal of Personality and Social Psychology*, 36, 1101–6.

Corey, S. M. (1937) Professed attitudes and actual behavior. *Journal of Educational Psychology*, 28, 271–80.

Cottrell, N. B. (1968) Performance in the presence of other human beings: mere presence, audience and affiliation effects. In E. C. Simmel, R. A. Hoppe and G. A. Milton (eds), *Social Facilitation and Imitative Behavior*, Boston: Allyn & Bacon.

Cottrell, N. B. (1972) Social facilitation. In C. G. McClintock (ed.), *Experimental Social Psychology*, New York: Holt, Rinehard & Winston.

Couch, A. S. and Carter, L. F. A. (1952) A factorial study of the rated behavior of group members. Paper presented at the annual meeting of the Eastern Psychological Association.

Coupland, N., Coupland, J., Giles, H. and Henwood, K. (1988) Accommodating the elderly: invoking and extending a theory. *Language in Society*, 17.

Coupland, N., Coupland, J., Giles, H. and Wiemann, J. M. (1988) My life in your hands: disclosure in intergenerational talk. In N. Coupland (ed.), *Styles of Discourse*, London: Routledge and Kegan Paul.

Coupland, N., Giles, H. and Wiemann, J. M. (in press). *The Handbook of Miscommunication*. Clevedon: Multilingual Matters.

Cowles, M. and Davis, C. (1987) The subject matter of psychology: volunteers. *British Journal of Social Psychology*, 26, 289–94.

Coyne, J. C. and Gotlib, I. H. (1983) The role of cognition in depression: a critical appraisal. *Psychological Bulletin*, 94, 472–505.

Crocker, J., Fiske, S. T. and Taylor, S. E. (1984) Schematic bases of belief change. In J. R. Eiser (ed.), *Attitudinal Judgment*, New York: Springer.

Crosby, F. (1976) A model of egotistical relative deprivation. *Psychological Review*, 83, 85–113.

Croyle, R. T. and Cooper, J. (1983) Dissonance arousal: Physiological evidence. *Journal of Personality and Social Psychology*, 45, 782–91.

Crutchfield, R. A. (1955) Conformity and character. *American Psychologist*, 10, 191–8.

Cunningham, J. D. and Kelley, H. H. (1975) Causal attributions for interpersonal events of varying magnitude. *Journal of Personality*, 43, 74–93.

Cushman, D. and Cahn, D. (1985) *Communication in Interpersonal Relationships*. Albany: State University of New York Press.

Czwartosz, Z. (1976) How previous experience may affect behaviour in a conflict situation. *Polish Psychological Bulletin*, 7, 187–96.

Daly, M. and Wilson, M. (1984) A sociobiological analysis of human infanticide. In G. Hausfater and S. B. Hrdy (eds), *Infanticide*, New York: Aldine.

Damon, W. (1977) *The Social World of the Child*. San Francisco: Jossey-Bass.

Dance, F. E. X. and Larson, C. (1976) *The Functions of Human Communication*. New York: Holt, Rinehart & Winston.

Dane, F. C. and Wrightsman, L. S. (1982) Effect of defendants' and victims' characteristics on jurors' verdicts. In N. L. Kerr and R. M. Bray (eds), *The Psychology of the Courtroom*, London: Academic Press.

Danziger, K. (1983) Origins and basic principles of Wundt's Völkerpsychologie. *British Journal of Social Psychology*, 22, 303–13.

Darley, J. M. and Batson, C. D. (1973) From Jerusalem to Jericho: a study of situational and dispositional variables in helping behavior. *Journal of Personality and Social Psychology*, 27, 100–8.

Darley, J. M. and Goethals, G. R. (1980) People's analyses of the causes of ability-linked performances. In L. Berkowitz (ed.), *Advances in Experimental Social Psychology* (vol. 13), New York: Academic Press.

Darley, J. M. and Latané, B. (1970) Norms and normative behavior: field studies of social interdependence. In J. Macaulay and L. Berkowitz (eds), *Altruism and Helping Behavior*, New York: Academic Press.

Darwin, C. (1871) *The Descent of Man and Selection in Relation to Sex*. London: Murray.

Darwin, C. (1872, 1896) *The Expression of the Emotions in Man and Animals*. New York: Appleton Century-Crofts.

Davidson, A. R. and Jaccard, J. J. (1979) Variables that moderate the attitude–behavior relation: results of a longitudinal survey. *Journal of Personality and Social Psychology*, 37, 1364–76.

Davies, J. C. (1969) The J-curve of rising and declining satisfactions as a cause of some great revolutions and a contained rebellion. In H. D. Graham and T. R. Gurr (eds), *The History of Violence in America: Historical and Comparative Perspectives*, New York: Praeger.

Davis, J. H. (1984) Order in the courtroom. In D. J. Müller, D. E. Blackman and A. J. Chapman (eds), *Psychology and Law*, Chichester: Wiley.

Davis, J. H., Kerr, N. L., Atkin, R. S., Holt, R. and Meek, D. (1975) The decision processes of 6- and 12-person juries assigned unanimous and two-thirds majority rules. *Journal of Personality and Social Psychology*, 32, 1–14.

Davis, K. E. and Todd, M. (1982) Friendship and love relations. *Advances in Descriptive Psychology*, 2, 79–122.

Dawes, R. M. (1980) Social dilemmas. *Annual Review of Psychology*, 31, 169–93.

Dawes, R. M., McTavish, J. and Shaklee, H. (1977) Behavior, communication and assumptions about other people's behavior in a commons dilemma situation. *Journal of Personality and Social Psychology*, 35, 1–11.

Dawes, R. M. and Smith, T. L. (1985) Attitude and opinion measurement. In G. Lindzey and E. Aronson (eds), *Handbook of Social Psychology* (vol. 1), 3rd edn, New York: Random House.

Deaux, K. (1985) Sex and gender. *Annual Review of Psychology*, 36, 49–81.

Deci, E. L. (1971) Effects of externally mediated rewards on intrinsic motivation. *Journal of Personality and Social Psychology*, 18, 105–15.

Deci, E. L. (1972) Intrinsic motivation, extrinsic reinforcement, and inequity. *Journal of Personality and Social Psychology*, 22, 113–20.

Deci, E. L. (1975) *Intrinsic Motivation*. New York: Plenum.

Deconchy, J. P. (1984) Systèmes de croyances et représentations idéologiques. In S. Moscovici (ed.), *Psychologie Sociale*, Paris: Press Universitaires de France.

De Jong-Gierveld, J. and Kamphuis, F. (1985) The development of a Rasch-type loneliness scale. *Applied Psychological Measurement*, 9, 289–99.

Dembroski, T. M. and MacDougall, J. M. (1982) Coronary-prone behaviour, social psychophysiology and coronary heart disease. In J. R. Eiser (ed.), *Social Psychology and Behavioural Medicine*, Chichester: Wiley.

De Montmollin, G. (1977) *L'Influence Sociale: phénomènes, facteurs et théories.* Paris: Presses Universitaires de France.

De Paolis, P., Carugati, F., Erba, M. and Mugny, G. (1981) Connatzione sociale de sviluppo cognitivo. *Giornale Italiano di Psicologia*, 8, 149–65.

DePaulo, B. M., Brown, P. L., Ishii, S. and Fisher, J. D. (1981) Help that works: the effects of aid on subsequent task performance. *Journal of Personality and Social Psychology*, 41, 478–87.

DePaulo, B. M. and Coleman, L. M. (1986) Talking to children, foreigners and retarded adults. *Journal of Personality and Social Psychology*, 51, 945–59.

DePaulo, B. M., Stone, J. I. and Lassiter, G. D. (1985) Telling ingratiation lies: effects of target sex and target attractiveness on verbal and nonverbal deceptive success. *Journal of Personality and Social Psychology*, 15, 247–52.

Deschamps, J.-C. (1973–4) L'attribution, la catégorisation sociale et les représentations intergroupes. *Bulletin de Psychologie*, 27, 710–21.

Deschamps, J.-C. (1977) Effect of crossing category memberships on quantitative judgements. *European Journal of Social Psychology*, 7, 517–21.

Deschamps, J.-C. and Brown, R. J. (1983) Superordinate goals and intergroup conflict. *British Journal of Social Psychology*, 22, 189–95.

Deschamps, J.-C. and Doise, W. (1978) Crossed category memberships in intergroup relations. In H. Tajfel (ed.), *Differentiation between Social Groups*, London: Academic Press.

Deutsch, M. (1958) Trust and suspicion. *Journal of Conflict Resolution*, 2, 265–79.

Deutsch, M. (1973) *The Resolution of Conflict: constructive and destructive processes.* New Haven: Yale.

Deutsch, M. and Gerard, H. B. (1955) A study of normative and informational influence upon individual judgement. *Journal of Abnormal and Social Psychology*, 51, 629–36.

Deutsch, M. and Krauss, R. M. (1960) The effect of threat upon interpersonal bargaining. *Journal of Abnormal and Social Psychology*, 61, 181–9.

Dewey, J. (1917) The need for social psychology. *Psychological Review*, 24, 266–77.

Diab, L. N. (1970) A study of intragroup and intergroup relations among experimentally produced small groups. *Genetic Psychology Monographs*, 82, 49–82.

Diamond, S. and Herhold, C. J. (1981) Understanding criminal sentencing: views from law and social psychology. In G. M. Stephenson and J. H. Davis (eds), *Progress in Applied Social Psychology* (vol. 1), Chichester: Wiley.

Diener, E. (1976) Effects of prior destructive behaviour, anonymity, and group presence on deindividuation and aggression. *Journal of Personality and Social Psychology*, 33, 497–507.

Diener, E. (1980) Deindividuation: the absence of self-awareness and self-regulation in group members. In P. Paulus (ed.), *The Psychology of Group Influence*, Hillsdale, NJ: Erlbaum.

Di Giacomo, J. P. (1985) *Rappresentazioni Sociali e movimenti collettivi.* Napoli: Liguori.

Dillehay, R. C. and Nietzel, M. T. (1985) Jury experience and jury verdicts. *Law and Human Behavior*, 9, 179–91.

Dillon, W. R. and Kumar, A. (1985) Attitude organization and the attitude–behavior relation: a critique of Bagozzi and Burnkraut's reanalysis of Fishbein and Ajzen. *Journal of Personality and Social Psychology*, 45, 33–46.

Dindia, K. (1987) The effects of sex of subject and sex of partner on interruptions. *Human Communication Research*, 13, 345–71.

Dion, K. (1979) Intergroup conflict and intragroup cohesiveness. In W. G. Austin and S. Worchel (eds), *The Social Psychology of Intergroup Relations*, Monterey, Calif.: Brooks/Cole.

Dion, K., Berscheid, E. and Walster, E. (1972) What is beautiful is good. *Journal of Personality and Social Psychology*, 245, 285–90.

Dittes, J. E. and Kelley, H. H. (1956) Effects of different conditions of acceptance on conformity to group norms. *Journal of Abnormal and Social Psychology*, 53, 100–7.

Di Vesta, F. J. (1959) Effects of confidence and motivation on susceptibility to informational social influence. *Journal of Abnormal and Social Psychology*, 59, 204–9.

Dohrenwend, B. S. and Dohrenwend, B. P. (1974) *Stressful Life Events: their nature and effects*. New York: Wiley.

Doise, W. (1976) *L'articulation psychosociologique et les relations entre groupes*. Brussels: de Boeck. Translated as *Groups and Individuals: explanations in social psychology*. Cambridge: Cambridge University Press, 1978.

Doise, W. (1986) Les représentations sociales: définition d'un concept. In W. Doise and A. Palmonari (eds), *L'Étude des représentations sociales*, Neuchâtel: Delachaux et Niestlé.

Doise, W., Deschamps, J.-C. and Meyer, G. (1978) The accentuation of intra-category similarities. In H. Tajfel (ed.), *Differentiation between Social Groups: studies in the social psychology of intergroup relations*, London: Academic Press.

Doise, W. and Mugny, G. (1984) *The Social Development of Intellect*. Oxford: Pergamon Press. First published as *Le Développement Social de l'intelligence*. Paris: Inter Editions, 1981.

Doise, W., Mugny, G. and Perret-Clermont, A. N. (1975) Social interaction and the development of cognitive operations. *European Journal of Social Psychology*, 5, 367–83.

Dollard, J., Doob, L. W., Miller, N. E., Mowrer, O. H. and Sears, R. T. (1939) *Frustration and Aggression*. New Haven: Yale University Press.

Doms, M. (1983) The minority influence effect: an alternative approach. In S. Moscovici and W. Doise (eds), *Current Issues in European Social Psychology*, Cambridge: Cambridge University Press.

Doms, M. and Van Avermaet, E. (1980) Majority influence, minority influence and conversion behaviour: a replication. *Journal of Experimental Social Psychology*, 16, 283–92.

Doms, M. and Van Avermaet, E. (1982) The conformity effect: a timeless phenomenon. *Bulletin of the British Psychological Society*, 35, 383–5.

Doms, M. and Van Avermaet, E. (1985) Social support and minority influence: the innovation effect reconsidered. In S. Moscovici, G. Mugny and E. Van Avermaet (eds), *Perspectives on Minority Influence*, Cambridge: Cambridge University Press.

Donaldson, M. (1978) *Children's Minds*. Fontana: London.

Donnerstein, E., Donnerstein, M., Simons, S. and Dittrichs, R. (1972) Variables in interracial aggression. *Journal of Personality and Social Psychology*, 22, 236–45.

Donnerstein, E. and Wilson, D. W. (1976) The effects of noise and perceived control upon ongoing and subsequent aggressive behavior. *Journal of Personality and Social Psychology*, 34, 774–81.

Dryden, C. and Giles, H. (1986) Language, social identity and health. In H. Beloff and A. Coleman (eds), *Psychology Survey* (vol. 6), Leicester: British Psychological Society.

Duck, S. W. (1973) *Personal Relationships and Personal Constructs: a study of friendship formation*. London: Wiley.

Duck, S. W. (1982) A topography of relationship disengagement and dissolution. In S. Duck (ed.), *Personal Relationships* (vol. 4), London: Academic Press.

Duck, S. W. (ed.) (1984) *Personal Relationships* (vol. 5). London: Academic Press.

Duck, S. W. and Gilmour, R. (eds) (1981–4) *Personal Relationships* (5 vols). London: Academic Press.

Duck, S. W. and Miell, D. (1984) Towards a comprehension of friendship development and breakdown. In H. Tajfel (ed.), *The Social Dimension* (vol. 1), Cambridge: Cambridge University Press.

Duncan, B. L. (1976) Differential social perception and attribution of intergroup violence: testing the lower limits of stereotyping of blacks. *Journal of Personality and Social Psychology*, 34, 590–8.

Duncan, S. and Fiske, D. W. (1977) *Face-to-Face Interaction*. Hillsdale, NJ: Erlbaum.

Dunkel-Shetter, C. and Wortman, C. B. (1982) The interpersonal dynamics of cancer: problems in social relationships and their impact on the patient. In H. S. Friedman and M. R. Dimatteo (eds), *Interpersonal Issues in Health Care*, New York: Academic Press.

Dunn, J. (1984) Early social interaction and the development of emotional understanding. In H. Tajfel (ed.), *The Social Dimension* (vol. 1), Cambridge: Cambridge University Press.

Dunn, J. and Kendrick, C. (1982) *Siblings, Love, Envy and Understanding*. London: Grant McIntyre.

Durkheim, E. (1898) Représentations individuelles et représentations collectives. *Revue de Metaphysique et de Morale*, 6, 273–302 (English trans. in Durkheim, E. (1974) *Sociology and Philosophy*. New York: Free Press).

Durkin, K. (1985) *Television, Sex Roles and Children: a development social psychological account*. Milton Keynes and Philadelphia: Open University Press.

Durkin, K. (1986) Language and social cognition during the school years. In K. Durkin (ed.), *Language Development in the School Years*, Beckenham: Croom Helm.

Durkin, K. (1987) Social cognition and social context in the construction of sex differences in human performance. In M. A. Baker (ed.), *Sex Differences in Human Performance*, London: Wiley.

Durkin, K. (in press) Minds and language: social cognition, social conflict and the acquisition of language. *Mind and Language*.

Durkin, K., Rutter, D. R. and Tucker, H. (1982) Social interaction and language acquisition: motherese help you? *First Language*, 3, 107–20.

Dustin, D. S. and Davis, H. P. (1970) Evaluative bias in group and individual competition. *Journal of Social Psychology*, 80, 103–8.

Duval, S. and Wicklund, R. A. (1972) *A Theory of Objective Self-Awareness*. New York: Academic Press.

Duval, S. and Wicklund, R. A. (1973) Effects of objective self-awareness on attributions of causality. *Journal of Experimental Social Psychology*, 9, 17–31.

Dweck, C. S. (1975) The role of expectations and attributions in the alleviation of learned helplessness. *Journal of Personality and Social Psychology*, 31, 674–85.

Dyson-Hudson, R. and Smith, E. A. (1978) Human territoriality: an ecological reassessment. *American Anthropologist*, 80, 21–42.

Eagly, A. H. and Chaiken, S. (1984) Cognitive theories of persuasion. In L. Berkowitz (ed.), *Advances in Experimental Social Psychology* (vol. 17), Orlando, Fla.: Academic Press.

Eagly, A. H. and Warren, R. (1976) Intelligence, comprehension, and opinion change. *Journal of Personality*, 44, 226–42.

Ebbinghaus, H. (1908) *Abriss der Psychologie*. Leipzig: Veit.

Eckhardt, G. (1971) Problemgeschichtliche Untersuchungen zur Völkerpsychologie der zweiten Hälfte des 19. Jahrhunderts. *Wissenschaftliche Zeitschrift der Friedrich-Schiller-Universität, Gesellschafts- und sprachwissenschaftliche Reihe,* 20, Heft 4, 7-133.

Edwards, J. R. and Giles, H. (1984) Applications of the social psychology of language: Sociolinguistics and education. In P. Trudgill (ed.), *Applied Sociolinguistics*, London: Academic Press.

Egeth, H. E. and McCloskey, M. (1984) Expert testimony about eye-witness behaviour: is it safe and effective? In G. L. Wells and E. F. Loftus (eds), *Eyewitness Testimony: psychological perspectives*, Cambridge: Cambridge University Press.

Ehrlich, I. (1982) The market for offences and the public enforcement of laws: an equilibrium analysis. *British Journal of Social Psychology*, 21, 107–20.

Eibl-Eibesfeldt, I. (1972) Similarities and differences between cultures in expressive movements. In R. A. Hinde (ed.), *Non-Verbal Communication*, Cambridge: Cambridge University Press.

Eibl-Eibesfeldt, I. (1973) *Der Vorprogrammierte Mensch: Das Erebte als bestimmender Faktor im menschlichen Verhalten*. Vienna: Molden.

Einhorn, H. J. and Hogarth, R. M. (1986) Judging probable cause. *Psychological Bulletin*, 99, 3–19.

Eiser, J. R. (1971) Enhancement of contrast in the absolute judgement of attitude statements. *Journal of Personality and Social Psychology*, 17, 1–10.

Eiser, J. R. (1975) Attitudes and the use of evaluative language: a two-way process. *Journal for the Theory of Social Behaviour*, 5, 235–48.

Eiser, J. R. (1980) *Cognitive Social Psychology*. London: McGraw-Hill.

Eiser, J. R. (1982) Addiction as attribution: cognitive processes in giving up smoking. In J. R. Eiser (ed.), *Social Psychology and Behavioural Medicine*, Chichester: Wiley.

Eiser, J. R. (1983) Attribution theory and social cognition. In J. Jaspars, F. D. Fincham and M. Hewstone (eds), *Attribution Theory and Research: conceptual, developmental and social dimensions*, London: Academic Press.

Eiser, J. R. and Bhavnani, K. K. (1974) The effects of situational meaning on the behavior of subjects in the prisoner's dilemma game. *European Journal of Social Psychology*, 4, 93–7.

Eiser, J. R. and Stroebe, W. (1972) *Categorization and Social Judgment*. London: Academic Press.

Eiser, J. R. and Tajfel, H. (1972) Acquisition of information in dyadic interaction. *Journal of Personality and Social Psychology*, 23, 340–5.

Ekman, P. (1985) *Telling Lies: clues to deceit in the marketplace, politics and marriage*. New York: Norton.

Ekman, P. and Friesen, W. V. (1969) The repertoire of non-verbal behavior: categories, origins, usage and coding. *Semiotica*, 1, 49–98.

Elwell, C. M., Brown, R. J. and Rutter, D. R. (1984) Effects of accent and visual information on impression formation. *Journal of Language and Social Psychology*, 3, 297–9.

Emler, N. (1984) Differential involvement in delinquency: toward an interpretation in terms of reputation management. In B. Maher (ed.), *Progress in Experimental Personality Research*, (vol. 13), New York: Academic Press.

Emler, N. and Hogan, R. (1981) Developing attitudes to law and justice: an integrative review. In S. Brehm, S. M. Kassin and F. X. Gibbons (eds), *Developmental Social Psychology: theory and research*, Oxford: Oxford University Press.

Emler, N., Reicher, S. and Ross, A. (1987) The social context of delinquent conduct. *Journal of Child Psychology and Psychiatry*, 28, 99–109.

Emler, N. and Valiant, G. L. (1982) Social interaction and cognitive conflict in the development of spatial coordination skills. *British Journal of Psychology*, 73, 295–303.

Emmerich, W., Goldman, K. S., Kirsh, B. and Sharabany, R. (1977) Evidence for the traditional phase in the development of gender constancy, *Child Development*, 48, 930–6.

Endler, N. S. and Magnusson, D. (1976) Toward an interactional psychology of personality. *Psychological Bulletin*, 83, 956–97.

Endler, N. S. (1965) The effects of verbal reinforcement on conformity and deviant behaviour. *Journal of Social Psychology*, 66, 147–54.

Endler, N. S. and Hunt, J. McV. (1968) Inventories of hostility and comparisons of the proportions of variance from persons, responses, and situations for hostility and anxiousness. *Journal of Personality and Social Psychology*, 9, 309–15.

Epstein, S. (1966) Aggression toward outgroups as a function of authoritarianism and imitation of aggression models. *Journal of Personality and Social Psychology*, 3, 574–9.

Eron, L. D. and Huesmann, L. R. (1980) Adolescent aggression and television. *Annals of the New York Academy of Science*, 347, 319–31.

Eron, L. D., Huesmann, L. R., Lefkowitz, M. M. and Walder, L. O. (1972) Does television violence cause aggression? *American Psychologist*, 27, 253–63.

Essock-Vitale, S. M. and McGuire, M. T. (1980) Predictions Derived from the theories of kin selection and reciprocation assessed by anthropological data. *Ethology and Sociobiology*, 1, 233–43.

Evans, G. and Crumbaugh, C. M. (1966) Effects of prisoner's dilemma format on cooperative behavior. *Journal of Personality and Social Psychology*, 3, 486–8.

Evans-Pritchard, E. E. (1937) *Witchcraft, Oracles and Magic among the Azande*. Oxford: Clarendon.

Eysenck, H. J. (1954) *The Psychology of Politics*. London: Routledge & Kegan Paul.

Farr, R. M. (1980a) *Homo loquiens* in social psychological perspective. In H. Giles, W. P. Robinson and P. M. Smith (eds), *Language: social psychological perspectives*, Oxford: Pergamon.

Farr, R. M. (1980b) On reading Darwin and discovering social psychology. In R. Gilmour and R. Duck (eds), The Development of Social Psychology, London: Academic Press.

Farr, R. M. (1986) The social psychology of William McDougall. In C. F. Graumann and S. Moscovici (eds), *Changing Conceptions of Crowd Mind and Behavior*, New York: Springer.

Farr, R. M. and Anderson, A. (1983) Beyond actor/observer differences in perspective: extensions and applications. In M. Hewstone (ed.), *Attribution Theory: social and functional extensions*, Oxford: Basil Blackwell.

Farr, R. M. and Moscovici, S. (eds) (1984) *Social Representations*. Cambridge: Cambridge University Press.

Farrington, D. P., Biron, L. and LeBlanc, M. (1982) Personality and delinquency in London and Montreal. In J. Gunn and D. P. Farrington (eds), *Abnormal Offenders, Delinquency and the Criminal Justice System*, Chichester: Wiley.

Farrington, D. P., Gallagher, B., Morley, L., St Ledger, R. J. and West, D. J. (1986) Unemployment, school leaving and crime. *British Journal of Criminology*, 26, 335–56.

Fazio, R. H., Chen, J., McDonel, E. C. and Sherman, S. J. (1982) Attitude accessibility, attitude–behavior consistency, and the strength of the object–evaluation association. *Journal of Experimental Social Psychology*, 18, 339–57.

Fazio, R. H. and Williams, C. J. (1986) Attitude accessibility as a moderator of the attitude perception and attitude–behavior relations: an investigation of the 1984 presidential election. *Journal of Personality and Social Psychology*, 51, 505–14.

Fazio, R. H. and Zanna, M. P. (1981) Direct experience and attitude–behavior consistency. In L. Berkowitz (ed.), *Advances in Experimental Social Psychology* (vol. 14), New York: Academic Press.

Fazio, R. H., Zanna, M. P. and Cooper, J. (1977) Dissonance and self-perception: an integrative view of each theory's proper domain of application. *Journal of Experimental Social Psychology*, 13, 464–79.

Feather, N. T. and O'Brien, G. E. (1986) A longitudinal study of the effects of employment and unemployment on school-leavers. *Journal of Occupational Psychology*, 59, 121–44.

Feinman, S. (1979) An evolutionary theory of food-sharing. *Social Science Information*, 18, 695–726.

Fellner, C. H. and Marshall, J. R. (1981) Kidney donors revisited. In J. P. Rushton and R. M. Sorrentino (eds), *Altruism and Helping Behavior*, Hillsdale, NJ: Erlbaum.

Felson, R. B. (1984) Patterns of aggressive interactions. In A. Mummendey (ed.), *Social Psychology of Aggression: from individual behavior to social interaction*, New York and Heidelberg: Springer.

Ferguson, C. K. and Kelley, H. H. (1964) Significant factors in overevaluation of own group's product. *Journal of Abnormal Social Psychology*, 69, 223–28.

Ferguson, T. J. and Rule, B. G. (1983) An attributional perspective on anger and aggression. In R. Geen and E. Donnerstein (eds), *Aggression: theoretical and empirical reviews* (vol. 1), New York: Academic Press.

Festinger, L. (1954) A theory of social comparison processes. *Human Relations*, 7, 117–40.

Festinger, L. (1957) *A Theory of Cognitive Dissonance*. Stanford: Stanford University Press.

Festinger, L. (1980) Looking backward. In L. Festinger (ed.), *Retrospections on Social Psychology*, New York: Oxford University Press.

Festinger, L. and Carlsmith, J. M. (1959) Cognitive consequences of forced compliance. *Journal of Abnormal and Social Psychology*, 58, 203–10.

Festinger, L. and Maccoby, N. (1964) On resistance to persuasive communications. *Journal of Abnormal and Social Psychology*, 68, 359–66.

Festinger, L., Riecken, H. W. and Schachter, S. (1956) *When Prophecy Fails*. Minneapolis, Minn.: University of Minnesota Press.

Festinger, L., Schachter, S. and Back, K. W. (1950) *Social Pressures in Informal Groups*. New York: Harper.

Fhanér, G. and Hane, M. (1979) Seat belts: opinion effects of law-induced use. *Journal of Applied Psychology*, 64, 205–12.

Fiedler, F. E. (1978) The contingency model and the dynamics of the leadership process. In L. Berkowitz (ed.), *Advances in Experimental Social Psychology* (vol. 12), New York: Academic Press.

Fiedler, F. E. and Potter, E. H. (1983) Dynamics of leadership effectiveness. In H. H. Blumberg, A. P. Hare, V. Kent and M. Davies (eds), *Small Groups and Social Interaction* (vol. 1), Chichester: Wiley.

Fiedler, K. (1982) Causal schemata: review and criticism of research on a popular construct. *Journal of Personality and Social Psychology*, 42, 1001–13.

Fincham, F. D. (1981) Developmental dimensions of attribution theory. In J. Jaspars, F. Fincham and M. Hewstone (eds), *Attribution Theory and Research* (vol. 1), London: Academic Press.

Fincham, F. D. (1985) Attributions in close relationships. In J. H. Harvey and G. Weary (eds), *Attribution: basic issues and applications*, Orlando, Fla.: Academic Press.

Fincham, F. D. (in press) Children's reactions to failure: implications for education. *European Journal of Educational Psychology*.

Fincham, F. D., Beach, S. R. and Baucom, D. H. (1987) Attribution processes in distressed and nondistressed couples. 4: Self–partner attribution differences. *Journal of Personality and Social Psychology*, 52, 739–48.

Fincham, F. D. and Jaspars, J. M. (1980) Attribution of responsibility from man the scientist to man as lawyer. In L. Berkowitz (ed.), *Advances in Experimental Social Psychology* (vol. 13), London: Academic Press.

Fincham, F. D. and Shultz, T. R. (1981) Intervening causation and the mitigation of responsibility for harm. *British Journal of Social Psychology*, 20, 113–20.

Firestone, I. L., Lichtman, C. M. and Colamosca, J. V. (1975) Leader effectiveness and leader conferral as determinants of helping in a medical emergency. *Journal of Personality and Social Psychology*, 31, 343–8.

Fischer, D. G., Kelm, H. and Rose, A. (1969) Knives as aggression-eliciting stimuli. *Psychological Reports*, 24, 755–60.

Fishbein, M. (1963) An investigation of the relationships between beliefs about an object and the attitudes toward that object. *Human Relations*, 16, 233–40.

Fishbein, M. (1967) A behavior theory approach to the relations between beliefs about an object and the attitude toward the object. In M. Fishbein (ed.), *Readings in Attitude Theory and Measurement*, New York: Wiley.

Fishbein, M. (1982) Social psychological analyses of smoking behaviour. In J. R. Eiser (ed.), *Social Psychology and Behavioural Medicine*, Chichester: Wiley.

Fishbein, M. and Ajzen, I. (1974) Attitudes toward objects as predictors of single and multiple behavioral criteria. *Psychological Review*, 81, 59–74.

Fishbein, M. and Ajzen, I. (1975) *Belief, Attitude, Intention, and Behavior: an introduction to theory and research*. Reading, Mass.: Addison-Wesley.

Fishbein, M. and Ajzen, I. (1981a) Acceptance, yielding and impact: cognitive processes in persuasion. In R. E. Petty, T. M. Ostrom and T. C. Brock (eds), *Cognitive Responses in Persuasion*, Hillsdale, NJ: Erlbaum.

Fishbein, M. and Ajzen, I. (1981b) Attitudes and voting behaviour: an application of the theory of reasoned action. In G. M. Stephenson and J. H. Davis (eds), *Progress in Applied Social Psychology* (vol. 1), Chichester: Wiley.

Fishbein, M. and Coombs, F. S. (1974) Basis for decision: an attitudinal analysis of voting behavior. *Journal of Applied Social Psychology*, 4, 95–124.

Fisher, J. D., DePaulo, B. M. and Nadler, A. (1981) Extending altruism beyond the altruistic act: the mixed effects of aid to the help recipient. In J. P. Rushton and R. M. Sorrentino (eds), *Altruism and Helping Behavior*, Hillsdale, NJ: Erlbaum.

Fisher, J. D., Nadler, A. and Whitcher-Alagna, S. (1982) Recipient reactions to aid. *Psychological Bulletin*, 91, 27–54.

Fisher, S. and Todd, A. D. (eds) (1983) *The Social Organization of Doctor-patient Communication*. Washington: Center for Applied Linguistics.

Fishman, J. A. (1972) The relationship between micro- and macro-sociolinguistics in the study of who speaks what language to whom and when. In J. B. Pride and J. Holmes (eds), *Sociolinguistics*, Harmondsworth: Penguin.

Fiske, S. T. and Taylor, S. E. (1984) *Social Cognition*. New York: Random House.

Fitzmaurice, C. and Pease, K. (1986) *The Psychology of Judicial Sentencing*. Manchester: Manchester University Press.

Fitzpatrick, M. A. (1984) A typological approach to marital interaction: recent theory and research. In L. Berkowitz (ed.), *Advances in Experimental Social Psychology* (vol. 18), New York: Academic Press.

Flament, C. (1982) Du biais d'équilibre structural à la représentation du groupe. In J.-P. Codol and J.-P. Leyens (eds), *Cognitive Analysis of Social Behavior*, The Hague: Nijhoff.

Flavell, J. (1963) *The Developmental Psychology of Jean Piaget*. New York: Van Nostrand.

Flavell, J. and Ross, L. (eds) (1981) *Social Cognitive Development: frontiers and possible future*. Cambridge: Cambridge University Press.

Foa, U. G. and Foa, E. B. (1972) Resource exchange: toward a structural theory of interpersonal communication. In A. W. Siegman and B. Pope (eds), *Studies in Dyadic Communication*, New York: Pergamon.

Foa, U. G. and Foa, E. B. (1975a) *Societal Structures of the Mind*. Springfield: Thomas.

Foa, U. G. and Foa, E. B. (1975b) *Resource Theory of Social Exchange*. Morristown, NJ: General Learning Press.

Fogelson, R. M. (1971) *Violence in Protest*. New York: Doubleday.

Folkman, S. and Lazarus, R. (1985) If it changes it must be a process: study of emotion and coping during three stages of a college examination. *Journal of Personality and Social Psychology*, 48, 150–70.

Foot, H. C., Chapman, A. J. and Smith, J. R. (1980) Patterns of interaction in children's friendships. In H. C. Foot, A. J. Chapman and J. R. Smith (eds), *Friendship and Social Relations in Children*, Chichester: Wiley.

Forgas, J. P. (1978) The effects of behavioural and cultural expectation cues on the perception of social episodes. *European Journal of Social Psychology*, 8, 203–13.

Forgas, J. P. (1983) Language, goals and situations. *Journal of Language and Social Psychology*, 2, 267–94.

Forsyth, D. R. (1980) The functions of attributions. *Social Psychology Quarterly*, 43, 184–9.

Forsyth, D. R. (1983) *An Introduction to Group Dynamics*. Monterey, Calif.: Brooks/Cole.

Fortin, A. (1985) Apprentissage social et conflit cognitif. *Cahiers de Psychologie Cognitive*, 5, 89–106.

Fowler, R., Hodge, R., Kress, G. and Trew, A. (1979) *Language and Control*. London: Boston & Henley.

Fox, J. and Guyer, M. (1977) Group size and others' strategy in an *n*-person game. *Journal of Conflict Resolution*, 12, 224–34.

Fraczek, A. (1974) Informational role of situation as a determinant of aggressive behavior. In J. DeWit and W. W. Hartup (eds), *Determinants and Origins of Aggressive Behavior*, The Hague: Mouton.

Fraser, C., Gouge, C. and Billig, M. (1971) Risky shifts, cautious shifts, and group polarization. *European Journal of Social Psychology*, 1, 7–29.

Freedman, J. L. (1984) Effect of television violence on aggressiveness. *Psychological Bulletin*, 96, 227–46.

Freedman, J. L., Levy, A. S., Buchanan, R. W. and Price, J. (1972) Crowding and human aggressiveness. *Journal of Experimental Social Psychology*, 8, 528–48.

Freedman, J. L. and Sears, D. O. (1965) Selective exposure. In L. Berkowitz (ed.), *Advances in experimental social psychology* (vol. 2), New York: Academic press.

Freud, S. (1933) *New Introductory Lectures in Psychoanalysis*. New York: Norton.

Freud, S. (1940) Collected works (18 vols). London: Imago.

Freud, S. (1953) Group psychology and the analysis of the ego (1921 original). In J. Strachey (ed.), *The Standard Edition of the Complete Psychological Works of Sigmund Freud* (vol. 18), London: Hogarth.

Frey, D. (1978) Die Theorie der kognitiven Dissonanz. In D. Frey (ed.), *Kognitive Theorien der Sozialpsychologie*, Bern: Huber.

Frey, D. (1986) Recent research on selective exposure to information. In L. Berkowitz (ed.), *Advances in Experimental Social Psychology* (vol. 19), Orlando, Fla.: Academic Press.

Frey, D. and Rogner, O. (1987) The relevance of psychological factors in the convalescence of accident patients. In G. R. Semin and B. Krahe (eds), *Issues in Contemporary German Social Psychology*, London: Sage.

Frey, D., Rogner, O., Schuler, M., Korte, C. and Havemann, D. (1985) Psychological determinants in the convalescence of accident patients. *Basic and Applied Social Psychology*, 6, 317–28.

Frey, D. and Rosch, M. (1984) Information seeking after decisions: the roles of novelty of information and decision reversibility. *Personality and Social Psychology Bulletin*, 10, 91–8.

Friedman, M. and Rosenman, R. H. (1959) Association of a specific overt behaviour pattern with increases in blood cholesterol, blood clotting time, incidence of arcus senilis and clinical coronary artery diseases. *Journal of the American Medical Association*, 169, 1286–96.

Friedrich-Cofer, L. and Huston, A. C. (1986) Television violence and aggression: the debate continues. *Psychological Bulletin*, 100, 364–71.

Fullard, W. and Reiling, A. M. (1976) An investigation of Lorenz's 'babyishness'. *Child Development*, 7, 1191–3.

Funder, D. C. (1987) Errors and mistakes: evaluating the accuracy of social judgment. *Psychological Bulletin*, 101, 75–90.

Furnham, A. (1986) Assertiveness through different media. *Journal of Language and Social Psychology*, 5, 1–12.

Furth, H. G. (1980) *The World of Grown-Ups: children's conceptions of society*. New York: Elsevier.

Fusilier, M. R., Ganster, D. C. and Mayes, B. T. (1986) The social support and health relationship: is there a gender difference? *Journal of Occupational Psychology*, 59, 145–53.

Gabler, H., Schulz, H.-J. and Weber, R. (1982) Zuschaueraggressionen: Eine Feldstudie über Fussballfans. In G. Pilz et al. (eds), *Sport and Gewalt*, Schorndorf: Karl Hofmann.

Gaes, G. G., Kalle, R. J. and Tedeschi, J. T. (1978) Impression management in the forced compliance situation: two studies using the bogus pipeline. *Journal of Experimental Social Psychology*, 14, 493–510.

Garber, R. M. and Maslach, C. (1977) The parole hearing: decision or justification? *Law and Human Behavior*, 1, 261–81.

Gardner, B. T. and Wallach, L. (1965) Shapes of figures identified as a baby's head. *Perceptual and Motor Skills*, 20, 135–42.

Garfinkel, H. (1967) *Studies in Ethnomethodology*. Englewood Cliffs, NJ: Prentice-Hall.

Gates, M. F. and Allee, W. C. (1933) Conditioned behavior of isolated and grouped cockroaches on a simple maze. *Journal of Comparative Psychology*, 15, 331–58.

Geen, R. G. and O'Neal, E. C. (1969) Activation of cue-elicited aggression by general arousal. *Journal of Personality and Social Psychology*, 11, 289–92.

Geen, R. G. and Stonner, D. (1971) Effects of aggressiveness habit strength on behavior in the presence of aggression-related stimuli. *Journal of Personality and Social Psychology*, 17, 149–53.

Gerard, H. B. and Hoyt, M. F. (1974) Distinctiveness of social categorization and attitude toward ingroup members. *Journal of Personality and Social Psychology*, 29, 836–42.

Gerard, H. B. and Mathewson, G. C. (1966) The effects of severity of initiation on liking for a group: a replication. *Journal of Experimental Social Psychology*, 2, 278–87.

Gerard, H. B., Wilhelmy, R. A. and Connolley, E. S. (1968) Conformity and group size. *Journal of Personality and Social Psychology*, 8, 79–82.

Gerbner, G., Cross, L., Morgan, M. and Signorelli, N. (1980) The 'mainstreaming' of America: violence profile no. 11. *Journal of Communication*, 30, 10–29.

Gergen, K. J. (1973) Social psychology as history. *Journal of Personality and Social Psychology*, 26, 309–20.

Gergen, K. J. (1978) Experimentation in social psychology: a reappraisal. *European Journal of Social Psychology*, 8, 507–27.

Gergen, K. J. (1985) Social psychology and the phoenix of unreality. In S. Koch and D. E. Leary (eds), *A Century of Psychology as Science*, New York: McGraw-Hill.

Gergen, K. J. and Gergen, M. M. (1983) Social construction of helping relationships. In J. D. Fisher, A. Nadler and B. M. DePaulo (eds), *New Directions in Helping. Vol. 1: Recipient reactions to aid*, New York: Academic Press.

Gergen, K. J., Morse, S. J. and Gergen, M. M. (1980) Behavior exchange in cross-cultural perspective. In H. C. Triandis and W. W. Lambert (eds), *Handbook of Cross-Cultural Psychology. Vol. 5: Social psychology*, Boston: Allyn & Bacon.

Gibbons, F. X. (1978) Sexual standards and reactions to pornography: enhancing behavioral consistency through self-focused attention. *Journal of Personality and Social psychology*, 36, 976–87.

Giddens, A. (1982) *Profiles and Critiques in Social Theory*. London: Macmillan.

Gilbert, S. J. (1977) Effects of unanticipated self-disclosure on recipients of varying levels of self-esteem. *Human Communication Research*, 3, 368–71.

Gilbert, S. J. and Horenstein, D. (1975) The communication of self-disclosure: level versus valence. *Human Communication Research*, 1, 316–22.

Gilbert, S. J. and Whiteneck, G. G. (1976) Toward a multidimensional approach to the study of self-disclosure. *Human Communication Research*, 2, 347–55.

Giles, H. (ed.) (1977) *Language, Ethnicity and Intergroup Relations*. London: Academic Press.

Giles, H. (1979) Ethnicity markers in speech. In K. R. Scherer and H. Giles (eds), *Social Markers in Speech*, Cambridge: Cambridge University Press.

Giles, H. (ed.) (1984) The dynamics of speech accommodation. *International Journal of the Sociology of Language*, 46, special issue.

Giles, H., Coupland, N., Henwood, K., Harriman, J. and Coupland, J. (in press). The social meaning of RP: an intergenerational perspective. In S. Ramsaran (ed.), *Studies in the Pronunciation of English: a commemorative volume in honour of A. C. Gimson*, London: Croom Helm.

Giles, H. and Farrar, K. (1979) Some behavioural consequences of speech and dress styles. *British Journal of Social and Clinical Psychology*, 18, 209–10.

Giles, H. and Fitzpatrick, M. A. (1984) Personal, group and couple identities: towards a relational context for the study of language attitudes and linguistic forms. In D. Schiffrin (ed.), *Meaning, Form and Use in Context: linguistic applications*, Washington, DC: Georgetown University Press.

Giles, H. and Hewstone, M. (1982) Cognitive structures, speech and social situations: two integrative models. *Language Sciences*, 4, 187–219.

Giles, H. and Johnson, P. (1981) The role of language in ethnic group relations. In J. C. Turner and H. Giles (eds), *Intergroup Behaviour*, Oxford: Basil Blackwell.

Giles, H. and Johnson, P. (1986) Perceived threat, ethnic commitment and inter-ethnic language behaviour. In Y. Kim (ed.), *Interethnic Communication: recent research*, Beverly Hills: Sage.

Giles, H. and Powesland, P. F. (1975) *Speech Style and Social Evaluation*. London: Academic Press.

Giles, H. and Sassoon, C. (1983) The effects of speaker's accent, social class background and message style on British listeners' social judgements. *Language and Communication*, 3, 305–13.

Giles, H. and Street, R. L., Jr (1985) Communicator characteristics and behavior. In M. L. Knapp and G. R. Miller (eds), *Handbook of Interpersonal Communication*, Beverly Hills: Sage.

Giles, H. and Wiemann, J. M. (1987) Language, social comparison and power. In C. R. Berger and S. Chaffee (eds), *Handbook of Communication Science*, Newbury Park, Calif.: Sage.

Giles, H., Wilson, P. and Conway, A. (1981) Accent and lexical diversity as determinants of impression formation and employment selection. *Language Sciences*, 3, 92–103.

Gilly, M. and Roux, J. P. (1984) Efficacité comparée de travail individuel et du travail et interaction sociocognitive dans l'appropriation et la mise en oeuvre de règles de resolution chez des enfants de 11–12 ans. *Cahiers de Psychologie Cognitive*, 4, 171–88.

Glass, D. C., Krakoff, L. R., Contrada, R. et al. (1980) Effect of harassment and competition upon cardiovascular and plasma catecholaminic responses in type A and B individuals. *Psychophysiology*, 17, 453–63.

Glasser, W. (1975) *Reality Therapy: a new approach to psychiatry*. London: Harper & Row.

Goffman, E. (1959) *The Presentation of Self in Everyday Life*. New York: Doubleday Anchor.

Goffman, E. (1963) *Behavior in Public Places*. New York: Free Press.

Goldfoot, D. A. and Wallen, K. (1978) Development of gender role behaviors in heterosexual and isosexual groups of infant rhesus monkeys. In D. J. Chivers and J. Herbert (eds), *Recent Advances in Primatology*, London: Academic Press.

Gordon, K. H. (1924) Group judgments in the field of lifted weights. *Journal of Experimental Psychology*, 7, 398–400.

Gottman, J. (1979) *Marital Interaction: experimental investigations*. New York: Academic Press.

Gottman, J. (1982) Emotional responsiveness in marital conversations. *Journal of Communication*, 32, 108–20.

Gottman, J. and Levenson, R. (in press) The social psychophysiology of marriage. In P. Noller and M. A. Fitzpatrick (eds), *Marital Interaction*, Clevedon: Multilingual Matters.

Gould, S. J. (1983) *The Panda's Thumb*. Canterbury: Chaucer.

Gouldner, A. W. (1960) The norm of reciprocity: a preliminary statement. *American Sociological Review*, 25, 161–78.

Gove, W. R. (1979) The relationship between sex roles, marital status and mental illness. *Social Forces*, 51, 34–44.

Grant, J. D., Grant, J. and Toch, H. (1982) Police–citizen conflict and decisions to arrest. In V. Konecni and E. Ebbeson (eds), *The Criminal Justice System: a social psychological analysis*, San Francisco: Freeman.

Graumann, C. F. (1976) Modification by migration: vicissitudes of cross-national communication. *Social Research*, 43, 367–85.

Graumann, C. F. (1983) Theorie und Geschichte. In G. Lüer (ed.), *Bericht über den 33. Kongress der Deutschen Gesellschaft für Psychologie* (Vol. 1), Göttingen: Hogrefe.

Graumann, C. F. (1986) The individualization of the social and the desocialization of the individual: Floyd H. Allport's contribution to social psychology. In C. F. Graumann and S. Moscovici (eds), *Changing Conceptions of Crowd Mind and Behavior*, New York: Springer.

Graumann, C. F. (1987a) History as multiple reconstruction, tributaries, and undercurrents. In G. Semin and B. Krahé (eds), *Issues in Contemporary German Social Psychology*, London: Sage.

Graumann, C. F. (1987b) From knowledge to cognition. In D. Bar-Tal and A. W. Kruglanski (eds), *Social Psychology of Knowledge*, Cambridge: Cambridge University Press.

Graumann, C. F. and Moscovici, S. (eds) (1986) *Changing Conceptions of Crowd Mind and Behavior*, New York: Springer.

Graumann, C. F. and Sommer, M. (1984) Schema and inference: models in cognitive social psychology. In J. R. Royce and L. P. Mos (eds), *Annals of Theoretical Psychology* (vol. 1), New York: Plenum.

Greenberg, M. S. (1980) A theory of indebtedness. In K. J. Gergen, M. S. Greenberg and R. H. Willis (eds), *Social Exchange*, New York: Plenum.

Greenberg, M. S., Wilson, C. E., Ruback, R. B. and Mills, M. K. (1979) Social and emotional determinants of victim crime reporting. *Social Psychology Quarterly*, 42, 364–72.

Greenstein, T. N. and Knottnerus, J. D. (1980) The effects of differential evaluations on status generalization. *Social Psychology Quarterly*, 43, 147–54.

Greenwald, A. G. (1975a) Does the Good Samaritan parable increase helping? A comment on Darley and Batson's no-effect conclusion. *Journal of Personality and Social Psychology*, 32, 578–83.

Greenwald, A. G. (1975b) On the inconclusiveness of 'crucial' tests of dissonance versus self-perception theories. *Journal of Experimental Social Psychology*, 11, 490–9.

Grice, H. P. (1975) Logic and conversation. In P. Cole and J. L. Morgan (eds), *Syntax and Semantics. Vol. 3: Speech acts*, New York: Academic Press.

Griesinger, D. W. and Livingstone, J. W. (1973) Toward a model of interpersonal motivation in experimental games. *Behavioral Science*, 18, 73–8.

Grush, J. E. (1979) A summary review of mediating explanations of exposure phenomena. *Personality and Social Psychology Bulletin*, 5, 154–9.

Grzelak, J. L. (1981). Social interdependence: do we know what we want to know? *Polish Psychological Bulletin*, 12, 125–35.

Grzelak, J. L. (1982) Preferences and cognitive processes in social interdependence situations. In V. Derlega and J. Grzelak (eds), *Cooperation and helping behavior: theory and research*, New York: Academic Press.

Grzelak, J. L. and Tyszka, T. (1974) Some preliminary experiments on cooperation in *n*-person games. *Polish Psychological Bulletin*, 5, 83–91.

Gudjonsson, G. and Clark, N. K. (1986) Suggestibility in police interrogation: a social psychological model. *Social Behaviour*, 1, 83–104.

Gudykunst, W. B. (ed.) (1986) *Intergroup Communication*. London: Edward Arnold.

Gudykunst, W. B. and Kim, Y. (1984) *Communicating with strangers: an approach to intercultural communication*. New York: Random House.

Guimond, S. and Dubé-Simard, L. (1983) Relative deprivation theory and the Quebec nationalist movement: the cognition–emotion distinction and the personal–group deprivation issue. *Journal of Personality and Social Psychology*, 44, 526–35.

Gurr, T. R. (1970) *Why Men Rebel*. Princeton, NJ: Princeton University Press.

Guyer, M. and Rapoport, A. (1972) 2 × 2 games played once. *Journal of Conflict Resolution*, 16, 409–31.

Haaland, G. A. and Venkatesan, M. (1968) Resistance to persuasive communications: an examination of the distraction hypotheses. *Journal of Personality and Social Psychology*, 9, 167–70.

Habermas, J. (1979) *Communication and the Evolution of Society* (trans. T. McCarthy). Boston: Beacon.

Haines, H. and Vaughan, G. M. (1979) Was 1898 a 'great date' in the history of experimental social psychology? *Journal of the History of the Behavioral Sciences*, 15, 323–32.

Hall, C. S. and Lindzey, G. (1968) The relevance of Freudian psychology and related viewpoints for the social sciences. In G. Lindzey and E. Aronson (eds), *Handbook of Social Psychology* (vol. 1), 2nd edn, Reading, Mass.: Addison-Wesley.

Hall, J. A. (1984) *Nonverbal Sex Differences*. Baltimore: Johns Hopkins University Press.

Halpin, A. W. and Winer, B. J. (1952) *The Leadership Behavior of the Airplane Commander*. Columbus: Ohio State University Research Foundation.

Hamburger, H., Guyer, M. and Fox, J. (1975) Group size and cooperation. *Journal of Conflict Resolution*, 19, 503–31.

Hamilton, D. L. (1979) A cognitive-attributional analysis of stereotyping. In L. Berkowitz (ed.), *Advances in Experimental Social Psychology* (vol. 12), New York: Academic Press.

Hamilton, D. L. (1981) Illusory correlation and stereotyping. In D. L. Hamilton (ed.), *Cognitive Processes in Stereotyping and Intergroup Behaviour*, Hillsdale, NJ: Erlbaum.

Hamilton, D. L. and Rose, T. (1980) Illusory correlation and the maintenance of stereotypic beliefs. *Journal of Personality and Social Psychology*, 39, 832–45.

Hamilton, D. L. and Trolier, T. K. (1986) Stereotypes and stereotyping: an overview of the cognitive approach. In J. Dovidio and S. Gaertner (eds), *Prejudice, Discrimination, and Racism*, New York: Academic Press.

Hans, V. P. and Vidmar, N. (1982) Jury selection. In N. L. Kerr and R. M. Bray (eds), *The Psychology of the Courtroom*, London: Academic Press.

Hardin, G. (1968) The tragedy of the commons. *Science*, 162, 1243–8.

Hardoin, M. and Codol, J.-P. (1984) Descriptions de soi et d'autrui: influence de l'ordre des descriptions sur les catégories de réponses utilisées. *Cahiers de Psychologie Cognitive*, 4, 295–302.

Harford, T. and Solomon, L. (1967) 'Reformed sinner' and 'lapsed saint' strategies in prisoner's dilemma game. *Journal of Conflict Resolution*, 11, 104–9.

Hargreaves, D. H. (1967) *Social Relations in a Secondary School*. London: Routledge & Kegan Paul.

Hargreaves, D. J., Molloy, C. G. and Pratt, A. R. (1982) Social factors in conservation. *British Journal of Psychology*, 73, 231–4.

Harris, M., Jones, D. and Grant, J. (1983) The nonverbal context of mothers' speech to infants. *First Language*, 4, 21–30.

Harrison, A. A. (1968) Response competition, frequency, exploratory behavior, and liking. *Journal of Personality and Social Psychology*, 9, 363–8.

Harrison, A. A. (1977) Mere exposure. In L. Berkowitz (ed.), *Advances in Experimental Social Psychology* (vol. 10), New York: Academic Press.

Hart, H. L. A. and Honoré, A. M. (1959) *Causation in the Law*. Oxford: Clarendon.

Hartley, E. L. (1946) *Problems in Prejudice*. New York: King's Crown.

Hartnett, D. and Bradley J. (1986) Sex roles and work. In D. J. Hargreaves and A. M. Colley (eds), *The Psychology of Sex Roles*, London: Harper & Row.

Harvey, D. J. (1965) The history of psychology as sociology of thought. *Journal of the History of the Behavioral Sciences*, 1, 196–202.

Harvey, J. H., Weber, A. L., Yarkin, K. L. and Stewart, B. E. (1982) An attributional approach to relationship breakdown. In S. Duck (ed.), *Personal Relationships. Vol. 4: Dissolving personal relationships*, London: Academic Press.

Harvey, J. H. and McGlynn, R. P. (1982) Matching words to phenomena: the case of the fundamental attribution error. *Journal of Personality and Social Psychology*, 43, 345–6.

Harvey, J. H., Town, J. P. and Yarkin, K. L. (1981) How fundamental is 'the fundamental attribution error?' *Journal of Personality and Social Psychology*, 40, 346–9.

Harvey, J. H., Wells, G. L. and Alvarez, M. D. (1978) Attribution in the context of conflict and separation in close relationships. In J. H. Harvey, W. Ickes and R. F. Kidd (eds), *New Directions in Attribution Research* (vol. 2), Hillsdale, NJ: Erlbaum.

Hastie, R. (1981) Schematic principles in human memory. In E. T. Higgins, C. P. Herman and M. P. Zanna (eds), *Social Cognition: the Ontario symposium* (vol. 1), Hillsdale, NJ: Erlbaum.

Hastie, R. (1984) Causes and effects of causal attribution. *Journal of Personality and Social Psychology*, 46, 44–56.

Hatfield, E., Utne, M. K. and Traupmann, J. (1979) Equity theory and intimate relationships. In R. L. Burgess and T. L. Huston (eds), *Exchange Theory in Developing Relationships*, New York: Academic Press.

Hawkins, R. P., Wiemann, J. M. and Pingree, S. (eds) (in press) *Convergence in Communication Research*. Newbury Park, Calif.: Sage.

Hearnshaw, L. S. (1964) *A Short History of British Psychology, 1840–1940*. London: Methuen.

Heider, F. (1944) Social perception and phenomenal causality. *Psychological Review*, 51, 358–74.

Heider, F. (1946) Attitudes and cognitive organization. *Journal of Psychology*, 21, 107–12.

Heider, F. (1958) *The Psychology of Interpersonal Relations*. New York: Wiley.

Hellpach, W. (1933) *Elementares Lehrbuch der Sozialpsychologie*. Berlin: Springer.

Helm, B., Bonoma, T. V. and Tedeschi, J. T. (1972) Reciprocity for harm done. *Journal of Social Psychology*, 87, 89–98.

Helson, H. (1964) *Adaptation-Level Theory: an experimental and systematic approach to behavior*. New York: Harper & Row.

Hemphill, J. K. (1961) Why people attempt to lead. In L. Petrullo and B. M. Bass (eds), *Leadership and Interpersonal Behavior*, New York: Holt, Rinehart & Winston.

Henchy, T. and Glass, D. C. (1968) Evaluation apprehension and the social facilitation of dominant and subordinate responses. *Journal of Personality and Social Psychology*, 10, 446–54.

Henderson, S., Byrne, D. G. and Duncan-Jones, S. (1981) *Neurosis and the Social Environment*. London: Academic Press.

Henshel, R. L. (1980) The purposes of laboratory experimentation and the virtues of deliberate artificiality. *Journal of Experimental Social Psychology*, 16, 466–78.

Herdt, G. H. (1981) *Guardians of the Flute: idioms of masculinity*. New York: McGraw-Hill.

Hewes, D., Graham, M. L., Doelger, J. and Pavitt, C. (1985) Second guessing: message interpretation in social networks. *Human Communication Research*, 11, 299–334.

Hewstone, M. (1986) *Understanding Attitudes to the European Community*. Cambridge: Cambridge University Press.

Hewstone, M. (1988) Attributional bases of intergroup conflict. In W. Stroebe, A. Kruglanski, D. Bar-Tal and M. Hewstone (eds), *The Social Psychology of Intergroup Conflict: theory, research and applications*, New York: Springer.

Hewstone, M. and Brown, R. J. (1986) Contact is not enough: an intergroup perspective on the contact hypothesis. In M. Hewstone and R. Brown (eds), *Contact and Conflict in Intergroup Encounters*, Oxford: Basil Blackwell.

Hewstone, M. and Giles, H. (1986) Social groups and social stereotypes in intergroup communication: review and model of intergroup communication breakdown. In W. B. Gudykunst (ed.), *Intergroup Communication*, London: Edward Arnold.

Hewstone, M. and Jaspars, J. (1982) Explanations for racial discrimination: the effect of group discussion on intergroup attributions. *European Journal of Social Psychology*, 12, 1–16.

Hewstone, M. and Jaspars, J. (1983) A re-examination of the roles of consensus, consistency and distinctiveness: Kelley's cube revisited. *British Journal of Social Psychology*, 22, 41–50.

Hewstone, M. and Jaspars, J. (1984) Social dimensions of attribution. In H. Tajfel (ed.), *The Social Dimension: European developments in social psychology* (vol. 2), Cambridge: Cambridge University Press, Paris: Maison des Sciences de l'Homme.

Hewstone, M. and Jaspars, J. (1987) Covariation and causal attribution: a logical model of the intuitive analysis of variance. *Journal of Personality and Social Psychology*, 53, 663–72.

Hewstone, M., Jaspars, J. and Lalljee, M. (1982) Social representations, social attribution and social identity: the intergroup images of 'public' and 'comprehensive' schoolboys. *European Journal of Social Psychology*, 12, 241–69.

Hewstone, M. and Ward, C. (1985) Ethnocentrism and causal attribution in Southeast Asia. *Journal of Personality and Social Psychology*, 48, 614–23.

Hiebsch, H. and Vorwerg, M. (1980) *Sozialpsychologie*. Berlin (GDR): Deutscher.

Higgins, E. T. (1980) The 'communication game': implications for social cognition and persuasion. In E. T. Higgins, C. P. Herman and M. P. Zanna (eds), *Social Cognition: the Ontario symposium*, Hillsdale, NJ: Erlbaum.

Higgins, E. T., Rhodewalt, F. and Zanna, M. P. (1979) Dissonance motivation: its nature, persistence, and reinstatement. *Journal of Experimental Social Psychology*, 15, 16–34.

Higgins, E. T., Ruble, D. N. and Hartup, W. W. (eds) (1983) *Social Cognition and Social Development*. Cambridge: Cambridge University Press.

Hill, C. T., Rubin, Z. and Peplau, L. A. (1976) Breakups before marriage: the end of 103 affairs. *Journal of Social Issues*, 32, 146–67.

Hill, R. et al. (1970) *Family Development in Three Generations*. Cambridge, Mass.: Schenkman.

Hinde, R. A. (1960) Energy models of motivation. *Symposia of the Society for Experimental Biology*, 14, 199–213.

Hinde, R. A. (1974) *Biological Bases of Human Social Behavior*. New York: McGraw-Hill.

Hinde, R. A. (1979) *Towards Understanding Relationships*. London: Academic Press.

Hinde, R. A. (ed.) (1983) *Primate Social Relationships*. Basil Blackwell: Oxford.

Hinde, R. A. (1984a) Why do the sexes behave differently in close relationships? *Journal of Social and Personal Relationships*, 1, 471–501.

Hinde, R. A. (1984b) Biological bases of the mother–child relationship. In J. D. Call, E. Galenson and R. L. Tyson (eds), *Frontiers of Infant Psychiatry* (vol. II), New York: Basic.

Hinde, R. A. (1986) Some implications of evolutionary theory and comparative data for the study of human prosocial and aggressive behaviour. In E. Olweus, M. Radke-Yarrow and J. Block (eds), *The Development of Antisocial and Prosocial Behavior*, London: Academic Press.

Hinde, R. A. (1987) *Individuals, Relationships and Culture*. Cambridge: Cambridge University Press.

Hinde, R. A. and Barden, L. D. (1985) The evolution of the teddy bear. *Animal Behaviour*, 33, 1371–3.

Hinde, R. A. and Stevenson-Hinde, J. (eds) (1973) *Constraints on Learning: limitations and predispositions*. London: Academic Press.

Hinde, R. A. and Stevenson-Hinde, J. (1987) Interpersonal relationships and child development. *Developmental Review*, 7, 1–21.

Hinde, R. A. and Tamplin, A. (1983) Relations between mother–child interaction and behaviour in preschool. *British Journal of Developmental Psychology*, 1, 231–57.

Hindelang, M. J., Hirschi, T. and Weis, J. G. (1981) *Measuring Delinquency*. Beverly Hills: Sage.

Hobfoll, S. (1986) *Stress, Social Support, and Women*. New York: Hemisphere.

Hoekstra, M. and Wilke, H. (1972) Wage recommendations in management groups: a cross-cultural study. *Nederlands Tijdschrift voor de Psychologie*, 27, 266–72.

Hogarth, J. (1971) *Sentencing as a Human Process*. Toronto: University of Toronto Press.

Hogg, M. (1985) Male and female speech in dyads and groups: a study of speech style and gender salience. *Journal of Language and Social Psychology*, 4, 99–112.

Holstein, J. A. (1985) Jurors' interpretation and jury decision making. *Law and Human Behaviour*, 9, 83–100.

Homans, G. (1950) *The Human Group*. London: Routledge & Kegan Paul.

Hood, R. (1962) *Sentencing in Magistrates Courts*. London: Stevens.

Hormuth, S. E. (1979) *Sozialpsychologie der Einstellungsänderung*. Königstein/TS: Verlagsgruppe Athenäum.

Horowitz, I. A. (1969) Effects of volunteering, fear, arousal, and number of communications on attitude change. *Journal of Personality and Social Psychology*, 11, 34-7.

Horwitz, M. and Rabbie, J. M. (1982) Individuality and membership in the intergroup system. In H. Tajfel (ed.), *Social Identity and Intergroup Relations*, Cambridge: Cambridge University Press.

Hosking, D. M. (1981) A critical evaluation of Fiedler's contingency hypothesis. In G. M. Stephenson and J. M. Davis (eds), *Progress in Applied Social Psychology*, Chichester: Wiley.

Hough, M. and Mayhew, P. (1983) *The British Crime Survey: first report*. London: HMSO.

House, J. (1980) *Occupational Stress and the Mental and Physical Health of Factory Workers*. Ann Arbor, Mich.: University of Michigan Survey Research Center.

Hovland, C. I. (1959) Reconciling conflicting results derived from experimental and survey studies of attitude change. *American Psychologist*, 14, 8-17.

Hovland, C. I., Janis, I. L. and Kelley, H. H. (1953) *Communication and Persuasion*. New Haven, Conn.: Yale University Press.

Hovland, C. I. and Sherif, M. (1952) Judgmental phenomena and scales of attitude measurement: item displacement in Thurstone scales. *Journal of Abnormal and Social Psychology*, 47, 822-32.

Howard, J. A. and Levinson, S. (1985) The overdue courtship between attribution and labelling. *Social Psychology Quarterly*, 19, 191-202.

Howard, J. W. and Dawes, R. M. (1976) Linear prediction of marital happiness. *Personality and Social Psychology Bulletin*, 2, 478-80.

Howe, C. (1981) *Acquiring Language in a Conversational Context*. London: Academic Press.

Hoyt, M. F., Henley, M. D. and Collins, B. E. (1972) Studies in forced compliance: confluence of choice and consequence on attitude change. *Journal of Personality and Social Psychology*, 23, 205-10.

Hraba, J. and Grant, G. (1970) Black is beautiful: a re-examination of racial preference and identification. *Journal of Personality and Social Psychology*, 16, 398-402.

Huesmann, L. R., Lagerspetz, K. and Eron, L. D. (1984) Intervening variables in the TV violence–aggression relation: evidence from two countries. *Developmental Psychology*, 20, 746-75.

Hughes, M. and Grieve, R. (1980) On asking children bizarre questions. *First Language*, 1, 149-60.

Huici, C. (1984) The individual and social functions of sex role stereotypes. In H. Tajfel (ed.), *The Social Dimension* (vol. 2), Cambridge: Cambridge University Press.

Hurtig, M.-C. and Pichevin, M.-F. (1985) La variable sexe en psychologie: donné ou construct? *Cahiers de Psychologie Cognitive*, 5, 187-228.

Huston, A. (1985) The development of sex typing: themes from recent research. *Developmental Review*, 5, 1-17.

Huston, T. L. (1983) Power. In H. H. Kelley, E. Berscheid, A. Christensen et al. (eds), *Close Relationships*, New York: Freeman.

Huston, T. L., Surra, C. A., Fitzgerald, N. M. and Gate, R. M. (1981) From courtship to marriage: mate selection as an interpersonal process. In S. W. Duck and R. Gilmour (eds), *Personal Relationships. Vol. 2: Developing personal relationships*, London: Academic Press.

Hutt, C. and McGrew, W. C. (1967) Effects of group density upon social behaviour in humans. Paper presented at the meeting of the Association for the Study of Animal Behaviour, Oxford, 17-20 July.

Hymes, R. W. (1986) Political attitudes as social categories: a new look at selective memory. *Journal of Personality and Social Psychology*, 51, 233–41.

Ilgen, D. R. and Fujji, D. S. (1976) An investigation of the validity of leader behavior descriptions obtained from subordinates. *Journal of Applied Psychology*, 61, 642–51.

Illich, I. (1976) *Limits to Medicine*. London: Marion Boyars.

Ingham, A. G., Levinger, G., Graves, J. and Peckham, V. (1974) The Ringelmann effect: studies of group size and group performance. *Journal of Personality and Social Psychology*, 10, 371–84.

Insko, C. A., Drenan, S., Solomon, M. R., Smith, R. and Wade, T. J. (1983) Conformity as a function of the consistency of positive self-evaluation with being liked and being right. *Journal of Experimental Social Psychology*, 19, 341–58.

Insko, C. A. and Oakes, W. F. (1966) Awareness and the 'conditioning' of attitudes. *Journal of Personality and Social Psychology*, 4, 487–96.

Irle, M. (1975) *Lehrbuch der Sozialpsychologie*. Göttingen: Hogrefe.

Irons, W. (1979) Cultural and biological success. In N. A. Chagnon and W. Irons (eds), *Evolutionary Biology and Human Social Behavior*, Mass.: Duxbury.

Irving, B. (1980) Police interrogation: a case study of present practice. Research study no. 2, Royal Commission on Criminal Procedure. London: HMSO.

Irving, B. (1987) Interrogative suggestibility: a question of parsimony? *Social Behaviour*, 2, 19–29.

Irving, B. and Hilgendorf, L. (1980) Police interrogation: the psychological approach. Research study no. 1, Royal Commission on Criminal Procedure. London: HMSO.

Isenberg, D. J. (1986) Group polarization: a critical review and meta-analysis. *Journal of Personality and Social Psychology*, 50, 1141–51.

Israel, J. and Tajfel, H. (eds) (1972) *The Context of Social Psychology: a critical assessment*. London: Academic Press.

Jaccard, J. J. and Davidson, A. R. (1972) Toward an understanding of family planning behaviors: an initial investigation. *Journal of Applied Social Psychology*, 2, 228–35.

Jackson, J. M. and Harkins, J. M. (1985) Equity in effort: an explanation of the social loafing effect. *Journal of Personality and Social Psychology*, 49, 1199–1206.

Jacobs, R. C. and Campbell, D. T. (1961) The perpetuation of an arbitrary tradition through several generations of a laboratory microculture. *Journal of Abnormal and Social Psychology*, 62, 649–58.

Jacobson, N. S. and Margolin, G. (1979) *Marital Theory: strategies based on social learning and behavior exchange principles*. New York: Brunner/Mazel.

Jaffe, Y. and Yinon, Y. (1983) Collective aggression: the group individual paradigm in the study of collective antisocial behavior. In H. H. Blumberg, A. P. Hare, V. Kent and M. Davies (eds), *Small Groups and Social Interaction* (vol. 1), New York: Wiley.

Jahoda, G. (1962) Development of Scottish children's ideas and attitudes about other countries. *Journal of Social Psychology*, 58, 91–108.

Jahoda, G. (1963) The development of children's ideas about country and nationality: the conceptual framework. *British Journal of Educational Psychology*, 33, 47–60.

Jahoda, G. (1983) European 'lag' in the development of an economic concept: a study in Zimbabwe. *British Journal of Developmental Psychology*, 1, 113–20.

Jahoda, G. (1984) Levels of social and logico-mathematical thinking: their nature and interrelations. In W. Doise, and A. Palmonari (eds), *Social Interactions in Individual Development*, Cambridge: Cambridge University Press.

Jahoda, G. and Woerdenbagch, A. (1982) The development of ideas about an economic institution: a cross-national replication, *British Journal of Social Psychology*, 21, 337–8.

James, W. (1890) *Principles of Psychology* (2 vols). New York: Holt, Rinehart & Winston.

Janis, I. L. (1967) Effects of fear arousal on attitude change: recent developments in theory and experimental research. In L. Berkowitz (ed.), *Advances in Experimental Social Psychology* (vol. 3), New York: Academic Press.

Janis, I. L. (1972) *Victims of Groupthink*. Boston: Houghton Mifflin.

Janis, I. L. and Mann, L. (1977) *Decision Making: a psychological analysis of conflict, choice and commitment*. New York: Free Press.

Jaspars, J. (1980) The coming of age of social psychology in Europe. *European Journal of Social Psychology*, 10, 421–8.

Jaspars, J. (1982) Social judgement and social behaviour: a dual representational model. In J.-P. Codol & J.-P. Leyens (eds), *Cognitive Analysis of Social Behavior*, The Hague: Nijhoff.

Jaspars, J. (1983) The task of social psychology. *British Journal of Social Psychology*, 22, 277–88.

Jaspars, J. (1986) Forum and focus: a personal view of European social psychology. *European Journal of Social Psychology*, 16, 3–15.

Jaspars, J., Hewstone, M. and Fincham, F. D. (1983) Attribution theory and research: the state of the art. In J. Jaspars, F. D. Fincham and M. Hewstone (eds), *Attribution Theory and Research: conceptual, developmental and social dimensions*, London: Academic Press.

Jaspars, J., Van De Geer, J. P., Tajfel, H. and Johnson, N. B. (1973) On the development of national attitudes. *European Journal of Social Psychology*, 3, 347–69.

Jellison, J. M. and Davis, D. (1973) Relationships between perceived ability and attitude extremity. *Journal of Personality and Social Psychology*, 27, 430–6.

Jellison, J. M. and Green, J. (1981) A self-presentation approach to the fundamental attribution error: the norm of internality. *Journal of Personality and Social Psychology*, 40, 643–9.

Jemmott, J. B. and Locke, S. E. (1984) Psychosocial factors, immunology mediation, and human susceptibility to infectious diseases: how much do we know? *Psychological Bulletin*, 95, 78–108.

Jennings, H. H. (1950) *Leadership and Isolation*. New York: Longman.

Jennings, S. M. (1971) *Self-Disclosure*. New York: Wiley-Interscience.

Jodelet, D. (1984) Représentations sociales: phénomènes, concept et théorie. In S. Moscovici (ed.), *Psychologie Sociale*, Paris: Presses Universitaires de France.

Johnson, R. C., Thomson, C. W. and Frincke, G. (1960) Word values, word frequency, and visual duration thresholds. *Psychological Review*, 67, 332–42.

Johnson, R. D. and Downing, L. L. (1979) Deindividuation and valence of cues: effects on prosocial and antisocial behaviour. *Journal of Personality and Social Psychology*, 37, 1532–8.

Johnson, T. E. and Rule, B. G. (1986) Mitigating circumstances: information, censure, and aggression. *Journal of Personality and Social Psychology*, 50, 537–42.

Jonas, K. (1987) Der Wert-Erwartungs-Ansatz in der Furchtappellforschung. Unpublished doctoral dissertation, Universität Tübingen.

Jones, E. E. (1979) The rocky road from acts to dispositions. *American Psychologist*, 34, 107–17.

Jones, E. E. (1985) Major developments in social psychology during the past four decades. In G. Lindzey and E. Aronson (eds), *Handbook of Social Psychology* (vol. 1), 3rd edn, New York: Random House.

Jones, E. E. and Aneshansel, J. (1956) The learning and utilization of contravaluant material. *Journal of Abnormal and Social Psychology*, 53, 27–33.

Jones, E. E. and Davis, K. E. (1965) From acts to dispositions: the attribution process in person perception. In L. Berkowitz (ed.), *Advances in Experimental Social Psychology* (vol. 2), New York: Academic Press.

Jones, E. E., Davis, K. E. and Gergen, K. J. (1961) Role playing variations and their informational value for person perception. *Journal of Abnormal and Social Psychology*, 63, 302–10.

Jones, E. E. and de Charms, R. (1957) Changes in social perception as a function of the personal relevance of behaviour. *Sociometry*, 20, 75–85.

Jones, E. E., Farina, A., Hastorf, A. H., Markus, H., Miller, D. T. and Scott, R. A. (1984) *Social Stigma: the psychology of marked relations*. New York: Freeman.

Jones, E. E. and Gerard, H. B. (1967) *Foundations of Social Psychology*. New York: Wiley.

Jones, E. E. and Harris, V. A. (1967) The attribution of attitudes. *Journal of Experimental Social Psychology*, 3, 1–24.

Jones, E. E. and McGillis, D. (1976) Correspondent inferences and the attribution cube: a comparative reappraisal. In J. H. Harvey, W. J. Ickes and R. F. Kidd (eds), *New Directions in Attribution Research* (vol. 1), Hillsdale, NJ: Erlbaum.

Jones, E. E. and Nisbett, R. E. (1972) The actor and the observer: divergent perceptions of the causes of behaviour. In E. E. Jones, D. E. Kanouse, H. H. Kelley, R. E. Nisbett, S. Valins and B. Weiner, *Attribution: perceiving the cause of behavior*, Morristown, NJ: General Learning Press.

Jones, E. E. and Sigall, H. (1971) The bogus pipeline: a new paradigm for measuring affect and attitude. *Psychological Bulletin*, 76, 349–64.

Jones, E. E. and Thibaut, J. W. (1958) Interaction goals as bases of inference in interpersonal perception. In R. Tagiuri and L. Petrullo (eds), *Person Perception and Interpersonal Behaviour*, Stanford: Stanford University Press.

Jourard, S. M. (1971) *Self-Disclosure: the experimental investigation of the transparent self*. New York: Wiley.

Judd, C. M. and Kulik, J. A. (1980) Schematic effects of social attitudes on information processing and recall. *Journal of Personality and Social Psychology*, 38, 569–78.

Kahneman, D. (1973) *Attention and Effort*. Englewood Cliffs, NJ: Prentice-Hall.

Kahneman, D. and Tversky, A. (1973) On the psychology of prediction. *Psychological Review*, 80, 237–51.

Kalin, R. (1982) The social significance of speech in medical, legal and occupational settings. In E. B. Ryan and H. Giles (eds), *Attitudes towards Language: social and applied contexts*, London: Edward Arnold.

Kalven, H., Jr and Zeisel, H. (1966) *The American Jury*. London: University of Chicago Press.

Kanter, R. M. (1977) Some effects of proportions on group life: skewed sex ratios and responses to token women. *American Journal of Sociology*, 82, 965–90.

Kantola, S. G., Syme, G. J. and Campbell, N. A. (1982) The role of individual differences and external variables in a test of the sufficiency of Fishbein's model to explain behavioral intentions to conserve water. *Journal of Applied Social Psychology*, 12, 70–83.

Karpf, F. B. (1932) *American Social Psychology: its origins, development, and European background*. New York: Macmillan.

Kassin, S. M. (1979a) Consensus information, prediction, and causal attribution: a review of the literature and issues. *Journal of Personality and Social Psychology*, 37, 1966–81.

Kassin, S. M. (1979b) Base-rates and prediction: the role of sample size. *Personality and Social Psychology Bulletin*, 5, 210–13.

Kassin, S. M. and Hochreich, D. J. (1977) Instructional set: a neglected variable in attribution research? *Personality and Social Psychology Bulletin*, 3, 620–3.

Kassin, S. M. and Pryor, J. B. (1985) The development of attribution processes. In J. B. Pryor and J. D. Day (eds), *The Development of Social Cognition*, New York: Springer.

Katz, D. (1967) The functional approach to the study of attitude. In M. Fishbein (ed.), *Readings in Attitude Theory and Measurement*, New York: Wiley.

Katz, D. (1978) Social psychology in relation to the social sciences. *American Behavioral Scientist*, 5, 779–92.

Katz, D. and Braly, K. W. (1933) Racial stereotypes of one hundred college students. *Journal of Abnormal and Social Psychology*, 28, 280–90.

Kaye, K. (1982) *The Mental and Social Life of Babies*. Brighton: Harvester.

Kayser, E., Schwinger, T. and Cohen, R. L. (1984) Laypersons' conceptions of social relationships: a test of contract theory. *Journal of Personal and Social Relationships*, 1, 433–58.

Keesing, R. M. (1982) Introduction. In G. H. Herdt (ed.), *Rituals of Manhood*, Berkeley: University of California Press.

Kelley, H. H. (1950) The warm–cold variable in first impressions of persons. *Journal of Personality*, 18, 431–9.

Kelley, H. H. (1967) Attribution theory in social psychology. In D. Levine (ed.), *Nebraska Symposium on Motivation*, Lincoln, Nebr.: University of Nebraska Press.

Kelley, H. H. (1972) Causal schemata in the attribution process. In E. E. Jones et al., *Attribution: perceiving the causes of behavior*, Morristown, NJ: General Learning Press.

Kelley, H. H. (1973) The processes of causal attribution. *American Psychologist*, 28, 107–28.

Kelley, H. H. (1979) *Personal Relationships: their structures and processes*. Hillsdale, NJ: Erlbaum.

Kelley, H. H., Berscheid, E., Christensen, A., Harvey, J. H., Huston, T. L., Levinger, G., McClintock, E., Peplau, L. A. and Peterson, D. R. (1983) *Close Relationships*. New York: Freeman.

Kelley, H. H. and Stahelski, A. J. (1970a) The inference of intentions from moves in the prisoner's dilemma game. *Journal of Experimental Social Psychology*, 6, 401–19.

Kelley, H. H. and Stahelski, A. J. (1970b) Social interaction basis of cooperators' and competitors' beliefs about others. *Journal of Personality and Social Psychology*, 16, 66–91.

Kelley, H. H. and Thibaut, J. W. (1978) *Interpersonal Relations: a theory of interdependence*. New York: Wiley.

Kelley, H. H., Thibaut, J. W., Radloff, R. and Mundy, D. (1962) The development of cooperation in the 'minimal social situation'. *Psychological Monographs*, 76, whole no. 19.

Kelman, H. C. (1961) Processes of opinion change. *Public Opinion Quarterly*, 25, 57–78.

Kendon, A. (1983) Gesture and speech: how they interact. In J. M. Wiemann and R. P. Harrison (eds), *Nonverbal Interaction*, Beverly Hills: Sage.

Kennedy, C. W. and Camden, C. T. (1983) A new look at interruptions. *Western Journal of Speech Communication*, 47, 45–58.

Kenrick, D. T. and Stringfield, D. O. (1980) Personality traits and the eye of the beholder. *Psychological Review*, 87, 88–104.

Kerr, N. L. (1982) The jury trial. In V. J. Konečni and E. B. Ebbeson (eds), *The Criminal Justice System: a social-psychological analysis*, San Francisco: Freeman.

Kerr, S. and Jermier, J. M. (1978) Substitutes for leadership: their meaning and measurement. *Organizational Behavior and Human Performance*, 22, 375–403.

Kidder, L. H. and Campbell, D. T. (1970) The indirect testing of social attitude. In G. F. Summers (ed.), *Attitude Measurement*, Chicago: Rand McNally.

Kiesler, C. A. and Pallak, M. S. (1975) Minority influence: the effect of majority reactionaries and defectors, and minority and majority compromisers, upon majority opinion and attraction. *European Journal of Social Psychology*, 5, 237–56.

King, M. (1986) *Psychology In and Out of Court: a critical examination of legal psychology*. Oxford: Pergamon.

Kinney, J. and Leaton, G. (1983) *Loosening the Grip: a handbook of alcohol information*. London: Masby.

Kitchener, R. F. (1986) *Piaget's Theory of Knowledge: genetic epistemology and scientific realism*. New Haven: Yale University Press.

Kitson, G. C., Babri, K. B. and Roach, M. J. (1985) Who divorces and why: a review. *Journal of Family Issues*, 6, 255–94.

Klineberg, O. and Hull, W. F. (1979) *At a Foreign University: an international study of adaptation and coping*. New York: Praeger.

Klugman, S. F. (1947) Group and individual judgments for anticipated events. *Journal of Social Psychology*, 26, 21–33.

Knapp, M. L. (1983) Dyadic relationship development. In J. M. Wiemann and R. P. Harrison (eds), *Nonverbal Interaction*, Beverly Hills: Sage.

Knapp, M. L. (1984) *Interpersonal Communication and Human Relationships*. Boston: Allyn & Bacon.

Knapp, M. L., Ellis, D. G. and Williams, B. A. (1980) Perceptions of communication behaviour associated with relationship terms. *Communication Monographs*, 47, 262–78.

Knight, G. P. (1981) Behavioral and sociometric methods of identifying cooperators, competitors and individualists: support for the validity of the social orientation construct. *Developmental Psychology*, 17, 430–3.

Knight, H. C. (1921) A comparison of the reliability of group and individual judgment. Unpublished master's thesis, Columbia University.

Koch, S. (1985) Foreword: Wundt's creature at age zero – and as centenarian. Some aspects of the institutionalization of the 'new psychology'. In S. Koch and D. E. Leary (eds), *A Century of Psychology as a Science*, New York: McGraw-Hill.

Kogan, N. and Wallach, M. A. (1964) *Risk Taking: a study in cognition and personality*. New York: Holt, Rinehart & Winston.

Kohlberg, L. (1966) A cognitive-developmental analysis of children's sex-role concepts and attitudes. In E. E. Maccoby (ed.), *The Development of Sex Differences*, Stanford: Stanford University Press.

Komorita, G. P. and Barth, J. M. (1985) Components of reward in social dilemmas. *Journal of Personality and Social Psychology*, 48, 364–73.

Konečni, V. J. (1975) The mediation of aggressive behavior: arousal level versus anger and cognitive labeling. *Journal of Personality and Social Psychology*, 32, 706–12.

Konečni, V. J. and Ebbeson, E. B. (1979) External validity of research in legal psychology. *Law and Human Behavior*, 3, 39–70.

Konečni, V. J. and Ebbeson, E. B. (eds) (1982) *The Criminal Justice System: a social-psychological analysis*. San Francisco: Freeman.

Kothandapani, V. (1971) Validation of feeling, belief, and intention to act as three components of attitude and their contribution to prediction of contraceptive behavior. *Journal of Personality and Social Psychology*, 19, 321–33.

Kramer, R. M. and Brewer, M. B. (1986) Social group identity and the emergence of cooperation in resource conservation dilemmas. In H. Wilke, D. Messick and C. Rutte (eds), *Experimental Social Dilemmas*, Frankfurt: Peter Lang.

Krantz, S. E. and Rude, S. (1984) Depressive attributions: selection of different causes or assignment of different meanings? *Journal of Personality and Social Psychology*, 47, 193–203.

Kraut, R. E. and Higgins, E. T. (1984) Communication and social cognition. In R. S. Wyer and T. K. Srull (eds), *Handbook of Social Cognition*, (vol. 3), Hillsdale, NJ: Erlbaum.

Kravitz, D. A. and Martin, B. (1986) Ringelmann rediscovered: the original article. *Journal of Personality and Social Psychology*, 50, 936–41.

Krebs, D. (1981) Gewaltdarstellungen im Fernsehen und die Einstellungen zu aggressiven Handlungen bei 12–15 jährigen Kindern – Bericht über eine Längsschnittstudie. *Zeitschrift für Sozialpsychologie*, 12, 281–302.

Krebs, D. and Groebel, J. (1979) *Die Wirkungen von Gewaltdarstellungen im Fernsehen auf die Einstellungen zu Gewalt und die Angst bei Kindern und Jugendlichen*. Aachen: Projektabschlussbericht.

Krueger, D. L. (1982) Marital decision-making: a language–action analysis. *Quarterly Journal of Speech*, 68, 273–87.

Kruglanski, A. W. (1975) The endogenous–exogenous partition in attribution theory. *Psychological Review*, 82, 387–406.

Kruglanski, A. W. (1979) Causal explanation, teleological explanation: on radical particularism in attribution theory. *Journal of Personality and Social Psychology*, 37, 1447–57.

Kruglanski, A. W. (1980) Lay epistemologic – process and contents. *Psychological Review*, 87, 70–87.

Kruglanski, A. W. and Ajzen, I. (1983) Bias and error in human judgment. *European Journal of Social Psychology*, 13, 1–44.

Kruse, L. (1975) Crowding: Dichte und Enge aus sozialpsychologischer Sicht. *Zeitschrift für Sozialpsychologie*, 6, 2–30.

Kruuk, H. (1972) Surplus killing by carnivores. *Journal of Zoological Society of London*, 166, 233–44.

Kuhlman, M. D. and Marshello, A. M. J. (1975) Individual differences in game motivation as moderators of preprogrammed strategy effects in prisoner's dilemma game. *Journal of Personality and Social Psychology*, 32, 912–31.

Kuhn, M. H. and McPartland, T. S. (1954) An empirical investigation of self-attitudes. *American Sociological Review*, 19, 68–76.

Kulik, J. A. (1983) Confirmatory attribution and the perpetuation of social beliefs. *Journal of Personality and Social Psychology*, 44, 1171–81.

Labov, W. (1966) *The social stratification of English in New York City*. Washington: Center for Applied Linguistics.

La Gaipa, J. J. and Wood, H. D. (1981) Friendship in disturbed adolescents. In S. Duck and R. Gilmour (eds), *Personal Relationships* (vol. 3), London: Academic Press.

Lakoff, R. (1975) *Language and the Woman's Place*. New York: Harper & Row.

Lalljee, M. (1981) Attribution theory and the analysis of explanations. In C. Antaki (ed.), *The Psychology of Ordinary Explanations of Social Behaviour*, London: Academic Press.

Lalljee, M. and Abelson, R. P. (1983) The organization of explanations. In M. Hewstone (ed.), *Attribution Theory: social and functional extensions*, Oxford: Basil Blackwell.

Lamb, T. A. (1981) Nonverbal and paraverbal control in dyads and triads: sex or power differences? *Social Psychology Quarterly*, 44, 49–53.

Lamm, H. and Myers, D. G. (1978) Group-induced polarization of attitudes and behaviour. In L. Berkowitz (ed.), *Advances in Experimental Social Psychology* (vol. 11), New York: Academic Press.

Landman, J. and Manis, M. (1983) Social cognition: some historical and theoretical perspectives. In L. Berkowitz (ed.), *Advances in Experimental Social Psychology* (vol. 16), New York: Academic Press.

Lange, F. (1971) Frustration-aggression: a reconsideration. *European Journal of Social Psychology*, 1, 59–84.

Langer, E. (1978) Rethinking the role of thought in social interaction. In J. H. Harvey, W. Ickes and R. F. Kidd (eds), *New Directions in Attribution Research* (vol. 2), Hillsdale, NJ: Erlbaum.

Langer, E., Blank, A. and Chanowitz, B. (1978) The mindlessness of ostensibly thoughtful action: the role of placebic information in interpersonal interaction. *Journal of Personality and Social Psychology*, 36, 635–42.

La Piere, R. T. (1934) Attitudes versus actions. *Social Forces*, 13, 230–7.

Larson, R. W. (1984) States of consciousness in personal relationships: a life span perspective. International Conference on Personal Relationships, Madison.

Latané, B. (1981) The psychology of social impact. *American Psychologist*, 36, 343–56.

Latané, B. and Darley, J. M. (1969) Bystander 'apathy'. *American Scientist*, 57, 244–68.

Latané, B. and Darley, J. M. (1976) *Help in a Crisis: bystander response to an emergency*. Morristown, NJ: General Learning Press.

Latané, B. and Nida, S. (1981) Ten years of research on group size and helping. *Psychological Bulletin*, 89, 308–24.

Latané, B. and Rodin, J. (1969) A lady in distress: inhabiting effects of friends and strangers on bystander intervention. *Journal of Experimental Social Psychology*, 5, 189–202.

Latané, B., Williams, K. and Harkins, S. (1979) Many hands make light the work: the causes and consequencies of social loafing. *Journal of Personality and Social Psychology*, 37, 822–32.

Latané, B. and Wolf, S. (1981) The social impact of majorities and minorities. *Psychological Review*, 88, 438–53.

Lau, R. R. and Russell, D. (1980) Attributions in the sports pages. *Journal of Personality and Social Psychology*, 39, 29–38.

Laycock, G. (1985) *Property Marking: a deterrent to domestic burglary?* London: Home Office.

Layden, M. A. (1982) Attributional style therapy. In C. Antaki and C. Brewin (eds), *Attributions and Psychological Change*, London and New York: Academic Press.

Lea, M. and Duck, S. (1982) A model for the role of similarity of values in friendship development. *British Journal of Social Psychology*, 21, 301–10.

Leavitt, H. J. (1951) Some effects of certain communication patterns on group performance. *Journal of Abnormal and Social Psychology*, 46, 38–50.

LeBon, G. (1895) *Psychologie des foules*. Paris: Alcan (English trans. *The Crowd*, London: Unwin, 1903).

L'Ecuyer, R. (1978) *Le Concept de soi*. Paris: Presses Universitaires de France.

Lee, M. T. and Ofshe, R. (1981) The impact of behavioral style and stutus characteristics on social influence: a test of two competing theories. *Social Psychology Quarterly*, 44, 73–82.

Leet-Pellegrini, H. M. (1980) Conversational dominance as a function of gender and expertise. In H. Giles, W. P. Robinson and P. M. Smith (eds), *Language: social psychological perspectives*, Oxford: Pergamon.

Lefkowitz, M. M., Eron, L. D., Walder, L. O. and Huesmann, L. R. (1977) *Growing Up to be Violent*. New York: Pergamon.

Lehman, D. R., Ellard, J. H. and Wortman, C. B. (1986) Social support for the bereaved: recipients' and providers' perspectives on what is helpful. *Journal of Consulting and Clinical Psychology*, 54, 438–46.

Lemaine, G. (1966) Inegalité, comparaison et incomparabilité: esquisse d'une théorie de l'orginalité sociale. *Bulletin de Psychologie*, 20, 1–9.

Lemaine, G. (1975) Dissimilation and differential assimilation in social influence. *European Journal of Social Psychology*, 5, 93–120.

Lemyre, L. and Smith, P. M. (1985) Intergroup discrimination and self esteem in the minimal group paradigm. *Journal of Personality and Social Psychology*, 49, 660–70.

Lepenies, W. (1977) Problems of a historical study of science. In E. Mendelsohn, P. Weingart and R. Whitley (eds), *The Social Production of Scientific Knowledge*, Dordrecht: Reidel.

Lepper, M. R. and Greene, D. (eds) (1978) *The Hidden Costs of Reward: new perspectives on the psychology of human motivation*. Hillsdale, NJ: Erlbaum.

Lepper, M. R., Greene, D. and Nisbett, R. E. (1973) Undermining children's intrinsic interest with extrinsic reward: a test of the 'overjustification' hypothesis. *Journal of Personality and Social Psychology*, 28, 129–37.

Leventhal, H. (1970) Findings and theory in the study of fear communications. In L. Berkowitz (ed.), *Advances in Experimental Social Psychology* (vol. 5), New York: Academic Press.

Levine, J. M. and Murphy, G. (1943) The learning and forgetting of controversial material. *Journal of Abnormal and Social Psychology*, 38, 507–17.

Levine, R. (1987) Waiting is a power game. *Psychology Today*, April, 24–33.

Levinger, G. (1983) Development and change. In H. H. Kelley et al., *Close Relationships*, New York: Freeman.

Levinson, S. (1983) *Pragmatics*. Cambridge: Cambridge University Press.

Lewin, K. (1948) *Resolving Social Conflicts: selected papers on group dynamics*. New York: Harper & Row.

Lewin, K. (1951) *Field Theory in Social Science: selected theoretical papers*. New York: Harper & Row.

Lewin, K. (1965) Group decision and social change. In H. Proshansky and B. Seidenberg (eds), *Basic Studies in Social Psychology*, London: Holt, Rinehart & Winston.

Lewis, C. (1986) Early sex-role socialization. In D. J. Hargreaves and A. M. Colley (eds), *The Psychology of Sex Roles*, London: Harper & Row.

Leyens, J.-P. (1983) *Sommes-nous tous des psychologues? Approche psychosociale des théories implicites de la personnalité*. Bruxelles: Mardaga.

Leyens, J.-P., Aspeel, S. and Marques, J. (1987) Cognition sociale et pratiques psychologiques. In J. L. Beauvois, R. V. Joulé and J. M. Monteil (eds), *Perspectives Cognitives et conduites sociales. 1: Théories implicites et conflits cognitifs*, Cousset: Delval.

Leyens, J.-P. and Fraczek, A. (1984) Aggression as an interpersonal phenomenon. In H. Tajfel (ed.), *The Social Dimension* (vol. 1), Cambridge: Cambridge University Press, Paris: Editions de la Maison des Sciences de l'Homme.

Leyens, J.-P. and Herman, G. (1979) Cinéma violent et spectateurs aggressifs. *Psychologie Française*, 24, 152–68.

Leyens, J.-P., Herman, G. and Dunand, M. A. (1982) Towards a renewed paradigm in movie violence research. In P. Stringer (ed.), *Confronting Social Issues: applications of social psychology*, European Monographs in Social Psychology, London: Academic Press.

Leyens, J.-P. and Parke, R. D. (1975) Aggressive slides can induce a weapons effect. *European Journal of Social Psychology*, 5, 229–36.

Liebert, R. M. and Baron, R. A. (1972) Some immediate effects of televised violence on children's behavior. *Developmental Psychology*, 6, 469–75.

Liebrand, W. B. G. (1984) The effect of social motives, communication and group size in an n-person multi-stage mixed-motive game. *European Journal of Social Psychology*, 14, 239–64.

Liebrand, W. B. G., Jansen, W. T. L., Ruken, V. M. and Cuhre, C. J. M. (1986) Might over morality: social values and the perception of other players in experimental games. *Journal of Experimental Social Psychology*, 22, 203–15.

Liebrand, W. B. G. and van Run, C. J. (1985) The effects of social motives on behavior in social dilemmas in two cultures. *Journal of Experimental Social Psychology*, 21, 86–102.

Light, P. (1983) Social interaction and cognitive development: a review of post-Piagetian research. In S. Meadows (ed.), *Developing Thinking: approaches to children's cognitive development*, London: Methuen.

Light, P. (1986) Context, conservation and conversation. In M. P. M. Richards and P. Light (eds), *Children of Social Worlds*, Oxford: Polity.

Light, P., Buckingham, N. and Robbins, A. I. (1979) The conservation task as an interactional setting. *British Journal of Educational Psychology*, 49, 304–10.

Light, P. and Glachan, M. (1985) Facilitation of individual problem solving through peer interaction. *Educational Psychology*, 5, 217–25.

Likert, R. (1932) A technique for the measurement of attitudes. *Archives of Psychology*, 140, 44–53.

Likert, R. (1967) *The Human Organization*. New York: McGraw-Hill.

Lind, E. A. and O'Barr, W. M. (1979) The social significance of speech in the courtroom. In H. Giles and R. N. St Clair (eds), *Language and Social Psychology*, Oxford: Basil Blackwell.

Linder, D. E., Cooper, J. and Jones, E. E. (1967) Decision freedom as a determinant of the role of incentive magnitude in attitude change. *Journal of Personality and Social Psychology*, 6, 245–54.

Lindner, G. A. (1871) *Ideen zur Psychologie der Gesellschaft als Grundlage der Sozialwissenschaft*. Vienna: Gerold.

Lingle, J. H. and Ostrom, T. M. (1981) Principles of memory and cognition in attitude formation. In R. E. Petty, T. M. Ostrom and T. C. Brock (eds), *Cognitive Responses in Persuasion*, Hillsdale, NJ: Erlbaum.

Linville, P. W. (1982) The complexity–extremity effect and age-based stereotyping. *Journal of Personality and Social Psychology*, 42, 193–211.

Lippman, W. (1922) *Public Opinion*. New York: Harcourt.

Liska, J. (1978) Situational and topical variations in credibility criteria. *Communication Monographs*, 45, 85–92.

Livesley, W. J. and Bromley, D. B. (1973) *Person Perception in Childhood and Adolescence*. London: Wiley.

Livingstone, S. M. (in press) The implicit representation of characters in 'Dallas': a multidimensional scaling approach. *Human Communication Research*.

Lloyd-Bostock, S. M. (1979) Common-sense morality and accident compensation. In D. P. Farrington, K. Hawkins and S. M. Lloyd-Bostock (eds), *Psychology, Law and Legal Processes*, London: Macmillan.

Lloyd-Bostock, S. M. (1984) Legal literature, dialogue with lawyers, and research on practical legal questions: some gains and pitfalls for psychology. In G. M. Stephenson and J. H. Davis (eds), *Progress in Applied Social Psychology* (vol. 2), Chichester: Wiley.

Loftus, E. F. (1974) Reconstructing memory: the incredible eyewitness. *Psychology Today*, August, 116–19.

Loftus, E. F. (1984) Expert testimony on the eyewitness. In G. L. Wells and E. F. Loftus (eds), *Eyewitness Testimony: psychological perspectives*, Cambridge: Cambridge University Press.

Lord, R. G. (1977) Functional leadership behavior: measurement and relation to social power and leadership perceptions. *Administrative Science Quarterly*, 22, 114–33.

Lorenz, K. (1950) Ganzheit und Teil in der tierischen und menschlichen Gemeinschaft. *Studium Generale*, 3(9).

Lorenz, K. (1963) *Das sogenannte Böse*. Vienna: Borotha-Schoeler (English trans. *On Aggression*, London: Methuen/University Paperback).

Louw-Potgieter, J. and Giles, H. (in press) Imposed identity and linguistic strategies. *Journal of Language and Social Psychology*.

Lück, H. E. (1987) A historical perspective on social psychological theories. In G. Semin and B. Krahé (eds), *Issues in Contemporary German Social Psychology*, London: Sage.

Ludwig, D., Franco, J. N. and Malloy, J. E. (1986) Effects of reciprocity and self-monitoring on self-disclosure with a new acquaintance. *Journal of Personality and Social Psychology*, 50, 1077–82.

Lujansky, H. and Mikula, G. (1983) Can equity theory explain the quality and stability of romantic relationships? *British Journal of Social Psychology*, 22, 101–12.

Lukens, J. (1979) Interethnic conflict and communicative distances. In H. Giles and B. Saint-Jacques (eds), *Language and Ethnic Relations*, Oxford: Pergamon.

Lukes, S. (1973a) *Individualism*. Oxford: Basil Blackwell.

Lukes, S. (1973b) *Emile Durkheim: his life and work. A historical and critical study*. London: Allen Lane.

Lumsden, C. J. and Wilson, E. O. (1981) *Genes, Mind, and Culture: the coevolutionary process*. Cambridge, Mass.: Harvard University Press.

Lumsden, C. J. and Wilson, E. O. (1982) Précis of *Genes, Mind, and Culture*. *The Behavioral and Brain Sciences*, 5, 1–37.

Lund, M. (1985) The development of investment and commitment scales for predicting continuity of personal relationships. *Journal of Social and Personal relationships*, 2, 3–23.

Lutkenhaus, P. (1984) Pleasure derived from mastery in three-year-olds: its function for persistence and the influence of maternal behavior. *International Journal of Behavioral Development*, 7, 343–58.

Lynch, J. J. (1977) *The Broken Heart*. New York: Basic.

Maass, A. and Clark, R. D. III (1984) Hidden impact of minorities: fifteen years of minority influence research. *Psychological Bulletin*, 95, 428–50.

Maass, A., Clark, R. D. III and Haberkorn, G. (1982) The effects of differential ascribed category membership and norms on minority influence. *European Journal of Social Psychology*, 12, 89–104.

Maccoby, E. E. and Martin, J. A. (1983) Socialization in the context of the family: parent–child interaction. In P. H. Mussen (ed.), *Handbook of Child Psychiatry* (vol. IV), New York: Wiley.

MacCrimon, K. R. and Messick, D. M. (1976) A framework of social motives. *Behavioral Sciences*, 21, 86–100.

MacKay, D. M. (1972) Formal analysis of communicative processes. In R. A. Hinde (ed.), *Nonverbal Communication*, Cambridge: Cambridge University Press.

Mackenzie, K. D. (1976) *A Theory of Group Structures* (2 vols). New York: Gordon and Breach.

Mackie, J. L. (1974) *The Cement of the Universe: a study of causation*. Oxford: Clarendon.

Maddux, J. E. and Rogers, R. W. (1983) Protection motivation and self-efficacy: a revised theory of fear appeals and attitude change. *Journal of Experimental Social Psychology*, 19, 469–79.

Maier, N. R. F. and Solem, A. R. (1952) The contribution of a discussion leader to the quality of group thinking: the effective use of minority opinions. *Human Relations*, 5, 277–88.

Maki, J. and McClintock, C. G. (1983) The accuracy of social value prediction: actor and observer influences. *Journal of Personality and Social Psychology*, 45, 829–38.

Manis, M. (1977) Cognitive social psychology. *Personality and Social Psychology Bulletin*, 3, 550–6.

Mann, L., Newton, J. W. and Innes, J. M. (1982) A test between deindividuation and emergent norm theories of crowd aggression. *Journal of Personality and Social Psychology*, 42, 260–72.

Mansell, J., Felce, D., Jenkins, J., de Kock, U. and Toogood, A. (1987) *Developing Staffed Housing for People with Mental Handicaps*. Tunbridge Wells: Costello.

Manstead, A. S. R., Plevin, C. E. and Smart, J. L. (1984) Predicting mothers' choice of infant feeding method. *British Journal of Social Psychology*, 23, 223–31.

Manstead, A. S. R., Profitt, C. and Smart, J. L. (1983) Predicting and understanding mothers' infant-feeding intentions and behavior: testing the theory of reasoned action. *Journal of Personality and Social Psychology*, 44, 657–71.

Manstead, A. S. R. and Semin, G. R. (1980) Social facilitation effects: mere enhancement of dominant responses? *British Journal of Social and Clinical Psychology*, 19, 119–36.

Mantell, D. M. (1971) The potential for violence in Germany. *Journal of Social Issues*, 27, 101–12.

Marchand, B. (1970) Auswirkung einer emotional wertvollen und einer emotional neutralen klassifikation auf die Schätzung einer Stimulus-Serie. *Zeitschrift für Sozialpsychologie*, 1, 264–74.

Markel, N. N., Long, J. F. and Saine, T. J. (1976) Sex effects in conversational interaction: another look at male dominance. *Human Communication Research*, 2, 356–64.

Markova, I. (1982) *Paradigms, Thought, and Language*. Chichester: Wiley.

Markova, I. (1983) The origin of the social psychology of language in German expressivism. *British Journal of Social Psychology*, 22, 315–25.

Markus, H. (1977) Self-schemata and processing information about the self. *Journal of Personality and Social Psychology*, 35, 63–78.

Markus, H. and Sentis, K. (1982) The self in social information processing. In J. Suls (ed.), *Social Psychological Perspectives on the Self*, Hillsdale, NJ: Erlbaum.

Markus, H. and Zajonc, R. B. (1985) The cognitive perspective in social psychology. In G. Lindzey and E. Aronson (eds), *Handbook of Social Psychology*, New York: Random House.

Marlowe, D., Frager, R. and Nuttall, R. L. (1965) Commitment to action-taking as a consequence of cognitive dissonance. *Journal of Personality and Social Psychology*, 2, 864–8.

Marques, J. M. (1986) Toward a definition of social processing of information: an application to stereotyping. Unpublished PhD dissertation, University of Louvain.

Marques, J. M., Yzerbyt, V. and Leyens, J.-P. (1987) The 'black sheep effect': judgemental extremity towards in-group members as a function of group identification. Unpublished manuscript, University of Louvain-La-Neuve.

Marrow, A. J. (1969) *The Practical Theorist: the life and work of Kurt Lewin*. New York: Basic.

Marwell, G. and Schmitt, D. R. (1975) *Cooperation: an experimental analysis*. New York: Academic Press.

Marx, K. and Engels, F. (1962) *Selected Works* (2 vols). Moscow: Foreign Languages.

Marx, M. H. and Hillix, W. A. (1979) *Systems and Theories in Psychology*. 3rd edn. New York: McGraw-Hill.

Maslach, C. (1978) The client role in staff burn-out. *Journal of Social Issues*, 34, 111–24.

Matthews, K. A., Glass, D. C., Rosenmann, R. H. and Bortner, R. W. (1977) Competitive drive, pattern A, and coronary heart disease: a further analysis of some data from the Western Collaborative Group study. *Journal of Chronic Diseases*, 30, 489–98.

Mausner, B. (1954) Prestige and social interaction: the effect of one partner's success in a relevant task on the interaction of observer pairs. *Journal of Abnormal and Social Psychology*, 49, 557–60.

McArthur, L. A. (1972) The how and what of why: some determinants and consequences of causal attributions. *Journal of Personality and Social Psychology*, 22, 171–93.

McArthur, L. Z. and Post, D. L. (1977) Figural emphasis and person perception. *Journal of Experimental Social Psychology*, 13, 520–35.

McCall, G. J. (1974) A symbolic interactionist approach to attraction. In T. L. Huston (ed.), *Foundations of Interpersonal Attraction*, New York: Academic Press.

McCall, M. (1970) Boundary rules in relationships and encounters. In G. J. McCall et al. (eds), *Social Relationships*, Chicago: Aldine.

McCarthy, E. D., Langner, T. S., Gersten, J. C., Eisenberg, J. G. and Orzeck, L. (1975) Violence and behavior disorders. *Journal of Communications*, 25, 71–85.

McClintock, C. G. (1972) Social motivation: a set of propositions. *Behavioral Science*, 17, 458–64.

McClintock, C. G. and McNeel, S. P. (1967) Prior dyadic experience and monetary reward as determinants of cooperative behavior. *Journal of Personality and Social Psychology*, 5, 282–94.

McClintock, C. G., Messick, D. M., Kuhlman, D. M. and Campos, F. T. (1973) Motivational basis of choice in three choice decomposed games. *Journal of Experimental Social Psychology*, 9, 572–90.

McClintock, C. G. and Van Avermaet, E. F. (1982) Social values and rules of fairness. In V. J. Derlega and J. L. Grzelak (eds), *Cooperation and Helping Behavior: theory and research*, New York: Academic Press.

McCord, J. (1978) A thirty year follow-up of treatment effects. *American Psychologist*, 33, 284–9.

McDougall, W. (1908) *Introduction to Social Psychology*. London: Methuen.

McDougall, W. (1920) *The Group Mind*. Cambridge: Cambridge University Press.

McGarrigle, J. and Donaldson, M. (1975) Conservation accidents. *Cognition*, 3, 341–50.

McGuire, W. J. (1964) Inducing resistance to persuasion: some contemporary approaches. In L. Berkowitz (ed.), *Advances in Experimental Social Psychology* (vol. 1), New York: Academic Press.

McGuire, W. J. (1969) The nature of attitudes and attitude change. In G. Lindzey and E. Aronson (eds), *Handbook of Social Psychology* (vol. 3), 2nd edn, Reading, Mass.: Addison-Wesley.

McGuire, W. J. (1985) Attitudes and attitude change. In G. Lindzey and E. Aronson (eds), *Handbook of Social Psychology* (vol. 2), 3rd edn, New York: Random House.

McGuire, W. J. (1986) The vicissitudes of attitudes and similar representational constructs in twentieth century psychology. *European Journal of Social Psychology*, 16, 89–130.

McShane, J. (1980) *Learning to Talk*. Cambridge: Cambridge University Press.

Mead, G. H. (1934) *Mind, Self and Society from the Standpoint of a Social Behaviorist*. Chicago: University of Chicago Press.

Mead, G. H. (1934) *On Social Psychology*. Edited by A. Strauss, Chicago: University of Chicago Press, 1977.

Meertens, R. W. (1980) *Groepspolarisatie*. Deventer: Van Loghum Slaterus.

Meeus, W. H. J. and Raaijmakers, Q. A. W. (1986) Administrative obedience: carrying out orders to use psychological-administrative violence. *European Journal of Social Psychology*, 16, 311–24.

Mehrabian, A. (1968) Relationship of attitude to seated posture, orientation, and distance. *Journal of Personality and Social Psychology*, 10, 26–30.

Mehrabian, A. (1972) *Nonverbal Communication*. Chicago: Aldine.

Meinefeld, W. (1977) *Einstellung und soziales Handeln*. Reinbek: Rowohlt.

Mellen, S. W. L. (1981) *The Evolution of Love*. Oxford: Freeman.

Messé, L. A. and Sivacek, J. M. (1979) Predictions of others' responses in a mixed-motive game: self-justification or false consensus? *Journal of Personality and Social Psychology*, 37, 602–7.

Messer, D. J. (1983) The redundancy between adult speech and nonverbal interactions: a contribution to acquisition. In R. M. Golinkoff (ed.), *The Transition from Prelinguistic to Linguistic Communication*, Hillsdale, NJ: Erlbaum.

Messick, D. M. and Brewer, R. M. (1983) Solving social dilemmas: a review. In L. Wheeler and P. Shaver (eds), *Review of Personality and Social Psychology* (vol. 4), Beverley Hills: Sage.

Messick, D. M. and McClintock, C. G. (1968) Motivational basis of choice in experimental games. *Journal of Experimental Social Psychology*, 4, 1–25.

Meyer, C. B. and Taylor, S. E. (1986) Adjustment to rape. *Journal of Personality and Social Psychology*, 50, 1226–34.

Meyer, J. P. and Mulherin, A. (1980) From attribution to helping: an analysis of the mediating effects of affect and expectancy. *Journal of Personality and Social Psychology*, 39, 201–10.

Michaels, J. W., Acock, A. C. and Edwards, J. N. (1986) Social exchange and equity determinants of relationship commitment. *Journal of Social and Personal Relationships*, 3, 161–75.

Michotte, A. E. (1946) *La Perception de la causalité*. Paris: Vrin (English trans.: *The Perception of Causality*, New York: Basic, 1963).

Miell, D. (1984) Cognitive and communicative strategies in developing relationships. Unpublished PhD thesis, University of Lancaster.

Mikula, G. (1980) On the role of justice in allocation decisions. In G. Mikula (ed.), *Justice and Social Interaction*, Bern: Hans Huber.

Mikula, G. and Petri, B. (1987) *Auslösende Bedingungen des Erlebens von Ungerechtigkeit: Erste Befunde*. Berichte aus dem Institut für Psychologie der Universität Graz.

Milardo, R. M. (1982). Friendship networks in developing relationships: converging and diverging social environments. *Social Psychology Quarterly*, 45, 162–72.

Milgram, S. (1963). Behavioral study of obedience. *Journal of Abnormal and Social Psychology*, 67, 371–8.

Milgram, S. (1965). Some conditions of obedience and disobedience to authority. *Human Relations*, 18, 57–76.

Milgram, S. (1974) *Obedience to Authority: an experimental view*. New York: Harper & Row, London: Tavistock.

Milgram, S., Mann, L. and Harter, S. (1965) The lost-letter technique: a tool of social science research. *Public Opinion Quarterly*, 29, 437–8.

Milgram, S. and Toch, H. (1969) Collective behavior: crowds and social movements. In G. Lindzey and E. Aronson (eds), *Handbook of Social Psychology* (vol. 4), 2nd edn, Reading, Mass.: Addison-Wesley.

Miller, D. T. and Holmes, J. E. (1975) The role of situational restrictiveness on self fulfilling prophecies. *Journal of Personality and Social Psychology*, 31, 661–73.

Miller, D. T. and Ross, M. (1975) Self-serving biases in the attribution of causality: fact or fiction? *Psychological Bulletin*, 82, 213–25.

Miller, G. A. and Cantor, N. (1982) Book review of Nisbett, R. and Ross, L. *Human Inference: strategies and shortcomings of social judgement. Social Cognition*, 1, 83–93.

Miller, L. C., Berg, J. H. and Archer, R. L. (1983) Openers: individuals who elicit intimate self-disclosure. *Journal of Personality and Social Psychology*, 44, 1234–44.

Miller, N., Brewer, M. B. and Edwards, K. (1985) Cooperative interaction in desegregated settings: a laboratory analogue. *Journal of Social Issues*, 41, 63–79.

Miller, N. E. (1944) Experimental studies in conflict. In J. McV. Hunt (ed.), *Personality and the Behavior Disorders* (vol. 1), New York: Ronald.

Miller, N. E., Sears, R. R., Mowrer, O. H., Doob, L. W. and Dollard, I. (1941) The frustration-aggression hypothesis. *Psychological Review*, 48, 337–42.

Milner, D. (1983) *Children and Race: ten years on*. 2nd edn. London: Ward Lock.

Milner, D. (1984) The development of ethnic attitudes. In H. Tajfel (ed.), *The Social Dimension: European developments in social psychology* (vol. 1), Cambridge: Cambridge University Press.

Mischel, W. (1973) Toward a cognitive social learning reconceptualization of personality. *Psychological Review*, 80, 252–83.

Moede, W. (1920) *Experimentelle Massenpsychologie*. Leipzig: Hirzel.

Money, J. W. and Ehrhardt, A. A. (1972) *Man and Woman, Boy and Girl*. Baltimore: Johns Hopkins University Press.

Monson, T. C. and Snyder, M. (1977) Actors, observers and the attribution process.

Journal of Experimental Social Psychology, 13, 89–111.

Montada, L., Dalbert, C. and Schmitt, M. (1987) Ist prosoziales Handeln im Kontext Familie abhängig von situationalen, personalen oder systemischen Faktoren? In H. W. Bierhoff and L. Montada (eds), *Altruismus: Bedingungen der Hilfsbereitschaft*, Göttingen: Hogrefe.

Montagner, H. (1978) *L'Enfant et la communication*. Paris: Stock.

Montagner, H. (1979) La genèse de comportement de l'enfant à partir de l'étude des interactions au sein de groupes à la crèche et à l'école maternelle. *Petits Groupes et Grands Systemes*, 5, 197–208.

Montagner, H., Restoin, A., Schall, B., Rodriguez, D., Ullman, V., Ladouce, I., Guedira, A., Viala, M., Godard, D., Hertling, E., Didillon, H., and Gremillet, H. (1981) Apport éthologique à l'étude ontogenetique des systèmes de communication de l'enfant. *Medecine et Hygiene*, 39, 3906–22.

Montagner, H., Restoin, A., Ullman, V., Rodriguez, D., Goddard, D. and Viala, M. (1984) Development of early peer interaction. In W. Doise and A. Palmonari (eds), *Social Interaction in Individual Development*. Cambridge: Cambridge University Press.

Moore, B. S., Sherrod, D. R., Liu, T. J. and Underwood, B. (1979) The dispositional shift in attribution over time. *Journal of Experimental Social Psychology*, 15, 553–69.

Moreno, J. L. (1934) *Who Shall Survive?* Washington, DC.: Nervous and Mental Disease Monograph no. 58.

Moreland, R. L. and Zajonc, R. B. (1977) Is stimulus recognition a necessary condition for the occurrence of exposure effects? *Journal of Personality and Social Psychology*, 35, 191–9.

Morland, J. K. (1969) Race awareness among American and Hong Kong Chinese children. *American Journal of Sociology*, 75, 360–74.

Moscovici, S. (1961) *La Psychanalyse: son image et son public*. 2nd edn 1976. Paris: Presses Universitaires de France.

Moscovici, S. (1972) Society and theory in social psychology. In J. Israel and H. Tajfel (eds), *The Context of Social Psychology: a critical assessment*. London: Academic Press.

Moscovici, S. (ed.) (1973) *Introduction à la psychologie sociale*. Paris: Larousse.

Moscovici, S. (1976) *Social Influence and Social Change*. London: Academic Press.

Moscovici, S. (1980) Toward a theory of conversion behavior. In L. Berkowitz (ed.), *Advances in Experimental Social Psychology* (vol. 13), New York: Academic Press.

Moscovici, S. (1981a) On social representations. In J. P. Forgas (ed.), *Social Cognition: perspectives on everyday understanding*, London: Academic Press.

Moscovici, S. (1981b) *L'Age des foules*. Paris: Fayard.

Moscovici, S. (1982) The coming era of representations. In J.-P. Codol and J.-P. Leyens (eds), *Cognitive Analysis of Social Behavior*, The Hague: Nijhoff.

Moscovici, S. (ed.) (1984) *Psychologie Sociale*. Paris: Presses Universitaires de France.

Moscovici, S. (1985a) Prefazione. In J. P. Di Giacomo, *Rappresentazioni sociali e movimenti colletivi*. Napoli: Liguori.

Moscovici, S. (1985b) Social influence and conformity. In G. Lindzey and E. Aronson (eds), *Handbook of Social Psychology* (vol. 2), 3rd edn, New York: Random House.

Moscovici, S. and Hewstone, M. (1983) Social representations and social explanations: from the 'naive' to the 'amateur' scientist. In M. Hewstone (ed.), *Attribution Theory: social and functional extensions*, Oxford: Basil Blackwell.

Moscovici, S. and Lage, E. (1976) Studies in social influence. III: Majority versus minority influence in a group. *European Journal of Social Psychology*, 6, 149–74.

Moscovici, S., Lage, E. and Naffrechoux, M. (1969) Influence of a consistent minority on the responses of a majority in a colour perception task. *Sociometry*, 32, 365–80.

Moscovici, S. and Nemeth, C. (1984) Studies in social influence. II: Minority influence. In C. Nemeth (ed.) *Social Psychology: classic and contemporary integrations*, Chicago: Rand McNally.

Moscovici, S. and Personnaz, B. (1980) Studies in social influence. V: Minority influence and conversion behaviour in a perceptual task. *Journal of Experimental Social Psychology*, 16, 270–82.

Moscovici, S. and Zavalloni, M. (1969) The group as a polarizer of attitudes. *Journal of Personality and Social Psychology*, 12, 125–35.

Mowrer, D. H. (1975) Foreword. In W. Glasser, *Reality Therapy: a new approach to psychiatry*, New York: Harper & Row.

Mugny, G. (1982) *The Power of Minorities*. New York: Academic Press.

Mugny, G. and Doise, W. (1978a) Socio-cognitive conflict and structuration of individual collective performances. *European Journal of Social Psychology*, 8, 181–92.

Mugny, G. and Doise, W. (1978b) Factores sociologicos y psicosociologicos del desarrollo cognitivo. *Anuario de Psicologia*, 18, 22–40.

Mugny, G. and Doise, W. (1979) Factores sociologicos y psicosociologicos del desarrollo cognitivo: une neuva ilustraction experimental. *Anuario de Psicologia*, 21, 4–25.

Mugny, G., Levy, M. and Doise, W. (1978) Conflict sociocognitif et developpement cognitif. *Revue Suisse de Psychologie Pure et Appliquée*, 37, 22–43.

Mugny, G. and Papastamou, S. (1980) When rigidity does not fail: individualization and psychologization as resistances to the diffusion of minority innovations. *European Journal of Social Psychology*, 10, 43–62.

Mulac, A., Wiemann, J. M., Widenmann, S. and Gibson, T. (1983) Male/female language differences and their effects in like-sex and mixed-sex dyads: a test of interpersonal accommodation and the gender-linked language effect. Paper presented at the 2nd international conference on social psychology and language, Bristol.

Mulder, M. (1960) Communication structure, decision structure and group performance. *Sociometry*, 23, 1–14.

Mulder, M. (1963) *Group Structure, Motivation and Group Performance*. Den Haag: Mouton.

Mummendey, A., Linneweber, V. and Löschper, G. (1984) Actor or victim of aggression: divergent perspectives – divergent evaluations. *European Journal of Social Psychology*, 14, 297–311.

Munsterberg, H. (1908) *On the Witness Stand: essays on psychology and crime*. New York: Clark Boardman.

Murnighan, J. K. and Roth, A. E. (1983) Expecting continued play in prisoner's dilemma game. *Journal of Conflict Resolution*, 27, 279–300.

Murstein, B. I. and Christy, P. (1976) Physical attractiveness and marriage adjustment in middle-aged couples. *Journal of Personality and Social Psychology*, 34, 537–42.

Murstein, B. I., MacDonald, M. G. and Cerreto, M. (1977) A theory and investigation of the effects of exchange-orientation on marriage and friendship. *Journal of Marriage and the Family*, 39, 543–8.

Myers, D. G. (1978) Polarizing effects of social comparison. *Journal of Experimental Social Psychology*, 14, 554–63.

Myers, D. G. (1982) Polarizing effects of social interaction. In H. Brandstätter, J. H. Davis and G. Stocker-Kreichgauer (eds), *Group Decision Making*, New York: Academic Press.

Myers, D. G., Wojcicki, S. B. and Aardema, B. S. (1977) Attitude comparison: is there ever a bandwagon effect? *Journal of Applied Social Psychology*, 7, 341-7.

Nadel, J. (1986) *Imitation et communication entre jeunes enfants*. Paris: Presses Universitaires de France.

Nadler, A. (1987) Determinants of help seeking behaviour: the effects of helper's similarity, task centrality and recipient's self esteem. *European Journal of Social Psychology*, 17, 57-67.

Nadler, A. and Mayseless, O. (1983) Recipient self-esteem and reactions to help. In J. D. Fisher, A. Nadler and B. M. DePaulo (eds), *New Directions in Helping. Vol. 1: Recipient reactions to aid*, New York: Academic Press.

Neisser, U. (1980) On 'social knowing'. *Personality and Social Psychology Bulletin*, 6, 601-5.

Nel, E., Helmreich, R. and Aronson, E. (1969) Opinion change in the advocate as a function of the persuasibility of his audience: a clarification of the meaning of dissonance. *Journal of Personality and Social Psychology*, 12, 117-24.

Nelson, K. (1985) *Making Sense: the acquisition of shared meanings*. New York: Academic Press.

Nemeth, C. (1982) Stability of fact position and influence. In H. Brandstätter, J. H. Davis and G. Stocker-Kreichgauer (eds), *Group Decision Making*, New York: Academic Press.

Nemeth, C. (1986) Differential contributions of majority and minority influence. *Psychological Review*, 93, 23-32.

Nemeth, C., Swedlund, M. and Kanki, G. (1974) Patterning of the minority's responses and their influence on the majority. *European Journal of Social Psychology*, 4, 53-64.

Nemeth, C. and Wachtler, J. (1974) Creating the perceptions of consistency and confidence: a necessary condition for minority influence. *Sociometry*, 37, 529-40.

Newcomb, T. M. (1953) An approach to the study of communicative acts. *Psychological Review*, 60, 393-704.

Newcomb, T. M. (1961) *The Acquaintance Process*. New York: Holt, Rinehart & Winston.

Newcomb, T. M. (1971) Dyadic balance as a source of clues about interpersonal attraction. In B. I. Murstein (ed.), *Theories of Attraction and Love*, Springer.

Newton, N. and Newton, M. (1950) Relationship of ability to breast feed and maternal attitudes toward breast feeding. *Pediatrics*, 11, 869-75.

Newtson, D. (1974) Dispositional inference from effects of actions: effects chosen and effects forgone. *Journal of Experimental Social Psychology*, 10, 489-96.

Nisbett, R. E., Caputo, C., Legant, P. and Maracek, J. (1973) Behaviour as seen by the actor and as seen by the observer. *Journal of Personality and Social Psychology*, 27, 154-64.

Nisbett, R. E. and Ross, L. (1980) *Human Inference: strategies and shortcomings in social judgment*. Englewood Cliffs, NJ: Prentice-Hall.

Noller, P. (1982) Channel consistency and inconsistency in the communications of married couples. *Journal of Personality and Social Psychology*, 43, 732-41.

Noller, P. (1984) *Nonverbal Communication and Marital Interaction*. Oxford: Pergamon.

Noller, P. and Fitzpatrick, M. A. (eds) (in press) *Marital Interaction*. Clevedon: Multilingual Matters.

Norman, R. (1975) Affective-cognitive consistency, attitudes, conformity, and behavior. *Journal of Personality and Social Psychology*, 32, 83-91.

Nuttin, J. M., Jr (1986) *Sociale Psychologie: vijftien inleidende lessen*. Leuven: Wouters.

Nuttin, J. M., Jr (1975) *The Illusion of Attitude Change: towards a response contagion theory of persuasion*. London: Academic Press.

Nye, R. (1975) *The Origins of Crowd Psychology: Gustave LeBon and the crisis of mass democracy in the Third Republic*. London: Sage.

Oaker, G. and Brown, R. J. (1986) Intergroup relations in a hospital setting: a further test of social identity theory. *Human Relations*, 39, 767–78.

Oakes, P. J. and Turner, J. C. (1980) Social categorization and intergroup behaviour: does minimal intergroup discrimination make social identity more positive? *European Journal of Social Psychology*, 10, 295–302.

O'Connell, L. (1984) An exploration of exchange in three social relationships: kinship, friendship and the market place. *Journal of Personal and Social Relationships*, 1, 333–45.

O'Connor, P. and Brown, G. W. (1984) Supportive relationships: fact or fancy? *Journal of Personal and Social Relationships*, 1, 159–75.

Oppenheim, A. N. (1966) *Questionnaire Design and Attitude Measurement*. London: Heinemann.

Orne, M. T. (1962) On the social psychology of the psychological experiment: with particular reference to demand characteristics and their implications. *American Psychologist*, 17, 776–83.

Orne, M. T. (1969) Demand characteristics and the concept of quasi-controls. In R. Rosenthal and R. L. Rosnow (eds), *Artifact in Behavioral Research*, New York: Academic Press.

Orvis, B. R., Cunningham, J. D. and Kelley, H. H. (1975) A closer examination of causal inference: the roles of consensus, distinctiveness and consistency information. *Journal of Personality and Social Psychology*, 32, 605–16.

Orvis, B. R., Kelley, H. H. and Butler, D. (1976) Attributional conflict in young couples. In J. H. Harvey, W. J. Ickes and R. F. Kidd (eds), *New Directions in Attribution Research* (vol. 1), Hillsdale, NJ: Erlbaum.

Osgood, C. E., Suci, G. J. and Tannenbaum, P. H. (1957) *The Measurement of Meaning*. Urbana: University of Illinois Press.

Osgood, C. E. and Tannenbaum, P. H. (1955) The principle of congruity in the prediction of attitude change. *Psychological Review*, 62, 42–55.

Osterhouse, R. A. and Brock, T. C. (1970) Distraction increases yielding to propaganda by inhibiting counterarguing. *Journal of Personality and Social Psychology*, 15, 344–58.

Ostrom, T. M. (1969) The relationship between the affective, behavioral, and cognitive components of attitude. *Journal of Experimental Psychology*, 5, 12–30.

Ostrom, T. M. (1977) Between-theory and within-theory conflict in explaining contrast effects in impression formation. *Journal of Experimental Social Psychology*, 13, 492–503.

Page, M. M. (1969) Social psychology of a classical conditioning of attitudes experiment. *Journal of Personality and Social Psychology*, 11, 177–86.

Page, M. M. and Scheidt, R. (1971) The elusive weapons effect: demand awareness, evaluation and slightly sophisticated subjects. *Journal of Personality and Social Psychology*, 20, 304–18.

Paicheler, G. (1976) Norms and attitude change. I: Polarization and styles of behavior. *European Journal of Social Psychology*, 6, 405–27.

Paicheler, G. (1977) Norms and attitude change. II: The phenomenon of bipolarization. *European Journal of Social Psychology*, 7, 5–14.

Paicheler, G. (1985) *Psychologie des influences sociales*. Paris: Delachaux & Niestlé.

Palmonari, A. (1980) Social differentiation processes and collective representation in adolescents. *Italian Journal of Psychology*, VII, 55–63.

Palmonari, A., Carugati, F., Ricci-Bitti, P. E. and Sarachielli, G. (1979) *Identita Imperfette*. Bologna: Il Murbio.

Palmonari, A., Carugati, F., Ricci-Bitti, P. E. and Sarchielli, G. (1984) Imperfect identities: a socio-psychological perspective for the study of the problems of adolescence. In H. Tajfel, (ed.), *The Social Dimension: European developments in social psychology* (vol. 1), Cambridge: Cambridge University Press.

Papousek, H. and Papousek, M. (1977) Mothering and the cognitive head-start: psychobiological considerations. In H. R. Schaffer (ed.), *Studies in Mother–Infant Interaction*, London: Academic Press.

Park, R. E. (1972) *The Crowd and the Public*. Chicago: University of Chicago Press (German original: *Masse und Publikum*, Bern: Lack & Gruner, 1904).

Parke, R. D., Berkowitz, L., Leyens, J. -P., West, S. G. and Sebastian, R. J. (1977) Some effects of violent and nonviolent movies on the behavior of juvenile delinquents. In L. Berkowitz (ed.), *Advances in Experimental Social Psychology* (vol. 10), New York: Academic Press.

Parkinson, B. and Manstead, A. S. R. (1981) An examination of the roles played by meaning of feedback and attention to feedback in the 'Valins' effect. *Journal of Personality and Social Psychology*, 40, 239–45.

Patterson, G. R., Littman, R. A. and Bricker, W. (1967) Assertive behavior in children: a step toward a theory of aggression. *Monographs of the Society for Research in Child Development*, 32, no. 5 (serial no. 113).

Patterson, M. L. (ed.) (1984) Nonverbal intimacy and exchange. *Journal of Nonverbal Behavior, 8*, no. 4 (special issue).

Paulus, P. B. (1983) Group influence on task performance and informational processing. In P. B. Paulus (ed.), *Basic Group Processes*, New York: Springer.

Paulus, P. B. and Murdoch, P. (1971) Anticipated evaluation and audience presence in the enhancement of dominant responses. *Journal of Experimental Social Psychology*, 7, 280–91.

Payne, S. (1951) *The Art of Asking Questions*. Princeton, NJ: Princeton University Press.

Peevers, B. H. and Secord, P. F. (1973) Developmental changes in attribution of descriptive concepts to persons. *Journal of Personality and Social Psychology*, 27, 120–8.

Pelz, E. B. (1965) Some factors in 'group decision'. In H. Proshansky and B. Seidenberg (eds), *Basic Studies in Social Psychology*, London: Holt, Rinehart & Winston.

Pepitone, A. (1981) Lessons from the history of social psychology. *American Psychologist*, 36, 972–85.

Peplau, L. A. (1983) Roles and gender. In H. H. Kelley et al., *Close Relationships*, New York: Freeman.

Peplau, L. A. and Perlman, D. (eds) (1982) *Loneliness: a sourcebook of current theory, research and therapy*. New York: Wiley-Interscience.

Peplau, L. A., Rubin, Z. and Hill, C. T. (1977) Sexual intimacy in dating relationships. *Journal of Social Issues*, 33, 86–109.

Perret-Clermont, A. -N. (1980) *Social Interaction and Cognitive Development in Children*. London: Academic Press.

Perret-Clermont, A. -N. and Brossard, A. (1985) On the interdigitation of social and cognitive processes. In R. A. Hinde, A. -N. Perret-Clermont and J. Stevenson-Hinde (eds), *Social Relationships and Cognitive Development*, Oxford: Clarendon Press.

Perrin, S. and Spencer, C. (1980) The Asch effect: a child of its time. *Bulletin of the British Psychological Society*, 33, 405–6.

Personnaz, B. (1981) Study in social influence using the spectrometer method: dynamics of the phenomena of conversion and covertness in perceptual responses. *European Journal of Social Psychology*, 11, 431–8.

Pessin, J. (1983) The comparative effects of social and mechanical stimulation on memorizing. *American Journal of Psychology*, 45, 263–70.

Peterson, C. and Seligman, M. E. P. (1984) Causal explanations as a risk factor for depression: theory and evidence. *Psychological Review*, 91, 347–74.

Petronio, S., Martin, J and Littlefield, R. (1984) Prerequisite conditions for self-disclosing: a gender issue. *Communication Monographs*, 51, 268–73.

Pettigrew, T. F. (1958) Personality and sociocultural factors in intergroup attitudes: a cross-national comparison. *Journal of Conflict Resolution*, 2, 29–42.

Pettigrew, T. F. (1971) *Racially Separate or Together?* New York: McGraw-Hill.

Pettigrew, T. F. (1979) The ultimate attribution error: extending Allport's cognitive analysis of prejudice. *Personality and Social Psychology Bulletin*, 5, 461–76.

Pettigrew, T. F. (1986) The intergroup contact hypothesis reconsidered. In M. Hewstone and R. Brown (eds), *Contact and Conflict in Intergroup Encounters*, Oxford: Basil Blackwell.

Petty, R. E. and Brock, T. C. (1981) Thought disruption and persuasion: assessing the validity of attitude change experiments. In R. Petty, T. M. Ostrom and T. C. Brock (eds), *Cognitive Responses in Persuasion*. Hillsdale, NJ: Erlbaum.

Petty, R. E. and Cacioppo, J. T. (1981) *Attitudes and Persuasion: classic and contemporary approaches*. Dubuque, Iowa: Wm C. Brown.

Petty, R. E. and Cacioppo, J. T. (1986a) *Communication and Persuasion: central and peripheral routes to attitude change*. New York: Springer.

Petty, R. E. and Cacioppo, J. T. (1986b) The elaboration likelihood model of persuasion. In L. Berkowitz (ed.), *Advances in Experimental Social Psychology* (vol. 19), Orlando, Fla.: Academic Press.

Petty, R. E., Cacioppo, J. T. and Goldman, R. (1981) Personal involvement as a determinant of argument-based persuasion. *Journal of Personality and Social Psychology*, 41, 847–55.

Petty, R. E., Wells, G. L. and Brock, T. C. (1976) Distraction can enhance or reduce yielding to propaganda: thought disruption versus effort justification. *Journal of Personality and Social Psychology*, 34, 874–84.

Piaget, J. (1928) *Judgment and Reasoning in the Child*. London: Routledge & Kegan Paul.

Piaget, J. (1932) *Le Jugement Moral chez l'enfant*. Republished as *The Moral Judgment of the Child*, Harmondsworth: Penguin.

Piaget, J. (1941) *La Genèse du nombre chez l'enfant*. Republished as *The Child's Conception of Number*, London: Routledge & Kegan Paul, 1952.

Piaget, J. (1942) *Classes, relations et nombres: essai sur les 'groupements' de la logistique et la reversibilité de la pensée*. Paris: Vrin.

Piaget, J. (1952) *The Child's Conception of Number*. London: Routledge & Kegan Paul.

Piaget, J. and Weil, A. (1951) The development in children of the idea of the homeland and of relations with other countries. *International Social Science Bulletin*, 3, 561–76.

Pittman, T. S. (1975) Attribution of arousal as a mediator in dissonance reduction.

Journal of Experimental Social Psychology, 11, 53–63.

Poliakov, L. (1980 *La Causalité Diabolique*. Paris: Calman-Lévy.

Poppe, M. (1980) *Social Comparison in Two-Person Experimental Games*. Tilburg: Van Spaendonck.

Porier, G. W. and Lott, A. J. (1967) Galvanic skin responses and prejudice. *Journal of Personality and Social Psychology*, 5, 253–9.

Potter, J. and Litton, I. (1985) Some problems underlying the theory of social representations. *British Journal of Social Psychology*, 24, 81–90.

Pruitt, D. G. (1967) Reward structure and cooperation: the decomposed prisoner's dilemma game. *Journal of Personality and Social Psychology*, 7, 21–7.

Pruitt, D. G. (1968) Reciprocity and credit building in a laboratory dyad. *Journal of Personality and Social Psychology*, 8, 143–7.

Pruitt, D. G. and Kimmel, M. J. (1977) Twenty years of experimental gaming: critique, synthesis, and suggestions for the future. *Annual Review of Psychology*, 28, 363–92,

Pryor, J. B. and Kriss, M. (1977) The cognitive dynamics of salience in the attribution process. *Journal of Personality and Social Psychology*, 35, 49–55.

Pyszczynski, T. A. and Greenberg, J. (1981) Role of disconfirmed expectancies in the instigation of attributional processing. *Journal of Personality and Social Psychology*, 40, 31–8.

Quattrone, G. A. (1982) Overattribution and unit formation: when behavior engulfs the person. *Journal of Personality and Social Psychology*, 42, 593–607.

Quattrone, G. A. and Jones, E. E. (1980) The perception of variability within ingroups and outgroups. *Journal of Personality and Social Psychology*, 38, 141–52.

Quine, L. (1981) Alone in the community. *New Society*, 11 June, 435–7.

Rabbie, J. M. (1982) Are groups more aggressive than individuals? Henri Tajfel lecture, presented at the annual conference of the social psychology section of the British Psychological Society, 24–6, September.

Rabbie, J. M. and de Brey, J. H. C. (1971) The anticipation of intergroup cooperation and competition under private and public conditions. *International Journal of Group Tensions*, 1, 230–51.

Rabbie, J. M. and Horwitz, M. (1969) Arousal of ingroup–outgroup bias by a chance win or loss. *Journal of Personality and Social Psychology*, 13, 269–77.

Rabbie, J. M. and Horwitz, M. (1982) Conflict and aggression between individuals and groups. In H. Hiebsch, H. Brandstätter and H. H. Kelley (eds), *Social Psychology*, revised and edited version of selected papers presented at the XXII international congress of psychology, Leipzig, no. 8.

Rabbie, J. M. and Lodewijkx, H. (1983) Aggression toward groups and individuals. Paper presented to the East–West meeting of the European Association of Experimental Social Psychology, Varna, Bulgaria, 17–20 May.

Rabbie, J. M., Lodewijkx, H. and Broeze, M. (1985) Individual and group aggression under the cover of darkness. Paper presented to the symposium on psychology of peace at the third European congress of the International Society for Research on Aggression (ISRA), devoted to multidisciplinary approaches to conflict and appeasement in animals and men, Parma, Italy, 3–7 September.

Rabbie, J. M. and Wilkens, G. (1971) Intergroup competition and its effect on intragroup and intergroup relations. *European Journal of Social Psychology*, 1, 215–34.

Radlow, R. (1965) An experimental study on cooperation in the prisoner's dilemma game. *Journal of Conflict Resolution*, 9, 221–7.

Radzicki, J. (1976) Technique of conjoint measurement of subjective value of own and other's gains. *Polish Psychological Bulletin*, 7, 179–86.

Ragan, S. L. and Hopper, R. (1984) Ways to leave your lover: a conversational analysis of literature. *Communication Quarterly*, 32, 310–17.

Rapoport, A. (1976) *Experimental Games and their Uses in Psychology*. Morristown, NJ: General Learning Press.

Rapoport, A. and Chammah, A. M. (1965) *Prisoner's Dilemma: a study in conflict and cooperation*. Ann Arbor, Mich.: University of Michigan Press.

Rapoport, A. and Chammah, A. M. (1969) The game of chicken. In R. Buchler and H. G. Nutini (eds), *Game Theory in the Behavioral Sciences*, Pittsburgh: Pittsburgh University Press.

Raven, B. H. and Haley, R. W. (1982) Social influence and compliance in hospital nurses with infection control policies. In J. R. Eiser (ed.), *Social Psychology and Behavioral Medicine*, Chichester: Wiley.

Reeder, G. D. (1982) Let's give the fundamental attribution error another chance. *Journal of Personality and Social Psychology*, 43, 341–4.

Reeder, G. D. and Brewer, M. B. (1979) A schematic model of dispositional attribution in interpersonal perception. *Psychological Review*, 86, 61–79.

Regan, D. T. and Fazio, R. H. (1977) On the consistency between attitudes and behavior: look to the method of attitude formation. *Journal of Experimental Social Psychology*, 13, 28–45.

Reich, J. W. and Zautra, A. (1981) Life events and personal causation: some relationships with satisfaction and distress. *Journal of Personality and Social Psychology*, 41, 1002–12.

Reicher, S. D. (1982) The determination of collective behavior. In H. Tajfel (ed.), *Social Identity and Intergroup Relations*, Cambridge: Cambridge University Press, Paris: Maison des Sciences de l'Homme.

Reicher, S. D. (1984) The St Pauls' riot: an explanation of the limits of crowd action in terms of a social identity model. *European Journal of Social Psychology*, 14, 1–21.

Reicher, S. D. and Emler, N. (1985) Delinquent behavior and attitudes to formal authority. *British Journal of Social Psychology*, 24, 161–8.

Reicher, S. D. and Emler, N. (1986) Managing reputations in adolescence: the pursuit of delinquent and non-delinquent identities. In H. Beloff (ed.), *Getting into Life*, London: Methuen.

Revans, R. (1964) *Standards for Morale: cause and effect in hospitals*. London: Tavistock.

Rice, M. E. and Grusec, J. E. (1975) Saying and doing: effects on observer performance. *Journal of Personality and Social Psychology*, 32, 584–93.

Ridgeway, C. L. (1978) Conformity, group-oriented motivation, and status attainment in small groups. *Social Psychology*, 41, 175–88.

Riess, M., Kalle, R. J. and Tedeschi, J. T. (1981) Bogus pipeline attitude assessment, impression management, and misattribution in induced compliance settings. *Journal of Social Psychology*, 115, 247–58.

Rijsman, J. B. (1983) The dynamics of social competition in personal and categorical comparison-situations. In W. Doise and S. Moscovici (eds), *Current Issues in European Social Psychology* (vol. 1), Cambridge: Cambridge University Press, Paris: Maison des Sciences de l'Homme.

Rijsman, J. B., Zoetebier, J. H. T., Ginther, A. J. F. and Doise, W. (1980) Sociocognitief conflict en cognitive ontwikkeling. *Pedagogische Studei*, 57, 125–33.

Ring, K. (1967) Experimental social psychology: some sober questions about some frivolous values. *Journal of Experimental Social Psychology*, 3, 113–23.

Roberts, J. V. (1985) The attitude–memory relationship after 40 years: a meta-analysis of the literature. *Basic and Applied Social Psychology*, 6, 221–41.

Robinson, D. N. (1980) *Psychology and Law: can justice survive the social sciences?* Oxford: Oxford University Press.

Robinson, J. P. and Shaver, P. R. (1969) *Measures of Social Psychological Attitudes.* Ann Arbor, Mich.: Survey Research Center, University of Michigan.

Robinson, W. P. (1972) *Language and Social Behaviour.* Harmondsworth: Penguin.

Robinson, W. P. (1984) The development of communicative competence with language in young children: a social psychological perspective. In H. Tajfel (ed.), *The Social Dimension* (vol. 1), Cambridge: Cambridge University Press.

Rodin, J. and Langer, E. (1980) Aging labels: the decline of control and the fall of self-esteem. *Journal of Social Issues*, 36, 12–29.

Roethlisberger, F. J. and Dickson, J. (1939) *Management and the Worker.* Cambridge, Mass.: Harvard University Press.

Rogers, R. W. (1975) A protection motivation theory of fear appeals and attitude change. *Journal of Psychology*, 91, 93–114.

Rogers, R. W. (1983) Cognitive and physiological processes in fear appeals and attitude change: a revised theory of protection motivation. In J. T. Cacioppo and R. E. Petty (eds), *Social Psychophysiology: a sourcebook*, New York: Guilford.

Rogers, R. W. (1985) Attitude change and information integration in fear appeals. *Psychological Reports*, 56, 179–82.

Rogers, R. W. and Mewborn, C. R. (1976) Fear appeals and attitude change: effects of a threat's noxiousness, probability of occurrence, and the efficacy of coping responses. *Journal of Personality and Social Psychology*, 34, 54–61.

Rokeach, M. (1948) Generalized mental rigidity as a factor in ethnocentrism. *Journal of Abnormal and Social Psychology*, 43, 259–78.

Rokeach, M. (1960) *The Open and Closed Mind.* New York: Basic.

Romer, D. (1979) Distraction, counterarguing, and the internalization of attitude change. *European Journal of Social Psychology*, 9, 1–17.

Rosch, E. (1978) Principles of categorization. In E. Rosch and B. B. Lloyd (eds), *Cognition and Categorization*, Hillsdale, NJ: Erlbaum.

Rosenbaum, M. E. and Blake, R. R. (1955) Volunteering as a function of field structure. *Journal of Abnormal and Social Psychology*, 50, 193–6.

Rosenberg, M. and Simmons, R. G. (1972) *Black and White Self-Esteem: the urban school child.* Washington, DC: American Sociological Association.

Rosenberg, M. J. (1968) Hedonism, inauthenticity, and other goads toward expansion of a consistency theory. In R. P. Abelson, E. Aronson, W. J. McGuire, T. M. Newcomb, M. J. Rosenberg and P. H. Tannenbaum (eds), *Theories of Cognitive Consistency: a sourcebook*, Chicago: Rand McNally.

Rosenberg, M. J. and Hovland, C. I. (1960) Cognitive, affective, and behavioral components of attitudes. In C. I. Hovland and M. J. Rosenberg (eds), *Attitude Organization and Change*, New Haven: Yale University Press.

Rosenberg, S. and Sedlack, A. (1972) Structural representations of implicit personality theory. In L. Berkowitz (ed.), *Advances in Experimental Social Psychology* (vol. 6), New York: Academic Press.

Rosenthal, R. (1966) *Experimenter Effects in Behavioral Research.* New York: Appleton-Century-Crofts.

Rosenthal, R. (1982) Conducting judgment studies. In K. R. Scherer and P. Ekman (eds), *Handbook of Methods in Nonverbal Behavior Research*, New York: Cambridge University Press.

Rosenthal, R. and Rosnow, R. L. (1975) *The Volunteer Subject.* New York: Wiley.

Ross, E. A. (1908) *Social Psychology*. New York: Macmillan.

Ross, L. D. (1977) The intuitive psychologist and his shortcomings: distortions in the attribution process. In L. Berkowitz (ed.), *Advances in Experimental Social Psychology* (vol. 10), New York: Academic Press.

Ross, L. D., Amabile, T. M. and Steinmetz, J. L. (1977) Social roles, social control, and biases in social-perception processes. *Journal of Personality and Social Psychology*, 35, 485–94.

Ross, L. D., Greene, D. and House, P. (1977) The false consensus phenomenon: an attributional bias in self-perception and social perception processes. *Journal of Experimental Social Psychology*, 13, 279–301.

Ross, L. D., Lepper, M. R. and Hubbard, M. (1975) Perseverance in self perception and social perception: biased attributional processes in the debriefing paradigm. *Journal of Personality and Social Psychology*, 32, 880–92.

Ross, M. and Fletcher, G. J. O. (1985) Attribution and social perception. In G. Lindzey and E. Aronson (eds), *Handbook of Social Psychology* (vol. 2), 3rd edn, New York: Random House.

Ross, M., McFarland, C. and Fletcher, G. J. O. (1981) The effect of attitude on the recall of personal histories. *Journal of Personality and Social Psychology*, 40, 627–34.

Rothbart, M. (1981) Memory processes and social beliefs. In D. L. Hamilton (ed.), *Cognitive Processes in Stereotyping and Intergroup Behaviour*, Hillsdale, NJ: Erlbaum.

Rubin, Z. (1973) *Liking and Loving: an invitation to social psychology*. New York: Holt, Rinehart & Winston.

Rubin, Z. and Peplau, L. A. (1975) Who believes in a just world? *Journal of Social Issues*, 31, 65–89.

Ruble, D. N. (1983) The development of social comparison processes and their role in achievment-related self-socialization. In E. T. Higgins, D. N. Ruble, and W. W. Hartup (eds), *Social Cognition and Social Development: a sociocultural perspective*, Cambridge: Cambridge University Press.

Rule, B. G., Dyck, R. J. and Nesdale, A. R. (1978) Arbitrariness of frustration: inhibition or instigation effects in aggression. *European Journal of Social Psychology*, 8, 237–44.

Rule, B. G. and Ferguson, T. J. (1984) The relation among attribution, moral evaluation, anger, and aggression in children and adults. In A. Mummendey (ed.), *Social Psychology of aggression: from individual behavior to social interaction*, New York: Springer.

Rule, B. G. and Nesdale, A. R. (1976) Emotional arousal and aggressive behavior. *Psychological Bulletin*, 83, 851–63.

Runciman, W. G. (1966) *Relative Deprivation and Social Justice*. London: Routledge & Kegan Paul.

Runkel, P. J. and McGrath, J. E. (1972) *Research on Human Behavior: a systematic guide to method*. New York: Holt, Rinehart & Winston.

Rusbult, C. E. (1980) Commitment and satisfaction in romantic associations: a test of the investment model. *Journal of Experimental Social Psychology*, 16, 172–86.

Rushton, J. P. (1975) Generosity in children: immediate and long-term effects of modeling, preaching, and moral judgment. *Journal of Personality and Social Psychology*, 31, 459–66.

Rushton, J. P. (1980) *Altruism, Socialization and Society*. Englewood Cliffs, NJ: Prentice-Hall.

Russell, D. W., Altmaier, E. and Velzen, D. van (1987) Job-related stress, social support, and burnout amongst classroom teachers. *Journal of Applied Psychology*, 72, 269–74.

Russell, J. (1979) Nonverbal and verbal judgments of length invariance by young children. *British Journal of Psychology*, 70, 313–17.

Rutte, C. G. and Wilke, H. A. M. (1983) Social dilemmas and leadership. In V. Allen and E. van der Vliert (eds), *Role and Role Transitions*, New York: Plenum.

Rutte, C. G. and Wilke, H. A. M. (1984) Social dilemmas and leadership. *European Journal of Social Psychology*, 14, 105–21.

Rutte, C. G. and Wilke, H. A. M. (1985) Preference for decision structures in a social dilemma situation. *European Journal of Social Psychology*, 15, 367–70.

Rutter, D. R. and Durkin, K. (1987) The development of turn-taking in mother–infant interaction: longitudinal and cross-sectional studies of vocalizations and gaze. *Development Psychology*, 23, 54–61.

Rutter, M. and Giller, H. (1983) *Juvenile Delinquency: trends and perspectives*. Harmondsworth: Penguin.

Ryan, E. B., Bartolucci, G., Giles, H. and Henwood, K. (1986) Psycholinguistic and social psychological components of communication by and with older adults. *Language and Communication*, 6, 1–22.

Ryen, A. H. and Kahn, A. (1975) Effects of intergroup orientation on group attitudes and proxemic behaviour. *Journal of Personality and Social Psychology*, 31, 302–10.

Sampson, E. E. (1977) Psychology and the American ideal. *Journal of Personality and Social Psychology*, 35, 767–82.

Sanders, G. S. (1981) Driven by distraction: an integrative review of social facilitation theory and research. *Journal of Experimental Social Psychology*, 17, 227–51.

Sanders, G. S., and Baron, R. S. (1977) Is social comparison irrelevant for producing choice shifts? *Journal of Experimental Social Psychology*, 13, 303–14.

Sanders, G. S., Baron, R. S. and Moore, D. L. (1978) Distraction and social comparison as mediators of social facilitation effects. *Journal of Experimental Social Psychology*, 14, 291–303.

Scarr, S. and Kidd, K. K. (1983) Developmental behavior genetics. In M. M. Haith and J. J. Campos (eds), *Mussen's Handbook of Child Psychology* (vol. II), New York: Wiley.

Schaap, C. and Buunk, B. (in press) Marital conflict resolution. In P. Noller and M. A. Fitzpatrick (eds), *Marital Interaction*, Clevedon: Multilingual Matters.

Schachter, S. (1951) Deviation, rejection and communication. *Journal of Abnormal and Social Psychology*, 46, 190–207.

Schachter, S. (1964) The interaction of cognitive and physiological determinants of emotional state. In L. Berkowitz (ed.), *Advances in Experimental Social Psychology* (vol. 1), New York: Academic Press.

Schachter, S. and Singer, J. (1962) Cognitive, social, and physiological determinants of emotional state. *Psychological Review*, 65, 379–99.

Schaffer, H. R. (1977a) Early interactive development. In H. R. Schaffer (ed.), *Studies in Mother-Infant Interaction*, London: Academic Press.

Schaffer, H. R. (1977b) *Mothering*. London: Open Books.

Schaffer, H. R. (1978) Lo sviluppo della competenza interattiva nell' infanzia. In A. Palmonari and P. E. Ricci-Bitt (eds), *Aspetti cognitive della' socializzazione in eta evolutiva*, Bologna: Il Mulino.

Schaffer, H. R. (1984) Parental control techniques in the context of socialization theory. In W. Doise and A. Palmonari (eds), *Social Interaction in Individual Development*, Cambridge: Cambridge University Press.

Schaffer, H. R. and Crook, C. K. (1979) Maternal control techniques in a directed play situation. *Child Development*, 50, 989–98.

Schank, R. and Abelson, R. P. (1977) *Scripts, Plans, Goals, and Understanding*. Hillsdale, NJ: Erlbaum.

Scheerer, M. (1954) Cognitive theory. In G. Lindzey (ed.), *Handbook of Social Psychology*, Cambridge, Mass.: Addison-Wesley.

Scherer, K. R. (1979) Voice and speech correlates of perceived social influence in simulated juries. In H. Giles and R. St Clair (eds), *Language and Social Psychology*, Oxford: Basil Blackwell.

Scherer, K. R., Abeles, R. P. and Fischer, C. S. (1975) *Human Aggression and Conflict*. Englewood Cliffs, NJ: Prentice-Hall.

Schlegel, R. P. (1975) Multidimensional measurement of attitude towards smoking marijuana. *Canadian Journal of Behavioral Science*, 7, 387–96.

Schlegel, R. P. and DiTecco, D. (1982) Attitudinal structures and the attitude–behavior relation. In M. P. Zanna, E. T. Higgins and C. P. Herman (eds), *Consistency in Social Behavior: the Ontario symposium* (vol. 2), Hillsdale, NJ: Erlbaum.

Schlenker, B. R. (1974) Social psychology and science. *Journal of Personality and Social Psychology*, 29, 1–15.

Schlenker, B. R. (1982) Translating actions into attitudes: an identity-analytic approach to the explanation of social conduct. In L. Berkowitz (ed.), *Advances in Experimental Social Psychology* (vol. 15), New York: Academic Press.

Schlenker, B. R. and Miller, R. S. (1977) Egocentrism in groups: self-serving biases or logical information processing? *Journal of Personality and Social Psychology*, 35, 755–64.

Schmidt, H.-D. and Schmidt-Mummendey, A. (1974) Waffen als aggressionsanbahnende Hinweisreize: Eine kritische Betrachtung experimenteller Ergebnisse. *Zeitschrift für Sozialpsychologie*, 5, 201–18.

Schneider, D. J. (1973) Implicit personality theory: a review. *Psychological Bulletin*, 79, 294–309.

Schönbach, P. (1985) A taxonomy for account phases: revised, explained and applied. Berichte aus der AE Sozialpsychologie (mimeographed reports). Fakultät für Psychologie der Ruhr-Universität Bochum.

Schopler, J. and Bateson, N. (1965) The power of dependence. *Journal of Personality and Social Psychology*, 2, 247–54.

Schriesheim, C. A. and Kerr, S. (1977) Theories and measures of leadership: a critical appraisal of current and future directions. In J. G. Hunt and L. L. Larson (eds), *Leadership: the cutting edge*, Carbondale, Ill.: Southern Illinois University Press.

Schroeder, D. H. and Costa, P. T., Jr (1984) Influence of life event stress on physical illness: substantive effects or methodological flaws? *Journal of Personality and Social Psychology*, 46, 853–63.

Schulz, U. (1986) The structure of conflict and preferences in experimental games. In R. Scholz (ed.), *Current Issues in West German Decision Research*, Frankfurt: Lang.

Schuman, H. and Kalton, G. (1985) Survey methods. In G. Lindzey and E. Aronson (eds), *Handbook of Social Psychology*, (vol. 1), 3rd edn, New York: Random House.

Schwartz, G. E., Fair, P. L., Salt, P., Mandel, M. R. and Klermann, G. L. (1976) Facial muscle patterning to affective imagery in depressed and nondepressed subjects. *Science*, 192, 489–91.

Schwartz, S. H. (1970) Elicitation of moral obligation and self-sacrificing behavior: an experimental study of volunteering to be a bone marrow donor. *Journal of Personality and Social Psychology*, 15, 283–93.

Schwartz, S. H. (1977) Normative influences on altruism. In L. Berkowitz (ed.),

Advances in Experimental Social Psychology (vol. 10), New York: Academic Press.

Schwartz, S. H. (1978) Temporal instability as a moderator of the attitude–behavior relationship. *Journal of Personality and Social Psychology*, 36, 715–24.

Schwartz, S. H. and Gottlieb, A. (1976) Bystander reactions to a violent theft: crime in Jerusalem. *Journal of Personality and Social Psychology*, 34, 1188–99.

Schwartz, S. H. and Howard, J. A. (1981) A normative decision-making model of altruism. In J. P. Rushton and R. M. Sorrentino (eds), *Altruism and Helping Behavior*, Hillsdale, NJ: Erlbaum.

Schwarz, N. (1985) Theorien konzeptgesteuerter Informationsverarbeitung. In D. Frey and M. Irle (eds), *Theorien der Sozialpsychologie. Vol. III: Motivations- und Informations-verarbeitungstheorien*, Bern: Huber.

Schwarz, N., Strack, F., Kommer, D. and Wagner, D. (1987) Soccer, rooms, and the quality of your life: further evidence on informative functions of affective states. *European Journal of Social Psychology*, 17, 69–80.

Scott, M. B. and Lyman, S. (1968) Accounts. *American Sociological Review*, 33, 46–62.

Seligman, C., Lambert, W. E. and Tucker, G. R. (1972) The effects of speech style and other attributes on teachers' attitudes toward pupils. *Language in Society*, 1, 131–42.

Seligman, M. E. P. and Hager, J. L. (1972) *Biological Boundaries of Learning*. New York: Appleton-Century-Crofts.

Selltiz, C., Wrightsman, L. S. and Cook, S. W. (1976) *Research Methods in Social Relations*. New York: Holt, Rinehart & Winston.

Selman, R. L. (1980) *The Growth of Interpersonal Understanding*. New York: Academic Press.

Semin, G. R. (1986) On the relationship between representations of theories in psychology and ordinary language. In W. Doise and S. Moscovici (eds), *Current Issues in European Social Psychology* (vol. 2), Cambridge: Cambridge University Press.

Semin, G. R. and Glendon, A. I. (1973) Polarization and the established group. *British Journal of Social and Clinical Psychology*, 12, 113–21.

Semin, G. R. and Manstead, A. S. R. (1979) Social psychology: social or psychological? *British Journal of Social and Clinical Psychology*, 18, 191–202.

Semin, G. R. and Manstead, A. S. R. (1983) *The Accountability of Conduct: a social psychological analysis*. London: Academic Press.

Sermat, V. (1967) The possibility of influencing the other's behavior and cooperation: chicken versus prisoner's dilemma. *Canadian Journal of Psychology*, 27, 204–19.

Shanab, M. E. and Yahya, K. A. (1978) A cross-cultural study of obedience. *Bulletin of the Psychonomic Society*, 11, 267–9.

Shantz, C. U. (1983) Social cognition. In P. H. Mussen (ed.), *Carmichael's Manual of Child Psychology. Vol. 3: Cognitive development* (eds J. H. Flavell and E. Markman), New York: Wiley.

Shapland, J. M. (1978) Self-reported delinquency in boys aged 11 to 14. *British Journal of Criminology*, 18, 255–66.

Shaver, K. G. (1981a) Back to basics: on the role of theory in the attribution of causality. In J. H. Harvey, W. Ickes and R. F. Kidd (eds), *New Directions in Attribution Research* (vol. 3), Hillsdale, NJ: Erlbaum.

Shaver, K. G. (1981b) *Principles of Social Psychology*. Cambridge, Mass.: Winthrop.

Shaw, M. (1932) A comparison of individuals and small groups in the rational solution of complex problems. *American Journal of Psychology*, 44, 491–504.

Shaw, M. E. (1964) Communication networks. In L. Berkowitz (ed.), *Advances in Experimental Social Psychology* (vol. 1), New York: Academic Press.

Shaw, M. E. (1981) *Group Dynamics: the social psychology of small group behavior.* 3rd edn. New York: McGraw-Hill.

Shaw, M. E. and Wright, J. M. (1967) *Scales for the Measurement of Attitudes.* New York: McGraw-Hill.

Sherif, M. (1935) A study of some factors in perception. *Archives of Psychology*, 27, no. 187.

Sherif, M. (1936) *The Psychology of Social Norms.* New York: Harper & Row.

Sherif, M. (1966) *Group Conflict and Co-operation: their social psychology.* London: Routledge & Kegan Paul.

Sherif, M., Harvey, O. J., White, B. J., Hood, W. R. and Sherif, C. W. (1961) *Intergroup Conflict and Cooperation: the robber's cave experiment.* Norman, Okla.: University of Oklahoma.

Sherif, M. and Hovland, C. J. (1961) *Social Judgment.* New Haven, Conn.: Yale University Press.

Sherif, M. and Sherif, C. W. (1953) *Groups in Harmony and Tension: an integration of studies on intergroup relations.* New York: Octagon.

Sherif, M. and Sherif, C. W. (1967) Attitude as the individual's own categories: the social judgment-involvement approach to attitude and attitude change. In M. Sherif and C. W. Sherif (eds), *Attitude, Ego-Involvement, and Change*, New York: Wiley.

Sherif, M., White, B. J. and Harvey, O. J. (1955) Status in experimentally produced groups. *American Journal of Sociology*, 60, 370-9.

Sherman, S. J. and Corty, E. (1984) Cognitive heuristics. In R. S. Wyer and T. K. Srull (eds), *Handbook of Social Cognition* (vol. 1), Hillsdale, NJ: Erlbaum.

Shiffrin, R. M. and Schneider, W. (1977) Controlled and automatic human information processing. II: Perceptual learning, automatic attending, and a general theory. *Psychological Review*, 84, 127-90.

Short, R. (1979) Sexual selection and its component parts, somatic and genital selection, as illustrated by man and the great apes. *Advances in the Study of Behaviour*, 9, 131-58.

Shweder, R. (1977) Likeness and likelihood in everyday thought: magical thinking in judgments about personality. *Current Anthropology*, 18, 637-58.

Sidowski, J. B., Wyckoff, L. B. and Tabory, L. (1956) The influence of reinforcement and punishment in a minimal social situation. *Journal of Abnormal and Social Psychology*, 52, 115-19.

Sighele, S. (1891) *La folla delinquente.* Torino: Fratelli Bocca.

Silberer, G. (1983) Einstellungen und Werthaltungen. In M. Irle and W. Bussmann (eds), *Marktpsychologie als Sozialwissenschaft, Enzyklopädie der Psychologie* (vol. 4), Göttingen: Hogrefe.

Simmel, G. (1908) *Soziologie – Untersuchungen über die Formen der Vergesellschaftung.* Leipzig: Duncker & Humblot.

Simon, B. and Brown, R. J. (1987) Perceived intergroup homogeneity in minority–majority contexts. Unpublished paper, Universität Münster.

Simon, H. A. (1976) *Administrative Behavior: a study of decision making process in administrative organizations.* New York: Free Press.

Simon, M. D., Tajfel, H. and Johnson, N. B. (1967) Wie erkennt man einen Österreicher? *Kölner Zeitschrift für Soziologie und Soziolpsychologie*, 19, 511-37.

Simons, L. S. and Turner, C. W. (1976) Evaluation apprehension, hypothesis awareness and the weapons effect. *Aggressive Behavior*, 2, 77–87.
Simpson, A. E. and Stevenson-Hinde, J. (1985) Temperamental characteristics of
three- to four-year-old boys and girls and child–family interactions. *Journal of Child
Psychology and Psychiatry*, 26, 43–53.
Singer, J. E. (1964) The use of manipulation strategies: machiavellianism and attrac-
tiveness. *Sociometry*, 27, 138–50.
Singer, J. L. and Singer, D. G. (1979) Television viewing, family style and aggressive
behavior in preschool children. In M. Geen (ed.), *Violence and the American Family*,
Washington, DC: American Association for the Advancement of Science.
Skevington, S. (1981) Intergroup relations and nursing. *European Journal of Social
Psychology*, 11, 43–59.
Skinner, B. F. (1953) *Science and Human Behavior*. New York: Macmillan.
Slater, P. E. (1955) Role differentiation in small groups. *American Sociological
Review*, 20, 300–10.
Smedslund, J. (1985) Necessarily true cultural psychologies. In K. J. Gergen and K. E.
Davis (eds), *The Social Construction of the Person*, New York: Springer.
Smith, E. R. and Miller, F. D. (1979) Attributional information processing: a response
time model of causal subtraction. *Journal of Personality and Social Psychology*, 37,
1723–31.
Smith, M. B., Bruner, J. S. and White, R. W. (1956) *Opinions and Personality*. New
York: Wiley.
Smith, P. K. (1986) Exploration, play and social development in boys and girls. In D. J.
Hargreaves and A. M. Colley (eds), *The Psychology of Sex Roles*, London: Harper &
Row.
Smith, P. M. (1985) *Language, the Sexes and Society*. Oxford: Basil Blackwell.
Smith, P. M. and Fritz, A. S. (1987) A person-niche theory of depersonalization:
implications for leader selection, performance and evaluation. In C. Hendrick (ed.),
Review of Personality and Social Psychology (vol. 8), Beverly Hills: Sage.
Smith, V. L. and Ellsworth, P. C. (1987) The social psychology of eyewitness accuracy:
misleading questions and Communicator expertise. *Journal of Applied Psychology*,
72, 294–300.
Snow, C. E. and Ferguson, C. A. (1977) *Talking to Children: language input and
acquisition*. Cambridge: Cambridge University Press.
Snyder, D. K. and Regis, J. M. (1982) Factor scales for assessing marital disharmony
and disaffection. *Journal of Counseling and Clinical Psychology*, 50, 736–43.
Snyder, M. (1974) The self-monitoring of expressive behavior. *Journal of Personality
and Social Psychology*, 30, 526–37.
Snyder, M. and Kendzierski, D. (1982a) Acting on one's attitude: procedures for linking attitude and behavior. *Journal of Experimental Social Psychology*, 18, 165–83.
Snyder, M. and Kendzierski, D. (1982b) Choosing social situations: investigating the
origins of correspondence between attitudes and behavior. *Journal of Personality*,
50, 280–95.
Snyder, M. and Swann, W. B. (1978) Behavioral confirmation in social interaction:
from social perception to social reality. *Journal of Experimental Social Psychology*,
14, 148–62.
Softley, P. (1980) *Police Interrogation: an observational study in four police stations*.
London: HMSO.
Sokolov, A. N. (1963) *Perception and the Conditioned Reflex*. Oxford: Pergamon.
Sonne, J. L. and Janoff, D. S. (1982) Attributions and the maintenance of behaviour

change. In C. Antaki and C. Brewin (eds), *Attributions and Psychological change*, London and New York: Academic Press.

Sorrentino, R. M., King, G. and Leo, G. (1980) The influence of the minority on perception: a note on a possible alternative explanation. *Journal of Experimental Social Psychology*, 16, 293–301.

Sparks, R. F., Genn, H. G. and Dodd, D. J. (1977) *Surveying Victims*. Chichester: Wiley.

Spence, K. W. (1956) *Behavior Theory and Conditioning*. New Haven, Conn.: Yale University Press.

Srull, T. K. and Wyer, R. S., Jr (1980) Category accessibility and social perception: some implications for the study of person memory and interpersonal judgments. *Journal of Personality and Social Psychology*, 38, 841–56.

Staats, A. W. and Staats, C. K. (1958) Attitudes established by classical conditioning. *Journal of Abnormal and Social Psychology*, 57, 37–40.

Staub, E. (1970) A child in distress: the effect of focusing responsibility on children on their attempts to help. *Developmental Psychology*, 2, 152–3.

Steiner, I. D. (1972) *Group Processes and Productivity*. New York: Academic Press.

Steiner, I. D. (1976) Task-performing groups. In J. W. Thibaut, J. T. Spence and R. C. Carson (eds), *Contemporary Topics in Social Psychology*, Morristown, NJ: General Learning Press.

Stephenson, G. M. (1978) Interparty and interpersonal exchange in negotiation groups. In H. Brandstätter, J. H. Davis and H. Schuler (eds) *Dynamics of Group Decisions*, London: Sage.

Stephenson, G. M. and Davis, J. H. (1986) Editorial. *Social Behaviour*, 1, 1.

Sternglanz, S. H., Gray, J. L. and Murakami, M. (1977) Adult preferences for infantile facial features: an ethological approach. *Animal Behaviour*, 25, 108–15.

Stewart, M. A., Ryan, E. B. and Giles, H. (1985) Accent and social class effects on status and solidarity evaluations. *Personality and Social Psychology Bulletin*, 11, 98–105.

Stogdill, R. M. (1948) Personal factors associated with leadership. *Journal of Psychology*, 23, 35–71.

Stokols, D. (1972) On the distinction between density and crowding: some implications for future research. *Psychological Review*, 79, 275–8.

Stoner, J. A. F. (1961) A comparison of individual and group decisions involving risk. Unpublished master's thesis, Massachusetts Institute of Technology.

Storms, M. D. (1973) Videotape and the attribution process: reversing actors' and observers' points of view. *Journal of Personality and Social Psychology*, 27, 165–75.

Stosberg, M. (1980) Klassische Ansätze in der Einstellungsmessung. In F. Petermann (ed.), *Einstellungsmessung/Einstellungsforschung*, Göttingen: Högrefe.

Stouffer, S. A., Suchmann, E. A., DeVinney, L. C., Star, S. A. and Williams, R. M., Jr (1949) *The American Soldier. Vol. 1: Adjustments during army life*. Princeton, NJ: Princeton University Press.

Street, R. L., Jr and Cappella, J. N. (eds) (1985) *Sequence and Pattern in Communicative Behaviour*. London: Edward Arnold.

Strickland, L. H. (1979) *Soviet and Western Perspectives in Social Psychology*. Oxford: Pergamon Press.

Stroebe, M. S. and Stroebe, W. (1983) Who suffers more? Sex differences in health risks of the bereaved. *Psychological Bulletin*, 93, 279–301.

Stroebe, W. (1980) *Grundlagen der Sozialpsychologie*. Stuttgart: Klett-Cotta.

Stroebe, W. and Frey, B. S. (1982) Self-interest and collective action: the economics and psychology of public goods. *British Journal of Social Psychology*, 21, 121–37.

Stroebe, W., Insko, C. A., Thompson, V. D. and Layton, B. (1971) Effects of physical attractiveness, attitude similarity and sex on various aspects of interpersonal attraction. *Journal of Personality and Social Psychology*, 18, 79–91.

Stroebe, W., Lenkert, A. and Jonas, K. (1988) Familiarity may breed contempt: the impact of student exchange on national stereotypes and attitudes. In W. Stroebe, A. Kruglanski, D. Bar-Tal and M. Hewstone (eds), *The Social Psychology of Intergroup Conflict: theory, research and applications*, New York: Springer.

Stroebe, W. and Stroebe, M. S. (1987a) Bereavement as a stressful life-event: a paradigm for research on the stress–health relationship. In G. R. Semin and B. Krahé (eds), *Issues in Contemporary German Social Psychology*, London: Sage.

Stroebe, W. and Stroebe, M. S. (1987b) *Bereavement and Health*. New York: Cambridge University Press.

Stroebe, W., Stroebe, M. S., Gergen, K. J. and Gergen, M. (1982) The effects of bereavement on mortality: a social psychological analysis. In J. R. Eiser (ed.), *Social Psychology and Behavioural Medicine*, Chichester: Wiley.

Stults, D. M., Messé, L. A. and Kerr, N. L. (1984) Belief discrepant behavior and the bogus pipeline: impression management or arousal attribution? *Journal of Experimental Social Psychology*, 20, 47–54.

Sullivan, H. S. (1938) The data of psychiatry. *Psychiatry*, 1, 121–34.

Sweeney, P. D., Anderson, K. and Bailey, S. (1986) Attributional style in depression: a meta-analytic review. *Journal of Personality and Social Psychology*, 50, 974–91.

Swingle, P. G. and Gillis, J. S. (1968) Effects of emotional relationship between protagonists in the prisoner's dilemma. *Journal of Personality and Social Psychology*, 21, 121–37.

Swingle, P. G. and Santi, A. (1972) Communication in non-zero-sum games. *Journal of Personality and Social Psychology*, 23, 54–64.

Tagiuri, R. and Petrullo, L. (1958) *Person Perception and Interpersonal Behavior*. Stanford: Stanford University Press.

Tajfel, H. (1969a) Social and cultural factors in perception. In G. Lindzey and E. Aronson (eds), *Handbook of Social Psychology*, Reading, Mass.: Addison-Wesley.

Tajfel, H. (1969b) Cognitive aspects of prejudice. *Journal of Social Issues*, 25, 79–97.

Tajfel, H. (1970) Experiments in intergroup discrimination. *Scientific American*, 223, 96–102.

Tajfel, H. (1978a) *The Social Psychology of Minorities*. London: Minority Rights Group, report no. 38.

Tajfel, H. (ed.) (1978b) *Differentiation between Social Groups: studies in the social psychology of intergroup relations*. London: Academic Press.

Tajfel, H. (1978c) Intergroup behavior. I: Individualistic perspectives. In H. Tajfel and C. Fraser (eds), *Introducing Social Psychology*, Harmondsworth: Penguin.

Tajfel, H. (1981) *Human Groups and Social Categories: studies in social psychology*. Cambridge: Cambridge University Press.

Tajfel, H. (1982a) Social psychology of intergroup relations. *Annual Review of Psychology*, 33, 1–30.

Tajfel, H. (ed.) (1982b) *Social Identity and Intergroup Relations*. London: Cambridge University Press.

Tajfel, H. (1984) Intergroup relations, social myths and social justice in social psychology. In H. Tajfel (ed.), *The Social Dimension: European developments in social psychology* (vol. 2), Cambridge: Cambridge University Press.

Tajfel, H., Flament, C., Billig, M. G. and Bundy, R. P. (1971) Social categorization and intergroup behaviour. *European Journal of Social Psychology*, 1, 149–78.

Tajfel, H. and Fraser, C. (eds) (1978) *Introducing Social Psychology*. Harmondsworth: Penguin.

Tajfel, H. and Jahoda, G. (1966) Development in children of concepts and attitudes about their own and other nations: a cross-national study. Proceedings of the XVIIIth international congress of psychology, symposium, 36, 17–33, Moscow.

Tajfel, H., Nemeth, C., Jahoda, G., Campbell, J. D. and Johnson, N. B. (1970) The development of children's preference for their own country: a cross-national study. *International Journal of Psychology*, 6, 245–53.

Tajfel, H. and Turner, J. C. (1979) An integrative theory of intergroup conflict. In W. C. Austin and S. Worchel (eds), *The Social Psychology of Intergroup Relations*, Monterey, Calif.: Brooks/Cole.

Tajfel, H. and Wilkes, A. L. (1963) Classification and quantitative judgment. *British Journal of Psychology*, 54, 101–14.

Tanford, S. and Penrod, S. (1984) Social influence model: a formal integration of research on majority and minority influence processes. *Psychological Bulletin*, 95, 189–225.

Tannenbaum, P. H. and Zillmann, D. (1975) Emotional arousal in the facilitation of aggression through communication. In L. Berkowitz (ed.), *Advances in Experimental Social Psychology* (vol. 8), New York: Academic Press.

Tarde, G. (1895) *Essais et mélanges sociologiques*. Lyon: Storck.

Tarde, G. (1901) *L'opinion et la foule*. Paris: Alcan.

Tate, P. (1983) Doctor's style. In D. Pendleton and J. Hasler (eds), *Doctor–Patient Communication*, London: Academic Press.

Taylor, D. M. (1981) Stereotypes and intergroup relations. In R. C. Gardner and R. Kalin (eds), *A Canadian Social Psychology of Ethnic Relations*, Toronto: Methuen.

Taylor, D. M. and Brown, R. J. (1979) Towards a more social social psychology? *British Journal of Social and Clinical Psychology*, 18, 173–80.

Taylor, S. E. (1981) A categorization approach to stereotyping. In D. L. Hamilton (ed.), *Cognitive Processes in Stereotyping and Intergroup Behaviour*, Hillsdale, NJ: Erlbaum.

Taylor, S. E., Crocker, J., Fiske, S. T., Sprinzen, M. and Winkler, J. D. (1979) The generalizability of salience effects. *Journal of Personality and Social Psychology*, 37, 357–68.

Taylor, S. E. and Fiske, S. T. (1978) Salience, attention and attribution: top of the head phenomena. In L. Berkowitz (ed.), *Advances in Experimental Social Psychology* (vol. 11), New York: Academic Press.

Taylor, S. E. and Fiske, S. T. (1981) Getting inside the head: methodologies for process analysis in attribution and social cognition. In J. H. Harvey, W. Ickes and R. F. Kidd (eds), *New Directions in Attribution Research* (vol. 3), Hillsdale, NJ: Erlbaum.

Taylor, S. E., Fiske, S. T., Etcoff, N. and Ruderman, A. (1978) The categorical and contextual bases of person memory and stereotyping. *Journal of Personality and Social Psychology*, 36, 778–93.

Taylor, S. E. and Koivumaki, J. H. (1976) The perception of self and others: acquaintanceship, affect, and actor–observer differences. *Journal of Personality and Social Psychology*, 33, 403–8.

Tedeschi, J. T., Lindskold, S. and Rosenfeld, P. (1985) *Introduction to Social Psychology*. New York: West.

Tedeschi, J. T. and Riess, M. (1981) Verbal strategies in impression management. In C.

Antaki (ed.), *The Psychology of Ordinary Explanations of Social Behaviour*, London: Academic Press.

Tedeschi, J. T. and Rosenfeld, P. (1981) Impression management theory and the forced compliance situation. In J. T. Tedeschi (ed.), *Impression Management Theory and Social Psychological Research*, New York: Academic Press.

Tedeschi, J. T., Schlenker, B. R. and Bonoma, T. V. (1971) Cognitive dissonance: private ratiocination or public spectacle? *American Psychologist*, 26, 685–95.

Terhune, K. W. (1968) Motives, situation, and interpersonal conflict within the prisoner's dilemma game. *Journal of Personality and Social Psychology, Monograph supplement*, 8, 1–24.

Tesser, A., Gatewood, R. and Driver, M. (1968) Some determinants of gratitude. *Journal of Personality and Social Psychology*, 9, 233–6.

Tetlock, P. E., Bernzweig, J. and Gallant, J. L. (1985) Supreme Court decision making: cognitive style as a predictor of ideological consistency of voting. *Journal of Personality and Social Psychology*, 48, 1227–39.

Tetlock, P. E. and Levi, A. (1982) Attribution bias: on the inconclusiveness of the cognition–motivation debate. *Journal of Experimental Social Psychology*, 18, 68–88.

Tetlock, P. E. and Manstead, A. S. R. (1985) Impression management versus intrapsychic explanations in social psychology: a useful dichotomy? *Psychological Review*, 92, 59–77.

Thakerar, J. N. and Giles, H. (1981) They are – so they speak: non-content speech stereotypes. *Language and Communication*, 1, 251–5.

Thibaut, J. W. and Kelley, H. H. (1959) *The Social Psychology of Groups*. New York: Wiley.

Thibaut, J. W. and Strickland, L. H. (1956) Psychological set and social conformity. *Journal of Personality*, 25, 115–29.

Thomas, E. J. and Fink, C. F. (1961) Models of group problem solving. *Journal of Abnormal and Social Psychology*, 63, 53–63.

Thomas, W. I. and Znaniecki, F. (1918) *The Polish Peasant in Europe and America*. Boston: Badger.

Thompson, P. R. (1980) 'And who is my neighbour?' An answer from evolutionary genetics. *Social Science Information*, 19, 341–84.

Thorndike, E. L. and Lorge, I. (1944) *The Teacher's Wordbook of 30,000 Words*. New York: Teachers College, Columbia University.

Thorpe, W. H. (1961) *Bird Song*. Cambridge: Cambridge University Press.

Thurstone, L. L. (1928) Attitudes can be measured. *American Journal of Sociology*, 33, 529–54.

Thurstone, L. L. (1931) The measurement of attitudes. *Journal of Abnormal and Social Psychology*, 26, 249–69.

Tinbergen, N. (1956) On the functions of territory in gulls. *Ibis*, 98, 401–11.

Tinbergen, N. (1963) On aims and methods of ethology. *Zeitschrift für Tierpsychologie*, 20, 410–33.

Ting-Toomey, S. (1986) Interpersonal ties in intergroup communication. In W. B. Gudykunst (ed.), *Intergroup Communication*, London: Edward Arnold.

Tognoli, J. (1975) Reciprocation of generosity and knowledge of game termination in the decomposed prisoner's dilemma game. *European Journal of Social Psychology*, 5, 297–312.

Tomasello, M. and Todd, J. (1983) Joint attention and lexical acquisition style. *First Language*, 4, 197–212.

Torrance, E. P. (1954) The behavior of small groups under the stress of conditions of survival. *American Sociological Review*, 19, 751–5.

Totman, R. (1976) Cognitive dissonance and the placebo response. *European Journal of Social Psychology*, 5, 119–25.

Totman, R. (1979) *Social Causes of Illness*. New York: Pantheon.

Totman, R. (1982a) Psychosomatic theories. In J. R. Eiser (ed.), *Social Psychology and Behavioural Medicine*, Chichester: Wiley.

Totman, R. (1982b) Philosophical foundations of attribution therapies. In C. Antaki and C. Brewin (eds), *Attribution and Psychological Change*, London: Academic Press.

Travis, L. E. (1925) The effect of a small audience upon eye–hand coordination. *Journal of Abnormal and Social Psychology*, 20, 142–6.

Trevarthen, C., Hubley, P. and Sheeran, L. (1975) Les activités innées de nourrisson. *La Recherche*, 6, 447–58.

Triandis, H. C. (1978) Some universals of social behavior. *Personality and Social Psychology Bulletin*, 4, 1–16.

Triplett, N. D. (1898) The dynamogenic factor in pacemaking and competition. *American Journal of Psychology*, 9, 507–33.

Trivers, R. L. (1971) The evolution of reciprocal altruism. *Quarterly Review of Biology*, 46, 35–57.

Trivers, R. L. (1974) Parent–offspring conflict. *American Zoologist*, 14, 249–64.

Turiel, E. (1983) *The Development of Social Knowledge: morality and convention*. Cambridge: Cambridge University Press.

Turke, P. W. and Betzig, L. L. (1985) Those who can do: wealth, status and reproductive success on Haluk. *Ethology and Sociobiology*, 6, 79–87.

Turner, C. W. and Goldsmith, D. (1976) Effects of toy guns and airplanes on children's free play behavior. *Journal of Experimental Social Psychology*, 21, 303–15.

Turner, C. W. and Simons, L. S. (1974) Effects of subject sophistication and apprehension evaluation on aggressive responses to weapons. *Journal of Personality and Social Psychology*, 30, 341–8.

Turner, J. C. (1980) Fairness or discrimination in intergroup behaviour? A reply to Braithwaite, Doyle and Lightbown. *European Journal of Social Psychology*, 10, 131–47.

Turner, J. C. (1981a) The experimental social psychology of intergroup behaviour. In J. C. Turner and H. Giles (eds), *Intergroup Behaviour*, Oxford: Basil Blackwell.

Turner, J. C. (1981b) Some considerations in generalizing experimental social psychology. In G. M. Stephenson and J. Davis (eds), *Progress in Applied Social Psychology* (vol. 1), Chichester: Wiley.

Turner, J. C. (1982) Towards a cognitive redefinition of the social group. In H. Tajfel (ed.), *Social Identity and Intergroup Relations*, Cambridge: Cambridge University Press.

Turner, J. C. (1983a) Some comments on 'The measurement of social orientations in the minimal group paradigm'. *European Journal of Social Psychology*, 13, 351–67.

Turner, J. C. (1983b) A second reply to Bornstein, Crum, Wittenbraker, Harring, Insko and Thibaut on the measurement of social orientations. *European Journal of Social Psychology*, 13, 383–7.

Turner, J. C. and Brown, R. J. (1978) Social status, cognitive alternatives, and intergroup relations. In H. Tajfel (ed.), *Differentiation between Social Groups: studies in the social psychology of intergroup relations*, London: Academic Press.

Turner, J. C. and Oakes, P. J. (1986) The significance of the social identity concept for social psychology with reference to individualism: interactionism and social influence. *British Journal of Social Psychology*, 25, special issue on the individual–society interface.

Turner, R. H. and Killian, L. M. (1972) *Collective Behavior*. 2nd edn. Englewood Cliffs, NJ: Prentice-Hall.

Tversky, A. and Kahneman, D. (1974) Judgment under uncertainty: heuristics and biases. *Science*, 185, 1124–31.

Tversky, A. and Kahneman. D. (1978) Causal schemata in judgments under uncertainty. In M. Fishbein (ed.), *Progress in Social Psychology*. Hillsdale, NJ: Erlbaum.

Tyszka, T. and Grzelak, J. L. (1976) Criteria of choice in *n*-person nonconstant-sum games. *Journal of Conflict Resolution*, 20, 357–76.

Ullian, D. Z. (1976) The development of conceptions of masculinity and feminity. In B. B. Lloyd and J. Archer (eds), *Exploring Sex Differences*, London and New York: Academic Press.

Ulrich, W. (1986) The uses of fiction as a source of information about interpersonal communication: a critical view. *Communication Quarterly*, 34, 143–53.

United Kingdom Central Council for Nursing, Midwifery and Health Visiting (1984) *Code of Professional Conduct*. 2nd edn. London: UKCCNMHV.

Upshaw, H. S. (1969) The personal reference scale: an approach to social judgment. In L. Berkowitz (ed.), *Advances in Experimental Social Psychology* (vol. 4), New York: Academic Press.

Valiant, G., Glachan, M. and Emler, N. (1982) The stimulation of cognitive development through cooperative task performance. *British Journal of Educational Psychology*, 52, 281–8.

Van Avermaet, E. F., McClintock, C. G. and Moskowitz, J. (1978) Alternative approaches to equity: dissonance reduction, prosocial motivation and strategic accommodation. *European Journal of Social Psychology*, 8, 419–37.

Vanbeselaere, N. (1983) Mere exposure: a search for an explanation. In W. Doise and S. Moscovici (eds), *Current Issues in European Social Psychology* (vol. 1), Cambridge: Cambridge University Press, Paris: Maison des Sciences de l'Homme.

Van den Berghe, P. L. (1979) *Human Family Systems: an evolutionary view*. New York: Elsevier North-Holland.

Van Hooff, J. A. R. (1972) A comparative approach to the phylogeny of laughter and smiling. In R. A. Hinde (ed.), *Non-Verbal Communication*, Cambridge: Cambridge University Press.

Van Knippenberg, A. and van Oers, H. (1984) Social identity and equity concerns in intergroup perceptions. *British Journal of Social Psychology*, 23, 351–61.

Vanneman, R. D. and Pettigrew, T. F. (1972) Race and relative deprivation in the urban United States. *Race*, 13, 461–86.

Vaughan, G. M. (1964) Ethnic awareness in relation to minority group membership. *Journal of Genetic Psychology*, 105, 119–30.

Vaughan, G. M. (1978) Social change and intergroup preferences in New Zealand. *European Journal of Social Psychology*, 8, 297–314.

Veen, P. and Wilke, H. A. M. (1984) De kern van de sociale psychologie. Deventer: Van Loghum Slaterus.

Veroff, J., Douvan, E. and Kulka, R. A. (1981) *The Inner American*. New York: Basic.

Vlaander, G. P. J. and Van Rooijen, L. (1985) Independence and conformity in Holland: Asch's experiment three decades later. *Gedrag*, 13, 49–55.

Von Cranach, M. and Vine, I. (1973) Introduction. In M. Von Cranach and I. Vine (eds), *Social Communication and Movement*. London: Academic Press.

Von Neumann, J. and Morgenstern, O. (1944) *Theory of Games and Economic Behavior*. Princeton: Princeton University Press.

Wales, R. J. (1974) Children's sentences make sense of the world. In F. Bresson (ed.), *Les Problèmes Actuels en psycholinguistique*, Paris: Presses Universitaires de France.

Walker, C. (1977) Some variations in marital satisfaction. In R. Chester and J. Peel (eds), *Equalities and Inequalities in Family Life*, London: Academic Press.

Walker, I. and Pettigrew, T. F. (1984) Relative deprivation theory: an overview and conceptual critique. *British Journal of Social Psychology*, 23, 301–10.

Walters, R. H. and Brown, M. (1963) Studies of reinforcement of aggression. III: Transfer of responses to an interpersonal situation. *Child Development*, 34, 536–71.

Warr, P. B. (1965) Proximity as a determinant of positive and negative sociometric choice. *British Journal of Social and Clinical Psychology*, 4, 104–9.

Watson, D. (1982) The actor and the observer: how are their perceptions of causality different? *Psychological Bulletin*, 92, 682–700.

Watson, J. B. (1928) *Psychological Care of the Infant and Child*. New York: Norton.

Watson, R. I. (1979) The history of psychology conceived as social psychology of the past. *Journal of the History of the Behavioral Sciences*, 15, 103–14.

Watzlawick, P., Beavin, J. and Jackson, D. D. (1967) *Pragmatics and Human Communication*. New York: Norton.

Weary, G. (1981) The role of cognitive, affective and social factors in attribution biases. In J. H. Harvey (ed.), *Cognition, Behaviour and the Environment*, Hillsdale, NJ: Erlbaum.

Weary, G. and Arkin, R. M. (1981) Attributional self-presentation. In J. H. Harvey, W. J. Ickes and R. F. Kidd (eds), *New Directions in Attribution Theory and Research* (vol. 3), Hillsdale, NJ: Erlbaum.

Weaver, F. M. and Carroll, J. S. (1985) Crime perceptions in a natural setting by expert and novice shoplifters. *Social Psychology Quarterly*, 48, 349–59.

Webb, E. J., Campbell, D. T., Schwartz, R. F., Sechrest, L. and Grove, J. B. (1981) *Nonreactive Measures in the Social Sciences*. Boston: Houghton Mifflin.

Webley, P. (1983) Economic socialization in the pre-adult years: a comment on Stacey. *British Journal of Social Psychology*, 22, 264–5.

Wegener, H., Losel, F. and Haisch, J. (eds) (in press) *Criminal Behaviour and the Justice System: psychological perspectives*. New York: Springer.

Wegner, D. M., Guiliano, T. and Hertel, P. (1985) Cognitive interdependence in close relationships. In W. J. Ickes (ed.), *Compatible and Incompatible Relationships*, New York: Springer.

Wegner, D. M. and Vallacher, R. R. (1980) *The Self in Social Psychology*. New York: Oxford University Press.

Weick, K. E. (1985) Systematic observational methods. In G. Lindzey and E. Aronson (eds), *Handbook of Social Psychology* (vol. 1), 3rd edn, New York: Random House.

Weigel, R. H. and Newman, L. S. (1976) Increasing attitude–behavior correspondence by broadening the scope of the behavioral measure. *Journal of Personality and Social Psychology*, 33, 793–802.

Weiner, B. (1979) A theory of motivation for some classroom experiences. *Journal of Educational Psychology*, 71, 3–25.

Weiner, B. (1985a) 'Spontaneous' causal thinking. *Psychological Bulletin*, 97, 74–84.

Weiner, B. (1985b) An attributional theory of achievement motivation and emotion. *Psychological Review*, 92, 548–73.

Weiner, B. (1986) Attribution, emotion and action. In R. M. Sorrentino and E. T.

Higgins (eds), *Handbook of Motivation and Cognition*, New York: Guildford.

Weiner, B., Nierenberg, R. and Goldstein, M. (1976) Social learning (locus of control) versus attributional (causal stability) interpretations of expectancy of success. *Journal of Personality*, 44, 52–68.

Weiner, B., Russell, D. and Lerman, D. (1978) Affective consequences of causal ascriptions. In J. H. Harvey, W. J. Ickes and R. F. Kidd (eds), *New Directions in Attribution Research* (vol. 2), Hillsdale, NJ: Erlbaum.

Weinreich-Haste, H. (1979) What sex is science? In O. Hartnett, G. Boden and M. Fuller (eds), *Women: sex role stereotyping*, London: Tavistock.

Wells, G. L. (1984) A reanalysis of the expert testimony issue. In G. L. Wells and E. F. Loftus (eds), *Eyewitness Testimony: psychological perspectives*, Cambridge: Cambridge University Press.

Wells, G. L. and Harvey, J. H. (1977) Do people use consensus information in making causal attributions? *Journal of Personality and Social Psychology*, 35, 279–93.

Wells, G. L. and Loftus, E. F. (1984) Eyewitness research: then and now. In G. L. Wells and E. F. Loftus (eds), *Eyewitness Testimony: psychological perspectives*, Cambridge: Cambridge University Press.

West, C. (1984) *Routine Complications*. Bloomington, Ind.: Indiana University Press.

Wetherell, M. (1982) Cross-cultural studies of minimal groups: implications for the social identity theory of intergroup relations. In H. Tajfel (ed.), *Social Identity and Intergroup Relations*, Cambridge: Cambridge University Press.

Wheeler, L., Reis, H. and Nezlek, J. (1983) Loneliness, social interaction, and social role. *Journal of Personality and Social Psychology*, 45, 943–53.

Wheeless, L. R., Barraclough, R. and Stewart, R. (1983) Compliance-gaining and power in persuasion. *Communication Yearbook*, 7, 105–45.

Whyte, W. F. (1948) *Human Relations in the Restaurant Industry*. New York: McGraw-Hill.

Wichman, H. (1972) Effects of isolation and communication on cooperation in a two-person game. In L. S. Wrightsman, J. O'Connor and N. J. Baker (eds), *Cooperation and Competition: readings on mixed-motive games*, Belmont: Brooks-Cole.

Wicker, A. W. (1969) Attitudes versus actions: the relationship of verbal and overt behavioral responses to attitude objects. *Journal of Social Issues*, 25, 41–7.

Wicklund, R. A. (1974) *Freedom and Reactance*. Potomac, Md.: Erlbaum.

Wicklund, R. A. (1975) Objective self-awareness. In L. Berkowitz (ed.), *Advances in Experimental Social Psychology* (vol. 8), New York: Academic Press.

Wieczorkowska, G. (1982) A formal analysis of preferences. *Polish Psychological Bulletin*, 13, 73–7.

Wiemann, J. M. (1977) Explication and test of a model of communicative competence. *Human Communication Research*, 3, 195–213.

Wiemann, J. M. (1985) Interpersonal control and regulations in conversation. In R. L. Street and J. N. Cappella (eds), *Sequence and Pattern in Communicative Behaviour*, London: Edward Arnold.

Wiemann, J. M. and Bradac, J. J. (in press a) Meta-theoretical issues in the study of communicative competence: structural and functional approaches. *Progress in Communication Sciences*, 9.

Wiemann, J. M. and Bradac, J. J. (in press b) *Communicative Competence: a theoretical analysis*. London: Edward Arnold.

Wiemann, J. M. and Kelly, C. W. (1981) Pragmatics of interpersonal competence. In C. Wilder-Mott and J. H. Weakland (eds), *Rigour and Imagination: essays from the legacy of Gregory Bateson*, New York: Praeger.

Wiemann, J. M. and Knapp, M. L. (1975) Turn-taking in conversations. *Journal of Communication*, 25, 75–92.

Wiemann, J. M., Mulac, A., Ziemmerman, D. H. and Mann, S. K. (1987) Interruption pattern in same-gender and mixed-gender dyadic conversation. Presented at the 3rd international conference on social psychology and language, Bristol, July.

Wiener, M., Devoe, S., Rubinow, S. and Geller, J. (1972) Nonverbal behaviour and nonverbal communication. *Psychological Review*, 79, 185– 214.

Wilder, D. A. (1977) Perceptions of groups, size of opposition, and influence. *Journal of Experimental Social Psychology*, 13, 253–68.

Wilder, D. A. (1984) Intergroup contact: the typical member and the exception to the rule. *Journal of Experimental Social Psychology*, 20, 177–94.

Wilder, D. A. and Allen, V. L. (1978) Group membership and preference for information about other persons. *Personality and Social Psychology Bulletin*, 4, 106–10.

Wilke, H. A. M. and Lanzetta, J. T. (1970) The obligation to help: the effects of amount of prior help on subsequent helping behavior. *Journal of Experimental Social Psychology*, 6, 488–93.

Wilke, H. A. M., Messick, D. M. and Rutte, C. G. (eds) (1986) *Experimental Social Dilemmas*. Frankfurt: Peter Lang.

Wilke, H. A. M., Rutte, C. G., Wit, A. P., Messick, D. M. and Samuelson, C. D. (1986) Leadership in social dilemmas: efficiency and equity. In H. Wilke, D. Messick and C. Rutte (eds), *Experimental Social Dilemmas*. Frankfurt: Peter Lang.

Wilkinson, S. (ed.) (1986) *Feminist Social Psychology: developing theory and practice*. Milton Keynes: Open University Press.

Williams, J. A. and Watson, G. (in press) Sexual inequality, family life and family therapy. In E. Street and W. Dryden (eds), *Family Therapy in Britain*, London: Harper & Row.

Williams, J. E. and Best, D. L. (1982) *Measuring Sex Stereotypes*. Beverly Hills: Sage.

Wills, T. A. (1982) Nonspecific factors in helping relationships. In T. A. Wills (ed.), *Basic Processes in Helping Relationships*, New York: Academic Press.

Wilson, D. W. and Schafer, R. B. (1978) Is social psychology interdisciplinary? *Personality and Social Psychology Bulletin*, 4, 548–52.

Wilson, E. O. (1975) *Sociobiology: the new synthesis*. Cambridge, Mass.: Harvard University Press.

Wilson, J. Q. and Herrnstein, R. J. (1985) *Crime and Human Nature*. New York: Simon & Schuster.

Wilson, W. and Kayatani, M. (1968) Intergroup attitudes and strategies in games between opponents of the same or of a different race. *Journal of Personality and Social Psychology*, 9, 24–30.

Wilson, W. R. (1979) Feeling more than we can know: exposure effects without learning. *Journal of Personality and Social Psychology*, 37, 811–21.

Winterhoff-Spurk, P., Hermann, T. and Weinrich, D. (1985) Requesting rewards: a study of distributive justice. *Journal of Language and Social Psychology*, 5, 13–32.

Wish, M., Deutsch, M. and Kaplan, S. J. (1976) Perceived dimensions of interpersonal relations. *Journal of Personality and Social Psychology*, 33, 409–20.

Woodward, W. R. (1980) Toward a critical history of psychology. In J. Brozek and L. Pongratz (eds), *Historiography of Modern Psychology*, Toronto: Hogrefe.

Worchel, S., Andreoli, V. A. and Folger, R. (1977) Intergroup cooperation and intergroup attraction: the effect of previous interaction and outcome of combined effort. *Journal of Experimental Social Psychology*, 13, 131–40.

Word, C. O., Zanna, M. P. and Cooper, J. (1974) The nonverbal mediation of self-fulfilling prophecies in interracial interaction. *Journal of Experimental Social Psychology*, 10, 109–20.

Worell, J. (1981) Life-span sex roles: development, continuity and change. In R. M. Lerner and Busch-Rossnagel, N. A. (eds), *Individuals as Producers of Their Development*, New York: Academic Press.

Wundt, W. (1900–20) *Völkerpsychologie* (10 vols). Leipzig: Engelmann.

Wundt, W. (1921) *Völkerpsychologie: Eine Untersuchung der Entwicklungsgesetze von Sprache, Mythus und Sitte. Vol. 1: Die Sprache.* 4th edn. Stuttgart: Kröner.

Wyer, R. S. (1974) *Cognitive organization and change: an information processing approach.* Potomac, Md: Erlbaum.

Wyer, R. S. and Srull, T. (eds) (1984) *Handbook of Social Cognition* (3 vols). Hillsdale, NJ: Erlbaum.

Yaffe, Y. and Yinon, Y. (1979) Retaliatory aggression in individuals and groups. *European Journal of Social Psychology*, 9, 177–86.

Yang, K.-S. and Bond, M. H. (1980) Ethnic affirmation in Chinese bilinguals. *Journal of Cross-Cultural Psychology*, 11, 411–25.

Young, L., Giles, H. and Pierson, H. (1986) Sociopolitical change and vitality. *International Journal of Intercultural Relations*, 10, 459–69.

Young, M., Benjamin, B. and Wallis, C. (1963) Mortality of widowers. *Lancet*, 2, 454–6.

Youniss, J. (1980a) *My Friends, My Parents and Me: a Sullivan-Piaget perspective.* Chicago: Chicago University Press.

Youniss, J. (1980b) *Parents and Peers in Social Development.* Chicago: University of Chicago Press.

Youniss, J. (1986) Development in reciprocity through friendship. In C. Zahn-Waxler, E. M. Cummings and R. Iannotti (eds), *Altruism and Aggression: biological and social origins*, London: Cambridge University Press.

Yuille, J. C. and Cutshall, J. L. (1986) A case study of eyewitness memory of a crime. *Journal of Applied Psychology*, 71, 291–301.

Zajonc, R. B. (1965) Social facilitation. *Science*, 149, 269–74.

Zajonc, R. B. (1968a) Attitudinal effects of mere exposure. *Journal of Personality and Social Psychology, Monograph Supplement*, 9 (2, part 2), 1–27.

Zajonc, R. B. (1968b) Cognitive theories in social psychology. In G. Lindzey and E. Aronson (eds), *Handbook of Social Psychology* (vol. 1), 2nd edn, Reading, Mass.: Addison-Wesley.

Zajonc, R. B. (1980a) Feeling and thinking: preferences need no inferences. *American Psychologist*, 35, 151–75.

Zajonc, R. B. (1980b) Compresence. In P. B. Paulus (ed.), *Psychology of Group Influence*, Hillsdale, NJ: Erlbaum.

Zajonc, R. B. and Nieuwenhuysen, B. (1964) Relationship between word frequency and recognition: perceptual process or response bias? *Journal of Experimental Psychology*, 2, 160–8.

Zander, A. (1971) *Motives and Goals in Groups.* New York: Academic Press.

Zani, B. (1987) The psychiatric nurse: a social psychological study of a profession facing institutional changes. *Social Behaviour*, 2, 87–98.

Zanna, M. P. and Cooper, J. (1974) Dissonance and the pill: an attribution approach to studying the arousal properties of dissonance. *Journal of Personality and Social Psychology*, 29, 703–9.

Zanna, M. P. and Fazio, R. H. (1982) The attitude–behavior relation: moving toward a third generation of research. In M. P. Zanna, E. T. Higgins and C. P. Herman (eds),

Consistency in Social Behavior: the Ontario symposium (vol. 2), Hillsdale, NJ: Erlbaum.

Zanna, M. P., Kiesler, C. A. and Pilkonis, P. A. (1970) Positive and negative attitudinal affect established by classical conditioning. *Journal of Personality and Social Psychology*, 14, 321-8.

Zanna, M. P., Olson, J. M. and Fazio, R. H. (1980) Attitude–behavior consistency: an individual difference perspective. *Journal of Personality and Social Psychology*, 38, 432-40.

Zavalloni, M. (1971) Cognitive processes and social identity through focused introspection. *European Journal of Social Psychology*, 1, 235-60.

Zillmann, D. (1971) Excitation transfer in communication-mediated aggressive behavior. *Journal of Experimental Social Psychology*, 7, 419-34.

Zillmann, D. (1979) *Hostility and Aggression*. Hillsdale, NJ: Erlbaum.

Zillmann, D. and Cantor, J. R. (1976) Effect of timing of information about mitigating circumstances on emotional responses to provocation and retaliatory behavior. *Journal of Experimental and Social Psychology*, 12, 38-55.

Zillmann, D., Johnson, R. C. and Day, K. D. (1974) Attribution of apparent arousal and proficiency of recovery from sympathetic activation affecting excitation transfer to aggressive behavior. *Journal of Experimental Social Psychology*, 10, 503-15.

Zillmann, D., Katcher, A. H. and Milavsky, B. (1972) Excitation transfer from physical exercise to subsequent aggressive behavior. *Journal of Experimental Social Psychology*, 8, 247-59.

Zimbardo, P. (1969) The human choice: individuation, reason, and order versus deindividuation, impulse, and chaos. In W. J. Arnold and D. Levine (eds), *Nebraska Symposium on Motivation* (vol. 17), Lincoln, Nebr.: University of Nebraska Press.

Zimmerman, D. H. and West, C. (1975) Sex roles, interruptions, and silences in conversation. In B. Thorne and N. Henley (eds), *Language and Sex: differences and dominance*, Rowley, Mass.: Newbury House.

Zuckerman, M. (1979) Attribution of success and failure revisited, or: the motivational bias is alive and well in attribution theory. *Journal of Personality*, 47, 245-87.

Zumkley, H. (1981) Der Einfluss unterschiedlicher Absichtsattributionen auf das Aggressionsverhalten und die Aktivierung. *Psychologische Beiträge*, 23, 115-28.

Contributors

Charles Antaki
University of Lancaster

Michael Argyle
University of Oxford

Hans W. Bierhoff
Universität Marburg

Rupert Brown
University of Kent

Jean-Paul Codol
Université de Provence

Kevin Durkin
University of Kent

Dieter Frey
Universität Kiel

Howard Giles
University of Bristol

Carl F. Graumann
Universität Heidelberg

Janusz Grzelak
University of Warsaw

Miles Hewstone
Universität Mannheim

Robert A. Hinde
University of Cambridge

Renate Klein
Universität Marburg

Klaus Jonas
Universität Tübingen

Jacques-Philippe Leyens
Université Catholique de Louvain

A. S. R. Manstead
University of Manchester

Amélie Mummendey
Universität Münster

G. R. Semin
University of Sussex

Dagmar Stahlberg
Universität Kiel

Geoffrey M. Stephenson
University of Kent

Wolfgang Stroebe
Universiteit te Utrecht

John M. Wiemann
University of California, Santa Barbara

Eddy van Avermaet
Katholieke Universiteit Leuven

Ad van Knippenberg
Rijksuniversiteit te Groningen

Henk Wilke
Rijksuniversiteit te Groningen

Author Index

Aardema, B. S. 371, 506
Abele, A. 138, 458
Abeles, R. P. 276, 407, 458, 515
Abelson, R. P. 63, 64, 102, 123, 458, 496, 515
Abrahamson, L. Y. 138, 458
Abric, J. C. 99, 302, 458
Acock, A. C. 230, 503
Adorno, T. W. 385, 386, 458
Agassi, J. 4, 458
Ajzen, I. 108, 113, 125, 127, 143, 144, 145, 158, 159, 160, 162, 163, 165, 170, 174, 182, 184, 418, 458, 479, 495
Alberts, J. C. 210, 211, 459
Alexander, R. D. 31, 38, 224, 459
Allee, W. C. 318, 482
Allen, A. 164, 463
Allen, V. L. 107, 355, 356, 357, 380, 459, 527
Alloy, L. B. 117, 118, 459
Allport, F. H. 10, 13, 459
Allport, G. W. 18, 142, 392, 459
Altmaier, E. 428, 514
Altman, I. 210, 214, 215, 276, 459
Altman, S. 422, 459
Alvarez, M. D. 486
Amabile, T. M. 126, 513
Amir, Y. 392, 459
Anderson, A. 129, 477
Anderson, C. 133, 459
Anderson, K. 138, 139, 520
Anderson, N. H. 94, 101, 102, 104, 169, 459, 460
Andreoli, V. A. 393, 527
Andrews, F. M. 281, 465

Andreyeva, G. M. 25, 460
Aneshansel, J. 157, 492
Antaki, C. 121, 124, 140, 220, 460
Apfelbaum, E. 303, 460
Archer, R. L. 214, 503
Arcuri, L. 93, 107, 398, 460
Argyle, M. 151, 201, 202, 203, 204, 205, 210, 211, 212, 226, 228, 229, 231, 232, 233, 234, 235, 236, 243, 244, 460
Aristotle 460
Arkin, R. M. 208, 525
Aronson, E. 63, 66, 72, 80, 83, 187, 460, 469, 506
Asch, S. E. 89, 90, 100, 352, 353, 354, 355, 356, 357, 361, 368, 372, 380, 388, 461
Aschenbrenner, K. M. 395, 396, 461
Ash, M. G. 15, 461
Ashmore, R. D. 399, 461
Aspeel, S. 102, 497
Atkin, R. S. 434, 472
Austin, G. A. 399, 410, 467
Averill, J. R. 173, 283, 287, 461

Babri, K. B. 199, 494
Back, K. W. 229, 478
Bagozzi, R. P. 145, 160, 461
Bailey, S. 138, 139, 520
Baker-Miller, J. B. 420, 461
Baldwin, J. 433, 461
Bales, R. F. 76, 77, 334, 335, 336, 337, 461
Ball, P. 206, 461
Bandura, A. 173, 174, 183, 256, 272, 273, 287, 461, 462
Barden, L. D. 35, 488
Bar-Hillel, M. 105, 462

Baron, P..H. 179, 180, 462
Baron, R. A. 179, 180, 272, 273, 276, 277, 280, 285, 287, 462, 498
Baron, R. S. 320, 322, 323, 370, 514
Barraclough, R. 204, 526
Barrows, S. 10, 11, 462
Bar-Tal, D. 52, 262, 462
Barth, J. M. 295, 494
Bartlett, F. 118, 399, 462
Bartolucci, G. 209, 514
Bass, B. M. 344, 462
Bates, E. 43, 200, 462, 468
Bateson, N. 251, 515
Bateson, P. 38
Batson, C. D. 247, 249, 472
Baucom, D. H. 129, 479
Baumeister, R. F. 208, 462
Baumrind, D. 22, 462
Baxter, L. A. 211, 213, 215, 230, 462
Beach, S. R. 129, 479
Beaudichon, J. 43, 462
Beauvois, J. L. 90, 93, 462
Beavin, J. 200, 203, 217, 221, 525
Bell, P. A. 276, 277, 462
Bell, R. Q. 25, 462
Bem, D. J. 25, 164, 187, 188, 462, 463
Bem, S. L. 56, 57, 463
Benelli, B. 43, 463
Benjamin, B. 528
Bennett, W. L. 432, 463
Bentler, P. M. 163, 463
Berg, J. H. 214, 503
Berger, C. R. 204, 214, 220, 463
Berger, J. 463
Berkman, L. S. 463
Berkowitz, L. 171, 172, 251, 253, 269, 270, 271, 273, 279, 280, 463, 464, 508
Berlyne, D. E. 169, 464
Bernzweig, J. 441, 522
Berscheid, E. 23, 124, 226, 227, 228, 229, 230, 244, 245, 464, 474, 493
Berti, A. E. 53, 54, 464
Best, D. L. 35, 527
Betzig, L. L. 33, 523
Bhavnani, K. K. 301, 476
Bickmann, L. 62, 464
Bierbrauer, G. 378, 464
Bierhoff, H. W. 246, 247, 249, 250, 252, 257, 259, 261, 262, 464
Billig, M. G. 65, 93, 386, 394, 395, 396, 409, 464, 481, 520
Bilsky, W. 255, 465
Binet, A. 13, 465

Biron, L. 437, 478
Bixensteine, V. E. 296, 465
Blakar, R. M. 200, 204, 209, 220, 465
Blake, R. R. 252, 256, 257, 258, 392, 465, 512
Blank, A. 103, 257, 496
Blazer, D. G. 199, 465
Blumenthal, M. 281, 465
Blumer, H. 10, 465
Blyth, D. P. 127, 458
Bombi, A. S. 53, 54, 464
Bond, M. 216, 234, 460, 528
Bonoma, T. V. 189, 256, 487, 522
Borden, R. J. 400, 434, 469
Bordens, K. S. 465
Borgida, E. 105, 130, 465
Bornstein, G. 395, 465
Bortner, R. W. 422, 501
Bourhis, R. Y. 217, 402, 465
Bovet, M. 52, 465
Bower, G. H. 108, 465
Bowlby, J. 25, 27, 28, 227, 465
Box, S. 431, 465
Boyd, R. 34, 465
Brackwede, D. 152, 466
Bradac, J. J. 206, 214, 215, 218, 219, 220, 466, 526
Bradbury, T. N. 120, 466
Bradley, C. W. 131, 466
Bradley, J. 56, 486
Bragg, B. W. E. 356, 459
Braly, K. W. 96, 493
Brandstaetter, J. 82, 466
Branthwaite, A. 395, 466
Bray, R. M. 442, 444, 466
Breckler, S. J. 145, 466
Brekke, N. 105, 130, 465
Brewer, M. B. 63, 66, 80, 83, 133, 310, 312, 392, 395, 396, 460, 466, 495, 503, 511
Brewer, R. M. 139, 502
Brewin, C. R. 138, 140, 466
Bricker, W. 272, 508
Brickman, P. 120, 260, 428, 466
Bringle, R. G. 234, 466
Brislin, R. W. 171, 466
Brock, T. C. 179, 180, 507, 509
Broeze, M. 285, 510
Bromley, D. B. 53, 499
Brossard, A. 25, 508
Brouwer, D. 205, 466
Brown, F. J. 395, 396, 467
Brown, G. W. 241, 421, 466, 507

Brown, M. 272, 525
Brown, P. 208, 466
Brown, P. L. 260, 473
Brown, R. 44, 126, 205, 386, 466, 467
Brown, R. C. 283, 467
Brown, R. J. 94, 207, 387, 388, 392, 393, 397, 398, 399, 401, 402, 403, 404, 405, 407, 410, 467, 473, 476, 487, 507, 517, 521, 523
Bruner, J. S. 42, 43, 90, 94, 100, 153, 399, 467, 518
Buchanan, R. W. 276, 481
Buckingham, N. 52, 498
Bundy, R. P. 394, 395, 396, 520
Burgess, R. L. 225, 468
Burgoon, J. K. 210, 468
Burgoon, M. 220, 468
Burke, P. J. 335, 468
Burnkraut, R. E. 145, 160, 461
Burnstein, E. 370, 468
Burt, C. 435, 468
Buss, A. H. 27, 468
Buss, A. R. 14, 122, 468
Butler, D. 227, 507
Butterfield, H. 4, 468
Buunk, B. 217, 234, 466, 514
Byrne, D. 223, 387, 388, 468
Byrne, D. G. 421, 487

Cacioppo, J. T. 143, 149, 150, 151, 177, 178, 181, 182, 184, 195, 468, 509
Caddick, B. 407, 468
Cahn, D. 210, 471
Calabrese, R. 214, 463
Calder, B. J. 151, 188, 468
Callan, V. 206, 461
Camaioni, L. 42, 43, 468
Camden, C. T. 205, 215, 216, 468, 494
Camino, I. 281, 468
Campbell, D. T. 70, 71, 76, 151, 352, 389, 468, 471, 490, 494, 525
Campbell, J. D. 55, 521
Campbell, N. A. 163, 492
Campos, F. T. 298, 501
Cantor, J. R. 284, 529
Cantor, N. 92, 108, 468, 503
Cantril, H. 407, 468
Caporael, L. R. 209, 468
Capozza, D. 107, 469
Cappella, J. N. 201, 519
Caputo, C. 119, 127, 506
Carey, M. 75, 469

Carlsmith, J. M. 63, 66, 80, 83, 185, 186, 187, 188, 190, 195, 460, 469, 478
Carraher, D. W. 25, 469
Carraher, T. N. 25, 469
Carroll, J. S. 123, 431, 442, 469, 525
Carter, L. F. A. 338, 471
Cartwright, D. 13, 15, 16, 346, 349, 469
Carugati, F. 51, 57, 473, 508
Carver, C. S. 164, 469
Cerreto, M. 225, 226, 505
Chadwick-Jones, J. K. 224, 469
Chagnon, N. A. 38
Chaiken, A. L. 114, 469
Chaiken, S. 133, 142, 145, 165, 174, 176, 177, 181, 184, 195, 469, 476
Chammah, A. M. 294, 295, 306, 511
Chandler, M. J. 20, 47, 469
Chanowitz, B. 103, 257, 496
Chapman, A. J. 480
Chapman, J. P. 90, 469
Chapman, L. J. 90, 469
Chapman, M. 49, 469
Charms, R. 114
Check, V. P. 218, 469
Chemers, M. M. 342, 469
Chen, J. 162, 478
Christensen, A. 23, 226, 229, 230, 245, 493
Christie, R. 386, 469
Christy, P. 228, 505
Cialdini, R. B. 400, 469
Clark, K. B. 405, 470
Clark, M. P. 405, 470
Clark, M. S. 108, 225, 470
Clark, N. K. 432, 485
Clark, R. D. 262, 360, 362, 363, 364, 367, 380, 500
Clarke, A. D. B. 36, 470
Clarke, A. M. 36, 470
Clore, G. L. 224, 470
Coates, D. 260, 428, 466
Coch, L. 345, 470
Cochran, S. 280, 463
Cochrane, R. 443
Codol, J. P. 95, 99, 304, 305, 370, 470, 485
Cohen, R. L. 239, 493
Cohen, S. 240, 241, 470
Cohn, E. 260, 428, 466
Colamosca, J. V. 259, 479
Coleman, L. M. 209, 473
Colman, A. E. 294, 311, 470
Colley, A. 56, 470
Collins, B. E. 190, 332, 470, 489

Commins, B. 397, 470
Comstock, G. 273, 470
Comte, A. 7, 470
Condor, S. 392, 403, 404, 467
Connolley, E. S. 356, 482
Connor, W. H. 253, 463
Contarello, A. 234, 460
Contrada, R. 423, 483
Conway, A. 206, 483
Cook, S. W. 151, 392, 471, 516
Cook, T. D. 70, 71, 471
Coombs, F. S. 145, 158, 479
Cooper, J. 114, 186, 187, 188, 189, 190, 193, 195, 217, 469, 471, 478, 498, 527, 528
Corey, S. M. 158, 471
Corty, E. 126, 517
Costa, P. T., Jr 515
Cottrell, N. B. 319, 320, 321, 323, 471
Couch, A. S. 338, 471
Coupland, J. 207, 209, 214, 471, 483
Coupland, N. 207, 209, 210, 214, 471, 483
Cowles, M. 74, 471
Coyne, J. C. 138, 471
Crocker, J. 129, 171, 471, 521
Crook, C. K. 43, 515
Crosby, F. 407, 471
Cross, L. 482
Croyle, R. T. 188, 471
Crum, L. 395, 465
Crumbaugh, C. M. 295, 477
Crutchfield, R. A. 354, 356, 471
Cuhre, C. J. M. 304, 498
Culbertson, G. H. 209, 468
Cunningham, J. D. 116, 117, 471, 507
Cushman, D. 210, 471
Cutshall, J. L. 438, 528
Czwartosz, Z. 306, 471

Dalbert, C. 255, 504
Dalton, C. A. 127, 458
Daly, M. 32, 471
Damon, W. 471
Dance, T. E. X. 200, 203, 472
Dane, F. C. 433, 441, 472
Daniels, L. R. 251, 253, 465
Danziger, K. 8, 472
Darley, J. M. 133, 246, 247, 249, 250, 251, 257, 258, 472, 496
Darwin, C. 472
Davidson, A. R. 145, 159, 472, 490
Davies, J. C. 407, 472
Davis, C. 74, 471

Davis, D. 370, 491
Davis, H. P. 387, 475
Davis, J. H. 419, 434, 472, 519
Davis, K. E. 113, 114, 118, 123, 130, 472, 492
Dawes, R. M. 145, 165, 233, 294, 304, 339, 472, 489
Day, K. D. 278, 279, 529
Dean, J. 201, 202, 203, 204, 210, 211, 212, 460
Deaux, K. 56, 472
De Beni, R. 54, 464
De Brey, J. H. C. 393, 510
De Charms, R. 492
Deci, E. L. 191, 192, 472
Deconchy, J. P. 97, 472
DeHaan, D. 205, 466
De Jong-Gierveld, J. 241, 472
De Kock, M. 421, 500
Dembroski, T. M. 423, 473
De Montmollin, G. 350, 473
De Paolis, P. 51, 473
DePaulo, B. M. 208, 209, 259, 260, 473, 479
Dermer, M. 124, 464
Deschamps, J. C. 393, 397, 398, 409, 467, 473, 474
Deshusses-Addor, D. 52, 465
Deutsch, M. 235, 236, 290, 296, 304, 308, 354, 355, 443, 473, 527
DeVinney, L. C. 420, 519
Devoe, S. 200, 527
Dewey, J. 473
Diab, L. N. 392, 473
Diamond, S. 441, 473
Dickson, J. 76, 344, 512
Didillon, H. 45, 504
Diener, E. 285, 384, 473
Di Giacomo, J. P. 98, 473
Dillehay, R. C. 473
Dillon, W. R. 145, 473
Dindia, K. 205, 474
Dion, K. 228, 392, 464, 474
DiTecco, D. 145, 161, 162, 515
Dittes, J. E. 355, 474
Dittrichs, R. 285, 474
Di Vesta, F. J. 355, 474
Dodd, D. J. 431, 519
Doelger, J. 215, 487
Dohrenwend, B. P. 421, 474
Dohrenwend, B. S. 421, 474
Doise, W. 25, 36, 49, 50, 51, 98, 306, 397,

398, 409, 473, 474, 505, 511
Dollard, I. 268, 503
Dollard, J. 268, 474
Doms, M. 353, 363, 365, 366, 474
Donaldson, M. 25, 51, 474, 502
Donnerstein, E. 275, 276, 285, 287, 474
Donnerstein, M. 285, 474
Doob, L. W. 268, 474, 503
Douvan, E. 240, 524
Dovidio, J. F. 262
Downing, L. L. 384, 491
Doyle, S. 395, 466
Drenan, S. 358, 359, 490
Driver, M. 256, 522
Dryden, C. 219, 475
Dube-Simard, L. 407, 485
Duck, S. 245, 496
Duck, S. W. 210, 213, 219, 222, 223, 229, 475
Dunand, M. A. 273, 498
Duncan, B. L. 111, 112, 114, 115, 117, 121, 475
Duncan, S. 205, 475
Duncan-Jones, S. 421, 487
Dunkel-Shetter, C. 199, 475
Dunn, J. 43, 45, 475
Durkheim, E. 7, 12, 98, 475
Durkin, K. 41, 43, 44, 56, 57, 475, 514
Dustin, D. S. 387, 475
Duval, S. 129, 164, 475
Dweck, C. S. 137, 139, 475
Dyck, R. J. 284, 513
Dyson-Hudson, R. 32, 475

Eagly, A. H. 174, 176, 177, 178, 179, 195, 476
Ebbeson, E. B. 419, 441, 442, 444, 495
Ebbinghaus, H. 5, 476
Eckhardt, G. 9, 476
Edwards, J. N. 230, 503
Edwards, J. R. 207, 476
Edwards, K. 392, 503
Egeth, H. E. 438, 476
Ehrhardt, A. A. 36, 503
Ehrlich, I. 431, 476
Eibl-Eibesfeldt, I. 20, 28, 45, 476
Einhorn, H. J. 116, 123, 476
Eisenberg, J. G. 273, 501
Eiser, J. R. 94, 102, 114, 147, 156, 209, 301, 303, 397, 409, 429, 443, 476
Ekman, P. 20, 28, 215, 476
Ellard, J. H. 199, 497

Ellis, D. G. 214, 494
Ellsworth, P. C. 66, 110, 440, 469, 518
Elwell, C. M. 207, 476
Embree, M. 280, 463
Emler, N. 49, 51, 52, 436, 437, 443, 477, 511, 524
Emmerich, W. 56, 477
Endler, N. S. 25, 355, 477
Engels, F. 6, 501
Epstein, S. 272, 477
Erba, M. 51, 473
Eron, L. D. 273, 477, 489, 497
Essock-Vitale, S. M. 477
Etcoff, N. 132, 521
Evans, G. 295, 477
Evans-Pritchard, E. E. 133, 477
Eysenck, H. J. 386, 477

Fair, P. L. 151, 515
Farina, A. 209, 492
Farr, R. M. 7, 8, 12, 99, 109, 129, 220, 477
Farrar, K. 206, 483
Farrington, D. P. 437, 438, 478
Fazio, R. H. 156, 159, 161, 162, 164, 165, 189, 190, 193, 195, 471, 478, 511, 528, 529
Feather, N. T. 421, 478
Feinman, S. 28, 478
Felce, D. 421, 500
Feldman, M. S. 432, 463
Fellner, C. H. 224, 478
Felson, R. B. 287, 478
Ferguson, C. A. 43, 518
Ferguson, C. K. 393, 478
Ferguson, T. J. 281, 282, 478, 513
Festinger, L. 14, 18, 75, 91, 95, 100, 154, 179, 181, 185, 186, 187, 188, 190, 195, 229, 370, 387, 400, 409, 423, 478
Fhaner, G. 168, 193, 478
Fiedler, F. E. 341, 342, 343, 478, 479
Fiedler, K. 118, 479
Fielding, G. 121, 460
Fincham, F. D. 52, 120, 121, 123, 129, 137, 139, 414, 466, 479, 491
Fink, C. F. 317, 331, 522
Firestone, I. L. 259, 479
Fischer, C. S. 276, 515
Fischer, D. G. 270, 479
Fisek, M. H. 463
Fish, D. 126, 467
Fishbein, M. 143, 144, 145, 158, 159, 160, 162, 163, 165, 170, 174, 182, 184, 418, 458, 479

Fisher, J. D. 259, 260, 473, 479, 480
Fisher, S. 205, 480
Fishman, J. A. 208, 480
Fiske, D. W. 205, 475
Fiske, S. T. 93, 94, 104, 108, 109, 118, 125, 129, 132, 133, 140, 157, 171, 205, 470, 471, 480, 521
Fitzgerald, N. M. 230, 489
Fitzmaurice, C. 435, 480
Fitzpatrick, M. A. 199, 217, 218, 220, 236, 480, 483, 506
Flament, C. 94, 95, 394, 395, 396, 480, 520
Flavell, J. 47, 480
Fletcher, G. J. O. 131, 141, 157, 158, 513
Foa, E. B. 204, 224, 300, 480
Foa, U. G. 204, 224, 300, 480
Fogelson, R. M. 384, 480
Folger, R. 393, 527
Folkman, S. 78, 480
Foot, H. C. 480
Forgas, J. P. 209, 210, 460, 480
Forsyth, D. R. 134, 325, 332, 349, 480
Fortin, A. 51, 480
Fowler, R. 204, 480
Fox, J. 297, 480, 485
Fraczek, A. 270, 281, 480, 498
Frager, R. 151, 501
Franco, J. N. 214, 499
Fraser, C. 17, 65, 208, 481, 521
Freedman, J. L. 181, 274, 276, 481
Freeman, S. 400, 469
French, J. R. R., Jr 345, 470
Frenkel-Brunswick, E. 385, 368, 458
Freud, S. 11, 40, 274, 481
Frey, B. S. 290, 297, 312, 327, 519
Frey, D. 154, 155, 165, 181, 426, 427, 481
Friedman, E. 215, 466
Friedman, M. 422, 481
Friedrich-Cofer, L. 274, 481
Friesen, W. V. 20, 28, 476
Frincke, G. 169, 491
Fritz, A. S. 337, 518
Fujji, D. S. 338, 490
Fullard, W. 35, 481
Funder, D. C. 25, 90, 463, 481
Furnham, A. 199, 228, 232, 233, 460, 481
Furth, H. G. 53, 54, 481
Fusilier, M. R. 421, 481

Gabler, H. 267, 481
Gaes, G. G. 190, 191, 481
Gallagher, B. 437, 438, 478

Gallant, J. L. 441, 522
Gallois, C. 206, 461
Ganster, D. C. 421, 481
Garber, R. M. 441, 482
Gardner, B. T. 35, 482
Garfinkel, H. 343, 482
Gate, R. M. 230, 489
Gates, M. F. 318, 482
Gatewood, R. 256, 522
Geen, R. G. 272, 275, 482, 519
Geller, J. 200, 527
Gerard, H. B. 72, 250, 251, 354, 355, 356, 395, 473, 482, 492
Gerbner, G. 274, 482
Gergen, K. J. 9, 80, 81, 82, 114, 130, 226, 250, 423, 424, 425, 482, 492, 520
Gergen, M. M. 226, 250, 423, 424, 425, 482, 520
Gerritsen, M. 205, 466
Gersten, J. C. 273, 501
Gibbons, F. X. 164, 482
Gibson, T. 216, 505
Giddens, A. 82, 482
Gilbert, S. J. 214, 482
Giles, H. 206, 207, 208, 209, 210, 214, 215, 216, 217, 218, 219, 220, 402, 404, 410, 465, 466, 471, 475, 476, 482, 483, 487, 499, 514, 519, 522, 528
Giller, H. 437, 514
Gillis, J. S. 296, 520
Gilly, M. 51, 483
Gilman, A. 205, 467
Gilmour, R. 210, 222, 245, 475
Ginther, A. J. F. 51, 511
Glachan, M. 49, 51, 498, 524
Glass, D. C. 320, 422, 423, 483, 487, 501
Glasser, W. 429, 483
Glendon, A. J. 65, 66, 516
Goddard, D. 45, 504
Goethals, G. R. 133, 472
Goffman, E. 25, 75, 483
Goldfoot, D.A. 36, 483
Goldman, K. S. 56, 477,
Goldman, R. 181, 182, 509
Goldsmith, D. 270, 523
Goldstein, M. 135, 526
Goodman, C. D. 94, 467
Goodnow, J. J. 399, 467
Gordon, K. H. 329, 483
Gotlib, I. H. 138, 471
Gottlieb, A. 258, 516
Gouge, C. 65, 481

Gould, S. J. 35, 484
Gouldner, A. W. 214, 252, 256, 283, 484
Gove, W. R. 241, 484
Gozman, L. J. 25, 460
Graham, J. A. 228, 460
Graham, M. L. 215, 487
Grant, G. 405, 489
Grant, J. 43, 431, 484, 486
Grant, J. D. 431, 484
Graumann, C. F. 3, 4, 12, 13, 15, 484
Graves, J. 490
Gray, J. L. 35, 519
Graziano, W. 124, 464
Green, J. 126, 491
Green, R. G. 287
Greenberg, J. 123, 510
Greenberg, M. S. 256, 431, 484
Greene, D. 130, 191, 192, 195, 497, 513
Greenstein, T. N. 336, 484
Greenwald, A. G. 81, 249, 484
Gremillet, H. 45, 504
Grice, H. P. 210, 484
Griesinger, D. W. 298, 484
Grieve, R. 51, 489
Groebel, J. 274, 495
Gross, L. 274
Grove, J. B. 76, 525
Grush, J. E. 169, 484
Grusec, J. E. 257, 511
Grzelak, J. L. 294, 296, 304, 485, 524
Gudjonsson, G. 432, 485
Gudykunst, W. B. 216, 485
Guedira, A. 45, 504
Guiliano, T. 424, 525
Guimond, S. 407, 485
Gurr, T. R. 407, 485
Guyer, M. 294, 297, 480, 485

Haaland, G. A. 179, 485
Haberkorn, G. 363
Habermas, J. 210, 485
Hager, J. L. 26, 516
Haines, H. 13, 485
Haisch, J. 429, 525
Haley, R. W. 416, 418, 511
Hall, C. S. 4, 485
Hall, J. A. 228, 485
Halpin, A. W. 337, 338, 485
Hamburger, H. 296, 311, 485
Hamilton, D. L. 90, 97, 399, 410, 485
Hane, M. 168, 193, 478
Hans, V. P. 433, 485

Hardin, G. 294, 485
Hardoin, M. 485
Harford, T. 296, 486
Hargreaves, D. H. 437, 486
Hargreaves, D. J. 52, 486
Harkins, J. M. 329, 490
Harkins, S. 328, 329, 496
Harper, L. V. 25, 462
Harriman, J. 207, 483
Harring, K. 395, 465
Harris, M. 43, 486
Harris, T. 241, 421, 466
Harris, V. A. 125, 492
Harrison, A. A. 169, 220, 486
Hart, H. L. A. 120, 123, 486
Harter, S. 151, 503
Hartley, E. L. 96, 486
Hartnett, D. 56, 486
Hartup, W. W. 488
Harvey, D. J. 5, 486
Harvey, J. H. 23, 127, 130, 140, 226, 227, 229, 230, 245, 486, 493, 526
Harvey, O. J. 390, 517
Hastie, R. 95, 123, 124, 486
Hastorf, A. H 110, 209, 492
Hatfield, E. 226, 486
Havemann, D. 426, 481
Hawkins, R. P. 220, 486
Head, K. B. 281, 465
Hearnshaw, L. S. 8, 486
Heider, F. 90, 95, 96, 100, 112, 113, 118, 119, 126, 132, 141, 156, 486
Hellpach, W. 16, 486
Helm, B. 256, 487
Helmreich, R. 187, 506
Helson, H. 156, 487
Hemphill, J. K. 339, 487
Henchey, T. 62, 320, 464, 487
Henderson, M. 228, 231, 232, 233, 234, 235, 236, 243, 244, 460
Henderson, S. 421, 487
Henley, M. D. 190, 489
Henri, V. 13, 465
Henshel, R. L. 396, 487
Henwood, K. 207, 209, 471, 483, 514
Herdt, G. H. 26, 487
Herhold, C. J. 441, 473
Herman, G. 273, 498
Hermann, T. 220, 527
Herrnstein, R. J. 429, 527
Hertel, P. 424, 525
Hertling, E. 45, 504

Herzlich, C. 460
Hewes, D. 215, 487
Hewstone, M. 55, 57, 99, 116, 117, 123, 126, 130, 131, 141, 209, 217, 392, 410, 483, 487, 491, 504
Hiebsch, H. 6, 487
Higgins, E. T. 188, 201, 210, 487, 488, 495
Hilgendorf, L. 432, 490
Hill, C. T. 30, 231, 488, 508
Hill, R. 224
Hillix, W. A. 15, 501
Hinde, R. A. 8, 22, 23, 25, 26, 28, 29, 31, 35, 36, 37, 38, 45, 222, 224, 230, 267, 488
Hindelang, M. J. 436, 488
Hirschi, T. 436, 488
Hobfoll, S. 241, 488
Hochreich, D. J. 120, 493
Hodge, R. 204, 480
Hodgetts, R. M. 422, 459
Hoekstra, M. 344, 488
Hogan, R. 52, 477
Hogarth, J. 488
Hogarth, R. M. 116, 123, 441, 476
Hogg, M. 216, 488
Holmes, W. H. 113, 305, 458, 503
Holstein, J. A. 432, 488
Holt, R. 434, 472
Homans, G. 239, 488
Honore, A. M. 120, 123, 486
Hood, R. 442, 488
Hood, W. R. 390, 517
Hopper, R. 215, 511
Horenstein, D. 214, 482
Hormuth, S. E. 145, 488
Hornstein, H. A. 443
Horowitz, I. A. 434, 465, 488
Horowitz, M. 74
Horwitz, M. 286, 394, 489, 510
Hosking, D. M. 342, 489
Hosman, L. A. 214, 466
Hough, M. 431, 489
House, J. 243, 489
House, P. 130, 513
Hovland, C. I. 143, 144, 147, 156, 160, 176, 183, 200, 512, 517
Howard, J. A. 121, 254, 255, 489, 516
Howard, J. W. 233, 489
Howe, C. 42, 489
Hoyt, M. F. 190, 395, 482, 489
Hraba, J. 405, 489
Hubbard, M. 105, 513
Hubert, S. 101, 460

Hubley, P. 523
Huesman, L. R. 273, 477, 489, 497
Hughes, M. 51, 489
Huici, C. 57, 489
Hull, W. F. 171, 494
Hunt, J. McV. 25, 477
Hurtig, M. C. 56, 489
Huston, A. 56, 489
Huston, A. C. 481
Huston, T. L. 23, 225, 226, 229, 230, 231, 236, 245, 468, 489, 493
Hutt, C. 276, 489
Hymes, R. W. 158, 490

Ickes, W. J. 140
Iizuka, Y. 234, 460
Ilgen, D. R. 338, 490
Illich, I., 421, 490
Ingham, A. G. 490
Innes, J. M. 285, 500
Insko, C. A. 172, 188, 358, 359, 395, 465, 468, 490
Irle, M. 490
Irons, W. 33, 38, 490
Irving, B. 432, 490
Isen, A. M. 108, 110, 470
Isenberg, D. J. 371, 490
Ishii, S. 260, 473
Israel, J. 14, 17, 94, 490

Jaccard, J. J. 145, 159, 472, 490
Jackson, D. D. 200, 203, 217, 221, 525
Jackson, J. M. 490
Jacobs, R. C. 352, 490
Jacobson, N. S. 235, 490
Jaffe, Y. 248, 490
Jahoda, G. 53, 54, 55, 490, 521
Jahoda, M. 386, 469
James, W. 491
Janis, I. L. 60, 183, 200, 371, 372, 380, 491
Janoff, D. S. 139, 518
Jansen, W. T. L. 304, 498
Jaspars, J. 17, 18, 55, 57, 101, 116, 117, 123, 130, 131, 487, 491
Jaspars, J. M. 121, 414, 479
Jellison, J. M. 126, 370, 491
Jemmott, J. B. 243, 491
Jenkins, J. 421, 500
Jennings, H. H. 491
Jennings, S. M. 229, 491
Jermier, J. M. 340, 341, 494
Jodelet, D. 99, 491

Johnson, N. B. 55, 491, 517, 521
Johnson, P. 207, 216, 402, 483
Johnson, R. C. 169, 278, 279, 491, 529
Johnson, R. D. 384, 491
Johnson, T. E. 284, 491
Jonas, K. 170, 183, 491, 520
Jones, D. 43, 486
Jones, E. E. 15, 18, 113, 114, 115, 118, 123, 124, 125, 127, 130, 141, 152, 157, 186, 190, 209, 250, 251, 399, 491, 492, 498, 510
Jourard, S. M. 214, 230, 492
Judd, C. M. 157, 158, 492

Kahn, A. 392, 514
Kahn, R. L. 281, 349, 465
Kahneman, D. 104, 105, 130, 132, 322, 492, 524
Kalin, R. 207, 492
Kalle, R. J. 190, 191, 481
Kalton, G. 63, 515
Kalven, H., Jr 433, 492
Kamphuis, F. 241, 472
Kanki, G. 261, 506
Kanter, R. M. 420, 492
Kantola, S. G. 163, 492
Kaplan, S. J. 235, 236, 304, 527
Karpf, F. B. 8, 18, 492
Karuza, J., Jr 260, 428, 466
Kassin, S. M. 52, 105, 120, 130, 492
Katcher, A. H. 278, 529
Katz, D. 13, 96, 153, 349, 492
Kayatani, M. 387, 527
Kaye, K. 41, 492
Kayser, E. 239, 492
Keesing, R. M. 26, 492
Kelley, H. H. 23, 25, 101, 115, 116, 117, 118, 120, 123, 125, 130, 141, 183, 200, 224, 225, 226, 227, 229, 230, 245, 303, 304, 307, 311, 355, 362, 393, 471, 474, 478, 489, 492, 507, 522
Kelly, C. W. 203, 218, 362, 526
Kelm, H. 270, 479
Kelman, H. C. 174, 494
Kendon, A. 200, 492
Kendrick, C. 43, 45, 475
Kendzierski, D. 164, 257, 518
Kennedy, C. W. 205, 494
Kenrick, D. T. 25, 494
Kerr, N. L. 191, 433, 434, 442, 444, 466, 472, 494, 520
Kerr, S. 340, 341, 342, 494, 515

Kidd, K. K. 27, 514
Kidd, R. F. 140
Kidder, L. 260, 428, 466
Kidder, L. H. 151, 494
Kiesler, C. A. 171, 363, 494, 529
Killian, L. M. 285, 524
Kim, Y. 216, 485
Kimmel, M. J. 295, 308, 510
King, G. 366, 519
King, M. 442, 494
Kinney, J. 429, 494
Kirsh, B. 56, 477
Kitchener, R. F. 47
Kitcher, P. 38, 494
Kitson, G. C. 199, 494
Klein, R. 247, 464
Klerman, G. L. 151, 515
Klineberg, O. 171, 494
Klugman, S. F. 494
Knapp, M. L. 205, 212, 213, 214, 215, 220, 494, 527
Knight, G. P. 494
Knight, H. C. 329, 494
Knottnerus, J. D. 336, 484
Knurek, D. A. 171, 172, 464
Koch, S. 16, 494
Kogan, N. 368, 494
Kohlberg, L. 56, 57, 494
Koivumaki, J. H. 119, 120, 521
Kommer, D. 108, 515
Komorita, G. P. 295, 494
Konečni, V. J. 275, 419, 441, 442, 444, 494, 495
Korte, C. 426, 481
Kothandapani, V. 145, 495
Krakoff, L. R. 423, 483
Kramer, R. M. 310, 395, 466, 495
Kramp, P. 247, 464
Krantz, S. E. 137, 495
Krauss, R. M. 290, 473
Kraut, R. E. 201, 495
Kravitz, D. A. 327, 495
Krebs, D. 274, 495
Kress, G. 204, 480
Kriss, M. 132, 510
Krueger, D. L. 200, 495
Kruglanski, A. W. 108, 114, 125, 133, 192, 495
Kruse, L. 276, 495
Kruskal, W. 151, 468
Kruuk, H. 32, 495
Kuhlman, M. D. 299, 304, 495, 501

Kuhn, M. H. 400, 495
Kulik, J. A. 127, 157, 158, 492, 495
Kulka, R. A. 240, 524
Kumar, A. 145, 473

Labov, W. 208, 495
Ladouce, I. 45, 504
La Gaipa, J. J. 235, 495
Lage, E. 360, 363, 364, 504, 505
Lagerspetz, K. 273, 489
Laicardi, C. 42, 468
Lakoff, R. 205, 496
Lalljee, M. 57, 123, 124, 131, 487, 496
Lamb, T. A. 205, 496
Lambert, W. E. 207, 516
Lamm, H. 369, 380, 496
Landman, J. 101, 496
Lange, F. 285, 496
Langer, E. 103, 122, 209, 257, 496, 512
Langner, T. S. 273, 501
Lanzetta, J. T. 225, 256, 527
La Piere, R. T. 158, 496
Larson, C. 200, 203, 472
Larson, R. W. 236, 496
Lassiter, G. D. 208, 473
Latane, B. 246, 249, 250, 251, 257, 258, 328, 329, 356, 364, 367, 472, 496
Lau, R. R. 123, 496
Laycock, G. 431, 496
Layden, M. A. 139, 496
Layton, B. 228, 520
Lazarus, R. 78, 480
Lea, M. 496
Leaton, G. 429, 494
Leavitt, H. J. 346, 347, 497
LeBlanc, M. 437, 478
LeBon, G. 10, 11, 284, 384, 497
L'Ecuyer, R. 95, 497
Lee, M. T. 336, 497
Leet-Pellegrini, H. M. 205, 497
Lefkowitz, M. M. 477, 497
Legant, P. 119, 127, 506
Lehman, D. R. 199, 497
Lemaine, G. 95, 405, 497
Lemyre, L. 401, 497
Lenkert, A. 170, 520
Leo, G. 366, 519
LePage, A. 269, 464
Lepenies, W. 5, 497
Lepper, M. R. 105, 191, 192, 195, 497, 513
Lerman, D. 135, 526
Levenson, R. 214, 484

Leventhal, H. 183, 497
Levi, A. 81, 131, 522
Levine, J. M. 157, 356, 357, 459, 497
Levine, R. 247, 497
Levinger, G. 23, 226, 228, 229, 230, 245, 490, 493, 497
Levinson, D. J. 385, 386, 458
Levinson, S. 121, 125, 489, 497
Levy, A. S. 276, 481, 505
Levy, M. 51
Lewin, K. 14, 394, 405, 417, 497
Lewis, C. 56, 497
Leyens, J. P. 90, 93, 94, 98, 102, 108, 270, 273, 281, 402, 465, 497, 498, 501, 508
Lichtman, C. M. 259, 479
Liebert, R. M. 273, 498
Liebrand, W. B. G. 296, 297, 299, 304, 498
Light, P. 46, 49, 51, 52, 498
Lightbown, N. 395, 466
Likert, R. 146, 148, 338, 498
Lind, E. A. 206, 498
Linder, D. E. 186, 498
Linder, G. A. 12, 498
Lindskold, S. 208, 282, 521
Lindzey, G. 4, 485
Lingle, J. H. 157, 158, 498
Linneweber, V. 287, 505
Linville, P. W. 93, 498
Lippman, W. 96, 499
Liska, J. 160, 499
Littlefield, R. 214, 509
Littman, R. A. 272, 508
Litton, J. 98, 510
Liu, T. J. 127, 504
Livesley, W. J. 53, 499
Livingstone, J. W. 298, 484
Livingstone, S. M. 235, 499
Lloyd-Bostock, S. M. 414, 431, 499
Locke, S. E. 243, 491
Lockwood, J. 397, 470
Loftus, E. F. 433, 438, 439, 440, 499, 526
Lodewijkx, H. 285, 286, 510
Long, J. F. 205, 500
Lord, R. G. 338, 499
Lorenz, K. 35, 266, 267, 274, 499
Lorge, I. 169, 522
Löschper, G. 287, 505
Losel, F. 429, 525
Lott, A. J. 150, 510
Louw-Potgieter, J. 216, 499
Lück, H. E. 12, 499
Ludwig, D. 214, 499

Lujansky, H. 226, 499
Lukaszewski, M. P. 209, 468
Lukens, J. 216, 499
Lukes, S. 6, 7, 12, 94, 98, 499
Lumsden, C. J. 34, 499
Lund, M. 230, 499
Lutkenhaus, P. 45, 499
Lyman, S. 122, 516
Lynch, J. J. 242, 500

Maass, A. 360, 362, 363, 364, 367, 380, 500
McArthur, L. A. 116, 501
McArthur, L. Z. 129, 501
McCall, G. J. 25, 501
McCall, M. 25, 501
McCarthy, E. D. 273, 501
McClintock, C. G. 294, 296, 298, 300, 304, 311, 500, 501, 502, 524
McClintock, E. 23, 226, 229, 230, 245, 493
McCloskey, M. 438, 476
Maccoby, E. E. 22, 500
Maccoby, N. 179, 478
McConville, M. 433, 461
McCord, J. 428, 502
MacCrimon, K. R. 298, 500
MacDonald, M. G. 225, 226, 505
McDonel, E. C. 162, 478
MacDougall, J. M. 423, 473
McDougall, W. 11, 12, 265, 502
McFarland, C. 157, 158, 513
McGarrigle, J. 51, 502
McGillis, D. 113, 114, 115, 130, 492
McGlynn, R. P. 127, 486
McGrath, J. E. 62, 63, 64, 513
McGrew, W. C. 276, 489
McGuire, M. T. 477
McGuire, W. J. 94, 145, 153, 174, 175, 176, 178, 179, 184, 502
MacKay, D. M. 200, 500
Mackenzie, K. D. 347, 500
Mackie, J. L. 123, 500
McLaughlin, M. L. 220
McNeel, S. P. 294, 296, 501
McPartland, T. S. 400, 495
McShane, J. 42, 502
McTavish, J. 304, 472
Madden, T. J. 163, 458
Maddux, J. E. 183, 500
Magnusson, D. 25, 477
Maier, N. R. F. 317, 500
Maki, J. 304, 311, 500
Malamuth, N. M. 218, 469

Malloy, J. E. 214, 499
Mandel, M. R. 151, 515
Manis, M. 101, 122, 496, 500
Mann, L. 151, 285, 371, 491, 500, 503
Mann, S. K. 205, 527
Mansell, J. 421, 500
Manstead, A. S. R. 69, 81, 82, 122, 163, 189, 191, 193, 320, 322, 323, 418, 500, 508, 516, 522
Mantell, D. M. 378, 500
Maracek, J. 119, 127, 506
Marchand, B. 397, 500
Margolin, G. 235, 490
Markel, N. N. 205, 500
Markova, I. 6, 9, 500
Markus, H. 91, 94, 157, 209, 492, 501
Marlowe, D. 151, 501
Marques, J. 102, 497
Marques, J. M. 93, 101, 501
Marrow, A. J. 14, 501
Marshall, J. R. 224, 478
Marshello, A. M. J. 299, 304, 495
Martin, B. 327, 495
Martin, J. 214, 509
Martin, J. A. 22, 500
Martin, P. 38
Marwell, G. 297, 501
Marx, K. 6, 501
Marx, M. H. 15, 501
Maslach, C. 428, 441, 482, 501
Mathewson, G. C. 72, 482
Matthews, A. 392, 403, 404, 467
Matthews, K. A. 422, 501
Mausner, B. 355, 501
Mayes, B. I. 421, 481
Mayhew, P. 431, 489
Mayseless, O. 260, 506
Mead, G. H. 400, 502
Meek, D. 472, 434
Meertens, R. W. 371, 502
Meeus, W. H. J. 378, 502
Mehrabian, A. 151, 205, 502
Meinefeld, W. 159, 502
Mellen, S. W. L. 31, 502
Messe, L. A. 191, 304, 502, 520
Messer, D. J. 43, 502
Messick, D. M. 298, 300, 312, 500, 501, 502, 527
Mewborn, C. R. 183, 512
Meyer, C. B. 426, 502
Meyer, G. 409, 474
Meyer, J. P. 252, 502

Meyers, D. G. 496, 506
Michaels, J. W. 230, 503
Michotte, A. E. 92, 132, 503
Miell, D. 219, 230, 475, 503
Mikula, G. 226, 283, 300, 430, 499, 503
Milardo, R. M. 219, 503
Milavsky, B. 278, 529
Milgram, S. 11, 61, 66, 68, 151, 372, 373, 375, 376, 377, 378, 379, 380, 416, 420, 432, 503
Miller, D. T. 130, 131, 209, 305, 492, 503
Miller, F. D. 133, 518
Miller, G. A. 108, 503
Miller, G. R. 220
Miller, L. C. 214, 503
Miller, N. 179, 180, 392, 462, 503
Miller, N. E. 201, 268, 474, 503
Miller, R. S. 131, 515
Mills, J. 72, 225, 470
Mills, M. K. 431, 484
Milner, D. 55, 405, 503
Mischel, W. 25, 92, 468, 503
Moede, W. 16, 503
Molloy, C. G. 52, 486
Money, J. W. 36, 503
Monson, T. 464, 503
Monson, T. C. 127
Montada, L. 255, 262, 504
Montagner, H. 45, 504
Moore, B. S. 127, 504
Moore, D. L. 320, 322, 323, 514
Moreland, R. L. 170, 504
Moreno, J. L. 95, 96, 504
Morgan, M. 274, 482
Morgenstern, O. 289, 525
Morland, J. K. 405, 504
Morley, L. 437, 438, 478
Morse, S. J. 226, 482
Moscovici, S. 7, 11, 12, 17, 98, 99, 109, 126, 358, 359, 360, 361, 362, 363, 364, 365, 366, 367, 369, 380, 420, 477, 484, 504, 505
Moskowitz, J. 300, 524
Mothner, E. 420, 461
Motley, M. T. 215, 468
Mouton, J. S. 392, 465
Mowrer, D. H. 429, 505
Mowrer, O. H. 268, 474, 503
Mugny, G. 25, 36, 49, 50, 51, 306, 363, 473, 474, 505
Mulac, A. 205, 216, 505, 527
Mulder, M. 348, 505
Mulherin, A. 253, 502

Mummendey, A. 287, 505
Mundy, D. 307, 493
Munsterberg, H. 415, 505
Murakami, M. 35, 519
Murdoch, P. 320, 508
Murnighan, J. K. 295, 505
Murphy, G. 157, 497
Murstein, B. I. 225, 228, 505
Myers, D. G. 369, 370, 371, 380, 505, 506

Nadel, J. 43, 506
Nadler, A. 260, 479, 480, 506
Naffrechoux, M. 360, 505
Naji, S. 124, 460
Nanni, R. 107, 469
Neisser, U. 94, 108, 506
Nel, E. 187, 506
Nelson, K. 52, 506
Nemeth, C. 55, 361, 363, 367, 368, 420, 505, 506, 521
Nesdale, A. R. 279, 284, 513
Newcomb, T. M. 24, 100, 387, 506
Newman, L. S. 160, 525
Newton, J. W. 285, 500
Newton, M. 158, 506
Newton, N. 158, 506
Newtson, D. 119, 506
Nezlek, J. 223, 526
Nida, S. 249, 257, 496
Nierenberg, R. 135, 526
Nietzel, M. T. 473
Nieuwenhuysen, B. 319, 528
Nisbett, R. E. 94, 104, 105, 110, 114, 127, 132, 192, 492, 497, 506
Noller, P. 208, 217, 221, 222, 506
Noonan, K. M. 31, 459
Norman, R. 160, 506
Norman, R. Z. 463
Nuttall, R. L. 151, 501
Nuttin, J. M., Jr 187, 378, 507
Nye, R. 10, 11, 507

Oaker, G. 403, 507
Oakes, P. J. 309, 401, 507, 523
Oakes, W. F. 172, 490
O'Barr, W. M. 206, 498
O'Brien, G. E. 421, 478
O'Connell, L. 225, 507
O'Connor, P. 241, 507
Ofshe, R. 336, 497
Olson, J. M. 164
O'Neal, E. C. 275, 482

Oppenheim, A. N. 79, 507
Orne, M. T. 73, 507
Orvis, B. R. 116, 227, 507
Orzeck, L. 501
Osgood, C. E. 100, 147, 148, 507
Osterhouse, R. A. 179, 507
Ostrom, T. M. 81, 145, 157, 158, 498, 507

Page, M. M. 172, 271, 507
Paicheler, G. 10, 12, 363, 507, 508
Pallak, M. S. 363, 494
Palmonari, A. 57, 58, 508
Papastamou, S. 363, 505
Papousek, H. 42, 508
Papousek, M. 42, 508
Park, R. E. 11, 508
Parke, R. D. 270, 273, 498, 508
Parkinson, B. 69, 508
Parrar-Dayan, S. 52, 465
Patterson, G. R. 272, 508
Patterson, M. L. 201, 508
Paulus, P. B. 320, 321, 322, 349, 508
Pavitt, C. 215, 487
Payne, S. 79, 508
Pease, K. 435, 480
Peckham, V. 490
Peevers, B. H. 53, 508
Pelz, E. B. 417, 508
Penrod, S. 364, 367, 521
Pepitone, A. 12, 13, 508
Peplau, L. A. 23, 30, 199, 226, 229, 230,
    231, 241, 245, 281, 488, 493, 508, 513
Perlman, D. 199, 218, 241, 469, 508
Perret-Clemont, A. N. 25, 49, 474, 508
Perrin, S. 353, 509
Personnaz, B. 365, 505, 509
Pessin, J. 318, 509
Peterson, C. 138, 509
Peterson, D. R. 23, 226, 229, 230, 245, 493
Petri, B. 283, 503
Petronio, S. 214, 509
Petrullo, L. 94, 520
Pettigrew, T. F. 131, 386, 387, 392, 407,
    509, 524, 525,
Petty, R. E. 143, 149, 150, 151, 177, 178,
    179, 180, 181, 182, 184, 195, 468, 509
Piaget, J. 16, 48, 49, 55, 252, 399, 509
Pichevin, M. F. 56, 489
Pierson, H. 207, 528
Pilkonis, P. A. 171, 529
Pingree, S. 220, 486
Pittman, T. S. 188, 509

Plevin, C. E. 418, 500
Plomin, R. 27, 468
Poliakov, L. 132, 510
Poppe, M. 309, 510
Porier, G. W. 150, 510
Post, D. L. 129, 501
Potter, E. H. 342, 343, 479
Potter, J. 98, 510
Powesland, P. F. 206, 210, 220, 402, 404,
    483
Pratt, A. R. 52, 486
Price, J. 276, 481
Profitt, C. 163, 500
Pruitt, D. G. 256, 293, 295, 308, 510
Pryor, J. B. 52, 132, 493, 510
Pyszczynski, T. A. 123, 510

Quattrone, G. A. 127, 399, 510
Quine, L. 421, 510

Raaijmakers, Q. A. W. 378, 502
Rabbie, J. M. 285, 286, 392, 393, 394, 489,
    510
Rabinowitz, V. C. 260, 428, 466
Radloff, R. 307, 493
Radlow, R. 295, 510
Radzicki, J. 298, 510
Ragan, S. L. 215, 511
Rapoport, A. 294, 295, 306, 485, 511
Raven, B. H. 332, 416, 418, 470, 511
Reeder, G. D. 127, 133, 511
Regan, D. T. 161, 162, 511
Regis, J. M. 232, 518
Reich, J. W. 240, 511
Reicher, S. 437, 443, 477
Reicher, S. D. 285, 384, 511
Reiling, A. M. 35, 481
Reis, H. 223, 526
Restoin, A. 45, 504
Revans, R. 425, 511
Reykowski, J. 262
Rhodewalt, F. 188, 487
Ricci-Bitti, P. E. 57, 508
Rice, M. E. 257, 511
Richerson, P. J. 34, 465
Ridgeway, C. L. 336, 511
Riecken, H. W. 75, 478
Riess, M. 134, 191, 511
Rijsman, J. B. 51, 309, 511
Ring, K. 414, 442, 511
Roach, M. J. 199, 494
Robbins, A. I. 52, 498

Roberts, J. V. 158, 511
Robinson, D. N. 442, 512
Robinson, J. P. 79, 148, 512
Robinson, W. P. 43, 203, 512
Rodin, J. 209, 257, 258, 496, 512
Rodriguez, D. 45, 504
Roethlisberger, F. J. 76, 344, 512
Rogers, R. W. 182, 183, 500, 512
Rogner, O. 426, 427, 481
Rokeach, M. 386, 387, 512
Romer, D. 179, 512
Rosch, E. 92, 512
Rosch, M. 154, 155, 481
Rose, A. 270, 479
Rose, T. 399, 485
Rosenbaum, M. E. 252, 256, 257, 258, 512
Rosenberg, M. 144, 405, 512
Rosenberg, M. J. 143, 160, 512
Rosenberg. S. 101, 512
Rosenfeld, P. 189, 190, 195, 208, 282, 521, 522
Rosenholtz, S. J. 335, 463
Rosenman, R. H. 422, 481, 501
Rosenthal, R. 63, 73, 74, 512
Rosnow, R. L. 74, 512
Ross, A. 437, 477
Ross, D. 272, 461, 462
Ross, E. A. 12, 513
Ross, G. F. 407, 467
Ross, L. 94, 104, 105, 110, 114, 119, 125, 126, 130, 132, 480, 506, 513
Ross, M. 130, 131, 141, 151, 157, 188, 468, 503, 513
Ross, S. A. 272, 461, 462
Roth, A. E. 295, 505
Rothbart, M. 399, 513
Roux, J. P. 51, 483
Ruback, R. B. 431, 484
Rubin, Z. 30, 231, 235, 281, 488, 508, 513
Rubinow, S. 200, 527
Ruble, D. N. 52, 488, 513
Rude, S. 137, 495
Ruderman, A. 132, 521
Ruken, V. M. 304, 498
Rule, B. G. 279, 281, 282, 284, 478, 491, 513
Runciman, W. G. 407, 513
Runkel, P. J. 62, 63, 64, 513
Rusbult, C. E. 230, 513
Rushton, J. P. 246, 261, 262, 513
Russell, D. 123, 135, 496, 526
Russell, D. W. 428, 514
Russell, J. 52, 514

Rutte, C. G. 300, 339, 340, 514, 527
Rutter, D. R. 41, 44, 207, 475, 476, 514
Rutter, M. 437, 514
Ryan, E. B. 206, 209, 514, 519
Ryan, K. 120, 466
Ryen, A. H. 392, 514

Sahakian, W. S. 19
Saine, T. J. 205, 500
St Ledger, R. J. 437, 438, 478
Salt, P. 151, 515
Sampson, E. E. 17, 514
Samuelson, C. D. 300, 527
Sanders, G. S. 320, 322, 323, 370, 514
Sanford, R. N. 385, 386, 458
Santi, A. 296, 520
Sarachielli, G., 57, 508
Sassoon, C. 207, 483
Scarr, S. 27, 514
Schaap, C. 217, 514
Schachter, S. 75, 97, 229, 278, 345, 423, 478, 514
Schaefer, R. E. 395, 396, 461
Schafer, R. B. 4, 527
Schaffer, H. R. 40, 41, 43, 514, 515
Schall, B. 45, 504
Schank, R. 64, 102, 515
Scheerer, M. 15, 515
Scheidt, R. 271, 507
Scherer, K. R. 206, 276, 515
Schlegel, R. P. 145, 161, 162, 515
Schlenker, B. R. 82, 131, 189, 193, 515, 522
Schliemann, A. D. 25, 469
Schmidt, H. D. 270, 515
Schmidt-Mummendey, A. 270, 515
Schmitt, D. R. 296, 501
Schmitt, M. 255, 504
Schneider, D. J. 90, 110, 515
Schneider, W. 133, 320, 517
Schönbach, P. 283, 515
Schopler, J. 251, 515
Schriesheim, C. A. 342, 515
Schroeder, D. H. 515
Schuler, M. 426, 481
Schulz, H.-J. 267, 481
Schulz, U. 298, 299, 515
Schuman, H. 63, 515
Schwartz, G. E. 151, 515
Schwartz, R. F. 76, 525
Schwartz, S. H. 253, 254, 255, 258, 516
Schwarz, N. 108, 157, 515, 516
Schwinger, T. 239, 493

Scott, M. B. 122, 516
Scott, R. A. 209, 492
Sears, D. O. 181, 481
Sears, R. R. 268, 503
Sears, R. T. 268, 474
Sebastian, R. J. 273, 508
Sechrest, L. 76, 525
Secord, P. F. 53, 508
Sedlack, A. 101, 512
Seligman, C. 207, 516
Seligman, M. E. P. 26, 138, 458, 509, 516
Sellitz, C. 151, 516
Selman, R. L. 53, 516
Semin, G. R. 65, 66, 81, 82, 122, 320, 322, 323, 500, 516
Sentis, K. 94, 501
Sermat, V. 296, 516
Shaklee, H. 304, 472
Shanab, M. E. 378, 516
Shantz, C. U. 47, 516
Shapland, J. M. 436, 516
Sharabany, R. 56, 477
Shaver, K. G. 79, 120, 149, 516
Shaver, P. R. 148, 512
Shaw, M. 330, 517
Shaw, M. E. 79, 347, 349, 517
Sheeran, L. 523
Sherif, C. W. 156, 390, 517
Sherif, M. 147, 156, 343, 351, 382, 389, 390, 391, 393, 410, 420, 423, 489, 517
Sherman, S. J. 126, 162, 478, 517
Sherrod, D. R. 127, 504
Sherwood, V. 42, 467
Shiffrin, R. M. 133, 320, 517
Short, R. 30, 31, 517
Shultz, T. R. 120, 479
Shweder, R. 132, 517
Sidowski, J. B. 306, 307, 517
Sigall, H. 152, 190, 492
Sighele, S. 11, 284, 517
Signorelli, N. 274, 482
Silberer, G. 145, 517
Simmel, G. 12, 517
Simmons, R. G. 405, 512
Simon, B. 399, 517
Simon, H. A. 517
Simon, M. D. 55, 306, 517
Simons, L. S. 270, 518, 523
Simons, S. 285, 474
Simpson, A. E. 518
Singer, D. G. 273, 518
Singer, J. 97, 423, 514

Singer, J.E. 228, 518
Singer, J. L. 273, 518
Sivacek, J. M. 304, 502
Skevington, S. 403, 518
Skinner, B. F. 40, 518
Slater, P. E. 334, 335, 336, 337, 461, 518
Sloan, L. 400, 469
Smart, J. L. 163, 418, 500
Smedslund, J. 82, 518
Smith, E. A. 32, 475
Smith, E. R. 133, 518
Smith, J. R. 480
Smith, M. B. 153, 518
Smith, P. K. 56, 518
Smith, P. M. 205, 337, 401, 497, 518
Smith, R. 358, 490
Smith, T. L. 145, 165, 472, 518
Smith, V. L. 440, 518
Snow, C. E. 43, 518
Snyder, D. K. 232, 518
Snyder, M. 114, 127, 164, 257, 503, 518
Softley, P. 432, 518
Sokolov, A. N. 151, 518
Solem, A. R. 317, 500
Solomon, L. 296, 486
Solomon, M. R. 358, 359, 490
Sommer, M. 15, 484
Sonne, J. L. 139, 518
Sorrentino, R. M. 262, 366, 519
Sparks, R. F. 431, 519
Speckart, G. 163, 463
Spence, K. W. 319, 519
Spencer, C. 353, 509
Sprinzen, M. 129, 521
Srull, T. 94, 104, 110, 519, 528
Staats, A. W. 171, 172, 519
Staats, C. K. 171, 172, 519
Stahelski, A. J. 304, 493
Stangor, C. 142, 145, 165, 469
Star, S. A. 420, 519
Staub, E. 259, 262, 519
Steiner, I. D. 316, 317, 324, 325, 326, 327, 328, 330, 331, 332, 338, 340, 345, 347, 348, 349, 519
Steinmetz, J. L. 126, 519
Stephenson, G. M. 388, 419, 519
Sternglanz, S. H. 35, 519
Stevenson-Hinde, J. 23, 26, 488, 518
Steward, M. A. 206, 519
Steward, R. 204, 526
Stewart, B. E. 227, 486
Stogdill, R. M. 337, 519

Stokols, D. 276, 519
Stone, J. I. 208, 473
Stoner, J. A. F. 368, 369, 519
Stonner, D. 272, 482
Storms, M. D. 127, 128, 129, 519
Stosberg, M. 149, 519
Stouffer, S. A. 420, 519
Strack, F. 108, 515
Street, R. L., Jr 201, 208, 483, 519
Strickland, L. H. 6, 355, 519, 522
Stringer, P. 444
Stringfield, D. O. 25, 494
Stroebe, M. S. 241, 423, 424, 425, 519, 520
Stroebe, W. 147, 149, 151, 156, 170, 228, 241, 290, 297, 312, 327, 423, 424, 425, 476, 519, 520
Stults, D. M. 191, 520
Suchmann, E. A. 420, 519
Suci, G. J. 147, 148, 507
Sullivan, H. S. 25, 520
Surra, C. A. 230, 489
Swann, W. B. 114, 518
Swedlund, M. 361, 506
Sweeney, P. D. 138, 520
Swingle, P. G. 296, 520
Syme, G. J. 163, 492
Syme, S. L. 242, 463

Tabachnik, N. 117, 118, 459
Tabory, L. 306, 517
Tagiuri, R. 90, 94, 100, 467, 520
Tajfel, H. 14, 17, 35, 55, 93, 94, 96, 97, 106, 107, 110, 216, 294, 295, 296, 297, 303, 309, 388, 389, 400, 401, 402, 404, 405, 407, 409, 410, 420, 430, 464, 465, 467, 476, 490, 491, 517, 520, 521
Tamplin, A. 45, 488
Tanford, S. 364, 367, 521
Tannenbaum, P. H. 100, 147, 148, 279, 507, 521
Tarde, G. 11, 284, 521
Tardey, C. H. 214, 466
Tate, P. 219, 521
Taves, P. A. 188, 471
Taylor, D. 210, 214, 215, 459
Taylor, D. M. 94, 521
Taylor, S. E. 93, 94, 104, 109, 118, 119, 120, 125, 129, 132, 133, 140, 157, 171, 216, 399, 426, 471, 480, 502, 521
Teasdale, J. 138, 458
Tedeschi, J. T. 134, 189, 190, 191, 195, 208, 256, 282, 283, 467, 481, 487, 511, 521, 522

Terhune, K. W. 295, 522
Tesser, A. 256, 522
Tetlock, P. E. 81, 131, 189, 191, 193, 441, 522
Thakerar, J. N. 207, 208, 522
Thibaut, J. 395, 465
Thibaut, J. W. 124, 224, 225, 303, 307, 355, 492, 493, 522
Thomas, E. J. 317, 331, 522
Thomas, W. I. 143, 522
Thompson, P. R. 28, 522
Thompson, V. D. 228, 520
Thomson, C. W. 169, 491
Thorndike, E. L. 169, 522
Thorne, A. 400
Thorpe, W. H. 27, 522
Thurstone, L. L. 14, 146, 522
Tinbergen, N. 21, 32, 522
Ting-Toomey, S. 216, 522
Toch, H. 11, 431, 484, 503
Tod, M. 472
Todd, A. D. 205, 480
Todd, J. 43, 522
Tognoli, J. 295, 522
Tomasello, M. 43, 522
Toogood, A. 421, 500
Torrance, E. P. 336, 523
Totman, R. 120, 418, 421, 426, 444, 523
Town, J. P. 127, 486
Traupmann, J. 226, 486
Travis, L. E. 318, 523
Trevarthen, C. 523
Trew, A. 204, 480
Triandis, H. C. 256, 523
Trimboli, L. 460
Triplett, N. D. 317, 318, 523
Trivers, R. L. 30, 252, 523
Troccoli, B. 281, 468
Trolier, T. K. 97, 485
Tucker, G. R. 207, 516
Tucker, H. 44, 475
Turiel, E. 523
Turke, P. W. 33, 523
Turner, C. W. 270, 518, 523
Turner, J. C. 216, 309, 387, 388, 392, 395, 396, 397, 398, 400, 401, 405, 407, 410, 414, 467, 507, 521, 523
Turner, R. H. 285, 524
Tversky, A. 104, 105, 130, 132, 492, 524
Tyszka, T. 294, 296, 485, 524

Ullian, D. Z. 56, 524

Ullman, V. 45, 504
Ulrich, W. 211, 524
Underwood, B. 127, 504
Upshaw, H. S. 156, 524
Utne, M. K. 226, 227, 486

Vacherot, C. 302, 458
Valenzi, E. 422, 459
Valiant, G. 49, 524
Valiant, G. L. 51, 477
Vallacher, P. R. 95, 525
Van Avermaet, E. F. 300, 311, 353, 363,
  365, 366, 474, 502, 524
Vanbeselaere, N. 169, 524
Van De Geer, J. P. 55, 491
Van den Berghe, P. L. 32, 524
Van Hooff, J. A. R. 29, 524
Van Knippenberg, A. 403, 524
Vanneman, R. D. 407, 524
Van Oers, H. 403, 524
Van Rooijen, L. 353, 524
Van Run, C. J. 299, 498
Vaughan, G. M. 13, 405, 485, 524
Veen, P. 336, 524
Velzen, D. van 428, 514
Venkatesan, M. 179, 495
Veroff, J. 240, 524
Viala, M. 45, 504
Vidmar, N. 433, 485
Vine, I. 200, 524
Vinokur, A. 370, 468
Vlaander, G. P. J. 353, 524
Volterra, V. 43, 468
Von Cranach, M. 200, 524
Von Neumann, J. 289, 525
Vorwerg, M. 6, 487

Wachtler, J. 363, 506
Wade, G. 392, 403, 467
Wade, G. S. 393, 467
Wade, T. J. 358, 359, 404, 490
Wagner, D. 108, 515
Walder, L. O. 477, 497
Wales, R. J. 51, 525
Walker, C. 238, 525
Walker, I. 407, 525
Walker, M. R. 400, 469
Wallace, W. 151, 468
Wallach, L. 35, 482
Wallach, M. A. 368, 494
Wallen, K. 36, 483
Wallis, C. 528

Walster, E. 228, 464, 474
Walster, G. W. 228, 464
Walters, R. H. 272, 525
Ward, C. 131, 487
Warr, P. B. 229, 525
Warren, R. 178, 179, 476
Watson, D. 127, 129, 525
Watson, G. 427
Watson, J. B. 40, 525
Watson, R. I. 4, 525
Watzlawick, P. 200, 203, 217, 221, 525
Weary, G. 134, 205, 525
Weaver, F. M. 431, 525
Webb, E. J. 76, 525
Weber, A. L. 227, 486
Weber, R. 267, 481
Webley, P. 54, 525
Wegener, H. 429, 525
Wegner, D. M. 95, 424, 525
Weick, K. E. 75, 525
Weigel, R. H. 160, 525
Weil, A. 55, 509
Weiner, B. 123, 124, 135, 136, 137, 525, 526
Weinreich-Haste, H. 56, 526
Weinrich, D. 220, 527
Weis, J. G. 436, 488
Wells, G. L. 130, 179, 180, 438, 486, 509,
  526
West, C. 205, 526, 529
West, D. J. 437, 438, 478
West, S. G. 273, 508
Wetherell, M. 397, 526
Wheeler, L. 223, 526
Wheeless, L. R. 204, 526
Whitcher-Alagna, S. 260, 480
White, B. J. 390, 517
White, R. W. 153, 518
Whiteneck, G. G. 214, 482
Whyte, W. F. 333, 526
Wichman, H. 296, 526
Wicker, A. W. 158, 526
Wicklund, R. A. 129, 164, 255, 475, 526
Widenmann, S. 216, 505
Wieczorkowska, G. 298, 526
Wieman, J. M. 203, 204, 205, 209, 210,
  214, 215, 216, 217, 218, 220, 221, 471,
  483, 486, 505, 526, 527
Wiener, M. 200, 527
Wiener, R. L. 123, 442, 469
Wilder, D. A. 107, 356, 392, 459, 527
Wilhelmy, R. A. 356, 482
Wilke, H. A. M. 225, 256, 300, 336, 339,

340, 344, 488, 514, 524, 527
Wilkens, G. 393, 510
Wilkes, A. L. 106, 397, 409, 521
Wilkinson, S. 420, 527
Williams, B. A. 214, 494
Williams, C.J. 156, 478
Williams, J. A. 392, 403, 404, 467, 527
Williams, J. E. 35, 527
Williams, K. 328, 329, 496
Williams, R. M., Jr 420, 519
Wills, T. A. 240, 241, 260, 262, 470, 527
Wilmot, W. M. 211, 462
Wilson, A. 215, 468
Wilson, C. E. 431, 484
Wilson, D. W. 4, 275, 474, 527
Wilson, E. O. 8, 34, 38, 499,527
Wilson, J. Q. 429, 527
Wilson, K. V. 296, 465
Wilson, M. 32, 471
Wilson, P. 206, 483
Wilson, W. 267, 527
Wilson, W. R. 169, 170, 527
Winer, B. J. 337, 338, 485
Winkler, J. P. 129, 521
Winterhoff-Spurk, P. 220, 527
Wisegarver, R. 206, 466
Wish, M. 235, 236, 304, 527
Wit, A. P. 300, 527
Wittenbraker, J. 395, 465
Woerdenbagch, A. 490
Wojcicki, S. B. 371, 506
Wolf, S. 356, 367, 496
Wood, H. D. 235, 495
Woodward, W. R. 5, 527
Worchel, S. 187, 393, 410, 471, 527
Word, C. O. 217, 527
Worell, J. 56, 528

Wortman, C. B. 120, 199, 466, 475, 497
Wright, J. M. 79, 517
Wrightman, L. S. 151
Wrightsman, L. S. 433, 441, 472, 516
Wundt, W. 528
Wyckoff, L. B. 306, 517
Wyer, R. S., Jr 104, 519
Wyer, R. S. 94, 110, 179, 528

Yaffe, Y. 384, 528
Yahya, K. A. 378, 516
Yang, K. S. 216, 528
Yarkin, K. L. 127, 227, 486
Yinon, Y. 284, 384, 490, 528
Young, L. 207, 528
Young, M. 528
Youniss, J. 25, 53, 252, 528
Yuille, J. C. 438, 528
Yzerbyt, V. 93, 501

Zajonc, R. B. 15, 64, 91, 108, 168, 169, 170,
    195, 318, 319, 501, 504, 528
Zander, A. 344, 346, 349, 469, 528
Zani, B. 421, 528
Zanna, M. P. 159, 161, 164, 165, 171, 188,
    189, 217, 471, 478, 487, 527, 528, 529
Zautra, A. 240, 511
Zavalloni, M. 94, 369, 505, 529
Zeisel, H. 433, 492
Zelditch, M., Jr 335, 463
Zillmann, D. 278, 279, 284, 287, 521, 529
Zimbardo, P. 285, 384, 529
Zimmerman, D. H. 205, 527, 529
Znaniecki, F. 143, 522
Zoetebier, J. H. T. 51, 511
Zuckerman, M. 131, 529
Zumkley, H. 284, 529

Subject Index

Page numbers for glossary entries in bold type

accentuation theory 106–7, 156
accounts 121–2, 283–4
achievement attribution 123–4, 130–1,
    134–7
actor–observer difference 127–30, **445**
adaptation-level theory 156
additive model 101–2
adolescence 53–5, 57–8, 431, 435–8
adversary system 432, **445**
affect 108, 138–9
affective–cognitive consistency 160–1
affiliative messages 203, **445**
aggression
    and anger 269, 278, 283
    and anonymity 285–6, 384
    attribution of 111, 282–4
    and crowding 275–6
    and cues 269–71
    definitions of 268, 280
    displacement of 266–8
    emergent norm theory of 285
    ethological theory 266–7
    and frustration 268–71
    and heat 276–7
    norm-enhancement hypothesis 286
    in psychoanalytic theory 265–6, 274
    in social learning theory 271–4
    and television 272–4
altruistic behaviour 28–9, 225, 228, 246–62,
    298, 300, 309, 369, 378, 414, **445**
    in emergencies 257–9, 428
    and modeling 256–7
    and norms 252–7
    receiving help 259–61, 427–9
anchoring 99, 105–6, 127

arousal
    and aggression 275–80
    misattribution of 188–9, 282–3
    and social facilitation 319–22
assimilation 156
assimilation-contrast theory 156
attention 132, 174–5
attitude **445**
    consistency-theories of 154–8
    definitions 143–5
    expectancy-value model of 144–5, 174,
        181–4
    formation 52
    functions of 153–8
    information processing 154–8
    measurement of 14, 146–52
    structure 145
    theories of 14
attitude and behaviour 158–64, 167–8,
    170–3, 191, 416, 437
    correspondence of 159–60
    direct experience 161–2, 167–8, 170–3,
        191
attitude change 14, 167–95, 378, 413, 416,
    434
attraction 80, 228
    in groups 388
attributional style 138–9, **445**
attribution of responsibility *see* responsi-
    bility attribution
attribution theory
    analysis of variance (ANOVA) model
        115–17, 125, 130, 133
    biases: cognitive 125–32; motivational
        114, 131

configuration 115, 117–18, 125, 362
consensus 115–17, 130, 362
consistency 116–17, 362
control 131, 134
and depression 138–9
distinctiveness 115–17
expectancies 114, 123, 130
functions 134–9
group-serving biases 131–2
and illness 425–6
internal vs. external 112, 119–20, 135, 139, 253
and motivation 134–7
processes 132–3
and social influence 362–3
audience effects 318–24
augmentation principle 117, 362, **445**
authoritarian personality 385–7
F-scale 386
autokinetic effect 351–2, **445**
availability 104, 127, 132–3, 161–2
averaging model 101–2

balance theory 23–4, 95–6, 156, 226–7, **445**
base rate (fallacy) 105, 130, **445**
behavioural control 162, 203–9
behavioural intention 143–4, 162–3, **445**
behavioural style 360–2
behaviour change, incentive-induced 167–8, 184–92
behaviourism 15–16, 40
belief 143–4, **445**
bereavement 199, 241, 423–5, 427
bias
    in attribution 125–32, 391, 394–5, 403, 441
    in social cognition 104–6
bogus-pipeline method 152, 190–1, **446**
boomerang effect 178, 255
burnout 428
bystander effects 249, 257–9

categorical differentiation 397–8, **446**
categorization 92–3, 96, 394, 397, 399, **446**
catharsis 266, 268, **446**
causal schemata 117–18, **446**
cautious shift 369
central route to persuasion 177–8, 181, 194, **446**
central trait 89, **446**
classical conditioning 171–2, 174, 177, 269–71, **446**

cluster analysis 230, **446**
co-action 318, **446**
co-adapted complex 29–30, **446**
coercive power 281–2, **446**
cognition 15, 56, 91–4, 130, **446**
cognitive conflict 230–1, 232–3, 288–312, 401, 408
cognitive consistency theories 23, 95–6, 156, **446**
cognitive development 42–57, 414
cognitive dissonance theory 7, 72, 100, 154–7, 185–9, 417–19, **446**, 448
cognitive miser 104–6, 132
cohesion 333–4, 372, 390, 392, **446**
collective psychology 7
communication **446**
    affiliation function of 209–17
    control function of 203–9
    defined 199–201
    doctor–patient 205, 219–20
    functional approach to 201, 203–17
    in groups 345
    intergroup 216–17
    interpersonal 199, 203–19, 413
    marital 199, 217
    relational 212–15
    verbal/nonverbal 20, 73–4, 76, 200–1, 214, 413
communication networks 346–9, 447, **446**
communicative competence 217–19, **446**
communicative control 203–9, **447**
compensatory model 428–9, **447**
competition 288–312, 387, 423, **447**
compliance 185, 355, 364–8, 416–17, 420, 432, **447**
comprehension 174–6
computer simulation 64, **447**
concrete operational stage 48, **447**
conflict 230–3, 288–312, 389–90, 401, 408
    of interests 289–301, 391, **447**
conformity *see* majority influence **447**
confounding 72, **447**
conservation 48–52, **447**
construct validity 72, **447**
contact hypothesis 392–3
control *see* Communication
control group 70–1, **447**
conversion 355, 364–8, **447**
cooperation **447**
    and communication 296
    and learning 306–7
    and payoff structure 289–96

and partner's strategy 295-6
and personal closeness 296
and size of group 296-7
and social orientations 298-305
and trust 308-9
coordination losses in groups 327-9, 348
coping 427-8
Coronary Heart Disease (CHD) 422-3, 424
correlational research 61-2
correspondent inference 113-15, 123, **447**
covariation principle 115-18, 362, **447**
cover story 73, **448**
counter-argumentation 179-80
counter-attitudinal behaviour 174, 185-92,
   447
crime
   committing 430-1
   investigating 431-2
   juvenile 435-8
   reporting 431
   as reputation management 437-8
criminal justice system 429-42
crowd behaviour 8, 10-12, 20, 382-3,
   384-5, 408
crowding 20
crowd psychology 8, 10-12, 408, **448**
cue arousal theory 269-70, **448**
culture 9, 17, 26-8, 32, 34, 81-2, 227-8,
   234, 243, 353, 378, 386, 396-7

death instinct 266
debriefing 69, **448**
decentring 48-9
deception 69
decision making 65, 289, 305-6, 419,
   429-31, 433, 435, 441
deindividuation 285-6, 384, **448**
demand characteristics 73, 395, **448**
dependent variable 69, **448**
depression 138-9, 199, 241-2, 425
descriptive research 61-2
desertion 356-7
developmental psychology 46-52, 435
developmental social psychology 47, 52, 59
deviancy in groups 345
dialectics 21, 24-5, 33-5, **448**
diffusion of responsibility 258-9, 261, 285,
   448
direct experience 161-2, 168-71, 191
discounting principle 117, 362, **448**
disidentification 405
displacement 268, **448**

dissonance theory *see* cognitive dissonance
   448
distraction 179-80, **448**
distraction-response conflict 320
divergence 402
divorce *see* marriage
dogmatism 363
dominant response 268, 319-20, **448**

elaboration 177, **448**
elaboration likelihood model 177-81, 184,
   448-9
emotion 108, 138-9, 423-4
equal appearing intervals scale 146-7, **449**
equilibrium hypothesis 201-3, 211-12
   eye contact 201-3
equity theory 224, 226-7, 300, **449**
ethics 76, 85, 152, 378
ethnocentrism 131
ethology 20-38, 44
evaluation apprehension 258-9, 320, **449**
evolution of human behaviour 7-8, 20-1,
   26-8, 252
excitation transfer theory 277-9, **449**
expectancy-value models 144-5, 174,
   181-4, **449**
expectation-states theory 335-6
experiment 60, 70-1, **449**
experimental games 289-94, **449**
experimental research 61-2, 64, 66-74, 440
   critique of 80-3
experimental scenario 66-7, **449**
experimental simulation 63, **449**
experimenter (expectancy) effects 73-4, **449**
external validity 74, **449**
eye witness testimony 415, 429, 432-3, 435,
   438-40

facial electromyogram (EMG) 151
factor analysis 145, 223, 337, **449**
false consensus bias 130, 304, **450**
fear appeals 182-3, **450**
field
   experiment 63, 390, **450**
   studies 62-3, 66, **450**
   theory 417, **450**
forced compliance 186-7, 190
formal theory 63, **450**
freedom of choice 186-7, 418
free-rider effect 328, **450**
friendship 53, 237, 228-9, 231, 233-5, 239,
   252

frustration 268, **450**
frustration-aggression hypothesis 268-9, **450**
functional attitude theories 153, **450**
fundamental attribution error 125-7, 129, 378, **450**

Galvanic skin response (GSR) 150, **450**
gender 56-7
gender stereotypes 21, 35-6, 57
generalizability 414-15, **450**
Gestalt psychology 14-15, 90
goal expectation theory 308
goals 232-3, 355, 385, 389, 405, 422
group
   decision-making 289, 305-6, 368-72, 417, 433-4
   maintenance 346
   motivation 327, 347-8
   norms 343-6, 348-9, 351-2, 363, 391
   performance 315-49, 351, 416
   productivity 316-17, 326-32, 338, 340, 344, 349
   structure 332-48, 391
   tasks 324-32
group mind 6, 11-12, 384, 392, **450**
group polarization 65-6, 368-72, 433-4, **450**
groupthink 371-2, **450**

happiness 240
Hawthorne effect 76, **451**
health 242-3
   and social psychology 183, 420-9
   and stress 423-5, 427
hedonic relevance 114, **451**
hedonism 7, **451**
helping behaviour *see* altruism
heritability 27, **451**
heuristic processing 177, 184, **451**
heuristics 104-6, 126-7, 132, 177, 306, **451**
historiography 3-5, 13
Homo oeconomicus (model) 289-301, 305, **451**
Hull-Spence drive theory 319
hypnotism 10
hypothesis 61, **451**

identification 174, 177
identity 95, 383, 399-408
   personal 95, 408
   social 4, 55, 383, 399-404

ideology 131-2, 404
illusory correlation 90, 97, 104, 399, **451**
implicit personality theories 90, 100, 127, **451**
impression formation 89-90, 100, 102-4, 369
impression management theory 134, 189-91, 193, 206, **451**
incentive structure
inclusive fitness 29, 32
independent variable 67, 70, 115, **451**
individualism 6-8, 13, 17, 388, 405, 441, **451**
individuo-centred approach 6, **451**
informational influence 354-9, 364, 370-2, **451**
ingroup 131, 390-403, **451**
   bias 131, 391, 394-5, 403
   cohesion 390, 391-2
   favouritism 391-7
innovation *see* minority influence **451**
instinct and aggression 265-8, 383-5, **452**
instrumental conditioning 271-2, 286, **452**
interaction process analysis 76-7, 334-5, 337, **452**
interdependence 288-95, 303-5, 391, **452**
interdependence (payoff) structure 209, **452**
intergroup
   antagonism 384, 393, 414
   attribution 131-2
   behaviour 17, 284-6, 381, 387-93, **452**
   communication 216-17
   comparisons 391, 400, 404-5
   competition 383, 387-8, 391-3
   conflict 381, 389, 390-2, 420
   cooperation 381-3, 392-3
   differentiation 397-9, 402-3
   discrimination 392-3, 395-8, 400
   relations 25, 131, 381-410, 413, 416
internal validity 71-2, **452**
interpersonal-intergroup continuum 387-9, **452**
interpersonal relationships 23, 44-6, 53, 90, 95-6
interviews 78-80, 439
intrinsic motivation 191-2
involvement 180-1

judgement task 63, **452**
juries 11, 369, 371, 433-4
justice, procedural 432-3

kin 224–5, 236, 239
kinesics 200, **452**

laboratory experiment 63, **452**
language acquisition 42–4
leaders 259, 337–42, 348, 372
  LPC-leader 342, **452**
  socio-emotional leader 334–5, 337, 340
  task-oriented leader 334–5, 337, 340
leadership 317, 337–43
  contingency model of 341–3
  dimensions of 337–8, 341
learned helplessness 138, **452**
least preferred coworker 342, **452**
liberalism 7
life events 241, 421, **452**
Likert scale 148–9, 160, **452**
loneliness 199, 241
lost letter technique 151–2, **452**

majority influence 351–9, 352, 364–8, 370,
  372, 379, 416, **447, 452**
male–female relationships 237
marriage 25, 199, 223, 225, 230–1, 234, 237,
  240, 242, 424
mass psychology 10–12, 284
mental contagion 10–12, 384, **453**
mental health 240–2, 420–1
mere exposure 168–70, **453**
message reception *see* reception
metacommunication 203, **453**
minimal group
  experiments 394–9, 401
  paradigm 394–6, 400, **453**
minority influence 17, 350–1, 359–68, 420,
  451, **453**
  consistency and 359–64
misattribution 188–9, **453**
mixed motive game (conflict) 291, **453**
modelling (observational learning) 173–4,
  256–7, 272–3, **453**
Moro reflex 29, **453**
mother–child relationships 22–3, 25,
  29–30, 36
motivation 7, 12, 108–9, 134–7, 139, 176–7,
  181
  gains in groups 331, 348
  losses in groups 327–8
multidimensional scaling 235–6, **453**

national categorization 55–6
non-common effects principle 113, **453**

nonreactive measures *see* attitudes,
  measurement of
norm
  of reciprocity 214, 252, 256, 283, 286,
  453
  of social responsibility 251, 253, **453**
normalization 421, **453**
normative influence 354–9, 364, 370–1, **453**
normative model 125, **453**
norms 35–6, 81, 162–4, 184, 252–7, 283–6,
  298, 334, 343–6, 348–9, 351, 385,
  396–7, 414, 423, **453**

obedience 61, 66–9, 71–2, 81–2, 351, 372–8,
  414, 416, 420, 432, **453**
objective self-awareness 164
observation 75–7, 80, 83, 390, 440
obtrusive measures 64, 73, 76, 151–2, **453–4**
one-shot case study 70, **454**
outgroup 390–1, 408, **454**
  homogeneity of 399
over-accommodation 209
over-justification 192, **454**

paralinguistics 200, **454**
parent–child relations 41–4, 385
participant observation 75, **454**
path analysis 223, **454**
peer pressure 376–7
peer relations 44–6
peripheral route to persuasion 177, **454**
personalism 114, **454**
personality traits 25, 385–6
persuasion 174–84, 193–4, 370–1, 413, 420,
  454
persuasive communications 151, 174–83,
  378, **454**
physical appearance
physical attractiveness 223, 228
placebo pill 188
pluralistic ignorance 258–9, **454**
polygyny 30, 32, **454**
positive distinctiveness 399–400
positivism 7, **454**
post-experimental enquiry 69, 73, **454**
post-test only control group design 70, **454**
power 235–6
power function 367
pragmatics 124–5, **454**
prejudice
  anti semitism 385–6
  ethnic 14, 17, 63, 150–1, 385–6, 389,
  392–3, 420, **455**

racism 21, 383
preoperational stage 48-9, **455**
primary effect 89, 100, 101, 106, **455**
priming 104, **455**
prisoner's dilemma game 291-4, 295
proattitudinal behaviour 185-9, 191-2, **455**
process losses 317, 348
process model **455**
   of altruism 254-5
   of attribution 132-3
   of persuasion 174-8, **455**
prosocial behaviour *see* altruism
prosodics 200, **455**
protection motivation theory 183, **455**
prototype 92, 104, **455**
psychoanalytic theory and aggression
   265-6
pure science model 414-19, 442-3, **455**

questionnaires 63, 78-80, 223

random allocation (of subjects to conditions) 67-8, **455**
rating scale 149-50
recency effect 89, **455**
reception 176-9, 181, **455**
reciprocity 224-5, 261, 367, 420
   norm of 214, 256
recovery from illness 425-6
reinforcement 7, 224, 229, 355
relational development and deterioration
   model of 212-14
relationships 22-5, 30-1, 222-45
   components 30, 231-6
   effects of 227, 239-43
   formation and decline 212-14, 224-6,
   228-31
   theories 223-8
   types 237-9
relative deprivation 407-8
reliability 79, **455**
representativeness 104-5, 127, 132
research strategies 62-6
response competition 169-70, 320
responsibility attribution 253, 255, 259-61,
   414, 425-6, 428, 431, 441
retention 174-5
Ringelmann effect 327, 329
risky shift 368-9, **455**
role(s) 333-4, 393, 416, 424, **455**
rules of relationships 233-4

salience 126, 129, 132, **455**
sample survey 63, **456**
schema 93-4, 117-18, **456**
   and attitudes 157-8
script 52, 102-4, 123, 257, **456**
selective exposure 154-5, 181, **456**
self-consistency 164
self-disclosure 214-15, 230, **456**
self-esteem 134-5, 225, 247, 252, 260, 401,
   404-5, 423, 432
self-monitoring 164
self-perception theory 187-9, 194, **456**
self-presentation 134, 190-1, 285
self-report measures 77-80, 84, 223
self-serving bias 130-1, 227, **456**
semantic differential 147-8, 171, **456**
sentencing 434-5, 440-2
sex differences 30-1, 35-6, 227-8
sexual anatomy 30-1
similarity and attraction 223, 229, 387-8
simulation 63, 433
snowball effect 363, 366
social categories 55-8, 388, 395, 397
social categorisation 93, 309-10, 399
   criss cross 398
social cognition 15, 52-8, 89-110
social comparison 52, 258, 309-10, 364-5,
   370-1, 400, 405, 420, 423
social construction 173, 250, 280-3
social desirability 73, 79, 113-14, 150
social development 39-59, 414
social differentiation 57-8
social dilemma 294, 299-300, 328, 339, **456**
social dimension 17, 219
social exchange theory 224-6, 230, **456**
social facilitation 13, 64-6, 318-23, **456**
social identification 308-10, 403-4
social identity 4, 55, 383, 399-409, 418, **456**
social impact 367
social influence 10, 12, 17, 281-2, 350-80,
   416
social inhibition 258-9, 318-23, **456**
social interaction and cognitive development 42-6, 49-51
socialization 5, 16, 28, 39-59, 227-8, 253,
   255-7, 385, 435
social learning *see* modeling
social loafing 328-9, **456**
social orientations 298-305, **456**
social representations 7, 17, 58, 98-9, 126,
   219, **456**
social science model 419-20, 442-3, **456**

social structure 17, 53–4, 57
social support 240–1, 356–8, 369, 421, 423, 424–5, 428, 432
socio-biology 20–37, 224–5, **456**
socio-centred approach 6, **456**
socio-cognitive conflict 51, **456**
socio-emotional behaviour 334–5, 405, 423
sociology 7, 10, 12, **457**
source credibility 180
speech accommodation 402, **457**
speech styles 205–10
status 334–6, 355, 372, 397, 404–5, **457**
stereotype/stereotyping 17, 21, 35, 96–7, 118, 171, 209, 228, 271, 369, 399, **457**
suggestion 10, 12, 384, **457**
superordinate goal 391–3, **457**
survey 63

television and violence *see* aggression
theory of reasoned action 162–3, 418, **457**
three-component model of attitudes 143–5, **457**
Thurstone's (equal appearing interval) scale 146–7

triangle hypothesis 304
two-factor model of persuasion 176–9, 184, **457**
type A syndrome 422–3

unobstrusive measures 64, 73, 76, 151–2, **457**
utilitarianism 7, **457**

validation 365
validity 71–4, 79, 83, 418, **457**
vandalism 285
variable perspective theory 156
violence *see* aggression
Völkerpsychologie 8–10, 12, **457**
volunteers vs. non-volunteers 74

work relationships 237–9

yielding 174–6, **457**

Zeitgeist 11, 363